OXFORD JUNIOR ENCYCLOPAEDIA

GENERAL EDITORS

LAURA E. SALT & GEOFFREY BOUMPHREY

ILLUSTRATIONS EDITOR: HELEN MARY PETTER

VOLUME II

NATURAL HISTORY

DOM MINA
INVS TIO
ILLV MEA

OXFORD UNIVERSITY PRESS

Oxford University Press, Amen House, London E.C.4

GLASGOW NEW YORK TORONTO MELBOURNE WELLINGTON
BOMBAY CALCUTTA MADRAS KARACHI
CAPE TOWN IBADAN NAIROBI ACCRA SINGAPORE

FIRST PUBLISHED 1949
REPRINTED WITH CORRECTIONS 1951 1955
1957

SET IN GREAT BRITAIN
AT THE UNIVERSITY PRESS, OXFORD
AND REPRINTED BY
MESSRS. WEBB. SON. & CO., LTD.. LONDON

OXFORD JUNIOR
ENCYCLOPAEDIA

VOLUME II
NATURAL HISTORY

PREFACE

IN authorizing the preparation of this work the Delegates of the Oxford University Press had foremost in mind the need to provide a basic book of reference for school libraries. In form it was to be a genuine encyclopaedia, in treatment and vocabulary suitable for the young reader. To many children (and indeed to many adults) reading is not a natural activity: they do not turn to books for their own sake. But they can be trained to go to books for information which they want for some particular purpose—and thus, very often, to form a habit which will be of lifelong value. Their capacity to read continuously for any length of time being limited, they can absorb knowledge better if they get it in small quantities: therefore they will often read reference books when they may reject the reading of more extended matter. Again, it is probably true to say of such readers that their approach is from the particular to the general, and from the application to the principle, rather than the reverse, that their main interest is in the modern world around them, and that since they are not very good at conceiving things outside their own experience, their capacity for grasping abstract ideas is limited. On the other hand, once their interest is aroused, they will often pursue a subject to remarkable lengths, so long as its development is logical and the treatment avoids dullness.

But such generalizations can easily be overdone: many children using the books will not be of this type. Moreover, it was evident from the first that a project involving so great an amount of work, however exactly it might meet its principal mark, would be fully justified only if it could be of service to a far wider circle of readers. Even for the age-group first in mind, anything like 'writing down to children' must plainly be taboo—but clear exposition and simple language are no bad qualities in writing for any audience. Here, then, it seemed was the opportunity to provide a work of reference suitable for many readers to whom the large, standard encyclopaedias are too heavy and technical, and the popular alternatives for the most part neither sufficiently complete nor authoritative. The fact that the plan allowed for an exceptionally large proportion of illustrations to text (between one-quarter and one-third of the total space) is an advantage to any reader, since pictures may, in many instances, save whole paragraphs of involved explanation. With these secondary aims well in mind, then, the General

Editors have ventured to hope that the encyclopaedia may find usefulness not only among certain younger children, but also among older students in clubs, libraries, and Young People's Colleges, and even to no small extent among their parents and other adults who may wish for a simple approach to some unfamiliar or forgotten subject.

SCOPE AND EMPHASIS. Within certain limits the OXFORD JUNIOR ENCYCLOPAEDIA purports to be reasonably comprehensive, though (in common with all general encyclopaedias) not exhaustive. Chief among these limits is that matter already easily available in school text-books is included only so far as its presence is necessary for the proper understanding of the subject under discussion. Thus, although an immense field of history is surveyed, it will be found mainly under headings dealing with its effects, or in the biographies of those who lived to make it. Purely technical or scientific subjects, also, are omitted except when they have some general interest. In natural history and kindred studies the immense variety of forms necessarily led at times either to their treatment by groups or to their omission on purely arbitrary decisions as to which species would, in all probability, never be looked for, or because there was nothing particularly interesting to say of them. In point of general balance the stress is laid rather on the modern world, though due space is given to the factors which have shaped it, no less than to those which are changing it.

ARRANGEMENT. The encyclopaedia is planned to consist of twelve volumes. Each is arranged alphabetically within itself, and each deals with a particular range of related subjects. Within its terms of reference, then, each volume is virtually self-contained, and, owing to the great number of single-line cross-references, can well be used alone. This arrangement, which has several incidental advantages (as of production, in difficult times, and of prompt revision later), arose mainly from one consideration. If articles were to be kept really short—and, in fact, few approach and almost none exceeds 2,000 words—many subjects could be dealt with comprehensively only by referring the reader to other relevant articles—itself a desirable thing to do. It was clearly preferable for these to be under his hand, rather than be dispersed through any of the twelve volumes at the caprice of the alphabet. This the present arrangement achieves to a great extent. If it has led to a small amount of overlapping, that again is not without its advantages.

Cross-references, then, play an indispensable part in the make-up of the encyclopaedia. They are of two kinds: references in the text to further articles amplifying the particular point under review, and references at the end of an article to others taking the whole subject farther. Therefore, a reader looking up any wide subject, such as ANATOMY, and following up its cross-references either in the text or at the end of the article, can discover under what main headwords the subject is treated. These, again, will refer him to any subsidiary articles, as also, in many cases, to those of a complementary nature. Thus he may be guided either from the general to the particular or vice versa. It is believed that the titles of the twelve volumes (see p. xii), in conjunction with their sub-titles, will usually lead the reader straight to the volume containing the information he wants. In selecting headwords, the rules generally followed have been to prefer the familiar, or even the colloquial, reserving the technical alternative for a single-line entry, and to group narrow subjects under a headword of wider scope. Thus, for POLLINATION, *see* REPRODUCTION IN PLANTS, section 5; for RHIZOME, *see* STEMS, section 2*b*; for LEPIDOPTERA, *see* BUTTERFLIES or MOTHS; for DUNLIN, *see* WADING BIRDS; and for GAZELLE, *see* ANTELOPE.

L.E.S., G.M.B.

OXFORD, 1949

LIST OF CONTRIBUTORS

VOLUME EDITOR

DR. M. BURTON, Deputy Keeper at the British Museum (Natural History).

CONTRIBUTORS

General Biology and Zoology

DR. M. BURTON, British Museum (Natural History).

JOHN BUXTON, Fellow of New College, Oxford.

T. J. S. ROWLAND, M.A.

Mammals

D. SETH-SMITH, F.Z.S., M.B.O.U., *Late* Curator of Mammals and Birds, Zoological Society. The 'Zoo Man' of the B.B.C. Children's Hour.

R W. HAYMAN, Senior Experimental Officer, Dept. of Zoology, British Museum (Natural History).

Fish

A. FRASER-BRUNNER, F.Z.S., Associate in the Dept. of Zoology, British Museum (Natural History).

Birds

D. SETH-SMITH, F.Z.S., M.B.O.U., Late Curator of Mammals and Birds, Zoological Society. The 'Zoo-Man' of the B.B.C. Children's Hour.

JOHN BUXTON, Fellow of New College, Oxford.

P. H. TRAHAIR HARTLEY, M.A., Dept. of Ornithology, Oxford.

Reptiles

DR. MALCOLM SMITH.

Crustaceans and Molluscs

F. MARTIN DUNCAN, F.Z.S., Gen. Ed. and Librarian of Zoological Society (1919-45).

Insects

A. J. A. WOODCOCK, M.Sc., F.R.E.S.

G. J. ARROW, F.Z.S., F.R.E.S., Late Deputy Keeper Dept. of Entomology, British Museum (Natural History).

L. HUGH NEWMAN, F.R.E.S., Author of *Wings in the Sun*; *Butterfly Haunts*, &c.

G. E. J. NIXON, B.A.

DR. B. M. HOBBY, D.Phil., Hope Dept. of Entomology, Oxford University Museum.

PROF. G. D. HALE CARPENTER, Hope Professor of Zoology (Entomology), Oxford (1933-48).

Spiders

THEODORE H. SAVORY, M.A., F.Z.S., Author of *The Biology of Spiders*; *Arachnida*, &c.

Plants

T. H. HAWKINS, M.Sc., M.ED., F.L.S.

L. J. F. BRIMBLE, B.Sc., F.L.S., Joint Editor of *Nature*.

Assistant Editor—NORA C. DAY.

Valuable help in the early stages of planning this volume and in the selection of authors was given by Brian Vesey-Fitzgerald, F.L.S., F.R.E.S., Editor-in-Chief of *The Field* (1938–46). The work of revising the Volume for the 1955 edition has been carried out by Dr. B. M. Hobby, D.Phil., Hope Dept. of Entomology, Oxford University Museum, and Miss S. M. Littleboy, Dept. of Botany, Oxford.

ACKNOWLEDGEMENTS

THE EDITORS wish to thank all those who have lent photographs, or allowed them to be used at reduced fees for this educational project. They have had particular assistance from Harold Bastin; S. Beaufoy, F.R.P.S.; Arthur Brook; G. A. Gibson-Hill; Eric J. Hosking, F.R.P.S.; G. K. Yeates, F.R.P.S.; and the Zoological Society of London. They would also like to express their thanks to the Hope Dept. of Entomology, Oxford University Museum, for providing the specimens for the colour plates, opp. pages 80 and 336.

COLOUR PLATES

PLAN OF VOLUMES

GENERAL INDEX VOLUME
Covering entries in all 12 volumes

HOW TO USE THIS BOOK

THIS VOLUME is one of twelve, each on a separate subject, the whole set forming what is called an encyclopaedia, or work from which you can find out almost anything you want to know. (The word comes originally from the Greek *enkuklios*, circular or complete, and *paideia*, education.) Each of the twelve volumes is arranged alphabetically within itself, as twelve dictionaries would be.

The difference between a dictionary and an encyclopaedia is that while the first gives you no more than the meanings and derivations of words, the second tells you a very great deal more about their subjects. For instance, from a dictionary you could learn that a SALAMANDER is a lizard-like animal, and little more; but an encyclopaedia will tell you where and how they live, and will give details of interesting species, such as the Giant Salamander of Japan or the Hell-bender of the Mississippi. Then a dictionary contains nearly every word in the language; but an encyclopaedia deals only with words and subjects about which there is something interesting to be said, beyond their bare meanings. So you should not expect to find every word in an encyclopaedia—every subject is there, but not every word.

To find any subject, you have first to decide in which of the twelve volumes it comes. Each of these has a title as well as a number, and also a list of general subjects to make the title clearer. All these are set out in the Plan of Volumes on the opposite page. Very often you will be able to tell from the title alone which volume contains the information you need; but if not, the list of sub-headings on the plan opposite will help to direct you. For example, if you want to find out about an animal or plant, you would look it up in Volume II, Natural History; but if you wanted to know how that animal or plant is used in something like farming, fishing, or trapping, you would find it in Volume VI. If your subject were something in nature that does not have life—such as the sun, or a particular country or river, or a kind of stone—you would find it in Volume III, with tides, earthquakes, the weather, and many other things. Matters connected with communication of any kind—of people, or goods, or even of ideas—are in Volume IV. So you would look there for languages, and printing, and broadcasting, as well as for ships, and trains, and roads. But if it is the engineering side of any of these things that interests you, Volume VIII, Engineering, is the place to try.

Business and trade are in Volume VII; and how we are governed and protected by the State, the law, and the armed forces is in Volume X. All kinds of sport and games, as well as acting, dancing, concerts, and musical instruments, are in Volume IX; and Volume XI deals with almost everything connected with our homes, from the building and furnishing of the house to the clothes and health of those who live in it. The titles of Volumes V and XII, Great Lives and The Arts, explain themselves; and a rather fuller account of the volume you are reading now is given on page xv.

To find your subject in the volume, think of its ordinary name, and then look it up as though you were using a dictionary—the As on the first page and the Zs (if there are any) on the last. If you cannot find it, try a more general word. For instance, if you want to read about the Bladder-Wrack and cannot find it under its name (as you cannot), try either ALGAE or SEAWEEDS—either of which will lead you to it. As you read any article, you will probably come across the title of other articles in some way connected with what you are reading. You will know that they are titles of other articles because they will be printed in capital letters. Either they will be followed by (q.v.) in brackets (this is short for the Latin *quod vide*, and means 'which see'), or else they themselves will be in brackets, with the word *see* in front of them. You can look up these other articles at once if you want to know more about the particular point dealt with, or you can save them up until you have finished the article you are reading. At the end of any article you may find the words 'See also', followed by one or more titles in small capital letters. If you look these titles up, they will tell you still more about the subject that interests you. These last 'cross-references' are very useful if you want to look up a particularly wide subject (such as ANATOMY or BIRDS), because they show you at once the titles of all the main articles dealing with it. You can then decide for yourself which to read.

WHAT YOU WILL FIND IN THIS VOLUME

THIS VOLUME IS ABOUT LIVINGS THINGS, PLANTS AND ANIMALS, WHICH EXIST IN A NATURAL STATE ON THE EARTH.

PLANTS. The thousands of different PLANTS in the world all belong to a number of big groups, such as FLOWERING PLANTS, CONIFERS, FERNS, SEAWEEDS, FUNGI, and BACTERIA. You will find articles on these groups but not on every individual plant. You can read about the various parts of plants, the FLOWERS, SEEDS, FRUIT, LEAVES, STEMS, and ROOTS, which all serve different and essential purposes, and about the GROWTH OF PLANTS, REPRODUCTION IN PLANTS, RESPIRATION IN PLANTS, and other such subjects. You can find out about plants which have special devices for living, by looking up headwords such as CLIMBING PLANTS, PARASITIC PLANTS, and PLANT DEFENCES; and others which prefer a certain type of environment such as DESERT PLANTS, SEASHORE PLANTS, and WATER PLANTS.

ANIMALS. There is a vast range of animal life in the world, from the highly specialized animals which include Man himself, as well as APES, ELEPHANTS, and CATS, to the simple creatures such as SPONGES and CORALS which hardly seem like animals at all, and the microscopic AMOEBA. This book describes the way of life and behaviour of all the better-known species of MAMMALS, BIRDS, FISH, REPTILES, INSECTS, and other animals. It also tells you about the ANATOMY OF ANIMALS, the different methods of GROWTH, REPRODUCTION, and MOVEMENT, and how the parts of the body, such as the BRAIN and the HEART, have developed. Animals respond to their environment through their SENSES, and are protected from their natural enemies by CAMOUFLAGE. Their song and courtship display are part of ANIMAL LANGUAGE, and the instinctive behaviour is directed in the higher animals by a dawning INTELLIGENCE.

The chart on the next page gives a simple picture of how by EVOLUTION plants and animals have developed into their many varied and complex forms; and it gives the general headings under which the plants and animals will be found.

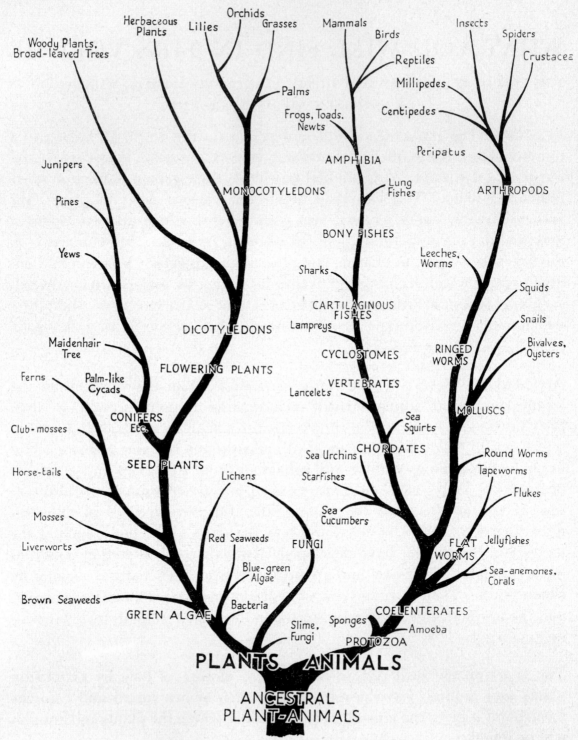

LIVING PLANTS AND ANIMALS

Designed by Dr. B. M. Hobby

This very much simplified evolution chart gives a guide as to what is to be found in this volume. It suggests how plants and animals may have grown up from the beginning. It might be compared with the chart in Vol. III, p. 139.

A

AARD-VARK (Dutch for earth-pig), or Ant-bear. This mammal is the only member of the order of animals called the Tubulidentata, and was at one time included with the ANT-EATERS, SLOTHS, and ARMADILLOS (qq.v.) in the order Edentata. It has no front teeth, and the rest of its teeth are simple and peg-like; but apart from the lack of front teeth, the long snout, and the habit of eating ants and termites, it bears little resemblance to these others. It is confined mainly to the open country of South and East Africa, and is an animal of very extraordinary, ungraceful appearance. It is large and heavy, 5 or 6 feet in length, including the long thick tail. It has a rounded back, long tubular snout, and ears which are very long and donkey-like, evidently adapted for picking up the slightest sound of approaching danger. In hot districts it is nearly hairless, in cooler districts its skin is covered with coarse, yellowish-brown hair—but this is short and sparse on the back and hardly noticeable at first sight. The Aard-varks dig themselves deep burrows with their powerful claws. They stay hidden in these until after dark,

when they come out to attack the nests of termites, picking up the insects with their long, sticky tongues. They are much esteemed as food by the natives, who dig them out of their burrows.

AARD-WOLF. This mammal of South and East Africa looks very like a small HYAENA (q.v.). It is about the size of a fox, but stands higher on account of its longer legs. It has a

yellowish or reddish-brown, shaggy, woolly coat, marked with about half a dozen vertical stripes on each side of its body. The tail is fairly long and bushy, and on the nape of the neck and along the back there is a distinct mane. The muzzle is more pointed and the ears longer than those of the hyaena.

The exact position of Aard-wolves in the animal world has been rather a puzzle to zoologists. They appear to be related to Hyaenas, but their way of life is very different. Unlike Hyaenas, Aard-wolves have weak jaws, and their teeth show that their diet is very different from that of ordinary flesh-eating mammals. Their main food seems to be termites (white ants), and other insects, fruit, and grubs. They live in burrows dug by themselves, several often sharing the one hole. Like most burrowing animals, they are timid and cowardly, and make off at a rapid pace when they are driven from their earths. They venture out only at night, and on this account are rarely seen.

ADDER (also known as the VIPER). The old English name of Adder is preferable, since there are many species of Viper (q.v.) (Viperidae) throughout the world. It is the only poisonous snake found in England, and can readily be distinguished from the Grass Snake or the Smooth Snake (qq.v.), the other two English kinds. It is a short snake, seldom more than 15 inches in length; it has a fairly thick body, a short tail, and a head very distinct from the neck. In colour it is brownish or reddish, with a dark zigzag stripe or series of spots down the middle of the back, which vary in distinctness, but are never absent. The belly is either dark greyish with light spots, or almost entirely black. Owing to the many colour variations, the adder has at times been given different names; but there is only one species. The particularly large red ones that are occasionally seen are always females, for the females grow to a larger size than the males.

The adder is widely distributed over most of Europe, and is found all over England and Scotland, usually in pine and heather country. It feeds mainly upon lizards and small mammals, and gives birth to from six to twelve living young at a time. The popular legend that the adder in time of danger will swallow its young, or allow them to crawl down its throat in order to protect them, still needs confirmation: for no one has been able to prove it by finding an adder with the young in its stomach. The bite of the adder is seldom fatal to human beings, but sheep and dogs not infrequently die from it.

See also Snake.

AGAMA. This is a lizard of the family Agamidae, found in the tropical and sub-tropical regions of Africa and Asia. Agamas differ from all other lizards in having their teeth fixed to the parapet of the jaw, and these can be divided roughly into incisors, canines, and molars. Except by their teeth, there is little to distinguish them from the Iguanas (q.v.). In the breeding season, many Agama males are very beautifully coloured. They are found living under all sorts of conditions, in desert country and among rocks, in the forests and in the open country.

An Indian species, known as the Bloodsucker, is found frequently in gardens on bushes and shrubs. It feeds on insects and grubs, and in spite of its name is harmless. In the breeding season, the male becomes bright red in colour—and this may have given rise to its name, for it certainly never sucks blood.

A FRILLED LIZARD
Zoological Society of London

The Frilled Lizard from the north of Australia is one of the largest members of the family. It has an expansion of skin on each side of the neck, which is its frill. This can be erected by means of special bones in the throat, which extend into the skin like the ribs of an umbrella. When the lizard is excited and standing at bay, the frill is spread out, giving it a formidable appearance. Another Australian species, known as the Moloch, was called by the early settlers Spiny Lizard or Thorny Devil. It grows to 8 inches in length, of which the tail forms nearly half. It has a small head, short limbs, and a flattened body, and is covered all over the upper surface with large, horny spines. It is quick and agile in its movements, and when kept as a pet has been found, for a lizard, to have considerable intelligence.

See also Lizards.

AGOUTI. This Rodent (q.v.), about the size of a rabbit, is related to the Cavies (q.v.) and lives in the forests of South America and in the West Indies. It has slender legs, looks rather like a small antelope, and can run very fast. Its colour varies greatly, but is usually olive-brown, with yellow-orange hindquarters. Whenever the animal is alarmed, the brightly coloured patch of hair opens out and becomes very conspicuous. This is regarded by some as a signal, warning other Agoutis of approaching danger, and indicating the direction they should follow—as when rabbits show the white undersides of their tails.

During most of the day Agoutis lie concealed in hollow trees or in burrows in their forest homes, and come out in the early morning or at night to eat leaves, plants, and fallen fruits— at which time they can sometimes be seen in the open. With their sharp incisor teeth they can pierce the shells of the toughest nuts. In cultivated districts they eat sugar-cane and bananas. They are active animals, either trotting or springing along at high speed; they swim well, but cannot dive. For most of the year the two sexes live apart, but at the mating season each male selects a female and follows her with squeaks and grunts, staying by her until after the birth of their offspring. She has her young in a lair or in a nest carefully made of leaves, roots, and hair, and she prevents the male from coming near them until some days after their birth.

Agoutis are hunted a great deal for their flesh. They live well in captivity, and have been bred in Zoological Gardens.

ALBACORE, *see* MACKEREL.

ALBATROSS, *see* PETREL.

ALGAE. Although by no means always the smallest, algae are in structure and organization the simplest of all plants. They include such plants as the unicellular plant called Protococcus, the green, powdery growth seen on damp wood and the bark of trees; the green threads of Spirogyra, seen as scum on ponds; and all the many kinds of seaweeds. These simple plants do not bear seeds, but usually reproduce themselves by swimming spores and other small reproductive bodies, which grow into new plants. (*See* REPRODUCTION OF PLANTS, Section 2.) The algae are closely related to FUNGI (q.v.), but, unlike the latter, contain green colouring matter or chlorophyll (often masked by other pigments), and are able to make their own food by the process known as PHOTO-SYNTHESIS (q.v.). They thrive only in moist situations.

If some of the green powdery Protococcus, found on trees and fences during mild and moist weather, is scraped off and examined under a microscope, it will be seen to consist of many tiny green cells, globular in shape, each a minute plant. It is one of the most abundant plants of temperate regions, and inside each single cell all the functions of life go on. Protococcus is largely responsible for the green tint of the leafless trees and shrubs at the end of a mild autumn, and is particularly abundant on the windward side of a tree trunk where the rain, beating with the wind, provides the damp surface necessary for its growth. The greener side of a tree trunk is said to face the direction of the prevailing wind.

Plants very similar to Protococcus are found in ponds and streams. Some of them, shaped like small eggs, have a pair of delicate whip-like protoplasmic hairs at one end, which, by their alternate straightening, bending, and swinging, enable the plants to swim about.

The Spirogyra is the commonest of the green thread-like plants which float on the surfaces of stagnant pools and ponds. The Spirogyra, when

Greatly enlarged

(*left*) PROTOCOCCUS, AND (*right*) SPIROGYRA

looked at under the microscope, is seen to be of striking beauty, each thread being a row of cells containing spirals of chlorophyll, from which spirals it gets its name.

Probably the best-known algae are, however, the seaweeds (*see* SEASHORE PLANTS). These are of three kinds—red, green, and brown. Green

BROWN SEAWEEDS: (*a*) Serrated Wrack (*Fucus serratus*) and (*b*) Bladderwrack (*Fucus vesiculosus*); GREEN SEAWEED: (*c*) *Enteromorpha compressa*; RED SEAWEEDS: (*d*) *Lithophylum versicolor* and (*e*) *Laurencia pinnatifida*

seaweeds are found in very shallow water and are exposed most of the time to the atmosphere. Brown seaweeds grow abundantly between tide-marks, where they are exposed at low tide. Red seaweeds, which are particularly beautiful, are the least frequently seen, because they occur in deeper water. Some seaweeds are very large, even reaching a length of more than a quarter of a mile—yet their organization is still simple, and they show no division into roots, stems, and leaves. The SARGASSO SEA (q.v. Vol. III), in the North Atlantic Ocean, is the centre of a vast eddy in which a particular brown seaweed accumulates. Here, it floats at the surface and used to be a great nuisance to navigation. Sea-weeds were once used as a source of iodine, but to-day are used mainly as manure or for making power alcohol, chiefly in Ireland. In recent years, 'agar', a jelly-like substance used widely in commerce, has been obtained from seaweeds.

ALLIGATOR, *see* CROCODILES.

ALPACA, *see* LLAMA.

ALPINE PLANTS. The 'alpine region' refers to land above the upper limit of coniferous trees —that is, about 5,000 feet or more above sea-level—as in the PYRENEES (q.v. Vol. III) and all the lofty mountains of central Europe. In alpine regions, with their high day temperature and dry atmosphere, the plants grow in compact cushions to suit the peculiar conditions under which they live. Because the soil is frozen there is a lack of moisture, and, in addition, the plants have to live under their warm covering of snow, in darkness, for a large part of the year. One of the peculiarities of alpine flora is, therefore, their tendency to 'rush into flower' at the earliest possible moment when the snow melts in spring-time, their short but brilliant flowering period being usually confined to this time. To carry them over the long period when they are buried under the snow, most of the plants are provided with some form of underground organs in which reserve stocks of food can be stored.

Many alpine flowers are dazzling blues— although not so many as the casual observer is inclined to believe—and these are specially noticeable because of the intense depth of colour and the large number of individual flowers. Among the many strikingly beautiful alpine flowers, the best known are the deep blue Gentians, Anemones, pale violet Soldanellas, Campanulas or Bell-flowers, many kinds of yellow-gold Saxifrages, and, of course, the well-known Edelweiss and the Alpenrose, after which so many Swiss inns are named, and which might be called the national flowers of Switzerland. As well as these there are many other less well-known gems. The weirdly shaped, vivid, rose-coloured Sempervivum is a wonderful example of adaptation to meet the demands of environment. When the soil is quite dry and the sun so hot that all other flowers have flagged, the Sempervivum stands erect and full of living sap. It has a supply of water in its thick rosettes of leaf-heads. These are covered with sticky hairs and hair-threads which form a net, like a cobweb, over the plant to hold in the moisture and counteract the effect of the sun. Lovers of the Alps or Dolomites also know the golden Alpine Poppy, the red cushions of Moss Campion, the unbelievable sky-blue of the rare Fairy Forget-me-not, the rose-red, purple-stamened Dolomites Potentilla, and a whole galaxy of others.

The Edelweiss, about which so much romance has been woven and which is commonly believed

SAXIFRAGA LYCHNITIS
Dr. G. Taylor

MECONOPSIS BELLA
Dr. G. Taylor

GENTIANA ACAULIS
Paul Popper

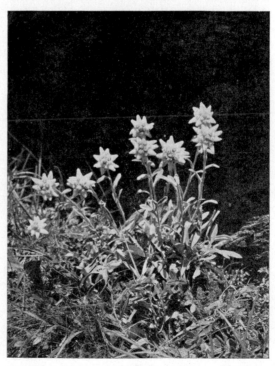

EDELWEISS
Paul Popper

ALPINE PLANTS

to grow only in places which even the most hardy mountaineer can barely reach, is a complete fraud: it is not a rare plant, indeed it is almost common. Every season huge masses of Edelweiss are gathered by the Swiss peasants, or even cultivated in the lowlands of northern Switzerland for sale to the tourist. The Edelweiss may be local in its distribution, but where it does occur, it grows freely. The characteristic whiteness—the word means 'precious white'—is due to a thick covering of long woolly hairs, which are really empty cells. The stem and leaves of the Edelweiss are in fact green, but the greenness is masked by these grey-white hairs. The leaves, like those of many alpine plants, are arranged in a rosette just above the soil. A single stalk springs from the centre of the rosette, bearing what appears to be a solitary flower, but is really a complicated structure consisting of several flower heads, as found in daisies and dandelions. Edelweiss grows in southern Europe, India, and Siberia.

The Alpenroses, of which there are two, the Common and the Hairy, are more common than the Edelweiss. Alpenroses are really small-flowered evergreen Rhododendrons, growing to a height of from 2 to 3 feet or more. They grow in great abundance on the higher pastures among the alpine thickets, or on the borders of the coniferous forests, especially where these fringe the margins of alpine lakes. The Common Alpenrose is easily recognized, because the undersides of the older leaves have a rusty-brown appearance, due to the presence of numerous scales, which protect the leaf pores or stomata, and so decrease the water-loss caused by TRANSPIRATION (q.v.) during their intense spring-flowering period. The Hairy Alpenrose, more common on limestone soils, is like the Common Alpenrose, except that all the leaves are green beneath and fringed with hairs along their margins.

See also Vol. III: ALPS; CARPATHIANS; PYRENEES.

AMOEBA. This is one of the simplest animals, consisting only of a single cell about a hundredth of an inch across. It is only one of the several thousands of simple, single-celled animals which are grouped together in the phylum (or sub-kingdom) PROTOZOA (q.v.); but its name has become almost a household word. In the 19th century, after DARWIN (q.v. Vol. V) had startled the world with his work *The Origin of Species*, the Amoeba was accepted by the biologists as representing what the first animal, from which all others were descended, probably looked like. To-day, with the advance of our knowledge, we

AMOEBA DIVIDING INTO TWO

The microscopic Amoeba multiplies by simply dividing into two. A 'waist' appears, which becomes narrower until it parts in the middle and there are two Amoebae where formerly there was one.

know that there are much simpler organisms still, such as bacteria and the viruses.

The Amoeba is important because it represents the pattern upon which all the different cells composing the bodies of all the million known species of animals are built. An understanding of the structure and behaviour of Amoeba helps us considerably to understand the structure of all animals. To take but one example, the white corpuscles of our blood, so essential to us in keeping the body healthy, are so like Amoebae that, if we found them wandering about outside our bodies, we should believe them to belong to a species of Amoeba.

Some species of Amoeba live in the mud of ponds and streams. A fresh-water Amoeba has a tiny body irregular in outline and almost transparent, although with the naked eye it can just be seen as a minute white speck. Under the microscope the body is seen to contain a central, slightly more opaque, spherical nucleus. This is the centre of control, and acts towards the rest of the cell as our brain does to our body. The protoplasm, known as the 'cytoplasm', surrounding the nucleus, is filled with microscopic grains, so that it looks on a minute scale like a gum after it has been stirred in a bottle with a stick, and is filled with minute air bubbles. Here and there are 'contractile vacuoles' which collect water from the cytoplasm. These grow almost as large as the nucleus and then burst, ejecting water to the exterior.

An Amoeba has no legs, but moves about by pushing a part of its body out like a finger. As this finger-shaped part grows outwards, the granules in the rest of the body are seen to flow towards it and into it, so that as the finger gets longer and longer, the rest of the body becomes correspondingly smaller and smaller. Soon another finger is pushed out, and then another, and so the Amoeba moves about with a somewhat erratic course, following its own fingers, so to speak. These fingers are spoken of as 'pseudopodia', or false feet. They are not permanent: they appear where wanted, and become merged in the rest of the body when their task is done.

An Amoeba has no sense-organs, but its whole body is sensitive to light, heat, and poisons, from which it will move away. It has no stomach or intestine, but simply flows round its food and takes it into its body. The undigested remains are got rid of by the simple process of leaving them behind as it moves away.

The animal multiplies as simply as it does

AMOEBA IN MOVEMENT (GREATLY ENLARGED)
An Amoeba is throwing out a pseudopodium, which flows away and gradually increases in size, carrying the rest of the animal with it.   *D. A. Kempson*

everything else. Both cytoplasm and nucleus split into two, producing two exactly similar Amoebae where previously there was but one. This splitting or asexual reproduction may go on many times, and is the only method of reproduction.

See also PROTOZOA.

AMPHIBIA. These are literally creatures which live both in the water and on land. In zoology, they form that class of the vertebrates which lies between the FISHES (q.v.), from which they developed, and the REPTILES (q.v.), to which they in their turn gave rise. The term includes all those animals commonly known as Salamanders, Newts, Toads, and Frogs. The vast majority have four limbs; but some have lost the hinder pair and others have lost all four, or perhaps never had them. They are classified according to the presence or absence of limbs and tail; so that there are three main divisions: the Caecilians with elongated, worm-like bodies and without limbs; the SALAMANDERS and NEWTS (qq.v.) with a tail and usually four but sometimes only two limbs; and the FROGS and TOADS (qq.v.) without a tail and always with four limbs.

All the Amphibia lay eggs, which hatch into larvae or tadpoles. These, with a few exceptions, live in the water, breathing chiefly by means of gills: some, such as the Siren and the Mexican Axolotl, never lose their gills. In some species, such as the Black Salamander of Europe, and certain frogs or toads living in South America and some of the Pacific Islands, development of the young takes place in or on the body of the mother: these are called 'viviparous'. The actual number of known species of Amphibia is not large when compared with the other great divisions of the vertebrates. Of the Caecilians there are some 50 or more species; of the Salamanders, 150; of the Frogs and Toads, 1,500; whereas there are some 40,000 species of fish, and some 5,300 of reptiles.

The Caecilians, the smallest group of Amphibia, are also known as the Apoda. They live in the tropical and wet regions of Asia, Africa, and America, and not very much is known about them because of their retiring habits. They have extremely short tails and only traces of eyes, generally so buried under the skin of the head that they are useless for sight. Some species have scales embedded in the skin, like certain fishes, and all are moist and slimy to touch. They live

A CAECILIAN

The female lays her eggs in an underground chamber and coils herself round them for their protection

in the ground near water, and the tadpoles continue to live underground, not taking to the water until they are almost mature. Some species are known to guard their eggs in the early stages.

ANACONDA, *see* Boa.

ANATOMY is the study of the organs of the body, the word itself meaning to cut up. The reason for its use in this connexion is, of course, that the organs cannot be studied in detail until they are artificially separated from the body. The different organs, such as heart and muscle, are dealt with elsewhere, each under its separate heading. Here we are making a comparative study of the anatomy of animals, and of how the anatomy becomes more elaborate the higher in the scale is the animal.

In the scale of animal life we see, on the one hand, the unicellular Amoeba (q.v.), with practically no special organs (even the organs of locomotion and digestion being transitory), and, on the other hand, the higher mammals, in which each organ has its special function. In other words, the anatomy of animals in its simplest form deals first with a single cell in which all the functions of living are carried out, and at the opposite end of the scale, a body composed of millions of cells, served by different organs, each having its separate function to perform. This transition from the unicellular to the multicellular animal is accomplished by a division of labour. No doubt in the first place a few Amoeba-like animals started to live together in a colony, each cell retaining its original shape and function. After a while, the cells began to take on different functions and, later, different shapes.

The situation can best be understood by comparing it with what has happened in human society. Primitive man, when he lived with his family alone in a cave, had to do everything for himself. He hunted his own food, fetched his own wood for the fire, made his own pots, tools, weapons, clothes, and so on. As the families came together to form communities, it followed that some men were better hunters, while others were better at making pots; and so the work would be divided, making a more efficient system. As time went on, and the human communities grew in size, the division of labour became more and more marked, until in a modern society this division of labour and the specialization that goes with it has reached a very high degree. Indeed, men who have specialized in certain trades or professions, and worked at these for many years, would find it difficult to work efficiently at anything else. In a precisely similar way, as the multicellular animals have developed, so their cells have become specialized.

We speak of a primitive society and a civilized (or specialized) society, the second growing out of the first as a result of the division of labour, or of specialization. In the same way we speak of primitive or specialized animals: the lower we go in the animal kingdom, the more primitive its members; the higher we go, the more specialized. If we compare the eyes of different animals, we can see the kind of thing that happens with all organs as we pass from the primitive to the specialized. An Amoeba has no eyes, yet it is not insensitive to light, and will move rapidly away if a strong beam of light is allowed to play on it. The response to light is vested in the whole body, which in this case is a cell. Certain other unicellular animals, especially among those known as the Flagellates, are light-loving, and these have a few grains of a dark, usually red, pigment which is sensitive to light. This is not an eye in the sense in which we usually speak, but it is the beginning of an eye—and the group of pigment granules is known as an eye-spot.

Some of the multicellular animals are without eyes or eye-spots, yet still react to light. It is found, for example, that Sponges (q.v.) grow best in a moderate light (although, being permanently fixed, they cannot alter their position once they have passed the post-larval stage); so, although they have no eyes, they clearly must be responsive to light stimuli throughout the tissues of the body. Other permanently fixed animals are also without eyes; and it soon becomes apparent, as might be expected, that the development of eyes goes hand in hand with locomotion. Moreover, the faster an animal moves—especially where speed of movement is needed for catching prey, as in insects, birds, and mammals—the better will be the eyesight.

The eyes of slow-moving worms are not obvious; but certain cells of the skin contain pigment cells, and these are scattered singly and evenly over the whole body. In other worms these cells are seen to be collected in groups, with slender nerve fibres running from them to the main nerve cord—here is the beginning of a retina. In other cases the pigmented cells are sunk in a pit in the skin—a sort of rounded chamber lined by pigmented cells. At this point we can see that the eyeball is foreshadowed— and, sure enough, other animals related to worms have developed a lens. It is not possible to describe every type of eye, nor to name the animals that possess them. Summarizing, however, we may say that, as we pass from the lowest to the highest animals, we see the eye develop, first as an eye-spot, then as a group of pigmented cells, and then, as the group of cells grows larger to form a retina, a lens is added, an optic nerve, and all the accessories seen in the eye of the highest mammal (*see* SIGHT).

In the same way we can follow the building up of a digestive system and a BLOOD SYSTEM (q.v.)—the one for taking in food, and the other for passing it round the body. For this purpose we need not go lower in the animal scale than the SEA-ANEMONES or HYDRA (qq.v.). A sea-anemone is nothing more than a cylindrical bag, with an opening or mouth at one end, surrounded by tentacles. The inside of the bag is capacious, and the wall is composed of only two layers of cells, the inner layer being purely digestive, the outer forming the skin. Food taken into this large digestive cavity is absorbed by the cells of the inner layer, and some is passed on to the cells of the outer layer. The important point is that no cell is so far away from the digestive cells that it cannot absorb

DIAGRAM OF ANATOMY OF RABBIT

food direct from it. The next stage in development after the sea-anemones and their relatives is seen in animals with a narrow tube for the digestion of food, the so-called alimentary tract. These animals have highly developed MUSCLES (q.v.). Muscles take up space, and so the digestive cavity grows smaller. This fact alone means that many cells in the body are too far away to have food passed direct to them. Blood-vessels are necessary, therefore, to carry the food round to all parts of the body.

As we go up the scale, and animals develop limbs and become more active, the need for muscles gets greater, the bulk of the body increases in proportion to the space occupied by the alimentary tract, and a more complicated system of blood-vessels becomes necessary. Also, the more active the animal, the more food is needed—and, again, this is an added reason for a more efficient blood system (*see* NUTRITION IN ANIMALS).

With a wider network of blood-vessels comes the greater need for an efficient pump to drive the blood through them. So, in the WORMS (q.v.), the heart is no more than the slightly dilated parts of some of the blood-vessels which, by having more muscular walls than the rest, are able to pulsate and drive the blood along. In the vertebrates, however, a very muscular heart appears, a simple S-shaped tube in fishes, a three-chambered heart in amphibia, and four-chambered in birds and mammals (*see* HEART).

No matter which of the organs we choose, whether the stomach, heart, BRAIN (q.v.), kidneys, or any others, it is possible to show how, as the animal becomes more specialized and complicated, so each organ becomes more elaborate. On the whole, however, there is an orderly pattern along which these specializations proceed, although there are, of course, many exceptions.

Perhaps the chief exceptions in this broad

DIAGRAM OF ANATOMY OF HYDRA

plan concern the NERVOUS SYSTEM, the skeleton, and the organs of RESPIRATION (qq.v.)—that is, gills and lungs. Two points are worth mentioning, however. Firstly, the nervous system of invertebrates is ventral and there is no true brain, while that of the vertebrates is dorsal and there is a brain. Secondly, the skeleton of invertebrates (with the exception of the SPONGES and CORALS (qq.v.)) is on the outside of the body and is called an 'exoskeleton' while that of the vertebrates is internal and is called an 'endoskeleton'. As to the respiratory system, the fact of whether an animal has gills or lungs depends mainly on whether it lives in water or out of it. But again there are exceptions to this, as in the LUNG-FISHES (q.v.) and others.

Briefly, then, the internal organs are, on the whole, built on a regular pattern which becomes more complicated as the animal becomes more specialized. Exceptions do occur, however—one large group, the INSECTS (q.v.), being particularly marked in its departure from the general plan, especially in the breathing and blood-systems. Insects have neither gills nor lungs, but tracheae (although some aquatic larvae have external structures which are called gills); and instead of blood-vessels in the form of a system of tubes, they have large blood spaces or sinuses.

ANCHOVY, *see* HERRING.

ANGEL-FISH, *see* CICHLIDS.

ANGLER-FISH. In shallow waters round the coasts of Britain and also those of Europe and America is found a curious fish which lies on the bed of the sea and catches smaller fishes by means of a 'rod and line'. Its head is broad and flat, and the wide mouth is armed with long, sharp teeth. Any small animal finding its way between these jaws will be unable to escape, for the teeth can be depressed backwards to form a barrier like a row of fixed bayonets. The 'rod' is the first ray of its first dorsal (back) fin, which is placed rather more forward than usual, near the nose, and is very long, with a tassel of skin at the end. The Angler-fish is so flat that when it lies on the sea-floor it is not easily seen. It also has a CAMOUFLAGE (q.v.) of small flaps of skin that resemble bits of weed. Hidden in this way, it waves its 'bait' to and fro—and when a small, unsuspecting fish approaches the tempting morsel, the great jaws close upon it with a snap. It does not rely entirely on its angling, however, but sometimes attacks sea-birds from below, dragging them down to the sea-floor. This Angler-fish, 2 or 3 feet long (brought to market under the name Monk-fish), is one of the several kinds of fish sold in shops as 'Rock Salmon'.

Related to the Angler-fish are the smaller Frogfishes; but the 'lure' on the nose is much smaller, and there are various hump-like growths on the back. Frogfishes get their name from the fact that the pectoral and pelvic fins have long, muscular bases, so that they can be used like legs, the fins themselves serving as feet. Thus the pelvic fins look like front legs, and the pectoral fins like hind legs, the fish, when seen from above, having the appearance of a rather queer frog. Most Frogfishes inhabit tropical shores, and have elaborate patterns of coloured patches, which help to make them invisible as they creep about among the weed. One kind, how-

ANGLER-FISH USING ITS BAIT TO ATTRACT THE PREY
A. Fraser-Brunner

ever, lives always upon the masses of floating weed in the Sargasso Sea (q.v. Vol. III) and elsewhere.

In the very deep sea, where it is very cold and the light of day does not penetrate, there are many kinds of Angler-fish of various weird shapes, with terrifying faces and even more frightful teeth. They are not flattened and do not lie on the bottom, but swim about in the blackness waving their 'baits', which are often very elaborate, and give off a bright light to attract their prey. Their stomachs are so elastic that they can swallow fishes larger than themselves—though this does sometimes result in their death (*see* Deep-Sea Fishes).

In some of these oceanic Anglers the male is very small and permanently fixed to the female. It has, in fact, no independent life and cannot even feed for itself, but gets all its nourishment from the blood of the female, which flows into its own blood-vessels. Not all the males are attached in this way—indeed, it is very difficult to understand how this curious thing comes about, or what purpose it serves. It is hard to study creatures living at these great depths, and we have still a lot to learn about them.

ANGLE-SHADES MOTH, *see* Night-Flying Moths.

ANIMAL AND PLANT DISTRIBUTION. By the 'distribution' of an animal or plant is meant those areas of the earth's surface which are the animal's natural home, but excluding any areas to which it has been introduced, whether intentionally or accidentally, by man.

In the latter part of the 19th century it was realized that the land masses of the earth could be divided into five regions, within each of which the majority of the land plants and animals formed a group more or less distinct from that of any other region. The names of these regions,

FEMALE DEEP-SEA ANGLER-FISH CARRYING HER LIGHT ON HER NOSE
Firmly attached beneath her are three parasitic 'husbands'.   *A. Fraser-Brunner*

established by the English ornithologist Sclater, are:
1. Holarctic, which may be divided into
   (i) Palaearctic, the northern region of the Old World.
   (ii) Nearctic, the northern region of the New World.
2. Ethiopian, including most of Africa and Arabia.
3. Oriental (or Indian), including those parts of Asia south of the Palaearctic region.
4. Australasian, the continent of Australia, New Zealand, and adjacent islands, including some of the East Indian Islands.
5. Neotropical, the continent and islands of America south of the Tropic of Cancer.

The map shows that the division between the Indian and Australasian region passes through some narrow straits between islands of the East Indies, as between Bali and Lombok. This line was named Wallace's Line by T. H. Huxley, after the great naturalist, A. R. Wallace (qq.v. Vol. V).

The names of these regions are useful, not only for grouping their fauna and flora, but as a short and comprehensive way of referring to the countries they comprise. Zoologists and botanists naturally prefer to use one word, such as 'palaearctic', in describing the distribution of an animal or plant rather than make a long list of all the countries in which it is found. These terms are instructive as well as convenient, because it is interesting to know of any animal

SHOWING ANIMAL AND PLANT DISTRIBUTION

or plant that is (or is not) found in association with any other which may be named.

The distribution of marine (or sea) animals bears some resemblance to that of land animals, but with certain important differences. To understand their distribution, it is necessary to remember that marine animals are divided into three kinds, according to habit. The 'planktonic' animals are those that float on the surface, but drift with the currents, such as jelly-fishes, as well as the teeming microscopic forms. The 'nektonic' animals are those that are free-swimming and capable of propelling themselves against a current. The 'benthic' animals are those which live on the bottom—either fixed, such as sponges and corals, or burrowing, such as worms and some shell-fish, or creeping about the bottom, such as starfish and most molluscs.

The distribution of the plankton is largely determined by the ocean currents, and that of the nekton is mainly governed by temperature. The distribution of the benthic animals, however, is closely similar to that of land animals.

This is a very simplified version of a very complicated subject. To begin with, there is no hard-and-fast line to be drawn between plankton, nekton, and benthos. For example, the larva of a coral is a free-swimming larva and therefore planktonic; but the adult is benthic. The larval fish is planktonic, and the adult nektonic. Moreover, we have outstanding exceptions, such as the large blue whales of the Antarctic. These are powerful swimmers, therefore nektonic; but they feed on krill, a minute shrimp-like animal which drifts in its millions with the currents. Thus the whales follow the krill and their distribution, which is planktonic.

ANIMAL LANGUAGE. Man alone is able to convey precise information to his fellows through speech. But although only he, when hungry, can ask for the particular food he wants, many other animals can show that they are hungry, and to that extent have a language or means of communication. Thus, when hungry, a lamb will bleat, a lion will roar, a dog will fawn upon his master. The difference between human and animal language is, therefore, that whereas an animal can show by voice, gesture, or other sign that it is in a certain emotional or physical state—such as hungry, tired, frightened, playful, and so on—man is able to express such feelings in precise terms, and to indicate not only that he is hungry, but what he wishes to eat, not only that he is afraid, but of what he is afraid.

Apart from speech, however, man still retains certain features of animal language. Laughter, usually considered as peculiarly human, is language of this sort: a Zulu, hearing an Englishman laugh, understands his feeling; though if the Englishman tried to describe why he laughed, the Zulu would probably not understand. So it is with tears, sobs, screams, and other primitive language sounds, as well as gestures and bodily movements: these are universal just because they are primitive, and because they indicate the emotional state of the person who makes them, without any further attempt at definition.

It is not only by such simple sounds as most of the mammals produce that animals can show their state of feeling: the song of birds, for example, is far more elaborate and highly developed. It is produced in the lower part of the larynx, in a portion known as the syrinx—a great variety of sounds resulting, continuous chirrups, raucous croaks, sweet and varied musical notes, cries of alarm, and shrieks of rage. True bird-song has two main purposes. Many male birds sing in order to warn off other males of their own kind from intruding into their breeding territory. Many also sing to attract a mate to the territory (see ANIMAL TERRITORY). Some birds, therefore, like the Nightingale, sing only during the breeding season; others, which sing all the year round, are at their best at this period. Song is most used by birds which would otherwise find it difficult to communicate with each other— birds living scattered in the woods, hedges, and fields, and small birds with inconspicuous plumage. Large conspicuous birds or those living in flocks do not usually sing.

Another form of animal language is that known as display. The strutting PEACOCK with his fanned and gorgeous tail, the magnificent BIRD OF PARADISE displaying his plumes in dance, the great crested GREBES shaking their fantastically adorned heads at one another, or the BLACKBIRD (qq.v.) with the feathers of his

rump raised up and his tail pressed on the ground—all these are showing their readiness to mate and breed. These displays are confined to this special use just as much as song is confined to its uses, or as other forms of display are employed to frighten off an intruder, to lure away an enemy, or even to submit to a superior. The ROBIN, for instance, will raise up his beak and sway from side to side, waving his red danger signal at a rival; a SNIPE disturbed at her nest will flutter away as if she were injured, with dragging wings, and so lure an inquisitive dog or man far from her eggs; and a JACKDAW will bow his head and expose the pale grey patch on his nape in submission, like a dog with his tail between his legs. Other forms of display are used when birds are looking for a site for their nest, when they are warning their chicks to hide, or inviting them to fly. The cock REDSTART (qq.v.) has a series of displays by which he induces the hen to begin the nest, which she alone builds, in a hole which he alone selects. If one of his displays fails, he will try the others.

Though these displays seem so clearly directed to achieve their end, it must not be supposed that the bird can perceive that end, or that he deliberately tries to bring it about. The displaying bird is doing no more than expressing his own emotional or physiological state. The hen responds because this expression brings something new into her environment, and her response is likewise no more than an expression of her state, though that may have been changed by her perception of the male's display.

The language of birds, because of the complexity of their lives, is more elaborate and more apparently purposeful than the language of other groups of animals. Yet it is no more remarkable than the language of many insects. In this, though sound plays some part, as with crickets and grasshoppers, and though some beetles make gestures with their armoured legs, and other insects with their wings or tails, the most elaborate displays are connected with scent and the sense of smell. This sense lies in the antennae, but the scent scales are situated in various parts of the body. In most British butterflies the male's scent scales are on the upper part of the wing. In some species, such as the GRAYLING (q.v.) (whose scent is like the wood of an old cigar-box), the male will stand before the female, waving his wings slowly to direct the scent towards her, and she will touch the scented patches

Blackcock displaying its tail feathers on the 'lek', or communal mating ground. *G. K. Yeates*

Above. The Ruff displaying before the Reeve (hen).
Harold Bastin

Right. Superb Bird of Paradise displaying.
Harold Bastin

Greyheaded Albatrosses courting. *C. A. Gibson-Hill*

MALE BIRDS DISPLAYING BEFORE THE FEMALES AS PART OF THEIR COURTSHIP with her antennae. Many female butterflies and moths have scents which lead the males to them, but these scents are not perceptible by man. The scents of the male, on the other hand, can be detected by man, and it is a surprising fact that most of them are pleasing to us as well as to the female insect.

It is not possible here to do more than suggest something of the immense variety of means by which animals of all classes communicate with one another. But it must be remembered that, since no animal except man has the power to reflect, and therefore the power to foresee, animal language is limited to the expression of an emotional or physiological state. They are not able to form ideas, or to define their needs or desires as we can; but by expressing their own feelings, they affect the consciousness of their companions, mates, offspring, or enemies, and so avoid the chaos which would ensue if they had no language.

See also VOICE.

ANIMAL TERRITORY. Many animals live in flocks, herds, or shoals, while others live a more or less solitary life for most of the year. But whether they live with others of their own kind or not, during the breeding season almost all animals keep their own small family isolated to some extent. This is more obvious in those which have only one mate, such as the fox, but is no less true of deer and seals, which are polygamous.

The segregation of a mated pair, or of a group of animals, is brought about because the male adopts an area which he regards as his own property or territory, and which he will defend against any intruder of his own species. The area defended may be extremely small, or it may cover a wide tract of land; but in either case it will be sufficient to secure freedom for its owner to breed without disturbance, and without the wasteful fighting which animals of all kinds (except man) have learnt to avoid. The supreme end of life for all living creatures, whether plant or animal, is the reproduction of their own kind, and their survival is, obviously, dependent on their success in achieving this. If, as was once supposed, male animals regularly fought for their mates, there would soon be very few males left. Where fighting does take place, it is usually for the sake of a territory, and not for a mate. The habit of holding a territory is

clearly related to the supply of food, and is therefore supremely important during the breeding season when the young are arriving—for not only do they require, proportionately to their size, a greater quantity of food, but they are also often unable to move about in search of it. Moreover, although the habit is most marked in birds, in certain mammals, and in such insects as dragonflies, it is obvious that to a lesser degree all species must have developed this habit of spacing themselves out—which is all the habit of holding territory amounts to.

As this behaviour was first noticed in birds, and has been most carefully studied in them, it may be as well to give examples from these. In spring, birds begin to return to the places where they will breed, either from overseas (*see* MIGRATION) or from the flock in which they gathered during the winter. The first to arrive, whether a Swallow or a Cuckoo from Africa, a Chaffinch from the flock in the neighbouring rick-yard, or a Lapwing from a flock in the meadows, will almost always be a male. And, often quite gradually, this male bird will settle down in some place where it is going to breed— at first, perhaps, returning for part of the day to the flock which it has just left, or associating with several other birds with which it arrived from migration. But soon, especially if the weather is fine, it will grow more and more intolerant of the presence of others of its kind. Now, if a Finch or Lapwing had to drive off all the trespassing Finches or Lapwings by fighting, it would soon become exhausted. Also, since the male has arrived first, some means must be found whereby the female, when she arrives, can find a mate. It is to meet these difficulties that male birds have developed their remarkable songs. The bird, once established in its territory, begins to sing, thereby warning other males of its kind not to trespass within hearing, at the same time informing arriving females where a mate of their own kind is to be found. Many birds, when singing, make themselves as conspicuous as possible—by perching on the topmost twig of a tree, like the Thrush, by flying high in the air over the fields, as the Skylark does. The Lapwing, which does not sing, often indulges in some aerobatic display.

Some birds of prey hold a territory covering many acres of moorland in which all the food for the pair and for their chicks will be found. The Finches and Thrushes of our gardens lay

claim, perhaps, to only an acre or less of territory, for these birds have a very varied diet, and
they can find all they require in a small area.
The Swallows and many sea-birds hold a territory covering only a few square feet about the
nest, for these birds range far and wide through
the air or over the sea for their food, and all they
require is space enough to lay their eggs without
disturbance. But the principle is the same in all.

Those birds with no song usually have a very
small territory, which they defend by visual
means. The Razorbill and Guillemot, for instance, defend their cliff territory by gesture and
display; Ducks can see any intruder coming over
the open water, and can warn them off by visual
means. Also, the pairing of these birds takes
place during the winter in the flock, so that there
is no question of the male needing to make his
presence known to the female.

Mammals achieve the same isolation during
breeding by much the same means. They have
no song, but the stag roars, and so warns off his
rivals, and other mammals, as well as reptiles
and fishes, make threatening sounds or gestures
which serve the same purpose as the song of
birds. Insects, too, often have their own territory, the grasshopper's reeling and the cricket's
chirrup serving to warn off rivals and to attract
mates.

Normally, territory is defended only against
animals of the same species. Thus in the same
garden, Blackbird and Thrush, Robin, Dunnock, and Wren, Chaffinch and Greenfinch,
Swallow and House Martin, may all have breeding territories overlapping one another, without
any rivalry between them. Tits of different
species, which all require holes in which to
breed, may quarrel over some particular hole or
nest-box, and contests of this sort do take place.
But for most birds any number of suitable places
are available, and if rivals of their own species
are kept away, no trouble arises from others.

When the breeding season is over and the
young are independent of their parents, territory is held no longer, except by a very few
species—of which, in Britain, the ROBIN (q.v.)
is the best known. Robins of both sexes hold
territory outside the breeding season, and the
hen Robin sings so that she may preserve it.
(Song is quite exceptional in hen birds of other
species.) After the breeding season, a hundred
or more seals may be seen basking together on
the same rock, huge flocks of Geese and Waders

come to our estuaries and feed peacefully side
by side, and in the stubbles and rick-yards the
little birds that sang so vigorously not long
before to segregate themselves from their fellows,
now peck about together without concern.

See also ANIMAL LANGUAGE.

ANOA, see BUFFALO.

ANT-EATER. This mammal belongs to the
order of animals called Edentata (without teeth),
which includes also the SLOTHS and ARMADILLOS
(qq.v.). All members of this order are to be
found only in South or Central America. All
Edentata have relatively small brains and are
without front teeth, or, like the ant-eater, have
no teeth at all.

Ant-eaters live in tropical forests or low, wet
lands near rivers. The best-known of them
(though none are at all common) is the Great
Ant-eater. This is a large animal, standing
about 2 feet high and measuring about 6 feet
from head to tip of tail. It is a most fantastic-
looking creature. It has an extremely long,
narrow head; its body is covered with dark grey
hair, marked with black bands margined with
white; it has an enormous mass of long, stiff hair
on its tail, making it appear like a huge brush;
its front legs are long and very powerful; and
its front feet have curved claws, one of which is
much longer than the others.

The Great Ant-eater lives entirely on the
ground, and only comes out by night. During
the day it curls itself up, covering its body with
its great tail, the hairs of which fall down on
either side, hiding it very effectively among the
tall grasses where it makes its lair. Its food consists chiefly of termites and ants and their larvae.
It rips open their nests with the long curved claw
of its front foot; then, when the ants rush out,
it licks them up with its immensely long, sticky
tongue, which goes in and out of its mouth with
lightning speed. Except during the mating season the ant-eaters generally live alone. They are
not at all aggressive animals, but, if cornered,
they are said to turn and attack fiercely, their
method of attack being to catch their enemies in
their great muscular arms and crush them by
hugging.

Another species, the Lesser Ant-eater (Taman-
dua), is only about half the size, and has a shorter
head, short, bristly hair, and a long, but not hairy,
tail. It spends most of its life in trees, and climbs

THE LESSER ANT-EATER
Booth Steamship Co.

with the use of its prehensile tail as well as its claws. It is rather more common than its larger relation and is sometimes seen abroad during the day. The third species, the Pigmy or Two-toed Ant-eater, is very much smaller, no larger than a rat. It lives only in the hottest forest regions of South and Central America, and because of its size, its nocturnal habits, and the fact that it lives in the trees, it is very rarely seen. It hangs on to the branches of trees with its curved claws and its prehensile tail, and sleeps by day in a hollow tree-trunk.

The AARD-VARK or Ant-bear and the PAN-GOLIN (qq.v.) used to be included in the order Edentata, but are now classified differently.

ANTELOPE. 1. Antelopes are among the most grace-ful animals in the world. They live in various types of country—plains, forests, mountains, and marshes. They are herbivorous—that is, they eat mostly grass and the leaves of trees —ruminating or chewing the cud in the same way as the DEER and CATTLE, SHEEP, and GOATS (qq.v.). Whereas deer shed their antlers annually, the ante-lope's horns are part of the skull itself and remain throughout its life, as in cattle and sheep. The horns vary a great deal in shape and size: with some species they are curved or twisted in spirals, with others they are quite straight. Those

of the handsome African Kudus are sometimes 4 feet long, whereas those of the Dickerboks are only from 3 to 4 inches. Antelopes also vary greatly in size, from the Eland, nearly 6 feet high, to the tiny Pigmy Antelopes of Africa, only 12 inches high and little larger than a rabbit. The following are some of the best-known.

2. The Gazelles are a large group of smallish, sandy-coloured antelopes, found in Africa and parts of Asia. One species, called the Gerenuk, has such a long neck that it is often likened to a miniature giraffe. Another species, the Spring-bok of South Africa, gets its name from its habit of suddenly leaping into the air when it is run-ning. Vast herds of Springboks used to migrate from one district to another, in masses so dense that if they met a flock of sheep, the sheep would be inevitably swept along with them. Now, the Springboks are comparatively rare.

3. The Gnus or Wildebeests are large, un-gainly antelopes, with short, broad heads, long, hairy tails and manes, and broad heavy horns, rather like those of a buffalo. Their eyes are small, and their general appearance is uncouth and ungainly. There are few uglier beasts. Large herds used to be seen on the veld in South Africa; but to-day only a few are kept in game preserves, though large herds are still found in East Africa. The Hartebeests of South,

WATERBUCK WITH MAGNIFICENT LYRATE-SHAPED HORNS. *Paul Popper*

East, and West Africa are also fairly large, about 4 feet high, with long, narrow faces, and horns curved sharply backwards.

4. The largest antelopes, the Elands, are found only in Africa. They stand nearly 6 feet high, and both sexes have twisted horns from 2 to 3 feet long. They live both in semi-desert and in wooded country. Among the small antelopes are the Steinboks, the Grysboks, and the Klipspringers, which live in the mountains of Africa. The Klipspringer, whose name means 'rock-jumper', is able to bound up the sides of very steep cliffs, and has very small hoofs which enable it to stand safely on narrow ledges. Indeed, the hoofs are so small that the animal can take advantage of a projection of rock no larger than a penny to obtain a foothold in leaping. The Marshbucks, or Situtungas, which also live in Africa, have long, spreading hoofs which enable them to walk on marshy land and on the soft banks of streams and lakes.

Of the Indian antelopes, the largest is the Nilgai, sometimes called the 'Blue Bull', from the colour of the adult males. It stands about 5 feet high, has a mane on its neck, and a fringed tail, and is a rather ungainly animal. Only the males have horns—short, curved, and very sharp.

See also CHAMOIS.

ANTENNAE, *see* INSECT; MOTHS.

ANTLER-MOTH, *see* NIGHT-FLYING MOTHS.

ANTS. These insects belong to one large family, the Formicidae, which, together with the Apoidea (BEES, q.v.) and the Vespoidea (WASPS, q.v.), is included in the order Hymenoptera.

About 8,000 different kinds of ants are known, most of which are found in the tropics. With very few exceptions, they are social insects, living in communities which may contain as few as a dozen individuals or as many as several hundred thousand. The colony is made up of one or more perfect females, usually called 'queens', a large number of imperfect females, called 'workers', and, at the right time of the year, many males. These three different forms of ants are known as 'castes'. The worker ant, like the workers of the Hive Bee, the Bumble Bees, and the Social Wasps, does not produce offspring. Many kinds of ants have two forms of the worker caste, simple workers and 'soldiers'. The soldiers have enormous heads, which seem out of all proportion to the size of the rest

WORKER   QUEEN

MALE   SOLDIER

of the body. Although these curious workers are called soldiers, their role is by no means only to protect the colony. The huge head has made possible the development of powerful muscles. These give great strength to the pair of large mandibles, with which the soldier is able to crush seeds and insects. Only the queens and males have wings, but the queens remove theirs immediately after the marriage flight. The workers and queens of some kinds of ants are armed with a sting, which they use for defence. There are also many species which have no sting, but are able, instead, to squirt formic acid from a special gland situated at the tail-end of the body. Such an ant is *Formica rufa*, the Wood Ant. If one of its large, dome-shaped nests, built as a rule out of pine needles, is disturbed, the acid squirted up by the seething mass of ants may be seen rising as a fine spray.

The Queen Ant lays eggs, which hatch into legless grubs or larvae. These larvae are looked after by the worker ants, who carry them about and place them in whatever part of the nest seems at the time best for them. The workers are very sensitive to warmth and humidity, both of which are necessary for the growth of the larvae. For warmth they rely very much on the heat brought by the sun's rays—which is why, in warm, damp weather, the ant larvae will be found near the surface of the soil; but in cold or very dry weather, the workers carry the larvae deep down into the ground, where the soil is moist and the temperature higher. The grubs receive either liquid or solid food from the workers. The liquid food is stored by the ants in their crop, and taken back to the nest to be shared out amongst the brood. During feeding,

AUSTRALIAN BIRDS IN COURTSHIP DISPLAY

1. The Satin Bower-bird decorates his 'bower' with shells
2. The Lyre-bird displays his magnificent tail to the female

the worker places its mouth against that of the larva, and forces up from its crop a droplet of liquid, which is eagerly swallowed by the grub. The solid food is cut up into small fragments and placed within reach of the grubs.

When the larvae become full grown, they change into pupae. The larvae of some kinds of ants, among which is the Wood Ant, spin a cocoon before pupating. (It is the cocoons of the Wood Ant which are sold for feeding Gold-fish, as 'ants eggs'.) Others make the change without any protection. After a time there emerges from the pupa an adult ant, which may be a queen, a male, cr a worker. It is important to notice that each individual ant-larva is not confined during its growth within a cell, like the larvae of the social bees and wasps. The absence of the cell-building habit in ants has certainly been useful to them, because, if for some reason a nesting site becomes unsuitable, many kinds of ants are able to move to a new one, taking with them their eggs, larvae, and pupae.

The marriage flight of ants in this country usually takes place on still, sultry days towards the end of summer. The flights that we are likely to observe will be those of the common Black Garden Ant (*Lasius niger*). The tiny males and huge females leave the nests in enormous numbers, flying into the air in clouds. Pairing takes place in flight, and afterwards the females drift slowly down, with the males still attached to their bodies. Once the female reaches the ground, she quickly throws off the male, re-moves her wings, and is then ready to set about the business of starting a home.

The methods by which queen ants make their homes are many, and only a few can be men-tioned here. The fertilized female or queen may found her colony without any help at all, just as the queen Wasp and the queen Bumble Bee do. Or she may rely on the help of ants from strange colonies, belonging to a different species from herself. Or she may return to the nest from which she first came, which now, having per-haps several queens, may become so populous that a number of smaller colonies are split or budded off from it.

Among the ants which found their colonies without help is the common Black Garden Ant, mentioned earlier. The fertilized queen burrows into the ground, and hollows out for herself a small cell or chamber. She carefully blocks the entrance to this cell, and does not leave it again until she has brought up her first brood of workers. For roughly 9 months she remains a voluntary prisoner, and takes no food at all. How, then, does she feed her small brood of larvae? It must be remembered that when our queen ant set to work to bring up a family, her body was plump and well nourished. Now, by drawing on these fat reserves, she is able to keep up a constant supply of the special saliva on which she feeds her larvae. True, these larvae produce undersized ants; but these are vigorous, and very soon tunnel their way through to the surface of the ground to find food for themselves and their mother.

More exciting and adventurous ways of start-ing family life are shown by the queens of those species of ants which must have help during this critical period of their lives. The queen of the Slave-maker Ant (*Formica sanguinea*) must seek out a nest of *Formica fusca* and steal some of its pupae. She hides these away in some little cavity in the ground, taking care of them until they become adult ants, capable of bringing up the offspring of their foster-mother. The queens of other species somehow manage to get them-selves accepted by the workers of an alien colony as members of the community. Such an ant is *Lasius fuliginosus*, a shiny, jet-black ant which is fairly common in Great Britain, and whose rather slow-moving workers march in long files to and from their nest. The fertilized queen enters the nest of *Lasius umbratus* (a yellow ant which spends most of its life underground), and is treated as a friend by the yellow ants. What happens to their own queen-mother is not quite clear; but after a while, black *fuliginosus* workers appear among the yellow ants. The two species, so sharply contrasted in colour, work peacefully together, until finally the yellow ants die out, and the colony consists only of the black *fuliginosus*.

Ants like a mixed diet, being especially fond of sweet things. They feed eagerly upon a secretion given out by Plant-lice or APHIDS (q.v.). If a plant infested with Aphids is looked at closely, the ants will often be seen crawling about over the dense mass of greenfly, gently tapping them with their antennae, and quickly sucking up the droplet of fluid which is ejected by the Aphids, from the vent at the end of their bodies. This fluid is rich in sugar. Ants also devour great numbers of insects, not seeming to mind whether an insect is dead or alive so long as it can be dragged or carried back to the nest. A few species feed almost entirely on the seeds of plants, while others get all the nourishment they need from certain kinds of fungus. Ants generally feed on whatever is available in the place where the particular species lives.

See also INSECTS.

ANTS, HABITS OF.

So varied are the habits of ants that no more than a few of them can be examined here.

In South America some of the most abundant ants are the so-called Umbrella, or Leaf-cutting Ants, known as *Atta*. They are to be seen in great columns, each ant carrying a large piece of leaf over its head. The Attas, it seems, are expert gardeners, and grow a fungus in large hollows which they dig out in the soil. But a fungus will grow only on dead and decaying organic matter, and so the ants chew up into tiny fragments the pieces of leaf, and with them make a kind of mushroom bed in which the spores of the fungus will germinate and grow. Certain parts of the fungus form the main diet of the ants and their larvae. Now the Attas usually live in dry desert regions, where food in the form of insects is not easy to obtain: by cultivating a fungus and getting their nourishment from it, they are not worried by a shortage of other kinds of food.

In the drier parts of the world, where plant as well as animal life is scarce, other kinds of ants have solved the food problem quite differently from the Attas. In the deserts of North America, for example, live the Harvesting Ants, known as *Pogonomyrmex*. Although they will eat insects whenever they can get them, they normally rely for food on the seeds of various plants, which they gather and store. Even more remarkable are the Honey-pot Ants, likewise inhabitants of desert regions in various parts of the world. These ants set aside some of their sister workers to become living reservoirs of food. They feed them with juices until their abdomens become enormously swollen—so much so, indeed, that in the case of one species living in North America, *Myrmecocystus horti-deorum*, the self-sacrificing workers are unable to move. They hang motionless from the roof of their underground chambers, like so many barrels of wine, waiting to be tapped when other sources of food dry up.

The three kinds of ants that have just been mentioned all nest in the ground. This habit is shared by most species of ants; but there are a great many kinds that make their homes only in trees and shrubs. Perhaps the best known of these is *Oecophylla smaragdina*, an ant to be found in numbers all over the tropics of the Far East. Its nest is just a mass of leaves, drawn together and held fast by means of fine silken threads. Now, no adult ant has spinning glands; but the larvae of *Oecophylla* spin cocoons, and so they are cleverly used by the worker ants as living tools for spinning together the leaves out of which the nest is made.

The Dorylina or Driver Ants of Africa have strange nomadic habits, and work together in an almost uncanny way. Except for short periods, when they settle down in one spot, they are ever on the move, marching in long files many thousands strong and sweeping every living thing out of their path. They are meat-eaters, and will devour any animal that, by sheer weight of numbers, they can torment to death. If a human dwelling happens to stand in the path of the moving column, the ants will enter it and quickly rid it of spiders, cockroaches, and beetles. The astonishing fact about these ants is that the workers of which this vast crawling army is composed are entirely blind—and yet they have no difficulty in keeping together, or in uniting their efforts for a particular purpose. They communicate with each other by means of sense organs of which we understand very little at present.

Some ants have acquired the habit of keeping other ants as slaves. Some kinds cannot live at all without their slaves; others need them only when their colonies are small, but can do without them when the colonies become sufficiently populous. Of the latter type is the large handsome *Formica sanguinea*, in appearance very much like the common Wood Ant, but much brighter in colour and more rapid in its movements. It usually lives in dry places, such as the sandy heaths of southern England, and can often be seen on hot sunny days running nimbly over the ground. It often makes its nest in the stump of a pine tree. If we break off a piece of the decayed bark, we may very likely find a great many ants, with their brood, crowded beneath it. They will come out in a flurry of angry excitement, and we shall notice that, in addition to the large numbers of pugnacious red-coloured slave-

HABITS OF ANTS

1. Worker of Tree Ant, using larva for spinning threads; 2. Head of Driver Ant, showing tong-like mandibles; 3. Head of Slave-maker Ant, showing sickle-shaped mandibles; 4. Workers of Tree Ant using larvae to fasten edges of leaves together; 5. Worker of Honey-pot Ant, showing swollen abdomen; 6. Fungus gardens of Leaf-cutter Ant.

makers, there are many smaller ants, bronzy black in colour. These are the slaves, and they belong to a species called *Formica fusca*. These timid workers are no worse off in the colony of *Formica sanguinea* than they would be in their own: they tend the brood, forage for food, and altogether take a full share in the running of the community. What is interesting about these slave ants is not that they settle down so peacefully among strangers, but the manner in which they have been brought into the strange colony—the details of the slave-raid itself. Scouts of the red slave-maker having discovered the whereabouts of a nest of *Formica fusca*, the raid is made on some warm summer's day. The *sanguinea* ants come out of their holes in great numbers and, forming themselves into a rather loose band, make their way towards the nest of the black ant. As soon as they reach it, they rush boldly in, scattering the inhabitants, who begin to flee in confusion. Each *sanguinea* ant seizes a cocoon of the *fusca* and at once makes for home with it. Should a bolder *fusca* worker attempt to prevent a raider from carrying off its booty, a savage bite from the powerful mandibles of the slave-maker quickly puts it out of action. From these stolen cocoons eventually emerge the adult *fusca* workers, who from that time live in complete harmony with their captors.

Another and much more thorough-going slave-maker, *Polyergus rufescens*, is to be found on the continent of Europe, but not in Great Britain. The workers of this species are able neither to dig their nest nor to look after their brood—in fact, they are scarcely able even to feed themselves. They have become parasitic upon the ants they enslave, and cannot live without them. These Amazons of the ant world are blood-red in colour and have long, sickle-shaped mandibles, well fitted to pierce the heads of the ants whose colonies they plunder and pillage. The timid, black *Formica fusca* is again usually the victim. The raids made by *Formica sanguinea* seem clumsy affairs by comparison with the extremely well-organized raids of *Polyergus rufescens*. Arriving in almost military formation at a nest of the *fusca*, the Amazon ants pour into it, killing or driving out the numerous *fusca* workers, and seizing their cocoons. The late August Forel, a great expert on ants, made a series of observations on a colony of the Amazons, and estimated that the number of slave-makers in it was round about 1,000, and that the number of cocoons of slave-ants taken by them in one season was not far short of 20,000. Of all these stolen cocoons, only a small proportion eventually produce adult ants, the others being either killed by rough handling or consumed as food.

One species of ant, occurring in north Africa, and called *Bothriomyrmex decapitans*, has a particularly interesting method of starting its colony. After her marriage flight, the queen *Bothriomyrmex* wanders about over the ground until she finds a nest of another ant, *Tapinoma nigerrimum*. She is seized at once by the workers of *Tapinoma* and dragged into their nest. They treat her roughly, and unless she can find a means of protecting herself, she is likely to be severely mauled. She therefore mounts on to the back of the much larger *Tapinoma* queen, where for some reason she is safe from further attack. But for the *Tapinoma* queen this unwelcome load means certain death. Slowly and deliberately the *Bothriomyrmex* female begins to saw off with her strong mandibles the head of her rival. By the time this murderous deed is accomplished, she has acquired the nest odour of the *Tapinoma* colony and now moves about among the workers without fear of being molested by them. The workers bring up her brood, and the colony eventually becomes pure *Bothriomyrmex decapitans* —for the *Tapinoma* population, having now no queen of its own, gradually dies out.

APES (Anthropoid). **1.** Under the term 'ape' might be included not only the anthropoid or manlike apes, but also all the MONKEYS (q.v.), which belong to the same order as Man—the Primates. But this article is concerned only with the manlike apes—the Chimpanzee, Gorilla, Orang-utan, and Gibbon. Structurally, these animals are very much like man. They have hands adapted for grasping, though their feet, in contrast to man's, are adapted for grasping as well as for walking—the big toe being opposed to the other toes, as man's thumb is opposed to his fingers. In contrast to monkeys, they have no tails or cheek pouches, and have larger and more developed brains than any other animal except man—but even then the relative size of the brain is half or less than half that of man. The skulls of the manlike apes are very little different in shape from those of the ape-men, the earliest ancestors of modern man (*see* EVOLUTION OF MAN, Vol. I). The apes have longer arms and shorter legs than man, because they are adapted to a greater (Orang-utan) or lesser (Gorilla) degree for life in trees. They produce only one young one at a birth, as do all kinds of monkeys except Marmosets.

2. CHIMPANZEES. Of all the large manlike apes, the Chimpanzee of west and central Africa comes nearest to man in bodily structure, and has been the longest known to Europeans. A fully grown male is not more than 5 feet high, and when standing upright his arms reach only a short distance below the knee. The young animal has a bare face which is nearly white, though it usually darkens and often becomes

CHIMPANZEE   *Harold Bastin*

completely black later on. Chimpanzees live in forests and keep together in family parties, building a resting platform rather low in the trees. They eat fruit, nuts, and many kinds of green food, and seem continually to shift their haunts in order to find fresh feeding-grounds. Sometimes they visit and pillage deserted native plantations. They utter loud cries, which may be heard resounding through the forest at all hours of the night. Young chimpanzees are affectionate and intelligent, though apt to become rather uncertain in temper as they grow older. They used to be regarded as delicate, and were given hot-house treatment in zoos, which caused them to die very early; but now that they are given normal conditions, they live healthily for many years, and prove to be comparatively hardy.

3. GORILLA. This is the largest of the manlike apes, a full-grown male being as much as 6 feet high and weighing 40 stone. Gorillas live in family parties in the densest parts of the forests of Equatorial Africa, travelling from district to district in search of food, such as wild fruits, the juicy stalks of wild celery, the roots of plants, and leaves. They walk on all-fours, with their hands closed and the knuckles resting on the ground. Until quite recently, this huge ape was regarded as being very savage, and was supposed to live in the trees. This myth has now been completely exploded—gorillas are now known to be rather playful, docile, and peaceful animals, never attacking a man unless they are wounded, or in order to defend their young. Moreover, they do not live in trees—indeed they very rarely climb high up in trees, but spend most of their time on the ground, making beds or nests at the foot of trees or in the shelter of dense growths.

4. ORANG-UTAN. This manlike ape is found only in the swampy forests of Sumatra and Borneo. Its name, a Malayan word, means 'Man of the Woods'. Its brain is more like that of man than any other ape; but otherwise it is less like a human being in structure than are the Gorilla and Chimpanzee, and is far better adapted than they are for a life in trees, its legs being short and weak, but its arms long and very strong. The adult male is nearly 5 feet high, and grows large, fleshy flaps from the side of his face. He has a long, thick, reddish-brown coat—unusual for an animal living in such a hot climate, but it probably serves to protect the ape against the deluges of rain in the wet seasons and also against mosquitoes. The Orang-utan never leaps or jumps, and never seems to be in a hurry: the idea that he will make his way overhead in the forest as fast as a man can run on the ground below is not confirmed by modern observers, who all agree that he is slow and deliberate. He eats various fruits and leaves, gathering them with his long arms as he swings from bough to bough. He collects branches and leaves and builds a large sleeping-platform in the trees. Orang-utans live well under modern zoo conditions, one having recently lived to be over 30 years old in the London Zoo.

5. GIBBONS. These, the smallest of the man-like apes, live in the forests of south-east Asia. There are about half a dozen species, the largest of which is not more than 3 feet high. Their arms are so long that, when standing upright, they can touch the ground with their fingers. They are the only apes which walk normally in an upright position. Sometimes they use their arms when walking; but they can walk perfectly well with their hands clasped behind their necks. Gibbons live in family parties in the trees, rarely coming to the ground. They are extraordinarily agile, and swing from branch to branch and tree to tree without seeming to make any effort. They move so fast that they often succeed in capturing birds flying among the trees. As well as birds, they eat fruit and leaves. Their cries in the morning are loud and almost unearthly. On the whole, tamed Gibbons have an amiable and affectionate nature, though they appear to take a mischievous pleasure, as children sometimes do, in doing what they know is forbidden. Despite the greatest care, they do not live long in captivity in Europe.

See also MONKEYS: LEMURS.

APHIS. Those who grow roses know only too well that, in early summer, the young shoots are often crowded with a dense mass of green insects of varying size, which do much harm to the rose trees. They appear very suddenly, apparently from nowhere, and increase in numbers with great rapidity. In the vegetable garden, also, the same thing happens on the broad beans; but the insects that appear here—with equal suddenness and crowded together in similar masses—are black in colour. These are two examples from a large group of insects called Aphides. Those that infest rose-trees are usually called Green-flies or Plant-lice, and the insect that attacks the broad bean is known as the Black Dolphin or Black Blight.

Aphides, like all bugs, have their mouth-parts arranged like a beak, for piercing tissues and sucking juices through the wound. All Aphides live upon plants and often do them serious damage in several ways. They suck the juices, so that the plant loses much valuable material; they may cause malformations, such as galls or curled and twisted leaves; they may clog the pores of the leaves by means of a gummy secretion, usually called 'honey-dew'; or they may convey disease from an unhealthy plant to a healthy one, when they puncture the tissues. Some species of Aphis secrete by glands in the skin a white waxy substance that gives them a powdery or mealy appearance; in others this waxy substance may be produced in considerable quantity, making up a white woolly mass beneath which the Aphides live. The insect called the Woolly Aphis, introduced from America, is usually first noticed when long streamers of waxy substance are found hanging down from the bark of an apple-tree.

The life-history of an Aphis exhibits a number of interesting features. In the first place, these insects are capable of 'parthenogenesis'—in other words, a series of generations is raised in succession from female parents alone, the male insect never appearing. Then they are also capable of 'viviparity', which means that for a number of successive generations the young Aphides are born alive, instead of being hatched from eggs. As a result of these two peculiarities, the Aphis can make almost fantastic increases in numbers. Another interesting feature is that the Aphis will sometimes spend part of its life upon one plant and the remainder upon a plant of an entirely different species.

As a rule, the winter is passed in the egg. In the autumn, male and female Aphides are found together on the same tree; and after pairing, the female lays her eggs in places of safety, such as chinks in the bark. These eggs hatch in the following spring, and the minute Aphides immediately attack the food-plant, puncturing its tissues and sucking its juices. They grow up quickly, and, when adult, are all wingless females. These rapidly produce offspring, which are born alive. Generation after generation of female Aphides may be produced in this way in rapid succession, and enormous numbers of Aphides of all sizes gather together on one particular stem or leaf. Then, in the midst of all these appear other youngsters, born parthenogenetically and viviparously, as described above. These grow up into winged females, and fly away to carry the infection to other plants, often in such enormous numbers that they make quite a dense mass. New colonies are thus founded in fresh situations; and further series of generations follow rapidly until, in late summer, males appear again, and eggs are laid as in the previous year.

Some species of Aphis are found, so far as we know, on only one species of plant. Others, when they fly away, travel to a different species from the one they left, and their descendants find their way back to the original kind of plants. Thus the black Bean Aphis produces, on the bean, winged females in the summer. These fly to the spindle-tree. Here they produce female offspring that are able to lay eggs. These females are joined by males that have also flown there from bean plants; eggs are laid, and the colony of adults dies out. In spring, the eggs on the spindle-tree hatch, and in the new colonies which soon develop there winged females appear and fly to the beans. These females, which reach the bean plants singly, are probably not noticed at first, but soon the young shoots are covered with masses of black Aphides. The

Leaf-curling Currant Aphis flies to lettuce and sow-thistles in June and July. The Currant-root Aphis spends autumn, winter, and spring on the elm, where it breeds. Most Apple and Plum Aphides seem to confine themselves to these trees; but one species, the Damson-hop Aphis, lays its eggs on plum or sloe trees, hatches there in the spring, and then, when winged forms appear, they fly to the hop, returning

ARCHER-FISH CATCHING PREY
A. Fraser-Brunner

to the plum-tree in the autumn. The Woolly Aphis seems to confine itself to the apple-tree, as does the Strawberry Aphis to the Strawberry plant.

The sweet sticky material, honey-dew, is very popular with ants, which may often be found running up the stems of aphis-infested plants in order to obtain their share. They even, it is said, stroke the aphides with their antennae to encourage them into supplying more liberal quantities (*see* ANT).

See also BUG.
See also Vol. VI: INSECT PESTS.

ARCHER-FISH. This is a small fish, rather like the PERCH (q.v.), usually 6 to 8 inches long, which inhabits the fresh waters of the East Indian region. It is yellow, with broad black bands or spots, and gets its name from its habit of lying just below the surface of the water beneath overhanging plants, on which it can watch for insects to settle. When its prey appears, it shoots a jet of water upwards along a groove in the roof of its mouth, knocking the insect into the water, where it is eaten. The fish can aim accurately over a distance of at least 5 feet.

ARGONAUT, *see* OCTOPUS.

ARMADILLO. This mammal, found only in South America, belongs to the same order as the ANT-EATER (q.v.). Armadillos are unique among mammals in possessing a more or less complete shield of bony scales in the skin, which forms an armour over the head, shoulders, back, and even legs and tail. The shield is made up of movable bands of scales, so that the armadillo can move its body freely or roll itself into a ball

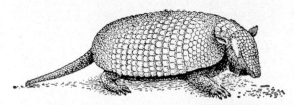

like a hedgehog. In some species a good deal of hair comes up between the scales—this is particularly true of the Long-haired Armadillo from Chile and Argentina, and of the Hairy Armadillo.

There are several kinds of armadillos living in various parts of South and Central America. They are mostly quite small: the largest, the

NINE-BANDED ARMADILLOS ON THE MARCH. *Paul Popper*

Giant Armadillo, which inhabits the forests of Surinam and Brazil, is only 3 feet from snout to base of tail. Traces, however, have been found of an extinct type reaching 6 or 7 feet in length. Armadillos are inoffensive creatures, living mainly on insects, especially ants. They dig into the ground with their very powerful claws and make burrows for their families. Except in the mating season, they usually live a solitary existence, and prefer flat, open country.

The smallest-known species is the Pichiciago (Fairy Armadillo), which is only 5 inches long, and has a pink scaled shield over its head and body and white fur underneath. It is to be found, though not at all commonly, in parts of Argentina, where it makes its burrow in the scorching hot sand. It hates both cold and wet.

ASH, *see* WOODLANDS, Section 4.

ASS. The Wild Ass or Donkey belongs to the same family as the HORSE (q.v.). The Abyssinian Wild Ass appears to be the direct ancestor of the domestic DONKEY (q.v. Vol. VI). It was domesticated in very early times by the ancient Egyptians, was brought to England in the 9th or 10th century, and is now used as a beast of burden in many parts of the world. Some of the domestic breeds, such as those produced in Spain, Italy, and the United States, are very fine, and much larger than the wild animal. There are only small numbers of African Wild Donkeys alive to-day. They are fine, strong, bluish-grey animals, large specimens standing about 12 hands at the withers. They move swiftly and gracefully, and their voice is the well-known bray.

The Asiatic Wild Ass, which is generally **a**

sandy-red colour, seems to be more or less untamable. It lives on open plains, often where there is little vegetation, its fleetness and sureness of foot enabling it to outrun most of its enemies. It is a remarkably silent animal, only occasionally uttering a stifled, suppressed bray. The largest species is the Kiang, which lives in Tibet and Mongolia, up to about 16,000 feet above sea-level. These are powerfully built animals, standing about 13 hands at the withers. They are never found far away from water, and, unlike the African ass, are strong and fearless swimmers, boldly crossing broad and swift-flowing rivers.

AUKS. 1. The Auk family (Alcidae) also includes the Razorbills, Guillemots, and Puffins. They all live in the cold regions of the northern hemisphere, some species migrating in the winter as far south as the Bay of Biscay or the coasts of Virginia. They all have heavy, compact bodies, and legs placed far back, with webbed feet. They feed on crustacea and small fish, and breed in colonies on rocky coasts, spending much of the rest of the year out at sea. All, except the Black Guillemot, usually lay only one egg.

The largest member of the family, the Great Auk, became extinct in the 19th century, after a relentless persecution for the sake of its feathers (*see* FEATHER HUNTING, Vol. VI). It was about the size of a goose, with such small wings that it could not fly. It was, however, an excellent swimmer and diver, and in winter carried out long migrations that way. The Little Auks, dapper little birds some 8½ inches long, fly each year in thousands from the Arctic regions, where they breed, down to the North Sea. Sometimes strong gales at sea force them close in shore, to escape the stormy waves.

2. THE RAZORBILL (or Lesser Auk) is often confused with the Guillemot, which it much resembles in size, build, and habits, and with whom it often lives. It differs from the Guillemot in being rather smaller (17 inches against 18 inches), in its characteristic thick

EXTINCT GREAT AUK

bill, and in certain of its habits. For instance, it feeds its young with small fish which it carries across the bill, several at a time—while the Guillemot carries one only, held lengthwise. The Razorbills congregate in large numbers at many points on the British coast and adjacent islands, generally preferring rough, stony ground, and sheer cliffs. They pair for life, and generally return to their last year's nesting site. Courtship is carried on by rubbing bills and nibbling at plumage, and the male shares in incubating and feeding the young. When the young Razorbill is about 3 or 4 weeks old, and before it can fly, its parents push it off its nesting ledge into the sea. As its nest may be as high as 500 feet above the sea, this leap is very perilous: its fluttering, weak wings may carry it clear of projecting rocks, but many come to grief.

3. THE GUILLEMOTS arrive in even greater numbers than the Razorbills to their nesting cliffs, crowding together so thickly that there seems to be no possible room for new-comers. But still more come, alighting on the backs of their fellows and waddling over them until they find a cranny into which to squeeze. This crowded community life gives them comparative protection from the attacks of their enemies, chiefly the Herring Gull. The Guillemots are true ocean birds, with legs so well adapted for swimming and diving that the birds are awkward on land and do not stand erect easily. They carry out an entertaining courtship, which involves odd bowing movements. The hen lays an egg (large for the size of the bird) on a bare cliff, with no attempt at a nest. During incubation she often holds the egg on her feet—after the manner of Penguins. The Black Guillemot is a smaller species, about 14 inches in length, which breeds on the rocky coasts of north Ireland, west Scotland, and the Scottish Isles.

4. THE PUFFIN is still smaller, about 12 inches, and is a strange-looking bird, with its grotesque, gaudy, orange and blue bill. It breeds on most rocky coasts of Britain, especially in the north and west. The Puffin lays her single egg in a burrow in the turf near the cliff top, and the male helps to dig the burrow, as well as to incubate and feed the young. He will fight fiercely for possession of his hole. Like most members of the Auk family, the Puffins are silent birds, but occasionally utter a deep, grumbling note.

AVOCET, *see* WADING BIRDS.

GUILLEMOTS ON RONA.   *Dr. F. Fraser Darling*

PUFFINS ON RONA.   *Dr. F. Fraser Darling*

B

BABOON. These grotesque-looking monkeys with their long, dog-like faces live in Africa and south-west Arabia. They are often very fierce, flying into a great rage if anything excites them. Instead of running away from a human being, as most animals instinctively do, they will turn round and face him with threatening gestures. The male baboons have most formidable tusk-like teeth—a baboon's bite is, in fact, almost as severe as a leopard's. As their arms and legs are about the same length, they feel much more at home on the ground than in trees, and though they can climb trees, most of them prefer homes in rocky places. On fairly flat ground they gallop almost as fast as a horse. They eat practically any food they come across—fruit, leaves, nuts, insects, young birds, and birds' eggs, and they frequently raid cultivated crops. They live in troops, with a powerful male as the leader. The baby baboon is at first carried by its mother, who holds it with one hand clasped to her breast, but later on it rides on her back as the troop moves from one place to another.

The Gelada of Abyssinia differs from the typical baboon in the shorter muzzle and in the structure of the skull. It is, however, a true baboon in its habits and general appearance. It is blackish-brown and has a massive mane on its shoulders. The Drill and the Mandrill are also large, powerful baboons, differing from the typical baboons in having very short tails and a greater inclination to resort to trees. They live in West Africa, and spend much of their time on the ground; but they are never far away from the forest trees, in which they sleep and take refuge from danger. The Mandrill is a gro-tesque-looking animal, having on its face large blue swollen ridges, a bright carmine-red nose, and a yellow beard. The hair on its hind-quarters is very scanty, showing rainbow-coloured skin underneath. The Drill has a shiny black, bare face, bordered with whitish fur.

See also MONKEY.

BACTERIA. The microscopic bacteria are, ex-cept for the VIRUS (q.v.), the simplest and lowliest of living organisms. They are usually classified with the plants and are probably most nearly allied to FUNGI (q.v.). They are generally colour-less, and are found everywhere—in the air, in the soil, in water, and in the bodies of all living things. Some are ball-shaped, 'cocci'; some are rod-shaped, 'bacilli'; and some are spiral-shaped, 'spirilla'. Some live almost motionless in jelly-like masses; others move by means of 'flagella' or hair-like projections. They reproduce by the simple method of splitting in two, or by forming spores, and can multiply with immense rapidity. Some are harmful in causing disease; others combat it; while others again perform valuable work in breaking down dead tissue (*see* SAPROPHYTES).

See also PARASITIC PLANTS; NITROGEN SUPPLY IN PLANTS; YEASTS; VIRUS.

See also Vol. XI: BACTERIAL DISEASES.

BADGER. The badger lives in most woods and forests in the British Isles, but only in small numbers. It belongs to the order CARNIVORA (q.v.), flesh-eaters. It is a thick-set, bear-like animal about 3 feet long, with thick, coarse, greyish fur, and a white face with broad black stripes. It is very keen of scent and hearing, and is an intelligent, courageous, and resourceful animal. Its skin is tough and loose, which enables it to wriggle round when seized and bite its aggressor.

Badgers live in deep burrows, called 'sets', in rocky hills and banks. The set has one or more chambers, with several entrance passages, and many workings on various levels. At the main entrance there is always a huge mound of excavated soil. Badgers are very clean animals: they bury their dung in an earth closet dug far away from the set, and clean their claws, like

A BADGER   *Harold Bastin*

cats, on a tree before going underground. At nightfall they come out to seek their food and also to play: to see them tumbling and rolling on the ground is a very amusing sight. They eat almost everything—roots, fruit, honey, slugs, snails, wire-worms, any kind of insect, moles, snakes, young birds, and rabbits.

In very cold climates badgers hibernate from November to March; but in England they sleep for short periods only in a deep set, bedded with dry bracken and grass. They block up the entrance to keep themselves warm; but they come out in mild weather, and sometimes even when there is snow on the ground. A regular spring-cleaning takes place about March, when they drag their bedding out into the sun, and make new chambers, lining them with fern and grass in preparation for the breeding season. Their two to four cubs are born in the spring or summer. These are silver-grey, and blind, and helpless at birth. They do not come out of the set for two months, during which time the mother washes them and looks after them most carefully.

Badgers are to be found in Asia and North America as well as in Europe. They are trapped for their fur, badger-hair being used for shaving-brushes. In Germany the small dachshund is used for driving the animal out of its set. If captured young, badgers are easily tamed and can make very good pets.

The Ratels of India and Africa, sometimes known as the Honey Badgers, belong to the badger family. They generally hunt in pairs, and are very bold for their size, attacking all sorts of animals, including poisonous snakes. They are very fond of honey (hence their name) and take no notice of the attacks of the bees. The Ratel, like the badger, soon becomes tame in captivity. It has the amusing habit of turning complete somersaults as it walks up and down its cage.

BAGWORMS. These caterpillars construct silken bags, strengthened with pieces of stick, leaves, lichen, or other objects, within which they live, and which protect them as they move over their food plants—the lichens on rocks, fences, and tree-trunks, and grasses, flowers, and leaves. The bags sometimes resemble the cases of the CADDIS-FLY (q.v.) (which, however, are found in water). The family of moths to which the Bagworms belong (*Psychidae*) is widespread, but

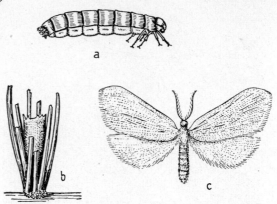

BAGWORM MOTH
(*a*) Typical wingless female; (*b*) Bag (or case);
(*c*) Typical male

only about 20 small species occur in Britain. The largest, found in Australia, makes bags 5 inches in length. The caterpillar eventually changes to a chrysalis, which has hooks enabling it to move within the bag and enabling the moth to make its escape. The males fly swiftly, chiefly by day, and have dull-coloured and very hairy wings, though some species, owing to imperfect scaling, have transparent wings. The females, the most degenerate of all moths, are without wings, and sometimes lack even antennae, mouth-parts, and legs. On hatching they remain inside the bag, where they are sought by the males, mate, and lay their numerous eggs. Some species appear to have no males, and the eggs develop without fertilization (*see* REPRODUCTION IN ANIMALS). The young caterpillars are sometimes blown considerable distances by the wind, the long strands of silk which they spin serving as parachutes. By this means the Bagworms colonize new areas, which might otherwise never be reached by an insect with a flightless female. The tiny lichen-feeding bagworms, for instance, to be found on the huge stones of Stonehenge, are $1\frac{1}{2}$ miles away from the nearest tree occupied by these moths.

BAMBOO, *see* GRASSES; *see also* Vol. VI, BAMBOOS.

BANDICOOT, *see* MARSUPIAL.

BARK, *see* STEMS SECTION 1e.

BARNACLE. This animal is now known, after close study of its life-history, to be a CRUSTACEAN

THREE STAGES OF THE BARNACLE
(*a*) 1st larval stage; (*b*) 2nd larval stage; (*c*) Adult acorn
Barnacles on rock

(q.v.); but the Acorn Barnacles are sufficiently like small limpets in appearance to have been originally classified as MOLLUSCS (q.v.). The Barnacle larva, with its minute triangular body, single central eye, and two pairs of jointed complex antennae, with which it swims freely through the water, is totally unlike its parent. After a while it reaches the second stage of its life-history, when the body and limbs are enclosed in a semi-transparent bivalve shell. Through this shell can be seen a pair of large compound eyes and six pairs of branched swimming feet; while in front, a pair of antennules, each bearing a sucker-like disc, project beyond the valves of the shell. After swimming about for a short period the larva becomes attached to some object, such as a rock or piece of submerged timber. It is held to its support by these sucker-discs, as well as by a cement secreted from glands at the base of the antennules, so that these fasten the front of its head to the support. The bivalve-shell is now cast off, and the beginnings of the shell-valves of the adult appear. The six pairs of swimming legs develop into graceful, feathery limbs, and the compound eyes disappear. The adult barnacle now remains for the rest of its life firmly attached by its head to the base it has selected, dwelling within the safe recesses of its shell and kicking its food into its mouth by means of the feathery legs, which serve as a most perfect casting-net for the capture of food.

The Goose or Ship Barnacles pass through a similar life-history, but choose floating timbers and the bottoms of ships, to which they attach themselves by a long muscular stalk—really the greatly elongated front part of the head. The body is enclosed in an oval shell composed of five separate pieces, hinged together to leave a slit through which the feathery-looking feet can be protruded. The Goose Barnacles gained their popular name from the once-prevalent idea that they finally developed into birds, the Barnacle GEESE (q.v.).

BASILISK, *see* LIZARDS; *see* FABULOUS CREATURES, Vol. I.

BAT. This is the only member of the order Chiroptera (hand-winged), and the only mammal which can really fly (*see* FLIGHT). Bats' wings are formed by a delicate membrane which connects up their enormously long fingers, and is carried back to join their hind limbs. On their toes are very sharp claws by which they hang downwards when resting. The hair may be either silky, woolly, or coarse—or, in some species, may be lacking entirely. In all but the Flying Foxes the eyes are small, and the sight is believed to be very poor. The insect-eating bats, however, have been shown to possess the remarkable power of finding their way about and of locating their insect food by echo-loca-

HEAD OF A BAT, SHOWING NOSE LEAVES AND EAR PETALS (probably used in echo-location)

tion. So, even if blindfolded, they can fly at a great speed without colliding with any obstacle, however small.

Bats frequently live together in large numbers. In the north-temperate zones they hibernate, mostly leaving their summer resorts in the winter, and retreating to caves or other shelters, where they hang upside-down by their feet with their wings wrapped round their bodies. Their temperature drops to that of their surroundings, and their breathing becomes light and slow (*see* HIBERNATION). In the summer many bats sleep most of the day and night, only coming out for food in the evening and morning. Others, however, fly through the night.

Once a year (about June or July in Britain)

one young is born, blind and naked. At its birth the mother turns head upwards and drops the young bat into a pouch made by bending her tail forward. Then she lifts it up, cleans it, and places it at one of the two teats on her breast. It clings on with its teeth, and holds on to its mother's fur with its thumbs and hind claws. There it stays for about a fortnight, without hampering her flight. After this time, however, she hangs it up by its feet in some safe place, while she goes away on a flight, replacing it at her breast on her return. Towards autumn the young bat begins to fly.

The order of bats (Chiroptera) is divided into two groups—the insect-eaters and the fruit-eaters: all British bats are insect-eaters, about 12 species having been seen at different times; but only the four described below—Pipistrelle, Long-eared Bats, Noctules, and Horseshoe Bats —are at all common. The first three belong to one family, the Vespertilionidae, called the 'typical' bats, members of which are found all over the world. They can bring their tails forward so as to form a pouch, into which they put large insects, leaving them there until they have been mastered.

The Pipistrelle, which has a wing-span of about 8 inches, is the most common bat in the British Isles. Large colonies live in church roofs and towers, and in any cranny in houses, trees, and rocks. The Long-eared Bats, which have a wing-span of about 10 inches, are also fairly common. Their ears are almost as long as their bodies, and so sensitive that they are kept constantly quivering. In warm weather they sleep

NOCTULE RESTING ON A POST
Harold Bastin

out, hanging from tree-trunks, and on colder days they take shelter in some warm spot. They hibernate, usually alone in hollow trees or in old buildings, from about mid-October to mid-April. They are the lightest sleepers of all British bats, and often come out in the winter, sometimes at mid-day, to drink. Noctules or Great Bats have a wing-span of from 13 to 15 inches, and live in many wooded districts of England and Wales. They make short flights, sometimes less than an hour. On their return they land head upwards, but at once turn upside-down and, hanging by one foot, perform an elaborate toilet. When this is over, they hang upside-down by both feet to rest. Their daily sleep in the summer is much like hibernation: it is very sound, their temperature falls, and their breathing becomes very short.

The Horseshoe Bats—the last of the common British bats—are a separate family. They derive their name from a growth of skin in the shape of a horseshoe on the face, which may be connected with the detection of obstacles or insects by echo-location. It has been seen in captivity that they do not put their prey in a tail pouch like the typical bats, but, instead, master large insects by pressing them with their mouths against their wings. Whether they do this in the wild is, however, not known. The females have two 'dummy' nipples on their groins as well as the two breast teats common to all bats. The mothers put the new-born young on to one of these dummies so that when she hangs head down, it is head up. She transfers it to the true teats for feeding only. There are two species, the Greater Horseshoe Bat (wing-span 13 inches), and the Lesser Horseshoe Bat (wing-span 8½ inches).

The so-called Vampires are small bats living in the forests of South and Central America and the West Indies. The appearance of some species, with their long, leathery ears and nose-leaf (an erect growth of skin of their face), is so hideous and diabolical that it fully accounts for their evil reputation. Some are purely insect-eaters, others live on a mixed diet of fruit and insects, and only one species lives entirely on the blood of other animals. The bloodsuckers attack their sleeping victims during the night, make slight incisions in the skin with their very sharp teeth, and then lap their blood. Some of them attack human beings whilst they are asleep.

The other large group of bats, the fruit-

A FLYING FOX   *Steven Henty*

eaters, are often called Flying Foxes on account of their fox-like heads. They live in Africa, southern India, and Australasia, and are typically much larger than insect-eating bats, some having a wing-span of 4 feet. During the day they hang by their toes from the branches of the forest trees, looking, with their wings wrapped round their bodies, rather like clusters of pears. At dusk they begin to move about amongst the branches with raucous squeaks and grunts. Presently, one flies off, to be followed by the whole party, which may number a hundred or more. Like a flock of large crows, they wing their way to some part of the forest where there is ripening fruit. Sometimes they have to travel several miles in their search, and in cultivated districts they cause, of course, immense damage.

The insect-eating bats are believed to be of value in helping to fight malaria by destroying mosquitoes. Sometimes, however, bats tend to be a nuisance because of the swarms of parasites they often carry.

BEAR. 1. Bears are found in most parts of the world, though in many countries they are now scarce and rarely found outside the large game reservations. They live in widely different climatic regions: the huge white Polar Bears live in Arctic regions; the Black and Brown Bears in the temperate zones; while in tropical countries are the oriental Sloth Bears and the Spectacled Bears. Those that live in cold climates hibernate through the winter (*see* HIBERNATION). Bears belong to the Order of CARNIVORA (q.v.), flesh-eaters, but in fact they eat a great variety of food—even the large Brown Bears eat great quantities of fruit and other vegetable food—and spend much of their time tearing to pieces old logs and digging in the ground in order to find grubs, worms, and insects. The female generally has a litter of two or three cubs, which are at first extremely small—Polar Bear cubs are only about a foot long.

2. POLAR BEARS. These are among the largest of the bears, often being as much as 9 feet long. They are provided with hair on the soles of their feet, which enables them to secure a good grip on the ice. If they are hungry they can be most formidable foes. In the winter they eat the flesh of seals and walruses, and in coastal districts a large amount of fish; but in the summer they keep to a vegetable diet. In autumn the female Polar Bear, having fed well and laid up a good stock of fat, retires to a cave beneath the snow and gives birth to her cubs in mid-winter. Polar Bears show a very strong love for their offspring: when starved and weak and living under the greatest hardships, they have often been seen carefully dividing among their cubs a small amount of food caught after long hours of hunting, keeping only a small piece for themselves.

3. BROWN BEARS. These are found in a few places in western and in most of eastern Europe, and in Asia and North America, their size and the shade of their coats varying according t where they live. In Alaska there are Brown Bears, called Kadiaks, which are sometimes as much as 10 feet long, and weigh over 1,500 lb.—the largest of all the bears. The Grizzly Bear of the Rocky Mountains is another huge animal, immensely strong. Although such enormous creatures, these giant brown bears are timid, inoffensive beasts, unless wounded, cornered, or protecting their young, and they will generally make every effort to escape man. The ferocity of the Grizzly has been greatly exaggerated; but once the Grizzly or the Alaskan Bear is aroused

BLACK BEAR CUBS CLIMBING A PINE-TREE IN SEARCH
OF A HONEYCOMB. *Paul Popper*

A POLAR BEAR
Dorien Leigh

and angered he is a dangerous and most deadly enemy. A Grizzly was once seen to break the neck of a bull bison with a single blow of its paw.

4. BLACK BEARS. The American Black Bear, a much smaller animal than the Brown Bear, still lives in many parts of Canada, and in some places in the United States; but it is now protected and may only be hunted at certain times. It is in general a shy, comparatively harmless bear, and in some of the National Parks has become tame enough to take food from visitors. In the Yellowstone Park in the U.S.A. Black Bears sometimes hold up cars to beg for food, and, if not given any, they have been known in their anger to try to tear the car to pieces. They rarely kill wild animals, but often become very destructive to sheep and raid farm-yards. They usually make their winter dens under the upturned roots of a fallen tree or beneath a pile of logs. They scrape together a few bushes or leaves to make a bed, and wait for the first snow-storm to complete the roof and fill in the remaining chinks.

There are Black Bears also in Asia—from Persia, right through the Himalayas, to China; and there is a smaller species in Japan. They live in the mountainous regions or forests, where they climb the trees in search of fruit. In Malaya are found the small Honey Bears or Sun Bears, which have short, sleek, black coats. They, too, are excellent climbers and in their search for honey are very clever at discovering the nests of bees.

5. TROPICAL BEARS. The Sloth Bear of India and Ceylon is a fairly large, shaggy animal, with a large white V mark on its chest. It has a passion for white ants (termites), and with its large, strong claws it tears the nests to pieces, then, blowing away the dust, it scoops up the insects with its long tongue and protruding lower lip. The young cubs are generally carried on their mother's back when the animals are on the move: it is an amusing sight to watch them dismount at the feeding ground and scramble back to their seats at the first alarm.

The only bear to be found in South America is the Spectacled Bear, which lives in the mountains of Peru and Colombia. It is a small inoffensive black bear, with a white breast and pale-coloured rings round its eyes, which give it a clownish appearance. It lives in remote areas, and avoids man as much as possible. Its food is fruit and other vegetable matter.

BEAVERS
'Picture Post' Library

BEAVER. This large, stout RODENT (q.v.) lives mainly in the water. He is about 2½ feet long—larger than an otter—and has a thick, warm, brown coat, the upper hairs of which form a waterproof covering to his woolly under-coat. It is this under-coat which is used in the fur trade (*see* FURS, Vol. VI). The beaver's hind-feet are webbed for swimming, and his tail, which is wide and flat, acts as a rudder. His front (incisor) teeth are very strong and sharp. There are still many beavers in North America, although they have been severely trapped for their fur (*see* FUR HUNTING, Vol. VI). In Europe they are found in Scandinavia, and also on the Rhone and Elbe, though they were once quite common even in England—there are many places in England, such as Beverley and Beaverbourne, which derive their name from the beaver.

The beaver shows almost incredible engineering skill and intelligence in constructing dams in the streams and rivers in which he lives. His main purpose in building the dam seems to be to ensure a sufficient depth of water around his house for him to swim in when the surface is frozen over in the winter. The way in which he seems to choose the very best spot for building the dam is almost uncanny.

Beavers obtain material to build their dams and also their houses (called 'lodges') by felling trees with their sharp teeth. If there are no suitable trees near the water, building material is often brought some distance over land. In this case the beavers usually construct canals to float down the material, since their heavy bodies, short legs, and webbed hind feet are not well adapted for carrying loads across country. They strip off the boughs, and cut up these and the trunk itself into convenient lengths. Most of the work is done at night, numbers of the beavers working together. The large logs form the base of the dam and the smaller wood is worked in later with turf and clay to form a watertight construction.

The beaver 'lodge' is a permanent house, with the entrance beneath the surface of the water, and the beaver lives there both summer and winter. The lodge usually contains two rooms, one used as a living-room, and the other as the pantry, where the beaver stores his winter food supply of twigs and branches. He also sinks food supplies in the water conveniently near the lodge, and in this way he is well provided for in the winter months, when ice and snow make it impossible to travel outside. In the autumn the beavers plaster their houses with mud, which, when frozen in the winter, forms a wind-proof and cold-proof covering, and protects them from their enemies—bears, wolverines, and foxes. At the close of winter or early in spring from three to four young are born in the lodge.

BED-BUG. This very unpleasant insect is now found only in human dwellings. Fully grown, it is reddish-brown, round, and flat, and about a quarter of an inch long. During the day it hides in the bedding, in cracks and crevices in the floor, walls, and ceilings, or under the wall-paper. At night it comes out to feed. Like many other bugs, it has a very unpleasant smell—indeed a bug-infested house has an odour all its own. It is usually found in dirty, ill-kept

× 3

houses, and once it has established itself it is most difficult to get rid of. The bed-bug is a blood-sucker. It is not strictly correct to call it a para-site, for it does not live upon man, but visits him when it needs a meal and returns again into seclusion when satisfied. It is said to be able to live for a year without taking any food, so it may live for a long time in an unoccupied house. It has been suspected as a possible carrier of disease from man to man, but there is no definite evidence of this.

The eggs are pearly-white, oval, and slightly curved. Each one has a little lid, which the young nymph pushes upwards as it emerges. The insect hatches in about a week after the egg is laid, and, except for its size and pale colour, looks very like its parents. It takes up to 6 months to become adult, and casts its coat five times during growth.

Three other nearly related bugs of similar shape and colour are found in Britain. Of these, one is found in dove cotes, another in swallows' nests, and the third is a parasite on various species of bat.

See also BUG.
See also Vol. XI, HOUSEHOLD PESTS.

BEECH, *see* WOODLANDS, Section 8.

BEE-EATER. This is the name of a large family of smallish birds, the species of which inhabit most of the tropical and sub-tropical parts of Africa, Asia, and Europe. They have long, curved beaks, long tails, and very brilliant colouring—predominantly blue and green, with black, yellow, and chestnut markings. They live on insects—principally, as their name suggests, on bees, which they catch in the open in full flight. The quick, darting flight of these vivid little birds in pursuit of their prey is an attractive sight. The European Bee-eater, a rather larger species, measuring 10 inches from beak to tail, not only takes its food on the wing, but also visits the bee-hives and captures the bees as they fly in or out. They visit southern Europe regularly in the summer, spending the winter in various parts of Africa, and breeding in central Asia. They have a peculiar cry, a single note repeated continuously. Like most Bee-eaters, they lay their glossy, white eggs at the end of long tunnels which they dig with their beaks, preferably in sandy river banks. These tunnels are generally fouled by the discarded indigestible parts of the bodies of bees and wasps.

The Swallow-tailed Bee-eaters of Africa measure about 8½ inches, and the Square-tailed Bee-eaters, species of which are also to be found in India and south Asia, are all rather smaller. Other species, such as the Bearded Bee-eaters, one of which has magnificent scarlet throat-

BEE-EATERS
C. K. Yeates, F.R.P.S.

feathers, inhabit the forests of the East Indies and other countries of southern Asia.

Related to the Bee-eaters are the Motimots of Central and South America. These are rather larger birds, some 15½ inches, with long beaks and very long tails. They are gaudy creatures, with magnificent green, blue, silver, and purple colouring. In the West Indies is another closely related family, the Todres, little green and red birds, which are now becoming rather scarce, because of the raids made on their burrows by mongooses, who eat their eggs.

BEES. 1. These are insects belonging to a huge group known as Hymenoptera, which includes also WASPS and ANTS (qq.v.). The Hymenoptera have on each side of the body two pairs of transparent wings, which are joined together by small hooks. They undergo, too, a complete METAMORPHOSIS (q.v.): out of the egg hatches a larva or grub (corresponding to the caterpillar of the butterfly or moth); when full grown, this becomes a pupa (corresponding to the chrysalis of the moth or butterfly); and from this emerges the full-fledged insect.

The females of all, except for the Stingless Bees, are able to sting. The 'drone' or male bee is a harmless creature, whose only job is to inseminate the female so that she may be able to lay fertile eggs.

The food of bees consists of honey and pollen.

Besides having jaws or mandibles to bite with, bees have tongues, with which they suck up nectar from the flowers. After the nectar has gone through chemical changes in the bee's stomach, it can be brought up again as honey. Pollen is used by the bees for feeding their young. The Lawn Bee, and a host of bees related to it, have very hairy hind legs, on which they collect the pollen grains; the Leaf-cutter Bees and Mason Bees collect pollen on the long hairs under their abdomens. Other bees, such as Bumble and Honey Bees, have a smooth, slightly hollowed-out surface on the outer side of the hind leg, called a pollen-basket, which is fringed with long hairs, and into which the bee packs the pollen until it forms a solid mass.

Little is known about the flight of bees. It has been discovered that the Honey Bee will rarely fly more than 2 miles in search of food. The celebrated French naturalist, FABRE (q.v. Vol. V), caught, marked, and then released forty Mason Bees 3 miles from their nest—and only nine were able to find their way home.

Bees are usually referred to as either 'social' or 'solitary' in habit. The social kinds are the Bumble Bees, the Honey Bees, and the Stingless Bees. The vast majority are solitary—in other words, the fertilized female provides food for her offspring, but otherwise takes no interest in them. She makes a cell for the egg in a burrow

Fig. 3. LEAF-CUTTER BEE, SHOWING THE LONG POLLEN-COLLECTING HAIRS ON THE ABDOMEN

in the ground, in an old tree-trunk, or often in the deserted burrows of other insects. She provisions each cell with a mass of pollen soaked with honey, known as 'bee-bread', and on this lump of food she lays an egg. She then closes up the cell, and pays no further attention to it. The social bees give much more attention to their offspring. The mother Bumble Bee, for instance, stays with her young throughout their lives, feeding them from day to day while they are still larvae. When they become adult, they help her to bring up further broods. In this way they build up a community, headed by the mother bee, the queen, and peopled by her children, the workers. These workers, like the queen but smaller, are the spinsters of the family—for, though female, they never have offspring.

2. SOLITARY BEES. A very common English solitary bee is the Lawn Bee. The female is a handsome little insect, having a black head, and the upper parts of the rest of the body clothed with deep, reddish, velvety hair. She usually makes her burrow in open grassy places, and, as numbers of females often make their burrows close together, the tiny mounds of earth thrown up by the diggers are quite conspicuous. The bees appear in spring, often in such numbers as to make themselves a nuisance to the owners of well-kept lawns. Solitary bees which make their burrows close together are said to be 'gregarious'. There are many gregarious species related to the Lawn Bee: their burrows are often only a few inches apart, and the bees appear in enormous numbers.

If an old and rotten tree-trunk, especially of willow, is broken up, there may often be found

Fig. 1. HIND LEG OF A SOLITARY BEE, *Panurgus*, SHOWING THE LONG POLLEN-COLLECTING HAIRS

Fig. 2. HIND LEG OF A HONEY-BEE, SHOWING THE POLLEN BASKET WITH SOLID LUMP OF POLLEN the remarkable cells of the Leaf-cutter Bees, brown bees in shape and size much like an ordinary hive bee. The female has powerful jaws which she can use as borers or scissors. She bores a long tunnel in the dry and crumbling wood, then lines it with tightly overlapping pieces of leaf, cut from rose and other kinds of leaves, and then closes each cell with a wad of smaller, circular pieces of leaf. The entire series of cells, laid bare, resembles a long thin cigar. If we separate them out, we see that the base of each cell fits very neatly within the projecting leaf-rim of the cell next to it (see Fig. 4).

There are many kinds of Leaf-cutter Bees all over the world, most of them much more brightly coloured than those in this country. Their relatives, the Mason Bees, make their cells,

Fig. 4. NEST OF LEAF-CUTTER BEE, SHOWING TUNNELS IN WOOD AND ROWS OF CELLS

not of leaves, but of cement composed of clay or fine particles of sand, made workable by saliva. One of the best known of these bees is the European Black Mason Bee, the bee about which Fabre has given us such a fascinating account. He tells us how the female bee will often build her cement cells on a large pebble, and how, when she has built side by side some six or eight cells, she covers the whole mass of them with a mortar of finer composition, to protect the delicate grubs inside from the blazing sun of summer and the extreme cold of winter.

A common British bee, *Osmia rufa*, also

Fig. 5. CELLS OF *Osmia rufa*, SHOWING PARTITIONS AND COCOONS IN CELLS

constructs its cells with mortar, usually clay, scraped up by the female with her mandibles from any damp spot, and moistened further with saliva. However, unlike her European relative, she does not build exposed cells, but makes use of some deserted insect-burrow, or any cavity with surfaces close enough to allow her just room to move between them—for instance, she may build in the disused lock of a door, which she enters through the key hole. She uses her mortar for the partitions separating one cell from another. (See Fig. 5.)

Other materials, besides pieces of leaf or grains of sand, clay, or earth, are used by solitary bees for making their nests. *Anthidium manicatum*, a fairly common British bee, uses a fibrous down that looks like cotton-wool, which she scrapes from the stalks and undersides of the leaves of certain plants. The female *Anthidium*, a rather sober-looking little black bee, touched up with yellow, makes separate cells in any convenient burrow out of this woolly material. Each cell contains a lump of bee-bread with a single egg on it, and is carefully sealed with more of the same wool.

Some solitary bees have no means of collecting pollen, and sip nectar from the flowers only for their own nourishment. They have come to lead a parasitic life and, instead of making their own nests, lay their eggs in other bees' cells, which have been stored with food by their rightful owners. In Europe, including the British Isles, most of these parasitic bees belong to the genus *Nomada*, and are small, black and yellow, or black and red bees, slender and wasp-like in appearance. Some of the tropical species are brilliant metallic green or gleaming like burnished copper. The *Nomada* lay their eggs in the underground cells of bees such as the Lawn Bee of the genus *Andrena*. Each species of *Andrena* usually has its own particular kind of *Nomada* living as a parasite on it.

3. SOCIAL BEES. The social bees of this

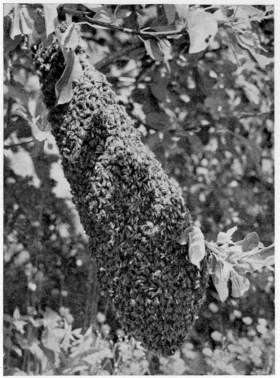

Fig. 6. A SWARM OF BEES
Eric J. Hosking, F.R.P.S.

the plates or segments of the underside of the abdomen. The queen Honey Bee is larger than the worker bee. She lacks the pollen baskets on the hind legs, her tongue is shorter, and she cannot secrete wax like the workers. In fact she is quite unfitted to live for any length of time without the attendance of her workers. (For a full account of honey-bee farming, see HONEY BEE, Vol. VI.)

Another group of social bees are the Stingless Bees of the tropics. They are known scientifically as *Meliponinae*, and most of the species occur in Africa and South America. The kind of community that these bees have developed is more elaborate than that of the Bumble Bee, and not very unlike that of the Honey Bee. Wax is secreted by the workers—and, oddly enough, by the males, too. Although the workers have no sting, they are not without means of defence; for it is said that if a nest is disturbed they will fly out at the intruder in great numbers, crawl into his eyes, ears, and hair, and smear him with a sticky substance, causing him to retreat in discomfort. The Stingless Bees, as producers of honey, have not so far been made use of by man.

BEETLES. 1. These form one of the largest of the main divisions, or orders, of insects. Nearly 4,000 kinds inhabit the British Islands alone, and in the whole world about a quarter of a million have been named. There are probably a great many more still undiscovered.

They are distinguished from other insects by the hardness of the first pair of wings. These are not used for flying, but as a protection to the second pair, which are folded beneath them when not in use. COCKROACHES and GRASS-HOPPERS (qq.v.), also, have the first pair hardened for the same purpose; but in beetles the difference between the two pairs is greater, and the first pair fit together closely along the middle of the back. Beetles begin life, like BUTTERFLIES and MOTHS (qq.v.), as eggs, then quite unlike the parents. The winged condition is only reached after a resting stage, generally passed in a cocoon made by the grub. When the skin is cast off all the organs of the adult beetle appear, enclosed in another skin and incapable of use. Not until this skin has been shed, which may be after some weeks or months, does the beetle reach its final form. This transformation is called METAMORPHOSIS (q.v.).

Owing to the special hardness and compact-

country are the BUMBLE BEE (q.v.) and the Honey or Hive Bee.

Although the Honey Bee (*Apis mellifera*) has been kept by man for a long time, it cannot be said to have become truly domesticated, for, whether kept in the old-fashioned skeps or in modern hives, it continues to follow the course of behaviour laid down by heredity. When a bee-keeper loses a swarm, it will settle down in a hollow tree, or perhaps in the space between the walls of a house, and may live there as successfully as in the hive or skep from which it came.

The Honey Bee (*Apis*) is the only one of the social bees to build the familiar honeycomb, with its double layer of six-sided cells. The combs built by the bees hang down vertically, with just enough space between them to allow the bees to move freely. The bees rear their brood in the middle and lower parts of the comb, and store their honey above and to the sides of the breeding zone. The wax, out of which the cells are made, is produced by the workers in the form of tiny scales, which appear between

HERCULES BEETLE OF SOUTH AMERICA—ONE OF THE LARGEST BEETLES. *E. O. Hoppé*

ness of their bodies and to their well-protected wings, beetles are able to live in abundance almost everywhere. The largest of them are as big as rats, while the smallest are almost invisible, except under a microscope. No beetles possess stings, and none injure man or domestic animals by biting. Some beetles, however, are harmful: the DEATH-WATCH BEETLE (q.v.), for instance, may bring great buildings to ruin by devouring the timber; and others, like the COLORADO BEETLE (q.v.), by attacking important crops, may threaten us with famine. On the other hand, there are many kinds which, by destroying other harmful creatures, are of great service to mankind. The LADYBIRDS (q.v.), for instance, feed upon other harmful insects; many CHAFERS (q.v.) act as scavengers; the STAG BEETLES (q.v.) help to clear woods and forests of dead trees, stumps, and logs. It is generally as grubs, when they are seldom seen, that beetles feed most, and are therefore of most importance to us.

Beetles have jaws which are often very strong and sharp, enabling them to bite through hard substances. Their eyes contain many lenses, sometimes several thousands, each joined by a nerve to the brain; and a few have another single eye on the top of the head. Although extremely sensitive to changes in the light falling upon them, which give them instant warning of any approaching danger, their eyes are not delicate organs like our own. A much more important sense than sight to most of them is that of smell, the organs of which are contained

in the feelers or antennae. It is by means of these that they are able to find, sometimes at a great distance, the proper food for themselves or their progeny, to recognize others of their kind, and to return, when necessary, to their own nests or burrows. Many beetles (*see* CHAFERS) have the end-joints of their antennae enlarged and placed side by side, like the leaves of a book: this both increases their scenting power and gives them protection. Some of these beetles expend weeks or months of exacting toil in providing for the well-being of their young; and, like BEES, ANTS, and WASPS (qq.v.), they often perform the most delicate operations in the complete darkness of their nests. Some of the little wood-boring beetles, known as Ambrosia Beetles, live in communities in extensive galleries, which by their united efforts they excavate in tree-stumps or logs. In their tunnels they cultivate a minute fungus, growing upon prepared soil, and this supplies the food for the young grubs, each of which may have a separate 'cradle' dug out of the wood.

Many beetles are able, by rubbing one part of the body against another, to produce chirping or squeaking sounds. This is generally done by scraping exceedingly fine and close ridges on one part of the body against hard ridges on some

BEETLE GALLERIES IN BARK OF ELM
S. Beaufoy, F.R.P.S.

other part, as a violin-bow scrapes the strings: the instrument may be played by quick movements of the head, the tail-end, the front or hind legs, or some other part. The grubs of a group of beetles called Passalids, which live, together with their parents, in the interior of tree-stumps, appear to have only four legs: the third pair are useless for walking, but serve as tiny hands to pluck fine ridges, whose vibrations make a chirping sound. The parent beetles also chirp by rubbing hard rough bosses against their folded wings. It has been said that parents and young communicate with each other by this means—but as we have no knowledge of any

organs of hearing in beetles, this is not at present certain.

2. WATER BEETLES. Although, like most other insects, they breathe air, a great many beetles spend almost all their lives in water—in rivers, streams, and even the smallest ponds. If these dry up, they are able to fly elsewhere. The wing-covers of most water beetles, besides protecting the wings, enclose a supply of air, which circulates constantly through their breathing-tubes as they swim. This makes them very light, so that when they cease to swim they come to the surface and, by poking the end of the body out of the water, renew the air-supply. They swim with the hind legs, which are fringed with stiff hairs and act like oars to drive the beetle rapidly through the water. The middle pair of legs is used for clinging to weeds or stones, and the front pair to grasp their prey—for most of them devour other aquatic creatures. The Great Carnivorous Water Beetle called *Dytiscus*, which is common in Great Britain and is amongst the largest of its tribe, is a fierce insect, destroying large numbers of other water-insects, and even young fishes.

Other water beetles, which are less active and live chiefly upon vegetable food, carry an air-supply beneath the body, where it is retained by fine silky hairs. One of these, the great shining black *Hydrophilus*, one of the largest beetles inhabiting Britain, makes a remarkable silken raft for its eggs, from which the young insects escape directly into the water. They feed upon water-snails, breaking their shells by squeezing them between the head and back.

A WHIRLIGIG BEETLE
G. J. Arrow

Whirligig Beetles are small shining black insects, often seen running in a kind of sociable dance over the surface of smooth water, each one gliding in and out of the throng faster than would seem possible for creatures with such short legs. They seize their prey with their forelegs, and with the other two pairs, which are like broad paddles, they skate over the surface of the water or swim rapidly beneath it. Since they live on the surface of the water, they are exposed to attack both from the air above and the water beneath. To meet this danger, they

GREAT WATER BEETLE
Above, larva; *below,* adult.
S. Beaufoy, F.R.P.S.

have four clusters of eyes, two on the top of the head to warn them of danger from the air, and two beneath it to watch for enemies in the water.

3. LAND BEETLES. Most of the many beetles to be found running swiftly over the ground or sheltering beneath stones also feed upon other insects. The prettily decorated Tiger Beetles, for instance, often seen in sandy places, hunt flies and other insects. Their eggs are laid in holes in the ground, and the young grub, on hatching, digs a perpendicular shaft, in which it lies in wait for its prey, its head exactly fitting the mouth of the shaft. As soon as an insect appears within reach, the Tiger-grub, by a sudden spring, grips it in its sharp jaws and drags it into its lair to be

AN EAST AFRICAN TIGER BEETLE *G. J. Arrow*

devoured. In winter-time the shaft is sealed up, its occupant remaining secure until spring-time. When fully grown it again seals its burrow, casts its skin, and, after another change of skin several weeks later, becomes a winged beetle. Its life may last 4 years or more in all. The great African Tiger Beetle, shown in the illustration, cannot fly, but hunts insects on the ground.

The common Ground Beetles, much more numerous than the Tiger Beetles, resemble them in their habits, some being even more voracious. In the grub-stage they generally live underground, and so are not often seen. Some of the beetles, when disturbed, are able to shoot from the hinder end of the body a drop of fluid, which explodes on meeting the air, making a puff of vapour capable of injuring, or at least shocking, the enemy, and so giving the beetle time to escape. Most beetles with this strange habit live in Africa and Asia—the only British ones being pretty little insects, half red and half blue, generally found beneath large stones near water, and known as Bombardier Beetles.

Many beetles burrow into the ground, either in search of food or to store provisions for their future offspring. The Burying Beetles, hand-some creatures, black with red or orange markings, bury the bodies of small animals and birds as food for their grubs. Their wonderful power of scent brings them quickly to a carcase. With their strong legs, they dig away the earth beneath the carcase until it is almost concealed in the hole. The females then lay their eggs upon it, and remain near the spot to feed the young grubs when the eggs hatch.

Most of the beetles which dig underground nests and provision them for their young are SCARABS or CHAFERS (qq.v.) of some kind. These industrious insects remove great quantities of decaying matter from the surface of the soil. According to the great naturalist FABRE (q.v. Vol. V), the horned Dor Beetle or Minotaur sometimes makes its nest as much as 5 feet below ground—the female digs out the earth, and the male carries it up the long shaft and ejects it. In India the stored cells made by a very large Chafer (*Heliocoptis*) have been found as deep as 8 feet.

Other beetles live in trees, depositing their eggs upon the trunks or branches, on which the grubs feed for months or years. A large group, the Longicorns (or Long-horns), have especially

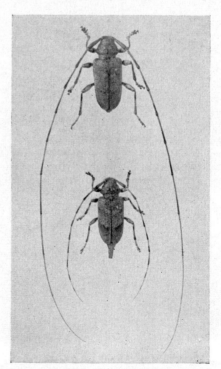

LONG-HORN BEETLES
Male (top) and female. *G. J. Arrow*

long antennae. The male of one species of Longicorn, sometimes found in felled pine-trees or wooden coal-mine props, has antennae four or five times as long as its body. Another common British Longicorn is called the Wasp Beetle, because it is decorated with bright yellow bands and has a fussy manner of flying. Its grubs feed inside decaying wooden posts or stumps.

A great many different kinds of beetles feed upon the leaves of plants. The common Tortoise Beetle feeds only upon thistles, and the Colorado Beetle only upon the potato and related plants. During their grub stage some members of this group live in cases, which they drag about with them and enlarge as they grow, changing to the beetle-shape before leaving the case. One of these (called *Clythra*) lives in its case within the nests of the large Wood Ant, and feeds upon the plant-fragments of which they are built. The ants will not allow the mother beetle to enter the nest, but she drops her eggs, each enclosed in a tiny case, near the nest, from a convenient tree or bush. The ants, for what reason we have no idea, carry them into the nest—perhaps they mistake them for some kind of food.

Many beetles have adopted the habit of living at the expense of ants or of the nest-building TERMITES (White Ants) (q.v.). Some of them are favourably treated by their hosts, and fed by them because they produce a sweet liquid, like the honey-dew of the APHIDES (q.v.), of which the ants are so fond. One of these beetles, called the Claviger (Club-bearer), because its feelers are like massive clubs, is found in Britain. It is quite blind, and entirely dependent upon the ants with which it lives, and which feed it with the greatest care. When they stroke it with their own feelers, it exudes a drop of sweet fluid, which they swallow greedily. They even allow others of these parasites to devour the helpless ant-brood, rather than drive them from the nest. Some beetles, however, are not so welcome in the ants' nest, and have to protect themselves in all sorts of ways. One remarkable group, called Paussids, can fire in the faces of the ants an explosive fluid, like the Bombardier Beetles.

A SOUTH AFRICAN PAUSSID BEETLE

G. J. Arrow

BELL-BIRD, *see* CHATTERER; HONEY-EATER.

BERRIES, *see* FRUITS, Section 3 *a*.

BIRCH, *see* WOODLANDS, Section 5.

BIRDS OF PARADISE. 1. There are at least fifty species of these tropical birds, which belong to the very large order of Passerine or perching birds. The family also includes the Australian Bower Birds, well known because of the strange constructions they build during the period of courtship.

Birds of Paradise are found mostly in the dense forests of New Guinea and the neighbouring islands, though there are a few in Australia. They vary in size from that of a starling to a large crow, and are remarkable for the adornment of the adult males, which carry plumes of eccentric shape and brilliant hues of scarlet, gold, violet, bronze, green, and many other colours. When plumes were in fashion, the Birds of Paradise were relentlessly hunted, and would have been exterminated had not a law been passed forbidding their import into America and Britain (*see* FEATHER HUNTING, Vol. VI). The birds were first brought to Europe by the survivors of Magellan's voyage round the world in 1521, when they were given their present name. The legend grew up that the birds were legless and therefore were not inhabitants of the earth, an idea that arose presumably because the skins brought to Europe had had the feet removed.

There is a wide variety in the types of plumes. The best-known species, the Great Bird of Paradise of the Aru Islands, near New Guinea, a bird about 23 inches long, has an abundance of long, golden-yellow plumes, which do not reach their prime until the bird is 7 or 8 years old. The Red Bird of Paradise has shorter flank plumes of a rich crimson, and the two middle tail-feathers are long, slender streamers, nearly 2 feet long. The Long-tailed Bird of Paradise has tail-feathers over 2 feet long and tinted a brilliant opal-blue. The Six-plumed Bird of Paradise has a set of three small black plumes on very long quills on each side of the head. Albert's Bird of Paradise, one of the most remarkable of the family, has a long streamer, twice the length of the body, coming from the head behind each eye. Each of the streamers is made up of thirty or forty squared lobes of feathers, light blue above and dusky below.

GREAT BIRD OF PARADISE DISPLAYING TO FEMALE
Harold Bastin

 at the top center and right:

to perform his dancing displays. The hen, however, appears to pay little attention to the bower, and builds a nest of the ordinary type in a bush or tree, often some distance away.

The Satin Bower-bird, so called because of its blue-black, shiny, satin-like plumage, constructs an elaborate bower. First he makes a twig tunnel, about 18 inches high, out of two parallel rows of twigs, their ends stuck in the ground and their tops nearly touching. All around this he places bones and coloured objects, such as shells, pebbles, feathers, and flowers—blue appearing to be a favourite colour. Then he paints the sticks of the bower blue with the blue juice crushed from a berry. The Gardener Bird of Papua builds perhaps the most remarkable bower. He makes a hut-like structure some 2 feet high, at the foot of a tree, and roofs it with orchis stems radiating from a central support, and with a mass of moss. In front of it he lays out a bed of moss, into which he fixes bright-coloured berries and flowers, which he replaces as they wither. (See coloured Plate.)

See also ANIMAL LANGUAGE.

This wonderful display of plumage in the male is presumably developed to attract the female; and the way in which the males use their plumage in their courtship display is most interesting. The males have their regular dancing places, either on the ground or in trees, where they display their plumes to entice the female. As the breeding season approaches the excitement of the cocks increases—and the sight of a dozen or twenty fully plumaged cocks together, raising their wings, stretching their necks, spreading their plumes, calling, and flying at intervals from branch to branch, is a sight not to be forgotten. The nest is usually placed high in the tree-tops, and generally two cream-coloured eggs are laid. Some species, however, appear to nest in holes in tree-trunks.

2. BOWER-BIRDS, mainly inhabitants of Australia, though two types are found in New Guinea and the Papuan Islands, are less spectacular in appearance than Birds of Paradise, though some of them have very handsome colours. They are so called because, at the mating season, the male constructs a 'bower' as part of his display to attract the female. He then uses the bower as a sort of 'playground' in which

BIRDS. This group of warm-blooded, vertebrate (backboned) animals, which usually, but not always, possesses powers of flight, has evolved in long-past ages from reptile ancestors (*see* EVOLUTION, CHART). Their anatomy more resembles that of reptiles than of mammals (which are, of course, also descended from reptiles). It is believed that the ancestor of birds was a small, tree-climbing, lizard-like creature.

The birds, with their powers of flight, have evolved skeletons distinguished at once for lightness and strength. The little Humming-bird, for instance, which is able to make a non-stop flight across the Gulf of Mexico, some 500 miles, weighs less than an ounce. The bird's skull is in remarkable contrast to the solid, heavy skull of the mammal. It consists of a box of thin bone to accommodate the brain, deeply hollowed at the sides to give room for the large eyes, and a light and flexible scaffolding of bony splints which supports the beak, palate, and lower jaw. Most of a bird's bones are hollow, with the interior webbed across by fine girders of bone to give added strength. The bones of the spine are flexibly connected in the neck, strongly bound together in the front part of the body, and united in the hinder part with the bones of the pelvis into a solid, rigid mass. The number of

Skull
Carpus
Metacarpus
Phalanges of the fingers
Radius
Ulna
Humerus
Cervical ribs
Clavical
Vertibrae
Coracoid
Spine
Ilium
Sternum
Ribs
Femur
Fibula
Pubis
Tibia
Tarso-metatarsus
Toes

SKELETON OF A BIRD

vertebrae in this rigid section varies in different species from ten to twenty-two. A small number of movable caudal vertebrae provide a support for the tail.

The large breast-bone or 'sternum', with its deep fore-and-aft keel, provides attachment for the powerful muscles which move the wings. The skeleton of the wings corresponds to the bones of the fore-limb (or arm) of other higher vertebrates. The number of bones in the 'wrist' and 'hand' is reduced (the fewer the moving parts, the greater the strength), and traces of only three fingers remain. The flight-feathers are carried on the bones of 'hand' and 'fore-arm'. The bones of the legs are comparatively little modified; the toes never number more than four, and the so-called 'knee' of a bird is a joint which somewhat resembles the ankle of a man.

The muscles which raise and lower the wings at each stroke are all attached to the lower side of the breast-bone. The down-stroke is made by a direct pull; but the wing is raised by a ten-don which passes from the upper side of the humerus, through a kind of pulley in the top of the shoulder girdle, and so downward to the muscles. The breast muscles may amount to as much as one-fifth of the total weight of the bird. The lungs of a bird are very important, for so large a mass of muscle, working at high speed, demands a good supply of oxygen. The lungs are so formed that the air is drawn into a system of air-sacs extending beyond the areas where oxygen is taken up by the blood. As a result, all the capillaries of the lung are in contact with freshly drawn air at each breath—a more efficient method of RESPIRATION (q.v.) than that of the mammals, in which the air in contact with the capillaries of the lungs is completely changed only once in several breaths.

In basic structure all birds are very much alike; but different ways of life have produced some outward differences. Beaks vary greatly with the uses to which they are put. The flesh-eating OWLS, HAWKS, and SHRIKES have beaks strongly hooked at the tip, while the fish-eating AUKS and diving DUCKS have sharp-edged or serrated beaks for grasping slippery prey. The beaks of SNIPE and WOODCOCK are long for probing and sensitive at the tip for finding hidden prey by touch. Seed and fruit-eaters, such as the FINCHES and NUTHATCH, have stout, strong beaks to enable them to tear open tough shells and crack hard stones; while many insect-eating birds, such as the FLY-CATCHERS (qq.v.), have sharp-pointed beaks, which make neat forceps for seizing small and agile victims. The feet, too, vary considerably—from the small feet of SWIFTS (q.v.), with all four toes set forward and used almost entirely as a set of hooks wherewith the bird can hang itself up, to the enormously long toes of the Jacanas and Lily-trotters of tropical regions, which enable the birds to walk across floating vegetation. Most swimming birds have their toes united by a web (COR-MORANTS, GEESE, GULLS) or flanged with lobes of skin (GREBES, COOTS, PHALAROPES) (qq.v.).

A bird's feathers are of two kinds, the large feathers of flight—on wings called 'remiges', and on tail 'retrices'—and the smaller contour feathers which make the general covering. In most birds the contour feathers do not grow evenly all over the body, but along certain feather tracts. All feathers are renewed by a process of moulting, in which the worn feather is dropped and replaced by a new one. The number of moults in the year, and the seasons of moulting, vary greatly between species, and sometimes between the two sexes of one species. At the moult the colours of a bird may be changed or made brighter. In some species, for example the Brambling (*see* FINCHES), certain colour-changes are effected by the wearing away of a feather tip, which is coloured differently from the rest of the feather.

The coloration of birds may serve to conceal them from their foes (*see* CAMOUFLAGE), or to advertise them to the other members of their own species. Brilliant or conspicuous colours may be used by birds in displaying to their mates (*see* ANIMAL LANGUAGE), and also in making the wearer look large and terrible to his opponents in battle. Where the sexes differ in colour the male is generally the more brilliant; for the more soberly coloured female, which performs the duties of incubation, needs to be as little conspicuous as possible. In a few species, such as the Red-necked Phalarope and Painted Snipe, the female is the brighter bird—and in these species it is the female which makes a courtship display to the male.

It used to be thought that most quarrelling between birds was for the possession of mates; but it is now known that much of the fighting between male birds (or of displays in place of fighting) is for the possession of a plot of ground in which the bird can breed (*see* ANIMAL TERRITORY). A bird without a territory, forced to lead a wandering life, is unlikely to retain a mate. The value of territory in helping to maintain the bond between the birds of a pair is undoubted. Many ornithologists believe that this habit of claiming a territory also prevents birds from crowding in upon a favourable area and over-taxing the supply of food. Song (the repetition of notes in accordance with some recognizable pattern for

each species) is one of the best known of bird habits, and serves to announce the ownership of a territory—a warning to rival males and a signal to hens in search of a mate.

The building of the nest may be the duty of one or both birds of the pair. Nests may be built of a variety of materials—often depending on what is most readily available in the bird's locality. They may be placed at the top of tall trees (CROWS and HERONS); in hollows among dense vegetation (as by many WADING BIRDS); in tunnels made by the bird in trees (WOODPECKERS), or in the ground (BEE-EATERS and KINGFISHERS) (qq.v.). Some water-birds, such as the GREBES and DIVERS (qq.v.), make no more than a mound of sodden plant material floating among reeds and rushes, and some waders scrape a shallow depression in the ground and line it with fragments of shell or bone. The African Palm Swift constructs only a little pad of down on a palm leaf—so small that it cannot support the egg, which must be glued to it by the parent bird. Some birds make bag-shaped nests with entrances at the top or on the side (GOLDCREST, Long-tailed TITS (qq.v.)). The Tailor-bird stitches together the edges of a suitable leaf with cobweb and cotton to make its hanging nest. Some species of WEAVER-BIRDS (q.v.)

NEST OF RED-THROATED DIVER.

G. K. Yeates, F.R.P.S.

NEST OF PENDULINE TIT.   *G. K. Yeates, F.R.P.S.*

construct a communal nest, within which many pairs of birds have their homes. One species of Swift builds a nest of its own saliva, which is eaten as a great delicacy in the Far East.

Some birds lay only one egg a year; others, such as some of the game birds, lay up to twenty. The incubation of the eggs is sometimes undertaken by the hen alone, sometimes shared between the parents. When the male is smaller and more dully coloured than the female, he usually takes the larger part in incubating the eggs and tending the young. When the young have hatched, they are either fed in the nest with food brought by one or both parents, or (in many wading and game birds) led forth to seek their own food. In most of those species in which the young remain some time in the nest, their droppings are collected and removed by the old birds—otherwise deep and hollow nests would become terribly fouled. The BRUSH TURKEY (q.v.) buries its eggs in a heap of dead vegetation, so that they are incubated by the heat of decay. Some birds bring up only one brood in a season, others as many as three.

It had been observed from ancient times that at certain seasons some species of birds were absent from their accustomed haunts. It used to be believed that the summer residents of the British Isles spent the winter in HIBERNATION (q.v.), sleeping in safe retreats until the spring, as do many species of mammals. When, however, in the late 18th and early 19th centuries, much more came to be known about the natural history of foreign lands, the truth about bird migration was established. Birds seen in Britain in the summer months were found to be inhabiting other countries during the winter, but not during the time of their residence in Britain. Migration seemed to be the only reasonable explanation—in fact, by regular movements to and fro about the world many species were able to inhabit areas which were suited to their needs for only part of the year. The routes which birds follow and the distances which they go have been much studied in the present century by the use of bird-ringing (or banding). A very light ring bearing an address and a serial number is clipped around the leg of the bird, and by the return of these rings from other lands, where the bird has been killed or found dead, it is possible to fix at least two points in its journeyings. (*See* MIGRATION.)

Because they can fly, birds are able to make long migrations relatively easily, for rivers or the sea do not present obstacles to them as they do to land animals. Some flightless birds, however, such as the PENGUINS (q.v.), perform long migrations partly by swimming and partly by walking over the ice. There was a tendency at one time greatly to exaggerate the speeds at which birds flew, more especially when on migration; but now it is known that speeds of more than 60 m.p.h. are rare, and that many small birds usually fly at speeds of between 20 and 30 m.p.h.

A hunting Barn Owl may fly as slowly as 14 m.p.h.

Birds have acute eyesight and good hearing, but little sense of smell (*see* SENSES). Though their senses closely resemble those of man, their mental processes are probably very different. They have a curious way of concentrating upon certain features of an object which engages their attention, and apparently neglecting others— they do not seem to look at the object as a whole. For example, the red breast of a ROBIN (q.v.) is a signal for another Robin to expel the intruder from his territory by battle (a stuffed Robin being just as fiercely attacked as a live one). A stuffed Robin with the breast discoloured, however, excites little attention; yet the red breast feathers alone, although not actually carried by a bird, will excite attack. Again, one of the American woodpeckers, the Flicker, distinguishes between the sexes by the presence or absence of a black moustachial streak, worn only by the male: a male Flicker will actually attack his own mate as though she were another male if she has an artificial 'moustache' glued to her plumage. That one small visual change seems to be sufficient to prevent his recognizing her. As soon as it is removed, however, he will greet her affectionately once again. The investigation of these problems of perception in birds has been one of the most rewarding lines of ornithological research in recent years.

BIRDWING BUTTERFLIES, *see* TROPICAL BUTTERFLIES, Section 2 *b*.

BISON. This huge animal is a member of the CATTLE family (q.v.), its main characteristics being short horns, a distinct beard under the chin, and high forequarters, which in winter are covered with a great mane of woolly hair. There are only two species, the European and the American Bison, which differ little from each other, and both of which are now protected in game preserves. In spite of their great size, bison are active animals, and can trot and gallop with great speed—they gallop with their heads close to the ground and their tails high in the air. During the breeding season they are fond of rolling in the dust, and the bulls fight fiercely amongst each other.

The European Bison or Wisent used to roam the large forests of Europe, and from fossil remains we know that it once inhabited Britain. Its numbers were gradually reduced by systematic hunting until it very nearly became extinct, and is now only to be found, protected, in eastern Europe. These bison feed mostly on the leaves, twigs, and bark of trees.

The American Bison lived in vast numbers, until comparatively recently, on the prairies of the United States and Canada. In 1871, a traveller estimated that a herd through which he had to pass covered an area of about 50 by 25 miles, and could not have numbered less than 4 million. The bison was to the Plains Indians of North America much what the camel was to the people of the Sahara, or the Yak to the people of Tibet—the provider of most of the necessities of life; and bison were hunted in every way possible (*see* AMERICAN INDIANS, NORTH, Vol. I). The decline in their numbers happened very quickly as the white man moved westwards, bringing horses and fire-arms with him. The massacre was completed when the building of the great railroads across the continent prevented the seasonal movements of the herds between north and south—a movement which had taken place from time immemorial. The vast armies employed on building the railway were supplied with buffalo beef ('buffalo' being the name quite inaccurately given by the European to the bison). One man, Buffalo Bill, with his troop of cowboys, entered into a contract to supply the meat, and consequently played a large part in practically exterminating the animals. An unusually fine bull may measure 5 feet 8 inches at the withers, but the average is considerably below this height. The cow does not breed till three years old, and sometimes produces two calves at a birth. American bison feed entirely on grass.

BITTERN, *see* HERON.

BLACK ARCHES MOTH, *see* TUSSOCK MOTHS.

BLACK BEETLE, *see* COCKROACH.

BLACKBIRD, *see* THRUSH.

BLACKCOCK, *see* GROUSE.

BLENNY. Most people who have examined a rock-pool on the coast after the tide has gone out will be familiar with Blennies. They are small

BUTTERFLY BLENNY. *A. Fraser-Brunner*

Blennies grow to quite a large size, inhabiting the open sea, and are of some value as food. The best-known of these are the Wolf-fishes, sometimes also called Cat-fishes, which have large and ugly heads, with very strong teeth, including canine or biting teeth in front of the jaws, and molars or crushing teeth at the back. Housewives are unwilling to buy such ugly-looking fish, so they are usually beheaded and skinned before being brought to market, where they are sold, along with other kinds, under the name 'Rock Salmon'.

fishes that lie in crevices in the rocks or among the weeds, and dart quickly from place to place. They seem to be able to withstand great variations of temperature; for when the cool waters of the sea have retreated, they survive in shallow pools exposed to the sun's rays, where the water may get quite warm.

There are very many different species of Blenny found on sea-shores throughout the world. All have rather long bodies, though the tropical species are usually shorter than those in the Arctic. The pelvic fins are placed far forward on the throat, and the two dorsal fins, the first of which has many spines, are usually joined together, extending right along the back. Most of them have little flaps of skin, tentacles or filaments, above the eyes, on the nose, or on top of the head.

Several different kinds of Blenny are found on the British coast, the best-known being the Common Blenny, which has tentacles over its eyes, and the Shanny which has none. The Butterfly Blenny is a handsome species, with a large and prettily marked first dorsal fin. Very similar kinds are found around America and Japan. All these, and many of the tropical species, have no scales; but there are also many kinds in which scales are present.

Most Blennies lay eggs, which they usually conceal carefully under stones or among sea-weed; but a few, such as the Viviparous Blenny of Europe, bear their young alive. A few

BLIND FISH. In the underground waters of limestone caves in the United States of America dwell a number of fishes, related to the ordinary freshwater fishes of that region, but having very small eyes. A prolonged existence in these dark surroundings has resulted in the complete loss of the sense of sight and the great development of special sense-organs in the skin, so that they can feel their way about the dark recesses of the caves and be aware of the presence of their prey. The best-known of these is the Kentucky Blind Fish from the famous Mammoth Cave, Kentucky.

Another group of fishes in which the eyes are very small, and which rely largely on their 'feelers' or barbels, namely, the CAT-FISHES (q.v.), have likewise found it possible to colonize caves and wells in the United States, Brazil, Trinidad, and Africa; while in the latter place, also, two or three relatives of the Barbel (*see* CARP) have taken up their abode in underground lakes.

The loss of all or most of their sight in these fishes is accompanied also by loss of colour, most of them being pale and translucent. Eyes are to see with, and coloration is largely for protection; but since neither of these is of value in total darkness, they have degenerated or disappeared. It has been shown, too, that the presence of light is necessary for the development of both eyes and pigment (the colouring matter of the skin). So in the very deep sea (the sun's rays being unable to penetrate beyond a depth of about 250

THE BLIND-FISH OF THE KENTUCKY CAVES AS IT IS SEEN BY TORCH-LIGHT
A. Fraser-Brunner

fathoms), many of the fishes are almost or quite blind, and, if blind, they are usually also colourless and provided with sensitive organs (*see* DEEP-SEA FISHES). Such are those belonging to a family called Brotulidae, to which the Cuban Blind Fishes belong. How these oceanic fishes came to be living in the underground freshwaters of Cuba is a matter of great interest: they must have been living among rocks at a time when these were raised up above the surface in a past geological age, and so have developed along with the caves, gradually becoming accustomed to living in fresh water.

The Blind Goby, found on the shores of southern California, spends its whole life under rocks or in the tunnels made by a species of burrowing shrimp. It is about 2 inches in length, pale pink in colour, with a smooth, naked skin. When very young, the eyes, though very small, can be used; but in the adult they are minute vestiges, and the fish is quite blind. It is, however, well supplied with sensitive organs on its head.

BLOODSUCKER LIZARD, *see* AGAMA.

BLOOD SYSTEM. In the majority of animals digested food and oxygen are carried to the living cells of the body in a fluid called blood. In a few very primitive animals, such as SPONGES, SEA-ANEMONES, and JELLY-FISH (qq.v.), the water in which they live is used for this purpose and there is no blood. In those animals which have blood, there is generally an arrangement for pumping it through the body. The pumping organ is the HEART (q.v.), and the canals by which the blood is carried away from it are known as the arteries. The blood returns to the heart through the veins. The pulse-rate (that is, the number of beats made by the heart in a minute) is usually measured by feeling the throbbing of the blood in one of the arteries. In the veins there is no such pulse.

The heart is a muscular organ, usually pear-shaped and, in the case of man, about the size of a closed fist. It is enclosed in a membranous bag, called the 'pericardium', which contains a lubricating fluid, enabling the heart to work smoothly and freely, without pressing against any adjacent organs. It is divided vertically into two halves by a wall or 'septum', and on each side is a thin-walled upper chamber, called the 'auricle', to receive inflowing blood, and a lower chamber, with a strong muscular wall, called the 'ventricle'. Valves between the upper and lower chambers prevent the blood from flowing back.

The left side of the heart always receives pure oxygenated blood from the lungs; the right side always receives impure blood returning from its

BLOOD SYSTEM OF EARTHWORM
Three main blood-vessels run the length of the body, connected just behind the mouth by five pairs of pulsatory tubes or 'hearts'.

journey through the body. When the heart contracts, pure blood flows out of the left ventricle by way of the main artery, called the 'aorta', and thence on, by a network of branching arteries, to all parts of the body. Having given up food and oxygen, the blood returns by way of the veins to the right auricle. At the same time as the left ventricle contracts, impure blood flows out of the right ventricle by way of the pulmonary artery to the lungs. On passing through the lungs, the impure blood gives up

Heart

Main artery

Main vein

BLOOD SYSTEM OF RABBIT
A number of arteries and veins run from the main artery and vein to all parts of the body

carbon dioxide and picks up a fresh supply of oxygen. Then it returns purified to the left auricle, by way of veins.

Thus there are two blood circuits: the body or systematic circulation, from the left ventricle to the top of the head and the tips of the toes, and back to the right auricle; and the lung or pulmonary circulation, from the right ventricle to the lungs, and back to the left auricle. As the left ventricle has to pump blood on a much longer journey, it is stronger and more muscular than the right ventricle, which is in comparison weak and flabby. About one gallon of impure blood is pumped into the lungs each minute in the body of an active human being. The same amount of pure blood is pumped to the body in the same time. When the body is at rest, the quantity may be reduced to one-half this amount.

The exchange of substances between the cells

of the body and the blood-stream takes place through very minute blood-vessels known as capillaries, into which the arteries branch out. This exchange does not take place directly, but through the lymph, a fluid which is a diluted form of plasma, the pale yellow liquid forming the fluid part of the blood. Floating in the plasma are red and white corpuscles. The red corpuscles are very small, round, elastic bodies, thicker at the rim than in the middle. They contain haemoglobin, a substance containing iron, which carries the oxygen. There are several kinds of white corpuscles, slightly larger than the red, and, unlike the red, all having nuclei (solid central parts). They are far less numerous than the red corpuscles, and their principal tasks are to feed on bacteria and to help in repairing damaged tissues. They can change their shape, or multiply by dividing into two, in the same way as an AMOEBA (q.v.).

BLOWFLY. There are two kinds of Blowfly—the Bluebottles which are dull blue, and their close relations, the Golden-greenbottles, which are brilliant metallic blue or green. These flies often enter houses, attracting attention by their loud buzzing noise. Their larvae feed on fresh or decaying meat, which is then, as every housewife knows, said to be 'fly-blown'. The maggots are like those of the HOUSE FLY (q.v.), but larger. They are often used for fishing bait, and are known as 'gentles'. Their life-history is similar to that of the House Fly, but takes longer to complete—a matter of about three weeks or a little more. They often lay their eggs in wounds: one of the Golden-greenbottles, which makes a habit of attacking sheep in order to lay its eggs, is called the Sheep-maggot Fly.

The maggots' habit of feeding on wounded animals has been made use of recently in surgery, with very satisfactory results. The larvae of the Golden-greenbottles, reared first under perfectly clean conditions, have been placed in wounds, and have cleared away pus-laden tissue and stopped the growth of bacteria in the wound.

See also FLIES.
See also Vol. XI, HOUSEHOLD PESTS.

BLUEBIRD (Blue Robin). This very well-known and favourite bird of North America is slightly larger than the European Robin, and is related to the WARBLERS on the one hand and the THRUSHES (qq.v.) on the other. The upper surface of the male is cobalt-blue, and the throat and underparts chestnut, while the female is an indeterminate blue-brown. The Bluebird winters in the southern States, and is one of the first birds to arrive in the Northern States in the spring, arriving as early as February or even January. The male arrives first, and greets the female on her arrival with a delicate bubbling song, to which she makes a low two-syllabled answer. They build a very simple nest of a few straws and feathers in a hole in a tree, and often in a nestbox. The hen lays four to six bluish-white eggs, and two or even three broods are produced in a year. Both male and female are excellent parents, feed their young on insect or vegetable food, and keep the nesting hole scrupulously clean.

BLUEBOTTLE, *see* BLOWFLY.

BLUES (Butterflies). There are eleven species of this large family of small butterflies in Britain. The Long-tailed and Short-tailed Blues visit Britain as rare migrants. The Mazarine Blue bred here in the last century, and became extinct about 1876, only occasional migrants having since been reported. In most species, the males have blue wings and the females brown, the undersides of the wings being peppered all over with various patterns of black dots. The caterpillars are shaped like wood-lice, and generally feed on leguminous plants, common on heaths and downs where Blues are usually to be found. Some species supplement their plant diet by preying on other species, and a few foreign species are entirely carnivorous.

The caterpillars of all the British species have a honey-gland on the back, which produces a sweet fluid very attractive to ants. The ants do not harm the caterpillars, but vigorously defend them against attack; so that both partners benefit from the association, one obtaining food and the other protection (*see* ANTS). The Large Blue, found only in North Cornwall, Devon, and the Cotswolds, has a very strange life-history. The eggs are laid in July on the buds of wild thyme, on the flowers of which the caterpillar feeds for about 20 days, augmenting its diet by attacking smaller individuals. Then it wanders, eventually being found by an ant, which strokes it until it yields some of the sweet fluid from its honey-gland. After an interval the caterpillar

suddenly hunches its back, a signal for the ant to carry it off to the nest; and there it remains for the rest of its caterpillar life, feeding on the ant larvae. It remains in the ants' nest as a chrysalis all winter, and emerges as a butterfly in early July. Both sexes of this butterfly are blue, with long white fringes to their wings.

The Small Blue is fairly well distributed over the chalk country and other regions of the British Isles, small colonies often being found in disused chalk-pits. The tiny females are dark chocolate-brown, and the males are faintly dusted with silvery-blue. Their wings are fragile, the scales coming off at the slightest touch. The caterpillars feed on kidney vetch, and generally live through the winter among the dead vetch flowers, which they exactly resemble. The butterflies emerge quite early in the summer.

The male of the Common Blue butterfly is pale violet-blue; usually the female is brown, but with some orange spots round the edges of her wings. Both sexes gather in the evening in long grass, where they rest head downwards. Two generations occur in southern England, in May and again in late August, though farther north there is only one generation, appearing during June and July. Isolation has produced distinct forms in Ireland and on one of the Scilly Islands. The caterpillars feed on bird's-foot trefoil, and hibernate when quite small, deep down in tufts of grass.

The Holly Blue is light blue, tinted with lilac, the female being distinguished by a deep border of black on the fore-wings, and a row of black dots round the edges of the hind-wings. This Blue hibernates as a chrysalis, attached by a girdle to the underside of an evergreen ivy leaf. It emerges very early in the spring, and, although a woodland species, is often seen in towns skipping over garden bushes, behaving more like a HAIRSTREAK (q.v.) than a Blue. The first brood lay their eggs chiefly on young shoots of holly. Some of these produce a more heavily marked second brood in July, while others hibernate and emerge the following spring. Occasionally there is a third brood, usually on the flower buds of ivy. The tiny, green, slug-like caterpillar eats its way into the centre of the bud as soon as it hatches, and remains hidden there until, having 'sucked' the bud dry, it moves to another one. The butterflies may sometimes be seen drinking at wet mud or moist dung.

The Chalk Hill Blue appears in August. The

male is 'Cambridge' blue, the female dusky, almost coffee-coloured, with a row of bright orange spots on the lower wings and fainter ones on the upper wings. The caterpillars feed on horseshoe vetch on the chalk downs of southern England, and can be found in the evenings crawling up out of thick grass tufts to feed.

The Adonis Blue is the most beautiful of the family. The caterpillars, which hibernate, feed only on horseshoe vetch. The butterflies are to be seen by May, a second brood appearing in late August, and in a fine autumn continuing even late into October. The Silver-studded Blue is fairly widely distributed in the south, in Norfolk and Suffolk, and in Wales, colonies often being found in rough meadows, on heaths and commons, and less frequently on the chalk. Distinct races occur on the mosses of north-west England and on the limestone cliffs of Caernarvon. The caterpillars feed on gorse, as well as on most low-growing leguminous plants, though the Caernarvon race eats rock rose. The winter is spent in the egg stage, the butterflies appearing in July and early August. The males are violet-blue with black hind margins; the females rich brown, often dusted with greyish-blue.

The Brown Argus is brown in both sexes, with a row of brilliant orange spots running round the edges of its wings. The Scottish race, possessing a white spot on the fore-wings, has only one generation a year, while the southern race is double-brooded. The two meet and interbreed in northern England, producing intermediates.

BOA. The Boa family of snakes is divided into two sub-families: the true Boas, which are found in tropical America and Madagascar, and the Pythons and Sand Boas, which inhabit Africa, Asia, and Australasia. The family includes the largest snakes now living, the Reticulated Python and the Anaconda, which reach a length of 28 or 30 feet. Such gigantic snakes have enormous strength, and can attack and overcome powerful animals, such as leopards and wild boars. Many Boas and Pythons are beautifully coloured with reds, greens, yellows, and blacks, and have a wonderful sheen on their scales when the skin has just been shed. Among the most beautiful are the Diamond Snake of Australia, the Royal Python of Africa, the Indian Python and the Reticulated Python of India, and the Boa Constrictor of South America.

GREEN TREE BOA
Zoological Society of London

The name Tree Boa is given to several species that live in trees. The Sand Boas inhabit the desert regions of south-west Asia and northern Africa, and spend much of their time buried in the soil; they have short, blunt-ended tails and are a dull uniform colour. The Anaconda, a dark greyish-brown above, with large black spots, lives in the dense forest regions of Brazil and the Guianas. It loves the water and spends much of its time in it. It feeds upon mammals and birds. The Blood Python, a small species found in Malaya, does not exceed 9 feet in length, but has a very thick body. It is brownish or red above, with large spots, the name Blood Python being a literal translation of its Malayan name.

See also SNAKE.

BOAR, *see* SWINE.

BOMBAY DUCK, *see* LANTERN FISH.

BONITO, *see* MACKEREL.

BOOKLOUSE. This very small, greyish-coloured creature looks rather like a minute animated dumb-bell. It belongs to a small group of insects containing some 800 species, of which about 50 occur in Britain. There are both winged and wingless species.

Booklice have jerky and uncertain movements, moving rapidly for a few moments and then suddenly stopping. When alarmed—and they are very easily alarmed—they run quickly into hiding with none of their previous indecision. They are quite common in houses, where they seem to prefer a shady room to a well-lighted one. They may be seen running over mantelpieces and the tops of furniture, and particularly along the shelves of libraries, to which they are attracted by the paste of the bindings. They will also eat any fragments of dry and decaying animal and vegetable refuse. Many are also found in the open, on the bark of trees or in moss, and seem to feed upon minute fungi. They are not particularly harmful in houses, apart from the damage they do to books; but they sometimes cause damage to stores of grain and flour. Like so many other wingless insects, their ability to get about from place to place is remarkable, while their minute size enables them to enter closed boxes, the contents of which would have been thought well secured.

× 14

It has been said that Booklice can make a tapping noise; but it is quite remarkable that so small an animal should be able to make so much noise.

BOWER BIRD, *see* BIRDS OF PARADISE, Section 2; Colour Plate facing p. 16.

BRACKEN, *see* FERNS.

BRAIN. This organ comprises the chief group of nerve cells found in the central NERVOUS SYSTEM (q.v.). In vertebrates it consists of the enlarged and highly developed front region of the spinal cord and is enclosed within and protected by the skull. In many invertebrates a group of cells in front of the mouth has a similar function to the brain, though this is very simple, consist-

ing only of a pair of cerebral ganglia or nerve-centres.

As soon as animals ceased to be sedentary and started to move about actively in search of food, the shape of the body changed from a radial pattern, such as we see in SEA-ANEMONES and STARFISHES (qq.v.), and took on a form known as 'bilaterally symmetrical', in which the left half of the body is the mirror image of the right. At the same time, one part of the body became the front or head end and the other the hind end. The front end, because it is what may be called the 'business' end—the end first to make contact with the outside world as the animal moves forward—became the lodging-place for the more important sense-organs, those of smell, sight, hearing, and taste. Since the NERVOUS SYSTEM is the means for receiving messages from the SENSES, and for transmitting the necessary instructions to the MUSCLES (qq.v.) and other organs, it is natural that there should be a great concentration of it close to the sense organs themselves. Just as in a telephone exchange there is a complicated mass of wires, so in the brain there is a complicated mass of nerve fibres.

In all Vertebrates the brain first appears in the developing embryo (the undeveloped animal before birth) as a swollen front end of the spinal chord. This is faintly divided into three parts, known respectively as the fore-brain, mid-brain, and hind-brain, each part being hollow. As the embryo grows, the brain unfolds along a definite pattern. The simplest brain is found in FISHES (q.v.): here the fore-brain becomes divided into three parts, a pair of olfactory or smelling lobes in front and the cerebrum or thinking part behind. The hinder part of the fore-brain bears the 'optic thalami' (the place where the

A   B   C   D

BRAINS OF (A) FISH, (B) AMPHIBIAN, (C) BIRD, (D) MAMMAL
The cerebrum or cerebral hemispheres (CH), the thinking part of the brain, develops enormously from the lower to the higher animal.
CB = cerebellum (controlling sense of balance)
OL = olfactory lobes (controlling sense of smell)
OPL = optic lobes (controlling sense of sight)

nerve emerges from the brain) and two glands called the 'pineal' and the 'pituitary'. The mid-brain gives rise to a pair of optic or seeing lobes; and the hind-brain becomes divided into two very important organs—the 'cerebellum', which is concerned with the control of all movements, and the 'medulla oblongata', which controls such functions as breathing, the circulation of the blood, swallowing, and feeding.

It follows that the shape and proportions of the brain vary according to the habits of the animal possessing it. Those depending largely on smell for their livelihood, as dogs and wolves do, have well-developed olfactory lobes; those depending on sight, as birds do, have large optic lobes. Intelligence is linked with the growth and size of the cerebrum, which is quite small in the fish but develops to an enormous size in human beings.

See also INTELLIGENCE.

BREAM, *see* CARP.

BRILL, *see* FLATFISHES.

BRIMSTONE BUTTERFLY, *see* YELLOWS (Butterflies).

BRISTLE FLY (or Tachinid). This is a stoutly built insect, about the size of the House-fly, though some are larger. They all have strong bristles on their abdomens. Their larvae are internal parasites in the grubs of moths, butterflies, beetles, and some other kinds of insects, which they kill when fully grown. Usually the Bristle Fly lays its egg on the body of the caterpillar, and the newly hatched maggot burrows through the caterpillar's skin. Some species however, lay their eggs on leaves, and so are eaten and hatch inside the body of the caterpillar. It often happens, during the summer, that a healthy-looking caterpillar will suddenly collapse, with its body bent into several short,

× 2

straight lengths. If the skin is slit from end to end, a number of whitish maggots will be found within. If the skin had not been slit open, the maggots would have bored their way out. After wandering about for a while, the maggots turn reddish-brown and become oval in shape—the new form being the puparia, from which Bristle Flies emerge in due course. Anyone who has opened up a collapsed caterpillar for the first time must have been struck with the completeness of the job done by the Tachinid maggots. There is practically nothing of the caterpillar left inside the skin—it is extraordinary that it is able to keep going so long.

Bristle Flies must exercise a very big effect upon the numbers of other kinds of insects. One species is believed to destroy as many as four-fifths of the caterpillars of the Small Tortoiseshell Butterfly in some years. The caterpillar of the Red Admiral Butterfly, the big furry caterpillar of the Tiger-moth, and the cream and red caterpillar of the Dagger Moth are also often severely attacked. Among Beetles, many weevil larvae are attacked by Bristle Flies; so also are the larvae of the burnished Golden Beetles, in particular the little green one found in summer on St. John's Wort. Usually, when these smaller insects are attacked, only one Bristle Fly comes out of each destroyed larva. Sometimes, with Butterflies and Moths, two different species of Bristle Fly develop from one parasitized caterpillar.

See also FLIES.

BRISTLE-WORM, *see* WORMS, Section 4.

BROWNS (Butterflies). This family is made up of brown or yellowish-brown butterflies, usually having somewhere on their wings black spots with white centres, resembling eyes. Most of them have a slow and feeble flight. There is usually one generation a year, and the winter is normally spent in the caterpillar state. They do not hibernate completely, but sleep intermittently, waking to nibble at grasses on warm winter days. The HEATHS (q.v.), described separately, also belong to this family.

The Meadow Brown, very common in the British Isles, is perhaps the laziest of all butterflies, and will almost allow itself to be trodden on before taking to wing. The females are more orange-brown than the males, and have much larger eye-spots on their forewings. Dis-

THE WALL BUTTERFLY SETTLING TO REST.

Left, The eye-spot in fore-wing is exposed. *Right,* The eye-spot is covered by the hind-wing. *S. Beaufoy, F.R.P.S.*

tinct races occur in Scotland, Ireland, and the Scilly Islands. The caterpillars are green, with a cream-coloured stripe above the legs. Like most Browns, they feed on grass under cover of darkness, and crawl down among the tufts of grass at dawn. The rich orange-brown Gatekeeper, sometimes known as the Hedge Brown, is to be seen commonly in country lanes, rough fields, on heather, in woods, and on commons.

The Grayling, found on dry heaths and downs, is the most alert and fast-flying of this family. On alighting, it displays for an instant the eyespots on the underside of the fore-wings, so diverting the attention of any watching enemies from its vulnerable body to the relatively unimportant wings. When the danger has passed, the conspicuous fore-wings are slid out of sight beneath the hind-wings, which so closely resemble the background in pattern that the butterfly becomes indistinguishable from it. Finally, the butterfly heels over at a steep angle from the sun, so that not even its shadow betrays its presence. It sits for long periods taking advantage of its perfect camouflage, but if disturbed, it is up and away in a flash. The females are more brightly coloured than the males on the upperside, and have cream-coloured splashes on all four wings. The caterpillars are brownish-grey, with darker lines running the length of the body. They pupate beneath the surface of the ground, making a rough cocoon, as certain moths do—a habit unique among British butterflies.

The Wall Butterfly sits with wings wide open on sunny walls—the reason, presumably, for its popular name. But it also frequents exposed hedgerows and the southern sides of hills, being an extremely restless butterfly, settling only for a few moments. The females lay their eggs on various grasses. The greenish caterpillars are long and thin, tapering towards the tail, and are quite inconspicuous amongst blades of grass. There are two distinct broods, in May and again in August.

WALL BUTTERFLY SPREADING ITS WINGS IN THE SUNSHINE
S. Beaufoy, F.R.P.S.

The Speckled Wood Butterfly avoids direct sunshine, preferring shady lanes and rather overgrown woodland ridings. Numbers of them may often be seen playing 'hide-and-seek' in and out of sunlit patches and shadows. The caterpillars, a clear green with a rather round green head, are continuously brooded from April to October. Strangely enough, only some of the caterpillars go into hibernation in September: the others pass the winter as chrysalises, hanging from withered grass stems and looking like large drops of greenish oil.

The Marbled White, a black and white butterfly with markings like a chess-board, differs markedly in some of its habits from the other members of the family. It lives in colonies on the rough grassy slopes of chalk downs or un-cultivated fields and waysides, never straying far from its breeding-ground. Unlike most other Browns, which seem to select with the greatest care a certain blade of grass for each egg they deposit, the females drop their eggs loose amongst the grass as they fly lazily to and fro. After eating the egg-shell, a source of protein food, the caterpillars hibernate until the spring, when they crawl up at dusk every night to feed on young grasses. They are greyish, with two yellow lines running the length of the body. Two famous specimens of this butterfly, a white one caught in 1843 and a black one taken in 1871, were sold at auction in 1943 for £110.

The Scotch Argus, though quite common in parts of Scotland, occurs in few places in England. It is a medium-sized butterfly, with rich brown wings, near the outer margin of which is a lighter band of rusty red, dotted with eye-spots. The caterpillars feed after dark on various grasses. The butterfly is on the wing throughout August, keeping to the lower slopes and valleys in mountainous districts. The Mountain Ring-let, much like the Scotch Argus but only about half the size, is the rarest of this family. Though more widely distributed in Scotland, it is found in England only above 1,800 feet, in little pockets in the mountainous districts of Cumberland and Westmorland. It is nowhere easy to find.

The Ringlet Butterfly, characteristic of wood-land rides, looks almost black from a distance, but at close quarters is a dark chocolate-brown. One variety has no rings round the eye-spots, and another has the spots much enlarged and almost pear-shaped. It, also, like the Marbled White, drops its eggs at random. The cater-pillars are small when they hibernate, and by the spring are brownish-grey and slightly hairy. They pupate on the ground in tufts of dead grass, and emerge in July.

BRUSH TURKEY. This bird is no relative of the Turkey, though it has a superficial resem-blance to it. It belongs to an Australasian group of birds, called Megapodes, which bury their eggs in mounds of sand, earth, or decaying vegetable matter, and allow them to be hatched by the warmth of the sun or by the heat generated by fermentation. The cock Brush Turkey spends a considerable part of the year in building a great mound of dead leaves and other rubbish, which he rakes up with his large feet, always working backwards. The hen-bird places her eggs in

tiers in a vertical position, the more pointed end downwards. During the period of incubation the cock-bird guards the mound against all intruders, and, when a chick is hatched, he care-fully scratches away the material to let it out. The chick emerges in a well-developed condi-tion and able to look after itself.

Closely related is the Maleo, a remarkable bird about the size of a domestic fowl, which inhabits North Celebes. It has dark brown upper plumage and salmon-pink underparts, with an almost naked head carrying a large, black, helmet-like protuberance. Several birds lay their eggs in the same place, burying them in the sand on the beach, where they are even-tually hatched by the warmth of the sun.

BUDGERIGAR, see PARROT.

BUFFALO. These wild CATTLE (q.v.) are all heavily built animals with thick, strong limbs, moderately long tails tufted at the end, short necks, very broad muzzles, and large ears. Their hair is often very thin, and in old age

OLD BULL BUFFALO PUSHING HIS WAY THROUGH THE BUSH AFTER HIS MUD BATH
Paul Popper

A HERD OF BUFFALO ON THE PLAINS OF MOZAMBIQUE
The white birds circling over the animals are Tickbirds (cattle herons), which pick vermin off the animals' backs.
Paul Popper

leaves the skin almost entirely naked. The main species are the African Buffalo, Indian Buffalo, and the Anoa or Pigmy Buffalo of Celebes in the East Indies. The North American 'buffaloes' are not buffaloes at all, but BISON (q.v.).

The largest African Buffaloes are found living in large herds in the reedy swamps of South and East Africa. The old bulls, who often live to some 30 years of age, often wander alone or in small parties. They are usually black, with horns which vary in size, but sometimes reach a span of nearly 50 inches between the two bends. A well-grown bull will stand about 5 feet at the shoulder. The calves are born, apparently never more than one at a birth, from January to March. The cow hides her calf in long grass, and for about ten days separates herself from the herd, to remain within a short distance of her offspring. A smaller African buffalo, known locally as the Bush Cow, lives in the forests of West and Central Africa. It is covered with bright orange-red, longish hair, and has long fringes on its ears. The bulls stand only about $3\frac{1}{2}$ to 4 feet high at the shoulder.

The Asiatic Buffaloes have larger heads and smaller ears than the African, and their horns are longer, though less massive at the base. They are very fond of water, and generally live in swamps. Wild Indian Buffaloes are nearly always found in herds of about fifty head. The calves are born in summer, and there are often two at a birth. The Indian Buffalo has been domesticated since very early times: it is bred to provide milk and used also as a beast of burden. One of its characteristics is that it always carries its head very low.

The Anoas or Pigmy Buffaloes, which live in the forests of Celebes, are the smallest wild cattle, being little over 3 feet high. They have almost straight, sharp-pointed horns, about a foot long. The males are fierce little creatures, and turn their sharp horns against any animal that interferes with them. The new-born calves have a fawn coat of woolly hair; but as they grow older the hair is gradually shed, until the bulls become quite bare, their skin shining as though it were polished.

BUFF-TIP MOTH, *see* PROMINENT MOTHS.

BUG. This word is used loosely, with many meanings. The entomologist uses the word for a large and important group of insects with special characteristics. The mouth part of a bug is formed into a 'beak' for piercing and sucking. This beak may be short or long (in some species even longer than the body); but it is always present, whether the insect is mature or immature. There are usually two pairs of wings, though many species are wingless. By comparing their wings, we can split up this very large group into two divisions. In the first, the tip of the fore-wing is soft and flexible, all the rest of it being stiff and horny. The fore-wings are used as 'elytra' or wing-cases, to protect the hindwings, which are folded beneath them when the insect is not in flight. This division includes the BED-BUG, the SHIELD BUG of woodlands, and the WATER-BOATMAN of ponds and streams (qq.v.). In the second division, though the fore-wings are often stiff, there is no flexible tip. This includes the APHIDES and FROG-HOPPERS (qq.v.). The METAMORPHOSIS (q.v.) of all bugs is incomplete, the nymph (or immature bug) resembling its parents except for the smallness of the wings. These increase in size at each cast of the skin until the adult stage is reached; only then are they of use in flight.

Bugs feed throughout life by piercing living tissues, either animal or plant, and sucking the juices. Most of them attack plants only, but others live on animal juices, and some of them cause very painful wounds.

ASSASSIN BUG
× 2

There are a great many kinds of bugs, including some very interesting and important insects. The Assassin Bugs in most instances live on other insects, though a few attack higher animals, including man. The British species are quite harmless—indeed one of the largest of them attacks the Bed-bug, flying into houses by night to do so. It chirps like a grasshopper, probably producing the sound by rubbing its beak against its body between the forelegs.

The Lace Bugs are pretty creatures, so called because of the gauze-like appearance of their wings and of the thin expanded parts of the thorax. The Capsid Bugs are a very numerous family, there being about 170 species in Britain alone. They are mostly soft-bodied, delicate creatures with long legs; and they are exceedingly active. They run with speed and, if alarmed, fall off their food plant, but soon fly back again. They used to be quite harmless; but, unfortunately, a few of them have recently altered their habits to attack fruit-trees and other crops, sometimes doing them serious damage. The Tarnished Plant-bug, for instance, does great harm to potatoes and is now known to be an almost world-wide pest of cultivated plants. The bright green Apple Capsid does great damage to fruit-trees. The Tea-bug, very destructive to the tea plants in Assam, is also a Capsid. The black and red Cotton-stainers or Red Bugs have for long been serious pests to cotton-growers, for they pierce the stems and bolls of the plants and suck the juices—and, worst of all, stain the cotton. The American Cinch-bug is very destructive to wheat and other cereals.

CAPSID BUG
× 5

Although most of these insects are found on land, some have taken to water. Besides the Water-boatmen and WATER-SCORPIONS (q.v.), there are the Water Measurers or Pond Skaters, and Water Striders. A Pond Skater has a velvet pile on the undersurface of the body which prevents it from becoming wet, and it usually creeps slowly on the surface of the water—to which habit it owes its name of Water Measurer. It has a slender body and a very long head. Its food seems to consist of such dead insects as it may find floating on the top of the water. Water Striders are shorter and stouter insects, with very long legs; and they move much more rapidly over the surface of the water. In still pools they may often be found in great numbers. They are capable of jumping from the water to attack insects that have fallen in and are struggling on the surface.

See also APHIS; BED-BUG; FROG-HOPPER; LANTERN-FLY; SCALE-INSECT; SHIELD BUG; WATER-BOATMAN; WATER-SCORPION.

BULBS, see STEMS, Section 2 d.

BULBUL. This bird is a little smaller than a thrush, with rather short legs and wings, and most species have crests. It is usually grey or brown, but many species have bright colours, either on the ear-coverts or under the tail-coverts. It is found in southern Asia, the East Indies, and Africa.

Green Bulbuls or Fruit-suckers have very much the same habits, but belong, in fact, to a different family. They have longer, stronger legs, green plumage, and no crest. They live on fruit, the nectar of flowers, and insects. The Golden-fronted Fruit-sucker is often kept as a cage-bird, and becomes extremely tame. The word Bulbul is also used in Turkey and Persia to describe the NIGHTINGALE (q.v.), and in this connexion has found its way into English poetry.

BULLFINCH, see FINCHES, Section 4.

BUMBLE-BEE (*Bombus*). This belongs to the group of insects called Hymenoptera, and is a member of the Bee family. It is one of the social bees, as is the Honey Bee (*see* BEES). Bumble-bees occur almost entirely in the cooler parts of the world, one species being found as far north as Lapland; while those few which occur in the tropics seem to be confined to high mountain ranges. There are some twenty-five different kinds in Britain, most of them black, with yellow bands and white-tipped abdomens. *Bombus lapidarius*, a very handsome bee, is closely covered with black hairs, and has a conspicuously red-tipped abdomen. A few species, among them the very common *Bombus agrorum*, are almost entirely brown.

The queen comes out of her winter sleep in the spring or early summer, and soon sets about the important business of founding her home. She likes a deserted mouse burrow, making herself snug and comfortable in the nest of grass and leaves left by the mouse. After working hard for about a month, gathering honey and pollen for

NEST OF BUMBLE-BEE
a. Empty cells used for storing honey.
b. Masses of growing larvae covered with wax and pollen.
c. Clumps of cocoons spun by larvae before pupating.

her growing family, she has usually brought up a small brood of some half a dozen workers, who then take over the task of running the little community. Henceforth, the queen devotes herself to egg-laying, and, with possible rare exceptions, never leaves the nest again. Towards the end of summer, males and perfect females (like the queen-mother) are reared by the workers from eggs laid by the queen. These fly from the nest for mating. After a short life the males die; but the young queens, as soon as they have been fertilized by the males, hide away in the ground or among leaves, and there they remain for their winter sleep until the following year.

Some Bumble-bees nest on the surface of the ground. They are called Carder Bees, from their habit of tearing dried blades of grass into fine threads, which they weave into their dome-shaped nests. They are the brown Bumble-bees referred to above; and the commonest of them, *Bombus agrorum*, is very frequently seen in gardens and often makes its nest in rough grass. The communities of Bumble-bees are usually small, rarely containing as many as 100 workers. On the whole the bees themselves are not aggressive: most of the species do not even attack when their nest is seriously disturbed. But *Bombus terrestris*, one of the commonest of the banded kinds, will sting fiercely in defence of its home.

Of particular interest are the Cuckoo-bees (*Psithyrus*). They are not Bumble-bees, but so closely resemble the true Bumble-bees that only an expert can tell them apart. However, like the bird which gives them their name, they are unable to feed and bring up their young themselves—so they get the Bumble-bees to do it for them. The female Cuckoo-bee (to whom we can hardly give the title of queen, since she does not produce worker bees) seeks out the nest of the Bumble-bee in early summer, and settles down in it. At first the *Bombus* workers try to drive her out; but, thanks to her thick armour plating, she is well protected against their stings, and is soon allowed to crawl about the nest unmolested. After a while she kills the *Bombus* queen, and usurps her role as head of the colony. The workers then tend and rear the brood of the Cuckoo female. Males and females eventually emerge and leave the nest for pairing, as do the *Bombus* males and females. After this the males soon die, and the females go into hibernation for the winter.

In the Bumble-bee community there is no elaborately constructed comb—the actual nest is formed merely by the accumulated mass of tough cocoons spun by the larvae before pupation. There are no sharp differences between queen and worker, except size and the inability of the worker to become fertilized and produce offspring. The queen is, in fact, a very capable worker, for she can collect honey and pollen and tend her brood, just as the workers do.

See also BEES.

BUNTING, *see* FINCHES, Section 7.

BURNET AND FORESTER MOTHS. These brightly coloured, day-flying moths are sometimes mistaken for butterflies, but may be distinguished by the antennae. The Burnets have dark, metallic greenish or bluish fore-wings with crimson spots and hind-wings, while the Foresters have golden green fore-wings and grey hind-wings. They move slowly, boldly displaying themselves on flowers, often in groups, their conspicuous colours serving to remind possible enemies that, in fact, they are unpleasant to taste. (*See* PROTECTIVE COLORATION.) Over 100 species are known, of which seven Burnets and three Foresters occur in Britain. One Burnet is restricted to the New Forest, and another to the mountains of Aberdeenshire. The Five and Six Spot Burnets are locally common in June among long grasses. Several species have thinly scaled and rather transparent wings. Blackish and yellow varieties are occasionally found, and, more frequently, specimens in which the crimson spots of the fore-wings have run together.

The black and yellow spotted green caterpillars are stout and somewhat hairy, and feed, without seeking cover, chiefly on trefoils and vetches. They hibernate as caterpillars, and in May they spin tough, yellowish, spindle-shaped

BURNET MOTHS. *S. Beaufoy, F.R.P.S.*

cocoons in which to pupate. Those of the Six Spot Burnet are sometimes found attached to such supports as twigs or fences, though more usually they choose grass stalks some distance above the ground—for birds find them more difficult to attack and break open from the slender swaying grasses. Both the caterpillar and the blackish chrysalis within the cocoon are thought to be distasteful to birds; but this fails to protect them in the breeding season, when there are numerous young birds to feed.

The Scarce Forester, attached to knapweeds, is found only on the Sussex and Kentish downs, while the Cistus Forester, which feeds on rockrose, occurs both on chalk and limestone, and extends as far as Yorkshire and Wales. The Common Forester is found locally in damp meadows and the outskirts of woods all over England, and less frequently in Wales, Scotland, and Ireland. The young caterpillar bores between the upper and lower surfaces of a sorrel leaf, soon making characteristic blotches by eating away the leaf until nothing is left but the transparent skin. After hibernation, it attaches its tough white cocoon low down on stems. The moths may be caught at the flowers of Ragged Robin in June.

See also Moth.

BURYING BEETLES, *see* Beetles.

BUSTARD. This bird belongs to the same order as the Crane (q.v.). It is a lover of open country, and the Great Bustard used to breed on Salisbury Plain and in stretches of East Anglia. Although it now occasionally migrates to Britain in the winter, more than a hundred years have passed since a nest was found. There are altogether about 30 species, all confined to the Eastern Hemisphere. The Bustard is a large, heavy bird, with stout legs and broad, rounded wings. A full-sized male may measure 4 feet from tip of beak to tail, and its wing-span may be as much as 8 feet. It is a handsome buff and brown bird, its back being marked with russet and black bars, and its underparts and wing-coverts white or grey. It has keen eyesight and can detect an enemy from afar. Its food is mainly vegetarian, though most species also eat reptiles, mice, or any other animal food that comes their way.

During the mating season the cock Bustard performs a remarkable courtship display. To

GREAT BUSTARD. *Harold Bastin*

attract the hen it inflates its neck and breast feathers, throws forward its tail, and spreads its wings. The cocks fight for the hens much as turkeys do, and even after the hens are sitting on their eggs the cocks often go on sparring— apparently for pleasure. (*See* Animal Language.)

There are several other birds closely allied to Bustards, among them the Indian Floricans, very long-legged black birds with more or less white wings. They are shy and wary, and not easy to approach.

BUTCHER-BIRD, *see* Shrike.

BUTTERFLIES. These belong to the same order of insects as Moths (q.v.), the Lepidoptera (scaly wings). All Lepidoptera have their whole surface, and particularly their wings, covered with minute scales, and they possess a sucking proboscis. Butterflies are to be found in most parts of the world: there are very many different species in the tropics, but fewer species in temperate climates. The British Isles have about sixty different butterflies, and there are altogether about 10,000 species known in the world—many fewer than moths, of which there are 2,000 in Britain alone.

The main groups of British butterflies are the Skippers, Whites, Blues, Hairstreaks, Browns, and the Nymphalidae (Fritillaries, Tortoiseshells, &c.) (qq.v.). The Duke of Burgundy and the Swallow-tail (qq.v.) are the only representatives of their families in Britain Some butterflies migrate to the British

Fig. 1. DIAGRAM OF BUTTERFLY

a. Clubbed Antennae; *b.* Compound Eye; *c.* Proboscis; *d.* Thorax; *e.* Abdomen; *f.* Femur; *g.* Tibia; *h.* Tarsus.

Butterflies can be distinguished from moths by their antennae, which are clubbed, and by the fact that, when they rest, they hold their wings vertically over their backs, exposing the underside, whereas most moths rest with wings folded down over the body. It is often said that butterflies fly by day and moths by night: yet though all British butterflies certainly are day-fliers, so are a number of moths. Generally speaking, butterflies are more brilliantly coloured than moths, though some moths, especially in the tropics, have magnificent colours.

A butterfly has two pairs of wings—fore and hind. These are composed of an upper and lower membrane stretched over a framework of hollow ribs or 'veins', much as an umbrella cover is spread over the frame. The way the 'veins' are arranged is an extremely important point in CLASSIFICATION (q.v.). The patterns and colours on the wings are due to minute scales attached by short stalks to the membrane. These scales are actually broad, flattened hairs, which overlap like slates on a roof and are so close together and so tiny that, until very closely examined, they appear to be one complete surface. Looked at through a microscope, the scales are seen to be of many different shapes and sizes, often varying on different parts of the wing, as well as on the wings of different species. The colour is, for the most part, pigment laid inside the scales during the stage in the insect's life when it is confined in a chrysalis. The underside of the wings usually has a different and much less conspicuous pattern than the upper-sides, so that the butterfly, when at rest with its wings folded over its back, remains hidden from view. The names of the different parts of a butterfly's body can be seen from Fig. 1.

Isles every year and stay to breed there: these include the Red Admiral and the Painted Lady of the Vanessinae family, and the Clouded YELLOWS (qq.v.). Occasional visitors to Britain are the MONARCH (q.v.) from North America, the Queen of Spain Fritillary, the Bath White, the Long and Short-tailed Blues from the Continent, and the Camberwell Beauty from northern Europe.

Most butterflies inhabit a particular kind of environment. The Cabbage White haunts gardens and allotments—as most gardeners know to their cost. Small Tortoiseshells and Peacocks also frequent gardens; and most people have seen the magnificent Red Admirals settled, with wings spread out, on buddleias or Michaelmas daisies, or feasting on over-ripe, fallen plums. Fritillaries, on the other hand, are to be found in the open clearings of woods, although some prefer rough, grassy uplands, where their strong, fast flight is in striking contrast to the rather slow, clumsy flight of the Browns, which are to be seen in most country lanes and fields. Blues are characteristic of chalk hills and downs. In the evening sunshine they will settle with wings outspread, looking like sapphire jewels, and then, as dusk descends, they gather, head down-wards, with wings closed, several together on a grass stem or flower head. The Hairstreaks and Skippers do not belong to any particular terri-tory—some frequent woods, others heaths and commons, while at least two of the Skippers seem particularly fond of grassy railway banks.

Fig. 2. PART OF THE WING OF A BUTTERFLY SHOWING THE ARRANGEMENT OF SCALES

A

B

C

D

Fig. 3. LIFE-CYCLE OF SMALL TORTOISESHELL BUTTERFLY, FROM (A) EGG, (B) LARVA, (C) CHRYSALIS, TO (D) ADULT
S. Beaufoy, F.R.P.S.

Male and female butterflies are often very different in appearance, the male usually carrying far more brilliant colours and taking the active part in courtship, though the female is often the larger. The male of a Common Blue is a beautiful violet blue; while the female is not blue at all, but a much less conspicuous reddish-brown. The female of the Orange-tip is without the gay orange tip which the male carries on its white wings. The male of the gigantic tropical Bird-wing has magnificent velvety, green, gold, purple, and black wings; but the female, often distinctly larger, is an inconspicuous brown or buff. The female's larger wing expanse no doubt enables her to carry better her heavier body distended with eggs, while her more sombre appearance gives her greater protection. Occasionally freak specimens occur in which one side is coloured like the male and the other like the female.

The courtship of a female by a male is one of the most interesting things a butterfly hunter can see. One of the world's most common butterflies, *Danaus chrysippus*, a near relative of the Monarch, and found everywhere in tropical and sub-tropical countries in the Old World, uses a remarkable piece of apparatus in courtship. The male hovers near the female, endeavouring to charm her with scent by protruding a powder-puff from the end of his body. The scent is produced by special scales in a particular patch on the hind wing, and the butterfly charges the powder-puff with scent by protruding it and wiping it on this patch. Special scent-producing scales are also found on British butterflies: the male Green-veined White has a scent like lemon-verbena, and the male Grayling has been seen to perform antics in front of the female in the endeavour to bring its scent patches into contact with her antennae. But only in tropical butterflies has complicated apparatus, such as the powder-puff, been evolved. (*See* ANIMAL LANGUAGE.)

A female butterfly may lay less than 100 or

Fig. 4. DANAIDAE
BUTTERFLY: POWDER-
PUFF APPARATUS

up to 3,000 eggs, the number as well as the size and shape of the eggs varying according to the family to which it belongs. Most butterflies lay their eggs singly, placing them on the leaves of a particular plant suitable for the food of the caterpillar when it emerges. How they select the right plant is a mystery; but one butterfly, the Painted Lady, has been observed drumming on various leaves with its front feet, presumably until it makes contact with a leaf of the right type. This contact stimulates it to cease drumming and to lay an egg. Butterflies certainly have highly sensitive taste-organs on their feet. Some species, in particular the Whites, lay large batches of eggs together on the food-plant. Unless conditions are abnormal in some way, an average of one or two eggs only out of a hundred reach maturity—the others fall victim at some stage to the butterflies' natural enemies. This is the way in which the balance of numbers is maintained. The ordinary cycle of a butterfly's life is from egg to larva (caterpillar), then to chrysalis (pupa), and then to adult butterfly (imago), a process called a complete META-MORPHOSIS (q.v.). Its adult life is generally very short—perhaps only a few weeks; though some species, particularly the Brimstones and members of the family Nymphalidae, sometimes live in a state of complete rest, neither eating nor moving, in a sheltered place all through the winter (*see* HIBERNATION). Butterflies feed on nectar from flowers, over-ripe fruit, and any other sweet food, which they suck up with their mouth-parts. A few imbibe juices from carrion or animal droppings. In the tropics, and occasionally in very hot summers in Britain, some species will swarm on damp patches of ground, where they drink freely. The sugars which constitute their normal food supply the necessary fuel to replace the energy expended in flight. But body-building foods are not a necessity to them in their short lives, as all growth takes place in the CATERPILLAR stage (q.v.)—in fact, some species have mouth-parts which will not open, so that they cannot feed.

See also CATERPILLAR; INSECT; METAMORPHOSIS; MIGRATION.

BUTTERFLIES AND MOTHS (Tropical).

1. 'Tropical' is a geographical term used for lands lying between the tropics of Cancer and Capricorn. But quite close to the Equator there are snow-capped mountains where, of course, no 'tropical' insects can live; and in other highlands within the tropical regions the climate is temperate, and so we find insects much like our own. A common Small COPPER (q.v.), for instance, very much like the British species, is found in the highlands of East Africa; and a form of our Large WHITE (q.v.) lives in Abyssinia. Here, however, we are concerned with butterflies and moths (Lepidoptera) living in lands with a hot climate. In the lower-lying hot lands of the tropics are found many spectacular and gaudy insects not to be seen in colder climates.

As in England, the favourite haunts of butterflies and moths are wooded lands and grass lands—clearings in forests, or openings made by roads or rivers, and the open savannahs. The insects appear in greatest numbers during or after a rainy season, and are not often seen in the dry season. Some butterflies, especially a relative of the Tortoiseshell in Africa, appear different according to whether they are caught in the wet or dry season. Most species feed chiefly on the nectar in flowers, and on fruit juices—they generally prefer rotting fruit, and an over-ripe bunch of bananas is good bait for many fine species. Decomposing animal matter or droppings attract certain species.

2. TROPICAL BUTTERFLIES. These often belong to the same families as British species; but the larger and more gaudy members of the family are to be found only in the tropics. Their brilliant colours are often a form of PROTECTIVE COLORATION (q.v.) called 'warning coloration', since they warn any insect-eating animal that this insect is unpleasant to the taste. The caterpillars, also, often carry warning colours. A characteristic butterfly of the Ethiopian region (Africa), an *Acraea*, for instance, has brightly coloured wings in red, yellow, and black, which would remind any animal that this insect is better avoided.

The tropical regions of the world include the Ethiopian (Africa), the Oriental (southern Asia), the Australasian, and the tropical American regions. Moths and butterflies show the same general distribution in those regions as do other animals (*see* ANIMAL AND PLANT DISTRIBUTION).

(*a*) Ethiopian Region. As well as the brilliant *Acraea* mentioned above, there are a great many kinds of BLUES (q.v.), many of which have caterpillars which are intimately associated with ants, as is the British Large Blue. Others have hairy caterpillars more like those of moths. One interesting African species successfully mimics a distasteful butterfly, and so acquires protection. A black and white butterfly called *Amauris*, found only in Africa, is a member of the same large family (Danaidae) as the American Milkweed butterfly, a noteworthy migrant (*see* MIGRATION). There are a great many SWALLOWTAILS (q.v.), and in the savannah lands the typical butterfly is the orange or purple-tipped *Coletis* of the White family.

(*b*) Oriental and Australasian Regions. These two regions have much in common, and produce the largest and most spectacular specimens. There are many lovely Swallow-tails, spangled with blue, green, and gold, one kind, the *Battus*, carrying red spots. Closely related to the Swallow-tails are the magnificent Ornithoptera, or Bird-wings, so called because of their great size. They are the largest of all butterflies: some of them measure up to 10 inches or more from one wing-tip to the other, and the shape of their wings when outspread gives the appearance of a bird in flight. Their brilliant colours range from green and gold to the most vivid purple, generally on a background of velvety black. They are found only in the Pacific Islands and north Australia, and are not easily seen, as they usually keep to the tree-tops. The females, often larger than the males, have none of the brilliant colouring, but are dark brown, streaked with buff or cream. The family Danaidae is well represented, the most common type having pale blue wings with a black network. The large, ghost-like *Idea*, a whitish butterfly with black spots and thinly scaled transparent wings, is only found in tropical Asia. Another whole section of the Danaidae, belonging only to these two regions, is particularly noticeable: the butterflies of this group have large velvety-black or brownish wings which in the male often carry a purple or bluish sheen. Another butterfly belonging only to Asia, particularly northern India, is the famous Dead-leaf Butterfly (*Kallima*) which, when at rest with its wings closed, looks exactly like one of the leaves of the plant on which it settles.

(*c*) Tropical America. This is a region in which Swallow-tails abound, especially the group called *Battus*, with their warning colours of red, green, and white. Other butterflies, found in greater numbers in America than elsewhere are the Riodinidae, smaller insects, many of which are so brilliantly coloured that they look like living jewels. There is a solitary representative of this family in Europe, the Duke of Burgundy Fritillary. One member of the family Danaidae, with wings marked with patterns of brownish-yellow and black, belongs exclusively to tropical America, as does also a group called Heliconiinae. These are medium-sized butterflies with elongated front-wings and rather small hind-wings, often marked beneath with flame-coloured, radiating streaks. The large metallic-blue Morphos are peculiar to the forests

CATERPILLAR OF THE ATLAS MOTH
G. A. Gibson-Hill

of tropical America: their brilliant wings are used in the manufacture of butterfly pictures and jewellery, for which industry the butterflies are bred in considerable numbers.

3. TROPICAL MOTHS. The greater number of these are little different in appearance from the common species of our gardens and woodlands, though some are much larger. The most spectacular are those which fly by day. Perhaps the most remarkable are the SILK MOTHS (q.v.) of the large family Saturnidae, the family to which the British EMPEROR MOTH (q.v.) belongs. The caterpillars are often very spiny, and some make a strong but rather coarse silk, from which the Chinese manufacture tussore silk. The long-tailed, pale green Moon Moth and the huge Atlas Moth are well-known Indian species. The Atlas Moth is the largest of all butterflies and moths, with a wing-span measuring sometimes over a foot from tip to tip. It has enormous strong fore-wings of a peculiar shape, and coloured every shade of rich brown, purple, and grey. Both fore and hind-wings are marked with large eye-like blotches, and the moth has a stout woolly body and feathered legs and antennae. Its caterpillar is very magnificent: it has a clear, rich green, velvety body, divided into well-marked segments which are marked with golden, rose-coloured, and sky-blue warts.

Some of the day-flying Uraniid moths, with their tailed hind-wings and resplendent gold and green colouring, are easily mistaken for Swallowtails. One family of tropical moths, called Limacodidae, have caterpillars with no visible legs. They move about like slugs, and are often provided with poisoned spines, which sting severely. Two representatives of the family, the Festoon and the Triangle, occur in Britain.

Tropical moths have been both friends and foes to man. Life in the hot countries seems to proceed with greater violence, so that ravages by pests are apt to be spectacular. For instance, the copra trade in Fiji in the Pacific Isles was almost destroyed because of a moth which fed on the leaves of the coco-nut palm, and multiplied without being checked by any natural enemy. A fly, however, was introduced from the East Indies, because it was known there to destroy moths of the same family—and this saved the situation. In Australia the prickly pear which had been imported from tropical America, and was spreading with such devastating rapidity that it was ruining the farming land, was finally checked by a small Argentine moth called *Cactoblastis*. The caterpillar of this moth burrows into the fleshy leaves of the prickly pear and kills the plant (*see* CACTUS). The moth, being transplanted from its natural home, was also removed from its natural enemies; and within 5 years (1927–32) it had reached large enough numbers to destroy the cactus plague. Now, the moth and the cactus control each other, for if the cactus dies out too much, the moth dies for lack of food. This use of one living organism to control another is known as BIOLOGICAL CONTROL (q.v. Vol. VI).

BUTTERFLY-FISH, *see* SEA PERCH.

BUTTERWORT, *see* INSECTIVOROUS PLANTS, SECTION 2.

BUZZARD, *see* HAWKS, Section 4.

C

CABBAGE MOTH, *see* NIGHT-FLYING MOTHS.

CABBAGE WHITE, *see* WHITES (Butterflies).

CACTUS. This word was first applied by the ancient Greeks to some prickly plant, and was later adopted by the famous Swedish botanist, LINNAEUS (q.v. Vol. V), as the name for a group of curious, succulent plants, most of them prickly, some of which produce beautiful flowers and are now popular in gardens. Cactuses mainly belong to the American continents; but one group has long been distributed on the shores of the Mediterranean and on the volcanic soil of Italy, while others are found in tropical Asia and Africa. Mostly, however, they grow in the hot, dry regions of tropical America.

Cactuses are extremely varied, and often fantastic in form, some being globe-shaped, some cylindrical, some columnar, and some flattened into thick joint-like divisions. Although some are quite smooth, the surface of most of these peculiar plants is either ribbed like a melon or covered with nipple-like protuberances. The great majority of species carry tufts of horny spines, some of which are exceedingly powerful. The flowers are large and showy, and often vividly coloured. Sometimes the flower has a long tube, as in the genus Cereus, or a very short one, as in Opuntia. At the base of the tube the ovary develops into a fleshy and often edible fruit—that produced by the Opuntias being known either as the Prickly Pear or the Indian Fig.

The fleshy stems and branches contain a store of water which thirsty travellers have been known to tap, while the juices of the edible fruits are sometimes used in cases of fever as a cooling drink. One cactus, a most beautiful hot-house plant, produces a purplish fruit resembling a gooseberry, which is good to eat, and the fleshy part of the stem, after the spines have been removed, is eaten as a vegetable. Probably the tallest cactus is the so-called Torch Thistle of Mexico, which has stems growing to a height of 70 feet. Its fruits are 2 to 3 inches long, and contain a crimson pulp from which the Indians prepare an excellent preserve.

Because of their prickly character, Opuntias (Prickly Pear) and other Cactuses are planted around Mexican houses as protective fences. In Australia, however, cactuses are not so popular —as the story of the spread of the Prickly Pear will explain. In 1839 and again in 1860, species of Prickly Pear were brought to New South Wales by settlers. Soon these plants escaped cultivation and began to flourish exceedingly. From 1900 onwards the spread became very rapid, and by 1925 about 50 million acres of Queensland and 10 million acres in New South Wales were affected. The dense growth of cactus choked all other growth and made the land unusable. Since the Australians could find no way of checking the Prickly Pear, they sent scientists to America to find some antidote. After experi-

PRICKLY PEAR, THE CACTUS WHICH OVERRAN AUSTRALIA
Dr. G. Taylor

THE STEMS AND FLOWERS OF THE PRICKLY PEAR
The stems are thickened to conserve water and are
protected with spines. *Harold Bastin*

menting with some 150 species of animals known
to eat cactus, some of which could not thrive in
Australia, while others would not restrict their
attacks to cactuses, they discovered an insect,
a moth-borer, with the name of *Cactoblastis
cactorum*, which showed promise of solving
their problem. Some 3,000 million insects were
released in Australia between 1928 and 1930,
and in a few years vast areas of prickly pear
were reduced to a decaying pulp. Indeed, by
1931 the *Cactoblastis* began to die out through
lack of food and the cactus made an alarming
revival. But the insect soon took charge again,
and by 1934 the areas were again under control. To-day, 95% of the area formerly devas-
tated by cactus is free once more.

See also DESERT PLANTS.

CAECILIANS, *see* AMPHIBIA.

CADDIS FLY. Most people know Caddis Flies
better in their earlier stages than as adults.
'Caddis-worms' attract attention by the cases
they live in and drag about the bottoms of ponds
and streams. The head and thorax of the larva,
or Caddis-worm, protrude beyond the mouth
of the case, so that the legs are outside; the
abdomen, meantime, grips the case by means of
a pair of hooks. The head and thorax, which
are thus exposed at times, are hard and horny;
but the abdomen is quite soft. The Caddis-
worm breathes through gills, which are supplied
with water by movements of its abdomen. The
water is drawn through the front of the case, and
flows out at the back.

The foundation of the case is a silk secreted
in the 'salivary-glands'. At first these are silk-
glands only; but during the pupal stage they are
transformed into the adult insect's digestive
glands. In addition to the silk foundation, the
materials which the Caddis-worm uses to make
its case vary, as a rule, with the different species:
so that in some the silken foundation is covered
with brown twigs, in others with stones or with
small shells. However, a Caddis-worm is obliged
to use only what is at hand, so that if the insect
has been deprived of a case of brown twigs and
then finds itself in water where grass only is
available, it will be moving about next morning
in a new case covered with short lengths of green
grass. Most Caddis-worms are vegetarian; but
some are carnivorous.

The pupa, which also breathes through gills,
has a protective case attached to a solid support.
To make it more secure, there are silken barriers
across the ends, to which fragments of stone are
often added—but never so as to exclude the free
passage of water through the case. The pupa
has movable jaws, by which it bites its way out
when the time has come to emerge. Its legs and
wings are also free, and when it has bitten its way
out it either crawls or swims to the surface of
the water. Those that swim have their middle
legs long and oar-like, and fringed with hairs.
In species living in fast-flowing rivers, the adult
emerges as soon as the pupa reaches the surface.

Adult Caddis Flies are moth-like, with very
hairy wings, and are generally brown. Though
they live near ponds and streams, they are
attracted by light at night, and so sometimes
enter houses. Their jaws are either very small
or absent altogether, and they seem able to take
food by sipping.

CAMBERWELL BEAUTY, *see* VANESSINAE
BUTTERFLY.

CAMEL. These most valuable beasts of burden
in desert country can travel long distances,
carrying heavy loads, with little food or water.
This is because they have special cells in their
stomachs which store water, and because they
can also store fat in their humps. When a camel
is in good condition and well fed, its hump is
large and firm; but when food is scarce and its
store of fat is getting used up, the hump becomes
flabby and may hang down. On their chests,

ARABIAN CAMEL

sandy ground where most animals would get stuck a camel can travel because of the cushion-like nature of the two widely spread toes of each foot, connected by a stout web of skin which prevents its feet from sinking into the sand. Besides using camels as transport animals, the ARABS (q.v. Vol. I) drink their milk, eat their flesh, weave their hair into cloth, and burn their dung as fuel—in fact, the camel supplies them with almost all the necessities of life.

Camels have been domesticated for so long that it is not known for certain where they originated, though Arabia is thought to be the most likely country. There are two distinct species—the Arabian or one-humped camel, found in the hot desert-lands of north Africa and south-west Asia (and later introduced into Australia), and the Bactrian or two-humped camel —a sturdier, shorter-legged animal, inhabiting the colder regions of central Asia. They both belong to the group of animals called RUMINANTS (q.v.), chewers of the cud.

There are several breeds of the Arabian camel.

ankles, and knees, camels have pads of hard skin on which they rest when lying down. Their peculiar swaying motion—not very pleasant for anyone riding them—is due to the fact that the two legs of one side move simultaneously, instead of alternately as with most animals. Over soft,

A GROUP OF ARABIAN CAMELS IN INDIA. *Paul Popper*

The lighter and swifter, known as Dromedaries, are used for riding, while the heavier breeds are used as baggage-carriers. Arabian camels are usually about 7 feet high and generally sandy-coloured, though sometimes they are white, various shades of brown, or black. They are powerful, ungainly-looking creatures, with a rather supercilious expression. They are stupid and, far from becoming attached to their masters, are often positively vicious. They have a habit, when passing a mounted man on a narrow path, of turning their heads suddenly round and trying to bite the rider's arm or shoulder. In the mating season the males have fits of almost uncontrollable rage, uttering a loud, unpleasant, bubbling noise. Arabian camels are fed mainly on grain; but they need a certain amount of green food, and to obtain it they will eat even the most thorny of branches. They dislike having to cross streams, and often have to be helped, for they are poor swimmers.

The two-humped Bactrian Camel is much better suited to rocky country than the Arabian Camel, as its shorter legs make it a better climber. In parts of central Asia droves of these animals are found living wild, and feeding chiefly on the bitter-tasting plants of the steppes, which most animals will not touch. They like salt and will drink the water of the salt lakes common in central Asia. When hungry they will devour almost anything—even blankets, flesh (including skin and bones), and fish. The mating season is from February to April, and one young camel is born 13 months later. The baby camel is very helpless at first, and has to be looked after with great care; but it soon gains strength, and is able to eat solid food after a week. In its third year it is ridden on short journeys, and

becomes fully grown in its fifth year. Bactrian Camels are said to be useful up to the age of twenty-five.

See also Vol. IV: BEASTS OF BURDEN.

CAMOUFLAGE. This word has come to be associated with modern warfare, as well as with natural history. In modern warfare it has become necessary, not only for the men of opposing armies to conceal themselves, but also to conceal their guns, tanks, and ships, and even camps, forts, and all buildings of military importance. Camouflage in the military sense achieves the same end and is based on the same principles as that found in the animal kingdom, and for precisely the same reasons—protection from the enemy, either in defence or attack. The only difference is that a man-made camouflage is, as a rule, less effective than that found in animals.

Camouflage may, then, be described as the taking on of deceptive appearances for purposes either of defence or offence and, except for a few of the very lowest forms of life, it is probably true to say that no animal is without its protective camouflage, either to conceal itself from its prey until the most favourable moment of attack, or to assist it to hide from its enemies. Since all animals either prey upon others or are preyed upon, it follows that camouflage is of prime importance and, by trial and error, it has been brought to a high pitch of perfection in the long evolutionary history. Warning colours also are a form of camouflage. Even armoured animals—such as the shelled molluscs—have their protective coating so designed or coloured that it harmonizes with its surroundings.

Animal camouflage is achieved either by having a particular colour pattern (the stripes on the tiger, or the mottled pattern on some kinds of deer); by some peculiarity of shape (such as the stick insects or dead-leaf butterfly); or by some trick of behaviour; or all three may be found in one animal. These have been given various names, such as protective coloration, protective resemblance, or mimicry—but they are all directed to the same end. Yet in spite of the many devices used, it still remains the fact that camouflage is only effective as long as the animal keeps still. Even with the most skilful disguise, movement will betray the presence of its possessor. This does not matter in the long run, for it is while the animal is at rest, that is to say, when it is not on the alert, that disguise is most needed.

BACTRIAN CAMEL

GIRAFFES IN KRUGER NATIONAL PARK

The broken pattern of their colouring helps to break up the outline of their bodies. In particular, the dark line on their necks is difficult to distinguish from the boughs of the trees. *South African Railways*

WOODCOCK NESTING

The speckled plumage of the bird is much the same colour as the sticks and lichen among which it nests. The eggs, also, have the same speckled pattern. *Eric J. Hosking, F.R.P.S.*

Colour is used in one of the following ways: to break up the outline of the body, or to make it harmonize completely with the background, or to provide obliterative shading. A good example of a colour pattern breaking up the outline of the body is found in many of the small song-birds. A wren, for example, with its mottled plumage of browns and grey, will be inconspicuous in a green hedge because of the broken pattern caused by the shadows among the foliage. An adder, because of its banding and mottling, does not strike the eye while it is among herbage, but becomes very conspicuous with its comparatively uniform pattern when it crosses a road.

Some animals have developed a mechanism for changing the colour pattern of the body according to the background. Certain spiders which frequent flowering plants will be red when resting on a red petal, green if on a leaf, yellow if on the centre of a daisy. The same spider will change from one colour to another as the occasion demands, the change usually taking a day or more to accomplish. The CHAMELEON (q.v.) is probably the best-known example of this kind of change; but FLAT-FISHES (q.v.), such as the plaice, also do the same. It should be noted that the ability to change colour in this way is found only in animals which stay motionless, or nearly so, for long periods on the same background. There is, obviously, no advantage in this for an animal moving quickly from one background to another.

Many animals have a dark colour on their backs, shading into a pale colour on the under-parts. This counteracts the effect of light falling from above, and produces the appearance of a flat and uniform surface, making the animal almost invisible against a background of the same tint. This type of colour concealment is seen particularly in land animals and in fishes. For fish there is an added advantage: a fish with a mottled back is almost invisible, viewed from above, against a background of weeds, mud, and stones; while viewed from below, its silvery belly tones in with the colour of the sky as seen through the water.

Reference has been made under PROTECTIVE COLORATION (Insects) to the *Kallima* butterfly, which so closely resembles a leaf. There are many other such—caterpillars resembling twigs, stick insects, and the like. There is a fish, *Mono-cirrhus*, living in the Amazon River, which has a body like a leaf, with a short stalk protruding forward from the lower jaw, which looks just like a leaf-stalk. The Frogfish of the SARGASSO SEA (q.v. Vol. III) has a body covered with leafy-looking outgrowths, so that it is difficult to distinguish it from the weed. Finally, among the many examples which could be quoted, is the Sea-dragon, a relative of the well-known SEA-HORSE (q.v.), the body of which bears a number of membranous streamers giving it perfect concealment when among seaweed.

Another kind of camouflage used by a variety of animals depends on tricks of behaviour. Among the best known of these tricks is that of 'shamming dead', a well-known trick of the OPOSSUM (q.v.), which has given rise to the expression 'playing possum'—a trick used also by many insects and spiders. There are many other kinds of camouflage depending on tricks of behaviour: the Spider Crab, for instance, decorates itself with seaweeds to disguise its presence; the Slender File-fish, with slender body and tail, mottled green in colour, stands on its head among eel-grass, so that the body and tail wave gently in the current like the blades of eel-grass; and some kinds of spiders decorate their webs with bands of silk, leaving gaps into which they themselves fit so that they look like a continuation of the bands.

See also PROTECTIVE COLORATION (Insects).

CANARY, *see* FINCHES, Section 1; *see also* Vol. IX, BIRD-KEEPING.

CAPERCAILLIE, *see* GROUSE.

CAPYBARA, *see* CAVY.

CARBON IN LIVING THINGS. Every living thing contains carbon. This can be shown by taking any dead organic matter (that is, matter derived from plants or animals), and burning it. Sugar, for example, turns black and gives almost pure carbon. Wood forms almost pure carbon, as charcoal. Coal is largely made up of carbon. The presence of carbon in organic substances has been so well recognized by the chemist that the branch of chemistry called 'organic chemistry' is sometimes also called the chemistry of carbon compounds (*see* CHEMISTRY, Vol. III).

The importance of carbon in Nature is enormous. There is a constant building-up and breaking-down of carbon compounds, so that a steady circulation is kept going. The chief build-ing-up process is PHOTOSYNTHESIS (q.v.), whereby plants make their own food (and, indirectly, food for all other living things). This cannot take place without carbon dioxide from the atmosphere. One of the breaking-down pro-cesses is RESPIRATION (q.v.) which, in plants and animals, liberates energy from food-stuffs, car-bon dioxide being evolved as a waste product. If the amount of carbon dioxide taken in during photosynthesis were equal to that given out during respiration, there would be a regular and balanced circulation of carbon in Nature. More carbon dioxide is taken in by photosynthesis, however, than is given out by the respiration of both plants and animals. Unless there were other processes in which carbon compounds were broken down, in time all the carbon dioxide in the atmosphere would be used up and photo-synthesis would come to a stop. This would mean the end of all life in the world.

But carbon compounds are also broken down by decay. This is largely carried out by bacteria in the soil; but, usually, before they begin their work, the remains of dead animals and plants—or humus—are acted upon by FUNGI and other plants called SAPROPHYTES (qq.v.), which, in-stead of building up their own food-stuffs from raw materials, obtain them from the dead remains or waste products of other plants or animals. The remains of the dead plants and animals are then acted upon by bacteria which cause final decay, and eventually the carbon compounds are reconverted to carbon dioxide, which can be used again by plants.

Perhaps the clearest illustration of the way in which the carbon of plant tissues is restored to natural circulation is given by COAL (q.v. Vol. III). During the Coal Age, some 250 million years ago, before flowering plants had been evolved (see EVOLUTION), the common plants were large tree-ferns and horsetails. These died, and in time their remains became buried hun-dreds of feet under the earth's surface. By com-pression, by the action of bacteria, and by other means, they became converted into an almost pure form of carbon, namely, coal. When coal is burnt, it is changed mostly into carbon dioxide, thus returning to circulation carbon which has been removed from the natural cycle for 250 million years.

CARDINAL FISH, see SEA-PERCH.

CARIBOU, see REINDEER.

CARNIVORA (Flesh-eaters). To this large order belong, typically, all those mammals whose most distinctive habit is eating the flesh of other animals. Not all Carnivora, however, live entirely on animal flesh: the extent to which they are flesh-eaters varies a great deal—most bears, for instance, live mainly on a vegetable diet. Neither are the Carnivora the only flesh-eating mammals: many of the INSECTIVORA and LEMURS eat animal flesh, and one group of MAR-SUPIALS (qq.v.) lives almost entirely on it.

The Carnivora have the following characteris-tics in common. The number of complete toes on each foot is never less than four, and is often five. All the toes have claws, and are generally sharp and curved, bearing no resemblance to nails. The first toe is never, like the human thumb, opposed to the others, and so they are not able to grasp. Most of them walk on their toes only, though not on the tips; but the bears and the badgers walk on the whole foot. The number of their teeth varies from 30, in the case of cats, to 42 in dogs; but all have strongly developed canine teeth, as weapons for seizing prey.

The order is divided into two sub-orders: (i) the Normal-footed Carnivora (Fissipedia), to which belong CATS, HYENAS, DOGS, WEASELS, BADGERS, OTTERS, RACOONS, BEARS (qq.v.), and others; and (ii) the Fin-footed Carnivora (Pinni-pedia), to which belong SEALS (q.v.), whose feet have been converted into swimming flippers.

CARP. This freshwater fish was originally a native of Persia, China, and the Malay Archi-pelago. It was introduced into Europe at an early date, and was known to be already under cultivation in Germany by 1258, though it was not referred to in England until the end of the 15th century. Carp in this country are now generally kept as interesting additions to orna-mental waters; but on the European continent, particularly in Germany, Poland, and Russia, Carp is a popular food, and great farms, with acres of breeding, rearing, and fattening ponds, supply a ready market.

Carp grow to about 2 feet long, get very tame, and live a long while—the greatest age for which we have reliable evidence is 40 years. Stories about Carp reaching the age of 200 years or more are not to be accepted. Two interesting varieties of the Common Carp are the Mirror Carp, with a row of large, silvery scales along each side, and the Leather Carp, with a few large leathery scales scattered on the body. There are also a Silver Carp and a Golden Carp, the latter not to be confused with the Goldfish, also a member of the Carp family.

The Carp and its relatives form probably the largest single family of fishes (the Cyprinidae). They include most of the freshwater fishes of Europe and Asia, and many of those of North America and Africa. In South America, however, their place is taken by the CHARACINS (q.v.). Members of the Carp family are recognized by having no teeth in the jaws (though they have special 'pharyngeal' or throat teeth attached near the gills). They have only one dorsal (back) fin, which has flexible rays, except for the first one, which is stiff and often has a saw-edge, as in the Goldfish; and they usually have distinct scales. They also have the air-bladder connected with the ear (see FISHES), a peculiarity they share with Characins and CAT-FISHES (q.v.). Most of them seem to feed on a mixed diet of small animals, such as worms, molluscs, and insect larvae, with a certain amount of vegetable matter.

The family includes many fishes familiar to the angler, such as Roach, Rudd, Dace, Chub, Gudgeon, Tench, Bream, and Barbel—also the ornamental Goldfish and Golden Orfe, and the small boy's friend, the Minnow or 'Tiddler'. The Golden Orfe is a domesticated variety of the Ide, another member of this enormous family, common in European rivers.

The Barbel is so called because of the 'barbels' or sensitive feelers on its lips, which help the fish to locate in the mud and stones the small animals on which it feeds. There are many different kinds found in freshwaters all over the Old World, especially in the tropics. Some are very prettily marked. They vary in length from 2 inches to several feet (as, for example, the Mahseer of India). One species is found in British freshwaters, where it affords sport to fishermen.

Another small member of the Carp family, the Bitter-

ling, about 2½ inches long, is found wild in the freshwaters of Europe, but not of Britain. It is interesting chiefly for its habit of laying its eggs inside the shell of the freshwater mussel, where they are safe from enemies. The female has at breeding time a long tube, called an

THE FANTAIL AND TELESCOPE-EYED MOOR, FANCY VARIETIES OF THE GOLDFISH. *A. Fraser-Brunner*

THE COMMON CARP. *A. Fraser-Brunner*

ovipositor, which she places between the two halves of the mussel-shell while it is open. The breathing of the mussel helps to aerate the eggs until they hatch out, which takes about a month. In return, the mussel casts its own young ones out of the shell—to fix themselves to the parent Bitterlings, who perforce carry them until they can fend for themselves. This saves the mussels from overcrowding. One good turn deserves another!

The Goldfish is the most popular of all ornamental fish (*see* AQUARIUM, Vol. IX). It is the domesticated form of a far-eastern member of the Carp family. The wild fish is an inconspicuous darkish green, and would have received little notice had it not produced an occasional 'sport' of bright reddish-gold, said to have been first noticed in China about A.D. 1200, and carefully fostered by breeding ever since. This golden variety is due simply to the absence of black colouring-matter (pigment), only the red and yellow being left. As bred by the Chinese, many fishes of curious shape and colour were evolved; but out of these, six main types have been selected for breeding. Although cultivated for so long, Goldfish still show signs of their wild ancestry. For some time after being hatched they have the natural colouring, and turn gold only when they are several years old. If left to breed for several generations in open water, they gradually revert to the wild form—a fact which caused great disappointment to a potentate from Madagascar who wished to beautify the waters of his own country by filling them with thousands of these enchanting fish. But the imported Goldfish soon reverted to their dingy wild colour—and incidentally ousted the only freshwater food-fish of the island.

A western relative of the Goldfish, which spread to Europe in remote times, is the Crucian Carp, sometimes called Prussian Carp. It is a rather deep-bodied, bronze-coloured fish with a rounded dorsal fin, and is sometimes kept in ornamental waters. Both Crucian Carp and Goldfish differ from true Carp in having no barbels, in having a saw-edge on the front ray of the dorsal fin, and in their smaller size.

CARPET MOTH, *see* LOOPERS.

CASE-BEARER MOTHS. The small caterpillars of the family Coleophoridae are the principal makers of cases among moths. Of nearly 1,000

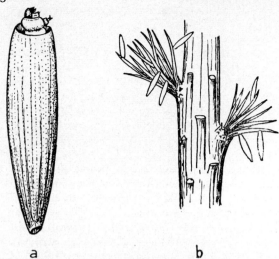

a   b

CASE-BEARER MOTH
a. Larva in case; *b.* Larch shoots showing the cases attached

known species, 110 occur in the United States, and 87 in Britain. The young caterpillar is a leaf-miner, which later constructs a distinctive case of silk, leaf-hairs, fragments of leaves, dead flowers, or seeds, according to its kind. The case, about $\frac{1}{4}$ inch in length, is attached in such a way to a leaf or seed-vessel that the caterpillar can push its head out and feed in all directions, without leaving the safety of the case. A pale blotch on a leaf, with a round hole in the centre of one side, is a sure sign of damage by a case-bearer.

Change to the chrysalis usually takes place inside the case in May, and the moths emerge in July. When fully expanded, they are about $\frac{1}{2}$ inch across, and have dark grey forewings, and white, yellow, brown, brassy, or bronzy hindwings, marked with various sprinklings and streaks.

See also CHINA-MARK MOTHS.

CASSOWARY, *see* OSTRICH, Section 2.

CATERPILLAR. This is the common name for the larva of BUTTERFLIES, MOTHS, and SAW-FLIES (qq.v.). The caterpillar represents the second stage in the complex life-history of these insects from egg to adult. It is during this stage that eating and, consequently, growth take place, and so the main function of the caterpillar is to eat and grow. Though some are gregarious, caterpillars generally live quite solitary lives,

A. Caterpillar; B. Geometrid Caterpillar;
C. Sawfly larva

concentrating on the task of eating. Some eat only by day, some only by night, and some all the time. They nearly always eat only one type of food plant—the PAINTED LADY larva, for instance, eats only thistles, the PRIVET HAWK MOTH larva privet leaves, and the RED ADMIRAL and PEACOCK larvae (qq.v.) nettles. Many of the smaller ones, such as LEAF-ROLLERS (q.v.) and Leaf-miners, roll leaves round themselves or tunnel in them. Some SAWFLIES make galls. A few are carnivorous (see BLUES). Some caterpillars live on, or beneath the surface of water, breathing oxygen from the water by gills (see CHINA-MARK MOTHS).

Some caterpillars move very little and slowly, depending either on CAMOUFLAGE (q.v.) or on bright warning colours to protect them from their natural enemies (see PROTECTIVE COLORATION). Others, on the other hand, will move very quickly, or drop suddenly, to take cover; while some have strange defensive movements, such as sudden jerkings up of their heads and front quarters, which a colony of caterpillars will do as a united action, when faced with danger. Sometimes they will wave unpleasant scent organs or spray poison at an approaching enemy (see PROMINENT MOTHS). Some live in protective cases which they carry about (see BAGWORMS, CASE-BEARERS). Sawfly caterpillars are sometimes covered with a white powder, others are slimy and resemble slugs. During their lives they cast their skins (moulting) at regular intervals, usually four times, to allow for growth. Caterpillars generally live about a month, though this varies a great deal, and in many species the caterpillars hibernate in a state of complete or partial rest in some sheltered place through the winter. Finally, however, they enter the pupal (chrysalid) stage, and many, especially caterpillars of moths and sawflies, prepare for this by spinning an elaborate cocoon of silk or of other materials (see SILK MOTHS).

The caterpillar is long and cylindrical in shape. It is made up of a head, followed by a body composed of thirteen ring-shaped segments, some of which bear legs. Its head is hard and firm, with strong jaws working sideways instead of up and down. The caterpillar of a butterfly or moth also has twelve minute and very simple eyes, whereas a sawfly caterpillar has only two. In front of these, on each side, are tiny antennae corresponding to the larger ones of the adult. It has also two tiny tubes, called spinnerets, from which comes a liquid that dries into silk. The first three segments of the body (the 'thorax') each carry a pair of legs, each leg ending in a single claw: these correspond to the three pairs of legs of the winged insect. In addition, caterpillars of butterflies and moths usually have five pairs of legs (commonly called 'prolegs') on the last segments of the abdomen, the last pair on the last segment of the body being called 'claspers'. These, unlike the thoracic legs, have fleshy soles for grasping, and are armed with many small hooks: they disappear after the larval stage. Looper caterpillars of the family Geometridae, however, have only two pairs of abdominal legs, and have therefore developed the peculiar gait from which they get their name. They hold on by their front legs while they draw up their hind legs, hitching their body into a loop. Then, holding on by the hind legs, they throw their body forward, and grasp again by the front legs (see LOOPER MOTHS).

The young caterpillars of NIGHT-FLYING MOTHS (q.v.) often have the first two abdominal legs undeveloped, so that they, too, walk like loopers; but the older caterpillars are normal, except in a few instances, such as the Silver-Y Moth, where the looping habit persists. Sawfly larvae usually have more than five pairs of legs on the abdomen, these being without the hooks so characteristic of Lepidoptera. They sometimes rest in a peculiar fashion, grasping the foliage with the front legs and holding the abdomen in the air.

Caterpillars breathe through nine pairs of openings on each side of the body, known as 'spiracles', which lead into branching tubes to carry the air to all parts of the body. The spiracles are often surrounded by conspicuous bright-coloured spots or other markings. A straight digestive tube runs down the whole body. The caterpillar's blood is often full of green colouring. Its skin is covered with hairs, sometimes so small that the caterpillar looks

A. LARVAE OF PRIVET HAWK MOTH
E. O. Hoppé

C. LOOPER CATERPILLAR OF THE PEPPERED MOTH
S. Beaufoy, F.R.P.S.

B. WOOLLY BEAR CATERPILLAR OF GARDEN TIGER
MOTH. *E. Syms*

D. LOBSTER MOTH LARVA REARING ITS HEAD IN DEFENSIVE
ACTION. *S. Beaufoy, F.R.P.S.*

LARVAE OF MOTHS

smooth or naked, sometimes so long and thick that it looks like a fur coat (*see* TIGER MOTHS). The Looper caterpillars have rough skins with raised knobs or warts, which make them resemble twigs. Some species carry large horns (*see* HAWK MOTHS), or have sharp and even poisonous spikes on their skins (*see* TUSSOCK MOTHS). The very largest caterpillars are sometimes as much as 7 inches long.

CATFISH. Many different species are to be found in the Catfish family, and we can mention only a few outstanding ones here. Nearly all the Catfish are freshwater fish; but a few live in the sea. They are found over the whole world, except for a few small islands and the very cold regions. They all have barbels or 'whiskers' round the mouth, often very long teeth in the mouth, only one dorsal (back) fin, with one stiff,

THE GIANT CATFISH, THE WELS, RISING FROM THE MUD IN PURSUIT OF A WATER-FOWL.
A. Fraser-Brunner

saw-like spine (the rest being flexible) which is followed by a low fleshy flap called the 'adipose fin'. Most Catfish have no scales; but some go to the other extreme and have a heavy suit of armour, formed of bony plates. Each breast-fin has usually a strong spine, like the one on the back, sometimes with a poison-bag, which makes them dangerous to handle.

Many Catfish are quite small, but some grow to several feet in length. Of the big ones, the best known is the Wels, which, next to the Sturgeon, is the largest river fish in Europe. It is not found in Britain, France, or Italy, but is common in the Danube. It spends a good deal of time in the mud, but will rise to the surface to seize such prey as water-birds and otters—for it is very voracious, and has been known to swallow a child whole.

Some of the little Armoured Catfish, from South America, are amusing to keep in a tropical AQUARIUM (q.v. Vol. IX), where they are useful as scavengers. A North American species, often called the Common Catfish, has been acclimatized to Europe and Britain, and is often kept in ponds and aquariums. The name Catfish is also given sometimes to one of the sea-fish called BLENNY (q.v.).

CATS. Of all the CARNIVORA (q.v.), or flesh-eating mammals, cats are the most highly developed, and the most perfectly adapted for a life of preying on other creatures. Their long, lithe bodies are agile as well as extremely strong, the larger cats being easily able to kill and drag away animals much larger than themselves. Other characteristics of the Cat family are their very short muzzles, their powerful canine and cutting teeth, and their strongly curved claws, which they can draw into sheaths for protection when not in use. All cats have rasp-like tongues, to enable them to lick the meat from bones, and perhaps also to help in cleaning their fur.

Some member of the Cat family lives in almost every part of the world, except Australia and the Arctic regions; but the large cats are found mainly in hot climates. The largest cats are the LIONS and TIGERS, and then the JAGUARS, LEOPARDS (or Panthers), and PUMAS (qq.v.); and there are a great number of smaller cats. Their fur is usually short; but those which live in cold climates, such as the Ounce and Lynx, grow fairly long coats, while the length of the Tiger's fur varies according to the climate. With few exceptions, the cat tribe has a great dislike for water. All the cats feed upon other animals and birds which they themselves have killed; a few hunt fish as well. The following are some of the more important wild cats which have not been dealt with in separate articles.

The Lynx is a wild cat about $2\frac{1}{2}$ feet long, with a whisker-like fringe of hair on its cheeks, and tufts of hair growing from its ears. In south-eastern Europe and Asia there are still a number of places where the smaller Lynxes live close to towns and villages. Very occasionally they make savage, unprovoked attacks on human beings; but they are generally looked upon as cowardly, timid animals, about as dangerous as a common fox or coyote. They prey on animals varying in size from a mouse to a sheep, and often kill more than they can devour. Their lairs are usually among rocks. They generally produce from two to five cubs at a birth. The Canadian Lynx is a more formidable animal, with a curious

CHEETAH KITTENS
These baby Cheetahs were found in Northern Rhodesia when they were 4 days old, and have been successfully reared in captivity. *Dorien Leigh*

habit of trailing a human being for miles—though this is apparently more through curiosity than with any idea of harming the man. Many of these animals do on occasions, however, make most vicious attacks.

There is only one wild cat in Britain—the European Wild Cat—which is found in the wild parts of Scotland, as also in various districts of the Continent. It is about the same size as the domestic cat, and marked very much like the fireside tabby; but its tail is shorter and ends bluntly instead of tapering to a point. It is probably one of the ancestors of the domestic cat, though there is considerable division of opinion on this. It is an expert climber, and its favourite home is in the most inaccessible mountainous woods. The females usually produce four or five kittens in a litter, and they have been known to bring them up in a deserted or captured nest of a large bird, although they normally use cavities among rock-piles. Even the kittens are most fierce and savage, and they will hiss and spit vigorously at intruders. Grouse, ptarmigan, rabbits, hares, fawns, and lambs are some of the creatures they destroy.

The Cheetah is a large, spotted, cat-like animal found in central India, Persia, and throughout the greater part of Africa. An adult is about 5 feet long, with a longish tail. It is lightly built, and has very long legs. For 500 yards it is able to run faster than any other living animal, but after that it tires and cannot keep up its high speed. It relies, therefore, on capturing its prey in one swift rush. Cheetahs are easily tamed, and in India are trained to hunt antelopes. The Cheetah is not a typical cat, and differs mainly in having blunt claws, which are only partially retractile (able to be drawn in).

See also Vol. IX: CATS; PETS.

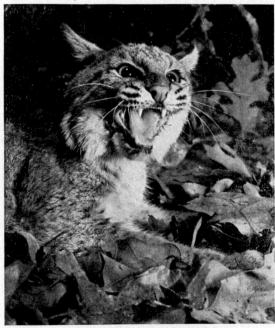

BOBCAT OR BAY LYNX (*Lynx rufus*)
Ewing Galloway, N.Y.

The American Bobcat is rather smaller than the Canadian Lynx, the other American species. It has shorter fur, and is more adaptable, taking a wider range of food. It therefore survives more easily in areas where man has settled.

CATTLE, WILD. This is the name applied to all members of the Ox Tribe, to which belong the BISON, BUFFALOES (qq.v.), Yaks, Gaurs,

Musk Oxen, and various other wild species. These are all members of the order Ungulata (hoofed beasts). The Cattle, together with the SHEEP, GOATS, and ANTELOPES (qq.v.) form a group known as the Hollow-horned RUMINANTS (q.v.), that is to say, animals which have hollow, unbranched horns and which are true 'chewers of the cud'. Cattle are mostly large and heavily built animals, and both sexes have permanent horns—in which respect they differ from the DEER (q.v.) whose horns (antlers) are shed and replaced annually.

The Yak is a very strong, hardy, and sure-footed animal, which lives in the high regions of Tibet and central Asia. It has been domesticated, and plays much the same part in the lives of the people of these regions as the camel does for the Bedouin Arabs: they drink its milk, eat its flesh, use its hide and hair for tent covers and clothing, and employ it as their main means of transport. It has such powers of endurance that it has been of great value on exploits such as the EVEREST Expeditions (q.v. Vol. III). The wild Yak stands about $5\frac{1}{2}$ feet high, and has long horns. It has a blackish-brown coat, with a long mane of hair on its throat and all along the underside of its body, reaching nearly to the ground. The herds often number hundreds or even thousands. When alarmed, the older bulls and cows place themselves on the outside of the herd with the calves in the centre, and, on the approach of the hunter, the whole herd takes flight, galloping away with heads down and tails in the air.

The Gaur, found in India, Burma, and the Malay Peninsula, is a very large species of wild Cattle, with massive horns, sleek, dark brown

A MUSK OX

coat, and whitish 'stockings'. The bulls are sometimes 6 feet high. Gaurs prefer hilly districts to plains, and generally wander about in small herds of about a dozen head, governed by one of the old bulls. This leader is in the end expelled from the herd by the younger bulls and cows, as he frequently causes trouble by objecting to any of the rising generation making advances to the cows in his herd. These solitary old bulls are extremely dangerous; but, having the finest heads and horns, they are most sought after by sportsmen (see Vol. IX, BIG-GAME SHOOTING). A domesticated race of the Gaur is known as the Gayal or Mithan.

Musk Oxen are a species of cattle to be found in the Arctic regions of north-eastern Canada, Greenland, and the adjoining islands. They stand about 4 feet high, and have a dark brown, hairy coat, which makes them look a good deal larger than they actually are. This coat reaches a long way down their massive legs, hiding their short tails. They have a light brown undercoat of fine, soft wool. In spring they shed their long winter coat in blanket-like masses. The adult bulls have large horns, generally about 2 feet long, which are broad and flat on their forehead, and then get narrow and grow downwards before turning up in sharp points. The horns of the young bulls and cows are very much smaller. All Musk Oxen have a large growth of hair between their hoofs, which enables them to secure a sure foothold on the frozen ground. They feed upon whatever sparse vegetation they can find in a barren land where the surface of the ground scarcely thaws. Their name is derived from the musky flavour of their flesh.

Our domestic cattle are descended from a wild species called the Aurochs, which once lived in Europe, including Great Britain, but became

A GAUR

TROPICAL MOTHS AND BUTTERFLIES

1. Atlas Moth (Himalayas). 2. Bird-wing Butterfly (New Guinea). 4 and 6. South American Nymphaline Butterflies (*Catagramma*). 7. African Blue. *Epitola* (Nigeria). Common British species for comparison. 3. Brimstone (male). 5. Garden Tiger Moth (male). 8. Common Blue (male). 9. Five-spot Burnet

(*about ⅗ nat. size*)

extinct about the 17th century. They were domesticated in ancient times, and are now one of the most useful and indispensable of all the animals man has tamed for his use.

See also Vol. VI, CATTLE, DOMESTIC.

CAVY. This South American family is a group of RODENTS (q.v.), differing from each other a good deal in appearance, but all having either very short tails or none at all. The true Cavies are probably the ancestors of the domestic guinea-pig; the Patagonian Cavies look rather like hares, and the Capybaras are the largest of all the rodents.

The true Cavies are a greyish colour. Their favourite haunts are marshes, where they live in the shelter of the vegetation; but they are also found occasionally on sandhills. They feed in the early morning and evening, eating roots and plants. Unlike domestic guinea-pigs, they breed only once a year, and have only one or two young. The best-known species are the Restless Cavy or Cutler's Cavy, which was domesticated by the INCAS of Peru (q.v. Vol. I), and from which it is thought the domestic guinea-pig was derived.

Patagonian Cavies, or Maras, are 2 feet 6 inches or more long, and rather over a foot high. They have long legs and ears, and are covered with thick grey fur, becoming yellow on their flanks and white underneath. They are shy and timid, and take to flight at the least alarm.

The Pacas or Spotted Cavies are about 2 feet long, and have coarse, dark brown fur, with rows of white spots. The natives hunt them for their flesh at all seasons, but especially in February and March, when the Pacas become extraordinarily fat: they first smoke them out of their burrows by lighting a fire at one of the entrances, and then chase them with dogs. The Pacas invariably make for water in their efforts to escape, since they can swim very fast.

The Capybaras, or Carpinchos, are 4 feet long and weigh about 98 pounds. On account of their large size, bristly hair, and grunting cries, they are often called 'water hogs'. Their hind-legs are a good deal longer than the front legs, and they have short webs between their toes. They love water and spend their time by the rivers and lakes, resting, or feeding on waterplants and the bark of young trees. Their principal enemies are jaguars and pumas. If there is any likelihood of attack, they plunge headlong into the water,

and travel for long distances below the surface. On land they trot slowly or progress by leaps.

See also AGOUTI.

See also Vol. VI, GUINEA-PIGS.

CEDARS, *see* CONIFERS.

CENTIPEDE, *see* MYRIAPODA.

CHAFER. This is a kind of beetle which includes Cockchafers, Rose-chafers, and many others. Their antennae or feelers have the end-joints flattened and arranged side by side, so that they can be opened and closed like the leaves of a book. These joints bear the organs of scent, and by their enlargement, and the protection gained by closing them when not in use, their sensitivity is much increased. In the south of France dogs and pigs are used, on account of their keen scent, to hunt for the underground edible fungi called truffles. But a little chafer, called *Bolboceras*, can find them with still greater exactitude. When it flies through the air, alights, and begins to scrape away the ground with its forelegs, a truffle is always to be found just beneath. A naturalist in Corsica, who had caught a female of another chafer, *Pachypus*, and put her into a box in his pocket, soon found himself pursued by males which had scented her from afar.

The truffle-loving beetle is closely related to another chafer of southern Europe, called the *Rebenschneider* or Vine-cutter, because it nips off tender shoots of the vine for its brood. A pair of the beetles dig a burrow in the ground, the male carrying away the soil dug by the female at the bottom of the shaft. The female then makes an oval cell opening out of the shaft, while the

COCKCHAFER LARVA
S. Beaufoy, F.R.P.S.

DOR-BEETLE *S. Beaufoy, F.R.P.S.*

male goes off to collect provisions. Biting off a shoot, he carries it back to the female, and returns for more. When the cell is packed full, an egg is laid in it; and then a few more cells are prepared and provisioned in the same way. Each young grub, on emerging from the egg, finds its food at hand, and by the time it has eaten it all up it has reached full size and is ready to undergo its transformation. The parents are said to guard the entrance to the nest and drive away intruders while the grubs are growing.

The Dor-beetles of English pastures and woods are related to the Vine-cutters, and have rather similar habits. They, too, work in couples, the male attending to the work of transport while the female labours in the burrow. The nest is provisioned with the droppings of rabbits, sheep, or cattle, brought by the male and packed into branch-tunnels by the female—who afterwards places an egg in each. Most of the spring and summer is occupied with these labours, although the family is a small one. Winter is spent below ground, and almost before it is past work begins again.

The male of one of the Dor-beetles, which the great naturalist FABRE (q.v. Vol. V) calls the Minotaur, has a pair of curious horns upon its back. Many other chafers carry horns of astonishing size and shape. The largest insects in the world, the Elephant-beetles and Hercules Beetles of South America, and the Goliath Beetles of Africa, also bear remarkable horns. The females are almost always without these large horns, the size of which would make their work impossible.

See also BEETLES.

CHAFFINCH, *see* FINCHES, Section 3.

CHALCID FLY. This is a minute insect related to the ICHNEUMON FLY and the GALL-FLY (qq.v.). Many are brilliant metallic-blue or green, and nearly all are either parasites on other insects or 'hyper-parasites'—that is to say, they live on the parasites of other insects.

The Fairy Flies, which include the smallest known insects, are Chalcids that spend their larval life inside the eggs of other insects, feeding on the contents. They make use of the eggs of Butterflies and Moths, and also sometimes of Bugs and Beetles. Most of these are black and lack the metallic brilliance of other Chalcids. One species of Fairy Fly feeds on the eggs of the aquatic bug called the WATER-BOATMAN (q.v.), and to reach them it swims under the water, using its wings as oars.

Those who grow tomatoes in glass-houses find one species of Chalcid Fly very useful, as it lives on the nymphs of the Greenhouse White Fly, a bug which has found its way here from America (*see* INSECT PESTS, Vol. VI). Fig Insects, which pollinate the flowers of the fig-tree, are also Chalcids. In one

Greatly enlarged.

kind of fig flower the female is able to reach the ovaries, in each of which she lays one egg. After the eggs are hatched, the white footless larvae attack the tissues of the ovaries, and convert them into 'galls' or growths of tissue on the plant. After the larvae have fed and pupated in the galls the Fig Insects emerge. The males are wingless, and it seems that they never leave the fig flower in which they were hatched. The females, however, do so, and as they pass out are dusted over with pollen. They then move to younger flowers, pollinating them as they seek to lay their eggs in the ovaries.

CHAMELEON. The lizards of this family are highly developed for life in trees. The hands and feet are modified for clasping, the digits being opposed to one another like the human thumb and fingers. The Chameleon's hand has two digits on the outside and three on the inside; in the foot this is reversed. The tail, which is also used for gripping, is generally long. The eyes can be moved independently. The tongue, of elastic tissue, is club-shaped at the tip and pro-

CHAMELEON IN THE ACT OF CATCHING A FLY BY SHOOTING OUT ITS LONG TONGUE. *E. O. Hoppé*

vided with a moist secretion. It can be shot out with great speed and accuracy to catch insects and grubs on which they feed: in fact, some species can stretch their tongues to a distance equalling their own length. With this marvellous weapon at its command, the Chameleon has no need to move quickly, and all its actions are slow and deliberate. The head is helmet-shaped, and often decorated with horns and bony outgrowths—altogether, the Chameleon is a very strange-looking creature. The power which it has of changing colour is proverbial, though popular legend claims much more than is actually justified.

The whole family is divided into four genera, with some 80 species. One species is found in the eastern Mediterranean, one in India; the vast majority live in Africa and Madagascar. Most Chameleons, so far as we know, lay eggs; a few species bring forth their young alive. The largest species, found in East Africa, grows to a length of 2 feet; but most of them are much smaller.

See also LIZARDS.

CHAMOIS. This sturdily built animal, living in the mountains of Europe and Asia, is often called a goat-like antelope. This is because GOATS and ANTELOPES (qq.v.) are structurally so alike that it is often difficult to draw a distinction between them, and chamois are sometimes classified with the one and sometimes with the other. Like goats and antelopes, they are, of course, RUMINANTS (q.v.)—that is to say, they ruminate or 'chew the cud'.

Chamois stand about $2\frac{1}{2}$ feet high at the shoulders; they have thick, chestnut-brown coats, and short horns which grow straight up from the forehead, ending in a sharp backward hook.

They have the most acute sense of sight, smell, and hearing, and are amazingly agile and sure-footed in moving about their mountain homes. A chamois is even able to stand with all four feet on the pinnacle of a rock hardly more than an inch in diameter. It is a shy and wary animal, and when alarmed it utters a shrill whistle, which sets the whole herd moving rapidly off. For most of the year, the herds, numbering from about fifteen to twenty head, live in the woods on the mountains, feeding on lichens and mountain grass. During the summer a few leave the herd and live for several weeks among the glaciers and snow-fields above the forests. A short spell of severe frost usually drives them back to shelter.

For most of the year the old males live apart; but during the mating season, in October and November, they join the flocks of females, driving away the young bucks and fighting fiercely amongst themselves. The fawns are born in May or June. When only a day old they can follow their dams almost anywhere. Their horns first show after 3 months, and at the age of 3 years they have attained their full size. It is believed that some chamois live to be 20 or even 25 years old.

Goral, Serows, and Takin are three other goat-like antelopes related to the chamois, which all live in the Himalayas. One of the Serows is also found as far south as Sumatra. Of the three, the Takin is the largest, standing about $3\frac{1}{2}$ feet high.

CHARACIN. This is the name given to the members of a large family of freshwater fishes found in South America and Africa. The fact that they are found only in these two places is one of the reasons why it is thought that these great continents were joined together a very long time ago—since these fish could never have crossed the Atlantic Ocean. Another example of this distribution is the CICHLID (q.v.).

There are a great many different kinds of Characin, most of them small and pretty, and, consequently, often kept in tropical aquariums (*see* AQUARIUM, Vol. IX). Others, however, are large and fierce, like the Dorado of South America and the Tiger-fish of Africa. The Piranha, or Piraya, is perhaps the most terrible fish found in South American rivers, for, although not very big—about a foot long usually—great shoals of them will attack bathers, very quickly biting away all the flesh with their sharp teeth.

THE PIRANHA OF THE AMAZON WATERS
A. Fraser-Brunner

Characins are related to the CARP family (q.v.), but they all have teeth in their jaws and have also a small, fleshy 'adipose fin' behind the back fin.

CHATTERER. This name is used for a group of tropical birds of central and South America, which belong chiefly to the forests of the Amazon. They vary in size from a sparrow to a crow, and many of the males have very gaudy plumage. The Cock-of-the-rock, for instance, is a fairly large bird, coloured bright orange-red, with a large, circular crest growing from each side of the head; and the Blue Cotinga, about the size of a lark, is bright blue, with black wings and tail. They have short, wide-opening bills, and feed principally on insects and fruits.

A remarkable-looking bird of the Chatterer family is the Umbrella Bird, a large, deep black bird, the male of which has a huge crest of feathers, which usually lies contracted, but which can be erected at will to form an umbrella-like covering to the head. He also has a long, feather-covered wattle growing from the throat. Umbrella Birds are very rarely seen, as they live in the upper branches of the dense Amazon forests; but their loud piping note is more often heard.

Another bird with a remarkable note is the Bell-bird, the two best-known species being pure white birds of south-east Brazil and the Guianas. Both are about the size of Jays, and utter frequently a series of metallic, bell-like notes. The Bell-birds of Australia and New Zealand are not Chatterers, but belong to the HONEY-EATER group (q.v.).

CHEESE-MITE, *see* MITES AND TICKS.

CHEESE-SKIPPER. This name is given to the larva of the Cheesefly, a small, shining black, two-winged fly that lays its eggs on cheese, and also upon the fat of ham and bacon. The Cheese-skipper is very like the maggot of the HOUSE-FLY (q.v.), broader at the hind end, tapering to the head, and without legs. It skips along by drawing its head and tail together until they nearly meet, and then suddenly straightening out the body. A Stilton cheese (preferably a good one, as the insect prefers the better sorts) will sometimes give an opportunity for seeing this remarkable display. It is not surprising that, when supplied with such rich material and needing no exertion to obtain food, the maggot is fully grown in under a week. It then skips out of the cheese to a quiet place and changes into a pupa. The pupa is enclosed in a golden-brown puparium, formed from the last larval skin.

See also FLIES.

CHEETAH, *see* CATS.

CHEVROTAIN (or Mouse Deer). These look very like some of the small DEER (q.v.), but in fact are quite different from them in structure. The Chevrotains are RUMINANTS (q.v.)—that is to say, they ruminate or 'chew the cud'; but their stomachs have only three compartments instead of the four of true ruminants. They have no antlers, but grow long upper tusks which stick out beyond their lower lips. They walk on the tips of their hoofs, making their legs look very stiff. They are shy animals and lie concealed in the grass of the jungle during the day, feeding only in the evening and early morning.

Most Asiatic Chevrotains are only from 10 to 13 inches high, and have brown and reddish coats, with white underparts. The Water

Chevrotain of Africa is a little larger, and has white spots and stripes on its olive body. It has large feet with wide-spreading toes, especially adapted for life in swampy ground.

CHIMAERA, *see* SHARKS AND RAYS, Section 4.

CHIMPANZEE, *see* APES.

CHINA-MARK MOTHS. Five British moths are remarkable in having aquatic caterpillars, four of which are China-marks, and the fifth a near relation. They have white wings, delicately traced with brownish markings. There are many other species, mostly belonging to the eastern tropics. In all China-marks the caterpillar constructs a case in which it remains concealed from its enemies, water-birds and fish.

The Small China-mark, rather less than an inch across the wings, occurs commonly in the British Isles near water covered with duckweed. The moths run about on the surface of the water, and lay their eggs, several together, on the underside of the weed, on which the velvety blackish-olive caterpillars feed. The caterpillar's body is covered with a coat of short fine erect hairs, which holds a layer of air and so keeps out the water. Young ones, until they have moulted twice, are not waterproof. The caterpillar's case is made out of fragments of duckweed, and contains a bubble of air which makes it float. Sometimes the caterpillar will go below the surface of the water, dragging the case with it, often leaving part of its velvety body protruding above the water and gleaming like silver. During the winter months the caterpillars shut themselves into their cases, not coming out to feed until mild days in April. They pupate in May in their cases.

The Brown, Beautiful, and Ringed China-marks belong to a different genus. They are common throughout most of the British Isles, though the Ringed China-mark does not extend farther north than Yorkshire. The Brown China-mark lays its eggs in a mass of jelly on the underside of the leaves of water-plants. The caterpillars make flattish, oval cases, about $1\frac{1}{2}$ inches long and $\frac{3}{4}$ inch wide. They cut out a piece from a leaf and fasten it with silk to the underside of another leaf, which is cut to match the first piece. As the leaves are concave, a space is enclosed in which the caterpillar lives, surrounded by air. When fully mature, it constructs a cocoon attached to a water-plant, sometimes

below and sometimes above the water. The Ringed China-mark builds a case below the surface, and depends, not on air, but on oxygen taken in from the water by gills. Every few minutes the larva makes rapid wave-like movements to drive out the foul water from its case and take in fresh.

The False-caddis Water-veneer, related to the China-marks, is more local than the others. The female moth has only rudimentary wings and uses its legs to swim below the surface of the water. Occasionally winged females appear at the end of the season. The males, which live about 2 days only, mate with the females on the surface of the water, and are often dragged down below to drown. The eggs are laid on submerged leaves, the caterpillars living at depths of 3 to 9 feet. They burrow into the food plant, and later make cases like those of the China-mark.

See also CATERPILLAR; CASE-BEARER MOTH.

CHINCHILLA. This is a small, squirrel-like RODENT (q.v.), with very long ears and a longish bushy tail, found in the Andes Mountains of

Chile and Bolivia. Large numbers live together in rock crevices and burrows, and are often seen about during the day-time running like mice in the shade thrown by the rocks and feeding upon the sparse vegetation. When feeding they sit up on their hind-quarters like squirrels and grasp their food between their fore-paws. Very few of them are now left, because they have been much hunted and trapped for their soft, silver-grey fur.

The Viscacha, another rodent, related to the Chinchilla, lives on the Argentine pampas. It is a heavily built animal, about 2 feet long. Its face is covered with mottled black and grey fur, which it combs with a bunch of stiff bristles growing on its hind foot. Viscachas usually live in parties of twenty to thirty, and form large warrens, each of which may contain from twelve to fifteen burrows, the whole covering an area of from 100 to 200 square feet. Some of these burrows open out into wide chambers from which tunnels radiate. Viscachas rarely leave their burrow before dusk, and feed upon grass, seeds, and sometimes roots. Just before they come out to feed and frolic, an old male usually mounts a mound of excavated earth heaped up outside the burrows, and takes a careful survey to see that no enemies lurk about the colony.

See also Vol. VI: Fur-farming, Section 7; Furs.

CHIPMUNK, *see* Marmot.

CHLOROPHYLL, *see* Photosynthesis.

CHOUGH, *see* Crow, Section 6.

CHRYSALIS, *see* Butterfly.

CICADA. This large bug is the noisiest of all insects. Generally, Cicadas chirrup only during bright sunlight—and the hotter the sun the greater the noise; but on hot tropical nights they may continue into the hours of darkness. Only the males are musical, and in tropical countries, where the largest and noisiest species occur, the effect is said to be deafening. They are insects of the forests and woodlands, and, like other bugs, they suck the juices from the roots and foliage of the trees. So far as is known, the nymphs always live underground, using their forelegs for

CICADA NYMPH

digging. There is only one species in Great Britain, and this is found only in the New Forest where it is a rarity. It is about $\frac{3}{4}$ inch long, with a wing expanse of just over 2 inches.

The organs of the male which enable it to sing are in the abdomen, and consist of a pair of drums, called the 'timbals', that bulge outwards. Large and powerful muscles pull these in and

then release them, in a continually repeated crackling noise. There are as well 'sounding-board' arrangements for increasing the noise, air-chambers, and methods of changing the air supply—altogether the most complicated mechanism for producing a sound found in any inrect. Yet the result is not to be compared with the variations of the human voice, produced by the very much simpler mechanism of our vocal cords. There are different opinions about the Cicada's music. The ancient Greeks are said to have kept the insects in cages for the pleasure of hearing them sing, and the Chinese and Japanese do so now; but the majority of people agree that the Cicada's song is a strident, monotonous, and unpleasant noise. Be that as it may, the important thing is that the male Cicada's music is favourably received by the female, who responds as best she can by making a crackling noise with her wings.

The American insect, called the Seventeen-year Locust or Periodical Cicada, is a Cicada bug, and not a locust at all. It is remarkable for the long time it takes to grow up. The eggs are laid in the twigs of trees, and the nymphs, which hatch out in about 6 weeks, drop down and go underground. They remain below, sucking the juices from the roots of the trees, for 17 years, when, fully grown, they come up again and become adults. As they all emerge about the

CICADA ADULT

same time, great numbers of their cast-off skins are to be seen clinging to the trunks of the trees. The males appear to start their shrill music almost at once and to keep it up for a few weeks, after which they all disappear again, and silence reigns for a further period of 17 years. More than twenty distinct broods of this insect are known in the United States, each of which has its own particular year for emerging above ground, so that one or more of these broods appears somewhere in the country each year. In the south there is a brood whose period below ground is 13 instead of 17 years.

See also Bug.

CICHLID. Like the Characins (q.v.), the fishes called Cichlids are found only in the fresh or brackish waters of South America and Africa,

THE MALE CICHLID FANS THE EGGS LAID OUT BEFORE HIM IN NEAT ROWS. THE FEMALE LOOKS FOR FOOD. *A. Fraser-Brunner*

with the exception of three species in India and Ceylon. They are Perch-like fishes—that is to say, the front part of the dorsal fin is supported by sharp spines (*see* PERCH). Unlike most fishes, they have only one nostril on each side. Many of them are very brightly coloured, and are favourites in the AQUARIUM (q.v. Vol. IX). In some Cichlids, when the eggs are laid, the mother takes them into her mouth and keeps them there until they hatch. Even then, should danger threaten, the baby fish will pop back into their strange hide-away, while the father swims round looking very fierce until all is safe again.

Perhaps the best-known Cichlid is the Angel-fish, found in the streams of Brazil and brought to Britain in large numbers as a favourite for the aquarium. It is silvery, with handsome dark bands, and its upper and lower fins are so long that its height is greater than its length—it is like a diamond-shape standing on one point. To add to its wonderful appearance, it has long streamers on the fins. It is so flat from side to side, that when seen in front it seems to be just an upright straight line. This is a useful protection, for if it is frightened, it darts away to a clump of weeds and, when it turns round to face the enemy, it immediately seems to disappear. The black stripes also help to make it invisible among water-plants. When it lays its eggs, it takes them in its mouth and sticks them to the leaf of a plant, or sometimes to a stone, where it fans them with its fins to aerate them until they hatch. Angel-fish are easy to keep in an aquarium if it is kept warm enough and there is a good supply of growing plants.

Another sort of Angel-fish found in tropical seas is related to the Butterfly fishes (*see* SEA PERCH).

CIVET. The Civet tribe is a group of flesh-eating mammals closely related to the CATS (q.v.), but with longer bodies, more pointed faces, and shorter legs. They are mostly between 2 and 3 feet in length, with longish tails. The chief members of the group, the true Civets, Genets, Palm Civets, and Binturongs, are found in Asia and Africa and two species in southern Europe also.

The African and the Indian Civets are very alike: they have greyish-brown hair, with darker streaks and spots on their bodies, and dark and light rings on their tails. The Indian Civet is very destructive, eating, as well as birds and small mammals, frogs, insects, eggs, fruit, and roots. Civets are not often seen, as they hunt only at night. Certain glands at the root of the tail secrete a scent which is used by perfumers (*see* PERFUMERY, Vol. VII).

Genets are chiefly found in Africa, the Common Genet being found also in southern Europe and south-west Asia. Genets are smaller than Civets, with shorter legs, more tapering tails, and soft, greyish or yellowish fur. When a Genet steals through the grass in chase of prey it presses close to the ground and stretches its long, lithe body to the utmost, so that it looks almost like a snake.

Palm Civets, except for one African species, live in Asia. They are also called Toddy Cats, because they are very fond of the palm-juice or 'toddy' which the natives in India and Ceylon collect in vessels suspended from the trees. The Indian Palm Civet, the best-known species, has blackish-grey, coarse fur. It spends most of its life in trees, and hunts for food during the night.

Binturongs or Bear Cats, which have long, blackish fur, are fairly common throughout the Malay Peninsula, East Indies, Assam, and Siam. These, in contrast to all the other members of the civet tribe, have long tufts of hair on their ears and tails. They can support their whole weight from the branches of the trees by their prehensile tails. They hide during the day, and climb in search of food only at nightfall.

CLAM. The true Clams lead sedentary lives in pools on coral reefs, where they can be a real source of danger to the unwary. This is particularly true of the Great Clam, for the power of its muscles is immense. Once the gaping valves of the great shell close upon the hand or foot of a man, it is practically impossible for him to free himself unaided from their vice-like grip, and, unless promptly rescued, he will be drowned by the returning tide. There are six or seven species of Clam, the Giant Clam being the largest. In the collection of shells at the British Museum (Natural History), there are two valves of the Great Clam weighing respectively 154 and 156 lbs. These great shells are broadly oval in form, and extremely massive and strongly ribbed; their edges are deeply fluted, and the interior is pure white. The animal inside may weigh upwards of 20 lbs., and the fleshy folds of its mantle are brilliantly coloured.

GIANT CLAM—ACTUAL SIZE 3 FT. × 2 FT.
Dr. S. Manton, F.R.S.

Under the general name of Clam are included the members of another family of bivalves, or twin-shelled molluscs, the Myidae—which are quite different, however, from the true Clams. They are found on some parts of our British coasts, where they are known as 'Gapers'. They never reach the size of the true Giant Clams, and their much smaller shells, greenish or yellow in colour, gape at each end, the right valve being a little larger than the left. They live in deep burrows in the sand or mud from about low-water mark to a depth of 25 fathoms. While their shells are of a dull colour, their remarkable long siphons, which are enclosed in a wrinkled skin and project far beyond the valves of the shell, are brightly tinted with red.

See also MOLLUSCS.

CLASSIFICATION OF ANIMALS AND PLANTS. In order to make the study of living creatures, whether plant or animal, more easily intelligible, it is necessary to arrange the different kinds in some logical system. The principle adopted by LINNAEUS (q.v. Vol. V) in the 18th century, which has become the standard arrangement throughout the world, is intended to show the relationship of different species to one another.

To classify animals or plants, they are arranged in groups, and these groups are repeatedly subdivided until we reach the single species (man, salmon, red admiral butterfly, yellow water-lily). The easiest way to explain classification will be by taking, as an example, man. It is convenient to start with the widest group, the 'phylum'. Man belongs to the phylum Chordata, animals with a hollow, dorsal nervous system and jointed spinal column. Within this phylum he belongs to the 'class' Mammalia, warm-blooded animals which have hair and suckle their young. Next, the mammals are subdivided into 'orders', where man is classed in the Primates, along with lemurs and monkeys and apes. The lemurs are excluded from the 'sub-order' Anthropoidea, but here man is still classed with the monkeys and apes. Man belongs to the 'family' Hominidae, which includes fossil and modern man only. His 'genus' is Homo, which includes species now extinct, such as Neanderthal man (*see* FOSSIL MAN, Vol. I), and his 'species' is *sapiens*—which includes all existing men, whether Caucasian, negroid, or mongoloid. Thus we arrive at man's scientific name of *Homo sapiens* (*see* SCIENTIFIC

NAMES). It will be seen, by working back through these groups, that we gradually discover man's different evolutionary relationships, which become wider and more numerous the farther back we go, just as in tracing the pedigree of an individual, we find two parents, derived from two different families, four grandparents from four, eight grandparents from eight families, and so on.

In classifying plants, similar groups are arranged to show relationships in a similar manner. Thus, the common daisy is one of the 'Phanerogams', plants in which there are true flowers with stamens and pistils. (In such plants as ferns, mosses, and fungi there are no true flowers, and they are known as 'Cryptogams'.) The daisy has seeds enclosed within a fruit, and is therefore a member of the tribe of 'Angiosperms'. (The 'Gymnosperms', in which the seed is naked, include the conifers, or cone-bearing trees.) Within the seed the embryo contains two 'cotyledons' or 'seed-leaves', and the daisy therefore belongs to the great class of 'Dicotyledons'. (Among the 'Monocotyledons', with only one seed-leaf, are orchids, lilies, grasses, and sedges.) More easily observed, but less certain distinctions between these two great classes are these: that in Dicotyledons the parts of the flower are in fours, fives, or eights, and the leaves have a more or less complex system of veining; while in the Monocotyledons the parts of the flower are usually in threes, and the veins of the leaf are usually simple and parallel. The daisy belongs to the great family of the Compositae, in which each 'flower' is in fact made up of a number of small, separate flowers; it is the only British member of the genus *Bellis*, and its specific name is *perennis* (everlasting).

A BRIEF CLASSIFICATION OF THE ANIMAL KINGDOM

Sub-kingdom: INVERTEBRATA

Phylum: Protozoa (Unicellular animals)
  „   Porifera (Sponges)
  „   Coelenterata (Jelly-fishes, Sea-anemones, Corals)
  „   Vermes (Worms)
  „   Polyzoa (Moss-animals)
  „   Brachiopoda (Lamp-shells)
  „   Echinodermata (Starfish, Sea-urchins)
  „   Mollusca (Shell-fish)
  „   Arthropoda

Class: Crustacea (Shrimps, Crabs, and Lobsters)
  „   Myriapoda (Centipedes and Millipedes)
  „   Insecta (Insects)
  „   Arachnida (Spiders, Scorpions, Mites)

Sub-kingdom: VERTEBRATA

Phylum: Protochordata (Primitive vertebrates)
  „   Chordata (Vertebrates)
Class: Pisces (Fishes)
  „   Amphibia (Frogs, Toads)
  „   Reptilia (Reptiles)
  „   Aves (Birds)
  „   Mammalia (Mammals)

A BRIEF CLASSIFICATION OF THE VEGETABLE KINGDOM

I. Cryptogams (seedless plants):
    Thallophyta (Seaweeds, Fungi, &c.)
    Bryophyta (Mosses, Liverworts)
    Pteridopyta (Ferns, Horsetails)

II. Phanerogams or Spermatophyta (seed-bearing plants):
    Gymnospermae (Conifers)
    Angiospermae (Flowering Plants)

CLEARWING MOTHS. The scales that clothe the greater part of the long narrow wings of these moths are loosely attached, and, except for a few round the margins and on the veins, are lost at the first flight. Their wings then resemble the transparent wings of wasps and bees. Their like-

HORNET CLEARWING MOTH

Its general shape and the black and yellow bands on its body make it so closely resemble a wasp that other animals leave it alone. *S. Beaufoy, F.R.P.S.*

ness to wasps and bees is increased by their banded bodies and, above all, by their swift flight in hot sunshine. Many are metallic-black or blue, marked with red or yellow. Some of the fifteen British species are rare, and the moths are not easy to find. The caterpillars, however, bore into tree-trunks, stems, and roots, and either they or the chrysalises can often be found (at least, of about six species). Even the covering of hard wood does not protect them completely from woodpeckers, which open up the galleries and eat the contents.

The largest and finest British species are the two Hornet Clearwings, one being found on poplars, the other on sallows. They measure $1\frac{5}{8}$ inches across, and have black and yellow bands on their bodies. The caterpillar takes two years to become fully grown, and then, still within its tunnel, it spins a weak cocoon and pupates. The pupa does not have the legs sealed down against the body, as do the pupae of most moths; and it possesses rows of spines which enable it to wriggle from the cocoon and screw along the tunnel to the thin cap covering the outlet. This it breaks through to allow the moth to escape. The moths emerge in summer, early in the morning, but the female does not normally fly until she has mated. Males assemble to virgin females (which can be used as decoys for the capture of specimens).

The commonest British species is the Currant Clearwing. The eggs are laid in early summer near the tips of pruned shoots of both red and black currants. The caterpillar bores down the centre of the shoot for several inches. It hibernates there, and completes its growth in the following April, often betraying its presence by pushing out brownish waste matter from the shoot. It pupates at the end of the burrow, and, just before the moth hatches, it forces its way out through the remaining thin layer of bark.

A Clearwing, known as the Peach Borer, is the most important peach pest in North America. The females lay several hundred eggs, either on the trunks of damaged or previously infested trees, or near them in cracks in the soil. The caterpillars burrow in the bark around the foot of the tree, where their presence is revealed by masses of waste matter embedded in gum. In many instances the trees die in the course of a few seasons.

CLEG, see HORSE-FLY.

CLIMBING PLANTS. Plants could not live if their shoots did not grow towards light. The leaves must present to the light the greatest surface possible, to assist the essential manufacture of food by PHOTOSYNTHESIS (q.v.). Most plants solve this problem fairly easily by developing stout herbaceous or woody stems which grow upwards towards the light. In others, however, the stem is so weak that the only way it can grow upwards is by making use of supports of all kinds. Many ingenious devices are used to achieve this end, and so to promote success in the struggle for existence. Sometimes their success is remarkable: pink flowers of the Blackberry have been seen forming a crown to a high Elm, for instance, while the hairy fruits of Traveller's-joy (Clematis) hang from many high trees in the autumn hedgerows.

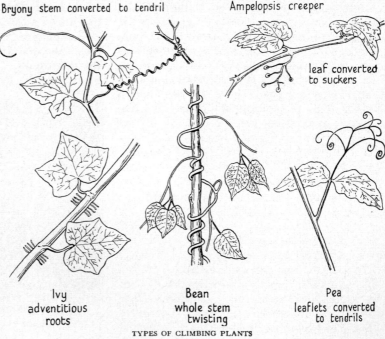

Bryony stem converted to tendril

Ampelopsis creeper

leaf converted to suckers

Ivy
adventitious
roots

Bean
whole stem
twisting

Pea
leaflets converted
to tendrils

TYPES OF CLIMBING PLANTS

In some cases the plant simply twines round a support. This may be a piece of string, placed by the gardener to help his Runner Beans, or the branch of a tree or post, round which the Honeysuckle can climb. Some plants, such as the French (or Kidney) Bean, Bindweed, or Gourd, climb in an anti-clockwise direction; while the Honeysuckle, Hop, and Black Bryony climb in a clockwise direction. In temperate regions climbing plants are usually herbaceous (that is, their stems do not contain much wood). In the tropics, however, the Lianas have woody stems which can twine round trunks and branches with such pressure that the limb of the tree becomes malformed. Honeysuckle will sometimes do the same in this country.

Other plants have developed special climbing organs. The Ivy, for instance, climbs by adventitious or stem ROOTS (q.v.), which fix themselves to the tree-trunk or wall. Traveller's-joy and the Garden Nasturtium twist their leaf-stalks round the stems of other plants. Goose-grass or Sticky Willie (Cleavers), so common in our hedgerows, climbs by means of small hooks on its stem. The Blackberry and the Rose scramble over other plants by the aid of curved woody prickles.

Probably the most important of the climbing organs, however, are tendrils. These are specialized parts of the stem, or leaves, or of portions of leaves. In the White Bryony, for instance, the twining tendrils are modified branch-stems; in the Virginian Creeper the stem-tendrils, instead of twining, develop flat, sticky disks at their tips, which stick to the walls. The tendrils of the Grape-vine are modified flower-shoots. In the Sweet Pea some of the upper leaflets of the compound leaf become modified as climbing tendrils. In the Yellow Vetchling the whole leaf is modified into a tendril, and to make up for the loss of the leaves certain outgrowths of the leaf, called 'stipules', become greatly enlarged to take over the normal food-manufacturing duties of the green leaf.

See also STEMS.

CLOTHES MOTH, *see* MOTHS; *see also* HOUSEHOLD PESTS, Vol. XI.

COBRA. This name is a Portuguese word meaning simply a SNAKE (q.v.)—any snake. Early settlers in India saw a snake which they called *Cobra di capello*, the hooded snake, and from that the name has come to be applied to any member of the small genus of poisonous 'hooded' snakes inhabiting tropical Asia and Africa. The two best-known species in Asia are the Common Cobra and the King Cobra. The so-called hood is, of course, in no sense a covering, but is an expansible portion of the skin of the neck, moved by ribs which are elongated for that purpose. The remarkable pose, with dilated hood, which the cobra adopts when alarmed, has made it known throughout the world. (When it is crawling about the hood cannot be seen.) The spectacled form (which is often illustrated) is found only in India: the cobras inhabiting Indo-China have 'monocles', and all-black individuals, with no marking on the hood, are not uncommon in both countries.

The Common Cobra, more common in India than anywhere else, seldom exceeds 5 feet in length. Annually many people die from its bite; but it is not an aggressive snake, and when disturbed usually makes off rapidly. It is more active at night, and will then bite more readily than in the day-time. When thoroughly roused, it will eject its poison to a distance of 3 feet or so, and with great accuracy, usually aiming at the face. On account of this habit, the term 'spitting cobra' has arisen; and one South African species, the Ringhals, is particularly given to it. The poison cannot harm unbroken skin, but if it enters the eyes it may cause blindness. The bite is generally fatal. The male and female cobra remain together after mating; the eggs are laid in a 'nest' which they make in the ground, and both parents take their turn to guard them until the young are hatched.

The King Cobra, or Hamadryad, is the largest poisonous snake known, reaching a length of 16 feet or more. It is a native of India and Malaya. The adult is dark brown all over; but the young are almost black, with distinct white cross-bars upon the body and tail. The King Cobra builds a nest of grass, twigs, and leaves; and the female (and possibly also the male) guards the eggs until they hatch out. The aggressive disposition of the King Cobra is well known, and there are many records of people having been attacked by it; but usually it makes off without delay when encountered. It feeds mainly upon other snakes.

The Crested Cobra or Crested Mamba is a legendary snake of Natal and Zululand, said to carry a crest of feathers which it spreads out like a fan when alarmed.

COCKATOO, *see* PARROT.

COCKCHAFER, *see* CHAFER.

COCKLE. If you look at a Cockle-shell end-wise, you will see that the two closely fitting valves of which it is composed are rather like a heart in shape, and it is from this resemblance that the Cockles have received their scientific name of *Cardium*. On any part of the sea-shore where there is plenty of soft and rather muddy sand Cockles abound. They are collected in large quantities, some being cooked and sent to market, but most being used for bait. The Cockle is a burrowing mollusc, which uses its long and strong foot for digging. Thrusting the pointed tip into the soft sand, the Cockle pushes its foot down as far as it will go, and then, bending the end of it into a hook like an anchor, drags itself, shell and all, beneath the surface. The Cockle also uses its remarkable foot to hop along the shore, by pressing it firmly against the sand, bending it, and then suddenly letting go, so that it acts as a spring. In this way the little mollusc jumps over the sands toward the incoming tide.

There are many species of Cockle, varying in size from barely that of a finger-nail to that of a closed hand, and ranging in colour from pure white to yellow, orange, red, and brown, often marked by waving lines of a darker tint. The largest British species is the Spiny Cockle which, when full grown, measures as much as 4 inches in length and just over 3 inches in breadth. It has a rather solidly built shell, with prominent, beautifully fluted ribs, which radiate in regular order on both valves, and are armed with

THE SPINY COCKLE PUTS OUT ITS LONG RED FOOT TO DIG IN
THE SAND

numerous sharp, polished spines. The shell has alternate concentric bands of yellowish and reddish-brown, grading off to a creamy-white at the beaks of the two valves. The Spiny Cockle

possesses a most remarkable and brilliant cardinal-red foot, which it can protrude some 4 inches beyond the edges of the valves of its shell.

See also MOLLUSCS.

COCKROACH. The Common Cockroaches, so often called 'Black-beetles', although they are neither beetles nor black, came here from the East. They are now found all over the world wherever there is human habitation, living in houses and bakeries. They move about only by night and, loving warmth, prefer the kitchen to any other part of the house. They have an unpleasant odour, which, when there are many of them, they may impart to the whole room. What their habits were before they became domesticated we can only guess. In our houses they are scavengers, eating anything of food value, but being especially fond of sweet and starchy foods.

The adult male has two pairs of wings: the forewings are narrow and shining brown, the hindwings small but wide, and folded fan-wise below the forewings. It hardly ever flies, but often spins round in a circle with both pairs of wings expanded. The female has two pairs of very short and quite useless wings. Her eggs are enclosed, sixteen at a time, in a horny brown case shaped like a purse, which she usually carries sticking out of the end of her body for some time before she cements it firmly in a sheltered position, such as the space between two floor-boards.

A much larger insect, the American or Ship's Cockroach, is also an immigrant. Both sexes are winged when adult, and the hindwings are relatively much larger than in the Common Cockroach, to which it has similar habits. It is not so widely found, but it has settled down here in a number of localities. Yet a third immigrant is the German Cockroach or Steam Bug, which is much smaller and paler than the Common Cockroach. It seems to have a preference for hospitals and the galleys of ships; but it sometimes swarms in other buildings, especially about radiators. A very pretty green Cockroach, often found among bananas, is a more rare visitor that has never established itself. Many of the tropical species are brightly coloured and live in foliage or under dead leaves.

Cockroaches and GRASSHOPPERS (q.v.) belong to the same group of insects; but whereas Grasshoppers are compressed from side to side and move chiefly by jumping, Cockroaches are very flat and are exceedingly swift runners.

See also INSECTS.

COD. With the exception of the Herring, the Cod is our most important food-fish. It abounds in the north Atlantic in numbers difficult to imagine: it has been estimated that about 400 million are caught each year—but these, of course, are only a small proportion of those actually swimming in the ocean. Such numbers are understandable, however, when we remember that a female Cod may lay about 6 million eggs at a time. It is true that most of these are eaten by various enemies, and that only six, on an average, grow to be adult fishes; but even at that rate the population would be trebled each year. So the numbers caught are easily replenished. In the north Pacific a closely allied species, called the Alaska Cod, is probably as abundant, and would be equally important if the fishing were as well developed. A good proportion of the Cod that are brought to Britain are salted for export to European markets. The livers yield an easily digested oil, containing important vitamins of great medical value.

Cod are voracious feeders; and with their strong, pointed teeth, they will eat almost anything. Among the curious things that have been found in their stomachs are a hare, various birds including a partridge, a bunch of keys, a long piece of tallow candle, and books! It is said that they feed mostly at night, guided by their sense of smell—though it is strange that a bunch of keys could smell appetizing!

A close relative of the Cod is the Haddock, which when smoked is the famous 'Finnan Haddie'. Like the Cod, it has a small 'barbel' or whisker on the chin; but whereas the Cod is greenish with a white lateral line, the Haddock has a black lateral line and a dark blotch near the shoulder. A smaller relative is the Whiting, which is silvery and has no barbel. All these have a short lower jaw, so that the mouth is more or less underneath. Two other well-known species, having a long lower jaw jutting forward somewhat beyond the upper, are the Pollack and Coalfish. Like the Cod, the Coalfish has a barbel on the chin and a white lateral line; but the fish is very much darker, almost black at times. It is caught in large numbers in the

COD-FISH
A. Fraser-Brunner

COMMON LING
A. Fraser-Brunner

Atlantic, and sometimes appears on the market. The Pollack, on the other hand, has no barbel, and is bronze-coloured. It has little commercial value, but is sought after by anglers who find it a good sporting fish. All these, and a number of smaller species, are peculiar in having three dorsal and two anal fins.

Allied to them are a number of species which have only two dorsal fins—the first fin short and high, the second extending for most of the length of the body—and a single long anal fin. These species include the Rocklings, small fishes inhabiting rock-pools, and often caught in lobster-pots, and the Ling, a large fish very much valued as food, but much less common than the Cod—rather curiously, as it lays even more eggs, sometimes as many as 28 million. Similar to the Ling is the Burbot, the only freshwater member of the family. This is found in rivers of Europe and England, as well as of America, where it is known also as the Lawyer.

The Hake has much the same arrangement of the fins, but has a more Pike-like head, with much more formidable teeth. It has no barbel and is silvery in colour, reaching a large size. It is found in the Atlantic and Mediterranean, and there are related forms in the Pacific. These, too, are good food-fishes—so that, on the whole, the Cod family is of the greatest importance to mankind.

See also Vol. VI, COD-FISHING.

COLEOPTERA, *see* BEETLES.

COLORADO BEETLE. This notorious insect was originally a native of the western part of North America, where it was not known to threaten any cultivated crop, but fed upon a wild plant related to the potato. Unfortunately it soon took to eating potato leaves—and at once began to multiply at an alarming rate, spreading across America. It reached the Atlantic coast about 1874, and half a century ago was found in Europe, at first in the south of France. It now ravages potato-crops over a large part of the Continent; but, although it is found from time to time in England, it has never established itself, thanks to the careful watch which is kept for it. It is a short, round-bodied insect about the size of a large cherry-stone, and decorated with alternate stripes of black and yellow. It is avoided by birds and other insect-eating creatures as it has a nasty taste, and its very conspicuous

GRUB OF COLORADO BEETLE

COLORADO BEETLE

pattern ensures that any inexperienced young bird which tries to eat it will not do so twice. It is because birds do not normally attack it that it spreads so rapidly. The grub is equally conspicuous—a soft-bodied, reddish insect, with two rows of small black spots on each side. The orange-yellow eggs are laid in the potato leaves.

See also BEETLES.
See also Vol. VI, INSECT PESTS.

COLORATION OF ANIMALS, *see* PROTECTIVE COLORATION (insects); CAMOUFLAGE.

COMMA BUTTERFLY, *see* VANESSINAE (Butterflies).

CONDOR. This large bird of prey belongs to the same order of birds as the VULTURE (q.v.)

which it closely resembles, although it is not, in fact, very closely related. There are ten species, all American birds, and the majority South American. They all have grotesque-shaped, naked heads, large hooked beaks, long claws, and huge wings. They are without the normal 'syrinx' or voice organ, and can utter only a kind of hiss. The largest of them is the black, grey, and white Condor of the Andes, the largest of all birds of prey, 4 feet long, and having a wing-span of some 9 feet. This great bird extends along the whole range of the Peruvian and Chilean Andes, at a height of from 9,000 to 16,000 feet, though some are also found on the rocky sea-coast. They breed on inaccessible mountain ledges, building no nest, but merely laying the two large white eggs on the bare rock. They feed mostly on carrion, but also frequently kill young goats and lambs, and are therefore persistently attacked by the natives, who have considerably reduced their numbers. When fully gorged, they become heavy and slow, and can often be lassoed or shot as they are roosting in trees.

The King Condor, though not so large, is brilliantly coloured, with a head and neck shading from orange to crimson and purple, cream shoulders and underparts, and black tail and wing feathers. This bird frequents forests rather than mountains, and ranges from Brazil to the southern states of the U.S.A. Another species, the Turkey-vulture, only about 2½ feet long, is a black and brown bird with a red head. It has a very wide range, and is quite common in the southern and middle states of the U.S.A. The Turkey-vultures are, like other Condors, scavengers, and though most unpleasing to look at when still, they have an exceedingly easy and graceful flight.

CONGER EEL, see EELS.

CONIFERS. This group includes well-known types such as Christmas-trees (Spruces and Firs), Monkey-puzzles, Pines, Yews, Larches, Cedars, and Cypresses. The only true natives of Britain are Scots Pines, Yews, and Junipers, but many others are planted in gardens or State forests, and a number of them have become naturalized. They are often quick-growing, and are valuable for their timber, and for the manufacture of WOOD PULP (q.v. Vol. VII) for paper-making.

SCOTS PINE
Eric J. Hosking, F.R.P.S.

SILVER FIR
Eric J. Hosking, F.R.P.S.

SPRUCE
Eric J. Hosking, F.R.P.S.

AUSTRIAN PINE
Eric J. Hosking, F.R.P.S.

Conifers are the simplest seed-bearing PLANTS (q.v.). Unlike the true FLOWERING PLANTS (q.v.), which also bear seeds, conifers have no true flowers, and bear their seeds exposed in cones instead of enclosed in seed boxes. The pollen grains are produced in similar but much smaller cones.

Conifers are usually large, and include some of the biggest and longest-lived of all trees. The Redwoods or Big Trees of California, for example, are so huge that a tunnel has been cut through the trunk of one of them, wide enough for a motor-car to drive through. One of the largest specimens is still growing on the south side of San Francisco Bay. Although its exact age is not known, records of it have been traced back to the first Spanish explorers of the 16th century. In 1777 it was already 137 feet high, with a trunk 15 feet in circumference. Now the circumference is 23 feet.

Although conifers are usually described as evergreens, the larch is deciduous—that is, it sheds its leaves completely in the autumn and renews them in the spring. Many evergreens such as the Holly, Ivy, Laurel, and indeed many tropical flowering plants, are not coniferous. It is quite untrue that evergreens never shed their leaves: they do—but the shedding, like the growth of new leaves, takes place all the year round, with the result that the tree never looks bare.

See also FLOWERING PLANTS, Section 4; REPRODUCTION OF PLANTS, Section 4.

See also Vol. VI, TREES, CONIFEROUS.

COOT, *see* RAILS.

COPPERS (Butterflies). The brilliant coppery-orange Small Copper is more closely related to the BLUES than to the HAIRSTREAKS (qq.v.), though all belong to the same family. It is common throughout the summer wherever its food plants, sorrel and dock, grow—that is, on uncultivated ground, in meadows and lanes, on heaths and commons, and sometimes in gardens. Like a number of birds, it guards its own territory, and when another butterfly passes by its flower-head it will suddenly dart out and pursue it for some distance before returning to keep watch once more (*see* ANIMAL TERRITORY). It generally has three generations a year, the eggs usually being laid singly on the underside of sorrel leaves. The young caterpillars eat channels in the leaves in which they lie hidden, and after the second moult make complete holes. They grow to resemble the leaves in colour, and are exceptionally difficult to see, as their flat shape, like wood-lice, casts little shadow. The last brood remain as caterpillars through the winter. The short, stout pupa hangs from its food-plant by tail hooks, and is supported by a silken girdle.

The British race of the Large Copper, a fiery copper-coloured butterfly, became extinct a century ago. It began to decline in numbers shortly before the draining of the fens, where it used to breed extensively. As it became scarcer and more localized it was much persecuted by collectors, who reduced its numbers. Attempts to introduce the German race into the fens in 1909 and again in 1926 failed, although another attempt succeeded in Ireland. In recent years, the Wicken Fen Trust has succeeded in establishing the Dutch form, which is very like the old English one, and under close protection it now flourishes. The caterpillars feed on the great water-dock, and can withstand prolonged flooding during hibernation. They have no honeyglands, but produce a sweet substance from scattered cells in the skin. This procures them attention from ants, and consequent protection from their enemies (*see* BLUES).

CORAL.

CORAL. This is a small marine animal, a polyp, closely related to the SEA-ANEMONE (q.v.). So similar are the two creatures in their external appearance that a Coral might be described as an Anemone which has taken to making a skeleton of carbonate of lime. Corals differ from Sea-anemones in two ways: they cannot move about when full-grown; and they possess a stony skeleton. Like the Anemones, they have a mouth surrounded by tentacles, armed with stinging-cells, each containing a coiled tubular thread, which acts like the stinging-hair of a nettle; these threads are used in the capture of the small organisms upon which the Corals feed. They multiply chiefly by budding. In some species the skeleton is in the form of a shallow cup, from the centre of which thin, vertical plates radiate at regular intervals. When the Coral is alive, the central plates and sides of this cup are concealed by the mouth, the tentacles, and the outer skin of the polyp.

The great coral reefs, so varied in form, are the work of the Reef-building Corals, which

A BRANCHING CORAL

multiply chiefly by a process of budding. The bud begins life as a slight prominence on the side of the body of the parent Coral, and, as it increases in size, a mouth forms at the free end, a circle of tentacles grows out round it, and the whole bud increases until it equals its parent both in size and shape. As the young Corals formed in this way do not become entirely separated from the parent stock, repeated budding on all sides results in the production of a colony numbering hundreds of thousands of individuals, and measuring many feet in length, breadth, and height. No matter what size such a colony may reach, all the polyps are intimately

DIAGRAM OF A SOLITARY CUP CORAL ILLUSTRATING SOFT TISSUES IN RELATION TO HARD STONY SKELETON

T. Tentacle; *O.W.* Thin layer of tissue covering outer wall of skeleton; *Sep.* Thin stony plate or septum; *M.* Soft lining tissue (Mesentery); *St.* Stomach; *Col.* Columella or central stony mass; *B.* The more solid stony base of the coral

A CORAL REEF   *Dr. S. Manton*

A CUP CORAL

never falls below 70° Fahr.—and there they grow at depths not exceeding 25 fathoms.

The so-called Precious or Red Coral is not a true Coral, but belongs to a closely related group of sea animals called Alcyonarians, which also include the Organ-pipe Coral and the Sea-fans. One of the outstanding differences between the true Corals and these Alcyonarians is in the number and appearance of their tentacles, those of the true Corals and Sea-anemones being simple, and usually numbering a multiple of six, whereas the Alcyonarians usually possess eight. Again, while some species of Corals live as single individuals, Alcyonarians form colonies. Many do not form a rigid stony skeleton; but their bodies are impregnated with countless

connected to each other, so that the colony really resembles a living sheet of animal tissue, fed and nourished by almost countless mouths and stomachs. It is by such simple processes of division and budding that all the varied forms of reef Coral are produced. Thus, when the Coral grows upwards and more or less outwards, budding as it grows, tree-like branches are formed; or, by symmetrical budding in all directions, the massive domes of the so-called Brain Corals result.

Besides these social or communal forms, there are many species of Corals, more particularly among those which live in colder seas than the reef-builders, which grow as solitary graceful cups, or as mushroom-shaped forms called Fungiacorals. One of these, less than an inch in diameter, lives attached to the shelving rocks in the deep pools on the coast of Devon and Cornwall. Reef-forming Corals, however, can only exist in the crystal-clear waters of tropical seas, where the mean temperature of the water for the year

BRAIN CORAL

BRANCH OF RED CORAL WITH EXPANDED POLYPS

spicules of lime, varying in shape and colour. The Red Precious Coral grows like a small shrub, the polyps, with their graceful, fringed tentacles, thickly covering the stem and branches, like tiny, pale bluish-white flowers. Red Coral grows on the rocky floor of the Mediterranean Sea, and its gathering used to be a small though flourishing industry.

The Organ-pipe Coral takes its name from the way it grows. It forms masses of slender, vertical tubes, which are joined at regular intervals throughout their length by thin cross-plates, giving added strength to the whole. The deep reddish-purple tubes are crowned with pale, lilac-tinted polyps, which, with their fully expanded tentacles, resemble little star-shaped flowers. It flourishes in warm and sub-tropical seas, masses of it adding to the wonderful colouring of the GREAT BARRIER REEF of Australia (q.v. Vol. III).

The Sea-fans are Alcyonarians, with horny, flexible stems growing in graceful branches covered with gaily tinted, tentacle-crowned polyps. They are found all over the world, in tropical as well as colder seas. Some species inhabit the great ocean depths and are luminescent.

See also Vol. III, CORAL ISLANDS.

CORAL SNAKE, *see* KRAIT

CORK, *see* STEMS, Section 1 *d.*

CORMORANT. This large, fish-eating bird belongs to the same order of birds as the GANNET (q.v.), and inhabits the seas around the coasts of the greater part of the world, including the British Isles. There are many species, all of which capture fish by diving, using their large webbed feet to swim beneath the surface of the water. They bring the fish to the surface, and then toss them in the air, catch, and swallow them. Young cormorants thrust their heads right down the throats of their parents to feed on the semi-digested fish in the crop.

The Common Cormorant is pitch black, glossed with bronze, with white on its cheeks and sides, and is nearly 3 feet in length. It nests in colonies, generally on sea cliffs or rocky islets, and lays its four to six bluish-white eggs in a nest consisting of a mass of seaweed, around which collect quantities of decaying fish and other refuse, producing a fearful stench. The Shag,

A PAIR OF CORMORANTS NESTING
Ralph Chislett, F.R.P.S.

or Green Cormorant, a slightly smaller bird, with glossy, greenish plumage and a crest on its head, also inhabits the coasts of Britain.

In eastern Asia Cormorants are tamed and used to catch fish for their owners. They are prevented from swallowing fish above a certain size by a ring which is placed around their necks. This sport was formerly practised in Britain, the Master of the Cormorants being an officer of the Royal Household (*see* VOL. VI, FISHING INDUSTRY, Section 3).

The tropical Darters, or Snake Birds, are related to the Cormorants, but are very much more slender in build, with long, snake-like necks, small heads, and long, pointed bills. They frequent large rivers and lakes, pursuing fishes under the water and spearing them with their sword-like bills. When on the surface with the body mostly submerged, the long, slender neck looks like a snake. They build their nests in trees.

CORM, *see* STEMS, Section 2 *c.*

CORNCRAKE, *see* RAILS.

COURTSHIP OF ANIMALS, *see* ANIMAL LANGUAGE.

COWRY. This type of MOLLUSC (q.v.) usually lives in shallow water on rock-strewn shores, where they may be seen slowly gliding over the weed-covered rocks or in the clear pools exposed at low tide. The common British species is about half an inch in length, not unlike a split pea in shape, and the shell is a pinkish white, sometimes marked with one or two dark-brown spots. If we turn the Cowry over we shall see that it is quite unlike most univalve (or one-piece) shells,

A BRITISH COWRY (*Cypraea europaea*)
a. Under surface of shell; *b.* Upper surface; *c.* The Cowry with body extended and mantle enclosing its shell

for the opening, instead of being circular, is a long, narrow slit running from end to end of the shell, and the lips of the slit are bluntly toothed and turn inwards. One would think that it must be a very thin and flat kind of animal that could comfortably pass in and out at such a door, but that is not so. When the Cowry begins to move it pushes out a long foot, which expands until it is twice as broad as the base of the shell; next appears a broad head with two long, straight tentacles; and finally, the folds of the mantle, or outer skin, project on each side and turn upwards, so that their two edges almost meet at the top of the shell. Moreover, the little animal is very gaily coloured: its large foot is golden or bright orange, marked with a long line of pale yellow; the long snout is scarlet; the tentacles light red, speckled with yellow; and the mantle a clear olive-green, splashed and dotted with black, and bordered with bright red.

Many of the Cowries living in tropical seas grow to a large size, and their shells are most beautifully coloured. The Tiger Cowry has always been a favourite with collectors on account of its brilliant markings, and it often measures a good 4 inches in length. The Orange Cowry, a good specimen of which may fetch as much as £40, is a rare tropical species, the shell being a bright orange colour, mottled with black spots, rather like a turtle-shell. The familiar little ivory-tinted Money Cowries, which come from the Indian and Pacific Oceans, were often used as money tokens in many parts of India and the Far East, and still pass as current coin among native tribes in parts of western Africa.

COYOTE, *see* WOLF.

COYPU. Also known as the Nutria or Beaver-Rat, the Coypu is a large RODENT (q.v.) which looks and behaves very much like a BEAVER (q.v.). It is found in the rivers and lakes of South America, especially in the Argentine. Its body is about 2 feet long, covered with long, dusty-looking, brownish-yellow fur, and ending in a long, rat-like tail.

Coypus generally make their burrows in the banks of rivers and lakes, nearly always choosing a quiet spot. If, however, the banks are not large enough, they build a platform-like nest among the reeds. They are usually seen in pairs; but large parties often come out in the evenings to swim in the water, uttering peculiarly mournful cries. The female takes her eight or nine offspring for a swim when they are a few days old. They are reluctant to learn, and try to find a safe place on their mother's back. The mother's teats are placed on the sides of her body, so that the young ones are able to reach them as they cling to her back, and in this position they are suckled. Coypus are awkward and ungainly on land. They eat the leaves, seeds, and roots of water plants.

Coypus are bred in captivity for their valuable fur, which in the trade is called nutria (*see* Vol. VI: FUR FARMING, Section 3; FURS).

CRAB. The true crabs make up a very large group of the CRUSTACEANS (q.v.). The majority inhabit the sea, though some species live in rivers, lakes, and swamps, and a few have established themselves on dry land, only returning to the sea for the breeding season. All are easily recognized by the broad 'carapace', or upper shell, the abdomen, which is reduced to a more or less triangular flap tucked under the body,

LARVAL STAGES OF THE COMMON SHORE CRAB
a. First or Zoëa stage; *b.* Megalopa stage; *c.* Young crab

the usually well-developed pincer-claws, and the four pairs of legs used for walking, digging, and sometimes for swimming.

The life-history of the Common Shore Crab is typical of the group. In the first stage the tiny larva has a helmet-like thorax, crowned by a long, tapering spine something like a dunce's cap, and with a second long spine sticking out in front, looking like a comical carnival nose. The eyes are large, but are not as yet carried on stalks, as they are in the full-grown crab; the abdomen is long and slender. The odd little creature swims in the sea by means of its 'maxillipedes' or jaw-feet. Gradually the larva increases in size, casting its skin from time to time, and passing through a series of changes until the second stage is reached. By now the eyes have grown out on short stalks, the ten legs have developed—the first pair as miniature claws—the dunce's cap spine has entirely disappeared, the long frontal spine has become reduced to a short triangular point between the eyes, and the slender abdomen is greatly shortened. The second-stage larva soon settles down on the floor of the sea, tucks its shortened triangular-shaped abdomen under its now-broadening carapace, and so acquires the adult form. Henceforward the crab does not change its shape, but as it grows it casts its shelly armour from time to time, and continues to do so at ever-lengthening intervals throughout the rest of its life.

The Common Shore Crab lives mainly under the weed-covered rocks between tide-marks. The large Edible Crab lives among rocks in deeper water, though young specimens are often found in the rock pools exposed at extreme low tide. On the Tasmanian coast is found the Giant Crab, which may measure fully 12 inches across its carapace, and has one of its claws developed into a very large and massive weapon. Several species of Swimming Crabs are to be found round the British coasts, the largest of which is the Velvet Fiddler Crab, measuring some 4 inches across the carapace. It is very like the Shore Crab, except that the last pair of legs is flattened and striped with blue, while the leg-joints are bright red. The popular names 'Fiddler' or 'Swimming' crab come partly from the shape of the flattened end-joint of the hind-leg, which is shaped rather like an old-fashioned viol, and partly from the half-scrambling, half-swimming movements of the legs when the crab is in the water.

An interesting British example of the burrow-

ADULT SHORE CRAB
Note the large right-hand claw used for holding and crushing food

i1̸g crabs is the Masked Crab, which has gained its popular name from the curious moulding of the back of its oval-shaped carapace, resembling a queer oriental mask. The body is about the size of a large walnut; the male has long and slender front legs, which terminate in small, blunt claws, while the same pair of limbs in the female are quite short and bear sharp-pointed claws. The long and stoutly haired antennae in both sexes serve as filters for the water passing down to the gills when the crab is buried in the sand. This strange-looking little crab is to be found on wide, sandy bays near low-tide mark, the only indication of its presence when the tide is out being the tips of the antennae, looking like a pair of short bristles, and just protruding from a slight hump on the surface of the wet sand.

The Spider Crabs are a particularly interesting family, not only because of their strange shapes, but also because of their curious habits. They are more or less oval in shape, with long slender legs and narrow claws, and both limbs and carapace bear a number of stout, short, curved spines. These crabs have the curious habit of dressing themselves up with pieces of living sponges, seaweeds, and other marine growths, which they gather with their claws and arrange on the carapace and legs, where they are held in position by little hooked spines. There the seaweeds and sponges continue to grow, so that the whole crab soon becomes

MALE CALLING CRAB

covered by a most effective disguise. As they are slow in their movements, this method of concealment undoubtedly saves the Spider Crabs from many hungry enemies. The Giant Spider Crab of Japan is the largest of the group. Its carapace may measure over 15 inches in length by 12 inches in width, and its claws may have a span of as much as 11 feet, when spread out. Another family of crabs which like to disguise themselves are the Sponge Crabs. They have adopted the habit of carrying a cloak, formed of a piece of living sponge, which is held in position on the back of the carapace by the last pair, or the last two pairs, of legs, these being specially modified for the purpose. Held in this fashion the living sponge continues to grow, so that the crab is completely hidden from view.

On the mud flats and salt marshes of tropical countries live the curious Calling Crabs, so named from the way in which they appear to beckon with one claw. While the females are quite normal in appearance, the males have one claw greatly developed—often larger than the crab's body, and sometimes brilliantly coloured. These gay colours probably serve to attract the female, and there is no doubt about the value of the great claws as weapons both for offence and defence, for the active and pugnacious males flourish them defiantly, and are always fighting. The Land Crabs, which have gills specially modified to serve for air-breathing, also inhabit tropical countries. Although they spend their adult life on land, their young stages are passed in the sea, so that the crabs have to go down to the shore for the breeding season. This MIGRATION (q.v.) takes place annually, the crabs marching across country in great companies, and as at this time they are in prime condition, considerable numbers fall victims to the many hungry foes who waylay them.

MALE MASKED CRAB

The Hermit Crabs, on account of their shape and varied habits, are a very interesting tribe. Nearly all of them are soft-bodied, and so they utilize the empty shells of MOLLUSCS (q.v.), such as winkles and whelks, as temporary homes, carrying them about with them in their wandering in search for food. Our Common Hermit Crab may often be found in the rock pools near low tide, scrambling about actively, the small ones carrying a winkle-shell, the larger a whelk-shell, into which they retreat when alarmed. It is not easy to extract a living Hermit Crab from his home without injury, for his body and some of his limbs are specially adapted for securing a firm grip inside the shell. His body is soft and twisted to fit the spiral shell; the pincer-claws of the first pair of legs are armoured and unequal in size, the larger of the two serving as a plug to the entrance of the shell; the next two pairs of legs are long and slender, and used for walking; while the last two pairs are short, and modified for gripping inside the shell and holding the soft-skinned defenceless body in place. House-hunting is almost an obsession in the life of the average Hermit Crab, for rarely will an unoccupied shell be passed without its possibilities as a convenient home being explored. Many Hermit Crabs live in close relationship with certain other marine animals—and here we have examples of that type of association between two quite different kinds of animals, in which the partners are rarely to be found separated, each

THE COCO-NUT CRAB (*Birgus latro*) IS A LAND-DWELLING RELATION OF THE COMMON HERMIT CRAB

benefiting more or less from the presence of the other. For example, full-grown Common Hermit Crabs, which live below low-water mark, frequently inhabit a large whelk-shell bearing a handsome Sea-anemone. The Sea-anemone benefits by sharing the fragments from the crab's meals, and the crab, while resting after the banquet, is protected by the outspread stinging tentacles of the Anemone. Sometimes a third partner is included in this curious association: a Bristle-worm may live in the upper whorls of the shell, and probably helps to keep the interior clean. It may be seen thrusting its head out at meal-times, to snatch morsels from the claws of its host. Another British Hermit Crab inhabits a spiral cavity in a living sponge. This association begins when the crab is still quite small and young, and living in a small winkle-shell on which the sponge settles. Though the winkle-shell soon becomes too small, the growth of the sponge keeps pace with that of the crab, and the latter, completely sheltered within the sponge, has no need to seek another home.

Species which may be called land Hermit Crabs, for they live almost entirely on land, are found on tropical beaches. They travel far inland and climb into low bushes in their search for food, only returning to the sea to breed. Like our British Hermits, they utilize the spiral shells of molluscs for their portable homes. The giant Coco-nut Crab, which actually climbs palm-trees to get at the young nuts, and grows to fully 12

HERMIT CRAB

Note the soft flexible body, and the small modified limbs adapted for holding on to the interior of the whelk or other univalve shell the crab may inhabit inches in body length, although belonging to the Hermit Crab tribe, does not make use of a portable shelter. Still more difficult to recognize at first sight as members of this family are the so-called Stone Crabs, of which one species, the Northern Stone Crab, is often caught by fishermen trawling in the North Sea. It looks much like a slender Spider Crab, but is easily distinguished because it has only three instead of four pairs of walking legs behind the pair of pincer-clawed legs. The fourth pair is actually there, but they are normally folded away out of sight in the gill chambers. Both its triangular-shaped thorax and its long, slender legs are covered with many short, sharp spines, while its unsymmetrical abdomen, carried tucked up beneath the thorax, is protected by shelly plates.

See also Vol. VI, CRAB AND LOBSTER FISHING.

CRANE. This large bird is related to the BUSTARD (q.v.), and is conspicuous for its very long legs and neck, and its powerful bill, with which it digs up roots, bulbs, and worms. Superficially Cranes resemble Storks, but their structure is different, and they never perch. There are about 19 species, found in all continents except South America, and most have predominantly grey or whitish plumage. Typical Cranes can sustain long flights. They migrate in flocks, flying at great heights in a **V** or **W** shape, each with its long legs stretched out behind. A migrating flock of Cranes can be an impressive sight, as was noticed by Jeremiah (Jer. viii. 8). The birds have a loud, trumpet-like call, which can be heard from two miles away. They are sometimes a menace to the farmer, for they will consume vast quantities of grain, but they are so vigilant and wary that they are difficult to shoot.

The Common Crane breeds in Europe, and winters in north and west Africa. At one time it was common in Britain, though it ceased to breed here many years ago. It frequents open country, especially swamps, where it constructs a large nest of grass and rushes on the ground. These large birds, up to 4 feet in length, perform an elaborate courtship dance, both sexes taking part, and bowing and turning before beginning the rather awkward skipping and hopping of the dance proper. They dance again at other times, sometimes when the eggs are laid—apparently for pleasure.

The White Crane of central and northern Asia is a lovely bird, with magnificent white plumage and red legs and face. It frequents wide expanses of shallow water and feeds on rushes and aquatic plants. The large Stanley Crane of South Africa is grey-blue, with a white crown and black markings. It lives on the open plains far away from water, and is carnivorous. The widely spread Demoiselle Crane, only about 2½ feet in length, is a purplish-grey, with long black breast-plumes and tufts of loose white feathers growing backwards from each side of the head. The Crowned Cranes of Africa have a fan-shaped crest of bristle-like feathers radiating from the top of the head.

In South and central America there are several groups of birds closely related to the Cranes. The Courlans of Brazil, chocolate-brown birds some 25 inches in length, live in swamps. The Sun-Bitterns are smaller birds, with long necks, long, pointed beaks, and a plumage marked with white, brown, and black—rather on the pattern of a butterfly's wing. They frequent the wooded banks of rivers, especially the Orinoco, and love to bask in the sun with their wings spread out, much like a butterfly. The Kagu of the island of New Caledonia is a remarkable-looking, grey-coloured bird, about the size of a domestic fowl, with a long crest of head-feathers drooping over its back. Although it has fairly well-developed wings, it seems incapable of flight, but lives on the ground, coming out at night to hunt for worms, molluscs, and insects.

CRANE-FLY (Daddy-long-legs). Crane-flies form a group of two-winged flies which must be known by sight to almost everybody. They are mostly of moderate or large size, and are easily recognized by their slender bodies and very long, fragile legs. The common Daddy-long-legs is a destructive pest. Its larva—called the 'leather-jacket' on account of its tough outer covering—lives underground, feeding on the roots of various grain crops and other grasses. The eggs are black, and are laid either on or in the ground. They hatch in about a fortnight, and the larvae feed throughout the year

CRANE-FLY

until the following spring, when they do their worst damage. The pupa is long and slender, usually with two horns on the forehead for breathing. It remains underground until the fly is ready to emerge, when it pushes itself partly out of the ground. The larvae of the different species have very varied habits—for while some, like the common Daddy-long-legs, are vegetarian, others are scavengers, others again are carnivorous; and while some live in the water, others live on land. The members of the Crane-fly family are often called Water Spiders.

See also FLY.

CRAYFISH, *see* LOBSTER.

CRICKET. This insect can be distinguished from its near relative, the Long-horned GRASS-

A HOUSE CRICKET

HOPPER (q.v.), by the way it carries its wings folded flat on its back. The outer edges of the fore-wings are bent down vertically along the sides, giving the body a flat, box-like appearance when viewed from above.

We have four species of Cricket—the House, Field, Ground, and Mole Crickets. The House Cricket, which is very common in many parts of the country, seems to keep entirely to houses and other well-heated buildings, especially bakeries. It is about ¾ of an inch long, and pale brown, with darker fore-wings. Its hind-wings, used in flight, are longer than its fore-wings, and quite pale. As they enjoy throughout the year a uniform high temperature, it is not surprising that House Crickets are to be found at every season of the year in all stages of their development. They will eat anything of food-value, and may be very destructive—for instance, at night to clothes drying in front of a kitchen fire:

woollen garments, especially, may be found riddled with holes next morning. They seem to be very thirsty insects—at all events they have a habit of collecting where water is stored, and water-cisterns have often been choked up with crickets that have fallen in and been drowned. In some places the House Cricket seems to be increasing greatly in numbers and becoming very much of a nuisance. It burrows into the walls, especially round kitchen fire-places and bakery ovens, staying in its tunnels out of sight, though not out of hearing, during the day-time, but coming out and often flying about the room at night. Its loud and not unpleasing chirruping can be distinctly heard by anyone passing a cricket-infested building at night. Their numbers, familiar haunts, and loud chirruping have caused crickets for centuries to be amongst our best-known insects. John Milton first used the phrase 'the cricket on the hearth' about 1630 in the poem *Il Penseroso*.

The Field Cricket, which is much rarer and a larger insect, is bulky and almost completely black, the male being shining black with a golden stripe across the base of each fore-wing. Field Crickets live in solitary seclusion, each in its own burrow below ground. They are very shy, retiring backwards rapidly into their burrows at the sound of approaching footsteps. They need hot sunshine, and may be found throughout the summer, in wild, rough pasturage, where they sing from May to July, both by day and by night.

The Mole Cricket, which is also rare, and much larger than our other crickets, is reddish-brown, and has short fore-wings which leave the greater part of the abdomen uncovered. It lives

A MOLE CRICKET

underground, having a preference for moist places such as the banks of streams and ponds. It owes its name to its burrowing habits, and to the likeness between the forelegs with which it digs and the hands of the mole. It feeds mainly on roots, and if it were common might be very destructive. It sings mostly on warm days in spring and summer. The Ground Cricket, which is rarely found, has a preference for walking about among dead leaves on dry banks in wooded districts.

The eggs of most crickets that live in the open are laid singly in holes in the ground. The ovipositor, or egg-laying tube, is slender instead of broad and sabre-shaped as in the Long-horned Grasshoppers.

CROCODILES. The Crocodilians form one of the four orders into which living reptiles are divided. They are to-day found only in tropical regions, but in the past they were more widely distributed, far more numerous, and more varied in form. Of that original vast horde, only four groups now survive, the true Crocodiles, the Alligators, the Caimans, and the Gharials.

Crocodilians differ from all other reptiles in having a four-chambered heart, and a muscular partition—not a true diaphragm—separating the heart, lungs, and liver from the abdominal cavity. Although in having four legs and a tail they resemble the lizards, they differ from them in many structural characters, and are, in fact, only distantly related to them. All Crocodilians also have a more or less well-developed bony armour covering the back, and in some species also the belly. Many people think the crocodile and the alligator are the same creature, but they are not, slight though the differences may be. Crocodiles generally have long, narrow snouts, alligators broad and bluntly pointed ones. In the crocodile, the fourth tooth in the upper jaw fits into a socket in the lower jaw, in the alligator it fits into a groove. Moreover, the two creatures occupy different regions of the world, and are never found living together.

All Crocodilians lay white, hard-shelled eggs, some burying them in the sand of river-banks, others building nests of reeds and grass. The female often keeps watch near her eggs until they are hatched. The home of the crocodiles is in the water; but on sunny days they will leave it to bask in the sun on the banks or upon logs. They have keen hearing and are sharp-sighted. They make a noise something between a loud bark and a bellow, but can also make a deep hissing sound. They have a well-developed tongue, which is, however, fixed to the floor of the mouth and cannot be put out.

CROCODILE

ALLIGATOR

CAIMAN

GHARIAL

TYPES OF CROCODILES

The Crocodilians eat only flesh, and will devour anything that they can overcome. As man-eaters they have a bad reputation, but only one species, the Estuarine Crocodile, really deserves it. The discovery of human ornaments or parts of human bodies in their stomachs does not necessarily mean that they have killed humans, for they have no objection to eating corpses. Crocodiles are hunted for the sake of their skins, which make good leather, but no other part of them is of value to man.

ALLIGATORS. *Zoological Society of London*

The true Crocodiles (with one exception which is found in central America) inhabit the eastern hemisphere, living in tropical Africa, Asia, the Malay Archipelago, and northern Australia. There are some ten different species, the largest being the dangerous Estuarine Crocodile, which sometimes grows to 30 feet and more. This is the largest of all living reptiles, and, like the rest of its group, continues to grow throughout its long life. It lives in brackish waters in the lower reaches of rivers, rarely being found above the tidal limit, but it is also quite at home in salt-water and has been found far out at sea. The common fresh-water species of India is the Mugger, of Africa the Nile Crocodile, and of Australia Johnston's Crocodile. All have been known to eat men, but none is so dangerous as the Estuarine Crocodile.

The Alligator was first seen by the early Spanish settlers, who called it 'una lagarta', a lizard—for it looked to them like an enormous lizard. From 'una lagarta' the English settlers produced 'alligator'. Two well-known species are the Mississippi Alligator, inhabiting the southern parts of North America, and the Chinese Alligator, living in the waters of the Chinese river, the Yang-tsze-kiang. In the past alligators flourished in all northern countries—indeed, the fossilized remains of one have been found in the London Clay.

The Caimans, or Jacaras, as they are called by the natives of Brazil, are the Crocodilians of Central and South America. Five species are recognized, and these differ from the true crocodiles and alligators in certain characters of the skull, and also in having a more strongly developed bony armour on both the back and belly. The largest species, the Great Caiman, grows to a length of 20 feet and has enormous bulk. On the Amazon and Orinoco rivers and their tributary waters and lakes they may be seen in huge numbers, particularly at the end of the dry season, when the receding waters confine them to certain areas. They seldom molest man and are therefore not greatly feared by the natives.

The Gharial, or Gavial, is the long-snouted crocodile of northern India, found mainly in the waters of the Indus, Ganges, and Brahmaputra, and subsisting mainly on fish. A specimen was shot some years ago in Upper Burma; but it is now very rare, if not extinct, in that part of the world. The male grows to a length of 20 feet or more and is distinguished from the female by having a large fleshy protuberance on the end of its snout. The name Gharial is said to have originated because this protuberance resembles a *ghara* or Indian earthenware pot.

Schlegel's Gharial, also known as the False Gharial, and now regarded as being closely related to the true Crocodiles, is a very rare beast and is restricted to Borneo and the Malay Peninsula.

CROSSBILL, see FINCHES, Section 5.

CROWS. 1. This family (Corvidae) of Passerine or perching birds includes many well-known
species, such as the Rook, Magpie, Jackdaw,
and Jay. They vary in size from the Raven,
over 2 feet in length and the largest of the
Passerine birds, to the Jay, which is only a little
more than half as big (13½ inches). They are
found in most parts of the world, and have, for
birds, a very highly developed intelligence. Most
crows pair for life, and the male shares in all the
duties of parenthood. Most members of the
family are disliked by the farmer or game-
preserver, as they steal other birds' eggs and
young, and raid the farmer's grain crops (see
BIRD PESTS, Vol. VI). Ravens will sometimes
kill a wounded sheep or attack a lamb. They
do, however, eat a great many harmful grubs
and insects.

2. CARRION CROW. This large, completely
black bird, about 20 inches in length, has the same
build as the Raven, but is smaller. Although war
has been waged upon it in Britain, it is still very
common, and does a good deal of damage. It
builds its large, rather untidy nest on a cliff
ledge on the coast, or high up in a tree. It
sometimes builds near a rookery, because, since
its own eggs hatch out earlier than the rooks',
it can steal rooks' eggs with which to feed its
young. It will eat anything that comes its way,
though it is a meat-eater by choice. It cracks
food such as shell-fish or nuts by dropping them
from a height

The Hooded Crow, apart from its grey back
and underparts, is very much like the Carrion
Crow in shape and habits. It is less common in
Britain, though a number migrate to eastern
coasts from Scandinavia and northern Europe,
where there are vast hordes of them.

3. THE RAVEN, the sacred bird of the Norse
god Odin and a character in many legends and
traditional tales, is perhaps the most intelligent
of all crows. It is a handsome bird, with its
glossy black plumage and fine size, but it also
has been relentlessly pursued because of its
depredations. It still breeds, however, in some
numbers on coastal cliffs and in mountainous
districts. It nests very early in the year, starting
to repair its old nest in January and producing
its young by the end of February. It is a very
strong flier, and during the courting season it
will perform gambolling flights, diving and

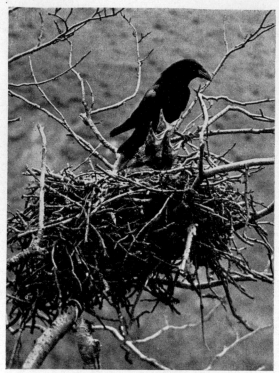

RAVEN AND YOUNG. *Arthur Brook*

tumbling from great heights, dropping a pebble
or twig and then diving after it, and closing its
wings and rolling round in the air. It uses these
tricks also to defend itself against attack by birds
of prey.

4. THE ROOK can be distinguished from other
crows by a bare white patch round the bill, which
is more pointed than that of other crows. It is
by far the most numerous of British crows, being
found anywhere where there are tall trees. It is a
gregarious bird, nesting in the tree-tops in great
colonies, called rookeries. These colonies are
very noisy, busy assemblies, especially during the
period of building the large, untidy, stick nests.
There is an old superstition that if the rooks
desert their rookery the heir to the estate will
die.

5. THE JACKDAW, the smallest of the four,
has a grey patch on the nape of its neck. It is,
perhaps, the most popular of the family, as it is
easily tamed and makes an amusing pet. It
is alternately quarrelsome, impudent, and
destructive, and is a most mischievous thief,
making off with and carrying to its nest any
bright thing which attracts its attention. This
characteristic has made it the subject of many

stories, including the famous story of *The Jackdaw of Rheims*. It builds its nest in holes in trees or cliffs, or in a building—often being responsible for blocking up a chimney.

6. The Chough is the least familiar of the crow family in Britain, being represented by one species only, the Cornish or Red-billed Chough. Though now quite rare in Cornwall, it is often to be found around the cliffs of Wales, western Ireland, and the Isle of Man. It is a vivacious bird, with a bright red bill and legs, and glossy black plumage; it has a buoyant flight and very fast run. But it is shy, and rarely permits anyone to approach it. The Alpine Chough, with a yellow bill, is an inhabitant of the mountainous districts of Europe and Asia, but does not appear in Britain.

7. The Magpie is well known everywhere because of its pied black-and-white plumage and long tail, and because of the superstitions which have grown round it. The old rhyme 'One for sorrow, two for joy' has various versions. In winter considerable gatherings of Magpies may be seen, but in spring and summer they are found in pairs. They build in the fork of a tree or bush, the structure of the nest differing from that of other crows. On a foundation of turf or clay is built a large nest of thorny sticks and twigs, the

sides of which continue up to form a complete dome with one side open. The nest is well lined with roots and dry grass. The six or more eggs are of the usual crow type—bluish-green and mottled. Magpies also can be tamed to make amusing pets.

8. The Jay is very different from the rest of the family in appearance, being one of the gayest of British birds, with its pinkish-brown plumage marked with white and black, and the bright blue, white, and black bars on the wing coverts. It has also a crest of upright feathers, whitish streaked with black. Most species of Jays are gaily coloured—among them the Blue Jay of North America, the Siberian Jay, grey with a bright, rust-coloured tail, to be found in the forests of northern Europe, and the crow-like Whisky-jack of Canada. Jays are noisy birds, except when near their nest, and they live in woods. They are wicked thieves of young birds and eggs, and so are shot without mercy by the game preserver. They have a very jaunty walk, including sideways hops—and this has led to the expression 'jay-walking'.

CRUSTACEA. This is the division of the animal kingdom which includes the Crabs, Lobsters, Prawns and Shrimps, Barnacles (qq.v.), Sand-hoppers, the Water-fleas (*Daphnia*) of the ponds, and a vast assemblage of small and less familiar creatures which are chiefly inhabitants of the sea except for a few species like the common Woodlouse (q.v.) of our gardens. They are extraordinarily diverse in size and shape, and many of them pass through most remarkable changes of form, or Metamorphoses (q.v.), before reaching the adult stage—changes as profound as those between a caterpillar and a butterfly. All, however, possess certain well-marked features by which they can be distinguished. The body and limbs are

MAGPIE WITH FLEDGLINGS WHICH ARE NEARLY READY TO LEAVE THE NEST
Arthur Brook

A SAND-HOPPER

divided into segments, and are covered entirely with a tough or a hard, lime-impregnated coat, which is pliable at the joints, allowing the limbs to move in certain directions. This outer skin, the cuticle, is incapable of growth, and in fact is like a suit of clothes which, as its owner grows, becomes too small, so that it has periodically to be cast off and replaced by a new garment. It is possible to watch this curious process taking place in a shore crab in an aquarium. First the shell splits across the back at the base of what is known as the 'carapace' or upper shell, and the crab slowly extricates its body and limbs, leaving the old suit quite complete down to the smallest detail. The new suit, which has been forming beneath the old one, is at first quite soft, and the crab for a few days is in a sorry plight, quite defenceless, and moving only with difficulty. Gradually, however, the shelly armour hardens, and when its new shell is compared with the discarded one, the crab will be seen to have made a sudden increase in size. Its whole growth, in fact, takes place in the interval between its emergence from the old and the hardening of the new suit. The sexes of Crustacea are distinct; and the young, on hatching from the eggs, are usually unlike their parents.

Most Crustacea are essentially sea creatures—even the land crabs seek the sea during the breeding season. In size they range from micro-

scopic forms to the giant lobsters and crabs. In habit they are equally varied: some act as natural scavengers, like the sand-hoppers, which help to break down and clear away the masses of sea-weed torn from the rocks and cast up on shore by the waves during heavy gales; a few species spend part of their lives as true parasites, feeding on the tissues of their unfortunate hosts. Vast numbers of small crustaceans which live in the surface-waters of the sea supply the natural food, not only of many kinds of fishes, but also

POLYCHELES, A LOBSTER-LIKE DEEP-SEA CRUSTACEAN

of the largest living mammals, the great whale-bone whales. Crabs, lobsters, shrimps, and prawns provide a popular and valuable food for mankind.

CRYPTIC COLORATION, see PROTECTIVE COLORATION, Section 2.

CUCKOO. Members of the Cuckoo family are found in most parts of the world, and are more numerous in tropical than in temperate climates. The tropical varieties are gaudy birds, much larger than the European Cuckoo, with brilliantly coloured plumage. The Plantain Eaters, or Touracos, of the forests of tropical Africa, for example, are sometimes as much as 3 feet long, and have green and blue plumage, with crests on their heads, and long tails.

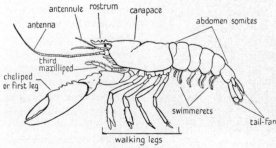

SIDE VIEW OF COMMON LOBSTER

antennule · rostrum · carapace · antenna · abdomen somites · third maxilliped · cheliped or first leg · swimmerets · tail-fan · walking legs

YOUNG CUCKOO REMOVING EGG FROM TREE PIPIT'S NEST. *Eric J. Hosking, F.R.P.S.*

MEADOW PIPIT FEEDING HER GREEDY FOSTER-CHILD. *Eric J. Hosking, F.R.P.S.*

The Common Cuckoo is about 12 inches long, with bluish-grey plumage on the upper part of its body, and white plumage with dark bars on the underneath. In flight it rather resembles a hawk—a likeness which apparently deceives small birds, which often mob it as they mob a hawk. It hunts for its food both in the trees and on the ground, at first living principally on beetles, but when caterpillars become plentiful, preferring them, especially the hairy ones. The Cuckoo does not winter in this country, but reaches Britain from Africa about the middle of April, the time of its arrival in different countries being suited to the time of the foster-parents' breeding. Soon the male's familiar 'cuckoo' song, which is delivered with bowing head and fanning tail, is heard incessantly all over the country. The hen's call is a quite different, bubbling sound. The note of the male is heard until the beginning of July, when the adult birds leave to make their way to Africa, the young following two months later.

The female Cuckoo, which is much less numerous than the male and therefore polyandrous (mated to several cocks) selects the nest of a bird such as the Meadow Pipit, Wagtail, Hedge Sparrow, Reed Warbler, or Sedge Warbler, and lays one egg in it before the owner of the nest has begun to incubate her own. Each female works a particular territory, confines her attentions to a particular species of foster-parent, and lays eggs of one type only—about twelve to twenty-four in a season. The foster-parent is the more deceived by the fact that the cuckoo egg is very small for the size of the bird, and more or less resembles the eggs of the chosen host. As a rule the Cuckoo removes one of the host's own eggs from the nest and swallows it. She lays her own egg in the nest and leaves it to the care of others. The young Cuckoo is hatched out about the same time as the young of its foster-parents, and when it is only a day or two old, and still blind, unfeathered, and otherwise helpless, it instinctively throws the other nestlings or any remaining eggs out of the nest. It works its way beneath them one at a time until they rest in the small hollow conveniently present in its back; then it climbs backwards up the side of the nest, and heaves them over. In this way the baby Cuckoo secures the whole attention of its foster-parents, who still do not appear to recognize that they are fostering an interloper, and do nothing to rescue the young which the Cuckoo has thrown out. They take such good care of the baby Cuckoo that it soon grows big and fills the nest. It often becomes so large that its foster-parent has to stand upon its back in order to put food in its mouth. In about 3 weeks it is able to fly; but its foster-parents feed it for a further 4 or 5 weeks before it leaves the nest, after which it very soon migrates. As there are no parent birds to show the young Cuckoo where to go, it follows the customary route purely by instinct (*see* MIGRATION).

The American Cuckoo is not a parasite on other birds, but builds its own nest, rather like that of a crow. In Africa, India, and as far as Australia are found Ground Cuckoos known as Coucals, much larger than the Common Cuckoo, and these, too, rear their own young. In India the Koël lays her eggs in the nests of Crows.

A CUTTLEFISH STRANDED ON A ROCKY COAST
F. Martin Duncan

A NEW ZEALAND SQUID
This torpedo-shaped animal is approximately 6 feet
Paul Popper

CUCKOO BEE, *see* BUMBLE BEE.

CUCKOO SPIT, *see* FROGHOPPER.

CURLEW, *see* WADING BIRDS, Section 2.

CUTTLEFISH AND SQUID. These belong to the same class (Cephalopoda) of MOLLUSCS as the OCTOPUS (qq.v.), though they differ from it in many ways. Their bodies are longer and more shapely, and the eight arms surrounding the mouth are covered with suckers throughout their entire length, and are much shorter than those of the Octopus. They have also two very long 'tentacles' or arms, which in some species are, when fully extended, quite three times the length of the creature's body. They are always without suckers, except at the club-shaped tips, where there are several suckers on the upper surface. These suckers have short stalks, and are surrounded by a hard, horny ring, the edge of which may be smooth or sharply toothed, making those of the larger species formidable weapons. The two long arms are used for the actual capture of prey; the short arms encircling the mouth hold the victim while it is being devoured. The Cuttlefishes have a flat, oblong shell of a chalky substance, which is entirely hidden beneath the skin of the mantle. The Squids have, instead, a slender, horny rod, often called the 'pen', embedded in the back. They are also different in shape, being more slender in build, for speed.

Both the Cuttlefishes and the Squids lead a much more active life than the Octopus, some species swimming far out in the open sea in large shoals numbering several hundred. They are great hunters, and the American mackerel fisheries are sometimes ruined by them. From the ink-bags of our British Cuttlefishes—for these creatures, like the Octopus, possess this organ of defence—the best quality of artists' sepia is manufactured.

Largest of all is the Giant Squid, which lives in the North Atlantic, and grows to a total length, including the long tentacles, of over 40 feet—a truly fearsome monster, with its great unwinking eyes, rather torpedo-shaped body, and strong, sucker-clad arms. It provides part of the food of the great toothed whales—and desperate encounters take place between these ocean giants, the whale's skin often being deeply scored by the armoured suckers of the Giant Squid.

See also Vol. VI, OCTOPUS, CUTTLEFISH, and SQUID FISHING.

D

DAB, *see* FLATFISHES.

DABCHICK, *see* GREBE.

DACE, *see* CARP.

DADDY-LONG-LEGS, *see* CRANE-FLY.

DAMSEL-FLY, *see* DRAGONFLY.

DEAD LEAF BUTTERFLY, *see* PROTECTIVE COLORATION, Section 3.

DEATH-WATCH BEETLE. Everyone is familiar with the little round holes (worm-holes) made by beetles in furniture or articles of wood that have been kept in a not very dry place; but the insects themselves are rarely seen. The beetle is a very inconspicuous, small, brownish creature, clothed with greyish hair. The female lays her eggs in little crevices in the wood, and when the tiny white grub hatches, it immediately burrows inwards, feeding upon the wood for a year or often longer. When fully grown it returns to near the surface and makes a cell, in which it undergoes its transformation from grub to beetle. In the spring or early summer, the winged beetle gnaws its way out through the remaining layer of wood. Each little hole shows where a beetle has emerged, and if we can see fresh wood-dust in or near it, mischief still in progress in the interior must be suspected. The beetle responsible for all this is the common Furniture-beetle, which usually attacks only deal, pine, or soft wood.

In hard woods, such as oak, bigger holes are sometimes found. These are the work of an entirely different species, the Death-watch Beetle, a larger insect, about a quarter of an inch long, with a mottled back. Many ancient roofs have been brought to ruin by this pest—for its work is often unsuspected for many years. The grub continues to burrow into and feed upon the timber for about 3 years, and the solid oak may at last be reduced to a condition in which it looks like a sponge. The name Death-watch is due to the beetle's habit of making ticking or tapping sounds which, to our superstitious ancestors, foretold a death. This is the beetle's method of communication. While clinging to the surface, the insect strikes its head on the wood several times in quick succession. In the spring, if we tap with the end of a pencil quickly about five or six times in some place where the Death-watch is known to be, a similar sound may be heard in reply from any beetle which happens to be sufficiently near—or better still, held captive in a small box. The beetles have no ears, but they probably feel through their feet the vibrations caused by the tapping.

See also BEETLES.

DEEP-SEA FISHES. Sunlight does not penetrate the water-layers of the sea beyond a depth of about 250 fathoms; so in the great ocean abysses (sometimes as much as 4 miles deep) the water is very cold and completely dark. At least, there would be complete darkness were it not for the fact that many of the inhabitants of these great depths carry their own lights around with them. These include various soft-bodied animals such as PRAWNS, SQUIDS (qq.v.), and fishes. This article is concerned only with the fishes.

The lamps carried by deep-sea fishes are of several kinds. Often they are arranged in rows along the sides of the fish, each kind having its own distinct number of lights, arranged in a particular way. This helps the fish to recognize another of its own species, so that shoals can keep together, and the male can find his mate. Without these 'recognition lights' they would, of course, be lost in the dark. The lamps are glands in the skin, each having a lens, behind which is a cavity where the actual light is produced; behind that, again, is a bright, silvery reflector; and finally there is a layer of black tissue that prevents any light from being lost to the rear. In fact, it is very much like a pocket-torch, except that the fish's light is produced in a different way. Two sorts of chemicals are poured into the cavity by cells—one a kind of fuel called 'luciferin', and the other an oxidizing agent called 'luciferase'. When the two come together, with a little oxygen from the blood, combustion

LUMINOUS DEEP-SEA FISHES

Top centre is an Angler-fish, that attracts prey with its luminous lure. On the right is the Gulper-eel, seen before and after swallowing a large fish. Bottom left is the Hatchet-fish, with tubular eyes for ever looking upward. *A. Fraser-Brunner*

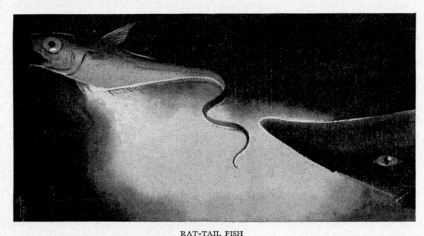

RAT-TAIL FISH

A luminous 'smoke screen' dazzles its enemy, while the Rat-tail makes its escape
A. Fraser-Brunner

looking deep-sea ANGLER-FISHES (q.v.). Most of these have a sort of lamp-bracket on the nose, which they wave about in the water. Little fishes, attracted by the light, swim towards it. As the bulb is very sensitive, the Angler feels the water movement before the fish can touch the bulb, and so opens its great jaws to engulf its prey. The Angler-fishes are nearly always black, so that they themselves are invisible; and as they live more by touch than by sight and do not swim in shoals, their eyes are very small. Yet another sort of light is found in certain deep-sea fishes known as Rat-tails. These have a gland under the body that can pour out a luminous slime. If the fish is attacked it puffs out this slime, which mixes with the water and forms a cloud of light. This dazzles the enemy, and so the Rat-tail can escape.

Other oceanic fishes get their light in a very strange way. Certain areas of the skin are set aside, so to speak, for the benefit of bacteria (very tiny, single-celled plants, like the 'germs' of disease). These bacteria live and feed in the tissues provided for them by the fish, and produce substances that glow with a bright light. Of course, as fast as they use up the tissues the fish grows some more. It is a sort of mutual-benefit arrangement—the fish feeds the bacteria, and in return they give the fish light. Often these wonderful shining patches are found in front of the eyes, like headlamps; but sometimes the whole head is lit up, or even the whole skin.

Deep-sea fishes belong to several different

takes place, and a bright light is obtained. Perhaps the most interesting thing about this light is that it is cold. Practically every sort of light we know is accompanied by heat (as, for instance, the heat of an electric lamp); but the fish's light wastes scarcely any energy on heat, and so is the most efficient light we know—indeed, could we master its secret, it might be very valuable to mankind. Fishes that have this kind of illumination naturally have large eyes, often very large, so as to make use of all the light available.

A second kind of lamp is used by the weird-families, having a variety of shapes and habits; but they all have certain things in common. For example, the tissues are always soft and fragile, and the bones are thin and papery. This is believed to be due to the lack of vitamin D, which needs sunshine for its formation; but it is no disadvantage, for it helps the fish to withstand the great pressure of the water at these depths. Again, they all feed on one another; there can be no vegetarians here, for plant life cannot flourish in the ocean abyss. Some of them can swallow fishes much bigger than themselves, unbelievable as it may seem. They are provided with specially elastic stomachs, and their jaws come apart at the hinges to make their mouths larger. Food is so hard to find in the darkness that they must make as big a meal as possible when the opportunity occurs. A wonderful example of this is the Gulper, an eel-like fish with a very small head but enormous jaws, and a little light on the end of its tail, perhaps used as a bait, as in the Anglers. Needless to say, nearly all deep-sea fishes have very strong teeth, and in many instances these hinge backwards, so that the prey, so difficult to obtain, may not be allowed to escape. Quite a number of species have tubular, upwardly directed eyes, so that they seem always to be gazing towards the surface.

A great deal remains to be learnt about the life of the deep sea, for observation is difficult. Very special apparatus is needed to catch specimens at such depths, so that collecting them is a costly business, and not done to any large extent.

See also ANGLER-FISH; BLIND-FISH; LANTERN-FISH.

DEER. 1. This large family, the Cervidae, members of the order Ungulata (hoofed beasts), are RUMINANTS (q.v.) or chewers of the cud, like ANTELOPES, CATTLE, SHEEP, and GOATS (qq.v.). They differ from Antelopes in that instead of horns they possess antlers, which are branching and solid, and are shed and grown afresh every year. Deer are found in almost all parts of Europe, Asia, and America. There were none originally in Australasia, though the Red Deer has been imported, and in New Zealand is now a serious pest. In Africa (the principal home of antelopes) there are no deer south of the Sahara. Deer have cloven hoofs, which make them very sure-footed and able to travel on soft ground. They generally live among trees, and eat shoots and leaves of trees, grass, young heather, moss,

and even sea-weed. They produce one, occasionally two, and in a few species three, young at birth. The young are always spotted, but the spots disappear, at any rate in the winter coat, in the adult, except in such species as the Spotted Deer.

The deer's antlers are of solid bone, attached to the skull only at the base. Once a year, about spring, the antlers drop off, but new ones soon sprout. At first they are covered with a substance called 'velvet', made of the skin, hair, and blood-vessels. This remains until the new antlers are fully grown, when it begins to shrivel and peel off—a process which the deer hastens by rubbing them against trees and rocks. The antlers grown by a stag in his first year are very small; but in each successive year they become larger and more branched, until their full development is reached. Some of the small deer have no antlers, but their upper canine teeth grow long and form tusks. In a few species the males have both antlers and tusks. With the exception of the REINDEER (q.v.) the females do not have antlers.

In the courting season, which takes place in the autumn, the stag uses his antlers as duelling weapons. He leaves the sheltered country in which he has been hidden, and roams boldly in the open, calling loudly to the females. Often his call is heard by another stag, who answers it with a bellowing roar of challenge. The two beasts hasten towards each other, and meet with a clash of their antlers. The struggle is furious and may last for hours, neither giving way until loss of blood or exhaustion causes one to collapse. The successful stag then proceeds to form a harem, sometimes collecting as many as a hundred females, sixty being the normal maximum, from whom he fights off any other rivals. But sooner or later, this first master-stag becomes so emaciated and exhausted that he retires before his strongest rival—who then inherits his place and herd. The second master-stag may, in turn, give way to a third. The hinds seem willing to accept whoever proves master.

There are a great many species of deer, varying considerably in size, colouring, and habitat. The Elk or Moose stands nearly 7 feet high, while the Muntjacs of India, China, and Borneo are only 18 inches in height, and the Pudu of South America and the CHEVROTAINS (q.v.) or Mouse Deer (not true deer) are even smaller. Some species live in hot, wet climates—such as

RED DEER STAG WITH HIS DOES AND YOUNG
Paul Popper

the Thamin from the swampy country of Burma and Malaya, the Chinese Water Deer from the reeds on the banks of the Yangtze River in China, and the Marsh Deer from the forests of Brazil and Argentina. Other species live in high mountains—such as the Musk Deer (again not true deer) from the Himalayas. Yet others inhabit cold, semi-arctic regions—such as the Caribou of North America and the Reindeer of Siberia, Lapland, and other parts of northern Europe and Asia. Those species which are found in the British Isles are the Red Deer, the Fallow Deer, and the Roe Deer. Fossil remains show that the Elk and Reindeer also once lived in these islands.

2. THE RED DEER, the largest of the British deer, live wild on the Scottish highlands, on some of the western Scottish Isles, on Exmoor, in Ireland, and in most countries on the Continent. The fully grown stag stands about 4 feet high, and has antlers, often 3 feet high or more, with at least six points or 'tines'. A stag with

twelve points is called a 'royal stag'. One stag killed in Transylvania is reported to have had 45 points. In summer the Red Deer has a reddish-brown coat; this changes to brownish-grey in the winter. The fully grown stags remain apart from the herds except during the mating season in the autumn. The stags (whose necks become swollen during these three weeks or so) then fight fiercely among themselves for the hinds, often goring their rivals to death. The white-spotted fawn, born about the end of May or June, is dropped in high heather and is subsequently visited by its mother from time to time. For about a week it is unable to stand, and lies motionless on the ground. It can gallop when it is two months old, but continues to follow its mother about for two years. The hinds can breed in their third year. Red deer live for about 12 years, although some have been known to live to an age of 20 years. In Scotland they are stalked on foot (*see* DEER-STALKING, Vol. IX), and in Devon and Somerset they are

A BULL MOOSE NEAR BANFF IN ALBERTA, CANADA
National Film Board, Canada

hunted with hounds—when they frequently try to escape by taking to the water (*see* STAG-HUNTING, Vol. IX).

3. THE FALLOW DEER, natives of the Mediterranean countries, were introduced into the parks of Britain and central Europe many years ago. They stand about 3 feet high, and have small heads, large ears, and relatively long tails. Their winter coat is usually fawn or yellowish-brown, with white underparts and a dark line running down the centre of the back; their summer coat is spotted white. Fallow Deer are restless creatures, rising and lying down often during the daytime. Like other deer, they eat grass and weeds, but are especially fond of horse-chestnuts. They soon become friendly and approach man without fear.

4. THE ROE DEER, the smallest of the British deer, being only just over 2 feet high, have reddish coats in the summer, changing in the winter to greyish-brown, with a white patch on the hindquarters. They can run very fast. Typical antlers have three 'tines' or points, and are about 8 inches long. There are many of these deer in parts of Scotland, and they are also found in wooded areas of south and east England; but they are difficult to see, as they are timid and hide in thick cover during the day. In winter

they retire into pine forests or the thickest undergrowth. The bucks, when they fight during the mating season, chase the does round and round, until they wear circular tracks in the grass.

5. THE MOOSE or ELK, of the northerly forests of North America and parts of northern Europe and Asia, is the largest of the deer, standing nearly 7 feet high. The male has huge, palmated (hand-like) antlers, often with a span of from 5 to 6 feet, and is coated with long, coarse hair and a slight mane. Both male and female have swollen muzzles, humped backs, and thick, woolly under-fur in their winter coats. Moose feed mostly on leaves and twigs, but also on lichen, moss, and water-plants. When ruminating, they lie with their tails to windward, relying on their sense of hearing and smell to warn them of danger from that direction, while using their eyes to watch for danger from any other quarter.

In summer, Moose usually live near swamps, rivers, or lakes, and wade deep into the water to eat the water-plants. In the winter they go to higher, thickly forested ground, and stay together in small parties. The adult male sheds his antlers in January, the new ones being fully grown by August. He then comes out of his swampy retreat to fight fiercely, often to death, with his rivals for the females. The fawns (one or two, but occasionally three) are born the following May in any place likely to be free from the attacks of wolves and bears. Moose have a long, swinging trot, faster than the pace of an ordinary horse. The bull's call is either a bellowing roar or a loud, long whistle. This the Indian hunters often imitate in order to draw their quarry within shooting range. Moose flesh is regarded as excellent venison.

Another North American deer, the Wapiti, is over 5 feet high, and is like a very large Red

Deer. In the 19th century they used to roam in herds of many thousands; but now they are quite rare.

See also REINDEER; CHEVROTAIN.

DESERT PLANTS. Deserts are found along the hot, dry, tropical belts of high pressure near the Equator. Here the vegetation is so scanty, and therefore so much sought after by grazing animals, that only plants which have special protections against their ravages can survive (*see* PLANT DEFENCES). The leaves and branches become modified into spiny structures: in species of the Butcher's Broom and Asparagus, which are common in deserts, the leaves are reduced to mere scales. As the development of water-storage tissue makes both leaves and stems tempting morsels, they are further protected by the development of bitter substances, disagreeable to the taste. The taller plants of desert regions are dependent on underground water, which they reach by their very long tap-roots. In places where the ground-water lies near the surface, such as depressions where a well can give a permanent supply of water, or along the banks of a river, like the Nile or the Euphrates, the vegetation shows the natural fertility of the desert soil. Here palms, especially date-palms, find congenial conditions; and, under their protection, other plants useful to human communities are cultivated.

Desert plants can be divided into two groups. First there are the annual plants, which run through the whole of their life-history very rapidly, though their seeds may remain dormant for years until some moisture reaches them. Then there are perennial plants, which adapt themselves to the peculiar conditions of the desert with its limited water-supply and great heat—the CACTUSES (q.v.) being the best-known of these. Contrary to the usual opinion, there is not a month in the year when no plants are in flower in the desert; but the great spectacular show of colour comes in the spring, when the rains cause the small, quickly developing annuals and the bulbous plants to flower.

Of all the peculiar desert plants, one of the most strange is Welwitschia, which is allied to coniferous plants (*see* CONIFERS), and occurs only in the coastal desert of South-West Africa, especially in the vicinity of Walvis Bay. Welwitschia is a unique plant, and botanists place it in a group of its own. It has a short, but thick, woody stem, not rising many inches above the rocky ground on which it grows, and narrowing below into a stout tap-root. The plant is said to live for a hundred years—but all this time, although the stem grows thicker, it never grows longer. The top of the stem is forked, with a hollow in the centre, and from its edges spring two gigantic leaves. These are never shed, but continue to grow at their bases while the tips wither and decay. The flowers appear in grooves on the top of the stem, the male or pollen-bearing flowers on one plant, and the female or egg-bearing flowers on another (*see* REPRODUCTION OF PLANTS). Pollination is effected by insects, and only takes place in 'wet' years.

In the same desert there is another peculiar plant, the Naras or Desert Melon. Unlike Welwitschia, which clings to the rocky hollows, this is a dune plant of the sand-hills. The Desert Melon obtains its water by means of a long and spreading root-system, sometimes stretching as far as 40 feet. The plant is a woody shrub, not more than 4–5 feet high, with green, well-protected branches, rudimentary leaves, and strong thorns. It produces rounded, grape-like 'Melons', which are greatly relished by the natives—and also by the jackals, which are mainly responsible for spreading the seeds.

ROSE OF JERICHO. (*a*) in flower, (*b*) in fruit

Another peculiar desert plant is the Rose of Jericho, quite common in Palestine. The fruits mature as the dry season comes on, the leaves drop off, and the dry branches curl inwards to form a ball of wickerwork protecting the pods. The ball remains in this position during the dry season until the rains come again, when it uncurls, allowing the seeds to escape. They are then washed away by the quickly flowing rivulets. But the plant has little hold on the sandy soil and is often detached by high winds and rolled away in its 'balled-up' form over the dry surface. If it reaches a moistened spot the branches uncurl and the liberated seeds have a chance to germinate.

See also DESERTS, Vol. III.

DEVIL FISH, *see* SHARKS AND RAYS.

DINGO, *see* DOG.

DIPPER (Water-Ouzel). This rather dumpy little bird, some 7 inches long, has a conspicuous white chest, and elsewhere dark plumage of chestnut-brown, with slaty-brown back, wings, and tail. It is a remarkable example of a Passerine or perching bird which has taken largely to an aquatic life. The Dipper is well known to those who frequent the hilly country of north or west Britain and is nearly always to be seen, for instance, on Highland burns or Yorkshire becks. It flits from stone to stone in a jerky manner, or stands on a rock in mid-stream, bobbing its body up and down. It does not swim at all, but sinks down under the water and walks on the stones and gravel at the bottom of the stream, hunting for food. How so light a body succeeds in keeping itself under water is difficult to understand. On coming to the surface again, it shakes the water out of its wings and is soon dry. (Another perching bird with the same habit is the Water Thrush of America.)

The Dipper nearly always builds a nest close to fast-flowing water—on a moss-grown bank just above the water, among the exposed roots of trees, under a bridge, or even on a rocky ledge under a waterfall. The covered nest is beautifully made of moss and grass, and has the entrance at the side. There are four or five white eggs, and two or three broods are reared in the same year. The bird generally returns to the same site the following year.

DISTRIBUTION OF ANIMALS AND PLANTS, *see* ANIMAL AND PLANT DISTRIBUTION.

DIVER. This family belongs to the same order of birds as the GREBE (q.v.). There are four species—the Red-throated Diver, which is the most common on British coasts, breeding on the banks of Scottish lochs and inland waters; the Black-throated Diver, a larger bird which also breeds in small numbers in the Scottish Highlands; the Great Northern Diver (or Loon) which frequently visits British coasts in the winter, but nests in Iceland, Greenland, and also Canada; and the White-billed Northern Diver, which rarely comes to Britain. These are large birds, the Great Northern Diver being more than $2\frac{1}{2}$ feet long, with a strong, sharply pointed bill and long, narrow head.

Divers are generally placed rather low in the scale of bird evolution, for they are much better adapted for life in the water than in the air or on land. They are strong fliers, but clumsy in rising and alighting and in changing direction. On land they are very awkward. In the water, however, their rather streamlined bodies cleave the water easily, and their powerful webbed feet make them strong and agile swimmers. They feed upon fish, diving after them and capturing them by chasing and spearing them below the surface. Except during the breeding season they spend much of their time out at sea, but they return to freshwater lochs and lakes to nest. The nest is merely a heap of weeds a few feet from the water's edge. Two eggs are laid, a rich greenish-brown, spotted and blotched, and the young take almost at once to the water. (*See* picture p. 45.)

DODO, *see* PIGEON.

DOG. Under this title are included all the animals known as WOLVES, JACKALS, FOXES (qq.v.), wild dogs, and, of course, all the domesticated breeds. It is not known for certain from which of the wild breeds the domesticated dog is descended—it may, in fact, be the product of several wild species.

The dogs are a very distinct group of animals (the Canidae). Among their points of structural similarity, all but certain specially bred domestic dogs have long, pointed muzzles, fairly long tails, and erect, pointed ears; and all but the African Hunting Dog have five toes on their forefeet and

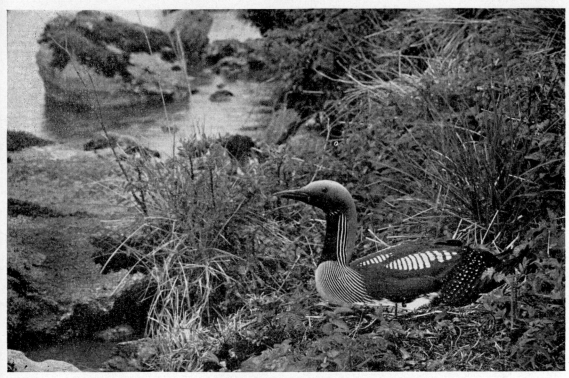

A BLACK-THROATED DIVER ON HER NEST
G. K. Yeates, F.R.P.S.

four toes on their hindfeet. They are more widely distributed over the world than any other flesh-eating mammal: some endure the Arctic cold and live mainly on fish; others live in Africa and India. Nearly all wild dogs hunt in large packs, following their prey chiefly by scent. They make their lairs in burrows, in the clefts of rocks, in caverns, or in hollow trees. Some dig their own burrows, while others seize holes deserted by other animals; some dig solitary burrows, others dig a number close together, forming a warren. The number of young in a litter varies from three to as many as a dozen, and the pups are believed always to be born blind.

The Dingo, the wild dog of Australia, is about as large as an Airedale Terrier, tawny, with erect, pointed ears, and a white tip to its rather bushy tail. It is not, however, thought to be a native of Australia, but may have been introduced by the aborigines from Asia. When the European settlers came it was to be found throughout the whole country; but to-day, although there are still many Dingoes in the backwoods, their numbers have been greatly reduced. They are so destructive to sheep and poultry, killing far more than they can eat, that the Government offered a reward of 5s. for each Dingo scalp. Large numbers are seldom found together, parties of a mother and her cubs being the most common. Each family is said to have a strictly defined territory, beyond which its members never venture and into which other families will not intrude (*see* ANIMAL TERRITORY). The young, usually from six to eight, are often born in the hollow of a tree-trunk.

The wild dogs of India and southern and central Asia, called Dholes, are pretty, fox-like animals with reddish coats. They hunt in packs at night, their prey being any animals up to the size of a deer. They run in a long, lobbing canter.

The African Hunting Dogs of South and East Africa look rather like hyaenas, for they are marked in patches of yellow, black, and white. They are about the size of small wolves, and have large ears and bushy tails. They kill cattle, sheep, and wild animals up to the size of large antelopes, but they rarely attack man.

THE DINGO; AN AUSTRALIAN WILD DOG
'Picture Post' Library

The South American wild dogs, called Bush Dogs, have long, dark-brown bodies, with short legs and ears, and grey necks and heads. Little is known about their life, as they are very scarce and keep hidden during the day. They eat any small animals.

See also Vol. VI: Dogs, Working.
See also Vol. IX: Dogs.

DOG-FISH, *see* SHARKS AND RAYS.

DOLPHIN, *see* WHALE.

DONKEY, *see* ASS.

DORMOUSE. This small RODENT (q.v.) is closely related to the MOUSE (q.v.), and is distributed over most of Europe, Asia, and Africa. The Common Dormouse, famous for its drowsiness and long winter sleep, is about the size of a mouse, and has a tawny coat and very striking, large, black eyes. It lives in trees, and sleeps during the day, only coming out at night, when it moves about with great agility. Like the squirrel, it sits up to eat, holding its food between the forepaws. It eats hard nuts, acorns, corn, haws and other wild berries, insects and grubs, and probably small birds and eggs. During the summer it puts on fat, which is used up in its winter sleep (*see* HIBERNATION).

Dormice hibernate from mid-October to mid-April, curled up in a ball, sleeping so soundly and becoming so cold and rigid that they can be rolled on a table without waking. On warm winter days, however, they will wake and eat

from the large stores of food they have laid up, before settling down again. They usually build their winter nests underground, but sometimes they use birds' nests. In the spring they build, for their day-time rest, small nests near the ground in a thicket or hedgerow, and larger nests for breeding. The nests are built of grass, moss, and strips of honeysuckle bark, and are lined and covered with leaves. There is a litter of two to four young ones in June. Sometimes the young are born in the autumn, but if so, they probably do not survive the winter. They are born blind and naked, but quickly develop, growing a first coat of grey, which does not change to tawny until they are 18 months old.

The Grey or Fat Dormouse, also known as the Edible Dormouse, is larger than the Common Dormouse. It was introduced from the Continent to Hertfordshire and Buckinghamshire, where it is now quite common.

THE COMMON DORMOUSE ON A WILD ROSE STEM
A. R. Thompson

DRAGONFLY. The brilliance of the Dragonflies' colouring and the beauty of the compound eyes of the larger species are unequalled in any other insects. Their colours fade, however, very rapidly after death, except in the case of metallic blue or green. In the sexes, the colours are sometimes so unlike that the female may appear to belong to a different species from the male.

ADULT DRAGONFLY. ⅔ nat. size
S. Beaufoy, F.R.P.S.

There are three types of Dragonfly: the large species, which are very rapid in flight and have slender bodies and big eyes meeting at the back of the head; those that are somewhat smaller, with shorter and flatter bodies, but equally fast on the wing; and others, often called Demoiselles, or sometimes Damsel-flies, which flutter in a weak, delicate manner along the banks of streams and rivers. These are usually much smaller, and have very slender bodies and eyes wide apart. Most are pale blue; but two belonging to this type have brilliant metallic blue or green bodies and wings with similar colourings.

Most people know our larger Dragonflies by sight, and often compare them to miniature aeroplanes. They are often thought to be dangerous, and the name of 'Horse-stingers' is common in many places; but Dragonflies sting neither horses nor anything else, and are, in fact, quite harmless. They feed on other insects, and our larger species will kill wasps and other insects of powerful flight like the Red Admiral Butterfly. They catch their prey in the air, and neatly strip off its wings before eating its body.

The early life of a Dragonfly is spent in the water. Some Dragonflies skim over the surface and dip the tip of the abdomen below it at frequent intervals, dropping eggs at random.

Others settle upon a water-plant and puncture the submerged stems, inserting an egg into each puncture. With some species, the male is in constant attendance upon the female, gripping her round the neck by the end of his abdomen, so that the pair fly 'tandem-wise'. The eggs may be dropped while they hover in this way over the water, or placed in the tissues of a water-plant while both are resting upon it, the female below with the tip of her abdomen submerged. On such occasions the colour differences between the sexes of certain species may be easily seen.

The young Dragonfly, which is called a nymph or naiad, eats different food at different ages, but is always carnivorous. It captures its food by means of an organ (called the mask, because it more or less covers the face when not in use) which has much the same movement as the human arm and forearm. In its resting position it is bent double at what corresponds to the elbow, and held between the limbs. It is broadest in front, where there are two movable hooks. When attracted to a prey, the nymph shoots out the whole organ to grip its victim, and to bring it back to the mouth to be eaten. As the nymph grows, the rudimentary wings increase in size after each casting of the skin; and at about the time of change into the adult, they stand out a little from the body. The large compound eyes, hitherto dull, may now begin to gleam. Up to this stage, breathing has been carried out by means of gills—three flat gill plates at the end of the body in the smaller species, and in the larger species, internal gills. But the gills now stop working, and the nymph breathes through its 'spiracles', or breathing-holes, holding fast to some support, such as a water-plant, with the front of its body out of the water. After resting this way for a time the nymph suddenly moves forward right out of the water—some go only a few inches, while others will travel some distance up a tree-trunk. The insect then remains fixed, until the nymphal skin splits along the back of the thorax. The head and thorax, legs and wings, are withdrawn from the skin, but the lower part of the abdomen remains inside. The body falls back and hangs down until the legs are strong enough to grip. A sudden movement then brings the body back again, the legs seizing either the empty skin or the support beyond it. The abdomen is now completely withdrawn, growing longer and narrower until it reaches its adult length (which is often much greater than that of the nymphal case from which it was withdrawn); the wings, which were quite small when first freed, expand to their full size. The Dragonfly is at first pale, and does not attain its full beauty until it has been on the wing for some time. It is now a denizen of the air. After mating and egg-laying, many of the larger kinds forsake the water altogether and seem to prefer woodlands, where they may be found during hot sunshine, hawking to and fro, often for long periods without a rest, and often remaining there until autumn is well advanced.

See also INSECTS.

DRINKER MOTH, see LACKEY MOTHS.

DROMEDARY, see CAMEL.

DRONGO. The King Crow, or Indian Black Drongo, is one of the most common birds in India, both in the hills and the plains. It is frequently to be seen perching on bare branches or telegraph-wires, and making quick, darting flights to catch insects. It has deep black plumage with a steel-blue gloss, and is about 11 or 12 inches in length, with a short bill and a forked tail. Other members of the family are to be found from Afghanistan to China, in Africa, and one species in Australia. The Racket-tailed Drongo, which lives in the forests of India, has a fine crest on its head, and the outer two tail-feathers are prolonged as wires ending in large racket-shaped plumes. All Drongos eat insects only and have a fine song.

DUCKS. 1. The Ducks, with the SWANS and GEESE (qq.v.), form the family Anatidae—web-footed birds of fresh or salt-water, found throughout the world. Although we commonly divide the family into these three groups, it is not always easy to say what is a duck and what a goose. Most of the family are omnivorous, eating grass, grain, insects, and grubs; but one group, the Mergansers, live entirely on fish, while the geese eat mainly grass. Some feed on land, like the Geese; others on the surface of the water or by up-ending, like the Swans; others again by diving. Ducks are found all over the world, but are more numerous in the colder regions of the northern hemisphere. Those of the northern hemisphere migrate, often very great distances, but those of the tropics make much shorter or no MIGRATIONS (q.v.).

In most of the ducks of the northern hemisphere the sexes have very different plumage, the drakes being much more brightly coloured, and also sometimes larger, than the ducks. But soon after the breeding season the drakes put on a dull-coloured 'eclipse' plumage, closely resembling that of the females, and do not regain their full plumage until early autumn. This strange fact is explained by the way ducks moult: they lose all their quills at the same time, and until a new lot has grown are unable to fly. They would, therefore, be easily caught by their enemies until the wing feathers grow again, if they did not assume a protective inconspicuous dress. In the Sheldrakes and many of the tropical species both sexes are alike and do not have this habit.

All the ducks have much the same courtship behaviour. The drakes woo the ducks by bobbing around them in the water, flirting their tails, raising and dipping their necks, and showing off their breasts. The Sheldrake leads off his mate to the nest, talking to her softly. Teals pretend to fight, and shoot through the water, showing off in front of the ducks. Ducks make simple nests, generally near water, though some nest in holes in the ground or in trees, often at some distance from the water. They line them with

THE TUFTED DUCK
G. K. Yeates, F.R.P.S.

down plucked from their breasts. The Tree-ducks of the tropical and sub-tropical world often nest in the fork of a large branch, and sometimes make use of a discarded crow's nest. Ten or twelve eggs are usually laid, and the ducklings, which are covered with down at hatching, are able to walk and swim as soon as they are dry.

2. The Duck family falls into two separate groups: the Surface-feeding Ducks and the Diving Ducks, including the Mergansers or Saw-billed Ducks. All Surface-feeding species have a patch of colour on the wings, known as the 'speculum', and this is often

AN EIDER DUCK NESTING

Her mottled plumage gives her a good camouflage in her natural surroundings.

G. K. Yeates, F.R.P.S.

the same in the two sexes. These patterns are useful in identifying the species. Of the Surface-feeding Ducks, the best known is the Mallard, or Wild Duck, which is found in the northern hemi-sphere from America to Siberia, wintering as far south as Panama and India. It is the most num-erous of all the ducks, and is the bird from which the many domestic kinds are derived (*see* DUCKS, Vol. VI). The handsome Sheldrake is found on the coasts, especially the sandy coasts of all temperate regions of the Old World (there is none in the Americas). One species, the Burrow-duck, is a resident of the British Isles. It nests in a burrow, often a rabbit-hole, making its nest sometimes 10 or 12 feet from the entrance. The Teal, another common species, is the smallest of the British ducks, about 14½ inches long. It is found throughout Europe and Asia, and a very similar species inhabits America. Its flight is full of sudden twists and turns and is very rapid, though not so rapid as that of the Garganey, sometimes called the Summer Teal. The Wigeon breeds in the north, but visits British shores in thousands in the winter, when it can be recognized by its swift flight and high-pitched, whistling cry. Less common, but similar in distribution, is the very handsome Pintail, with its long, pointed tail and rapid

flight; and the dull-coloured Gadwall may be seen at all times of the year in East Anglia and occasionally elsewhere. The Shoveler is easily recognized by the broad, ungainly bill, serrated along the edges, with which it sifts small animals from the surface of the water, in much the same way as the Baleen Whales. It is spread over the whole northern hemisphere, nesting principally within the Arctic Circle, and wintering farther south. There is also a species in South America, one in Africa, and two in Australia.

3. The Diving Ducks usually have shorter bodies and legs than the Surface-feeding Ducks, and spend almost all their time in the water. The Pochard and Tufted Duck have both in-creased considerably as breeding species in Britain within the last 50 years. Larger than either of these is the Golden-eye (19 inches), which breeds in northern Europe and visits Britain in the winter; its relative the Buffle-headed Duck of America, has occasionally strayed across the Atlantic. Many of the Diving Ducks, including the Eider, are birds of the sea-coasts. The Eider, which lives on northern coasts of Europe, including Britain, and America, is well known for the beautifully warm and elastic down which the female plucks from her breast to line her nest. In Scandinavia and

RED-BREASTED MERGANSER
An expert diver which feeds upon trout, young salmon, and other small fish. *Paul Popper*

Iceland, the down is carefully collected, but the birds are very strictly protected by law. The Eider Ducks become as tame as domestic ducks, and show no objection to a portion of their down being taken when they are incubating, and the rest when the ducklings are hatched. The Black Scoters are sea birds, and very gregarious, except during the nesting season. They nest far north, and in September and October migrate southwards, often appearing on British coasts in huge black flocks. The Common Scoter (length 20 inches) breeds in small numbers in Scotland; while the Velvet Scoter, a larger bird with a white patch on its wings and head, is a visitor from the north. An American species, the Surf Scoter, has been met with off the British coasts on a few occasions. The Scaup, not unlike the Tufted Duck, breeds in some of the Scottish islands, but is mainly a winter visitor; and the extremely handsome and graceful Long-tailed Duck is only a winter visitor.

The Mergansers or Saw-bills are a small group of Diving Ducks distinguished by the very narrow beak with a hook at the end, and by the serrations on the bill which enable them to hold fish. Two species, the Goosander and the Red-breasted Merganser, breed in Scotland; in winter, the Merganser is more often seen on salt-water, and the Goosander on fresh-water lakes and reservoirs. The small Smew is a bird of northern Europe which visits this country in small numbers in winter. Another member of this group, the Hooded Merganser, with its remarkable crest of stiff, hairlike feathers, white edged with black, has occasionally crossed the Atlantic from its native America.

DUKE OF BURGUNDY FRITILLARY. Despite the name, this small speckled brown and black butterfly is not a Fritillary, but is the only European representative of the family Riodinidae, chiefly found in South America. It looks, however, rather like a Fritillary, and so the name has stuck. The hairy caterpillars, which feed on primrose or cowslip leaves, hide during the day and only come up to feed after dark. The chrysalis is unlike that of any other butterfly, being hairy all over. It remains in this stage the whole of the winter, the butterfly emerging in May. In the British Isles it is occasionally found in clearings in woods, or on rough, uncultivated pastures where primroses grow. It rarely visits flowers, but frequently rests, after short, rapid flights, on twigs or leaves a few feet from the ground.

DUNLIN, *see* WADING BIRDS, Section 3.

E

EAGLE. This great bird of prey belongs to the same family as the FALCON, HAWK, BUZZARD, and VULTURE (qq.v.). There are a great many different species to be found in all parts of the world. They vary in size from the Bateleur Eagle of central and southern Africa, the male of which is only 21 inches long, to the magnificent Steller's Sea Eagle of eastern Siberia, north China, and Japan, which is nearly 3½ feet long. The female is generally larger than the male. The True Eagles, to which group the Golden Eagle belongs, feed on game-birds such as grouse, hares, rabbits, small mammals, and carrion, and will also attack a sickly lamb. Sea-Eagles eat fish and water-fowl also. The Buzzard-eagles and Serpent Eagles of southeast Asia feed mainly on snakes and other reptiles. The handsome Monkey-eating Eagle of the Philippines is said to live principally on the Macaque monkeys. Most Eagles, especially the magnificent Golden Eagle, contrary to the general idea, are not bold or courageous, and are often driven off their food by smaller birds or animals. A Golden Eagle has been observed to be attacked and routed by a pair of Skua Gulls. They are cowardly even in defence of their nest, and will fairly readily desert if disturbed. They are rather lethargic birds, appearing to prefer a meal of carrion which can be obtained without effort, to making their own kill. Their flight, too, though very powerful, is generally slow, and includes much sailing and circling. The Golden Eagle is, however, capable on occasions of a faster flight than any other bird (*see* FLIGHT).

Eagles usually build their 'eyries' or nests on rocky crags or on tree-tops, though sometimes

A GOLDEN EAGLE FEEDING HER YOUNG WITH GROUSE IN HER EYRIE ON A CRAGGY LEDGE
Arthur Brook

they build in low growing trees or even on the ground. They generally return each year to the same eyrie, and build on to the old nest. A White-tailed Sea Eagle, for instance, has been known to use the same nest for 20 successive years, building on to it each year until it became a very large construction, some 6 or 7 feet in diameter and 5 or 6 feet high. A Golden Eagle's nest in Colorado grew to 7 feet in height. Golden Eagles as a rule nest in two places, returning to each eyrie every alternate year. Generally two eggs are laid—large, dull white, and thinly speckled with irregular markings. The parents go on feeding their young for some five months after incubation.

Two species, the Golden Eagle and the White-tailed Sea Eagle, used to breed regularly in several places in the British Isles; but they were destroyed, largely by the use of poisoned meat, because of their attacks on game birds. Now, the Golden Eagle nests in some places in the Scottish Highlands, and probably a few in the more remote mountains of Ireland, while the Sea Eagle is only an occasional visitor. They are both very fine-looking birds, with strong wings reaching nearly to the end of their tails, strong curved claws, and straight beaks ending in a deep hook. The Golden Eagle, of which the female is almost 3 feet long (the American species being as much as 3 feet 5 inches), is a tawny golden-brown, shading to nearly black, and has feathered legs. The Sea Eagle has a greyer head, white tail-feathers, and legs of which only the upper part is feathered. It has a loud, shrill, yelping cry.

Of the many other species, one of the most spectacular is the great Harpy Eagle of the forests of central and South America, called by the Aztecs the 'winged wolf'. This bird will attack and kill animals much larger than itself, and can often be seen wheeling in circles high up over the forest. The much smaller African Bateleur Eagle is very different in appearance. It has a handsome maroon, black, and grey plumage, with short tail and wings, and voluminous crest. It prefers open mountainous country, and is quite common in some parts.

EARTHWORM, *see* WORM, Section 2.

EARWIG. This is one of the comparatively few insects that give maternal care to their eggs and young. Having laid her eggs in a batch, the female rests upon them. If the eggs are scattered, she searches them out and collects them together, and then resumes her position. The newly hatched Earwigs remain beneath her, and she looks after them until they are fit to scatter and take care of themselves.

Very few people know that Earwigs have wings—and indeed it is only very rarely that they have been seen to fly. The fore-wings are short and leathery, but the hind-wings are large, and beautifully folded away beneath the fore-wings. When they are unfolded they prove to be semi-circular and capable of being refolded fanwise. Further foldings of the inner and outer halves of the closed fan reduce it to a quarter of its original size, when it can be tucked away under the fore-wing. There is a variety of opinions as to the use of the forceps at the hind end of the body. It has been suggested that the Earwig uses them to pack its wings away; but the way in which the unfolded wing tends to fold up again 'of its own accord' suggests that the Earwig has no more trouble in this respect than any other insect. When alarmed, the Earwig often raises the hind end of the body and separates the forceps. The attitude is certainly a threatening one—so it may be that the forceps are weapons of defence and offence.

EARWIG
One hind-wing is expanded and the other folded away beneath the fore-wing. × 2

It is said that the insect got the name of Earwig because it crawls into the human ear. It is true that Earwigs are active only at night, hiding away in any dark hole or corner during the day-time; and so, provided the ear was conveniently placed, it might happen that an Earwig would use it as a place of retreat. On very rare occasions this has happened; but the idea that it is a habit of Earwigs to enter the ear may be dismissed as a myth. It is also suggested that the name is a corruption of 'earwing', on account of the shape of the wing, which is certainly ear-like. This, however, is most improbable, for the name must have been used before it was known that Earwigs had wings at all.

ECHIDNA. The Spiny or Porcupine Ant-eaters, as the Echidnas are often called, together with the Duck-billed PLATYPUS (q.v.), constitute the order Monotremata, being the only mammals which lay eggs. They live in rocky districts in Australasia, subsisting almost entirely on ants. They are from 18 inches to 2 feet or more in length, and have thick spines covering their bodies, short, round heads, small, toothless mouths, and long, slender beaks for snouts. They also have the long, worm-like tongue typical of all ant-eaters. On their short, sturdy legs they have strong claws, which they use for digging and for tearing open ants' nests. During the breeding-season—usually in May, which is at the beginning of the Australian winter—the female develops a nursing pouch on the underside of her body. She lays one egg and places it in the pouch by means of her beak. When it is ready to hatch, she breaks the shell with a heavy blow of her beak. She has no teats but, like the Platypus, she ejects the milk through pores in her skin into a hollow in her abdomen. She removes her offspring from her pouch after it has grown to a certain size, but puts it back again from time to time for suckling.

There are two species of Echidnas. The Common or Five-toed Echidna lives in Australia,

A NEW GUINEA ECHIDNA

Tasmania, and Papua—the Tasmanian Echidna being the largest, and exceptional because its spines are completely hidden by its fur. The Three-toed or New Guinea Echidna, found in the north-west of New Guinea, has fur almost completely concealing the spines. It is the larger of the two species, measuring 2 feet or more in length, and has fewer and shorter spines.

ECOLOGY OF PLANTS.

1. This is concerned with the study of plants in relation to their natural surroundings. Certain plants, for instance, will grow only in woods, others in marshes, and others on sand-dunes. The seed of a wild plant has no choice in the place where it settles. If it is fortunate in arriving at a suitable spot, the plant becomes established; if, on the other hand, the plant finds itself in an unfavourable place, it either perishes or develops poorly. On a sand-dune we find those plants which are adapted to grow in a shifting environment with little water; we do not expect to find these plants in marshes. In the same way we search for bluebells not on moorlands but in oak-woods. For in the course of time plants have developed special characteristics which fit them to live in some habitats, but not in others.

With cultivated plants it is possible, up to a point, to provide artificially the conditions in which the plants may flourish out of their natural homes. In the greenhouse it is possible to regulate the temperature of the atmosphere, and even to control the temperature of the soil. Thus, by controlling conditions, man has been able to make plants grow in places which would otherwise be unsuitable to them. In nature plants have become adapted to particular types of environment. In some this is so marked that it is possible to tell by looking at them the kind of habitat from which they have come. Ecology, then, is the study of plants in their natural communities, how they are affected by one another or by animal neighbours, the succession of plants according to the seasons, and so on.

2. PLANT ASSOCIATIONS. A good method of studying colonization by plants is to watch the gradual invasion of a newly exposed piece of soil. A great deal of information can be obtained by watching the newly made banks of roads and railway cuttings. Records should be kept over several seasons of the type of plant, the time that it arrives, the percentage of different plants, and similar facts. The first arrivals are plants which develop quickly from spores and not from seeds. These will include FUNGI, MOSSES AND LIVERWORTS, and FERNS (qq.v.). Spores, being microscopic in size, are easily carried in the air, and are always present in millions in the atmosphere. These are followed by the short-lived and annual flowering-plants which are common in the neighbourhood. And so a community of plants begins to be built up. Since the land we are observing has no established perennial plants, it is still open to new-comers, and is called an 'open community'. Then come the hardy perennials, such as grasses, thistles, plantains, and dandelions. Competition between the plants is keen: the community is in danger of becoming over-crowded, and survival goes only to the fittest. The weaker plants are choked out and die, and the hardier ones become more firmly established. Finally, only those plants which are most suited to that soil and climate remain; and the community is then said to be closed. Such a community of plants, living in harmony with each other, allowing only those new-comers which can compete with them to remain, and choking out any new-comers that are unsuited, is called a 'plant association'.

The struggle is not only for a place in the sun: there is also competition among the roots for a place in the soil. Root competition is chiefly due to the search for an adequate water-supply—and the depth to which some roots go shows the keenness of the competition.

The study of ecology need not be confined to natural vegetation. Slum-clearance areas, coal-tips, and lawns are also excellent places for observation. The effects of lime can be studied by watching the growth of plants under the lines of a marked football or hockey pitch. During the Second World War the colonization of bombed areas by such plants as the London Rocket and the Rose-bay Willow Herb was a constant source of wonder because of the rapidity with which they appeared and spread. The natural succession of plant communities was well illustrated after the eruption of the island KRAKATAU (q.v. Vol. III) in the Dutch East Indies in 1883. This tropical island was split in half, and one half disappeared into the sea, causing a gigantic tidal wave which swamped the rest and drowned 30,000 people. Practically all the plant life of the island was destroyed by hot volcanic material. Within 20 years, however, through seeds borne by wind and sea, the land had recovered, and the former tropical vegetation was practically restored.

3. DOMINANT PLANTS. No plant association is absolutely stable, since, when it appears to be settled, influences like disease epidemics, harmful animals, or the needs of man will come along and upset it. It also often happens that one or more plants tend to dominate the association. These are called the 'dominant plants'. In beech-woods, for instance, the dense foliage of the dominant Beech lets through little light; therefore few light-loving herbs can belong to an association in which the beech is the dominant plant. In some communities the plants are complementary to one another, each taking something different from the soil or occupying different levels in the soil and atmosphere. Thus, in an oak-wood the trees are tall and the roots go deep. The floor or carpet plants, such as Primroses and Ferns, are low-growing plants, with roots near the surface. Between these two there are shrubs, like the Hazel, which have shoots and roots between those of the tree and floor plants. This kind of complementary arrangement allows an abundant and mixed vegetation.

The study of plants in their natural surroundings is proving to be of great practical value in the planting up of newly developed areas. Fresh information about the most suitable plants for arable and grazing land is being obtained, and the ecologist is also providing the scientific knowledge to combat the grave problem of SOIL EROSION (q.v. Vol. III), which exists in so many countries. Among the more interesting plant communities found in Great Britain are those of WOODLANDS, HEATHS AND MOORLANDS, GRASS-LANDS, HEDGEROWS, WATERPLANTS, and SEA-SHORE PLANTS (qq.v.).

EDELWEISS, *see* ALPINE PLANTS.

EELS. Despite their snake-like appearance, Eels are true fishes, differing from most others only in the absence of pelvic fins. Most Eels live in the sea, but a few species spend a great part of their lives in rivers and ponds of Europe or of the Atlantic side of America, being therefore known as Freshwater Eels.

It is only in the last 40 years that the wonderful life-story of the Freshwater Eels has been made known. Before that time naturalists were puzzled, because although fully grown Eels were to be found in fresh waters all the year round, no one ever found any eggs or young ones—and some very queer guesses were made to account for this. But, as so often happens, the facts were stranger than the fictions. While living in fresh-water, the Eels are of a dull yellowish colour, and have rather small eyes; the females grow to a much larger size than the males. When at least 8 years of age a remarkable change comes over some of these 'yellow eels', as they are called:

larger species, that does not enter fresh water, though it may be found at river mouths. It usually lurks among rocks, or between the piles of piers, ready to dart out at likely food. When caught on hook and line, it often attacks the fisherman, like a dog, with its many strong, sharp teeth. There is a story that a Conger once bit the heel off a fisherman's heavy sea-boot. Females grow to a length of about 6 feet and a weight of about 60 pounds, males being much smaller. This species breeds far out at sea, but does not make such a wonderful journey as the Freshwater Eel. A Conger can be distinguished from a Freshwater Eel by the dorsal (back) fin, which begins just above the tip of the pectoral fins, whereas in the Freshwater Eel it begins much farther back.

Numerous kinds of Eels are found throughout the seas, some being very small and worm-like, others large and fierce. The Morays are large Eels of which many elaborately coloured varieties are found in the warmer waters. They lurk among rocks or coral, darting out to attack any unfortunate creature that appeals to their appetite. They have no pectoral fins, and the skin is thick and leathery, often covering the dorsal and anal fins so that the rays are not visible.

The snake-like appearance of Eels serves one of the tropical species in good stead. This fish, an inhabitant of the coral reefs of the East Indies, is very long, and has alternate stripes of black and pale yellow, which give it a striking resemblance to a very poisonous sea-snake that lives in the same region. The Eel, of course, is not poisonous; but it is no doubt mistaken for the snake by would-be enemies, and so avoided.

By far the strangest Eels, however, are those called Snipe-eels, which are found in the open ocean. Their jaws are long and slender, and curved away from each other so that it would appear that they cannot be brought together, even though they are armed with many small teeth. Yet one of these fishes has been taken with a large prawn in its stomach. Snipe-eels are exceedingly long and thin, with delicate fins, and sometimes with a sort of whip-lash on the end of the tail. They are sometimes found swimming, with swift undulations, close to the surface of the sea, though they seem to be equally at home in the great depths.

See also Vol. VI: EEL FISHING.

EGG, see REPRODUCTION IN ANIMALS.

EGGAR MOTH, see

EGRET, see HERON.

EIDER DUCK, see D

ELAND, see ANTELOP

ELECTRIC FISHES.
able to generate elec
light small bulbs, or
motor, is almost unbeli
of fishes are able to
enough, they are not e
This strange power ha
separately, by fishes be
families.

Perhaps the best kno
or Torpedoes, of which s
warm seas. These poss
head behind the eyes, a
of a number of hexago
like a honeycomb. The
jelly-like substance, and
electric plates. One sid
each plate is supplied wi
nected with a main nerv
lobe of the brain. It has l
rent passes from the uppe
organ, downwards to th
Generally it is necessary

THE TORPEDO, OR ELECTRI
A. Fraser-Br

A BOMBED SITE NEAR ST. PAUL'S, LONDON
The Ragwort (*Senecio squalidus*) and Rose-bay Willow Herb are quickly taking possession, springing up wherever any soil is to be found. *John Markham, F.R.P.S.*

the eye grows much larger, the nose more pointed, and the sides become silvery instead of dull yellowish—in fact, there is such a difference that at one time these 'silver eels' were thought to be a different species from the yellow. As soon as they get this bright new uniform the Eels make their way down to the sea. As they are often in small out-of-the-way ponds this means that they have to journey overland to the nearest river; but they manage this by wriggling through damp grass at night. They do not breed as soon as they get to the sea, but instead, they set off on a long journey, sometimes as much as 4,000 miles, to a small area in the western Atlantic, which is their breeding-ground. Here, in the deep sea, they lay their eggs, and then die.

The eggs float for a while, and the young, when they hatch out, in the spring, live near the surface, drifting north-eastwards with the Gulf Stream. These larvae are curious-looking creatures, very thin and broad, like transparent leaves, with tiny heads and long needle-like teeth, with which they seize minute animals for food. It is not surprising that, when they were first discovered, they were not recognized as Eels at all. For about 2½ years they move slowly towards the European coasts, growing all the time; and when eventually they approach their destination, they are about 3 inches long. Now a change comes over them: their substance seems to shrink together, so that they become slender and round instead of broad and flat, and they exchange their larval teeth for a new set more like the adult. At this stage they become

recognizable
still transpar
Glass-eels.

Now they
bers, and sw
Scarcely anyt
and they read
wriggling thr
parents did on
invasions by u
as 'Eel-fares',
earliest times,
whence they
guessed that E
that these Elv
that had left t
actually, the
our rivers to-c
previously, an
long and hazar
in quiet inlan
eels'. In cours
the return jour

An interestin
breeds in very
Atlantic as the
to understand a
up. But the An
stage much m
towards Europe
before it was tir
water habitat, a
European larv
America much
lessly ashore, or

A CONGER EEL
Large Conger-eels often lurk between the piles of jetties. *A. Fraser-Brunner*

to grow to 12 feet. Like the Hard Fern, it produces two kinds of leaves, the fertile leaves bearing clusters of spores at their upper ends. It grows best on the banks of rivers or streams.

FERRET, *see* WEASEL.

FIELDFARE, *see* THRUSH, Section 2.

FIGHTING FISH, *see* LABYRINTH FISH.

FINCHES. 1. The finches form a large family of small birds belonging to the Passerine or perching order of birds. There are altogether some 200 species, distributed over most cold or temperate regions of the world, with a few tropical species. They include some of the commonest of British birds, such as Chaffinches, Linnets, Yellow Hammers, and the common House-Sparrow. They all have much the same general pattern of behaviour; but they vary greatly in plumage. Some, like the Linnet and Corn-Bunting, wear a comparatively sober dress; others, like the Goldfinch and Bullfinch, are handsomely coloured; while some of the tropical species, such as the crimson-red Cardinal Finch of Mexico and central America, and the Rose Finch of Asia, are very gaudy. They are characterized by their strong, hard beaks, specially suitable for breaking into the seeds which form their principal food—the Hawfinch has so stout a bill that it can crack cherry-stones. Finches eat other food besides seeds: in summer they catch insects, on which the fledglings are mostly fed, and the Bullfinches in particular are a nuisance to the fruit-grower by eating the buds of his fruit-trees. They search for their food mainly on the ground, where they move by hopping. Most finches have an inconspicuous and not very melodious song; but there are exceptions, such as the Goldfinch and Linnet, and the wild Canary of the Canary Isles, from which has been bred the domestic Canary with its much more varied song. Many of them build most beautifully constructed nests, those of the Chaffinch and Goldfinch being lovely little cups of moss and wool, lined with hair and feathers. They generally build in hedges, shrubs, or the low boughs of trees, though some species, particularly the Buntings, often build on the ground. From four to six eggs are most usual.

2. GREENFINCHES AND HAWFINCHES. These finches have very stout beaks, deep at the lower

end. The Greenfinches or Green Linnets are common residents of the British Isles, even as far north as the Orkneys. A great many more arrive in the autumn from colder regions to winter in the east of England. They are also found over all Europe, north-west Africa, and much of Asia, as far as China and Japan. Their near relatives, the Grosbeaks and Red Cardinals, are found in most parts of the Americas. Greenfinches differ from other finches in building rather untidy nests ; the eggs are greenish-white marked with reddish-brown speckles. They have been known to mate with Goldfinches or Linnets, and to produce hybrids. In

A HAWFINCH

captivity they will mate with Canaries or Bullfinches. Hawfinches are easy to recognize because of their large, heavy bills and their thick-set build; but they are shy birds, and therefore not easy to see. They generally frequent the edges of woods, especially where there are hornbeams, the seeds of which are a favourite food; and they can be seen during the summer making their rapid undulating flight among the trees and bushes of gardens and orchards. They generally build in trees, and lay greenish-white eggs marked with spots and streaks of greyish- and greenish-brown.

3. CHAFFINCH, GOLDFINCH, AND SISKIN. The Chaffinch is one of the commonest of British birds and is a typical finch. Its numbers are increased considerably in winter by immigrants to the British Isles. In the summer the birds are seen about in pairs; but in the autumn, like many other species of finches, they become more gregarious, the sexes generally keeping to separate flocks. The eggs, laid in a beautifully constructed little nest, are a pale purplish-grey, spotted and streaked with shades of red. The

TROPICAL FISHES OF AUSTRALIAN SEAS

Above: Superb Trigger-fish
Below: Adorned Trunk-fishes, male (left) and female (right)

A CHAFFINCH

Brambling is a near relative of the Chaffinch, with a nest and eggs much alike. It comes to Britain in winter, but nests farther north.

The Goldfinch is one of the loveliest of British birds, and since the trapping of them as cage-birds has been forbidden, they have become much more common. They will now quite often appear in gardens to feed on the flower seeds, especially the seeds of Michaelmas Daisies, and serve a useful purpose in eating large quantities of weed seeds, being particularly fond of thistle seeds. In full spring plumage, the cock has vivid crimson cheeks and head, a white throat, and wings barred with gold and black. The female is only a little less brightly coloured. The nest, built generally in shrubs or trees not very high up

A GOLDFINCH

from the ground, is a most perfect construction, and contains bluish-white eggs, mottled, mainly at one end, with purple-red. The Siskin is a near relative with similar habits, and is also a good songster. It nests, generally in fir-woods, freely in north Scotland and parts of Ireland, and less freely farther south.

4. THE BULLFINCH is a quite unmistakable little bird, and has been very popular as a cage-bird. The male in his full spring plumage is very handsome. He has a stubby, slightly hooked beak, glossy black head and tail, black wings barred with white, a back shaded from black to blue and white, and a bright cherry-red throat, chest, and underparts. The female is inconspicuously coloured. Bullfinches almost certainly mate for life, and generally produce two broods, sometimes three, in a season. Their nest, a shallow cup of roots and hair, on a platform of twigs, is placed in a hedge or near the end of a low bough and the eggs are greenish-blue, spotted and streaked with purple, mostly at the large end.

5. THE CROSSBILL is a brightly coloured finch, not very common in England except after occasional invasions from northern Europe—though it has recently established itself in Norfolk and Suffolk. It breeds in parts of Scotland where there are pine forests. It has a remarkable beak of which the points are elongated and crossed to make an effective 'pair of scissors', capable of dealing with the hard seeds of the conifers on which it chiefly feeds. A legend relates that the bird twisted its beak in pulling out the nails from the Cross, and that its blood-red colour is a mark of the service it rendered.

6. LINNETS AND TWITES. These form a distinct group of the finches, with different appearance and habits. In many species their otherwise inconspicuous plumage is brightened by patches of red, especially on the head. They frequent commons with gorse and broom bushes, very often building their nests in gorse bushes, usually not far from the ground. The eggs have purple and red markings on a bluish-white background. The Mountain Linnet, or Twite, is a more slender bird, which is quite common on the moorlands and mountains of Scotland, Ireland, and Norway, but does not come very far south. The Lesser Redpoll is a smaller Linnet with dark plumage, a red forehead, and carmine breast. It breeds mainly in the northern part of the British Isles, but is found also in the south-eastern counties.

7. BUNTINGS. These also form a distinct group of the finches, the most typical being the Corn-Bunting, a bird rather like a Lark in appearance —though it can be quickly distinguished by its finch-like 'seed' beak. During autumn and winter it feeds almost entirely on corn, eating

GOLDFINCH AT ITS NEST IN AN APPLE-TREE
Eric J. Hosking, F.R.P.S.

drawn-out wheeze. The Cirl Bunting is comparatively rare, and very local—usually to be found in chalk districts.

There are other species of Buntings which occasionally visit the British Isles, among them the Ortolan, a handsome bird, with a greenish head and 'moustaches', which used at one time to be prized as a table delicacy. There are several species of Buntings in America, the best known being the Indigo Bird, and the Bobolink, whose cheerful song is a favourite in spring-time in the United States.

The House-sparrow, which is also a member of the finch family, is described under the headword SPARROW (q.v.).

See also Vol. IX: BIRD KEEPING.

FIREBRAT, *see* SILVERFISH.

FIRE-FLY. Beetles endowed with the strange power of giving light have for many centuries excited wonder and admiration. But the nature of the light and the way in which the insect controls it are still little understood. Fire-flies rarely show themselves in the day-time, only coming forth to flash their lovely lights as the daylight fades. In the warm climates in which most of them are found, firework displays of wonderful beauty may be enjoyed at the proper season, for the Fire-flies generally congregate together in large numbers, sometimes even flashing their lamps in unison as if to the beat of a conductor's baton. Britain has, unfortunately, no Fire-flies but only their relation, the common GLOW-WORM (q.v.). Unlike that insect, both male and female Fire-flies are torch-bearers. The light is produced from the hinder part of the body, as in the Glow-Worm, and can be switched on and off in the same way. In the Fire-flies of Italy and southern Europe it is of a golden colour.

Certain beetles of another kind, found in Tropical America and the West Indies, are also known as Fire-flies, and in South America as Cucujos. They show light of two colours, and

insects the rest of the year. It makes its nest, a loose cup of dry grass and roots, in a well-concealed hollow in the ground, and lays a typical Bunting egg, a faintly purplish-white with blotches and long streaks of purple. It has a very distinct song, a series of abrupt, hard notes, ending in a confused jumble which sounds rather like the jingling of a bunch of keys. The Reed Bunting is common in swampy, marshy country and along streams with banks overgrown with willows, alders, and reeds. It makes its nest in clumps of reeds or coarse grass, or near the roots of waterside trees.

The most common Bunting is the Yellow-hammer, a rather smaller bird, with bright yellow and brown plumage, common all over northern Europe and to be seen in almost every hedgerow in many parts of England. It has a persistent and characteristic song, consisting of a series of quick, hard notes, ending in a long are sometimes carried as a kind of living jewellery in the ladies' hair or dresses. They are larger than the true Fire-flies, some of them being more than an inch long, and belong to another family, that of the Click-beetles (*see* Wire-worms). Upon the back, just behind the head, they carry two pale round spots, like head-lamps, from which proceeds a strong greenish light—so strong, indeed, that if the beetle is held in the fingers, it is quite easy to read a book by it. When the beetle flies, its body is moved in such a way that it shows another lamp beneath it, giving a reddish light. Click-beetles are common in most parts of the world and are of many different kinds; but the luminous Cucujos are few in number, and are found only in America.

See also Beetles.

FIR-CONES, *see* Reproduction of Plants, Section 4.

FIRS, *see* Conifer.

FISHES. 1. Definition of a Fish. The name 'fish' is often used quite inaccurately: people speak of shell-fish, when they mean mussels, winkles, and scallops (which are molluscs), or crabs, lobsters, and shrimps (which are crustaceans). A common mistake is to think of Whales (q.v.), dolphins, and porpoises as fishes; whereas they are mammals—suckling their young—and are shaped like a fish only because that is the shape most suitable for a life in the water. What then constitutes a true fish?

We must remember that, over an enormous period of time, living things have evolved from minute, single-celled creatures, like Amoeba (q.v.). As they grew bigger and

more active, some sort of framework for the attachment of muscles and for stability became necessary. Some animals, such as insects, developed a hard outer covering, or external skeleton, for this purpose; others—small, jelly-like animals that lived in the waters of some distant period—developed a supporting rod (called a 'notochord') through their bodies. That was the beginning of an inside framework, or internal skeleton. In time, small plates of gristle grew along the notochord to strengthen it further, with special plates at the front end to protect the brain: animals with these features still exist at the present time (*see* Lampreys). Then new

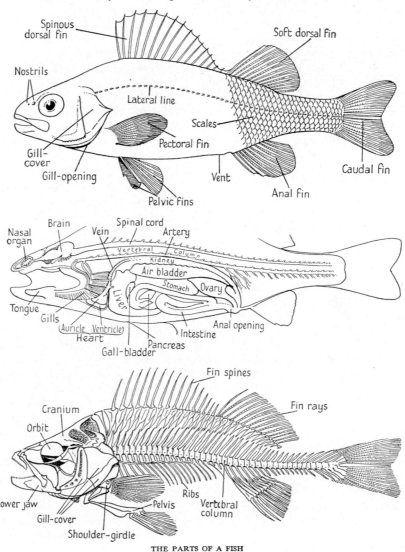

THE PARTS OF A FISH
Above, the outside parts; *Centre*, the internal organs; *Below*, the skeleton

types grew up, with much more gristle, forming a much stronger skeleton, with a complete skull and jaws and supports for the fins, which made it possible for them to grow much larger and more powerful. These were the Selachians, the SHARKS and RAYS (q.v.). In time, the gristle became further strengthened with lime, to form the first 'bony' skeleton, and the animals that possessed this were the true fishes, grouped in the class called Pisces. Once this strong frame-work had been developed, an enormous variety of types became possible. Moreover, certain of them became capable of breathing dry air; the bony supports of their fins became modified as walking limbs; and eventually reptiles were developed. From these evolved on the one hand the birds, and on the other the mammals—the last to appear being man himself (see EVOLUTION). A fish is the lowest kind of animal with a bony skeleton, representing the ancestors of all the higher types of vertebrate life.

2. STRUCTURE OF FISH. All fishes breathe by means of gills, which extract oxygen from the water that bathes them, though in a few special cases they can breathe ordinary air as well (see LUNGFISH, LABYRINTH FISH). The gills are carried on a framework of bones, protected by a movable cover of bony plates, just behind the mouth. Water is taken in at the mouth, passes over the gills, and is expelled through the gill-opening.

The heart of a fish has only two chambers, an auricle and a ventricle. Blood that has done its work comes into the auricle, bearing much waste (carbon dioxide): it then passes into the ventricle, which pumps it into the gills; here the carbon dioxide is given off in exchange for oxygen, which the blood carries away (see HEART). Fishes are often called 'cold-blooded' animals: their blood, in fact, is not always cold, but it is generally colder than ours. It is usually about the same temperature as the surrounding water, so that in cold weather it will be cold, but when the temperature of the water goes up, the blood will get warmer too. In the 'warm-blooded' animals (birds and mammals), on the other hand, the blood is kept at the same high temperature, whatever the weather may do. When the water, and the blood, are warm, a fish is active and needs a lot of food; but when it turns cold, a fish retires to deep water to lie quiet, and will not feed at all. It may even sleep for a whole winter.

Though many fishes have no teeth, others are provided with an amazing array of them, not only in the jaws, but often on the roof of the mouth and the tongue as well, together with certain special ones in the throat on some of the gill-bones. The teeth, of course, differ in shape and arrangement according to the kind of food the fish requires. The digestive organs are similar to our own, though somewhat simpler.

Most fishes possess a 'swim-bladder', occupying the middle of the body, at its centre of gravity. This bladder is supplied with gases which enable the fish to float easily in the water: it can vary the amount of gas at will, expelling some when it wishes to sink to the bottom, or adding more when it needs to rise.

Fishes have a simple brain, sharp hearing (though of a somewhat different kind from ours), and a keen sense of smell, the majority having two nostrils on each side. Their eyes are usually large and well adapted for seeing through water; but sometimes they are feeble, and a few fishes are quite blind (see BLIND-FISHES). Along each side of the body there is nearly always a 'lateral line', a special organ for detecting vibrations and changes in pressure in the water, which serves to warn the fish of the approach of other creatures or of its nearness to some solid body. It is a kind of 'sixth sense'.

A fish's muscles are fairly simple, being nearly all concerned with wriggling the body or moving the jaws, but they are often very powerful. Most fishes have an outer covering of scales, usually small and thin and arranged in rows, but sometimes large and bony.

The great majority of fishes possess fins (each with their own special bones), which serve to propel them through the water and to maintain balance. They are thin membranes, supported by movable 'rays', so that they can be closed like a fan, and are of two kinds. The first kind, known as the vertical fins, stand upright along the back (dorsal fins), at the end of the tail (caudal fin), and underneath the tail (anal fin). The second kind are known as paired fins, as there is one on each side, one pair just behind the gill-cover (pectoral fins), and a pair beneath the body (pelvic fins). These correspond to the limbs of higher animals, the pectoral fins corresponding to the arms, and the pelvic fins to the legs. Usually all these fins, paired and unpaired, can be seen on the same fish; but in some species one or more of them may be absent: in a very few kinds, such as certain rare eels, all the fins have been lost.

3. HABITS OF FISH. There may be about 40,000 species of fishes in the world, and new ones are being discovered each year. The variety of their forms and manner of life is almost endless, with wonderful adaptations to meet the differences of environment. There is scarcely any water on the earth's surface where they are not to be found.

Those that roam far and wide near the surface of the great oceans are called 'pelagic fishes' (from the Greek word *pelagos*, the ocean). They include swift creatures, like the MACKEREL, that swim in great shoals, feeding on the young of various other fishes, which in turn feed on the multitude of larval and invertebrate creatures forming the 'plankton' or floating life of the sea. The mackerel themselves are hunted by still larger fish, such as TUNNY and SHARKS (qq.v.). Down in the depths, in the dark and cold, dwell many fantastic fishes that feed on one another, and can sometimes swallow prey much larger than themselves (*see* DEEP-SEA FISHES).

The coasts abound with an endless variety of forms—fishes brilliantly coloured to match the coral among which they live, fishes drab and stone-like from the sombre rocky shores; some long and slender, some short and deep, others with tassels and flaps to resemble sea-weed—all

for concealment from prey or enemies (*see* CAMOUFLAGE). Many are armed against their enemies with strong armour-plating, or poison spines (*see* POISON FISH), or even by being able to puff themselves up with air. Some feed on lowly plant-life which they scrape from rocks, some have powerful teeth that can crush hard mollusc-shells or crabs, some eat worms; but most devour their smaller brethren.

Similarly, the fresh waters are everywhere inhabited by fishes—great lakes, mere ditches, water-holes in the desert, even the very edges of waterfalls, where the fish have special fins to prevent them, by suction, from being swept over. Insects form a large part of the diet of freshwater fishes, which in swampy country play a part in keeping down the mosquitoes.

The majority of fishes lay eggs that either lie at the bottom, or, as in many sea-fish, float at the surface. Some sea-fishes, like the Cod and Halibut, lay and then leave to their fate millions of tiny eggs, most of which are eaten by other creatures, possibly about six from each batch reaching the adult state. On the other hand, some freshwater fishes lay very few, large eggs, and take great care of them, fanning them with their fins, driving away enemies, even in some cases keeping them in their mouths as a protection. Some fishes go so far as to construct a sort of nest. There are certain fishes, both marine and freshwater, that bear their young alive (in other words, the eggs hatch inside the mother, and are not released into the water till the young are able to swim and feed). Some kinds of fish change in the most remarkable way as they grow up, so that the connexion between young and adult is difficult to see. Sometimes, too, the female is so different from the male that in the past they have been thought to be separate species.

4. DISTRIBUTION OF FISH. No one kind of fish is to be found everywhere: generally each species can thrive well in only one particular set of conditions. Most of the freshwater fishes cannot live in the sea, and very few sea-fishes can live in fresh water. Among sea-fishes, those that live near coasts.

PORCUPINE FISH

In the background a Porcupine fish swims normally, while the one in front is puffed out, with the sharp spines raised. *A. Fraser-Brunner* in shallow water, are used to particular temperatures; so, with some exceptions, those in the tropics cannot move far north or south, and those of the colder seas do not travel far towards the Equator. East and west travel is hindered for most sea-fishes by the great continents, so that the same species does not live in both the Atlantic and Pacific Oceans, or in the Atlantic and Indian Oceans; but some of the Indian Ocean species pass into the Pacific by way of the East Indies.

The distribution of fishes is governed by several things. We have already touched on the importance of temperature; the ocean currents also play a large part in distributing marine fishes. Although many adult shore-fishes do not travel far, in their immature stages, either as eggs or larvae, they may be carried wherever the currents take them, since they float helplessly near the surface. So, if we find West Indian fishes on the coast of West Africa, or East Indian fishes at Madagascar, the explanation lies in the great currents that move between these places. Geology also helps to explain the present-day distribution. We must remember that fishes lived in the seas long ago, when the arrangement of the land masses was quite different from what it is to-day. This is the only explanation why some North Atlantic fishes, such as Hake and certain dogfishes, have close relatives in the South Atlantic, with no connexions whatever in the vast area that lies between. It seems certain that they did inhabit the area near the Equator at a time when conditions were quite different; but as these conditions changed, the fish retreated, some to the north and some to the south, while other kinds arose to occupy the space between.

Each of the great river systems of the world has its own kinds of fishes, isolated by the great mountain or desert barriers, or the oceans in between. The distribution of freshwater fishes is difficult to understand if we consider things only as they now exist. For instance, there are two great families of freshwater fishes, known as CHARACINS and CICHLIDS (qq.v.), that are confined almost entirely to the rivers of South America and Africa. Since they could not possibly have crossed the ocean from the one continent to the other, the only explanation of their presence in these two widely separated places alone must lie in the fact that in a past geological age South America and Africa were

joined together, and were divided from the rest of the world by a great sea.

FLAMINGO. Although related to the GEESE (q.v.), and not very distantly, the Flamingo is classed in an order by itself, in which there are six species, distributed over most of the warmer regions of the world, but not Australia. A few individuals have, from time to time, wandered as far north as Britain, while the European Flamingo breeds by the salt-marshes and lagoons at the mouth of the Rhone, in Spain, and in other places. Flamingoes are large birds, a full-grown adult varying from 5 feet to over 6 feet in height. They are characterized by their extremely long, thin, pinkish-red (or occasionally yellow) legs, their very graceful swan-like necks, and their peculiar heavy bills, the lower part being much heavier and larger than the upper. Their colour varies from rose-tinted white to full scarlet, with black wing quills and some black markings. One South American species is a light vermilion, with brighter wing coverts.

Flamingoes generally live in flocks. On the lakes of North India these flocks sometimes number tens of thousands, and are a wonderful sight, either massed on the water or rising in a great rosy cloud. Although they prefer wading, they can swim powerfully. When they fly, they stretch their long necks out in front and their legs behind, and generally utter a 'gaggling' cry, much like that of geese. They feed mostly on water-plants, but also eat quantities of small molluscs. When hunting for these they turn their heads the wrong way up, so that the bent beak forms an excellent instrument for scooping up the muddy water. This they sift through the sifters on the edge of the bill, and so select the molluscs. They make nests on circular heaps of mud, fairly close to one another, near swamps or river estuaries. They generally lay one or sometimes two eggs, and these have greenish-blue shells, which are covered with a chalky covering.

FLASH-COLOURS. *See* COLOUR PLATE opp. p. 336.

FLAT-FISHES. Although quite a number of fishes are flattened in some way or another, the name Flat-fishes is reserved for a certain large group, all related to one another, which usually

A FLAMINGO NESTING COLONY
Some of the eggs are already hatched out and the little fledgelings are beginning to leave their flat mud nests
G. K. Yeates, F.R.P.S.

lie on one side on the bed of the sea, and have both eyes on the other, uppermost, side. They are extremely flat; so that when they lie in the sand there is hardly a bump to show that they are there—only the two watchful eyes, which are somewhat raised up and protected by over-hanging fleshy lids, covered with scales; and even these are easily mistaken for pebbles. Most Flat-fishes are coloured to match the ground on which they lie; and if they move on to a different surface, say, from sand to pebbles, they can change their colouring to match. So their CAMOUFLAGE (q.v.) is very complete, and they are not easily found by their enemies. Only one side of the body, the side that lies uppermost, is so coloured—the other side being usually white.

It has been suggested that the Flat-fish are Perch-like fishes (see SEA PERCH) which, having formed this curious habit of lying on one side, have developed a peculiar structure to fit them to this way of life—in other words, the eye on

the undermost side has moved over to lie on the upper side, and the colour underneath has been lost. But a study of these fishes from the time of hatching suggests another explanation. When first hatched, the young Flat-fish swims upright near the surface of the sea, and has an eye on each side of the head, just like any other fish. It is not until it is half an inch or more long that the skull begins to twist, so that one eye passes over the top of the head to the other side, and the mouth tends to move in the opposite direc-tion. When this occurs the fish sinks slowly to the sea-bed—and it appears that the twisting of the skull alters the balance of the creature: it is unable any longer to swim like an ordinary fish, and falls to one side. As colouring matter can only develop in the presence of light, the side of the fish that is buried remains colourless—in fact, if a Flat-fish is put in a glass-bottomed tank with a bright light underneath, the blind side will soon become coloured. Even in nature, we sometimes come across a Flat-fish with both sides coloured—these specimens usually occurring where the twisting of the head is not complete, so that the fish swims more or less normally.

Generally, a particular kind of Flat-fish will have the eyes and colour always on the same side (though reversed examples are known). Thus, the Halibut, Plaice, Dab, Flounder, and Smear Dab (or 'Lemon Sole') are right-sided, while the Turbot and Brill are left-sided. Owing to the twisting mentioned above, the mouth

THE SOLE, showing both eyes on one side of the head
A. Fraser-Brunner

comes to lie more on the blind side, and the teeth are usually better developed on that side. This is most convenient for the fish, which feeds mostly on bottom-living creatures, such as molluscs and small sea-urchins. When moving from one place to another Flat-fishes swim with the eyed side uppermost, and are propelled by wavy movements of the dorsal and anal fins, which form a margin to the body.

The largest of the Flat-fishes is the Halibut, which may grow to a length of 10 feet and a weight of 600 lb. It inhabits the northern parts of the Atlantic and Pacific Oceans, and is an important food-fish. In recent times the oil from its liver has become important in medicine, as it is rich in vitamin D. Related to the Halibut is the Brill, which has smooth sides, and the Turbot, with a number of wart-like tubercles scattered on the body.

Another well-known and important food-fish is the Plaice. This is captured by means of the trawl, the best catches being at night, since at that time the fish are feeding above the surface of the sand (see TRAWLING, Vol. VI). A near relative, the Flounder, is common near estuaries, and often travels a long way up rivers; a smaller kind, the Dab, is found close inshore, and is the kind usually caught by anglers from the end of piers. Another of these right-sided species, the Smear Dab, is caught in large numbers by trawlers in deeper water, often being sold in shops as 'Lemon Sole', though it is not a true Sole. The common Sole is a left-sided Flat-fish, and is one of the most valued food-fishes. It can always be distinguished from the other species mentioned by its having the snout and

A FLAT FISH

Sketches of Plaice, showing how, as the young fish grows, one eye moves over the top of the head to join the other. In the first two stages there is an eye on each side, like any other fish. In the last stage both eyes are on the right side, and the back fin has grown forward on the head upper lip overhanging the lower jaw, which also does not jut forward as in the other kinds; the mouth is very small, and the eyes are close together, with no bony ridge between them.

Altogether, about 450 species of Flat-fish are known, though most of them are smaller and less important than the ones mentioned; they are found in almost all seas.

FLAT-WORM. *See* WORM, Section 6.

FLEA. There are at least forty-six different species of fleas in Great Britain. They are all small and, when adult, are external parasites upon birds and mammals, piercing the skin and sucking the blood of the animals upon which they live. Like many other insects parasitic on higher animals, they are wingless. The body of

FLEA. Greatly enlarged

the flea, however, is deep and narrow, whereas the bodies of all other insect parasites are broad and flat. Fleas go through all the four stages of a typical INSECT (q.v.). The eggs—oval in shape and white in colour—are laid among the fur and feathers of the animal upon which the parent feeds, and they drop off upon the ground. A neglected kitten, troubled with fleas, will often leave a hundred eggs or so on the chair on which it has been sleeping. The larvae look like tiny caterpillars, and are not parasites. They are devoid of feet and move by wriggling. We find them in places where their parents abound: hen-houses, not kept properly clean, are infested with the larvae of the domestic fowl flea; those of the flea found on man will occur in cracks in the floor and under carpets; those of the rat flea are found in barns and granaries. They are all scavengers. The larva casts its skin twice during its growth period, and then spins a silken cocoon in which it changes into the pupa. When the fully developed fleas have come out of these cocoons, they have to find their own way to the

particular kind of animal they live on, and seem to be remarkably successful in doing so. Until they do, they cannot feed; but they seem able to live a long time before taking their first meal.

When an animal dies any fleas upon it at once leave it and look for another animal upon which to feed. Generally speaking, each flea has its own particular preference—so that the fleas found, for example, on rat, dog, hedgehog, cat, rabbit, and man, are all different species of insect. Nevertheless, if need be, they will turn to other animals. Thus the flea common to the rabbit has been found on cats which hunt rabbits, and the rat flea is known to transfer its attention to man: in fact, bubonic plague—a rat disease—is communicated to human beings by certain kinds of fleas which desert the dead body of the rat, carrying the disease with them.

The Jigger or Chigoe is a tropical flea that attacks a number of different animals, including man, in Africa, central America, and the West Indies. At first the Jigger lives the usual active life of a Flea; but later, the females burrow under the skin, and their abdomens become distended with eggs, swelling up to the size of a pea. On man these insects chiefly burrow into the toes. The result is a serious sore, which may involve the loss of a toe or even of a leg.

See also Vol. XI: HOUSEHOLD PESTS.

FLESH FLY. This is a large, grey or silvery fly, with coral-red eyes, dark longitudinal lines on its thorax, and dark and light draught-board markings on its abdomen. It is a common insect, fond of settling on the ground in woods, in pastures, along country roads, and on moorlands. Like most two-winged flies, it is most often seen during the hours of hot sunshine. It often comes into houses in rural districts.

There are many different kinds of Flesh Fly,

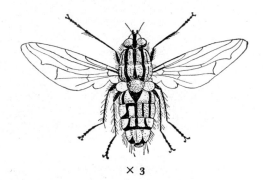

× 3

all of which look much alike, and about twenty of which are found in Great Britain. So far as we know, they never lay eggs: they generally drop their larvae, usually in a not very advanced stage of development, upon decaying vegetable or animal matter, upon which the maggots then feed. One species of Flesh Fly has been seen to do this accurately from a height of over 2 feet. Flesh Flies also drop their larvae on open wounds on animals, and even on human beings, and these often cause much harm to the animal or person. Many of these larvae are internal parasites of scorpions, snails, earthworms, and insects; the very large caterpillars of the Emperor, Oak Eggar, and Drinker Moths are, for instance, often selected as victims. In this respect they closely resemble their near relatives, the BRISTLE-FLY (q.v.).

See also FLY.

FLIGHT. There are three main classes of animals which can fly—bats, birds, and insects; and each has achieved the power of flight in a different way. There are also a number of other creatures—squirrels, lizards, fish, spiders—which are able to glide or float through the air for a limited distance; but they have not achieved true flight, since they can remain airborne only for so long as the impetus received from the initial launching lasts. The Flying Squirrel has a broad membrane of skin stretched between the legs, and the Cobegos or Flying Lemurs, as well as some tree-haunting lizards, have a similar parachute, which enables them to take flying leaps among the trees where they live. The Flying Fish has greatly enlarged pectoral fins, which enable it to make long glides over the surface of the sea to escape its enemies. Young spiders are borne for long distances by threads of gossamer, but have little more control over their movement than has thistledown. In true flight, however, the flying animal can remain airborne as a result of repeated muscular movement, and has normally complete control over the direction of flight.

The wing of a bat consists of a fold of skin stretched out on greatly lengthened fingers, and attached behind to the hind limb. In some ways bats are more efficient fliers than birds, in that they achieve as proportionately a good result with much smaller wing muscles. They also have a greater manoeuvrability. (See BATS.)

In BIRDS (q.v.), on the other hand, the whole

BIRD

BAT

FLYING FISH

THREE TYPES OF FLIGHT

body is made very light by the hollowness of the bones, the lightness of the feathers, and the presence of air-sacs inside the body itself. The back is rigid, and the wings, hinged against the backbone, are actuated by powerful muscles stretched over the keel or breastbone. Birds' flight, like that of bats, is normally effected by a flapping movement of the wings—that is, by movements which are apparently up and down —though, in fact, the tip of the wing describes a figure of eight, because the action is similar to that of an oar in rowing. But many birds, especially sea-birds, are able to glide for very long distances (see GULL, ALBATROSS, PETREL); and others can soar to great heights and for long periods (see HAWK, VULTURE, STORK). Gliding differs from soaring in that a gliding bird tends to lose height, and must flap to regain it, while a soaring bird does not. Birds that glide frequently have long, narrow wings, while those that soar generally have broad wings: both have larger wings than birds that merely flap. In both gliding and soaring, birds make use of air-currents (see GLIDING, Vol. IX). Off shore,

GULLS (q.v.) will usually follow in the wake of a ship; and they are commonly to be seen passing forwards and upwards beside the ship in the strong air currents created as the ship moves forward, and then circling back, and losing height, as the calmer air astern of the ship is reached.

Some birds, such as the KESTREL (q.v.), are able to hover (or remain motionless in the air) by making use of the air-currents, holding wings and tail meanwhile in such a way as to give buoyancy; others, such as the HUMMING BIRD (q.v.), hover by a rapid beating of the wings. Most birds, however, are unable to hover, and consequently, below a certain speed must stall like an aeroplane, and come to earth. The stalling speed is very low in most birds, because they are provided with slots in their wings (now copied on aircraft) which guide the air smoothly round the end of the wing. These slots are plainly to be seen when rooks are in flight. Normally birds steer with their tails.

The wings of INSECTS (q.v.) are not limbs, like those of bats and birds, but are extensions of the covering of the body. They are of many kinds and shapes and may be in one or two pairs. But in all insects the method of flight is by flapping, sometimes alternated, in species with large wings, by short glides. Many insects are able to hover, and this they do by an extremely rapid beating of the wings.

The fastest British bird is the Golden EAGLE (q.v.), with a maximum speed of 120 m.p.h., followed closely by swifts and swallows with 70–100 m.p.h. Ducks and geese fly at 40 to 60 m.p.h., crows and starlings at from 30 to 50 m.p.h., and the smaller birds at 20 to 35 m.p.h. Not only do birds excel in speed: they are also capable of great endurance in flight. The Arctic Tern, for instance, breeds in the Arctic and winters in the Antarctic, and so flies many thousands of miles every year; the Manx Shearwaters that breed off the coast of Britain go to the North coast of Spain to feed; and the tiny swallow winters in South Africa, doing the 5,000-mile journey there and back every year of its life—no small achievement for an animal weighing less than an ounce.

See also MIGRATION.

FLOUNDER, *see* FLAT-FISHES.

FLOWERING PLANTS. 1. STRUCTURE. Flowering plants first appeared about one hun-

dred million years ago (*see* EVOLUTION, CHART). To-day there are at least a quarter of a million species, without counting the hybrids and varieties which have been developed by horticulturists. They have penetrated to all parts of the world, including the frozen wastes of the Arctic, the dry zones of the desert, and the hot, humid jungles of the tropics. They propagate by seeds contained in capsules, or seed-cases—in contrast to plants such as CONIFERS (q.v.), which have naked seeds, or ALGAE, FUNGI, MOSSES AND LIVERWORTS, and FERNS (qq.v.) which reproduce by spores. The seeds of flowering plants have a double protection against unfavourable conditions, such as drought, heat, or cold, because they are protected not only by their own tough coats, but by the seed capsules in which they first develop.

Each seed consists of an outer protective coat containing a young plant complete with the beginnings of a root, known as the 'radicle', and a tiny shoot, the 'plumule'. Attached to this young plant are one or two special seed-leaves or 'cotyledons' containing a store of food for the young seedling, to feed it until it gets established. Some flowering plants have only one cotyledon, and are known as 'monocotyledons'; others have two, and are known as 'dicotyledons'. (*See* SEEDS.) Other differences between these two big groups are in the structure of the flowers and leaves and in the kind of foodstuffs which they build up. All flowering plants, although so different, are built to the same plan, the main features of which are the root, stem, leaves, and flowers. The extent to which each is developed, however, differs greatly from plant to plant.

The ROOT-system (q.v.) serves to fix the green plant firmly in the ground, and also to take from the soil water containing the dissolved mineral salts. The main function of the STEM (q.v.) is to support the leaves and display them to the sunlight, an end achieved in many different ways. Also, the stem conducts the water from the roots to the leaves. The LEAVES (q.v.) are the food-factories, and in them food-stuffs are made up from the raw materials taken in by the roots and from the atmosphere. They contain the green colouring matter, 'chlorophyll', which has the unique property of being able to absorb radiant energy from sunlight and convert it into chemical energy, this being stored at first as food. (*See* PHOTOSYNTHESIS.) Lastly, there are the FLOWERS (q.v.) which produce seeds.

2. HERBS, SHRUBS, AND TREES. A plant with a thick woody stem or trunk is called a tree. A small plant with a stem which contains little wood and which is usually green is called a herb. Plants intermediate between the herb and the tree, with much wood but with no main trunk or bole, are called shrubs. The elm and ash are trees; the daisy and sunflower are herbs; the privet, bramble, and gorse are shrubs. There is, however, no hard-and-fast line to be drawn. The hawthorn, for example, in some places grows with a well-developed trunk, and would have to be described as a tree; in other places it has many woody branches coming straight from the ground and seems to be a typical shrub.

3. LENGTH OF LIFE. Herbs are generally much shorter-lived than shrubs or trees. In contrast to trees, some of which are reputed to be several thousands of years old, some herbs complete their life-histories so quickly that their offspring can also complete their life-histories in the same season. There may even be three or four generations within the same year. Because their lives are so short, such plants are called 'ephemerals' (from a Greek word meaning short-lived). Many weeds, such as groundsel, are ephemerals—as the gardener, who suffers from their rapid propagation, is only too well aware.

Many herbs live only for one season. In Great Britain we sow our seeds in spring; and in the autumn, when the crops are ripe, we gather in the harvest, taking good care that there are enough seeds to sow again in the following spring. These one-year plants are called ANNUALS (q.v. Vol. VI), and include all our cereals, such as wheat, and all those flowers like the marigold, sweet pea, and nasturtium, the seeds of which we have to sow afresh each spring.

Many plants, such as the carrot, seldom complete their life-history, because we lift them to eat at the end of their first year of growth. If left in the soil, carrots would go into a resting condition in the winter; in the following spring they would throw up tall shoots with leaves and flowers; these would draw upon the food supply in the swollen root, and, after seeds had been produced, the whole plant would die. The carrot thus takes two years to complete its life-cycle, and is described as a BIENNIAL (q.v. Vol. VI). Many of our common 'root' plants, such as the swede, turnip, mangold, beetroot, and parsnip, are biennials.

Other plants, the grasses, daisies, buttercups, bluebells, crocuses, hollies, pines, oaks, and so on, live longer than annuals or biennials, their length of life ranging from a few years to many centuries. Some of these PERENNIALS (q.v. Vol. VI) are herbs, which store up food in underground parts during the growing season. In the cold season they pass into a resting condition, the delicate stem and leaves dying down. Growth is renewed in the next season at the expense of the food stored underground.

4. TREES. Trees and shrubs store up food in

THE BIG TREE OF TULE—A MEXICAN CYPRESS—THE OLDEST TREE IN THE WORLD
Ewing Galloway, N.Y.

their shoots as well as their roots, and grow new shoots and roots each year. They can live to a very great age. The great Dragon's-blood Tree (so named because of the red resin that it

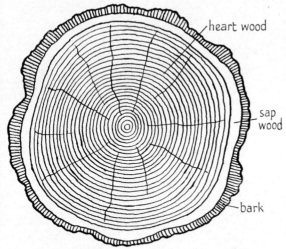

SECTION OF TREE TRUNK SHOWING ANNUAL RINGS

yields) which was blown down in Teneriffe in 1869 was said to be over 6,000 years old. Possibly the oldest tree living to-day is a bald cypress growing near Mexico, called the 'Big Tree of Tule'. It is between 6,000 and 7,000 years old and was already a big tree when the ancient Pyramids of Egypt were being built. Its circumference a yard or so from the ground is no less than 35 yards.

We can be sure of the age of a tree by counting the number of annual rings. If a tree is sawn down, the stump is seen to be made up of two kinds of wood. In the middle is wood of a darker colour called the 'heart-wood', and surrounding it lighter-coloured wood known as 'sap-wood'. Water containing dissolved mineral salts, which goes by the name of 'sap', passes through the tubes of the sap-wood to the leaves from the roots. The heart-wood is older, and dry, and contains no sap. Each year, during the growing season (which, in temperate countries like Great Britain is from spring to autumn), the tree grows a thin layer of wood which is added on to the outside of the already-existing sap-wood. No new wood is formed during the winter. Because more sap rises in the spring than in the autumn, the tubes which are produced in the spring are bigger than those produced in the autumn. Then comes the winter when no tubes are produced.

The following spring more big tubes grow, followed by small ones in the autumn, and so on. The difference in size between the small and big tubes causes the appearance of alternating light and dark rings, called 'annual rings', which can be counted to tell the approximate age of the tree. Experienced botanists can go even farther than that and, by examining the size of the tubes, can tell us, for instance, whether it was a fine or wet autumn in the year that Queen Anne died.

FLOWERS. The flower is responsible for the production of the seeds, which carry the species on from one generation to another. Before one generation dies the seeds of another must be sown. Certain parts of the flower, the stamens and the carpels, are concerned only with reproduction, while other parts, the sepals and the petals, serve for protection or for attracting the insects to pollinate the flowers. REPRODUCTION OF FLOWERS (q.v.) is sexual—fundamentally the same as that in all animals, including man.

The flower is really a condensed shoot in which the leaves have become modified to take on other work than manufacturing food. In a simple type of flower, such as the Buttercup, these are arranged in nearly concentric circles, called 'whorls'. The outermost are five green, leaf-like 'sepals', which protect the flower in bud. Inside the sepals are five usually heart-shaped 'petals', each with a small flap at its base making a little sac or nectary in which the sweet nectar is produced. The nectar serves to attract insects, and some of it later becomes converted into honey by bees. Both sepals and petals are attached to the swollen end of the flower-stalk, called the 'receptacle', which projects like a cone into the flower.

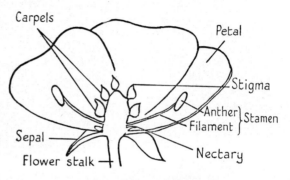

FLOWER PARTS OF A BUTTERCUP

Rose
(Rosaceae)

Orchid
(Orchidaceae)

Buttercup (Ranunculaceae)

Daisy
(Compositae)

Pea
(Leguminosae)

Cow Parsley
(Umbelliferae)

Iris
(Iridaceae)

Violet (Violaceae)

Lily (Liliaceae)

Wallflower
(Cruciferae)

COMMON FLOWER FAMILIES

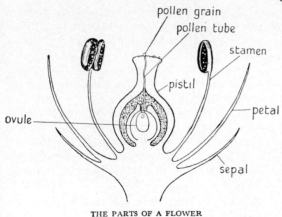

THE PARTS OF A FLOWER

Above the sepals and petals come those parts of the flower which are essential in reproduction. First, there are numerous 'stamens', or male reproductive organs, each consisting of a stalk-like filament and a head, called the 'anther'. The anthers contain compartments called 'pollen sacs' which, when they are ripe, contain the yellow pollen. Each pollen grain contains one male reproductive cell. At the top of the receptacle are many kidney-shaped 'carpels', each having a projecting beak or 'stigma' at the upper end. The lower, expanded part of the carpel is called the 'ovary', and contains the 'ovule' within which the egg, or female reproductive cell, is produced.

Most flowers are built on some such plan as this; but there are wide variations, not only in size, shape, and colour, but also in the numbers of the different parts. The Tulip, for instance, shows no distinction between sepals and petals, but has six brightly coloured floral leaves called 'perianth leaves'. In the Poppy there are only two sepals, while in the Lesser Celandine there are three. Petals are often entirely missing, a condition seen in the Willow flower. Sometimes, instead of being free, as in the Buttercup, the petals are joined to form a tube, as in the Primrose. In other flowers, such as those of the Pea family, the petals in the same flower may take on different shapes and have different uses.

In the stamens and carpels, too, there is great variation. Such flowers as the Deadnettle and Wallflower, instead of having an indefinite number of stamens and carpels, have a constant number. In flowers like the Hazel, Willow, and Poplar, the stamens and carpels are borne on separate flowers. Then again, in the Buttercup the stamens are carried on the receptacle, while in the Primrose the stamens are joined to the petals. There are similar variations amongst the carpels. In many flowers, as in the Buttercup, the number of carpels is indefinite, and they are all separate; in other flowers the number is constant, and often they are fused together. Thus, the Gooseberry has two carpels which are intimately joined, and the Primrose has five which are joined in a different way.

Flowering plants are classified into families according to these many differences. The basis of all flowers is, however, that they produce male and female reproductive cells which, after fusion, develop into the seeds from which new plants grow. All other parts of the flower are incidental to this fundamental process of sexual reproduction. (*See* REPRODUCTION OF PLANTS: *see also* INDEX, p. 63.)

FLY. The two-winged flies, of which the HOUSE-FLY (q.v.) is doubtless the best known, are an immense group of insects, over 5,000 species occurring in Great Britain. The front pair of wings is usually well developed for rapid flight, but the hindwings are reduced to a pair of stalked knobs called 'halteres' or balancers. The two halteres are clearly seen in the CRANE FLY (q.v.) or Daddy-long-legs; but in flies like the House-fly, each is covered over and hidden by a scale. During their life-history flies go through the four distinct stages of egg, larva, pupa, and imago or adult (*see* INSECTS).

Most flies lay their eggs in places suited to the habits of their larvae, which in most cases have to look after themselves. Some species, however, nourish their larvae internally, one at a time, sometimes until fully grown, when they are dropped and at once pupate. The KED, a common skin parasite on sheep, and the TSETSE FLY

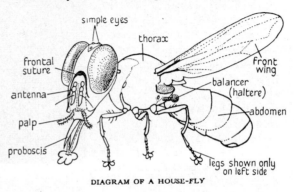

DIAGRAM OF A HOUSE-FLY

(qq.v.) of tropical Africa nourish their larvae in this way.

Fly larvae, many of which are commonly called 'maggots' and 'gentles', are legless. No other larvae in the insect world have such a variety of habits as those of the flies. Fly larvae may live in the water, underground, in the leaves, stems, or roots of plants; they may be active above ground, or live as internal or external parasites of other insects or of the higher animals. So many of the fly larvae living as parasites on man cause serious results that the special name of *myiasis* is used to include all the wounded conditions they produce. The varied habits of fly larvae are dealt with in the articles on the particular flies.

There are two ways in which pupation takes place. In one, the larval skin splits along the back, liberating the pupa. In the other, the adult larva, when it has stopped feeding, now a soft, white, legless grub, very large and blunt behind, but tapering to a narrow head, wriggles away from its food-supply, and soon becomes oval in shape, usually turning brown or reddish, and becoming hard in texture. The outer covering thus formed out of the larval skin is called a 'puparium', and the pupa is inside, generally immobile. In due course, after it has neatly removed the top or 'lid', the fly escapes. Many pupae not enclosed in puparia—aquatic pupae especially—are able to make considerable movements. The pupae of mosquitoes, for instance, swim vigorously.

One group of flies which pupates in a puparium has on the front of its face a narrow slit called the 'frontal suture'. This is in the shape of an inverted V or U, and passes upwards between the eyes and the antennae, bending over just above the latter. Traced into the head, this slit is found to lead into a closed sac. When the fly is about to escape from its puparium, this sac is forced 'inside-out' through the slit by fluid pressure in the head, forming a balloon-shaped structure in front of the head. This presses on the top of the puparium till the latter gives

way. Soon after the fly has escaped, the balloon is drawn back by muscles through the frontal suture into the head again, and is of no further use.

Though most flies are active by day, and especially in bright sunshine, their flight leads them to very different food-supplies. Many visit flowers for the nectar; others are blood-suckers, amongst them Mosquitoes, Gnats, Midges, Horse Flies, and Tsetse Flies, with mouth parts for piercing the skin as well as for sucking the blood. There are also many scavengers, such as House Flies and Blowflies.

See also Blowfly; Bristle Fly; Cheese Skipper; Crane Fly; Flesh Fly; Horse Fly; House Fly; Hover Fly; Humble-Bee Fly; Ked; Midge; Mosquito; Stable Fly; Tsetse Fly; Warble Fly.

FLY-CATCHERS. These are small Passerine or perching birds, feeding principally upon flying insects, which they catch on the wing. There are a number of species distributed over most countries of the Old World, including Australia, with a separate family found only in America. There are two British species, the Spotted Fly-catcher and the Pied Fly-catcher, which arrive

THE SPOTTED FLY-CATCHER TAKING A FLY TO THE NEST
Arthur Brook

in late April or early May to breed, and migrate farther south in September.

The Spotted Fly-catcher, which is spotted most when young, is an inconspicuous bird, quite common in all parts of Britain except the very north, and often seen in London parks. It has favourite perches on which it waits for insects, and from which it makes sudden little dashing flights to snap up its prey. It builds a neat little nest in a crevice in a wall, tree, or building, or in a creeper or shrub, and lays four to six greenish-white eggs clouded with rusty markings. The Pied Fly-catcher has black and white on the head and wings, so that it is more conspicuous; but it is far less common. It lays six to nine pale blue eggs, occasionally speckled with red.

The Fly-catchers of tropical and semi-tropical countries are much more showy. The Paradise Fly-catchers are found from Africa eastwards to Japan. The males of most of these have long streamers in the tail, and for part of the year the plumage is mainly white with a glossy blue crown. These birds are portrayed in many Chinese and Japanese paintings. In India are the lovely blue Niltavas. In Australia there are several species, including a Black and White Fly-catcher known as 'Willie Wagtail', the Flame-breasted 'Robin', and the gorgeously coloured Blue 'Wren', a small, long-tailed bird with purple and azure plumage. The little Black Fantail Fly-catcher of Australia builds a beautiful cup-shaped nest, often on a branch overhanging a stream. The nest, made of grass, strips of bark, and roots, is covered over with cobwebs, so that the whole thing looks like a knot of wood on the branch.

The King-bird belongs to the Tyrant Fly-catchers of Central and South America, and goes to the eastern states of the U.S.A. to breed. It is very bold in defence of its nest, fiercely attacking any other bird that comes near.

FLYING-FISHES. On any voyage across the ocean one is almost certain to see a shoal of Flying-fishes, and a very beautiful sight it is. These fishes, which are rather herring-like in shape, have very large wing-like, pectoral fins, and in some kinds large pelvic fins, too; so they are classed in two groups, popularly called two-winged and four-winged species. They are gliders, and do not fly by flapping their wings, as birds do. Generally they swim near the surface, and when they are attacked from below by Barracuta, Dolphin-fish, or other large enemies, they leap above the waves. As they leave the water they give a final flip of the tail (the lower part of the caudal fin is large for this purpose) which drives them high in the air, and then, spreading their fins wide like the wings of an aeroplane, they glide. There are many upward currents of air above the surface of the sea, due to the difference in temperature between the water and the atmosphere—and by skilfully taking advantage of these, the Flying-fish is able to glide along rapidly for a considerable distance.

The Flying-fish makes a sort of nest, too. The eggs, unlike those of so many oceanic fishes, are heavier than water and would sink were they not laid in a bunch of floating weed bound together with tough white threads. Since the SARGASSO SEA (q.v. Vol. III), a part of the western North Atlantic, has such abundant floating weeds, it is a favourite breeding-place for Flying-fish.

These familiar species are not the only fishes that fly, however; in tropical seas we find the fantastic Flying Gurnards—heavy-looking, bony headed creatures, with enormous, gaily coloured 'wings'; while one or two freshwater fishes have also learned to fly. The freshwater Flying-fishes are the CHARACINS (q.v.) from the Amazon region. They are, perhaps, more bird-like than any of the others, for they can flap their 'wings', having, like birds, a large keel for the support

FLYING FISHES TAKE TO THE AIR. *A. Fraser-Brunner*

of the huge pectoral muscles. In BIRDS (q.v.), however, the keel is on the breast-bone, while in these fishes it is part of the shoulder-girdle.

See also FLIGHT.
See also Vol. VI: FLYING-FISH FISHING.

FLYING FOX, *see* BAT.

FOOTMAN MOTH, *see* TIGER MOTH.

FORAMINIFERA, *see* PROTOZOA.

FOREST FLY, *see* KED.

FOX. This member of the Dog family is well known to those who enjoy FOX-HUNTING (q.v. Vol. IX), or to farmers and game-preservers who have suffered from its depredations (*see* PESTS, ANIMAL, Vol. VI). Foxes are related to WOLVES, DOGS, and JACKALS (qq.v.). Different species are to be found in most parts of the world, but not in Australia and New Zealand.

The most common fox generally is the Red Fox. The English Red Fox is reddish-brown, with a white belly and throat, a white tip to the tail, and black patches behind its ears. The North American Red Fox includes two colour varieties: a beautiful silver, and also a cross— a reddish-black fox, both much sought after by the fur-hunter, and bred by the fur-farmer (*see* FUR FARMING, Vol. VI). Another species is the Arctic fox, some of which remain bluish-grey the whole year round, while others turn white to suit their snowy surroundings during the winter. The smallest-known fox is the beautiful little sand-coloured Fennec Fox of the Saharan Desert, which is distinguished by its large ears.

THE BLUE ARCTIC FOX OF ALASKA AT THE ENTRANCE TO HIS DEN. *E. O. Hoppé*

Foxes hunt mainly by night, and hide during the day in holes or burrows, called 'earths' (often taken over from rabbits or badgers), in ravines, or among thick undergrowth. They are usually silent; but on a winter night the yapping scream of the vixen or the yelping bark of a dog-fox may often be heard. They hunt hares, rabbits, ground birds (particularly partridges), and frequently make raids on poultry-yards; they will carry off young lambs, and have even been known to kill a pony foal. When food is scarce they will eat rats, worms, beetles, frogs, fish, and almost any other animal, dead or alive.

All foxes are very intelligent, as every fox-hunter knows, and their cunning is proverbial. They use a number of ingenious devices for concealing from the hunter their strong scent, which is secreted in a gland beneath the tail. They will double back on their tracks, leap sideways, climb trees, take to water, mingle with sheep, roll in muck, and even put up another fox to side-track their pursuers. They use as varied a number of devices in their own hunting. Rabbits have often been deceived by watching a fox gambolling and rolling over and over with an apparent innocence of intention. The rabbits, reassured, draw near to watch—whereupon the fox pounces. Foxes can swim well, can climb trees, and can get out of almost any enclosure.

Except for the Fennec Foxes, which are social, foxes live solitary lives, save during the breeding season. Several dog-foxes will often fight fiercely over a vixen. They breed in early spring, and generally have a litter of four to six cubs.

FRIGATE BIRD. This ocean bird belongs to the same order as the CORMORANT, GANNET, and PELICAN (qq.v.)—all lovers of water. Frigate Birds inhabit the open sea, the Great Frigate Bird ranging the warmer regions of the Atlantic, Pacific, and Indian Oceans, and the Lesser Frigate Bird confining itself mainly to the Indian Ocean. They come to land in order to roost in trees and to breed on inaccessible cliff ledges or on the shores of little-inhabited islands; but they spend much of their time on the wing, making long, powerful, graceful flights, soaring to such heights that they have been called 'sons of the sun'. In build they are well fitted for such a life. They have slender bodies and very short legs, but long pointed wings and a long, deeply forked tail. Their hooked beaks are long and powerful,

A FEMALE FRIGATE BIRD FROM CHRISTMAS ISLAND IN THE PACIFIC. *C. A. Gibson-Hill*

and they have a remarkable pouch of scarlet skin beneath the throat, which they can inflate with air to a considerable size.

Frigate Birds catch fish for themselves on the surface of the sea; but they also depend largely for food on attacking other birds, such as Gannets and Terns, and making them disgorge their catch. Gannets returning from a feeding-ground in the evening will be assailed by two or three Frigate Birds, who will chase them relentlessly until the exhausted Gannets disgorge some of their fish. The Frigate Birds immediately dive for the morsel, catching it in mid-air. Sometimes they will seize their victims and shake them to make them disgorge.

FRILLED LIZARD, *see* AGAMA.

FRITILLARY. BUTTERFLIES. These orange butterflies, which generally live in woods, have black markings on the upperside of their wings, and often silver patterns on the underside. They belong, with the ADMIRALS, TORTOISE-SHELLS, and PURPLE EMPERORS (qq.v.), to the family Nymphalidae, which use only four legs for walking, their small forelegs being tucked up against their bodies. The larvae have small heads and long, thornlike spines. The pupae hang by tail-hooks only, and have sharp spines supposed to protect them from injury should they strike anything as they swing in the wind. They often have silver and gold spots, on account of which the name 'chrysalis', meaning 'golden', came to be used for the pupae of all butterflies.

The Pearl-bordered, probably the commonest of all the British Fritillaries, can be seen in most southern, dry, wooded districts in May and early June. It has seven border 'pearls',

and two other silver spots on the underside of its hindwings. The Small Pearl-bordered occurs more commonly in wet woods, and even marshes, in the same locality, and is the only Fritillary found in the north of Scotland. The two are often difficult to distinguish; but the undersides of the smaller species are more richly coloured and have more silver spots, and it emerges a little later than the larger species. The females of both these butterflies lay their eggs on the leaves of Dog-violet, or on pieces of trailing bracken near-by, and the black, spiny caterpillars hibernate amongst the fallen leaves.

The Silver-washed, the largest British Fritillary, has silver stripes and spots on the underside of its wings, the male usually being a lighter orange than the typical female. The variety *valezina*, restricted to females, is dark olive-green, and is fairly frequent in the New Forest, but rare elsewhere. The females lay their eggs singly in the crevices of tree trunks, where the young caterpillars hibernate all the winter, subsisting only on their egg-shell, which they eat when they hatch. When the weather turns warm in the spring, they drop to the ground in search of violets. They are purplish-brown, with two yellowish stripes along the back—these divert attention from their real shape and make them very difficult to find. The butterflies emerge in July, and may be seen in many of the larger woods in the southern counties, as also in Wales and Ireland. They feed freely at bramble flowers.

The Marsh Fritillary has a misleading name, as it occurs as much on hilltops as in marshy meadows. The colouring is very varied, no

MALE SILVER-WASHED FRITILLARY ON BRAMBLE FLOWERS *S. Beaufoy, F.R.P.S.*

other British butterfly having so many distinctive forms for the localities it frequents. The females lay large batches of yellow eggs on the under-side of scabious leaves, and these take much longer to hatch than most butterflies' eggs—nearly a month instead of ten days or a fortnight. The black, spiny caterpillars live together in thick webs, which they weave amongst the leaves and grass stems. They hibernate when about half-grown, and come out again in the first warm days of spring. When disturbed, they all jerk up their heads—this kind of collective movement being common among caterpillars which have a disagreeable taste, for it serves to remind would-be enemies of previous unpleasant experiences.

The Heath Fritillary is another butterfly with an even more misleading name, as it occurs only in woods, and never on heaths. It is easily distinguished from the other Fritillaries in having no silver or black dots on the underside of its wings. The tiny, black, shiny caterpillars hibernate in little groups of five or six in dead leaves on the ground. Their favourite food-plant is cow-wheat, a tiny yellow-flowered weed which grows best in the newly cut-down parts of a wood. The butterfly breeds only where its food-plant grows, and so is continually changing its headquarters. It is now restricted to Kent, Devon, and Cornwall, except for colonies in Essex and Sussex where it has recently been re-introduced.

The Glanville Fritillary breeds in the British Isles only in the Isle of Wight, where it is found mostly in sheltered spots on steep cliffs in May and June. The black, spiny caterpillars have reddish-brown heads and feed on plantain. They weave webs and live beneath them in large colonies throughout the winter, starting to feed, still in colonies, in the spring. When they have cast off several coats and are in the last skin, they begin to feed singly, nibbling the narrow-leaved plantain leaves which grow between the shingle within a few feet of high tide. They are named after a Lady Glanville, who, in the 17th century, was accused of lunacy because she collected butterflies!

The Dark Green Fritillary is a fast-flying butterfly, seen on the wing in July. Unlike most Fritillaries, it seems to prefer hill-sides and rough wild country to woods, a fine large and dark race occurring in the Hebrides. On the underside of its wings it has a regular pattern of silver spots on a greenish-brown background. The female lays her eggs on violet plants, especially those growing under bushes. The caterpillars hatch in about a fortnight, and at once go into hibernation, without feeding. The High Brown, usually found in sunny glades and ridings of woods, looks very like the Dark Green when seen on the wing. The undersides of their wings are, however, slightly different, the High Brown having a row of reddish-brown spots, with silver eyes along the edge. Like the Dark Green, the female lays her eggs amongst the leaves of violet plants, but they do not hatch until the following spring. The chrysalis of both the Dark Green and High Brown Fritillaries is sheltered in a tent made of leaves. Both the High Brown and the Silver-washed Fritillaries have the habit of resting in trees overnight and on dull days.

The Queen of Spain is a rare immigrant to this country from the Continent, where it is common. It has been known to breed in the British Isles, but it cannot survive the winter, and so dies off until fresh immigrants arrive. It has a number of large silver spots on the underside of its wings.

The Duke of Burgundy (q.v.) resembles Fritillaries in colour, but belongs to another family.

FROG. It is easy to distinguish frogs from Toads (q.v.) in England, for the frogs have a smooth, slimy skin, while the toads have a dry and warty one. But there is also a difference in the skeleton, and this distinguishes them all over the world. In frogs, the two front halves of the shoulder-girdle meet in the midline and form a firm bar; in the toads, they overlap. Strictly speaking, therefore, all those with a firm bar should be called frogs, and all the others, toads —and some naturalists have tried to apply this definition. But popular names do not grow up in that way, and the terms 'frog' and 'toad' are often interchanged. For instance, the Green Tree Frog of Europe, with its smooth and slimy skin, is structurally a toad. On the other hand, there is a large genus of Tree Frogs in Asia (such as Wallace's Flying Frog) which is externally very similar to the Tree Frog of Europe, but anatomically is a frog. The term 'frog' is much more often mis-applied than the term 'toad'.

The Common Frog is found throughout most of Europe and northern Asia, and its spawn and tadpoles are familiar to everyone. Most of its

A TREE FROG

life is spent on land, where in fields and gardens it is most useful in destroying insects and slugs. During the spring the croaking of frogs may be heard in ponds and ditches.

Closely related to the Common Frog is the Edible Frog, which is widely distributed over the whole of Europe, but in England is restricted to a few places in the east and south of the country (it can be found within a few miles of London). It may not be a native of Britain, but was possibly introduced by French monks several hundred years ago to add to their diet. Many colonies have been imported from Europe in the past 100 years and released in southern England; but most of them have disappeared. The Edible Frog is green to bronzy-brown on top, with black spots and three more or less distinct stripes down the back, and a green stripe flanked by two yellowish ones along the spine. The general colours, however, are very variable. In the breeding season the males can be very noisy; when croaking, they inflate sacs on either side of the head. Only the hind legs of the frog are eaten. The flesh, which is white and is served up fried, tastes like young chicken. Another well-known European frog is the Fire-bellied Frog, of which there are two species. They live in hilly districts, and are about $1\frac{1}{2}$ to 2 inches in length. Their general colour is dark grey to blackish, except for the belly and the under part of the limbs, which are conspicuously marked with red in one species, and with yellow in the other. When first caught, these frogs adopt a peculiar threatening attitude, throwing back their heads and turning their limbs upwards so that the bright colours of the under parts are shown.

The name Tree Frog covers a large number of frogs and toads which live in trees. They have adhesive pads to their fingers and toes, with which they cling to the bark or leaves. Many of them are green in colour. One large family of Tree Frogs, known as the Hylidae, which in structure are really toads, are to be found all over the world, and are represented in Europe by the well-known Green Tree Frog. Another large family, the Rhacophoridae, are true frogs, and are restricted to tropical Asia and tropical Africa. Most of the Hylidae spawn in the water like ordinary frogs; but the Rhacophoridae make 'nests', whipping the gelatinous substance which surrounds the eggs into a foam so as to enclose them completely. This mass is then laid over the water. The early larval stages are passed in the foam; but after a time, the wriggling tadpoles drop into the water, and then continue their development in the usual way. The European Tree Frog has been imported into England on several occasions: one colony has now lived for over 20 years in the Isle of Wight, and breeds there.

The best-known Flying Frog, Wallace's Flying Frog, is a species of Tree Frog of the genus Rhacophorus. It is some 3 inches in length, has a green back, and large black webs between the fingers and toes. It spends the greater part of its life at the tops of high trees, where, with its webbed digits expanded, it can glide through the air from one tree to another. Wallace's Frog lives in Borneo; but there are several other species, with equally broad webs, found in other parts of the Malayan region. The Hairy Frog is a species found in West Africa. The flanks and thighs of the male are covered with blackish growths, resembling hairs, which provide an additional means of breathing during the breeding season.

A FLYING FROG

The name 'Bull Frog' is applied indiscriminately to many frogs with a particularly noisy croak.

FROG-HOPPER. On the stems and leaves of many plants during the summer months a white frothy substance, called 'cuckoo-spit', can often be seen. In the middle of this is a little white grub, rather lively if disturbed, and possessing the beginnings of wings. This is the 'nymph' or early form of a plant-sucking bug called a Frog-hopper. After it has grown up it no longer remains in the froth, but sits on a leaf or stem with the front of its body raised, looking absurdly like a very small frog. If alarmed, it will jump smartly out of harm's way. Most Frog-hoppers are small, and are coloured in various shades of brown and yellow; but one British kind is about half an inch long, and is brilliantly arrayed in black and scarlet.

The nymphs do not leap like the adults. They are reasonably safe while bathed in the froth, though enemies, such as wasps, have been seen to pull them out. If removed during hot sunshine, they dry very quickly and die. The liquid required for the froth is passed out from the hind end of the body, and blown into foam by air forced out of a special air-chamber.

See also BUGS.

FRUITS. 1. The botanist uses the term fruit in a different sense from the housewife or greengrocer. To a botanist, Rhubarb is simply a swollen leaf-stalk, the Strawberry is not a true fruit but a collection of fruits, whereas the Tomato and the Peapod with its peas are true fruits. The fruit is the complete structure formed by the ovary and neighbouring parts of the flower after fertilization has taken place (*see* REPRODUCTION OF PLANTS); and it contains the seeds, which develop from the ovules after fertilization.

The fruits of flowering plants take on many shapes and sizes, and may be formed from one carpel or from many. Each fruit may contain one or a number of seeds, which may be distributed direct from the plant or, more often, shed from the fruit after it has left the plant. Many fruits are modified in structure to ensure that they and their seeds are widely distributed (*see* SEEDS).

Fruits are of three kinds—simple, aggregate, and composite. Simple fruits, such as those of the Sweet Pea and Poppy, are formed from one carpel or from a number of carpels joined to form a single structure. Aggregate fruits, of which the Buttercup is a good example, are formed when each carpel gives rise to a fruitlet, and the fruit is therefore made up of a number or aggregate of fruitlets. Composite fruits, of which there are not many, are formed, not from a single flower, but from a number of flowers, as in the Fig, Pine-apple, Mulberry, and Hop.

Aggregate of fruits (Buttercup)

It is convenient to divide simple fruits into two groups according to their condition when ripe: dry fruits, and succulent or fleshy fruits. Dry fruits can be either 'dehiscent' or 'indehiscent', according to whether they possess a mechanism allowing them to open to distribute their seeds or not. (*See* SEEDS, Section 2.)

Composite fruit (Mulberry)

2. DRY FRUITS. (*a*) 'Achenes' are fruits which are dry, indehiscent, and one-seeded. In the Buttercup, for instance, each carpel ripens after fertilization into a separate fruitlet, the whole collection of fruits being described as an aggregate of achenes. After fertilization, the carpellary wall undergoes no special change, so that each fruit is simply a single seed surrounded by the hardened carpellary wall; and before it can germinate, the fruit wall, or 'pericarp', must be ruptured to allow the radicle and plumule to emerge.

Other examples of achenes are found in the Dock, Sorrel, and also in the Rose-hip, where the receptacle is red and cup-shaped and encloses the achenes. The fruit of the Strawberry,

Achene (Rose hip)

Samara, Winged fruits (Sycamore)

whether the cultivated variety or the Common Wild Strawberry, is a greatly swollen, red, fleshy receptacle, bearing scattered achenes (the pips).

(b) 'Samaras' (Winged Fruits) are achenes in which the hardened carpellary wall grows into a long, flattened, wing-like structure, adapted for dispersal of the fruit by wind. A good example of the samara is the fruit of the Ash, which hangs from the tree in large bunches after fertilization. The fruit of the Elm might be described as a double samara, while in the Sycamore two and sometimes three samaras fuse slightly at their swollen bases.

Nut (Hazel)

(c) 'Nuts' are dry, in-dehiscent, one-seeded fruits, closely related to the achene. They may or may not be formed from one carpel. Unlike the achene, the carpel-lary wall of the nut be-comes hard and woody. The term 'nut' is usually applied to all large or hard-coated achenes, although some are not nuts at all: for example, the Brazil-nut and Horse-Chestnut are seeds; the Walnut, Almond, and Coco-nut are 'drupes'. Among true nuts are the Hazel, Oak, Beech, and Sweet Chestnut.

In the Hazel or the Filbert (which is a culti-vated Hazel), the shell is the hardened car-pellary wall and the kernel is the seed. The nut lies in a large green leafy cup formed from the small leaves immediately behind the flower, but which have persisted after fertilization. In the Beech and Oak the nut is formed from three carpels, but only one seed develops. In the Beech and Sweet Chestnut the nuts are com-pletely enclosed in a cupule formed of bracts. It is easy to see that fruits, and not seeds, are enclosed, because the remains of the style and

Horse - chestnut fruit

Nut enclosed in a cupule (Sweet Chestnut)

stigma can be seen on the nut. In the case of the Horse Chestnut and Sweet Chestnut, the brown-coloured bodies, which superficially re-semble each other, are in the former case seeds and in the latter case fruits.

(d) 'Schizocarp' is a dry, indehiscent fruit formed from two or more carpels which, when ripe, splits into portions, each portion containing one seed. The schizocarp of the Mallow or Hollyhock is a stout ring which splits into wedge-like segments. The schizocarp of the Geranium is formed from five joined carpels, and splits at the base into five one-seeded portions.

(e) 'Caryopsis' is the characteristic grain or fruit of all grasses and cereals, such as Oats, Maize, Wheat, and Barley. It is a dry, in-dehiscent fruit, in which the pericarp, or fruit wall, is so closely joined to the seed-coat that the seed cannot be taken out of its case. What appears to be the 'seed' of cereals, therefore, is really the fruit. In many cases, the fruit or grain is covered by the persistent bract which forms a husk around it. Cereal grains will live in a dormant condition up to perhaps about 100 years, though claims that 'mummy wheat' grains taken from the tombs of Ancient Egypt are still alive have been proved to be without foundation.

(f) 'Follicles', such as the fruits of the Marsh Marigold, Monkshood, and Larkspur, are one of the simplest kinds of dry, dehiscent or split-ting fruit. Each follicle is formed from a single, free carpel, containing several ovules. When the seeds are ripe the follicle splits along the whole length of the inner seam which bears the seeds, so that the seeds are exposed for distribution. The aggregate fruits of many members of the Buttercup family consist of collections of follicles.

(g) 'Pods' or legumes are dry, dehiscent fruits, like follicles in that they are formed from a single, free carpel, containing several ovules which later become the seeds; but un-like follicles, the pod, when ripe, splits, not only along the inside seam, but also along the outside seam or midrib. The pod is the characteristic fruit of the Pea family.

(h) 'Siliquas', the characteristic fruit of the Wallflower family, are dry, dehiscent fruits, which are formed from two carpels. The

Pod or Legume (Pea)

Siliqua
(Wallflower)

Capsule
(Poppy)

Scarlet Pimpernel
'Pyxidium'

siliqua appears to be two-chambered, because of the growth of a false partition between the two carpels. The fruit is long and cylindrical, and when ripe, the two parts split from the bottom upwards, exposing the seeds, which are attached to the false partition. In some members of the Wall-flower family—Honesty, for instance—the fruit is short and flat. When the fruit splits the seeds are left exposed on the oval, flattened, false parti-tion, which looks like silvery parchment.

(*i*) 'Capsules' are a form of dry, dehiscent fruit, which show many variations. They are many-seeded, formed from two or more carpels, and may be one-valved or many-valved. Although they vary greatly in the way they split, most of them split the whole length of the capsule, the number of splits corresponding to the number of carpels that formed the 'valves' or segments. The Iris, for example, splits along the midribs into three valves; the capsules of Willow and Poplar split into two valves, and the Willow-herb into four. Many capsules which split lengthwise split down only a little way, and are said to open by teeth. These teeth are only open in dry weather, remaining closed on wet days. The number of teeth is either the same, or twice as many, as the number of carpels. The Primrose capsule, for instance, opens by five teeth and the Campion by ten, both fruits being formed from five carpels.

Capsules sometimes open by pores. This is seen in the Poppy and Snapdragon, where a number of pores are formed by a breaking away and bending back of tissues at the top of the ripe fruit. In the capsule of the Canterbury Bell and other Campanulas, however, large pores are formed at the base of the fruit. Some capsules split crossways—a good example of this being the fruit of the Scarlet Pimpernel, which looks like a little box and is called a 'pyxidium'. The whole top of the capsule comes off readily, like a little lid, exposing the seeds attached to the central core. The cone-shaped fruit of the Plan-tain is also a pyxidium.

3. FLESHY FRUITS. (*a*) 'Berries' are one of the simplest types of fleshy or succulent fruits, in which the whole of the fruit wall is pulpy or fleshy. The seeds, which are usually hard, are embedded in the pulp. Common berries are the Tomato, Grape, Currant, Banana, Orange, Lemon, Grape-fruit, Gooseberry, Pomegranate, and Cucumber.

The Tomato is formed by the union of two carpels. When ripe, the fruit wall, a mass of tissue with a thin tough skin, becomes thick and juicy, and a sticky fluid is given off into the ovary cavity. The Tomato is a native of South America, first brought to Europe by the Spaniards, and originally called the 'love-apple'. As a vegetable, it has only been popular in Great Britain for about 70 years. The Grape is also a berry, formed from two joined carpels, in which the fruit-wall becomes fleshy. Dried currants, raisins, sultanas, and muscatels are all dried forms of Grapes and are, therefore, berries. True Currants, black, white, and red, are the berries of small deciduous shrubs. The Banana is also a berry, though highly cultivated Bananas, which are now successfully propagated by cuttings, do not develop seeds, the only sign of them being a brown dustiness sometimes to be seen in the centre of the fruit.

Oranges, Lemons, and Grape-fruit, all closely related tropical plants, produce berries, each of which is composed of six or more fused carpels, in which the fruit-wall is divided into a tough outer skin containing many oil-glands, and a fleshy inner part. In the Gooseberry and Pome-granate, the pulp or ed-ible portion of the berry is derived largely (in the case of the Gooseberry)

Berry
(Gooseberry cross-section)

Pericarp
Seeds

or entirely (in the Pomegranate) from the outer coats of the seeds. The Date is a most interesting berry, easily mistaken for a drupe. The stone or seed of a Date has no kernel, as has the stone of a drupe, but is hard all through, because the reserve food is stored up as cellulose. This seed

Drupe (Plum)   Drupe (Walnut)

is completely surrounded by the fleshy fruit-wall.

(*b*) 'Drupes' (Stone fruits) are succulent, one-seeded fruits, examples of which are the Plum, Cherry, Peach, Apricot, Coco-nut, Walnut, and Almond. In the drupe the fruit is formed from either one carpel or three joined carpels. Whereas in the berry the whole fruit-wall or pericarp becomes fleshy, in the drupe the fruit-wall swells and becomes divided into three distinct layers—the 'epicarp' or outer skin; the 'mesocarp' or middle region, usually a thick, fleshy and often edible portion, and the 'endocarp', the hard inner part or 'stone', which encloses and protects the seed.

The Walnut is not easily recognizable as a drupe, because what we crack to eat is the stone only. In green pickled walnuts, however, the drupe-like character of the fruit is clear. The fruit is formed from two fused carpels, and consists of a thin epicarp, a fleshy, green mesocarp, and a woody endocarp (or stone), containing the seed. As it ripens, the two large seed-leaves or cotyledons, which form the mass of the kernel, become divided by a thin partition, and sometimes also by thin cross-partitions. The Almond is another example of a fruit of which the portion used for food is only the seed. The actual drupe is composed of a fruit-wall divided into three layers—an epicarp, which is green and velvety, a tough, downy mesocarp, and the stony shell or endocarp. There are two types of almond—the sweet, which is produced from the pink-flowered almond plant, and the bitter, which is produced from the white-flowered plant. The bitterness of the latter is due to the presence of a complex organic chemical. The Coco-nut, too, has its epicarp and mesocarp removed before it is offered for sale in the shops, and

Collection of drupes (Blackberry)

we see only the woody endocarp with the contained seeds—though traces of the mesocarp occasionally remain as fibrous tufts, for here the mesocarp is not fleshy but fibrous.

(*c*) 'Pomes'. In the Apple, the Pear, and other fruits derived from some members of the Rose family, the succulent 'fruit' called a Pome is formed, not from the ovary, but from the greatly swollen stem or receptacle. The true fruit is the membranous core. The ovary of the flower is formed from five fused carpels, and is intimately fused with the surrounding receptacle. After fertilization of the flower, this receptacle swells greatly to form the fleshy part of the fruit.

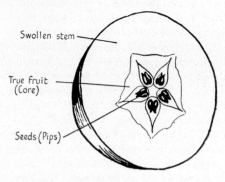

Pome (Apple)

The carpels themselves become tough and form the core, which contains the small brown pips or seeds. Among other pomes are the Quince, Medlar, Rowan (Mountain Ash), Cotoneaster, and Hawthorn.

(*d*) Pine-apple. This is an interesting 'fruit' because it is not really a fruit at all. It is a swollen stem, where the fleshy axis and the flowers have all fused together. In the ripened 'fruit' the diamond-shaped areas on the surface mark the remains of the fertilized flowers. Seeds are rarely formed. At the top of the stem is a tuft of green foliage leaves. The name 'pine-apple' was given by Spanish explorers, who found it in America and thought the 'fruit' resembled a pine-cone.

FUNGI. Just as some people are revolted by such creatures as spiders and centipedes, other people shrink from members of the plant world called Fungi. The reason is probably that, lacking green colouring-matter, or 'chlorophyll', fungi are often unhealthy-looking; and they sometimes have an unpleasant smell. Some people are repelled by these plants, too, because they associate them with death and decay: the word fungus brings to mind such unpleasant thoughts as dry-rot in furniture and poisonous toadstools. Not all fungi are harmful, however—indeed many people will always be grateful to the mould fungus from which the valuable drug, penicillin, is produced. The common fungus, YEAST (q.v.), plays an essential part in making bread rise. Many fungi are edible, in addition to the well-known MUSHROOMS (q.v. Vol. VI), morels, and truffles.

Truffles grow only in a few localities in Great Britain, and are therefore expensive in this country; but on the Continent they are cultivated and are a popular food. A curious feature of truffles is that the edible part, as well as the rest of the plant, grows underground. To know where to dig for them, farmers who cultivate truffles keep pigs, which can smell the plants and root them out with their snouts from under the soil. Years ago, a certain variety of dog was bred for the same purpose, even in Britain.

Morels, used for food for thousands of years, and now usually dried and used for flavouring, have, when they are fresh, brownish-yellow caps and short white stems, grooved at the base. The commonest morels are found in spring-time in hedges or garden borders. They seem to like ground which has been disturbed or burnt, and have especially flourished on bombed or shelled areas in France. At one time in Germany, countrywomen had to be stopped from burning

land in order to encourage the growth of morels. The morel is the only fungus which the Indian Moslems will eat, all others being considered impure food.

Among the other edible fungi are the Chantarelle, the Blewit, the Shaggy Ink Cap, the Giant and Common Puff-Ball, and the Boletus. The Boletus is much prized in Russia, and was always sought after at the great fungus market which used to be held in Moscow during the first three days of Lent, and which was attended by dealers from all parts of Europe. All these edible fungi are quite distinct in appearance, and not at all likely to be confused with poisonous species.

Probably the most valuable function of fungi, however, is the work done by those which are SAPROPHYTES (q.v.)—that is, plants which get their nutrition from dead organic matter. By causing decay, these plants rid the world of the useless remains of dead animals and plants, which would otherwise accumulate to such an extent that they would interfere seriously with the life of succeeding generations.

It has to be admitted, however, that of the 50,000 different fungi known, many are our enemies. Among the smaller ones are the MOULDS (q.v.), which form delicate lace-work on the surface of moist substances, such as bread, jam, cheese, and leather. Others live as PARASITES (q.v.) on living plants and animals, and often cause serious diseases. For example, it has been stated that nearly half a million pounds of

SPECIES OF BRITISH FUNGI
Left, Puff-balls. *Right, Amanita mappa,* a fungus of the Death Cap type. *Harry Meyer*

Fly Toadstool
A. R. Thompson

Shaggy Caps or Lawyers' Wigs
Harry Meyer

Jew's Ear Fungus
Eric J. Hosking, F.R.P.S.

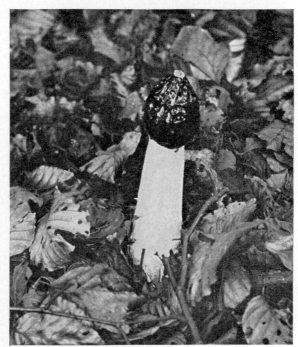

Stinkhorn Fungus
A. R. Thompson

SPECIES OF BRITISH FUNGI

oranges imported from Palestine to England used to be lost every year because of the work of a mould fungus. The failure of the potato crop in Ireland in 1846, which led to the death of so many thousands, was due to a fungus disease called potato blight. All the main foods of the world, such as rice, wheat, oats, barley, and millet, are subject to attacks by fungal diseases, and so also are crops like fruit and timber. These diseases are so serious that almost every country has laws dealing with the introduction of plants from other countries, and with the notification and treatment of disease (*see* Fungus Diseases, Vol. VI).

Many fungi are mildly poisonous, but only one British species, the Death Cap, is deadly poisonous. This fungus is common in woods and adjoining pastures in late summer and early autumn. In its earliest stages it looks much like an egg half-buried in the soil, but, as the cap emerges, it flattens out and takes on a characteristic olive or yellowish-green, with a darker centre. The white stem is often tinged with green, and has a well-marked, large, white or greenish ring. When fresh, the flesh is practically tasteless and without smell, but becomes fetid as it decays. The Death Cap is responsible for over 90 % of the recorded cases of fungus poisoning, more than 50 % of them being fatal.

Closely related to the Death Cap, but not nearly so poisonous, is the beautiful Fly Agaric, the typical toadstool of children's stories and pictures. The sticky cap of the Fly Agaric is scarlet or orange-red, shiny, and dotted with thick white or yellowish wart-like patches. It is common in woodlands in autumn, especially under birches and pines. When chopped up in sugar or milk, the fungus is used as a trap for flies, and is still commonly used for this purpose in Poland, Czechoslovakia, and Roumania. There are other poisonous fungi in Britain, including the mildly poisonous yellow staining

mushroom which is easily mistaken for the edible mushroom. When bruised, its skin turns a brownish-yellow. Many fungi, poisonous to man, can be safely eaten by animals. Rabbits, for example, are not usually affected even by the Death Cap, while slugs actually thrive on it.

Among the larger fungi are the familiar mushrooms and toadstools which are found in meadows and damp woods. The well-known fairy rings are sometimes made by the Fairy-ring Mushroom or Champignon, which is more delicious than the common Edible Mushroom and, though not common in Great Britain, is eaten a good deal in Italy and France. Most fairy rings are, however, caused by poisonous toadstools. The rings are formed by the outward growth of the fungal threads, which spread rather as ripples spread when a stone is thrown into a pond. The deeper colour of the grass inside the ring is due to the presence of the decaying fungal threads, which fertilize the soil. At a certain time, the young threads at the edge of the rings throw up the fruiting bodies (the mushrooms or toadstools themselves) to form a circle. Some fairy rings are said to be 300 or 400 years old.

Other interesting fungi are the conspicuous brackets projecting from the trunks of trees which they have doomed to death and decay. One of the most common of these is the Dryad's Saddle. The puff-balls, too, which pour out clouds of spores when they are ripe, are also fungi. The Giant Puff-ball, which sometimes appears on lawns and meadows, often attains the size of a football in a few days.

Fungi reproduce themselves, not by flowers and seeds, but asexually by single-celled spores. They also reproduce by 'vegetative propagation' —in other words, part of the white fibrous matter called the 'spawn' breaks off from the parent plant and forms an independent plant (*see* Reproduction of Plants).

G

GADFLY, *see* HORSE-FLY.

GALL-WASP. During the summer months, bright red and yellow growths, usually called oak-apples, may be found upon our oak-trees. They look like fruit, but anyone who has tasted them has found them 'bitter as gall'. When an oak-apple is cut open, it is found to contain several small, whitish grubs, each in a little cavity of its own. In late summer the grubs turn into pupae, and from these emerge insects, which tunnel through the substance of the oak-apple to the open air. These Gall-wasps, as they are called, are brown and about a twelfth of an inch long. The males have two pairs of wings; the females are wingless, and have a pointed structure at the end of the abdomen, which is an 'ovipositor' or egg-laying organ.

Men were for long puzzled to know how the maggots got into the oak-apples. The way the adult Gall-wasp comes out later in the year is quite clear, but there is no way in or out earlier in the summer. In the days before we were sure that all living things were produced by a parent, and in no other way, many animals were thought to spring 'from corruption' or out of vegetable matter—and Gall-wasps were quoted as examples. The following is, however, what really happens. The females, having mated, travel down the tree until they reach the root, which they puncture in a number of places, placing an egg in each. Around each puncture grows a round, hard, and woody 'gall', inside which is a single maggot, hatched from one of the eggs. These galls grow throughout the autumn and, as they are often close together, they may merge with one another. The insect inside each bores its way out sometime during winter or early spring. It looks very different from the one that laid the egg: it is larger, brown and black, always a female, and has a longer ovipositor. Before the buds have burst, it has crawled up the tree, bored into the buds, and laid a number of eggs in each puncture. Around these punctures grow the oak-apples of the following summer, with their numerous inhabitants.

Another very well-known oak-gall is the marble-gall, which is about the size of a marble, almost completely spherical, brown, and very hard on the outside. Each contains a single maggot, and this grows into a brown, winged Gall-wasp that is always female. This gall has only been known in England since about 1830, when it was first found in Devonshire; but since then it has spread all over the country. A common gall on the rose-tree is the pincushion-gall, which is attached to its stem. It is reddish, with a mossy appearance, and inside it is a series of hard kernels containing the grubs of a Gall-wasp. Both males and females occur in these galls.

Galls grow on many different plants, varying very much in shape; but each particular kind is produced by, and for the advantage of, a particular species of parasite that lives within it. The three species already mentioned are members of the large family of Gall-wasps; but many other insects, such as APHIDES (q.v.), as well as other creatures, produce plant-galls. The larvae of the small, often minute, gnat-like insects we call Gall-midges, live within swellings on a great variety of plants, the galling of the plant occurring in the buds, fruit, leaves, stem, or root, according to the species of midge. One of our best known Gall-midges is the Pear-midge, which is very destructive indeed to the young fruit.

The larvae of some species of Gall-midge have

OAK-APPLE-GALL　　　　ROSE-PINCUSHION-GALL

two ovaries, one on each side of the body. These produce from five to seventeen larvae inside the body, which feed upon the parent tissues until they have destroyed them. They then eat their way out through the dead skin, and continue to grow. Each of these may breed in the same way, bringing about its own destruction—and so on for many generations extending over a period of 2 or 3 years. But in the end, there arises a generation of larvae that grow normally, and ultimately become midges.

See also INSECTS.

See also Vol. VI: INSECT PESTS.

GANNET (Solan Goose). These are large, somewhat goose-like, white sea-birds with straight, sharp-pointed bills, long wings with black wing-quills, and wedge-shaped tails. They belong to the same order as the CORMORANT, PELICAN, and FRIGATE BIRD (qq.v.). They are to be found in great numbers, especially on the west coasts of Ireland and Scotland, in the Orkneys and Hebrides, and on the shores of North America. They sometimes range as far south as the tropics in the winter, but breed farther north. The Gannets on the Bass Rock at the mouth of the Firth of Forth have often been described. The Boobies, the Gannets of the southern seas, also breed in vast numbers on rocky islands.

The Common or Northern Gannet is the largest and most powerful flier of all British sea-birds. All round our coasts, the Gannet may be watched in spring, summer, and autumn, patrolling the seas. It is most at home on the sea or in the air, rarely coming to land except during the nesting season. It can often be seen dropping like a stone from a height to dive after a fish, which it catches with its beak. The Gannet is equipped for diving with air-sacs on either side of its neck, which are inflated before the dive. Also it has no external nostrils. The bird rests for a few seconds after the dive, then shakes itself, and flies off low above the surface, mounting gradually and gracefully into the air, ready to dive again. Gannets feed almost entirely on fish, and cause great devastation on the shoals of herrings.

GANNET NESTING COMMUNITY ON THE ISLAND OF GRASSHOLME OFF THE PEMBROKESHIRE COAST OF WALES
C. A. Gibson-Hill

CAPE GANNET FROM BIRD ISLAND, SOUTH AFRICA
C. A. Gibson-Hill

The Gannets breed in colonies on islands off the coast, sometimes on ledges and precipitous cliffs. The nests are made of seaweed and any rubbish available, and usually only one egg is laid—a pale blue with a whitish, chalky covering. At birth the young are naked, but they soon grow a covering of white down. This is replaced by a dark brown plumage with white-spotted feathers. The adult white plumage is not fully assumed until the birds are 4 or 5 years old. Young Gannets grow slowly, being nearly 3 months old before they take their first flight, to which they are forced by hunger—for their parents have by then deserted them.

GARFISH. This is a long-bodied fish, perhaps reaching 6 feet in length. It has both jaws lengthened to form a slender beak, which is armed with strong teeth. Garfish occur on British coasts, and relatives are found in tropical and temperate seas, the American kinds often ascending rivers. They are quite good to eat, although the housewife is sometimes put off because their bones are bright green.

Similar to these is the little Skipper, which moves in great shoals and forms the prey of many large mackerel-like fishes, and the curious tropical Half-beak, which is vegetarian, and has only the lower jaw prolonged. All these fishes are closely related to the FLYING-FISH (q.v.), having the habit of leaping from the water when attacked by enemies from below.

GAUR, *see* CATTLE.

GAZELLE, *see* ANTELOPE.

GECKO. This is a lizard of the family Geckonidae, of which there are more than 300 species.

Geckos inhabit tropical and sub-tropical regions, and the species best known to us are those which live in houses and can be seen after dark running up and down the walls and even across the ceiling in search of food. They are able to do this because they carry special plates (*lamellae*), with adhesive powers, on the under-surfaces of the fingers and toes. Some species have not this adaptation, and live on the ground. The main classification of the family is based upon the way their fingers and toes are formed. The eye is usually large, and in most species is covered with a transparent membrane, as in snakes; but a few species have well-developed eyelids. The skin is usually soft, and covered with tubercles or small grain-like projections: only a few species

A TOOKAY

have scales. The tail is fragile and very variable in shape. All the Geckos have voices. Usually they make a soft chirruping or clucking sound, such as we can make with our tongue; but some of the large Malayan species (Tookays) have a

A NEWLY HATCHED HOUSE GECKO, AND TWO EGGS SOON TO HATCH. ABOUT TWICE NATURAL SIZE. *C. A. Gibson-Hill*

loud cry that can be heard a long way off. Many of them squawk when caught. They feed chiefly on insects; but some of the larger species will devour small animals. The House Geckos are frequently transported in ships' cargoes, and the wide distribution over the world of some of the species is due to this. Nearly all the Geckos lay eggs, usually two in number; one species inhabiting New Zealand produces living young.

The Tookay, or Tuktoo, is one of the largest of the Geckos. It is a native of Malaya, but has been introduced into Calcutta and the Dutch East Indies. It is common in the towns, and is well known to the people of southern Indo-China and Malaya on account of its loud call—from which comes its name. For a Gecko, it is a handsome creature, being pale grey above with large pinkish or reddish spots. It bites fiercely when caught.

See also LIZARD.

GEESE. These large, web-footed birds belong to the same family as the SWANS and DUCKS (qq.v.), though most of them are land-birds and grass-feeders. There are many species, most of which belong to America; but some species of both Grey and Black Geese visit the British Isles, and the Grey Lag Goose breeds in decreasing numbers in Scotland. Geese mate for life, and tend to return year after year to the same breeding area. They have a strong but rather heavy flight, many species making long migratory journeys.

The Grey Lag Goose is the species from which domestic GEESE (q.v. Vol. VI) are derived. They live in flocks during the winter, frequenting marshes, lakes, and open country near water, and often going to the coasts in hard weather. They have a harsh, discordant cry, well known to all keepers of domestic geese. Other grey geese which visit Britain are the White-fronted Goose, a rather smaller bird with a white patch

CANADA GEESE AT LOCKHART GADDY'S WILD GOOSE REFUGE AT ANSONVILLE, NORTH CAROLINA. *Paul Popper*

on the forehead; the Pink-foot Goose, which breeds in Spitzbergen; and, much less common, the Bean Goose, which breeds far north and winters over much of Europe and Asia.

Most Black Geese are smaller and more marine in their habits. The Brent Goose inhabits the coasts of Arctic Europe and northern Asia, and visits chiefly the east coasts of England and Ireland in the winter. Those of America nest in Greenland and winter sometimes as far south as Texas. The Barnacle Goose, a visitor to the west coast of Scotland and north Ireland, was so called because, according to the old legend, it was supposed to have developed from a BARNACLE (q.v.). Other wanderers to Britain are the strange-looking Red-breasted Goose from the tundras of Siberia, and the white snow Geese from Arctic America. The Canada Goose and the Egyptian Goose have both been introduced into Britain, and breed in the wild state in some parts, the former even more freely than the Grey Lag. Other exotic species to be seen on ornamental waters are the Muscovy Ducks, natives of tropical America, and—also from America—the brilliantly coloured Mandarin Ducks with their gaudy head-plumage—though neither of these are typical geese or ducks.

An extinct flightless goose is known to have existed formerly in New Zealand. This was related to the Australian Cape Barren Goose— a large, stoutly built goose, with a short neck and a large greenish swelling at the base of its short beak—which lives almost entirely on land.

GENTIAN, *see* ALPINE PLANTS.

GERMINATION, *see* REPRODUCTION OF PLANTS, Section 7.

GHOST MOTH, *see* SWIFT MOTH.

GIBBON, *see* APE.

GIPSY MOTH, *see* TUSSOCK MOTH.

GIRAFFE. These, with the OKAPI (q.v.), are the only existing members of a family which is intermediate between the DEER and CATTLE families (qq.v.). With their immensely long necks and legs, giraffes are by far the tallest of all the mammals, the largest of them being 18 feet high. But despite its size, a giraffe, standing motionless among trees, is almost invisible, its orangered skin, mottled with darker spots, blending

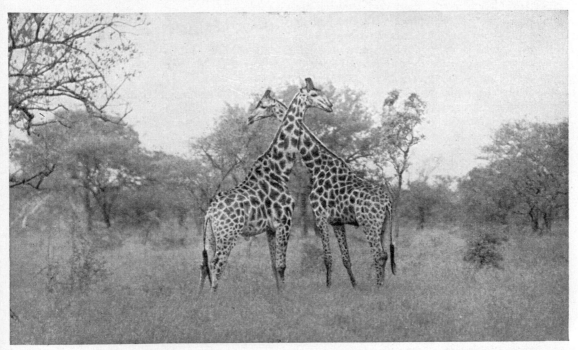

GIRAFFES STANDING IN A CHARACTERISTIC POSITION IN KRUGER NATIONAL PARK, TRANSVAAL
South African Railways

perfectly with the patches of sunlight and dense shadows of leaves. On its long, delicately shaped head are small blunt horns, covered with skin and surmounted by tufts of black hair. Some species have a second pair of rudimentary horns, merely bony lumps, at the back of the head; others have a single third horn on the forehead between the eyes. The body is proportionately short, and slants towards the tail. In its long tail, ending in a tuft of long hair, the giraffe has an invaluable fly-whisk, an essential weapon against the poisonous flies and stinging insects of central Africa.

Giraffes are found only in Africa, in dry regions south of the Sahara. They are most numerous to the north of the Kalahari Desert, in very dry country. It is a curious sight to see giraffes drinking water, for in spite of their long necks they cannot reach the water without straddling their legs wide apart. They have the same difficulty if they want to pick up a leaf from the ground, or when they graze, which they rarely do. They normally feed on leaves from trees, especially mimosa or acacia, and with their long tongues they can strip branches as much as 20 feet from the ground. Herds of giraffe vary in number from fifteen to as many as eighty. Their acute sight and hearing are useful means of defence, and with their great height they can see their enemies from a long distance. They defend themselves with their very powerful kick—the female defends her calf in this way against any attacks by flesh-eating foes, while the males kick fiercely when they fight in the mating season. Giraffe fawns are born singly in May or June, and after three days can trot by the side of their mothers.

Giraffes have great speed and endurance: big-game hunters say that it takes a good horse to run them down, and if the wind is favourable they will carry on for miles. They run with a peculiar gait like an awkward gallop, carrying their tails twisted like corkscrews over their backs.

GLASS SNAKE, *see* Slow Worm.

GLOW-WORM. The Glow-worm is the British representative of the Fire-flies (q.v.) of warmer climates and belongs to the same family of beetles—the Lampyridae. Only the female insect deserves the name; for the male, which flies about at night and sometimes enters houses,

attracted by the lights, is only very slightly luminous. The female when seen by day is unattractive enough, being a flat, crawling, grub-like creature, found in the hedgerows or near the ground; but after dark, when she displays her pale green light, she seems a different creature altogether. The light sometimes shines brightly and sometimes fades or goes out, to return again in all its beauty. It proceeds from the lower surface of the body, a little in front of the hinder end; so that it is best seen when the insect climbs above the ground on bank or herbage. Both males and females in the grub-stage closely resemble the mature female, and are found in the same places, where they feed upon snails, entering their shells and not leaving them until the occupant has been entirely devoured.

In tropical America there are insects, related to the Glow-worm, which carry a row of lamps along each side of the body. These give a beautiful green light, while the head glows with a fiery red. Only the female is capable of this wonderful display, which she can control in the same way as the Glow-worm. She is even more sluggish than the Glow-worm, while the male is an active winged insect, but not luminous.

See also Beetles.

GNAT, *see* Mosquito.

GNU, *see* Antelope.

GOAT. There are about ten species of wild goats, often called Ibexes, living in Europe, central Asia, Egypt, and Abyssinia. It is not always easy to distinguish between wild sheep, antelopes, and goats; but male goats always have a strong smell, and generally a beard on their chins. Both sexes have horns, those of the males being much the larger. They curve upwards and backwards, and are twisted in various shapes. Like the sheep, they are mountain animals, usually living in the most rugged districts. They are among the most sure-footed of animals, running up and down rocks and cliffs with the greatest ease. As well as grass, they eat any young shoots and leaves of trees and shrubs within their reach. They masticate this food when resting, by ruminating or 'chewing the cud' (*see* Ruminants). Nearly all wild goats live in herds, only some of the males leading a solitary life.

GOAT AND LEOPARD MOTHS. These primitive moths, belonging to the small family Cossidae, range in size from 1¼ to over 10 inches. They are found all over the world, but especially in temperate deciduous forests, and three species occur in Britain.

The Goat Moth is so called because the caterpillar has a strong goat-like smell, coming from a yellow oil secreted by glands in the head. The full-grown caterpillar, 3 to 4 inches long, is brownish-red above and yellowish-pink at the sides, with a shiny black head and black marks on the next segment. It is found in Britain much more commonly than the large brownish moth, and usually when wandering about before constructing its cocoon. The cocoon is made of tough silk, plastered with numerous particles, and the caterpillar overwinters within, not pupating until the following spring. The night-flying moth emerges in the summer and, although its mouth-parts are degenerate, it is attracted to sugar. Several eggs are laid together on tree trunks, and the young caterpillars begin to tunnel between the bark and the wood, later boring deeply into the heart wood. They can digest only the sugar and starch in the wood, of which there is so little that they have to remain sometimes as much as 4 years in the caterpillar stage, eating great quantities of wood, before they have made enough growth. In captivity, however, beetroot will supply all they need in a single season. The fermenting sap given off from trees wounded by these caterpillars attracts many insects, including Red Admirals and wasps.

The Leopard Moth, common in southern England, is 2½ to 3 inches across, and has thinly scaled whitish wings with bluish-black spots. The antennae of the female are thread-like, but those of the male are combed at the base. The female lays her eggs singly from June to August in cracks on the stems or branches of young trees, including fruit trees. The yellowish-white caterpillar has a brown head and is spotted with black. It tunnels in the wood for 2 or 3 years, causing the leaves of infested branches to wither, turn yellow, and be liable to break in the wind. The caterpillar pupates within a cocoon strengthened with particles of wood. The adult moth is attracted to light. The brownish and smaller Reed Leopard is restricted in Britain to the Cambridgeshire fens and to Dorset, where the caterpillar burrows in the stems of reeds, feeding for 2 years upon the pith.

DOMESTICATED GOAT OF THE SWISS ALPS
Paul Popper

The Markhor, a goat living in Afghanistan and the western Himalayas, is 3 ft. 8 in. high, and has horns twisted like a corkscrew. Markhors are wary animals, greatly prized by sportsmen. The Persian wild goats or Pasangs, found in south-west Asia, are very active animals, about 3 ft. high. They often appear near roads, but always take care to post a sentinel to warn the herd of danger. The Spanish wild goats are smaller still, about 2 ft. 2 in. high. As a rule the old bucks stay all the year round on the highest and most exposed peaks of the mountains, regardless of the snow and cold. The does, however, live on the southern slopes, and in the depths of winter approach close to the villages. The kids, by the time they are a few days old, are able to follow their mothers over the roughest ground; but while they are still young, the mothers keep to the southern slopes and warmer parts of the mountains, carefully shielding them from cutting winds.

Domestic goats are descended from the Persian wild goat. They were domesticated by the prehistoric inhabitants of the Swiss lake-dwellings, and were also kept by the ancient Egyptians.

See also Vol. VI, GOATS.

GOBY. Round sea-shores practically through-out the world, in rock-pools and coral-reefs, Gobies swarm in great abundance and variety; and many are found also in fresh waters. They are small fishes, rarely longer than 6 inches, and usually very much less. One of them, found in the Philippine Islands, is the smallest vertebrate animal in the world, the adult being only ½ inch long.

Gobies are distinguished by having two dorsal fins, no lateral line, eyes placed near the top of the head, and, in most species, pelvic fins joined together at the base to form a sucking disc on the breast, by which they can attach themselves to the rocks. Some Gobies can live out of water for some time, the most interesting of these being the so-called Mud-skipper, or Walking-fish, which lives on mud flats in the East Indies, using its fins like legs and skipping about in pursuit of its insect prey. This fish has even been observed to climb about over the roots of mangrove trees.

Male Gobies often fight fiercely in the breed-ing season, the winner displaying his colours proudly to the female. Even in northern waters they are often prettily coloured, while in the tropics they are frequently brilliant; a few, how-ever, such as the Transparent Goby of British seas, are colourless and glass-like. Generally, they take some care to protect the eggs by hiding them under stones or among seaweeds; and sometimes the male will make a sort of nest by turning over an empty shell and digging a pit underneath it.

A few Gobies live inside sponges, or even in the gill-chambers of larger fishes, while one kind lives in the tunnels of burrowing shrimps, and is quite blind (*see* BLIND FISHES).

See also FISHES.

GODWIT, *see* WADING BIRDS, Section 3.

GOLD AND PURPLE MOTHS. These brilliant, metallic, day-flying insects, formerly classified together in one family, measure only a ¼ to ½ inch across the wings. They have attracted much attention as being by far the most primitive of all Lepidoptera, and as throw-ing much light on the evolution of the Order. About a hundred species are known, most occur-ring in Europe and New Zealand, but some belonging to South Africa, Indo-Malaya, Aus-tralia, and North America—such world-wide distribution being characteristic of ancient groups. Gold moths have jaws and feed on pollen, but they have no 'proboscis' or sucking organ. In Purple Moths, however, a short pro-boscis has evolved, and the jaws are correspond-ingly reduced.

Purple Moths, of which nine species occur in Britain, lay their eggs in a slit in a leaf, usually birch, sometimes hazel, oak, or chestnut. The legless caterpillar feeds on the inner tissues of the leaf, making a characteristic blotch, and when mature pupates in a tough cocoon in the ground. The pupa is remarkable for its comparatively large, toothed jaws, with which it bites its way out of the cocoon through the soil to the surface.

One of the five British species of Gold Moth occurs commonly in May and June in butter-cups, often many individuals being together in one flower. The caterpillar, which probably feeds on mosses, has eight pairs of jointed abdominal legs, conspicuous antennae, and eight rows of peculiar globular appendages. The pupa has mov-able legs and jaws.

There are so many differences between Gold and Purple Moths that it is best to consider the Purple Moths as the most primi-tive Lepidoptera, and place the Gold Moths in the separate Order Zeugloptera, more ancient in origin than the Lepidoptera.

THE WALKING GOBY OR MUD-SKIPPER IN A MANGROVE SWAMP
A. Fraser-Brunner

GOLDCREST (Golden-crested Wren). The name Wren—given,

presumably, because of the bird's tiny size—is quite inaccurate: the Goldcrest is a WARBLER (q.v.), the smallest European bird. It is very gaily coloured, with olive-green plumage and a bright yellow and black crest. It is resident in the British Isles, frequenting plantations of conifers. Sometimes in autumn great flocks of immigrants from Scandinavia are to be seen, while in other years they are less noticeable.

Goldcrests are sociable little birds, often hunting for their insect food in company with Tits and Creepers. The nest is generally built on the underside of a conifer branch. It is a beautiful little bag, made of moss, wool, spiders' webs, and such material, and lined with feathers. The eight or more eggs are tiny, less than ½ inch long, and white with reddish specks.

The Firecrest is very much like the Goldcrest, but the crest is redder and there are whitish streaks round the eye. It is more local, not common in the British Isles, but occurring quite frequently in some regions. The American species is called the Rubycrest.

GOLDFINCH, see FINCHES, Section 3.

GOLDFISH, see CARP.

GOPHER, see SQUIRREL.

GORILLA, see APE.

GOSSAMER, see SPIDERS.

GRASSES. This group of flowering plants is one of the largest and most valuable, since it includes the cereals. Both man and the hoofed animals are dependent on them for their staple foods (see GRASSLANDS, Vol. VI). There are five thousand different species of grasses. Indeed, wherever flowering plants can exist, grasses of some sort will be found.

Most grasses are herbs (see FLOWERING PLANTS), and have fibrous root-systems (see ROOTS, Section 2); but some tropical forms, such as Bamboos, grow to more than 100 feet in height. Although most cereals and some grasses are annuals, a few cereals and the majority of grasses are perennials, and reproduce by the spread of underground stems, as with the Couchgrass, or with runners, as with the Common Bent (see STEMS). In most cases the stems are hollow, but in the Maize they are solid. The leaves are

TYPICAL GRASSES

characteristically long and narrow, and are arranged along the stem alternately in two ranks. Few grasses have stalked leaves, but each leaf has a sheathing base that surrounds the stem and more or less conceals it. The stem, with the leaf-sheaths, is known as the 'culm'. The leaves are usually smooth and often glossy, the outer cells containing a certain amount of silica (a hard white mineral, which, when the grass leaves are burnt, is usually enough to leave a distinct skeleton of the leaves). In several of the tropical bamboos a white opal-like substance called 'tabasheer', mainly composed of silica, and much prized by the natives as an ornament, is found in the joints. In one East Indian aquatic grass, the wide leaf-sheaths are much dilated and serve as floats.

The grasses of temperate regions rarely branch at the upper parts of the culm, but bamboos and many tropical grasses branch freely. In many bamboos these upper branches are long and spreading, or drooping and much-branched; in others they are merely hooked spines. One bamboo, a native of Malay, climbs over trees which are 100 feet and more in height. Grass-culms, especially bamboo culms, grow rapidly: a bamboo sometimes grows as much as 100 feet in 2 or 3 months. Some grass-culms can grow 3 feet or even more in 24 hours. In cool countries grasses are able to form turf, and they can do this because they produce in shallow soil a great mass of fibrous roots.

The flowers are borne in groups called 'spikelets', which are enclosed in leaf-like structures called 'glumes'. There are no petals or sepals in the flowers. The stamens are usually conspicuous, and there are generally three of them. Each anther, or pollen-containing box, is carried on a long stalk. There is one carpel with two feathery styles, and after fertilization the single-chambered ovary develops into the typical fruit or grain. In some bamboos, however, the fruit is thick and fleshy, forming a berry, often as large as an apple. The appearance of grasses when fruiting varies according to whether the stalks of the spikelets are long and spreading outwards from the stem, as in the Oat or Quaking Grass, short, as in the Meadow Fescue, or absent, as in Wheat or in Perennial Rye Grass. Each flower in the spikelet is protected by two structures (palea) of which the outer, in some cases, bears a long bristle (awn). This is very prominent in some grasses, especially in the cereals Oat, Barley, and Bearded Wheat.

In most cases grasses are pollinated by wind, though in the majority of cereals self-pollination takes place. The fruit is also usually light enough to be disseminated by wind. The awn helps in the distribution of the fruits by making them stick to animals or birds (*see* SEEDS 2(b) Animal Dispersal). The awn is also of use in burying the fruit in the soil: in the Oat, for instance, and other grasses, at the base of the glume is a sharp point, which easily penetrates the ground and cannot easily be withdrawn, because of the short, stiff, upwardly

pointing hairs above. The long awn, which is bent and closely twisted below the bend, reacts strongly to moisture in the atmosphere, the coils untwisting when damp and twisting up again when dry. When the upper part of the awn has become fixed in the earth, or caught in the surrounding vegetation, the repeated twisting and untwisting drives the point deeper into the ground. Such grasses often cause harm to sheep by catching in the wool and boring into the skin.

Of the British wild grasses, some of the most common are the Fescues. The Meadow Fescue grows 1 or 2 feet high, and bears its flowered spikelets in close, nodding clusters 8 to 10 inches long. It is a good pasture grass. The Tall Fescue grows along river banks and in wet places, and reaches a height of 3 feet. The clusters or spikelets are only 3 to 6 inches long. Some Fescues, especially when growing on mountains, reproduce themselves in a curious way. Instead of the usual flower spikelets, there are small, leafy shoots. These develop adventitious roots at their bases, and these eventually fall off and take root in the soil (*see* ROOTS, Section 5).

The Quaking or Quake Grass grows in dry pastures, especially among taller grasses, and comes into flower during June and July. The many-flowered spikelets, which shiver at the end of long thin stalks, have given the grass the

FOREST OF GIANT BAMBOO GRASSES ALONG A RIVER BANK IN BURMA

popular name of 'Shivery-shakes'. Cocksfoot, a valuable pasture grass, bears groups of flowers which are distinctly branched and form dense tufts. Yorkshire Fog, a perennial grass, common in meadows, pastures, and waste places throughout Britain, has a short awn, and the flowers are pinkish-grey. Marram Grass grows in tufts on sea-shores, especially on sand-dunes (see SEA-SHORE PLANTS). It has long, ridged leaves, covered with a pale green bloom. This grass is often deliberately planted on dunes and elsewhere in order to bind the wind-swept sand. Couch-grass is an abominable weed in gardens and on farmlands, because it spreads by long, tenacious, underground stems which are difficult to eradicate. A small portion of such a stem, if left in the ground, will send up shoots and begin to spread.

Besides the cereals and the Sugar-cane, the most interesting foreign grasses are the tropical Bamboos, which grow in large clumps and spread rapidly by means of underground stems. Some Bamboos flower annually, others at longer intervals, and others once only before they die. The Pampas Grass, with its long, dark, arching leaves and its enormous white plumes carried at the end of long, straight stalks, is a native of Argentina and Brazil, but it is often seen in this country in our larger gardens and parks.

See also Vol. III: GRASSLANDS.
See also Vol. VI: GRASSES; GRASSLANDS.

GRASSHOPPER AND LOCUST. Three
closely related insects—the grasshopper, locust, and CRICKET (q v.)—are similar in general appearance. Their mouth-parts are used for biting; they have hardened, elongated fore-wings, with the hind-wings folded fanwise beneath them; the hind-legs are very long, with enlarged femurs; the males, and sometimes the females, are provided with sound-producing organs, and in both sexes there are organs for the reception

of sound. The METAMORPHOSIS (q.v.) is incomplete, the immature insects or nymphs resembling the adults, except that their wings are rudimentary.

Grasshoppers can be separated into two distinct groups—the Short-horned and Long-horned Grasshoppers. The first of these includes all the small Grasshoppers so common throughout the British Isles, and also the large Locusts, whose periodic swarms have throughout history spread destruction over vast areas of fertile country (see MIGRATION). The members of the second group have much more in common with the CRICKETS (q.v.) than they have with the Short-horned Grasshoppers.

Two very obvious characteristics of all these insects are their sound-producing capacity and their powers of movement by leaping. In the Short-horned Grasshoppers and Locusts sound is produced by working the hind-leg upon the fore-wing so that the fore-wing vibrates. The sound-receiving organs are two tightly stretched membranes, each surrounded by a horny ring, situated one on each side of the first segment of

BODY OF LOCUST WITH WINGS REMOVED SHOWING 'EAR'

the abdomen. In the Long-horned Grasshoppers and Crickets sound is produced by the friction of one fore-wing upon the other. A pair of similar sound-receivers is situated on the surface of the tibia of each fore-leg. These membranes vibrate in response to the chirrup of a neighbouring insect, and the vibrations are interpreted as sounds by means of the nervous system. As the various sounds produced by insects are usually shrill and strident, their production is called 'stridulation'. Grasshoppers and Crickets may chirrup for various reasons. The males chirrup to attract the attention of the females during courtship, and also in rivalry with each other. Warmth or sunshine will often arouse a solitary

GREAT GREEN GRASSHOPPER

FRONT TIBIA OF FORE-LEG OF GRASSHOPPER SHOWING 'EAR'

Grasshopper or Cricket to a long-sustained musical effort. One of the most insistent chirrupers is a North American Long-horned Grasshopper, which has brilliant green, leaf-like fore-wings, and is called the Katydid, because its notes suggest that it is constantly repeating 'Katy did, she did'.

If we look at the hind-legs of these insects from the side, the enlarged femur is very obvious. Above is the big muscle which straightens the leg. If it contracts quickly, the insect will jump. Below it is a much narrower muscle which bends the leg again. Large Grasshoppers do not jump nearly so well as the small insects, the best performers of which have been known to jump a length of up to 6 feet. There is a Long-horned Grasshopper, not uncommon in the south of England, called the Great Green Grasshopper, which when adult is about 2 inches long. The small immature specimens found during summer can make very good leaps; but when they become adults they can jump no higher than the nymphs, and always finish with a heavy flop.

Short-horned Grasshoppers and Locusts have short and not very obvious 'ovipositors' or egg-laying tubes. With her ovipositor the female excavates a hole, usually in the ground, and places in it anything up to 100 eggs. She then pours upon them a fluid, which hardens into a protective covering. This means of protecting the eggs resembles that used by her relatives, the Cockroaches (q.v.). She may be capable of egg-laying for as long as two months, during which time she deposits several batches of eggs. The nymphs cast their skins from five to eight times during growth, and there may be either one or two generations in a year. The Long-horned Grasshoppers have stout, curved ovipositors, sometimes as long as the rest of the body. Because of the shape of these organs, the insects are often called the Sabre-tailed Grasshoppers. Sometimes the eggs are laid in the ground, but more often in the tissues of plants. The Short-horned Grasshoppers are vegetarian, whereas many members of the Long-horned group are carnivorous.

See also Crickets.
See also Vol. VI: Insect Pests (Locusts).

GRASS SNAKE. (Sometimes also called the Ring-necked Snake.) This is the commonest of the three British snakes, being found all over England, Wales, and south-eastern Scotland, as well as throughout Europe. There are several colour varieties, each with its own geographical range. In England it is normally greyish, olive, or brownish above, usually with black spots or narrow cross-bars on the back and vertical ones on the flanks; it has a yellow or orange collar on the neck, bordered behind with black; the belly is chequered with black and grey or white, or may be entirely black. In old females the orange collar and the black markings on the back have sometimes disappeared. Males seldom exceed 3 feet in length; females grow larger, and a specimen measuring 5 feet 10 inches has been recorded. Such a size, however, is most unusual in Britain, although in southern Europe it is not uncommon.

COMMON GRASS SNAKE, ABOUT 3 FEET LONG
J. J. Ward, F.R.E.S.

The Grass Snake lives in hedgerows and open woodland country. It is fond of water and can swim well. When caught, it does not bite, but gives out a nauseous-smelling fluid from the vent. In captivity it soon becomes tame, and if properly cared for will live for several years. Its main food is frogs, but it will also eat toads, newts, and fish. Eggs are laid in June, July, and early August, manure heaps being favourite places for them, or they may be hidden under dried leaves or in holes in walls. The young emerge some two months later.

Closely allied to the English Grass Snake, and much like it in general appearance, though it is without the yellow collar, is the Tessellated Water-snake. It has a wide range in Europe, and is sometimes sold in England as a pet.

See also Snakes.

GRASS-VENEER MOTHS. These small, brownish, yellowish, or whitish moths, sometimes streaked with silver, are very abundant almost everywhere in summer in long grasses—thirty-seven species occurring in Britain. They rest with their long 'palpi' or feelers projecting forwards and their long, narrow wings so folded that they appear cylindrical, their form and colour making them difficult to distinguish among the dry grass stems. They fly at twilight or by night, and, when disturbed during the day by anyone walking in the grass, they soon settle again. The eggs are either scattered freely or attached to grasses, and the caterpillars either bore into the stems or crowns of grasses or cereals, or live about the roots. Many construct silken galleries, a habit which has earned them the American name Webworm. Several species are serious pests—notably the Oriental Rice Borer, which causes enormous losses in southern and eastern Asia, and the Sugar-cane Borer of the West Indies and United States. Much remains to be discovered about the biology even of British species.

GRAYLING BUTTERFLY, *see* BROWNS.

GREBE. The Grebes are water-birds related to the DIVERS (q.v.), but more inclined to frequent fresh water. They are found over a great part of the world in temperate or sub-tropical climates, and are fairly familiar British birds. They have legs placed very far back, close thick plumage, and lobes on the toes, all fitting them for an aquatic rather than a terrestrial life. Some species fly well, with their necks stretched out before them; but all prefer water to air, and the Dabchicks, in particular, are unwilling to fly, always escaping from an enemy, if they can, by diving, rather than by flight. They are expert divers, and swim long distances under water. They seek concealment often by sinking under the water and staying with only the tip of the beak showing. How so light a body can keep itself submerged without exerting great force is a mystery—like that of the DIPPER (q.v.), which can walk underwater on the floor of a stream. Grebes breed by fresh-water lakes, broads, and meres, where there are reeds in which they like to nest. The nest is often a floating construction, and the mass of decomposing vegetable matter of which it is made produces a good deal of heat —so much in fact that, by covering them up, the birds can leave the eggs for 6 hours at a time without harm. The chicks take to the water almost at once, and hang on to their parents'

GREAT CRESTED GREBE ON NEST
G. K. Yeates, F.R.P.S.

plumage or climb on their backs when they need to rest. They feed on frogs, small fish, molluscs, and water-insects, and also on the shoots and seeds of aquatic plants.

The largest and most handsome of the Grebes is the Great Crested Grebe, about 21 inches long. It has a grey, chestnut-brown, and white plumage, darker in the summer than winter, with large tufts of feathers making a frill round its neck, and with a double crest. (In fact, the word 'grebe' comes from a Celtic word for a comb, though most of the family are without anything like a 'comb'—and even this species loses its crest in the winter). The smallest member of the family, and the most familiar, is the Dabchick or Little Grebe, found on streams, ponds, and lakes throughout the British Isles, though less commonly farther north. Other species which breed occasionally in Britain or are winter visitors are the Red-necked Grebe, the Slavonic Grebe, and the Black-necked Grebe.

GREENFINCH, *see* FINCHES, Section 2.

GREENFLY, *see* APHIS.

GREENSHANK, *see* WADING BIRDS, Section 3.

GROUSE. There are some thirty species of this family of game-birds of the order Gallinae, which are found for the most part in the northern half of the northern hemisphere. They have, in general, stout, compact bodies and strong legs with curved claws, with which they can run quickly and scratch efficiently. The legs, and often also the toes, are feathered. The males are generally larger and more brightly coloured than the females. Most of them have a loud cry, in some species produced by the inflating and deflating of air-sacs on the side of the neck. Grouse build nests on the ground, generally in hollows in heather or grass or under cover of a bush, lining them scantily with grass or moss. Even those species, such as the Blackcock and Hazel-hens, which prefer woods to open moorland, nest on the ground. Most species lay seven to twelve eggs or even more, the Prairie-hens of the Mississippi valley reaching, not infrequently, as many as twenty. The chicks are hatched well developed and covered with thick down, and become fully grown in a few weeks. Grouse are sedentary birds, rarely wandering from their breeding area.

Many species of Grouse make elaborate courtship displays (see ANIMAL LANGUAGE). The Red Grouse cocks fight in the spring, the victor often rising to a height of some 20 feet in the air and crowing before descending to claim the hen. Red Grouse and their near relatives, the Ptarmigans, have one mate only. The Blackcock and their relatives, the Capercaillies, both of which are polygamous, perform excited courtship dances, the Capercaillie in its favourite pine-tree, and the Blackcock on its display grounds, in which a number of cocks gather and display against each other. Two Blackcocks will approach each other in a crouching attitude, their throats vibrating with their bubbling cries. They will go forwards and backwards several times, and then suddenly rush at each other and, almost interlocked, rise a little way into the air, striking at each other with their feet and uttering a high, hissing note. The Prairie-hens of America assemble in the early morning on high, dry hillocks and, inflating their orange air-sacs and raising their long neck-tufts, they utter their loud courting-cry.

The Red Grouse, the game-bird of British moorlands, is the best known of the family. This is the only bird which is found in the British Isles and nowhere else, though it has a relative

RED GROUSE AND NEWLY HATCHED FLEDGLINGS
Eric J. Hosking, F.R.P.S.

CAPERCAILLIE NESTING ON HEATHER ON THE EDGE OF A PINE FOREST
Eric J. Hosking, F.R.P.S.

very much like it, the Willow Grouse, which is found in Europe and North America. The Red Grouse, unlike the Willow Grouse, never turns white in winter. It has, however, remarkable colour variations, ranging from phases of entirely black (which is rare) to chestnut-red, and to spotted white. Its main food is heather, but it also eats bilberry, crowberry, various seeds, and caterpillars and insects. Grouse are subject to serious epidemics of grouse-disease, the first recorded outbreak being in 1815. The hen generally sits very close on her nest in the heather, relying on the good camouflage of her plumage to protect her.

The Ptarmigan is a mountain bird, found at high altitudes over a wide area of northern Europe, Asia, and America, including the Scottish Highlands. In summer it has a grey-brown plumage, with a red comb over the eye, while in winter the plumage becomes almost purely white—a perfect camouflage when the Ptarmigan is roosting in the snow. It has the strongest flight of any game-bird, and the chicks are able to fly when they are only 10 days old.

Blackcock, the hens of which are called Greyhens, inhabit woods near moors or rough land, and perch in trees. The cock is bluish-black, with some white on the wings and under the tail, and the hen is brown and grey. They are most common in Scotland, but are found locally in Wales and north and south-west England.

The Capercaillie, a near relative of the Blackcock, is like it in many ways, but is much larger. It is the largest of the Grouse, the cock being nearly as large as a turkey. The females are much smaller. Capercaillies inhabit the pine forests of northern Europe, north and central Asia, and the Pyrenees, Alps, and Carpathian mountains. They became extinct in Scotland about 1770, but were reintroduced successfully in 1837, and are now thriving.

See also Vol. IX: GAME SHOOTING.

GROWTH OF ANIMALS. 1. LENGTH OF LIFE. The average expectation of life for human beings is usually reckoned to be 70 years, the biblical threescore years and ten. The greatest or maximum age is much more difficult to arrive at. It is probably about 108; for, although we sometimes read reports of somebody having lived to the age of 140, these reports always come from countries where a register of births and deaths is not very carefully kept. Even in Britain, where very careful records are kept, we can only say that the average age is somewhere about 70, and the maximum somewhere about 108 years.

It is not possible to discuss length of life without using the word 'longevity', a word difficult to define, but meaning broadly the maximum length of life of the longest-lived individuals of a species. Thus, when we talk of longevity in human beings, we refer, not to the average age of 70, but to those men and women who go on living far beyond the average, say, 90 or 100 years or more.

In animals, records of longevity are even more difficult to arrive at, and are only to be had from domesticated animals or from wild animals kept in captivity. Indeed, we know less about the rate at which they grow, or the length of time they live, than any other single thing about them. Unfortunately the records of longevity of animals kept in captivity are an indication only of how long members of that species are capable of living under the most favourable circumstances. In the wild an aged animal is apt to be an easy prey to enemies, or to suffer in competition with its fellows for food and shelter. The fact that an elephant has been known to live to the age of 75 in a zoo, where everything is done to protect it, does not mean that this age is, of necessity, ever attained in the wild state.

The figures given for the ages of animals are often very exaggerated. Elephants have been said to live to an age of 200 years, or even, some people have said, to 500 years. In fact, the Indian elephant may live to be 70 years and the African elephant to 40 to 50 years only. Other animals about which excessive estimates have been made are the large tortoises, some of which are said to reach an age of 500 years. The most reliable record we have is of the famous Marion's Tortoise which was taken from the Seychelles to Mauritius in 1766. In 1918, blind with age, it fell down a well and died. Thus it must have been well over 150 years—probably 160 or so.

On the whole it may be said that the smaller an animal the shorter its expectation of life. Thus the shrew, the smallest British mammal, lives only up to 18 months, while a rat may live to 4 years of age, a squirrel to 14 years, and a horse to 60 years. However, this ratio between size and longevity is not invariable.

2. STAGES IN GROWTH. All living things pass

through an infancy, youth, or childhood, during which growth in size is fairly rapid, and then reach maturity, when they are said to be adult, or grown-up. At that stage, usually known as sexual maturity, bodily growth all but ceases, and the animal is capable of producing offspring. The end of this period of maturity, old age, or senility, is marked by a slight decrease in size and a noticeable decrease in energy and strength. In human beings we speak of infancy, childhood, youth, manhood or womanhood, middle age, and old age. In animals we speak simply of the young, the adult, and the old.

Just as we are ignorant of the longevity of most species of animals, so we know little about the times taken to reach maturity. This is partly because of a lack of accurate observation, but also because there is a fair degree of variation in the times taken by individuals of a given species. For legal purposes, we usually speak of persons being adult when they reach the age of 21; but most people are physically mature well before this. A youth, however, will sometimes stop growing in height when in other respects he is still not fully developed, while another youth may attain all the development associated with manhood at an early age and then suddenly start to grow more in height. What determines these irregularities in growth is not fully known. In some cases it may be heredity factors, but more often the causes are environmental—that is, governed by the conditions under which the person lives. So it is with animals, the greatest influence on growth being probably exerted by food. With the lower animals in particular, however, growth is affected by such conditions as temperature, the amount of oxygen present, the intensity of light, overcrowding, and so on. When all conditions are most favourable, we say the animal is growing under 'optimum conditions'. For example, some marine animals grow best in a moderate light; but if grown in a bright light or in darkness they not only take longer to reach maturity but attain a much smaller size than when grown under optimum conditions. With all animals there are optimum conditions of the environment—conditions of light, temperature, humidity, oxygen, and so on. With some animals, unfavourable conditions may bring about a condition of suspended growth. A French scientist, who had joined his regiment on the outbreak of war in 1939, found on returning to his laboratory in 1946 that in the hurry of his departure he had left the larvae of some mites in a corked tube. These were still alive after 7 years, and ultimately grew to maturity when fed again. Instead of the usual year, these mites had lived for 8 years, owing to adverse conditions, namely, starvation, which had interrupted their normal growth-rate.

Rate of growth and size are governed also, of course, by HEREDITY (q.v.), which determines the size for the species or race. Of the two species of elephant, for example, the Indian elephant, when fully grown, averages about 9 feet high at the shoulder, while the African elephant averages 10 feet 6 inches. For all species there is an average maximum size, not only for the body as a whole but for the component parts of the body—and these are inherited. Individuals of the lower invertebrates, however, will often vary greatly from the average for the species, especially where food is particularly abundant.

GROWTH OF PLANTS. If a living cell were placed in circumstances where growth could proceed without interruption, the cell would grow evenly in every direction and eventually form a sphere. Plants and animals are seldom spherical, because growth takes place more at some points than at others. The term 'growth' means a permanent increase in size and shape. Temporary increase in either size or shape can take place for reasons other than growth. When a root-hair absorbs water from the soil it increases in size, an increase due to a swelling of the cell with extra water. Similarly, when a plant absorbs water rapidly, much of it may enter the leaf-cells and make them swell so much that the leaf area is increased, and the general shape altered; but later the leaf will return to its original shape—so no growth has occurred. A plant can only be said to have grown when it has permanently increased in size, and consequently in bulk. In plants, growth takes place by the use of energy which has been released from food by respiration; and growth is, therefore, one of the important results of NUTRITION (q.v.).

Growth is the product of two sets of opposed forces which go on in the plant. Some processes, of which PHOTOSYNTHESIS (q.v.)—the production of food-stuffs by green leaves in the presence of sunlight—is the most important, build up new tissues for the plant. Other processes, of which RESPIRATION (q.v.) is the most important, break down the built-up food substances to release energy, and this is again used in the building-up processes. So the two apparently opposed forces are really interdependent, and if the building-up process predominates, growth takes place. When the breaking-down process takes place faster than the building-up process, growth ceases. The sum of the two processes is known as 'metabolism'.

Active growth takes place in plants in two regions—at the extreme tip of the shoot and just behind the tip of the root. In the root the tip itself consists of a root-cap, a layer of cells which bears the brunt of the friction caused as the root forces its way through the earth. Although the outer layers are constantly being worn away by this friction, new cells are as constantly being formed, and the delicate growing-point is permanently protected. The growing-point itself consists of a number of active cells, regularly and rapidly dividing to produce new cells, and so increasing the length of the root.

The rates of growth in different plants vary considerably. In most FLOWERING PLANTS (q.v.) in Britain, the growth is usually so small each day that it is scarcely noticeable; but in Ceylon certain Bamboo stems normally grow 16 inches in a day. The most rapid growth in plants, however, takes place in small structures like fungal threads, flower-stamens, and pollen-tubes. These grow 40, 60, and even 150 times faster than bamboo shoots. The fruiting body of the Stinkhorn fungus, for example, will grow from beneath the soil to its full height of about 6 inches in just over an hour. The force produced by growing plants is often considerable. Some shoots have been found to exert an upward force of 82 lb. per square inch, and growing roots have often forced rocks and banks apart, and even caused houses to tumble down.

It is very difficult to measure growth in plants accurately, since they spread in three directions, and growth in length may not be accompanied by a corresponding growth in thickness. In some trees the shoot ceases to grow in length by early summer, but continues to grow in girth. If increase in weight were taken as a test of growth, this would be considerably affected by the amount of water present in the plant, and therefore by whether or not the roots had been recently absorbing water, and whether the leaves had been giving off water by TRANSPIRATION (q.v.). Generally, growth in plants is measured by their increase in dry weight; but to do this the plant has to be killed, and so cannot be used to compare dry weight at different times. There is no one way of measuring growth, and different methods have to be used in different circumstances.

Since the growth of a plant depends upon the combined effects of the various processes which nourish it, such as food-manufacture, absorption of water, and loss of water, and since these are all influenced by external conditions, growth, too, will be dependent on conditions such as temperature, light, and the available water-supply. As with respiration and other plant processes, there are two extremes of temperature above and below which no growth takes place. A plant will go on respiring at a much lower temperature than it will go on growing. Generally, the rate of growth is doubled for each 10 degrees rise of temperature, falling off at about 30° C. and ceasing altogether at about 35° C. The effect of temperature on growth is seen when plants are grown in hot-houses. In this way flowers and vegetables of all kinds can be given an artificially made temperature, and so be 'forced' to grow out of season.

Light affects growth in many ways. For instance, the shoot and root of a green plant grow more rapidly in length at night than during the day, whereas growth in area of the leaf-blade is much reduced by the absence of light. This effect of darkness in developing stems is made use of by gardeners in growing Rhubarb, Celery, and Sea-kale. If plants like the House-leek, which normally has a rosette habit of growth, are grown in the dark, the stem lengthens considerably, so that each leaf has a well-marked piece of stem between it and the next. The rate at which a stem grows in length is not the same throughout the whole period of development: at first its rate of lengthening is small, then it increases to a maximum, and finally slows down before it ceases altogether.

During the last 20 years crop-breeders have been experimenting on the effect of varying periods of light on certain plants. It was noticed that a certain tobacco plant in America, called Maryland Mammoth, produced no flowers at certain latitudes; but at other latitudes, where the days were shorter and the nights longer, it blossomed. It was then found that some plants produce flowers and fruit of better quality more quickly if they are illuminated for periods of less than 12 hours daily. These are called 'short-day' plants. Others have been found to do better with light-periods of more than 12 hours, and have been called 'long-day' plants. A considerable amount of experimental work, especially in Russia and America, is proceeding along these lines, particularly in the introduction of new crops in new territories. Chrysanthemums are short-day plants: that is why they thrive during the autumn.

PLANT HORMONES. Plants need the correct external conditions—water, light, warmth, for example—for normal growth. In addition to these, however, growth is also influenced by internal factors. The shoot of a plant, for instance, will bend upwards towards the light, and the root will bend downwards; but if the tip of the shoot or root is cut off, then these movements will not take place. This is because the tips are producing a substance, called an 'auxin' or 'plant hormone', which affects the growth of the regions below them. This substance, when extracted from stem or root tips, always seems to be the same; and so, strangely enough, the same auxin makes roots turn downwards towards gravity, and stems turn upwards away from gravity. This auxin has a very important effect on the life of the plant, for it ensures that roots grow down into the soil and that stems grow up towards the light.

Other substances have been found recently which also have an effect on the growth or development of plants. Some varieties of apple-trees, for example, have caused great anxiety to fruit growers because most of the fruit tends to drop off long before it is ripe. A hormone has been found which, if sprayed on the trees at the right time, prevents the fruit from falling until it is ripe. Other substances, extracts of which can now be bought by gardeners, encourage cuttings to grow roots. Hormone weed killers, if used on lawns, make the broad-leaved plants, such as plantains, dandelions, and daisies, grow so fast that eventually they outgrow their strength and die.

See also MOVEMENT OF PLANTS.

GUILLEMOT, see AUK, Section 3.

GUINEA-FOWL. This African group, named after the Guinea Lands of West Africa, belongs to the order of game-birds. There are several species, the predominant colours being black, pale blue, and white, and some species carrying handsome crests. They are gregarious birds, and collect in large flocks in grass-covered plains near forests. But they are very shy, and make their escape by running at great speed through the grass. They were already domesticated in the days of the ancient Greeks, our domesticated Guinea-fowl coming from one of the West Indian species (see GUINEA-FOWL, Vol. VI).

GUINEA-PIG, see CAVY.

GULLS. 1. These sea-birds of the order Lariae include the typical Gulls and the Terns, Skimmers, Kittiwakes, and Skuas. Although they are all essentially sea-birds, some gulls often come a long way inland and will breed on inland waters. The Herring Gull, for instance, can often be seen following the plough on an inland farm, in search of worms. Gulls are to be found over much of the world, though in fact no gulls proper inhabit the great area lying between South America and Australia—only Terns. They are mostly gregarious, noisy birds, powerful fliers and good swimmers, though few of them dive to catch fish. Their food is principally fish and refuse, though they will eat almost anything. Their plumage, except for the Skuas, is predominantly white, their wings are long, and their feet webbed. They have long bills, the upper half being longer than the lower, and bent over at the tip. They generally nest in colonies, some species choosing ledges on cliffs, others inland swamps, sand-dunes, or coarse grass. The

LESSER BLACK-BACKED GULL AT NEST
G. K. Yeates, F.R.P.S.

A HERRING GULL PAUSING IN THE AIR
C. A. Gibson-Hill

WHITE TERN IN FLIGHT
C. A. Gibson-Hill

order is divided into two families, the Gulls, Terns, and Kittiwakes in the one and the Skuas in the other.

There are between forty and fifty species of typical gulls, the smallest being the Little Gull, common in Mediterranean countries and a visitor to the British Isles, and the largest the Glaucous or Greater White-winged Gull, an Arctic bird measuring fully 32 inches, which comes farther south only in winter. The comparatively small Black-headed Gulls are the most common in Britain, preferring flat shores in winter and breeding in marshes. They are, in fact, nearly as much inland as sea birds. The Common or Mew Gull visits England mainly in winter, breeding throughout northern Europe and Asia, and in Ireland and Scotland and locally in England. The Herring Gull, a larger bird, measuring 23 inches or more, frequents all British coasts and those of northern Europe and North America, reaching as far as North Africa in the winter. It nests on broad cliff-ledges, the eggs varying widely in colour. Herring Gulls are so named because they follow the shoals of herrings, hovering above them before plunging for their catch. They are magnificent fliers, gliding, soaring, and riding on the gusts of wind. Another resident in Britain is the Black-backed Gull, though that and the Great Black-backed Gull are found more often in the north. The Great Black-backed Gull, the 'vulture of the seas', preys on other birds, and will even attack a young lamb or wounded animal, killing it after first pecking out its eyes. Perhaps the most beautiful of the gulls is the snowy-white Ivory Gull, which breeds in Spitzbergen and other far-northern regions.

2. TERNS (or Sea Swallows) have long, pointed wings, deeply forked tails, slender bodies, and short legs. They rarely rest on the water, but fly skimming over it, generally with their bills pointed downwards, scanning the surface for small fish on which to plunge. Most Terns are spring and summer migrants to Britain, returning farther south for the winter. They make practically no nest, but lay their two to three eggs on shingle beds or in sand-dunes or dry grass. They generally breed in large communities. They will defend their nests with great boldness, flying in the face of intruders and even killing other birds or animals. There are several species, ranging from the Little Tern, which is 9 inches long, to the Sandwich Tern, which is 16 inches. The Arctic Tern is famous for the tremendous range of its migratory flights (*see* MIGRATION). The tropical Noddy, a dusky black tern, nests in vast quantities in islands off the coast of Florida and many other tropical lands.

3. KITTIWAKES, close relatives of the Gulls, breed on ledges on cliffs, often only a few feet above the water, and are altogether more completely sea-birds than the Gulls. Unlike other members of the family they are expert fishers,

BLACK-HEADED GULL WITH 8-DAY OLD CHICK.   *F. Vear*

diving skilfully after their prey. There are only two species, the North Atlantic and North Pacific Kittiwakes. They are very strong fliers, being known regularly to cross the Atlantic.

4. SKIMMERS. These close relatives of the Terns are like them in most respects; but they have very remarkable beaks, which have led to their being called 'Scissor-bills'. The beak is elongated and compressed to a knife-like shape, with the upper half much shorter and more flexible than the lower. There are three species, belonging to India, the Red Sea and Nile, and North America respectively. The North American bird has been observed skimming over the water with the long lower half of its bill beneath the surface—doubtless catching food.

5. SKUAS. These residents of north Scotland, the Scottish Isles, and other northern regions, have strong, hooked claws and sharp, hooked beaks. They are the pirates of northern waters, rarely fishing for themselves but attacking other birds and making them disgorge their catch. The Skua then swoops after the falling morsel so swiftly that it generally recovers it in mid-air. Two species breed within the limits of the British Isles, the Great Skua, a bird some 25 inches long, which leads a solitary life, generally out at sea, and the Arctic Skua, a more common and gregarious bird. Three species are found in the southern hemisphere, dispersed as widely as from the coasts of South America to those of New Zealand and the Indian Ocean.

GURNARD, *see* SCORPION FISH.

H

HABITAT, *see* Animal and Plant Distribution; Animal Territory.

HADDOCK, *see* Cod.

HAG-FISHES, *see* Lamprey.

HAIR. All mammals except the whales, porpoises, and dolphins have a covering of hair—and even whales, when they are young, have a few bristles on the snout, though these disappear later. A hair grows from a small depression or tube in the skin called a 'hair follicle'. This is formed by the 'epidermis' (or outer skin) growing down into the 'dermis' (or true skin). A tiny 'papilla' or outgrowth appears at the bottom of the follicle, and the cells of this then divide and grow rapidly, until the young hair projects beyond the surface of the skin.

Each hair has a fibrous interior and an outer horny coat. A blood-vessel at the root supplies food material, and a gland opening on the side of the follicle supplies a kind of oil or fat to keep the hair soft and pliable. The follicle is in a slanting position, so that the hair usually lies

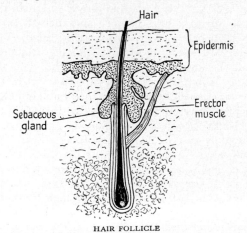

Hair

Epidermis

Erector
muscle

Sebaceous
gland

HAIR FOLLICLE

down one way. At the root of the hair is a tiny muscle, and when this contracts it pulls the hair upright. Cats, dogs, and animals with manes are able to use this muscle to make themselves look bigger and more ferocious; but in man the muscle has practically ceased to function, so that fright no longer causes the hair to stand on end. Colour granules give the hair its tint; but in people who are in ill health or who are elderly, tiny air-bubbles take the place of the granules and the hair becomes white or grey.

Hair may be fine, coarse, straight, curly, long, or short. The wool of sheep, the fur of seals, the manes of lions, and the spines of hedgehogs or porcupines are all different kinds of hair. The horns of the rhinoceros and the armour-like skin of the armadillo are just cemented masses of hair.

Nails and Claws, as well as Hoofs (qq.v), are produced in the same way as hairs. Instead of a small follicle we find a mass of cells making a nail-bed, so that a wide horny outgrowth comes from the broad root. Feathers (q.v.), which are peculiar to birds, are produced in just the same way as hairs.

HAIRSTREAKS. These butterflies, members of the same family as the Blues and Coppers (qq.v.), are called 'Hairstreak' because of the delicate white lines on the undersides of their wings. The males have special scales which distribute alluring scents during courtship. These are grouped into bands on the front wings, whereas the Blues and Coppers have them scattered. Four of the five British species are named after their distinguishing colours: green, purple, brown, and black. All but the Green Hairstreak have at the angle of each hind-wing a tiny, slender tail, which may deflect the attention of enemies away from the vulnerable head. The caterpillars are shaped like woodlice, and lie flat, casting little shadow.

The Green Hairstreak, the most common species, is seen in May and June almost everywhere in the British Isles where dogwood grows. The caterpillars eat a variety of other plants, such as broom, bramble, rock-rose, and whortleberry, and also are carnivorous. The stout pupa, which is capable of making a creaking sound, lies under a few silken threads at the foot of its food plant from July until the following May. The butterfly has entirely green undersides, the colour being due to the structure of the scales and not to pigment. Since this colouring

FEMALE PURPLE HAIRSTREAK BUTTERFLY RESTING ON AN OAK TWIG. *S. Beaufoy, F.R.P.S.*

is such good camouflage when the butterfly rests with wings closed on the green leaves, it is strange that it is not more common.

The White Letter Hairstreak, restricted to midland and southern counties, has white hairstreaks forming a definite letter 'W' on the hindwings. The female lays her eggs only on elm twigs. Generation after generation will breed on one large tree in a group of elms, nothing short of the felling of their tree inducing them to move to another. The butterflies are sometimes found in great abundance in July and August at the flowers of privet and bramble.

The Purple Hairstreak has ashy-grey under sides, but rich purple upper sides. The female is about as brilliant a purple as the male PURPLE EMPEROR (q.v.). These Hairstreaks can often be seen flitting round the outer branches of old oak trees during July and early August, but usually well out of reach. The larvae, descending from the oak to pupate in late May, may be found in the litter beneath the trees.

Brown Hairstreaks, not uncommon in many southern, western, and midland counties, fly high over tree-tops during August and September, but can sometimes be seen when they descend to suck nectar from flowers or to lay eggs on the twigs of low-growing blackthorn saplings. The caterpillar hatches in the following spring, and pupates in June on the underside of a leaf, the old larva-skin holding the pupa in place, for it has no tail hooks.

The Black Hairstreak, the rarest resident butterfly in Britain, is restricted to blackthorn thickets in the woods of Huntingdonshire, Northamptonshire, and the Oxfordshire–Buckinghamshire border. The females fly in June and July, and nearly always select the highest spikes of old bushes on which to lay their eggs. The caterpillar emerges in the spring, and in June changes into a pupa easily mistaken for a bird-dropping.

HAKE, *see* COD.

HAMSTER, *see* MOUSE.

HARE. This rodent belongs to the same family as the RABBIT (q.v.), and is found in most parts of Europe, Asia, Africa, and North America. Unlike the rabbit, the hare is a native of Britain, not introduced by man. Both the hare and the rabbit belong to the order of double-toothed RODENTS (q.v.), and have teeth especially adapted for gnawing. The hare has a divided upper lip, which has led to the expression 'hare-lipped'.

The common Brown Hare is a great enemy to the farmer and gardener (*see* PESTS, ANIMAL, Vol. VI), and would probably have been exterminated were it not preserved for sport (*see* HARE-HUNTING, Vol. IX). It lives on grass, young corn, roots, and bark. The hare is an unsociable animal. It does not live in burrows, but in the open, and selects convenient places, called 'forms', where it lies crouched and concealed during most of the day and night. Hares will sometimes allow themselves to be almost trodden on before stirring. When forced to move, they will run to a safe distance and then sit up on their hind-legs, with ears erect to listen. They have a very acute sense of hearing and smell, but, because of the position of the eyes, it is thought that their forward vision is limited. This weakness of sight, as well as their habit of following regular runs, makes them easy to snare or net.

Hares show much cunning in escaping from pursuers and in laying a baffling scent. They will elude a faster pursuer by 'jinking', or swerving at high speed. When hunted, they use most of the same tricks as the Fox (q.v.): in particular, they double back on their tracks and then make a series of long, sideways leaps before continuing their run. It is said that, when coming to or from their form, they will take two very long leaps (about 15 feet) to break the scent. They move by a series of jumps with their long hind-legs and skip with their forelegs: the faster they go the longer are the jumps. They can jump up on to a 5-foot wall, and can swim well.

The main courting season is February and March. The jacks (as male hares are called) in their pursuit of does get very excited, and run about, kicking, bucking, and jumping—from which has come the expression 'mad as a March hare'. The doe has two litters in a year, producing at a birth two to five young 'leverets', which she cares for very well and in whose protection she will fight fiercely. The leverets are born in the open, and soon after their birth the mother finds separate 'forms' for each leveret, visiting each in turn by night to suckle it. The tiny leverets, therefore, go a remarkably long time without food, much longer than most large animals. In about a month's time they are able to fend entirely for themselves.

The Brown Hare is rarely found on hills and moors, or far north, where the Blue Mountain or Alpine Hare takes its place. This hare is rather smaller, and is bluish-grey in the summer, gradually changing in the autumn and winter to white. It is duller in colour than the brown hare, and its flesh is much poorer in flavour. The Scottish Mountain Hare belongs to this group. The Irish Hare, much like the Blue Hare in most ways, is rather larger, and much more gregarious: as many as 200–300 have been seen in droves. The American Prairie Hare is most usually called the Jack Rabbit (a shortening of Jackass Rabbit). It is a large hare, with very long ears and legs, and it makes enormous, kangaroo-like bounds. In Arctic regions, the American hare, which is white in winter, is known also as the Snowshoe Rabbit, from the thickly furred soles of its feet that enable it to move on soft snow.

HARRIER, *see* HAWK, Section 5.

HARTEBEEST, *see* ANTELOPE.

HARVESTMAN. This is a member of the same class of animals as SPIDERS (q.v.)—the Arachnida. It is distinguished by the absence of the narrow waist (which in spiders separates the two portions of the body), by the great length of its legs, and by the possession of two glands in the

head, which secrete an evil-smelling fluid. There are about three thousand known species, twenty of which can be found in Britain, the rest being distributed all over the world, except in the polar regions.

In this country Harvestmen are most conspicuous in the autumn, to which fact they doubtless owe their popular name. Although a few species are frequently active in the sunshine, most of them come out by night. Using the long, second pair of legs as sense-organs, they detect their prey by touch, and seize it in their pincer-like jaws. They do not possess venom-glands. Many Harvestmen live near water or in moist surroundings: they have a constant thirst for water, and die in a short time if they cannot get it. Harvestmen very often shed their legs if they are grasped; but, unlike all other Arachnida, they are unable to grow them again. Since they have five or six legs, they do not seem to be seriously inconvenienced by the loss of one or two. If, however, they lose both legs of the second pair, they are seriously handicapped and usually do not live long.

The female lays her eggs underground in the autumn in clumps of twenty or more. They hatch in the spring, and the young ones, which resemble their parents except in size, grow during the summer, with periodic castings of the skin. A few exceptional species are to be found as adults at all times of the year.

Harvestmen normally feed on insects and other small creatures; but they will also eat a variety of other foods. They have been seen feeding on dead moles, on the patches of 'sugar' used by moth-collectors, and on the marmalade of a picnic party. Only in rare circumstances are they cannibals—in which they differ from most other members of their class. They are easy to keep under observation in captivity, and there is still much to be learnt about their habits.

HAWFINCH, *see* FINCHES, Section 2.

HAWK. 1. The Hawk tribe forms a very large group of the Birds of Prey, to which also belong the FALCONS and EAGLES (qq.v.). Its members are distributed throughout the world. The

COCK SPARROW-HAWK AT NEST
Arthur Brook

common Sparrow-hawk of Britain is a typical Hawk. The larger Goshawk is now only a rare visitor to the east coast, though it used to be much more common in Britain, and was a great favourite with falconers (*see* FALCONRY, Vol. IX). The Hawk tribe also includes the Kites, the Buzzards, and their near relatives, the Harriers.

2. The SPARROW-HAWK, one of the smaller members of the family, is distinguished from a Falcon, to which it is closely related, by its shorter, rounded wings and its long tail, which it holds at a downward angle when in flight. It is an elegant-looking bird, about 13 inches long, with very sharp eyes and a hooked beak. It is a bold robber. Its flight is swift and dashing rather than long-sustained, and it attacks its prey by a sudden rush, generally from behind, instead of (as with a Kestrel) from above. Sparrow-hawks build nests of sticks in trees, and lay five or six handsome eggs, with orange and brick-red markings on a whitish ground— typical of the family.

3. KITES are larger birds, about 2 feet long, with long narrow wings. They used to be common, and were often to be seen flying in circles or hanging in the air above the streets of London and other European cities, where they acted as scavengers. They were consistently attacked by sportsmen, farmers, and gamekeepers, because of their depredations on young birds, until by 1895 they were practically extinct. Now, a few

pairs of Red Kites have been successfully re-established in the mountains of South Wales. They are magnificent fliers, appearing to hang in the air for long periods, with hardly any movement of the wings. They feed on carrion and garbage of any sort, and although they will attack young or weakling birds, they are not bold robbers. The Honey-buzzards (Bee-hawks), relatives of the Kites (not the Buzzards), are now practically extinct in Britain. These large, rather un-hawklike birds, so called because they will dig out the nests of bees and wasps with their claws to feed on the grubs, are found over northern Europe and much of Asia.

4. BUZZARDS are rather more like lesser Eagles than Hawks, being some 2 feet in length and lacking the dash of Hawks and Falcons. They are not a danger to gamekeepers, for they feed mainly on field-mice and such small mammals, or even on insects and worms. They are found in remote districts in Wales, the Lake District, the Scottish Highlands, and elsewhere, and make bulky nests of sticks in high trees or on craggy ledges. At times, especially in the breeding season, Buzzards will soar in circles high in the air, uttering at intervals their shrill, whistle-like cry. Species of Buzzards are to be found over most of the world.

5. HARRIERS, relatives of the Buzzards, used to be more common in Britain than they are now. The Hen-harrier breeds on the wilder

THE MALE BUZZARD (RIGHT) ARRIVES WITH FOOD FOR THE FAMILY. *Arthur Brook*

MONTAGU'S HARRIER AND YOUNG
Arthur Brook

a proboscis twice this length. Many of these moths fly at night or at twilight, and the flowers dependent upon them for pollination are often white and therefore conspicuous in the dark. Humming-bird Hawk Moths fly in the sunshine, their size (1¾ inches in expanse), colour (greyish-brown fore-wings, and orange hind-wings), and behaviour so strongly suggesting HUMMING-BIRDS (q.v.) that experienced travellers are often deceived. Bee Hawks also fly by day. The colour of their hairy bodies, and their transparent wings give them a mimetic resemblance to humble bees (*see* PROTECTIVE COLORATION).

The Death's Head Moth, a robust insect with a wing spread of 4¾ inches, has dark fore-wings, brownish-yellow hind-wings with two black bands, and a yellowish blotch suggesting a skull and crossbones on the thorax. It ranges across Europe to north Africa, through central and southern Asia to Japan, and reaches Britain as an immigrant, though not every year nor in large numbers. It enters bee-hives for the honey, and squeaks like the queen bee, the sound being made by forcing air from the gut over a vibrating fold in the mouth. The full-grown caterpillar, which usually feeds on potatoes or nightshade, measures about 5 inches in length. It may be brown, yellow-green, yellow-purple, green-blue, or yellow-blue. The seven oblique side-stripes, so characteristic of Hawk Moth larvae, are bluish or purplish, and the horn near the rear end also characteristic of the family, is short, rough, and bent back at the tip. When about to pupate, the caterpillar first wanders, and then burrows a few inches into the earth, where it constructs a cell made of particles of soil held together by a gummy liquid which it secretes, and a little silk. Caterpillars in this stage grind their jaws together, making a noise resembling the winding of a watch. The caterpillar changes to a red-brown pupa usually in July and August, about 10 days after it has ceased to feed.

Other species found commonly in Britain are the greenish Lime Hawk, the greyish Poplar Hawk recognized by the rusty red patch on the

moors of Wales and Scotland; but the Marsh-harrier and Montagu's Harrier are found regularly in East Anglia only. They are slender birds, with long legs, tails, and wings, and they feed mainly on field-mice, lizards, frogs, birds, eggs, and larger insects. They have a characteristic flight when hunting. They quarter the ground very carefully, flying low over it with alternate flapping and gliding. When gliding, they hold their wings tilted up, instead of horizontally like most birds. The male passes the prey in mid-air to the female, who catches it in her talons and takes it to the nest.

HAWK MOTHS. These powerful moths, many of which are very large, occur in most parts of the world. Of 900 known species, 17 occur in Britain, though only 9 of them habitually breed, the others being immigrants of greater or lesser frequency. They have long fore-wings, small hind-wings, and hooked antennae. The proboscis or sucking organ varies greatly in size: in some species it is very small and almost useless; but in others it is much lengthened, notably in those which hover on the wing and, without alighting, probe the depths of long tubular flowers for nectar. The Convolvulus Hawk, which occurs throughout the Old World and in many Pacific Islands, and is an immigrant to Britain, has a proboscis about 5 inches in length, more than the wing expanse; while there is a tropical American species with

EYED HAWK MOTH CATERPILLAR AND ADULT MOTH
The Moth is showing his eyes because he has been disturbed. *E. Syms & S. Beaufoy, F.R.P.S.*

POPLAR HAWK MOTH
S. Beaufoy, F.R.P.S.

ELEPHANT HAWK MOTH ON SPRAY OF ROSEBAY WILLOW-
HERB. *S. Beaufoy, F.R.P.S.*

hind-wing, the black, grey, and pink Privet Hawk, the brownish Eyed Hawk which has an eye-like spot on each hind-wing, and the rosy-pink Elephants, Large and Small. The caterpillars of the first three feed on the plants from which they take their names. The magnificent larva of the Privet-hawk is bright green with seven pairs of oblique white and lilac stripes. The Eyed Hawk caterpillar, also green, but with only white stripes, is sometimes a pest in apple orchards. The Elephant Hawk caterpillar, found on willow-herb, bedstraw, or fuchsia, is normally blackish or brownish and bears several eye-like markings in front which the insect dis-

plays if molested. When full grown and fully extended, it is nearly 3 inches long and tapers strongly towards the head, reminding one of an elephant's trunk. The large green caterpillar of the Convolvulus Hawk may be found occasionally on bindweed in cultivated fields on the coast. It changes to a chrysalis in which the proboscis stands out from the body as does a handle from a jug. The Pine Hawk, formerly found mainly in Suffolk and Dorset, is now more abundant and more widely spread. The Oleander, Spurge, Bedstraw, and Striped Hawks are migrants apparently unable to complete their life-cycle in Britain in the open. In America

Hawk Moth caterpillars are known as Horn-worms. One of the most injurious pests of tobacco plants is the green and white striped Tobacco Hornworm.

See also MOTH.

HAZEL, *see* FRUITS, Section 2 c.

HEARING, *see* SENSES, Section 3.

HEART. The simplest animals have no blood. The flow of water around or through their bodies, from which food and oxygen are obtained, takes the place of a blood stream. As animals became more highly organized, special organs for supplying the cells with food were evolved, and a pump, in the form of a heart, for the transport of food became necessary.

The WORM (q.v.) has a closed circuit of real blood-vessels, containing red blood, but no lungs. One large blood-vessel runs along the back, and from it smaller ones communicate with another large blood-vessel along the belly. Near the head, these are connected by five pairs of swollen blood-vessels that encircle the gut. These may be called hearts because, by contracting and expanding, they force the blood along.

In INSECTS (q.v.) there is a tubular heart above, and a method for making the blood circulate. A series of cone-like chambers, with openings in their sides, runs along the back of the insect. These chambers are full of blood, and they communicate with spaces, or sinuses, filled

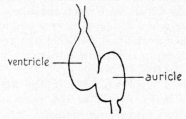

FIG. 1. TWO-CHAMBERED HEART OF FISH (SIDE VIEW)

with blood, between the cells of the animal's body. As the chambers contract and dilate, blood is forced out and drawn in, so being kept continually on the move. The blood carries food but not oxygen, which gets directly into the blood by means of air passages opening at the sides of the body. This kind of circulation is known as an 'open circuit'.

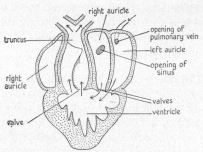

FIG. 2. THREE-CHAMBERED HEART OF FROG (FRONT VIEW)

The FISH (q.v.) has a two-chambered heart with an 'auricle', or upper chamber, a 'ventricle', or lower chamber, and valves to control the flow of blood. The blood is pumped from the heart to the gills, where it receives oxygen, and then on round the body and back to the heart (*see* Fig. 1). The FROG (q.v.) goes a step farther, with a three-chambered heart made up of two auricles and one ventricle. The right auricle receives de-oxygenated blood from the body, and the left auricle oxygenated blood from the lungs. Thus the ventricle contains mixed blood which is pumped to the cells of the body (*see* Fig. 2).

MAMMALS (q.v.), including man, have a four-chambered heart, which gives the most efficient blood circulation. It is really two pumps in one, and two blood circuits which operate at the same time. One circuit, from the left ventricle, sends pure blood to the cells of the body and back to the right auricle. The other circuit, from the right ventricle, sends impure blood to the lungs

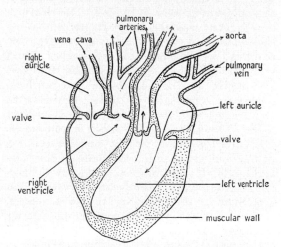

FIG. 3. FOUR-CHAMBERED HEART OF MAMMAL

for purification. Having received fresh oxygen, this returns to the left auricle—ready to repeat the journey round the body (*see* Fig. 3).

See BLOOD SYSTEM.

HEATH (Butterfly). The Small Heath, which belongs to the same family as the BROWNS (q.v.), is one of the commonest butterflies in the British Isles, and is a familiar sight on commons and heaths in all parts except the Scillies, Orkneys, and Shetlands. It is normally light brown, but may be deeper or lighter in tint, and very rarely creamy-white. Some forms have a large, clear eye-spot on the upper side of the fore-wing, but in others this is either faint or entirely absent. The Heath is an inactive butterfly, generally flying only when disturbed. The female lays her eggs in early summer singly on blades of grass, on which the striped green caterpillars feed. They either hibernate or yield a second brood in the autumn, of which the larvae always overwinter.

The rarer Large Heath resembles the Small Heath, except that it is about half as big again; but it is a more active butterfly. The green-and-white striped caterpillars are well camouflaged on the food plant, beaked rush, and are found up to an altitude of 2,000 feet. They hibernate during the winter. The Large Heath does not breed in southern England, but has been found on rough pastures, bogs, and mosses, in the Lake District, parts of Yorkshire, Lancashire, Cheshire, and Shropshire, in Wales, Scotland, the Hebrides, Orkneys, and even the Shetlands, where it is the only indigenous butterfly. It is also common in parts of Ireland. This distribution suggests that the Large Heath established itself in Britain before the separation from the mainland of Ireland and the smaller island groups. The Mountain Ringlet (*see* BROWNS) also occurs in Ireland. These two northern species are represented by distinct British forms and are probably the butterflies longest resident there. The Large Heath shows a continuous gradation from dark, heavily ringed specimens in England, through intermediates in Cumberland, to light, indistinctly spotted forms in Scotland. Intermediates also occur in Wales. This gradation in the characteristics of a species, through a range involving considerable change in climatic or other factors, is called a 'cline', and is typical of animals tending to remain in the districts in which they were born.

HEATHER, *see* HEATHS AND MOORLANDS.

HEATHS AND MOORLANDS. These occur on gently undulating land which is exposed at higher altitudes to sun and wind. Moorland is characterized by wet peat, which is brown in colour, acid in reaction, and often of considerable depth, whereas heaths are found on shallow soils which are generally sandy or gravelly.

Heath soils do not retain water, and in the course of time the soluble mineral salts have been washed out from them. They are therefore poor, dry, and unsuitable for the growth of most plants, those that do grow there having special characteristics which enable them to survive. Among the heath-plants are the Ling, Bilberry, Bell-heather, and Broom. In all these the leaves are greatly reduced and have thickened surfaces, and the 'stomata' or pores through which water-loss or TRANSPIRATION (q.v.) takes place are especially well protected, so that the plants can conserve as much as possible of the water which has been absorbed by the roots. Bracken is found also on heaths—and it is significant that the leaves of these heath brackens are much thicker and stouter-looking than those of the graceful brackens found in woods. Besides the sandy soils and the lack of water and of mineral salts, other difficulties against which heath plants must contend are exposure to high winds, the recurrence of fires (caused by people's carelessness), and interference by animals.

The peat of moorlands is due to the accumulation of plant remains over long periods under conditions which were unfavourable to decay. Peat, which usually contains much humic acid, when once established, becomes independent of the underlying rocks. In places it may be as thick as 30 feet.

There is great variation in the amount of water to be found in different moorlands, and this accounts for the wide range of plant populations. Dry moors usually occur on high ground, and may extend over the summits of hills. Ling is the dominant plant here, while the Bilberry, common Mat Grass, and Bell-heather also occur. Other plants found in the dry peat areas are the orange-berried Cloudberry and the Crowberry. Cotton-grass also occurs on these moors and, where the peat is wetter, it becomes the dominant plant. On the uplands of Wales, north England, and Scotland, the soil is composed of

Fine-leaved Heather

Cross-leaved Heather

Bog Asphodel

Cotton Grass

Ling

HEATH AND MOORLANDS PLANTS

the supply of oxygen is limited, it gets what it needs from the air passing through numerous air-canals which extend throughout the plant. Various rushes and sedges also grow on grass moors, as well as the lovely Bog Asphodel, Cross-leaved Heath, and Sweet Gale.

See also Vol. III: MOORLAND AND MARSH.

HEDGEHOG. This very common little member of the INSECTIVORA (q.v.), or insect-eating mammals, is found throughout the whole of Europe, in Asia, and in Africa. He is about the size of a large guinea-pig, and has a pig-like snout and extremely short legs. His protective coat of sharp spines grows only on the upper part and sides of his body, the rest

glacial clays left by the retreating glaciers of the ICE-AGE (q.v. Vol. III). The peat, about 6 inches in depth, overlies the water-holding clay, making the soil sour and sometimes waterlogged, although in summer the surface layers may become dry. Because the water drains more readily here than on the moors where the peat is very thick, there is more oxygen dissolved in it; and in consequence, the Purple Moor Grass, which demands more oxygen than the Cotton Grass, is often the dominant plant. The Purple Moor Grass has a great many roots, some penetrating quite deeply and others remaining short, by which the plant absorbs water readily. The roots are invaded also by fungal threads, called 'Mycorrhiza', which break down the decaying humus and pass on the nitrogen compounds to the plant, so making up for the deficiency of nitrates in the soil. In summer the leaves of the Purple Moor Grass are withered at the tips, and in winter the withered leaves bend before the wind, giving the appearance of waves. Since this grass grows in situations where

being covered with coarse hair which offers little protection against the sharp teeth of his natural enemies, such as the fox or badger. But when the hedgehog rolls himself up, the unprotected parts of his body are tucked away, together with his head and feet, inside the prickly ball, leaving sharp spines sticking out in all directions. The hedgehog has a most acute sense of smell and hearing. On sensing danger, he stops and listens, then drops his head between his forefeet, erects his spines, and if, further alarmed, rolls himself up into a tight ball. The badger sometimes manages to tear open the prickly ball with his long, strong claws, and the fox is said to have many clever tricks to make a hedgehog unroll.

Hedgehogs are usually seen waddling slowly along the ground; but they can run quite fast. Down steep slopes they either roll, or drop like a ball, landing on their spines, and in water they are very good swimmers. The adults occasionally emit a subdued grunt or cough-like snort, and the young have a shrill squeak. They spend

HEDGEHOG AND FAMILY.   *A. R. Thompson*

most of the day hidden in hedges and shrubberies, or in holes, and hunt for food during the
night—though in summer and autumn they
quite often venture out before dusk. Besides
insects, they eat a great deal of animal food,
such as slugs, frogs, young birds, rats, and mice,
and they will taste almost anything. A hungry
hedgehog will sometimes make a meal of a snake
—even a poisonous viper or adder. He makes a
swift snap at the snake's back to break the backbone and cripple his enemy. Then instantly he
rolls himself up into a prickly ball, at which the
snake strikes in vain, inflicting severe injury on
itself. When at last the reptile lies dead, the
hedgehog crushes its bones and, beginning at
the tail, devours it all.

During the summer and autumn, the hedgehog eats as much as he can to put on fat. Then,
late in November or December, he retires to
hibernate in a warm bed of mossy leaves. He
sinks into a deep sleep, his heart almost ceases
to beat, and he scarcely breathes. During his
hibernation he uses up the fat he has stored in
his body, so that when he wakes up in the spring,
he is quite thin and very hungry (*see* HIBER-
NATION).

The sow has two litters a year, of from four to
seven young. They are born blind, with tiny
soft spines which take about three weeks to
harden, during which time the babies are
defenceless.

HEDGEROWS. Although these are artificial
barriers introduced by man, and not natural
features of the vegetation of a country, hedgerows are interesting plant associations (*see*
ECOLOGY OF PLANTS), because they show so
many communities. Usually a hedge includes
three things: the hedge itself, the bank, and the
ditch at the bottom. The plants in these different
positions have their own characteristics, and
vary according to the nature of the soil, its
dampness, and their exposure to the sun. The
direction in which the hedge runs has a strong
effect upon the vegetation, a hedge extending
from north to south, thus presenting east and
west aspects, having a much richer plant population than one running from west to east. The
plants on the two sides also differ from one
another, particularly in the case of a hedge
running from west to east, and can be broadly
divided into shade-loving and light-loving
plants.

The vegetation of the ditch at the bottom of
the hedge depends upon the water-supply. In
a dry ditch, plants like Silverweed, Colts-foot,

and Red and White Dead-nettles are typical. If the ditch is damp, even for part of the year, tall plants like Stinging-nettles, Horsetails, and Hogweed occur. In a ditch where fresh water is standing most of the year, the characteristic plants are Brooklime, Figwort, Meadowsweet, Wild Celery, and various Mints.

The bank of the hedge shows many variations, but the soil is generally dry. The typical plants are Thale-cress, Ivy-leaved Speedwell, and Chickweed. These are annual plants which flower early in the spring, when moisture is still present, and set their seeds before the drought of summer. Other plants germinate in the autumn, and spend the winter as seedlings, before completing their development in the spring. Seedlings which can be seen in the winter include Cleavers (Goosegrass, Sticky Willie, or Bobby-buttons), Garlic-mustard (Jack-by-the-hedge), and Shepherd's Purse. Many plants of dry hedgebanks have a rosette habit, the leaves spreading close to the ground and keeping the soil moist. Among these are the Daisy, Dandelion, Plantain, and Cat's Ear and Mouse Ear Hawkweed. On the light side of the banks are prostrate plants, like the Creeping Buttercup and Wild Strawberry; while the non-climbing shade plants, such as Woodsage, Yarrow, and Heath Stitchwort, usually have long, narrow, and much-divided leaves, adapted to making the most of the rays of light which penetrate the hedge. The shade plants proper include the Wood-violet, Primrose, Ground-ivy, and Cuckoo-pint, and, if the atmosphere is moist enough, ferns such as the Harts-tongue.

The hedge proper consists of shrubs and bushes, such as Hawthorn, Hazel, Elder, Maple, and Sloe, together with small trees of Elm, Oak, Ash, and Willow. Sometimes a hedge is formed wholly of trees which are kept cut—Beech and Hornbeam being often used. To thicken a hedge, the shrubs are cut back regularly, as this causes dormant buds at the base to grow into branches, which can be 'laid' into position by the farmer (see HEDGES, Vol. VI). The original planted hedge soon becomes colonized by other species, most of them being climbers or scramblers, using any available means of support to grow up to the light. (See CLIMBING PLANTS.) Some of these, such as the Bindweed, Black Bryony, and Honeysuckle, have twining stems. Clematis has twining leaf-stalks, while the White Bryony and Vetches have tendrils. The Ivy has adventitious roots, which adhere firmly to the bark of shrubs or trees. Of the scramblers the most common are Cleavers, the Rose, and the Bramble, which scramble by means of hooks or thorns. Besides exposing their leaves to light, climbing plants also display their flowers for pollination and their fruits for dispersal by wind. Many of these hedge-top plants, such as the Hawthorn, Rose, Bramble, Elder, Ivy, and Bryony, have juicy fruits attractive to birds—who thus help to disperse their seeds. (See also ECOLOGY OF PLANTS.)

See also HEDGES, Vol. VI.

HEDGE SPARROW, see THRUSHES, Section 5.

HERBS, see FLOWERING PLANTS.

HEREDITY. It is a matter of common observation that the offspring resembles the parents. We do not expect a cat to have a litter of puppies or a cow to throw a foal. In all species, young are produced which, even though they may differ markedly from the parents at first, will eventually grow to resemble them. This is expressed in the well-known saying that like begets like. The process of heredity goes farther than this, however, for if a pair of tabby cats mate, we expect to see tabby kittens; and from black parent cats we shall expect black kittens, and so on. Sometimes, in spite of this, however, a pair of pure black cats will have one kitten or more not pure black. Obviously there is some mechanism by which the uniformity of the species is maintained, and by which the individual characteristics of the parents appear once more in the offspring. This mechanism has been very extensively investigated during the last hundred years, and although there is a multitude of questions still unsolved, considerable progress has been made in understanding it. Nevertheless, it is a difficult thing to understand, and the subject is best approached from the early beginnings.

If we watch a unicellular animal, such as AMOEBA (q.v.), we shall see that sooner or later it will divide in two, by simply splitting across the middle. The two Amoebas are, so far as we can see, exactly alike; yet one is the parent and one the offspring. Such a division is known as asexual reproduction. Not only does the body of the cell, the cytoplasm, divide, but the nucleus also. All multicellular organisms, except those produced by non-sexual methods such as budding, begin life as a single cell, the ovum. This, after fertilization, begins to divide by a splitting very like that seen in Amoeba; but the two halves, instead of separating, remain together, and by continued division of the cells a multicellular body is built up. Some of the cells go on to form the tissues of the body, and are known as 'somatic cells'; others are concerned only with reproduction, and are known as the germ-cells or 'gametes' (*see* REPRODUCTION).

In fertilization, a 'spermatozoon', or male gamete, unites with the 'ovum', or female gamete. The spermatozoon consists practically of nucleus only. The resulting offspring shows a mixture of characters from both male and female parents. It is a simple deduction, therefore, to suggest that the mechanism for the inheritance of the parental characters must be carried in the nucleus and not in the 'cytoplasm', or body of the cell.

We know that the nucleus of any cell will take up a stain or colour more rapidly than the cytoplasm, and that if a cell is immersed in colouring matter and then examined under a microscope, the nucleus will be seen to contain a network of deeply stained protoplasmic thread, which has been called 'chromatin' (from the Greek word *chroma*, meaning colour). The first sign that a cell is about to divide is that the chromatin network of the nucleus breaks up into lengths, each length or piece being called a 'chromosome'. If the cell is a somatic or body-building cell, each chromosome splits into two, each half passing into the nucleus of each of the two cells formed by the division. In a dividing gamete or reproducing cell, however, the chromosomes sort themselves out into pairs, and only one of each pair goes to each nucleus of the cells resulting from the division. In this way, all somatic cells have the same number of chromosomes; but the gametes or germ-cells have only half this number. This is a very important part of the mechanism of heredity. If, for example, the number of chromosomes characteristic of a given species is twelve, all the somatic cells will have this number, but the gametes will have six only. At fertilization, however, when the ovum and spermatozoon come together to form a single cell, there will be twelve chromosomes, six being contributed by the spermatozoon and six by the ovum. Thus the number of chromosomes is kept constant for all members of a species.

There are cases known, however, particularly among cultivated plants, where the chromosomes have failed to divide and the offspring have double, treble, or quadruple the number of chromosomes—and in consequence new varieties are formed (*see* REPRODUCTION IN PLANTS).

Experiment has shown beyond doubt that the factors controlling heredity are carried in the chromosomes—in other words, the chromosomes carry the mechanism which decides how an animal shall develop and what its characteristics shall be. We are, however, very much in the dark as to precisely how this mechanism works, or what exactly it is. It is suspected that each chromosome carries a number of small bodies or particles, to which the name 'gene' has been given. Although the structure of these genes is still largely unknown, we can just see them with the electron microscope, and we can find out how they behave by studying the characteristics they control.

Although the mechanism of heredity has here been dealt with first, it was actually the behaviour of this mechanism which was first investigated. An Austrian monk, Gregor MENDEL (q.v. Vol. V), born in Silesia in 1822, experimented in the middle of the 19th century on garden peas. He noted that the seeds of some peas were round and smooth when ripe, while others were angular and wrinkled. He artificially united the two by cross-fertilizing the flowers of the round-seeded variety with the pollen of the wrinkled-seeded variety. The seeds resulting from this cross were sown, and the plants they gave rise to all bore pods containing nothing but rounded, smooth seeds. When this first generation of seeds was in its turn sown, the plants resulting produced smooth, rounded seeds and wrinkled, angular seeds in the proportion of three of the former to one of the latter. The reason for this was not at the time understood; but now, thanks to Mendel's patient work, and many further experiments, we know the explanation to be as follows.

In the chromosomes of the pea bearing rounded seeds was a gene governing the quality of roundness; in those of the pea bearing the wrinkled seed was a gene governing the quality of wrinkledness. Therefore, when the flower of the first was pollinated from the flower of the second, each seed would have chromosomes containing the genes governing both roundness and wrinkledness. Yet all the seeds produced were rounded. This is because the gene for roundness is 'dominant' or overpowering, and that for wrinkledness is 'recessive' or retiring. In other words, if the genes for roundness and wrinkledness are both present in the nucleus of a fertilized ovum, the gene for roundness will dominate or overpower the gene for wrinkledness, and all the hybrid seeds will show the rounded quality.

The second generation grown from these hybrid seeds will bear ovules and pollen; and, because of the reduction division in the gametes, they will bear the genes for roundness and wrinkledness in equal proportions. At fertilization, therefore, one-quarter of the seeds will receive two genes for roundness and will be round; two quarters will receive one gene for roundness and one for wrinkledness, and will also be round, because the gene for roundness will be dominant; in the remaining quarter the seeds will bear two genes for wrinkledness and will be wrinkled. Of every four seeds, therefore, three will be round and smooth and one wrinkled and angular. This is precisely how it worked out in Mendel's experiments. To quote the figures obtained in one of his tests, 5,474 were round and 1,850 were wrinkled, giving a ratio of 2·96 to 1. Over a larger number the result would be more nearly 3 to 1.

The examples given of Mendel's work are in a simple form; but the study of genetics—that is, the science dealing with the mechanism of heredity—has advanced enormously since his day, and is a very complicated matter. Enough has been said, however, to show that the offspring inherit characters from the parents according to simple arithmetical formulae. Moreover, these formulae can be of great assistance, not only in the elucidation of scientific problems, but in the selective breeding of domestic animals and plants (*see* STOCK BREEDING, Vol. VI).

In such selective breeding, the keeping of pedigrees is of the utmost importance, depending on the question, already mentioned, of dominant and recessive characters. In the second generation derived from the crossing of two strains, whether rounded peas and wrinkled peas, black rabbits and white rabbits, or whatever pair of characters we may take, the offspring will show the respective parental characteristics in the proportion of 3 to 1. Thus, if a pure-bred black rabbit is crossed with a pure-bred white, the hybrid offspring will be black, with the white

DIAGRAM SHOWING HOW THE PARENTAL CHARACTERS ARE INHERITED IN THE OFFSPRING IN A REGULAR ARITHMETICAL PROPORTION

recessive. In the next generation, bred from these, there will be three black to one white; but whereas the white will breed true (that is, if crossed with another white will give only white offspring), the blacks are divisible into one pure-bred black and two which are black but have the white recessive. Of these latter, the pure blacks will breed true; but the two hybrid blacks if crossed with one another, will have litters containing pure black, black hybrid, and pure white babies. If, then, a breeder, whether of dogs, sheep, rabbits, or cattle, wishes to maintain pure stock—that is, one that will breed true—he must know the past history for generations back of the animals he is proposing to mate.

A very simple example of a recessive character can be seen in human beings, namely, the possession of red hair. It often happens that a mother and father, both with brown hair, may have a son or daughter with red hair and a pronounced tendency to freckles. Red hair, which is linked with a tendency to freckles, is recessive to brown in hair; and where the situation arises such as we have just described, it will be found that both of the parents have a slight tendency to freckles and, what is more striking, the hair, which appears a normal brown, will be seen in certain lights to have a distinct touch of red in it. In both parents, the genes for brown hair and red hair are present, with the brown dominant and the red recessive.

It is a matter of common observation that, as a rule, the son will inherit more of the characters of the mother, and the daughter may equally resemble either parent, though this is by no means invariable, and there will be found many exceptions to it. There are certain diseases which are inheritable, the best known of which is haemophilia, the tendency to bleed profusely and uncontrollably from even a small cut. The disease manifests itself only in the males, but is passed on by the females, and is one of a large number of characters which are called 'sex-linked'. In this case, the male suffers from the disease because of a gene passed on by his mother, in whom the character is recessive.

HERMIT CRAB, *see* CRAB.

HERON. This group of birds includes the typical Herons, Egrets, and Bitterns, and also the STORKS (q.v.). There are about 70 species, found in most parts of the world, but not in the extreme north, the majority preferring warm or hot climates.

The common Heron stands some 3 feet 6 inches or more high, with a wing-span of nearly 6 feet. Most of its height is made up by its very long neck and legs, its total weight being only from 3 to 4 lbs. Its grey-brown plumage shades to pale bluish-white down the front. It is a powerful flier, but neither very fast nor skilful in manœuvring. In consequence it is rather defenceless against the attacks of birds such as Rooks and Terns, which often set upon it if it

THE COMMON GREY HERON AT ITS LARGE UNTIDY STICK-NEST
IN A TALL TREE. *G. K. Yeates, F.R.P.S.*

flies too near their nests. Herons always live near water—inland lakes and marshes or quiet sea-locks—and feed on fish or any kind of small water-animal. They fish principally in the early morning and evening, standing for long periods in the fishing-ground, and making no movement at all until some prey comes within reach. Then, one quick movement of the long neck—and the prey is caught in the sharp bill. A heron will swim from one fishing-ground to another to avoid the trouble of flight.

Herons nest in heronries on the tops of tall trees, building large, flat nests of sticks, in which they lay three or four bluish-green eggs, and often produce two broods in a season. They return year after year to the same heronry, adding to the nests, which often become very large constructions. In olden days, when Herons were protected, because they were popular game for the sport of FALCONRY (q.v. Vol. IX), there were many great heronries in Britain, especially in southern Lincolnshire. In that county, the famous heronry of Cressy Hall had as many as eighty nests. Even now, 4,000 pairs nest regularly in England and Wales, the largest heronries containing 100 nests. In Britain Herons generally choose tall oaks or elms for nesting; in North India they select the magnificent plane trees, in which they nest in great numbers. Closely related to the Grey Heron are the Purple Heron, common in many parts of Europe, and the Giant or Goliath Heron, a much larger bird, found mostly in Africa.

The Egrets, smaller birds, about 25 inches long, and the larger White Herons are found in Mediterranean countries and through southern Asia, and also a rather different form in Australia and New Zealand. They have beautiful pure white plumage and black legs and beaks. Egret plumes, much sought after by feather-hunters, are often marketed as 'ospreys', though their correct name is 'aigrette' (*see* FEATHER HUNTING, Vol. VI).

The Bitterns, shorter-legged relatives of the Herons, are occasional breeders in eastern Britain, and spread over most of the warmer countries of the world. They are essentially birds of the swamps, their mottled buff, brown, and black plumage harmonizing with the reeds and flags among which they live and nest. They often stand erect and still among the reeds, looking very much like a pointed stump. They have a booming cry, especially in the mating season.

THE TARPON, A GIANT HERRING, LEAPING FROM THE WATER
A. Fraser-Brunner

HERRING. Of all fishes, the Herring family are probably the most important as food for man, for not only do they appear with almost unfailing regularity in vast shoals, but also the flesh contains more nourishment than that of any other fish except Salmon. The common Herring is found in great schools, often numbering millions of individuals, throughout the North Atlantic—though the schools do not travel the immense distances they were once supposed to do. They are divided into a number of local races, which inhabit definite limited regions and always spawn in the same area. The eggs are 'demersal' —that is, they lie on the bed of the sea, among gravel and rocks, unlike those of most other sea fishes, which float near the surface. The Herring and some of its American relatives, such as the Alewife, may sometimes enter rivers, and when they get cut off from the sea, adapt themselves to life in fresh water; while the Shads, belonging to the same family, swim up rivers to lay their demersal eggs in fresh water. The Herring family is known by its very typical 'fish-shape', and has silvery scales that come off very easily. None of the fins has any stiff sharp spines. There is but a single short dorsal fin on the back, while the pelvic fins are far behind the pectoral fins; and there is usually a sharp edge along the middle of the lower surface, which is often made saw-like by the scales.

Closely related to the Herring is the Sprat, a smaller species, with a stronger 'saw' on the belly, and no teeth on the roof of the mouth. This fish lays eggs of the floating type. It is common off Norway, where it is caught in large numbers and canned as 'brisling', after the manner of 'sardines'. (The real 'sardine', however, is the young of the Pilchard, a more southern fish, which is the subject of an important industry in Portugal and southern France. Other species are found round America and Japan.) An easy way to tell the difference between a Herring, a Sprat, and a Pilchard is to hold them up by the dorsal fin (the one on the back). A Herring will balance evenly; a Sprat will hang head downwards, because the fin is nearer the tail; while the Pilchard will tilt with tail downwards, as the fin is nearer the head.

Another near relative of the Herring is the Anchovy, a small fish with a rather long nose jutting forward over the mouth. It has a very strong, peculiar flavour, and when salted is greatly valued for savoury dishes. Other interesting relatives of the Herring are the Gizzard-shads of American rivers, which have small mouths with no teeth, and feed mainly on mud. The stomach forms a strong muscular gizzard something like that of a fowl. The last ray of the dorsal fin is elongate and whip-like, similar to that of the Tarpon, a giant herring of tropical waters which affords great sport to anglers (*see* BIG GAME FISHING, Vol. IX). The Tarpon often takes great leaps out of the water, especially when caught by a hook and line; and it is said that the long last ray of the dorsal fin clings to one side of the fish, bending the fin to that side, like a rudder, in order to direct the flight of the fish. The enormous scales of the Tarpon are often made into ornaments.

See also FISHES.
See also Vol. VI: HERRING FISHING, q.v.

HIBERNATION (from a Latin word meaning 'winter'). When the frosts come and the days shorten, many animals with which we are familiar are no longer seen. Bats flit round no more at dusk; frogs, newts, and lizards are no longer to be found; dormice, field-mice, and others retire to their nests; snails no longer come out in the evening to feed. All are asleep until the warmer weather of spring shall rouse them. During hibernation, animals come very near to death; for, if disturbed, they appear lifeless and take a long time to rouse themselves. The heart

HIPPOPOTAMUS (River-horse). This huge African animal is a distant relative of the SWINE (q.v.), and no relation at all to the horse: it would, therefore, be more accurately called 'Suopotamus' or River-pig.

There are two species, the Common Hippo and the Pigmy Hippo. The Common Hippo used to be very common in all the large rivers and lakes of Africa; but its numbers have been greatly reduced by sportsmen and farmers, to whose crops it is a serious menace. It is nearly 5 feet high, 12 to 14 feet long, and weighs close on 4 tons. Its ugly head would seem to be too large and heavy for its body, since the animal is often seen resting its muzzle on the ground, as if to relieve its neck of the weight. Its upper and lower incisors grow into long tusks. It has short legs, and feet with pad-like soles and four well-developed toes encased in rounded black hoofs. Its skin is naked, rough, and warty, and enormously thick.

Hippos spend the greater part of their life in the water, where they move more naturally and faster than on land. Although they can run with ease at the bottom of a river or lake, they do not normally stay under water for more than five minutes at a time. On coming to the surface they spout up columns of water by violently blowing out air through their nostrils. Hippos usually dive hindquarters first, instead of going into the water head first. However, when on a high bank and suddenly frightened, they will not hesitate to plunge headlong into the water. They spend most of the day in a drowsy, yawning state, taking very little notice of their surroundings. But an hour after sunset, they set out on food-gathering excursions overland, and do not return until dawn. During the night they utter loud snorts and grunts, which can be heard at least a mile away. The size of their stomachs— 11 feet long when extended—gives an idea of the huge amounts of food they require. In uncultivated districts they eat grass and water plants; but where there is neighbouring land under cultivation, they cause great damage by trampling down, as well as eating, the crops.

The dam gives birth to a single offspring at any season of the year, having carried it for 8 months. She looks after it carefully, letting it stand on her back, and protecting it from the male, who is often evilly disposed towards it. Though the males are quarrelsome and bad-tempered with each other, even attacking a wounded comrade, hippos are as a rule fairly

HIPPOPOTAMI TAKING TO THE WATER. *'Picture Post' Library*

timid towards humans. If, however, a boat should run unexpectedly into the middle of a sleeping herd, or close to a solitary hippo at night, there is little chance of escape. Hippos used to be hunted for the ivory of their tusks; but now they are sought only for their hide, fat, and flesh. Their hide is used for making whips, and their feet make an excellent stew.

The Pigmy Hippo, which lives in parts of West Africa only, is a very much smaller animal, about $2\frac{1}{2}$ feet high, $5\frac{1}{2}$ feet long, and weighing only 400 pounds. It spends much less time in the water, but is extremely fond of a mud bath. It wanders for great distances in the woods, moving amazingly quietly considering its bulky body.

HOATZIN. This pheasant-like bird, sometimes called the Stink-pheasant because of its strong odour, is found near the Amazon and other rivers or lakes of north-western South America. It spends its life almost entirely in trees, eating an enormous quantity of leaves. Although it has long wings, it has a very poor flight. Its plumage is olive with white markings above, and dull red below. Its long, loose crest and the tips of its long, rather square tail are yellowish. Its skeleton is peculiar, the lower part of the breast-bone, on which the bird often supports itself when resting, being broad and flattened.

The Hoatzin builds a nest of sticks in bushes or low boughs overhanging the water. When the nestlings are hatched, they immediately begin to climb about actively, like little reptiles, among the branches, holding on not only by their beaks and clawed feet, but also by their wings. If they fall or dive into the water, which they often do, they can swim to the side and soon climb back safely to their branches. The wings of these nestlings are an interesting survival of an earlier form of limb belonging to ancestors of birds which lived entirely in trees, and used their wings (or arms) for climbing rather than for flying. The 'hand' part of the wing is relatively long, and is provided with finger-like ends and long claws. Before the nestling grows feathers, the wing-quills begin to develop, and these grow in such an order that they do not impede the use of the wing as a hand until the wing-feathers are grown enough to be able to carry the weight of the body. The adult Hoatzin uses its wings, though not very effectively, as other birds do.

See also BIRDS.

HOBBY, *see* FALCON.

HOLLY, *see* PLANT DEFENCES.

HONEY-BEE, *see* BEES.

HONEY-EATERS. This group of birds belongs to Australia, New Zealand, and the islands of the South Pacific. They are distinguished by their long tongues, which have brush-like tips and can be formed into a tube for sucking honey from flowers, especially from the various species of Eucalyptus. They vary considerably in colour, some being plain brown or greenish, while others are more brightly coloured, and one, the Blood Honey-eater or Soldier Bird of Australia, is deep black and brilliant scarlet.

The Parson Bird or Tui is a common bird in New Zealand, and well known for its lovely and varied song, in which the sound 'tui' is frequent. The male is a shining greenish-black, with white spots on the wings and two tufts of white feathers

SPINEBILL HONEY-EATER OF AUSTRALIA
Australian News & Information Bureau

at the throat. The Stitch Bird, also named because of its note, carries bright, canary-yellow wing feathers, which were so much sought after for decorating the robes of Maori chiefs that the bird has been almost exterminated. Another Honey-eater is popularly called 'Four o'clock', and the Hawaiian species is called by the natives the 'O-o'—in both cases because of the cry. The now rather uncommon New Zealand Bell-bird is well known in that country because of its bell-like note.

HOOF. This is the horny cap, corresponding to a finger- or toe-nail, on one or two toes in the hoofed animals, or 'ungulates'. In these animals the limbs are used only for running and walking, and the fingers have become unusually long and reduced in number. In cloven-hoofed ungulates there are two functional toes to each foot; but in horses there is only one, although remains of the others are seen in the splint bones. The way the horse's hoof has evolved is shown on page 138.

See also NAILS AND CLAWS.

HOOPOE. This bird is so called because of its cry. It is a little larger than a thrush, and has

HOOPOE AT ITS NESTING HOLE
Arthur Brook

sandy-coloured plumage, with vivid markings of black and white bands, and on its head a striking long crest, which it can open like a fan. It has a long, slender, and slightly curved bill, and broad wings. There are six species of Hoopoe, three of which are confined to Africa and Madagascar, and a fourth to India and Burma. The typical Hoopoe spreads over most of Asia, and central and southern Europe, wintering in Africa and India. It very occasionally visits

Great Britain, but practically never breeds here. It feeds on insects, grubs, and worms, which it collects mainly from the ground. It has a weak and laboured flight, fluttering rather like a butterfly. Hoopoes generally nest in hollow trees. The female sits very closely during the period of incubation, being fed regularly by the male, and leaving the nest for very short periods only. The nest gets very dirty and acquires a most unpleasant smell.

The Wood Hoopoes of Africa, a different family, are shy and wary birds, living in trees and seldom coming to the ground. They are rather larger, darker in colour, and have no crest.

HORMONES, PLANT, *see* PLANT GROWTH.

HORNBILL. This tropical bird of the Old World, of which there are some sixty species, is mainly conspicuous for its fantastic beak—as its name suggests. Hornbills vary in size from that of a pigeon to the Great Pied Hornbill of Asia, which measures nearly 5 feet in length. They generally have mainly black and white plumage, with fairly long tails. The majority of species have enormously developed, long beaks, along the top of which is a casque or helmet of a light, spongy, but very strong, texture. Most Hornbills are forest birds, living in trees and feeding on fruit and small animals caught among the trees. The African Ground Hornbills, however, live mainly in the open plains, hunting for food, such as reptiles, on the ground. Groups of them will attack and kill snakes.

Hornbills are particularly interesting because of their nesting habits. They nest in hollows in tree-trunks. When the period of incubation starts, the male shuts the female into the nesting-chamber by building a clay wall over the entrance, leaving open only a slit through which he can provide her with food. The female makes use of this period of imprisonment for completing her moult. When the eggs hatch, the male breaks down the wall with his powerful beak, and releases his family. By the end of the incubation period, the nests are generally filthy and give forth a fearful stench, and the female is wasted and dirty, being for a time hardly able to fly. Hornbills have an odd habit of tossing up into the air and catching again in their bills every piece of food which they pick up. They are noisy birds, noisy in their heavy flight, and in their characteristic cry, which is somewhere between a bray and a shriek.

HORNBILL

HORNET, *see* WASPS, Section 3.

HORNS AND ANTLERS. Many mammals carry on their heads more or less conspicuous weapons, usually in pairs—for the UNICORN (q.v. Vol. I) is a mythical beast—which are generally referred to as horns. Those of cattle, sheep, goats, giraffes, and other RUMINANTS (q.v.), except deer, are produced by the skin, and are, therefore, the same kind of growth as HAIR (q.v.). They are made of a nitrogenous compound called 'keratin', and the animal that possesses them carries them throughout its life. (In the newly born animal they are normally not present.) The antlers of the deer family, on the other hand, are bony extensions from the skull of the animal, and are usually shed each year and regrown. The horn of the rhinoceros consists of matted hair. The 'horn' of the narwhal is made of ivory and is, therefore, a kind of TUSK (q.v.).

Horns and antlers are primarily used as weapons; the female reindeer, who retains her antlers throughout the winter, after the male has shed his, protects her young with them. Some animals also use them as tools; cattle, for instance, will tear up turf with their horns.

HORSE. Horses belong to the order Ungulata, or hoofed beasts, as do CATTLE, SHEEP, and DEER (qq.v.); but they differ from most members of the group in being one-toed, and in not chewing the cud. The genus, *Equus*, includes also the DONKEYS and ZEBRAS (qq.v.). In prehistoric times, wild horses roamed all over Europe and Asia. To-day, however, the only real wild horses are those living in Mongolia. These are small, dun-coloured animals with a single dark stripe along the back. The so-called wild horses of America and the Brumbies of Australia are both descendants of imported domestic horses which have run wild. The evolution of the horse has been an interesting study for zoologists. The present horse has evolved in a series of gradual transformations, lasting for 50 million years, from a quite small, four-toed animal (*see* EVOLUTION). Horses have been domesticated since very early times, but not so early as the dogs, oxen, or asses. They were not known at all in America until the Europeans came in the 16th century, and not until two centuries later in Australasia.

See also Vol. IV: HORSE TRANSPORT.
See also Vol. IX: HORSES; RIDING.
See also Vol. VI: HORSES, FARM.

HORSE-FLY. About twenty-one species of these flies (also called Gad-flies and Breeze-flies) are found in Great Britain. They have very large eyes, which extend outwards so as to make the head wider than the front of the thorax. The abdomen is flat, and usually has more or less parallel sides. Most species are dark in colour, with grey or yellowish mottlings, but

ABOUT NATURAL SIZE

some are yellow-banded, looking like Hover-flies. Some species are among the biggest of our British flies. During hot summer weather they can be very troublesome to horses and cattle in fields, and to ourselves. Only the females 'bite'; the males suck only water, honey-dew, or the nectar of flowers. The small species, called Clegs, are dark brown and have mottled wings. In hot weather they attack fiercely. They are very quiet in their approach—usually the first evidence the victim has of their presence is when he feels the pain caused by the puncture in his skin.

Although these flies may be found in woods and dry pastures, they lay their eggs on plants growing in water or wet places. The larvae are carnivorous, feeding on any insect larvae and other aquatic creatures they find about them. Clegs are usually more common, and therefore more of a nuisance, in wet pastures.

See also FLIES.

HOUSE-FLY.

The House-fly and the Lesser House-fly are familiar to everybody. The larger species is found wherever there is human habitation, and seems to be able to adapt itself to all sorts of climates and temperatures. The higher the temperature, however, the better it flourishes and the greater its numbers.

The eggs are laid in batches of anything up to 150, a single female laying as many as 2,000 in its short lifetime of about a month. (Individual House-flies may live for two months in the adult state.) The eggs are usually laid in stable

LARVA. × 2

manure, but may also be laid in an uncovered dustbin or on meat. They hatch in about 19 hours; the first casting of the larval skin takes place about 24 hours later; the second occurs after another 24 hours; and the third and last, 3 or 4 days later still—when the pupal stage begins. After about 4 days as a pupa, the adult fly emerges. These times may be lengthened during cold weather, or speeded up during very hot spells. In an ordinary summer, an average of 10 to 11 days from egg-laying to the emergence of the adult fly is usual. The larva is a typical fly maggot, with a long, soft, whitish body, very narrow at the head, and thick at the back. The pupa is contained within a typical brown, horny puparium, consisting of the last larval skin.

Because of their feeding habits, House-flies are carriers of disease. In nearly all our two-winged flies the gullet divides into two tubes as it passes back through the neck into the thorax. The upper tube is the intestine, and the lower leads to a blind sac, the food reservoir, in the lower part of the abdomen. On taking a meal, the fly fills this reservoir, and later sends its contents back into the intestine for digestion. In the House-fly, however, when the reservoir is emptied, the food is actually passed out of the mouth to be re-eaten. In this way it makes vomit-spots, which disfigure our window-panes in the summer, and may infect all kinds of food. Sometimes a dead House-fly is seen on a window-pane surrounded by a white halo. This fly has been killed by a fungus which has digested away the contents of its abdomen, and the halo is a mass of fungus spores thrown off by minute fruiting bodies that have pushed their way out from the carcase.

The Lesser House-fly is not really very closely related to the House-fly, nor very like it in appearance. It is the insect with a queer jerky flight that loves to fly in little groups, preferably just below the light in the middle of a room. It appears earlier in the year than the House-fly, and disappears when it arrives. The larva of the Lesser House-fly is flat, with a double row of spines along each side and along the back. It grows up in much the same places as the larva of House-flies.

See also FLIES.
See also Vol. XI : HOUSEHOLD PESTS.

HOVER-FLY.

This fly is so called because it hovers for a long period in one spot, with its wings vibrating rapidly, and then darts with great speed to another spot, where it again hangs motionless. In colour and shape, as well as in their loud humming note, Hover-flies resemble WASPS and BEES (qq.v.) in a very remarkable way. If looked at carefully, however, they can be recognized easily enough as harmless flies by their single pair of wings and large eyes, which often almost meet on the top of the head.

There are large and small Hover-flies. One, a particularly handsome fly, with a rich mahogany thorax and black and bright golden-yellow bands on its abdomen, is an inch long, whereas most others measure less than ¼ inch. Some are slim, banded or spotted with yellow on a black, blue, brown, or metallic background. Others are much more bulky; and some are densely covered with fur, with yellow and black bands, or black with a red tip to the abdomen. Most Hover-flies frequent flowers, and they are the chief pollinators of the little blue speedwells.

BRAMBLE HOVER-FLY
About natural size

The habits of the larvae are very varied. A very handsome, black Hover-fly, with a white band across the top of its abdomen, passes its early days cleaning up the nests of bees and wasps, and then spends most of its adult life on bramble-blossom. Other Hover-fly larvae are aquatic, or live in decaying matter or filth. These include the Rat-tailed Maggot, which has a long breathing-tube, like a rat's tail, at its rear end, capable of being extended to several times the length of the body. The larvae of other Hover-flies feed on APHIDES (q.v.), sometimes eating one every minute, and moving rapidly over the leaves like a 'looper' caterpillar, in search of their prey.

Very few Hover-flies are harmful; but two species, called the Narcissus Flies, are destructive during their larval life to various kinds of bulbs.

See also FLIES.

HUMBLE-BEE FLY (Bee Fly). This beautiful insect should be looked for on the brightest and hottest days of spring and early summer. Its body is densely covered with brown and golden fur, and its long forked tongue stretches straight out in front. Its wings are spotted or bordered with brown. Its body is broad behind, but in front tapers rapidly to the head; there is no noticeable nipping-in to mark off the head, thorax, and abdomen from each other. The body is, in fact, streamlined, and the insect flies very fast. When visiting low-growing tubular flowers, such as those of ground ivy, it does not settle, but hovers very daintily over them, inserting its tongue into the flower-tube—thus behaving like a tropical HUMMING-BIRD (q.v.). When visiting primroses, however, Humble-bee Flies settle lightly upon the flowers. On a sunny day in early spring, when they will often be present in large numbers, they may be seen to leave the primrose bank and settle lightly upon the bare earth or on a sunlit wall, their wings outspread.

The eggs of the Humble-bee Flies are laid on the ground, and the larvae find their way into the nests of solitary bees. At first they feed upon the pollen stored there for the larva of the bee; but, later, they devour the larva itself.

See also FLIES.

HUMMING-BIRD. There are a great many species of these little birds, inhabitants of South and central America and the West Indies. Some of them migrate northwards as far as Canada in the summer. The majority are very small, the largest, the Great Humming-bird of the Andes, being about 8 inches long, and the smallest little larger than a bumble-bee. They mostly have brilliant plumage of metallic green, purple, cinnamon, black, and other colours. Some carry crests on their heads, others have long, fantastically shaped tails. They have long, slender bills, some straight and others curved, and they all possess long, tubular tongues, which they thrust down into flowers to suck up the nectar on which they feed (*see* COLOURED PLATE facing p. 208).

Humming-birds have long wings, with very strong wing-muscles which enable them to sustain for long periods the extremely rapid wing-beats necessary for their hovering flight. The little birds do not settle on flowers while extracting the nectar, but hover over them with such a rapid wing-motion that the wings become almost invisible, and produce a distinct 'hum'. Slow-motion films have shown that the wings

TINY HUMMING-BIRD IN ITS NEST BUILT ON A LARGE TROPICAL LEAF. *Booth Steamship Co.*

move almost horizontally, and for the back-stroke the wing is turned almost upside-down. When not hovering they make very quick darting flights, and perform strange contortions in the air as they catch the tiny insects which also form part of their diet. The beautiful, long tail-feathers of the Long-tailed Humming-bird are fascinating to watch during these rapid evolutions.

During the courting season, Humming-birds are vicious fighters, flying at each other with such violence that they sometimes blind each other with their beaks. The nests are beautifully constructed, fairly deep, little cups, some being hardly more than an inch across, woven out of soft materials such as vegetable down and spiders' webs. Two eggs are laid, white, and oval in shape.

Humming-birds are found only in America; but other birds of the same type which suck nectar from flowers inhabit the Old World. The HONEY-EATERS (q.v.) belong to Australasia; and in Africa and tropical Asia the Sunbirds form a large group of brilliantly coloured, small, elegantly shaped birds, which feed upon the sweet juices of flowers and small flying insects. Neither of these groups, however, hover while they feed.

HYAENA. This carrion-feeding beast represents a type of CARNIVORA which appears to link the CATS and the CIVETS (qq.v.). It is found in the countries of southern Asia and in Africa, and fossil remains show that it once also inhabited Europe, even as far north as Britain. It is entirely absent, however, from America and Australasia. There are three species now existing, the Striped, the Spotted, and the Brown Hyaena. They are all about the size of a wolf, and have greyish or yellowish-brown, coarse, shaggy coats, marked with darker stripes or spots. Their disproportionately short hind-legs give them an ungainly appearance. They are extremely strong, especially in their jaws and teeth, which are powerful enough to crack open the bones of the largest animals. Their necks also are strong; and it has been claimed that they can carry off a full-sized ass, though this has not been proved.

Hyaenas are mainly scavengers, eating dead animals in any stage of decomposition; but they also kill and devour dogs, sheep, and goats, which they hunt in packs. They will cripple other creatures, it seems out of sheer cruelty, and

HYAENA

they will lie in wait and pounce on young kids and lambs even when they are not hungry. They live wherever there is suitable cover, spending the daytime in dark caves or ruins, or occasionally in burrows, and coming out at nightfall to hunt for food. They are greatly dreaded in inhabited districts, as they often enter villages and camps to raid the domestic animals, occasionally attacking even human beings. They have been known to rob graves, eating a part of the corpse on the spot, and dragging the rest to their den. When out hunting, hyaenas utter uncanny, maniacal laughter and hair-raising howls. Strangely enough, in captivity they often become quite docile, and both in India and Africa they have been tamed and used as dogs.

HYDRA. This small animal, from $\frac{1}{8}$ to $\frac{1}{4}$ inch long, lives in not too stagnant freshwater ponds, clinging by its foot to stones, sticks, or water plants. It is a close relative of JELLY-FISH, SEA-ANEMONES, and CORALS (qq.v.)—among the simplest of multicellular animals. The body consists of a hollow cylinder, with the foot at one end, and six fine waving tentacles surrounding a conical mouth at the other. The walls of the body and the tentacles consist of two layers of cells, an outer one and an inner digestive layer.

Hydra feed on minute water-animals. When these come in contact with the tentacles, they are paralysed and held by the stinging cells, which are scattered over the surface, especially on the tentacles. Later they are pushed into the mouth by the tentacles, the mouth often stretching considerably to receive them. In the hollow cavity of the body the prey is digested, the indigestible parts being ejected, again through the mouth. Hydra reproduce both sexually, and asexually by budding. A bud appears on the side of the parent body. It grows, and produces a mouth and tentacles, which help to obtain food for the joint body. If food is plentiful, the Hydra produces several buds, and these may grow secondary buds, forming a temporary colony. Eventually the buds become detached and start an independent life. The Hydra is 'hermaphrodite'—one individual producing both male and female cells. The sperm is liberated into the water, where it swims freely until it reaches a Hydra with a mature ovum. The sperm then enters the ovary, and unites with the ovum, thus achieving fertilization. The young Hydra develops and finally drops off the parent.

HYRAX. This small, rabbit-like animal, an inhabitant of Africa and south-west Asia, has puzzled zoologists. It is in no way related to the rabbit or any other rodent. Its molar teeth and much of its skeleton show likeness to the rhinoceros, its lower incisor teeth to the hippopotamus; the structure of its feet resembles the elephant; and it has more pairs of ribs than any animal except the sloth. Professor Huxley finally placed it in an order of its own, the Hyracoidea. The Hyraxes are active little creatures, about 12 to 18 inches long, with blunt muzzles, small round ears, and thick, soft, greyish-brown fur. They feed on leaves and young shoots.

There are two kinds of Hyraxes: the Rock Hyraxes, which live in colonies among rocks and on cliffs, and the Tree Hyraxes, which use hollow trees for shelter and are sometimes called Tree Bears. Although they have hoof-like claws, which cannot grasp like the hands of a monkey, and have no prehensile tails, yet they climb up the smooth trunks of trees and over rocks. Apparently the naked soles of their feet, like those of the GECKO (q.v.), adhere to smooth surfaces. They are very timid—and with good reason, for they are favourite food for leopards and large birds of prey; but they are gentle and can easily be tamed. When feeding, they are said to place one of their number, usually an old male, to keep guard, and he gives notice of danger by uttering shrill squeaks, which send the whole colony to shelter.

I

IBEX, *see* Goat.

IBIS, *see* Storks.

ICHNEUMON AND BRACONID FLIES. If cabbages in a garden have been attacked by caterpillars of the Large White Butterfly, it is most likely that, late in the summer, one will find on the palings, walls of the tool-shed, or similar places, masses of about a hundred or more small golden-yellow cases, and perhaps amongst them the dead body of one of these caterpillars. If these are kept under observation, it will be found that, in about a month's time, one end of each case will be neatly removed from the inside, and out will come a very lively little black fly, with four wings and long slender antennae. This is the Braconid Fly, and after a moment's hesitation, it will fly away. The adult fly may survive the winter, and the following year will seek out newly hatched caterpillars in which to lay its eggs. Large species will insert one egg in the body of each host insect, and small species as many as 100 or 150. When the eggs hatch, the young larvae commence to feed on the fat of the host, but avoid the vital organs. To all appearance a caterpillar that has been 'ichneumonized' goes on feeding and moving about in the usual way—until suddenly it collapses. At this point, the larvae of the Braconid escape through its skin, each to spin a white silken cocoon, which soon turns golden.

This parasite in the Large White Butterfly is one of a group of insects called Ichneumoid Flies, closely related to the Bees and Wasps (qq.v.). As larvae they are all internal parasites, most of them in the caterpillars of butterflies and moths, though other insects and also spiders are attacked. The attacks of such parasitic flies are often devastating. Thus, on one occasion, of a batch of 100 caterpillars of the Large White

Butterfly, only four survived to enter the chrysalis state. All Ichneumon Flies have slender bodies, rounded heads with long antennae, a very narrow 'waist' and, in the female, a slender ovipositor, by means of which the eggs are laid within the body of the creature attacked. The majority are either black or amber-brown; but they vary greatly in size. Some of our British species are an inch or an inch and a quarter long, whereas others are very small indeed. One handsome species, black with small yellow spots, is actually longer than the Giant Wood-wasp (q.v.), the insect that it parasitizes, and is remarkable for the way it seeks out its victims. The larva of the Wood-wasp burrows through the timber of pine-trees; but even here the Ichneumon Fly succeeds in locating it, and then drills through the wood until it reaches its victim.

Ichneumon Flies are very active insects, taking readily to flight; they may often be seen running

over the window-panes in houses. It seems that their antennae play an important part in selecting the victims for egg-laying, as they are perpetually a-quiver, apparently testing everything they approach.

There are other insects which have similar habits to the Ichneumon Fly—such as the Bristle-fly, Chalcid-wasp, and Flesh-fly (qq.v.).

IGUANA. This lizard of the family Iguanidae is found in tropical America and Madagascar. The name Iguana is wrongly used for the Monitors (q.v.) of the Old World, which are not related. The true Iguanas usually live in trees; but they are good swimmers and take readily to water. Although they will devour insects, they feed mainly upon young leaves,

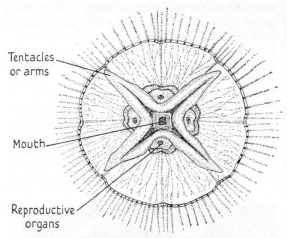

Tentacles
or arms

Mouth

Reproductive
organs

FIG. I.   UNDER-SURFACE OF ADULT JELLYFISH

the under-surface of the body, is a four-sided
opening, surrounded by four long and delicate
tentacles, and leading into a capacious stomach
(*see* Fig. 1). The eggs, when ripe, are discharged
through the mouth into the sea, where they are
fertilized. Each egg then develops into a hollow,
oval larva, covered with hair-like organs by
means of which it swims through the water. On
coming to rest on the floor of the sea it attaches
itself at one end to a suitable base, the lower
half of its body becoming rather slender. It then
gradually acquires the cup-shaped form of a

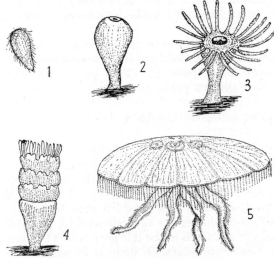

FIG. 2.   LIFE-HISTORY OF THE COMMON JELLYFISH
1. Free-swimming larva; 2. Larva, fixed to a base, develops into a small polyp; 3. Polyp develops a mouth
surrounded with tentacles; 4. Polyp develops 'waists';
5. Full-grown Jellyfish

small polyp, with a stomach and mouth encircled
by waving tentacles used for capturing food.
After a time, the little polyp, which has increased slightly in height, begins to show a series
of transverse constrictions, or waists, and the
creature grows to look like a pile of miniature
saucers. In time these saucers detach themselves,
turn over, swim away, and become full-grown
jellyfishes, whose offspring again will develop into
cup-shaped, anchored polyps. Thus, in the life-
history of the Common Jellyfish (*see* Fig. 2) we
have an example of the phenomenon called the
'alternation of generations', or the alternate occurrence of two different forms in one life-history
—the fixed polyp, and the free-swimming jellyfish which develops from it. In the plant world
the same phenomenon occurs in the life-history
of FERNS (q.v.).

Although milky-blue is the dominant colour,
some tropical species are brightly tinted, and
grow to a great size. Shoals are sometimes to be
seen during calm summer weather, drifting with
the tide or slowly moving up and down in the
water by rhythmic contractions of their bodies.
On a calm, dark, summer night, from the deck
of a ship, jellyfishes can often be seen, faintly
illumined by their own light, passing in an endless procession. Their food consists of small
crustacea, fish and the like, which are rendered
helpless by the stinging cells in the tentacles.
Nevertheless, some young fishes, such as young
whiting and horse-mackerel, find safe temporary
shelter inside the umbrella-shaped bodies of certain species—though whether the association is
in all cases of entirely mutual benefit has yet to
be proved.

See also CORALS; HYDRA; SEA-ANEMONES.

JERBOA. This RODENT (q.v.), often called the
Jumping Mouse, lives in the deserts of Asia and
North Africa, where its sandy colouring makes
it difficult to detect. It has long hind-legs, but
very short front ones—the disproportion being
greater even than in Kangaroos. Like Kangaroos, it makes enormous bounds, using its long
muscular tail to help it, and sometimes making
jumps in such rapid succession that it appears to
be flying. Jerboas live together in large numbers,
often in company with sand-grouse, desert larks,
and lizards. They use their fore-feet to dig
burrows in the hard ground. Just before sundown, they come out to eat leaves, fruit, and
insects, and quite often sit near the mouth of

THE JOHN DORY SURPRISES ITS PREY BY STRETCHING FORWARD THE JAWS LIKE A TELESCOPE. *A. Fraser-Brunner*

acquired a thick layer of fat, so that its weight is more than half as much again, it hibernates in its burrow, rolling itself into a tight ball to sleep (*see* HIBERNATION).

JOHN DORY. This fish, found in most temperate seas, is a useful food-fish, sometimes to be seen in fish-shops in Britain. It gets this curious name from the legend that the large black spots on each side of its body are the marks made by St. Peter's finger and thumb when he took a piece of money from the fish's mouth (Matt. XVII. 24–7). This association with the keeper of the Gate of Heaven caused the Italians to call it '*Janitore*' (a doorkeeper), the name John Dory being what the English tongue has made of it.

their holes during the day, though at the slightest sound they dive down their burrows. In hot weather they become very torpid, and fall into a long sleep.

Widely distributed over North America is a close relative of the Jerboa family, the Labrador Jumping Mouse. It is the smallest of the family, measuring about 5 inches, and its tail is much longer than its body. It lives near woods and shrubby places. In winter, having

As the John Dory is very flat from side to side, it is scarcely visible when seen from the front. This allows it to approach quite close to its prey without causing alarm. Having got within striking distance, it suddenly shoots its jaws forward, like a telescope, and sucks the unfortunate victim down.

JUNGLE FOWL, *see* PHEASANT.

K

KANGAROO. This, the best known of the MARSUPIALS (q.v.) or pouched animals, is to be found only in Australia, Tasmania, and New Guinea. There are many different species, the smaller ones being known as Wallabies. Their general appearance—their long, strong, hind-legs, with peculiar elongated feet, their short front legs, thick, muscular, tapering tails, and small heads—is well known to everyone. When the Kangaroo is not moving, it sits up on its hind-legs, supported by its tail, with its short fore-legs hanging like arms in front. It uses its fore-legs only when moving slowly to graze; when travelling at speed, it moves by enormous leaps, propelled by its hind-legs and balanced by its tail.

Young kangaroos are born one at a time, and, like all marsupials, are very small and un-developed at birth, those of the larger species being only about 1 inch long. As soon as it is born, the tiny creature works its way with its front claws into its mother's pouch, where it becomes firmly attached to her nipple; and, as it has not the power to suck, milk is pumped into its body by the mother. When developed enough to move by itself, it becomes detached from the teat, but remains in the pouch until it can run by its mother's side. At the approach of danger, however, the mother will pick up her young and thrust it into her pouch for safety.

The larger kangaroos are as tall as a man, while some of the smaller are no bigger than a rabbit. The two largest species are the Great Grey Kangaroo, which lives in forest country, and the Red Kangaroo, of the open plains. When travelling at full speed, these animals can leap 25 feet at a bound, and clear objects 6 feet high. In the mating season the males fight one another, striking forward with their hind-legs and inflicting serious injury with their formid-able claws. Another well-known species is the stout, heavily built Wallaroo, which has long, thick, grey fur.

Kangaroos are vegetarians, feeding mainly on grass, young heather, and other green plants. They are timid creatures, with acute sight, hearing, and sense of smell. Like those of hares, kangaroos' eyes seem to be set in such a way that their forward vision is limited, so that the animals may blunder into something directly in their path. Kangaroos always go about in droves, following a leader. The various droves keep to their own districts and have their own particular feeding-grounds. They feed in the early morning, at twilight, and during the night, and lie up by day in damp, scrubby gullies in summer, or on dry, sandy ridges in winter.

Quite distinct from the typical Kangaroos are the Tree Kangaroos found in the dense tropical forests of New Guinea and northern Australia. These have front legs very nearly equal in length to their hind-legs, and they spend most of their time climbing among trees, aided by their strong claws, and using their long furry tails to balance them.

The Rat Kangaroos are little larger than rabbits. They have small, rounded ears and long, furry tails, which are generally prehensile at the tips. Some of them use their tails to carry grass and other materials for their nest-building, curving the tip of the tail down below the bundle. They lie hidden in their nests in the grass during the day, and go out only at night.

KEA, see PARROTS.

KED. This insect, sometimes wrongly called the 'sheep-tick', is a very common skin parasite on sheep, and may be found clinging to the wool with its claws. It is a blood-sucker, and has a very hairy, reddish or grey-brown body with a flat abdomen. It has no wings, but in other ways it so closely resembles the two-winged flies that it must be grouped with them. Keds, there-fore, belong to a degraded division of two-winged flies called Louse Flies, all of which (with one exception, the Bee Louse) are parasites on birds and mammals, produce their young alive in an advanced stage of larval development, and pupate in a 'puparium' (the last larval skin).

Like so many external parasites, the Ked is spread by contact, and so passes from sheep to sheep; but it may occasionally be found crawling about the ground near sheep pasturage. Some-

KANGAROO WITH HER YOUNG IN HER POUCH
'Picture Post' Library

times it finds its way upon sheep-dogs or other animals. The larvae are born one at a time, at intervals of several weeks. They are dropped in the sheep's wool, and then burrow deep down amongst it. In about twelve hours they change into pupae, the pupal state lasting for about three weeks.

Some Louse Flies, such as the Forest Fly, a parasite on the horse, are fully winged, others have imperfectly developed wings, and others, like the Ked, have no wings. Some cast off their wings after they have arrived upon their hosts. The female of one of this last kind (a parasite on bats, found in Queensland and in some of the East Indies) embeds herself in the skin under a bat's ear, and then casts off both wings and legs. The Bee Louse, which is very minute, and has neither eyes nor wings, is found clinging to the thorax of the queen or of drones. Unlike the other members of its group, the female Bee Louse lays eggs; and the larvae, which are typical fly-maggots, feed in the brood-cells of the honey-comb upon the material stored there. They pupate in the honeycomb, and, when adult, make their own way on to the bees.

See also FLIES.

KENTISH GLORY MOTH. This moth, the only European representative of the family Endromidae, is a near relative of the domestic Silk Moth. Its name dates from the 18th century, when in England it was found only in Kent. Now, it is most abundant in Scotland and Wyre Forest, Worcestershire, where it frequents moors and woods containing young birches. The male, recognized by its combed antennae, has a wing-span of quite 2 inches, the fore-wings being brown, the hind-wings orange. The pale smoky-white female is even larger. Both sexes have white streaks and spots, two black lines edged with white across the fore-wings, and a single line on the hind-wings.

Freshly emerged unmated females give off scents which are attractive to the day-flying males: indeed, in Sussex, 118 males were once known to assemble to a single female. The some-what cylindrical eggs are laid on birch twigs in double rows. The young black larvae con-gregate together near the tip of the twig, and, clinging by the abdominal legs, hold up their heads and fore parts so that they closely resemble little stumps on the twig. They become green on moulting, and then so closely resemble a group of birch catkins as almost to defy detec-tion. As they grow larger, their resemblance to catkins is less striking, and they gradually become more leaf-like in colour and attitude. The mature caterpillar lives alone and is mainly green, with a dark central line. In June or July, shortly before pupation, it becomes reddish-brown, and so is not very conspicuous when it abandons the birches to spin its blackish-brown silk cocoon among moss and leaves on the ground, or just below the surface. The pupae, which often spend 2 years in this stage, work their way out of their cocoons in March or April, a week or so before they hatch.

KESTREL, *see* FALCON.

KING CROW, *see* DRONGO.

KINGFISHER. These brilliant birds are to be found all over the world, the majority of species belonging to tropical countries. There are two main sub-families: those which feed entirely on fish and live near rivers and lakes, and those, often living some way from water, which have a mixed diet including fish.

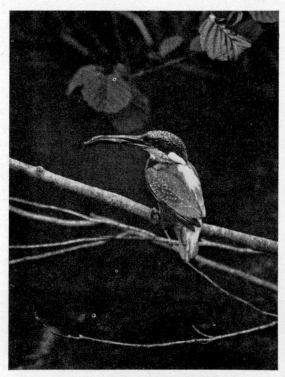

KINGFISHER WITH A MINNOW IN ITS BEAK
G. K. Yeates, F.R.P.S.

The common Kingfisher, a resident of the British Isles, is the most brilliantly coloured of European birds. It has a stocky body and short tail, and an unmistakable, long, dagger-shaped bill. Its back and wings are a dazzling blue-green, its throat and underparts salmon-pink and chestnut, and its feet bright red. It is a comparatively common bird where conditions are suitable, and is becoming more common now that it is no longer pursued for its feathers. It can be seen skimming over the surface of the water like a blue flash, or perching upon some branch, post, or rock over the water, watching for a fish or water-insect. On sighting its prey, it plunges headlong, and on securing its fish, it returns to its post, beats its victim on the perch until it is dead, and then swallows it head-first.

The Kingfisher makes a burrow for itself in the bank of a stream, digging out the earth with its strong beak, and making a tunnel horizontally into the bank for a distance of from 18 inches to 3 feet. The tunnel ends in a circular chamber where the six or seven round, glossy, white eggs are laid in a nest consisting of no more than a few half-digested fish-bones. By the end of the incubation period the nest is fouled with disgorged fish-bones and other refuse. This nesting habit is very different from that described in the Greek legend of the Halcyon (or Kingfisher), which was supposed to build a floating nest on the surface of the sea. According to the legend, Alcyone, the daughter of Aeolus, King of the Winds, was changed into a Kingfisher. She was granted two weeks' calm weather at the winter solstice, so that she might brood in peace. For this reason all sailors on the Mediterranean enjoyed a period of tranquillity during the 'Halcyon Days'.

The second sub-family of Kingfishers, which eat reptiles, crabs, and various insects, are often found in forest or bush country. The largest group is that of the Wood Kingfishers, of which there are about seventy species, the best known being the White-breasted Kingfisher, a bird found over all southern Asia and the greater part of Africa. Another well-known and larger species is the Laughing Kingfisher or Laughing Jackass of Australia.

KITE, *see* HAWK, Section 3.

KITTEN MOTH, *see* PROMINENTS.

KITTIWAKE, *see* GULLS, Section 3.

KIWI. This bird belongs to New Zealand only. It is a member of the section of flightless birds, to which also belongs the OSTRICH (q.v.). The bones of the wings are very small and slender, the whole wing being entirely concealed by the plumage of the back. But though Kiwis cannot fly, they can run very fast. They are robustly built, and have strong legs and feet, with which they scratch up the worms and insects on which they feed. They have long slender bills, useful for probing into soft ground and under leaves or moss. Their feathers are long and rather hair-like, reddish or grey in colour, streaked with a darker shade. They have no tails. They are little larger than a domestic hen.

Kiwis are night-birds, spending the day hidden in burrows or hollow logs, or under thick vegetation. They nest in some such hidden spot, laying one or two whitish eggs, remarkably large for the size of the bird. The incubation and care

A FAMILY OF NEW ZEALAND KIWIS
The New Zealand Herald

of the chicks is carried out almost entirely by the male, who generally will not allow the female to come near the nest after she has laid the eggs. Kiwis are now very scarce, and are carefully protected by the New Zealand government.

THE KOALA, OR NATIVE BEAR OF AUSTRALIA
E. O. Hoppé

KOALA (Australian Bear). This animal is not a bear, but belongs to the same family of MARSUPIALS as the KANGAROO (qq.v.). Its tubby shape and soft, greyish-brown, woolly coat has made it popular as a model for 'Teddy-bear' toys. It is about the size of a large poodle-dog, and has large, rounded ears and a prominent, black, india-rubber-like nose. In its cheeks it has pouches for storing food, like many monkeys.

Koalas live chiefly in the trees, climbing by means of the long claws on their feet. They are rather sluggish creatures, and move awkwardly on the ground, always making for a tree if pursued. They are not seen very often, as they stir very little until nightfall. They feed chiefly on the leaves of gum-trees; but sometimes they descend to the ground at night to dig up roots.

One young Koala is born at a time, and, like all young marsupials, it is reared in its mother's pouch, which, unlike that of a kangaroo, opens backwards. When it is a few months old, the mother carries it on her back. Koalas used to be common in eastern Australia, but they have been so much hunted for the sake of their fur that they are now scarce in most districts. They are rarely kept in zoos outside Australia because of the difficulty of supplying them with their natural food.

KRAIT. This genus of poisonous snakes, found in India and Indo-China, is most nearly related to the COBRAS (q.v.), but it differs from them in having no hood. Kraits have highly polished scales, with an enlarged series down the middle of the back. They are particularly abundant in India, where many people die every year as a result of their bite. There are thirteen species, the two best known being the Indian Krait, which is black with white cross-bands and grows to a length of 4 feet 6 inches, and the Banded Krait, which has broad yellow bands and has been known to reach 7 feet in length. Other species are the Ceylon Krait, the Black Krait of Assam, and the Yellow-headed Krait of the Malayan Region.

Another group of poisonous snakes closely related to the Kraits is the Coral Snakes, remarkable for the beauty of their colour. They may be red, pink, yellow, brown, black, or purple, and banded, spotted, or striped, with an equal variety of colours. Their scales are highly iridescent, but they are without the enlarged series down the back. They inhabit the tropical regions of America, India, and Australia.

See also SNAKES.

L

LABYRINTH-FISHES. Many kinds of fishes are able to breathe air, as well as the oxygen dissolved in water. Outstanding among these are the Anabantoids, or Labyrinth-fishes, so called because, above the gills, there has developed a special breathing-chamber, which is sometimes very complicated, like a labyrinth. All the Labyrinth-fishes are inhabitants of the fresh waters of Asia and Africa. To the group belong the Climbing Perch, the Fighting Fish, the Paradise Fish, and the Gouramies, many of which are popular as aquarium-fishes, and have therefore been well studied. Some of these fishes are so dependent on dry air that they cannot live without it, and will drown if forced to stay below water all the time. They inhale air in gulps at the surface, and this passes into the complicated labyrinth organs, which are richly supplied with blood-vessels for the absorption of the oxygen, the used air then passing out through the gill-openings.

Most Labyrinth-fishes have very interesting breeding habits. They build a nest of air-bubbles, which are blown at the surface and held together with a special sticky substance. The female turns upside down, and lays the eggs in this floating nest, after which the male guards them fiercely against danger.

The Climbing Perch of India often comes out of the water, moving from one pond to another at night, and after a heavy shower of rain, it sometimes enters gardens in search of earthworms. It travels over the ground by means of the lower part of its movable, sharp-prickled gill-covers, assisted by a row of spines at the anal fin. From the earliest times this fish has been credited with the habit of climbing trees, its discoverer in 1797 having actually found one in a cleft in the bark of a palm near a pond. A good deal of evidence has been produced to support this statement: it has been said that the fish only ascends during heavy rain, when water is pouring down the trunk of the tree, this being a natural result of its habit of moving up rapid streams against the current. But the story has been generally disbelieved by scientists; and the latest theory, put forward by an Indian naturalist, is that when travelling over land, the fishes are often seized by birds, such as crows or kites, which place them in the trees to be eaten later. It is certainly difficult to guess why a fish should want to climb trees in any case.

The natives of India and Malaya find the Climbing Perch useful, since, being able to live out of water, it can be kept alive for days in damp, clay pots, to be used as food when desired. There are a number of species of Climbing Fishes in Africa as well as in India. None of them is brightly coloured.

The Fighting-fishes are native to Siam. Long ago it was discovered that if two males were put in the same small tank together, they would immediately become angry and fight to the death. Since then, they have been carefully bred and selected for their fighting prowess, much like fighting cocks. In Bangkok, the capital, at least a thousand people breed them for contests, on the results of which large sums are wagered. Males are kept separately, in special glass jars, until the time for the fight arrives; then they are placed together in a bowl or jar. They at once approach each other, spreading their fins and gill-membranes, and watching for an opening. Then, with great rapidity, they attack again and again, with short intervals between the sallies. Gradually

SIAMESE FIGHTING-FISH IN COMBAT
A. Fraser-Brunner

CLIMBING PERCH OF INDIA
The fish moves over land by using alternately the spiny gill-cover and anal fin.   *A. Fraser-Brunner*

their fins are torn, or their gills are injured, until at last one of them gives up the fight, and tries to escape the attacks of its adversary. The one that is anxious to go on fighting is judged the winner. A wild fish will rarely fight for more than about 10 minutes, whereas a pedigree champion has been known to attack for 6 hours!

Fighting-fish are popular as ornamental fish for the AQUARIUM (q.v. Vol. IX), and for this purpose have been bred in a variety of lovely colours, with long, graceful fins. The males obviously have to be kept apart; but they may be allowed to see each other now and then through the glass, when they make a fine display, spreading their large and brilliant fins. Females are smaller and less brightly coloured than the males, and do not fight. These Labyrinth-fishes make bubble-nests, as do most of their relatives.

LACE BUG, *see* BUG.

LACEWING. From man's point of view this delicate insect is extremely useful, as it destroys large numbers of APHIDES (q.v.) found on plants. During the day-time, it may be seen on walls, tree-trunks, and herbage; it flies with a fluttering motion, generally in the evenings. Its body is slender and bright green; its wings appear to be the same colour also, but, in fact, only the network of 'veins' (to which the insect owes its name) is green, the rest being colourless. Its eyes are a brilliant, metallic gold. Many Lacewings have a very unpleasant smell.

They have a complete METAMORPHOSIS (q.v.)—that is to say, they go through each of the stages: egg, larva, pupa, and adult. The larvae are found on leaves infested with Aphides; they force their long, sickle-shaped jaws deeply into the insects and suck their juices. One Lacewing can destroy up to 400 Aphides during its period of growth. Usually the larvae cover themselves with the skins of dead Aphides, keeping them in position by hooked hairs on the back of their bodies. When it is ready to pupate, the larva spins a dense silken cocoon on the underside of a leaf. The pupa has movable jaws, with which it bites its way out of the cocoon.

Before laying an egg, the female Lacewing deposits a drop of fluid on a leaf; then she raises her body so as to draw the fluid out into a sticky thread, on the top of which she places her egg. The thread hardens, so that the egg is attached to the leaf by a long, slender stalk.

LACKEY MOTH. Lackeys, Eggars, Lappets, the December, Fox, and Drinker Moths all belong to the family Lasiocampidae, of which about 1,400 species are known, chiefly from tropical forests of Asia, Africa, and South America. The moths have heavy bodies, and are various shades of brown, with lighter or darker bands crossing the wings. Both sexes have combed antennae, and a very small proboscis. The large, hairy caterpillars of some species attract attention by their bright colours, and by their habit of living together in groups. They spin webs—indeed, those of the destructive Tent Caterpillars of North American forests may

A CLUSTER OF LACKEY MOTH LARVAE ROUND A HAWTHORN TWIG (×2). *S. Beaufoy, F.R.P.S.*

cover whole trees. One species, the Syrian silk-moth, used to be reared by the Greeks, especially on the Island of Cos, for the sake of the silk produced by the caterpillar. It was still bred in Italy up to the 19th century, but is now replaced by the Chinese Mulberry Silkworm, a species closely allied to the KENTISH GLORY (q.v.) (*see* SILKWORMS: Vol. VI).

The small Common Lackey lays its grey-brown eggs in July and August, in a ring-like cluster of 100–250, completely encircling a twig, often of hawthorn. The bluish caterpillars, with white and orange stripes along their backs, and brown hairs, hatch in April or May. They make conspicuous tents, in which they live in colonies, completely stripping the leaves from neighbouring shoots. After moulting, they move on to construct another and more elaborate tent elsewhere. In June they pupate within a double oval cocoon. The Ground Lackey is found only locally in Britain, on salt marshes. The Pale Oak Eggar, attached to hawthorn and sloe, and the Small Eggar, with its tent-making caterpillar, are common in woods in southern England, and less common farther north. The rather transparent greyish December Moth is frequently attracted to light in November and December, and sometimes in October. The caterpillar rests by day in cracks in the bark of trees, which it closely resembles, climbing the tree at night to eat the leaves. The magnificent yellowish-brown female Oak Eggar, with a wing-expanse of quite 3 inches, and the smaller rich chocolate-brown male, are common in July and August along the margins of woods and hedgerows. The dark moorland form, characteristic of Scotland and northern England, takes two years to complete its life-cycle. The males, flying by day in bright sunshine, are attracted in large numbers to the scent given off by an unmated female. The eggs, scattered freely over the food-plants as the female flies in circles, hatch in late summer, and the caterpillars overwinter when still small. The full-grown caterpillar, which curls up when disturbed, is brown, with deep velvet-black rings and a white stripe at the sides. It pupates in a hard, yellowish-brown silk cocoon suggestive of an egg, hence the common name Eggar. The Smaller Grass Eggar, a local species flying in August, is best known from sandhills on the coast, its caterpillar usually feeding on grasses.

Fox Moths, named from their reddish-brown

colour, are about 2½ inches in expanse, and have
two pale lines crossing the fore-wings. The males
can be commonly seen flying wildly over heaths
in May and June sunshine. The brown eggs are
laid in groups on stems, and the caterpillars feed
until October, when they hibernate, coming out
on fine days to bask in the sun, and not pupating
until March or April. They are magnificent
insects, 3½ inches in length, and velvety-black
with golden-brown hairs.

The Drinker, so called because the caterpillar
was observed as early as the 17th century to
drink dew, is a common moth, measuring 2–2½
inches across, the female being yellowish and
the male reddish-brown, both sexes having two
white spots on each fore-wing. The caterpillar
is slaty-grey, with two rows of yellowish spots
on the back, orange spots and tufts of white
hairs at the sides, and a pointed tuft of black
hairs at each end. It feeds on reeds or coarse
grasses by rivers, ditches, and marshes. The
yellowish cocoon, about 1½ inches in length, is
attached to stems a foot or so from the ground.

The Lappet is so called because the caterpillar
has fleshy flaps at the sides, effective in reducing
shadow as it rests on a branch of sloe, hawthorn,
or apple. The whitish eggs are laid, a few at a
time, on the undersides of leaves in July and
August, and the caterpillars hibernate when
nearly an inch in length, resuming feeding in
the spring. A full-grown female reaches about
4 inches in length, the males being smaller.
Their actual colour-pattern depends upon that
of their surroundings during growth—the general
colouring being dark grey or brown with some
white markings suggesting lichen. The beautiful
reddish-brown moth has scalloped outer margins
to the wings, and rests with its hind-wings
projecting in front of the fore-wings so that it
closely resembles a bunch of dead leaves.

The Small Lappet, attached to bilberry, is
very rare in Britain.

See also MOTHS.

LADY-BIRD.

LADY-BIRD. In Britain, as well as in other
countries, Lady-birds are amongst the best
known of all the beetles, because of their
abundance, their bright colours, and their
pretty patterns. They are also amongst the
most useful of all insects, feeding, as they do,
upon other insects which destroy our crops.
They lay their eggs in neat little packets upon
plants infested with these noxious pests, espe-

FEMALE LADY-BIRD LAYING HER EGGS ON A PLANT
INFESTED BY GREENFLY. *E. O. Hoppé*

cially the APHIDES (or 'green-fly') and the
SCALE-INSECTS (qq.v.), which are found in such
numbers and multiply so fast. The little, ugly,
crawling lady-bird grubs, on emerging from the
egg, set to work immediately to clear the plants
of these pests. At times, in various parts of the
world, important crops, such as apples and
oranges, have been menaced with destruction
which would have brought ruin to large
numbers of people; but the importation of the
right kind of Lady-bird from another country
has saved them.

Lady-birds are themselves rejected as food by
birds and other creatures, because of their nasty
taste—and their bright warning colours and
patterns are useful in making them immediately
recognizable, and so sparing them the risk of
being eaten by accident (*see* PROTECTIVE
COLORATION). In consequence they multiply
very fast, and are sometimes seen in vast
swarms. These sometimes migrate from their
birth-place and appear suddenly in another

country—even crossing the sea. In April 1939 a well-known naturalist noticed upon the coast of the Egyptian desert an immense number of little Eleven-spot Lady-birds, which had been drowned in the Mediterranean and washed up along its margin. They formed a bright-coloured band more than a foot wide, piled up about 6 inches high. He actually traced the long line of red-and-black beetles for 13 miles along the shore, without reaching its end. As he estimated that each foot of length contained about 70,000 insects, the total number of the swarm must have been unimaginably vast (see Migration).

See also Beetles.

LAMPREY. Lampreys and their relatives, the Hag-fishes, are the lowest type of vertebrate (back-boned) animal possessing anything that can be truly called a skull, and are therefore of interest because they show us what the ancestors of fishes and of the higher animals must have been like. The skull consists of a number of plates of cartilage (gristle), which do not form a complete box for the brain; there are no jaws; a complicated arrangement of rods of cartilage forms a sort of basket for the protection and support of the gills, which are in pouch-like gill-chambers; and the spinal column consists only of the primitive 'notochord' (or rod of gristle) and a series of isolated pieces of cartilage on each side of the spinal cord. So, having only the beginnings of a skeleton, they are placed in a class by themselves (called Marsipo-branchii, meaning pouch-gills), lower down on the tree of life than the Sharks or Fishes (qq.v.).

The Hag-fishes seem to be even more primi-tive than the Lampreys, the mouth being simply an opening, in front of which are four pairs of short tentacles. The single 'nostril' is connected with the back of the mouth. The eyes are very small and feeble. A strong, rasp-like tongue is set with horny teeth, by which the Hag-fish bores its way into the bodies of larger animals, such as an injured or dead Shark or other big fish, eating away the flesh and leaving only the skin and bones. The catches made by fishermen are often ruined by the attacks of Hag-fishes. When not feeding, these creatures live in the mud at the bottom of the sea, in rather deep water, and are able to swim very rapidly. They can exude an amazing amount of slime from

SEA LAMPREYS SEEN IN AN AQUARIUM
One of them has attached itself to the glass by its suckerlike mouth, showing its many horny teeth. *A. Fraser-Brunner*

special pores along their sides, and if placed in a bucket, will fill it with slime in a few minutes. There are two families of Hag-fish: one kind found in the North Atlantic and in the Pacific off Japan and Chile, the other on the Pacific side of America, around New Zealand, and off the Cape of Good Hope.

Lampreys have a somewhat stronger 'skeleton' than Hag-fishes, a better brain, more useful eyes, and other features that approach more nearly to fishes. There are seven gills, each with its own outer opening, and the 'nostril' is not connected with the mouth. The mouth is surrounded by a disk capable of powerful suction, and is armed with horny rasping teeth (in addition to those on the tongue). By means of this disk, Lampreys attach themselves to the body of a larger fish and rasp away the flesh with the horny teeth, while the victim, in its attempts to escape, carries them about.

Young Lampreys are so different from their parents that they were once thought to be different animals, and were named *Ammocoetes*. This young stage, still referred to as the *Ammocoete* stage, lasts for about three years, during which time the creature, being blind and without teeth, lives and feeds in the mud, like a worm. After this it undergoes a change, or 'metamorphosis', which takes about three weeks, and becomes like the adult.

Several species of Lamprey are known. The Sea Lamprey, large, with a marbled colour-pattern, spends its *Ammocoete* stage in rivers, migrating to the sea in order to become adult. The Lampern is sometimes called the River Lamprey, although it seems to spend most of its time in the sea, moving up the rivers to spawn. It is smaller than the Sea Lamprey, and was at one time abundant in the River Thames. Still smaller is the Brook Lamprey, which spends all its time in fresh water.

Lampreys were at one time much sought after as food, and still are in some parts of the world; but in Britain at least they are no longer of any commercial importance. They are not as common as they were, probably owing to the pollution of rivers by industry.

LANCELET. This creature offers a clue to the way in which the backboned animals have developed from the lower kinds. It possesses many features that are more suggestive of worms than of higher forms; but it has a very primitive

THE LANCELET, RESEMBLING THE EARLY ANCESTOR OF FISHES
A. Fraser-Brunner

sort of backbone, a slender rod of gristle called a 'notochord'. There is no skeleton other than this—no skull, no jaws; a spinal cord is present, but no brain and no eyes. The simple mouth is a lengthwise slit beneath the front end (we can hardly say 'head'), and water is taken in through many gill-slits into a longer chamber that has its exit far back on the underside of the body. There is a fringe of tentacles on each side of the mouth.

Lancelets are small, transparent creatures, of which there are a number of species, the smallest being only $\frac{1}{2}$ inch long, the largest 4 inches. They inhabit the warmer seas, living mostly in shallow water, buried in sand. Like many lowly organized animals, such as worms, they are not easily killed, and will live on after being partly cut up.

LANGUAGE OF ANIMALS, *see* ANIMAL LANGUAGE.

LANTERN-FISH. This name is given to the little oceanic fishes, usually about 2 inches long, belonging to the family Myctophidae, distantly related to the SALMON (q.v.). They all have large mouths, rather large eyes, and a small 'adipose fin' behind the dorsal fin on the back. Their most interesting feature is the series of luminous organs arranged in definite patterns on the body and head. About two hundred species of Lantern-fish are known, and each one has its own special arrangement of these 'lamps', enabling members of the species to recognize each other in the darkness of the deep ocean. Lantern-fishes, indeed, spend most of their time in darkness. During the day they remain in the deep waters of the ocean, beyond reach of the sun's rays, which would injure their large, sensitive eyes. At night, however, they often come nearer the surface, and, curiously enough, may be attracted by a bright light put over the side of a ship. Many have been caught in this way; for, although they are darkness-loving creatures, they seem to be fascinated by the light, just like moths round a lamp, and are easily netted. The eyes of Lantern-fishes are large in order to take advantage of every ray of light given out by the luminous creatures in the gloomy waters they inhabit; for only in this way are they able to keep together in shoals, to distinguish sexes in order to mate, and to find food, which consists for the most part of small luminous prawns that swarm in the deeper waters.

The so-called Bombay-duck, found in the Indian Ocean, and used, after drying and salting, as an accompaniment to curry, is related to the Lantern-fishes.

See also DEEP-SEA FISHES.

LANTERN FLY. This great Brazilian insect is called the Lantern Fly because, as long ago as 1705, it was said to be luminous. This belief has proved to be mistaken; but the Lantern Fly is quite remarkable in other ways. It has a wing-expanse of nearly 6 inches, and there is a large and very noticeable 'eye-spot' on each hind-wing. On its head there is a forward growth of a hollow, bladder-like structure, where the luminosity was supposed to occur. Viewed sideways, this looks like the head of some very fearsome reptile, and black markings upon it produce the illusion of eyes and nostrils. It has been suggested that it produces a terrifying effect, so that enemies are warned off by this deception.

Another similar fly is the Chinese Candle Fly, which also was assumed, without foundation, to be luminous. Certain species of this group of bugs excrete a white, feathery, waxy substance, which streams behind them when they fly. The Chinese collect this material and use it to make candles.

See also BUGS.

LAPWING, see WADING BIRDS, Section 5.

LARCH, see CONIFERS.

LARK. This brown or sand-coloured bird is a ground bird, nesting on the ground and very seldom perching on trees. It runs along instead of hopping. It is conspicuous for its song, the European Skylark being one of the best songsters in the family. There are a great many species, found especially in deserts and open plains of Asia, Africa, and Australia. Europe has several species, two of which breed in the British Isles and others being occasional visitors.

The Skylark is a common bird in most parts of Europe. Large numbers, breeding in northern Europe, migrate to Britain in the Autumn, while others, which have bred in Britain, emigrate to warmer climates for the winter. The Skylark is well known for its habit of circling high in the air with rapid wing-beats, singing all the while. It makes a simple nest in a tussock of coarse grass, and three to five speckled grey and brown eggs are laid.

The Woodlark, somewhat smaller than the Skylark, is more common in most of Europe than in Britain, where it is confined to certain districts in the south. It is an exception to the rest of its family in that it perches on the upper branches of trees to sing. Its song is rich and sweet, though less sustained than that of the Skylark.

The Crested Lark, so called from its small pointed crest, is common on the Continent, where it usually becomes very tame. The Shore Lark, a yellowish buff and black bird, which might well be called the Mountain Lark, for it breeds high in the mountains of Scandinavia and North America, sometimes visits the east coast of Britain on migration. Other species, including the Black Lark from Russia and the large-billed Calandra Lark from the Mediterranean, are very occasional visitors to Britain.

LEAF-INSECT, see STICK INSECT.

LEAF-ROLLERS (Tortricoidea). This very large group of small, wide-winged moths produce caterpillars which live concealed in their food-plant. Some live in the roots, fruits, or stems on which they feed; others, which are leaf-feeders, roll an edge of the leaf into a tube. Many are serious agricultural pests—such as the world-known Codling Moth, the larva of which lives in the core of the apple, the Peach Moth, and another species which attacks grapes (see INSECT PESTS, Vol. VI). Others attack trees, such as pines, larches, and oak-trees.

One of the most spectacular is the Green Oak-roller or Oak Tortrix. The moth is bright green with grey hind-wings. The caterpillars, lengthy for their size, and slightly hairy, attack the leaves of oak-trees in such numbers that, in dry years, whole forests of trees may be stripped of leaves even to the point of being killed. The caterpillars spin strands of thread across the part of the leaf to be rolled. As the silk threads dry, they shrink, drawing over the leaf-edges. This process is continued until a complete tube has been formed. These caterpillars, if disturbed, will drop out of their leaf-tubes and hang by a silk thread. Anyone passing through an oak wood in a dry May will soon find himself walking into them, as they hang all round him on their long threads. When ready to pupate, they either remain in the folded leaf, or drop by their threads to a chink in the bark or other suitable crevice.

The foxy-red Larch Tortrix moth lays eggs on the tip of a young larch shoot. The Pine-gall Tortrix larvae feed within the stem of a pine leaf-bud. As they tunnel into the stem, a drop of resin is exuded, and this forms a gall-like bulge on the twig, which increases in size as the caterpillar tunnels. The insect passes its pupal stage within this 'gall'. This excrescence should not be confused with the real gall made by the GALL-FLY (q.v.). The Light Brown Apple Moth is a serious defoliator of apple-trees in Australia and New Zealand.

See also MOTHS.

LEATHER-JACKET, see CRANE-FLY.

LEAVES. 1. FUNCTION. The main function of foliage leaves is that of PHOTOSYNTHESIS (q.v.), by means of which the green leaf is able to take raw materials and, in the presence of sunlight, convert them into food materials to nourish all parts of the plant. The work done by the green leaf, therefore, is responsible, directly or indirectly, for all life in the world. Since photosynthesis in the leaves depends upon sunlight, the stems that bear them grow in such a way as to present the greatest possible surface of leaf-blade to the light. Most leaves have their blades almost parallel to the ground, and it is interesting to see, in creeping and climbing plants, as well as in trees, how little overlapping there is. The leaves are so arranged that those growing below fit into the spaces left by those above, making not only a beautiful pattern, but also an efficient sun-trap. This leaf-pattern, or leaf-mosaic as it is called, is especially pro-

nounced in trees with a dense canopy, and in smaller plants growing in the shade. It can be seen by standing under a Beech or Elm, and looking upwards, and is well demonstrated by the young branches of Ivy and Sycamore.

2. LEAF STRUCTURE. Although there is an unknown number of different types of leaves, each plant has its own typical leaf-shape. The Privet, for example, has one of the simplest of leaves—a leaf-blade in one piece, and a simple leaf-stalk. The Banana plant has also a simple leaf, but a very great deal larger—anything from 1 to 3 yards long, though this frequently becomes broken up. The leaf-blade of the Horse-chestnut is divided into many leaflets, and is far from simple; but, like the Privet and the Banana and all other leaves, it is typical of its species. Between the simple leaf of the Privet and the compound leaf of the Horse-chestnut, there are leaves of intermediate kinds, ranging from those with jagged or serrated edges, like that of the Elm, to those with a deeply indented edge, like the Oak leaf. Leaf-shape, therefore, affords a good way of identifying a plant.

Most leaves are composed of a leaf-stalk and a leaf-blade. The leaf-stalk widens at the base, where it joins the stem into what is called the leaf-base. Sometimes this is merely a thicker structure, as in the Horse-chestnut, sometimes it is elongated into a sheath, as in the Buttercup. The flattened portion of the leaf—the leaf-blade—is sometimes joined to the leaf-base without the intermediate leaf-stalk. The thicker lines on the leaf-blade are veins or channels for conducting water to, and food from, the leaf. From the main vein, or midrib, side veins are given off, and these go on branching until the tiny vein-endings cover the whole leaf-blade. Most leaves have this net-veined lace-work; but the blade-like leaves, such as those of Grasses, Lilies, Irises, and Daffodils, have several main veins running parallel to one another instead of a mid-rib.

Compound leaves are easy to confuse with stems bearing several simple leaves. But there is usually a leaf-bud in the angle which a leaf-stalk makes with the stem. No matter how many leaflets there are in the compound leaf, there is only one leaf-bud; whereas, when several separate leaves are attached to a stem, there will be several leaf-buds (see STEMS). In the type of compound leaf to which the Horse-chestnut

Simple leaf (Coltsfoot)

Compound leaf (Rose)

Leaf converted to spines (Barberry)

Leaf with food storage (Lily)

Climbing leaf with part converted to tendril (Vetch)

Flower

Leaf converted to a flattened flower-bearing stem or phyllode (Butcher's Broom)

TYPES OF LEAVES

Leaves also become modified for storage purposes, sometimes as water-reservoirs and sometimes as food reserves. Those that store water are generally found in plants growing in dry regions, so that the water-supply in the leaves makes up for the scarcity in the soil (*see* DESERT PLANTS). The House-leeks and Stonecrops, which grow on rocks and walls, are good examples of this, and so are the succulent Samphires, which grow on cliffs. The Ice-plant, too, which, though not a native, grows freely by the sea in the south of England, stores water in its swollen leaves. In the fleshy leaves which form bulbs (*see* STEMS, Section 2(*d*)) food is stored. Leaves are also modified as tendrils for climbing purposes (*see* CLIMBING PLANTS); while, in some very peculiar plants, the leaves are modified as bladders and pitchers to trap insects (*see* INSECTIVOROUS PLANTS).

The Australian Acacias and Myrtles show an extraordinary kind of leaf modification: the blade often disappears completely, and the stalk becomes flattened to carry out the normal work of the leaf. The probable explanation of this is that it saves the leaves from over-exposure to the excessive light and heat of a tropical climate. Whereas the normal leaf-blade is arranged horizontally to face the sun, these flattened leaf-stalks grow vertically, exposing only their edges to the sun, and thus avoiding direct contact with its rays. Such flattened leaf-stalks are called 'phyllodes'. Among British plants, the Grass Vetch possesses well-developed phyllodes.

4. LEAF-FALL. One of the vital problems which plants, like human beings and all other living things, have to solve is how to obtain an adequate supply of water. The plant normally absorbs all the water it needs from the soil through its roots. In a tropical country, where there is little difference in climate between the seasons, absorption through the roots takes place as readily in winter as in summer. In temperate countries like Great Britain, however, plants are

and Lupin belong, the leaflets stretch out somewhat like fingers spread out, and the leaf is described as 'palmate'. Another type of compound leaf is the 'pinnate' (feathered) leaf, such as the Rose and the Vetch, where the leaflets are arranged in pairs along the midrib of the leaf.

3. LEAF MODIFICATIONS. Leaves develop special modifications to suit different circumstances, just as do roots and stems. The sharp spines of the Barberry, for example, represent foliage leaves which have become reduced, presumably as a means of protection against browsing animals (*see* PLANT DEFENCES). Here the whole leaf has become reduced to a spine; but in the Holly only the leaf-margin forms a series of spines. However, the belief that most holly trees bear more spines on the lower leaves within easy reach of animals, and less on the upper branches, can be disproved by anyone who uses his eyes. In a young Gorse plant it is possible to see all the stages between the whole leaf with its three leaflets and the spines into which it becomes modified. Some branch stems of the Gorse produce spines, too. Since buds grow in the axils of leaves, we thus get long 'stem' spines growing out of the axils of shorter 'leaf' spines.

most active during the warm summer, and practically come to a standstill, carrying on only essential processes, during the winter. The slowing-down of plant activities is due, not so much to the cold itself, as to the plant's inability to absorb water from the cold winter soil. Plants, therefore, must conserve water as much as possible during the winter. As plants give off water chiefly by TRANSPIRATION (q.v.) through the leaves, it is natural that some trees with thin, delicate leaves get rid of their leaves in the autumn. These trees are called deciduous. The few evergreen trees that occur naturally in Britain have their leaves specially thickened and modified to prevent their losing water, as happens in the leaves of deciduous trees. In herbaceous plants, the problem scarcely arises, because the shoot itself dies down before winter.

The autumn leaf-fall of deciduous trees is by no means haphazard. Before it begins, the green leaves gradually lose their colour and take on the characteristic shades of yellow, brown, and red, which we associate with the autumn. These colour changes are due to a chemical breaking-down of the green colouring matter, chlorophyll—which means that food manufacture can no longer go on in the leaf. At this time, some layers of cells at the base of the leaf-stalk become separated from one another and form a point of weakness, leaving the leaf-stalk attached to the twig only by a vein. By the weight of the leaf, or by the action of wind and frost, the vein is broken and the leaf falls. If this were the only process that had been taking place, the stem, of course, would be left with an open wound, which might soon be infected. A row of cells, however, underneath those at the base of the leaf-stalk, has been forming cork, and, by the time the leaf falls, this has spread right across the wound, sealing it off and leaving a healthy scar.

Leaf-fall, therefore, is an active process carried out by deciduous trees to get rid of structures which might otherwise cause them to lose too much water. Some experts say also that waste products are passed into the leaf before it falls, and that the tree uses this as one way of getting rid of waste matter formed during its life-processes. It is interesting to note that if a branch dies, or hangs broken from a tree, its leaves wither and curl up, but do not fall: this makes it still more evident that leaf-fall is a living process.

LEECH, *see* WORMS, Section 5.

LEMMING, *see* VOLES.

LEMUR. These are smallish, monkey-like animals, with pointed, fox-like faces, thick, woolly fur, and, as a rule, long, bushy tails. They belong to a sub-order of the Primates, the highest order in the animal kingdom, to which belongs man himself; but they are less highly developed—in the brain, for instance—than APES and MONKEYS (qq.v.). Some species of Lemurs are found in south and central Africa, in southern Asia, and in the East Indies; but by far the majority belong to Madagascar, where they are very common indeed.

Lemurs live in trees, very rarely coming to the ground. Some species are active only during the night; but others start hunting for food at dusk, uttering loud cries which resound through the forest. They feed on fruit, leaves, birds' eggs or small birds, reptiles, and insects.

The Mouse Lemurs of Madagascar are the smallest of the family, some being no larger than a mouse. They have large eyes and ears, and hunt at night, stalking moths and beetles,

A RING-TAILED AND A RED-FRONTED LEMUR
Harold Bastin

SLENDER LORIS OF ASIA
Paul Popper

fur, large round eyes, and either a short tail or no tail at all. They are unable to leap, but move about the forest trees slowly and deliberately, grasping the branches with their feet and hands. They are generally silent; but when angry, and especially when about to bite, they give a fierce growl.

The Aye-aye is a strange Lemur, about the size of a cat, which lives in the Madagascar forests. It differs from other Lemurs in having teeth like a RODENT (q.v.), which it uses, together with its peculiar, long middle finger, for digging out grubs from under the bark of trees or in decaying wood. Its large ears enable it to detect the grubs by listening. Its strong teeth are used for opening nuts on which it also feeds.

The Tarsiers of the East Indies also belong to the Lemur group, though they are in some ways more like monkeys. They are especially interesting to zoologists, being regarded by some as the most closely related of all living animals to the stock from which man is descended. They are weird-looking creatures, about the size of a small rat, with enormous eyes, very long ankle-bones, and fingers and toes equipped with sucker-like disks which enable them to cling firmly to the branches of trees. Like OWLS (q.v.), they can turn their heads round to face backwards without moving their bodies. They hunt insects and small reptiles, and take enormous leaps from bough to bough among the trees.

and making long jumps from branch to branch. During the very dry, hot season, when food is scarce, they lie asleep in their nests in the hollows of tree-trunks, living on the great amount of fat which is stored in their tails.

The Galagos, popularly known as Bush Babies, are a group of small Lemurs living in tropical Africa. Some are as large as a rabbit, others as small as a dormouse. They are night-hunters, taking enormous leaps from one tree to another. They have huge, naked ears which are extremely sensitive, and which they can fold up close to their heads so that they are not injured when they are hunting through thick foliage or going to sleep in wet surroundings.

The Lorises of Asia, about the size of a squirrel, have thick coats of very close, woolly

The Colugos or Flying Lemurs are not now regarded as members of the Lemur family, but as a separate order, related to the INSECTIVORA (q.v.). They are about the size of small cats, and have a very effective parachute made by a membrane of skin stretching between the neck and forelimbs and beyond to the hind-legs and tail. When they stretch out their legs, this enables them to glide from one tree to another. One kind lives in the Philippines and another in the Malay States, Siam, and Borneo.

LEOPARD (Panther). Although not as powerful, these big cats are in many ways more dangerous than tigers, for they are easily provoked. They are found throughout southern Asia, Ceylon, Java, and Africa. In India they are usually called 'Panthers'. The average leopard is 4 feet long, with a 3-foot tail, and stands 2 feet at the shoulder, though some are

THE TARSIER OF THE EAST INDIES
Paul Popper

A LEOPARD IN THE KRÜGER NATIONAL PARK
South African Railways and Harbours

much larger and some much smaller. Their coat is usually a tawny-yellow, marked with black spots arranged in rosettes; but black leopards are common in the hills of southern India, Asia, and the Malay Peninsula. They are very active, agile beasts, able to make tremendous leaps and bounds and to climb trees with the ease of a monkey.

The leopards' favourite strongholds are on rocky, scrub-covered hills, from which they can watch the surrounding country. Keeping to the cover of the rocks, they descend at sunset to cut off stragglers from the herds and flocks returning to some neighbouring village. During the night they climb over walls and native huts, and raid goat-folds and calf-pens. They will eat any flesh, but bullocks are about the largest animal they can kill. They seize their prey by the throat, and cling with tenacious claws to its neck until they succeed in breaking its spine or, if the bones are too strong, in strangling their victim. They have a peculiar liking for dog-flesh, and leopards in hill-stations have on occasion swooped down in broad daylight and carried off dogs from before their owners' eyes. There are very few man-eating leopards; but they frequently make attacks on children. There are usually from two to four cubs in a litter. Young leopards are generally more difficult to tame than young lions and tigers, and the adults are uncertain and morose in captivity.

The Snow Leopard or Ounce, which lives in the Himalayas, has long grey fur, marked with black rosettes. It is smaller and less powerful than the common leopard, and hunts comparatively small animals. As a rule it does not thrive in captivity, although it becomes very tame.

The Clouded Leopard of south-western Asia is greyish-brown, beautifully marked with darker blotches bordered with black. It is much smaller than the leopard, and has an exceptionally long tail. Most of its life is spent in the trees, where it preys on birds and tree-climbing animals.

See also CATS.

LEOPARD MOTHS, *see* GOAT AND LEOPARD MOTHS.

LEOPARD SNAKE, *see* SMOOTH SNAKE.

LEPIDOPTERA, *see* BUTTERFLIES; MOTHS.

LILIES. It is a remarkable fact that, although one of the most popular of garden flowers, no true lily is found growing wild in Great Britain. Even the Lily of the Valley is not a true lily, although it belongs to the lily family; while the so-called Arum and Water-lilies do not even belong to this family. The word 'lily' is, in fact, loosely used in connexion with many plants which are not really lilies. It is almost certain, for example, that the New Testament 'lilies of the field', which surpassed 'Solomon in all his glory', were really red anemones, a common flower in Galilee in the spring-time. In Great Britain, the lily family is represented by a miscellaneous collection of wild plants, including the common Bluebell and rarer plants like the Bog Asphodel, Autumn Crocus, and Solomon's Seal.

Perhaps the most typical of these wild 'lilies' is the Bluebell. It produces a typical bulb; it also propagates by seeds—but these take 3 years from the time of germination until their bulbs are large enough to develop flowering shoots. The leaves are characteristic of those plants which have only one cotyledon in the SEED (q.v.): they are long and narrow, pointed at the tips, with parallel veins, and sometimes reach a length of 18 inches. The bell-like, blue flowers grow in pendulous clusters, so that all the flowers seem to be hanging from one side of the flower-shoot. There are six to twelve flowers in each cluster. The flower is typical of the lily family in having its parts in threes or groups of three. There is no distinction between petals and sepals, and the six blue perianth leaves, as they are called, are joined to form the familiar bell. The six stamens are attached each to the inside of one of the perianth leaves. The ovary is three-chambered, and bears a long style at the top, carrying the stigma, which is shaped like a pin's head. As in many members of the lily family, the flowers droop and thus protect the pollen from the rain; but after fertilization, the fruit stands upright, so that the seeds are shaken out and spread a reasonably wide distance.

The little Bog Asphodel, with its clusters of star-like, golden-yellow flowers, grows on wet moors and in bogs, and flowers from June to August. It makes its way through the water-logged soil by means of thick underground stems. Its leaves are rigid and strong, noticeably ribbed, and ending in an extended point. Although the flowers are very conspicuous, they contain no nectar, and therefore are frequently self-pollinated.

The Lily of the Valley grows wild in Britain, but it is not common. It is shade-loving and

Bog Asphodel

Autumn Crocus

Aloe

Fritillary

Tiger Lily

VARIETIES OF LILIES

grows in woods, where it spreads by means of a thick, underground stem, each branch of which produces a few scales and one pair of foliage leaves each year. Thus a well-established plant, which has been spreading for some years, produces a mass of broad, lance-shaped leaves. In the wild state, the tiny white flowers appear during May and June. They are carried in clusters of six to twelve, and are frequently hidden behind the canopy of leaves. In structure, the flower is similar to the bluebell; but the fruit is a spherical red berry.

Solomon's Seal is sometimes found growing wild in woods. Its name comes from the fact that the annual shoots, when they die away, leave curious, seal-like markings on the thick underground stem. The leaves, oblong and pointed, grow alternately on arched stems, 2 to 3 feet long, and the groups of greenish-white flowers hang from the stem at intervals of about 12 inches. The fruit, a black berry, is rarely seen.

The Autumn Crocus or Meadow Saffron resembles the ordinary cultivated Crocus (which belongs to the Iris family) in forming a similar

underground storage organ or 'corm'. In the early summer, the corm of the Autumn Crocus produces smooth, lance-shaped, dark-green leaves. These are followed in the autumn by a large, solitary, purple or lilac flower, which forces its way through the soil above, remaining attached to the corm without an intervening stalk. Although comparatively rare in England, these Autumn Crocus flowers are sometimes found locally in meadows in purple masses. The leaves are poisonous to animals; but a chemical substance called colchicine, which is extracted from the seeds, has a peculiar tonic effect on other plants.

Others of the less common British flowers belonging to the family of lilies are the white and yellow Star of Bethlehem, the Snakeshead or Fritillary, and the strong-smelling Garlic or Ramsons. One British member of this family, the Butcher's-broom, which has flattened, leaf-like shoots, and grows in shady places in the south of England, is an evergreen shrub.

It is in tropical countries that wild lilies reach real magnificence, and many of these are cultivated in our gardens or hothouses (*see* LILIES, Vol. VI). One of the best-known in this country is the Tiger-lily, which grows wild in China and Japan. It has several varieties, one with orange, trumpet-shaped flowers, and another with scarlet flowers marked with black spots. Another favourite Japanese lily is the Golden-rayed Lily, which bears large, white trumpets in bunches at the end of long, leafy stems. The Orange Lily is a native of several semi-tropical countries. This produces in the axils of its leaves tiny bulblets, from which the plant can reproduce itself. The Turk's-cap Lily of the eastern Mediterranean countries has vivid scarlet flowers; the Meadow Lily of the U.S.A. has brilliant yellow and orange flowers; *Lilium Grayi*, also found in North America, has flowers which are deep crimson outside and yellow, blotched with purple, inside. Our garden tulips, too, belong to the lily family. They are natives of north temperate regions, and at one time there was a wild British tulip. To-day they are found wild in great profusion on the steppes of central Asia.

A few relatives of the lily in other countries grow like trees, the most notable being the Dragon's-blood Tree of Mexico, so called because of the red resin it yields, and the Aloe of South Africa, which yields the purgative juice called

FRITILLARIES OR SNAKESHEADS
John Markham, F.R.P.S.

aloes. Yucca or Adam's Needle, another Mexican tree-like lily, has a short, thickened stem crowned with a tuft of long, thick, sword-like leaves, and large, hanging, creamy, bell-shaped flowers, growing in a bunch on a stem which sometimes rises up for 5 feet above the tops of the leaves. This plant can be pollinated by one insect only, the night-flying YUCCA MOTH (q.v.).

A well-known relative of the lily is the Asparagus, quite a common wild plant in the drier, warmer parts of Europe and Asia. One wild variety is sometimes found in western England. The plant spreads by means of thick, creeping, underground stems, which send up the erect shoots used as a vegetable.

The Aspidistra is also a member of the lily family, hailing from eastern Asia. It rarely blooms under cultivation, and, when it does, the flower grows so close to the ground and is so insignificant, that it is often overlooked.

LIMPET. The familiar conical shell of the Common Limpet varies a good deal in colour and ruggedness with the age of the animal: old shells usually have a more rounded contour and a less roughened surface, while the colour may be greyish, olive-green, or yellow, obscurely marked with narrow rays of dark grey or chocolate-brown.

It requires some skill to dislodge a Limpet from its position on the rock, for the power of adhesion exerted by the strong muscular foot is quite extraordinary. In fact, one has to follow the tactics of the gulls and oyster-catchers who, before delivering the sudden glancing blow with their beaks which generally knocks off the mollusc from the rock, always look to make certain that the shell is raised just a little way from the rock—a sure sign that the Limpet is relaxing his hold and, for the moment, at a disadvantage. Having successfully detached the Limpet from the rock, one can take a look at its under-surface, the centre of which is occupied by the broad, muscular foot. In front of the foot can be seen a distinct head, with a small, round mouth and two small, horn-like tentacles, each with a bright eye at its base; while around the whole of the body is the edge of the yellowish-coloured mantle, and between the mantle and the foot, a frill of gill-plates. The Limpet's most remarkable organ is its long 'radula' or tongue, which is armed with row upon row of minute teeth, estimated to number 1,920 or more. By means of this rasp-like tongue, the Limpet scrapes from the surface of the rocks the delicate seaweeds upon which it feeds. The Limpet has a remarkable homing instinct, and after its excursions in search of food, it returns regularly to its own particular resting-place on the rock. This home-spot is a shallow depression which the Limpet has worn in the surface of the rock, and into which the margin of its shell exactly fits. This perfect fit is of prime importance, for any space between the rock and the base of the shell would render impossible that firm grip upon which the animal depends for safety. No two Limpet shells are so exactly alike that they would fit into the same depression.

There are several varieties or local races of the Common Limpet, which in the past have received distinctive names; but the differences are chiefly in size, shape, or colour, and are now regarded rather as interesting examples of adaptation to local conditions. Large quantities of Limpets are used as bait in line-fishing, and they used to be a popular food.

See also MOLLUSCS.

LING, *see* COD.

LINNET, *see* FINCHES, Section 6.

LIONS. Lions are the largest of the great cats. They are found to-day in many parts of Africa south of the Sahara, but have practically disappeared from Asia. In India, they are now found only in one large game reserve in Gujerat. The various forms of the African lion differ to some extent in size and appearance: the Somali race is particularly small, and the Senegal lions grow practically no mane; while the now extinct

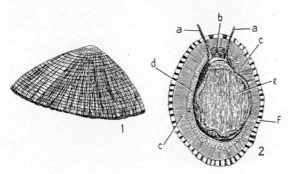

SIDE VIEW AND UNDER SURFACE OF LIMPET
(a) Tentacles; (b) Mouth; (c) Mantle; (d) Gills; (e) Foot;
(f) Shell edge

LION AND LIONESS IN KRUGER NATIONAL PARK
The Lioness, when she settles down, becomes almost lost in her surroundings
South African Railways and Harbours

lions of the Cape and Algeria grew particularly fine manes. Indian lions, generally, do not have such fine manes as the African lions.

African lions live in nearly all districts where there are large numbers of their natural prey—antelopes, zebras, and wild swine. Like most of the large cats, they hunt at night, lying asleep during the day in thick beds of reeds or among thickets and bushes in dry districts. Their colouring blends extraordinarily well with their surroundings. At sundown they begin their nightly prowl, being most active on dark and stormy nights, and very cautious in bright moonlight, especially when going to their drinking-place. As a rule, they begin to roar at nightfall and continue all through the night, reaching a climax when several troops approach the watering-place at the same time, and roar defiance at each other. The vibrating sound of the roar is often intensified by the habit they have of putting their mouths close to the ground.

African lions may be met alone or in pairs; but they very often, especially in the interior, hunt in companies numbering anything from four to twelve. They frequently join company in order to attack large animals, such as buffaloes, which would be difficult to overcome single-handed. Unlike TIGERS (q.v.), which always kill large prey by dislocating their necks, lions seem to have many methods of attack. They have been seen to kill antelopes by biting their throats, and horses and zebras by a bite on the back of the neck. It is said that a lion sometimes breaks the neck of a buffalo by springing on its shoulder, seizing its nose with one paw, and giving the neck a sudden wrench. No matter how plentiful game may be, lions will almost always feed on any dead animal left by a hunter. They frequently eat carcasses in a very advanced state of decomposition, although it would be little trouble to make a fresh kill.

When lions get old and feeble, and less successful in the chase, they will eat any small animal they can catch, and even grass. Such beasts often become a menace to humans, attacking domestic animals and frequently becoming man-eaters. In many districts, if a man is killed, the whole neighbouring population is roused and hunting parties immediately go out. Even if the lion escapes, it is so scared that it quickly leaves the district. Young lions, and particularly lionesses with cubs, will also become man-eaters if food is very scarce. Any lion if roused is a formidable foe, and a wounded animal is especially dangerous. The lion will conceal itself amazingly well in the long grass or thick cover, and will then rush upon its pursuer with lightning speed, uttering a coughing roar. Many a sportsman has taken refuge in a tree—for the lion, unlike other cats, does not normally climb. He will wait below the tree, however, ready to pounce should his prey try to descend or fall from exhaustion.

When a male lion has selected his mate, they stay together for most, if not all, of their lives. Wild lionesses never have litters of more than two or three cubs, but in captivity there may be up to six. The lioness is a very devoted mother. She guards her cubs carefully while they are still helpless, hiding them when she goes out to hunt for food. She will brave any danger to satisfy their hunger. When they get a little older, she brings back small live animals, and with these she begins to teach them to hunt for themselves. The young lion cubs are marked with dark stripes and faint spots. Their mane begins to grow at the age of 3, and stops growing when they are 6 years old. Lions in captivity often live to be 20 years old. If caught young, they are easily tamed, and are much more reliable in captivity than tigers.

See also CATS.
See also Vol. VI: BIG-GAME HUNTING.

LIVERWORTS, *see* MOSSES AND LIVERWORTS.

LIVER FLUKES, *see* Vol. IX: PARASITIC PESTS.

LIZARDS (Sauria or Lacertilia). These are reptiles of the same order as SNAKES (q.v.), from which they differ in having four well-developed limbs, eyes with movable eyelids, and a broad fleshy tongue. This short list of differences will cover the vast majority of lizards; but there are many exceptions. Some, like the SLOW-WORM (q.v.), have lost their limbs and have acquired

an elongated body; others, like the GECKOS and certain of the SKINKS (qq.v.), are without eyelids; and the MONITORS (q.v.) have a snake-like tongue. In their bodily structure the lizards show enormous variation. The CHAMELEONS (q.v.), and the Flying Lizards, each in their own particular way are built for living in trees; many of the Skinks have lost their limbs and live a subterranean life; the Geckos have developed adhesive pads to their digits, with which they can climb trees and the walls of houses; and the Sea Lizards of the Galapagos Islands live on rocky shores, feeding on sea-weeds, and dashing into the waves in time of danger.

The skin of lizards is normally covered with scales, the outer layer of which is shed periodically. It usually comes off in flakes; but in those species which have a greatly elongated body it may be shed in one piece, as with snakes. In some families there are small, bony plates in the skin. Most lizards lay eggs; but some produce their young alive. The egg-shell of the Geckos contains lime and is brittle; of other lizards it is parchment-like, as in snakes' eggs. The tail may or may not be fragile; a broken tail is always regrown, but can usually be recognized by its stumpier appearance. Young lizards are usually more brilliantly coloured than their parents, and sometimes their colour-pattern is so different that they have been regarded as different species. The brilliant colours which the IGUANAS and AGAMAS (qq.v.) develop in the breeding season are of quite a different nature: they are dependent

THE BEARDED LIZARD OF SOUTHERN AUSTRALIA
Paul Popper

A SAND LIZARD

upon stimuli of various kinds, and in moments of intense excitement may sweep over the creature like a wave. The sight of an enemy—for in the breeding season many lizards fight for their own particular territory—may produce quite as brilliant a colouring as the sight of a mate (*see* ANIMAL TERRITORY). These colours are always most vivid in the males.

Some 2,500 species of lizards are known. They are divided into many families, the best-known of which, apart from the Lacertids or typical lizards, are the Geckos, the Agamas, the Iguanas, the Chameleons, and the Monitors (all of which are described in separate articles). Another important family are the Skinks—rather small, harmless lizards, of which some 600 species are known, distributed over the tropical and sub-tropical regions of the world. The majority of these are ground lizards, common in the compounds and cultivated areas of the tropics; but a few species live in trees, and some live underground, having lost their limbs and developed long, snake-like bodies.

Two species of lizard are found in England: the Viviparous or Common Lizard, and the Sand Lizard. The Viviparous Lizard is common all over the British Isles and Europe. It lives on heaths and commons, in wooded areas, and in hedgerows. In colour it is variable, being brownish, greyish, or reddish above, with lighter or darker spots, and sometimes with dark lines down the back and sides. The underparts of the male are orange or red with black spots, in the female yellower and with the spots less distinctly marked. It grows to 6 inches in length, of which the tail forms one-half. As its name implies, its young, from six to twelve in number, are born alive. When born, they are enclosed in a more or less transparent membrane, which they break through at once. The Viviparous Lizard is one of the hardiest of reptiles: in Europe, it ranges farther north and at greater altitudes than any other species, having been found in latitude 63 N. in Russia, and in the Alps at a height of 10,000 feet.

The Sand Lizard is not uncommon in the heather country of Hampshire, Dorset, and Surrey, and is found also in the sandy parts of Lancashire, bordering the sea. It is bigger than the Viviparous Lizard, reaching 8 inches in length, of which the tail forms nearly one-half. Its upper parts are greenish or greyish in colour, with rows of black and white-eyed spots along the sides of its back and tail. In the breeding season, the male takes on a brilliant green hue, when it is sometimes mistaken for the Green Lizard (which, however, does not live in a wild state in this country). The Sand Lizard does well in captivity, and if properly looked after and given the right place in which to hibernate, will live for several years. It quickly becomes tame and learns to feed from the hand. Mating takes place in May and June, and the eggs, five to eight in number, are hatched in July and August. The Sand Lizard is found all over Europe and in western Asia.

The common Green Lizard of Europe is one of the largest of the European species, the male reaching a length of 16 or 17 inches, of which about one-half is the tail. It is most common in countries on the eastern and northern shores of the Mediterranean. It is bright green above (with or without black specks), greenish-yellow on the flanks, and yellow on the belly. In the breeding season, the throat of the male is blue. The young are marked above with one or two longitudinal yellowish stripes. This beautiful lizard is often kept in captivity in England; but although it feeds well, it does not usually live long. Attempts have been made to get it to live in a wild state in North Wales and the Isle of Wight; but after some years the colonies have always disappeared. Closely allied to the Green Lizard is the Eyed Lizard, an inhabitant of western Europe. It differs in colour, for the sides of the body are adorned with some two dozen blue, black-edged spots or 'eyes', the intensity of the blue and of the green of its body varying with the sex and with the time of year. It is a voracious creature, and will devour other lizards, or even snakes and mice.

A FLYING LIZARD

Another Lacertid lizard, the commonest of all the lizards in southern Europe and the islands of the Mediterranean, is the Wall Lizard, a small creature, not more than 7 inches in length. The upper parts of its body are brown or grey, sometimes with a bronzy sheen, and with black spots and streaks that vary greatly in size, intensity, and arrangement. Each particular region, sometimes each island, has its own special form, its main interest to naturalists being the great number of races and sub-species which can be recognized. No other lizard in Europe is so variable.

Some lizards (of the genus *Draco*) are known as Flying Lizards, because they can glide from one tree to another by means of a wing-like, membranous expansion from the side of the body, supported on extensions on the ribs. The distance travelled depends upon the height from which they have started; but they have been seen to cover between 40 and 50 yards. They live entirely among trees, and for that reason are not often seen, although in some places in the East they are common. When they are resting or climbing about in search of food, their wing-membrane is folded back along the sides of the body and is hardly visible. In many species it is beautifully coloured with red or yellow, and barred or spotted with black. The throat of the male has a membranous pouch (the female also has one, but much smaller) and in courtship this is often blown out like a paper bag. Some forty species of *Draco* are known. They are found mainly in Indo-China and Malaya; but one species inhabits India.

The only poisonous lizard known is the Gila Monster, which is a native of Mexico and the neighbouring countries, and lives in the desert. It is a thick, heavily-built creature, nearly 2 feet long, with a bulbous tail. It is barred and mottled with dark brown, pink, and orange. Its poison gland is in the lower jaw, and this

A MEXICAN HORNED LIZARD OR HORNED TOAD

carries a venom powerful enough to produce severe symptoms in man—though death from the bite is very rare. When in captivity, which it stands well, it is very fond of eggs.

Certain lizards of North America, called Horned Toads, have the remarkable habit, when caught, of spurting little jets of blood from the eyes. The blood, which comes from the veins of the eyelids, and is ejected by a sudden contraction of the muscles covering them, can be thrown for a distance of 15 inches, often several times in succession. Horned Toads are about 5 inches long, the head, back, and tail being covered with horny spines. They live mainly in sandy regions.

Among the burrowing lizards is the Amphisbaena family, which includes some 70 species of degenerate, worm-like creatures, inhabiting

A BASILISK LIZARD

northern and central Africa and tropical America. Most of them live in burrows, but some inhabit ant-holes. In form and structure they are well adapted for underground life: their eyes are concealed under the skin; they have small mouths, no ears, and, except for one species, no limbs; their skins are covered with squared plates arranged in regular rings; and their tails are short. They can move both backwards and forwards (their name, from the Greek, means one who can go in either direction). They feed on small insects and worms.

The Basilisk is a harmless lizard of tropical America, distinguished by a pointed casque on the back of its head, and a high crest of skin along its back to the base of the tail. It lives in trees, generally near water, into which it plunges when frightened. It feeds mainly on leaves, fruit, and flowers. The fabulous basilisk of the ancients was a reptile with a withering gaze, hatched by a serpent from a cock's egg (*see* FABULOUS CREATURES, Vol. I).

LLAMA. These animals, inhabitants of South America only, are RUMINANTS (q.v.), or chewers of the cud. They are related to the CAMEL (q.v.), but are far smaller and lighter in build, and have no humps. Llamas are found only in captivity, their domestication dating back to very early times, when the ancient Peruvians used them not only for transport, but also for their wool, milk, and flesh. They have very thick, woolly coats. Like camels, they have an expression of supercilious aloofness and calm contempt. They are extremely sure-footed, and their soft, padded, almost claw-like toes seem to adhere like suckers to the rocks. It is a common sight to see a herd of Llamas grazing on the precipitous side of a mountain so steep that the native Indians can hardly find a foothold. They are most useful transport animals, able to carry loads in high altitudes, in extreme cold, but they are not very strong, and will refuse to carry a load too heavy for them. (*See* BEASTS OF BURDEN, Vol. IV.)

The Alpaca—the other domestic member of the Llama family—is smaller than the Llama, and is specially bred for its wool, which is very fine and long, sometimes reaching almost to the ground. Alpacas are kept in herds on the high plateaux of Bolivia and southern Peru, and are driven down to the villages only once a year, at the shearing season. The flesh both of the Llama and the Alpaca is excellent to eat.

There are two wild relatives of the Llama: the Vicuña, and the larger Huanaco (or Guanaco), from which both the domestic Llama and the Alpaca are believed to be descended. The Huanaco is swift of foot, but not nearly so fast as the lightning-like Vicuña. Herds of these wild Llamas, sometimes numbering several hundred, live on the arid deserts, high plateaux, and mountain defiles of the Andes, and feed on the sparse vegetation. They have the curious habit of spitting at any intruder who goes near them. The Vicuñas can often be seen at play, racing around in circles, playing leap-frog, and even turning somersaults; but at the first sign of danger, they vanish in a cloud of dust. Strangely enough, nothing will induce them to cross, leap over, or push through a barrier, no matter how flimsy it may be. The Vicuña fawns are born singly in February, and from the beginning are remarkably swift and strong. Young males remain with their flock until they are full grown, when they are expelled by the dams. They then band themselves together in groups of twenty to thirty. Incessant fights take place between these male flocks in the mating season, when they utter a peculiar neighing sound which can be heard from a very long distance. The victorious males become leaders of flocks numbering from six to fifteen females. The male always remains a few paces behind his flock. If he sees danger, he utters a shrill warning whistle, whereupon the flock collects, and gallops off swiftly, with the male at the rear, stopping now and then to observe the foe.

THREE STAGES IN GROWTH OF THE LOBSTER
(1) Early larval stage; (2) Late larval stage; (3) Adult

CRAWFISH OR SPINY ROCK LOBSTER

LOBSTER. The Common Lobster is a CRUSTA-CEAN (q.v.), living in the shallow off-shore waters all round the coasts of Britain and western Europe. It shelters in crevices in the rocks, crawling forth at night in search of food, and, when alarmed, shooting swiftly backwards through the water by powerful strokes of its broad tail-fan. The two great claws differ in size and shape, the larger having the blades armed with blunt knobs for crushing, while the smaller has saw-edged blades for holding and tearing its prey. When alive, the Lobster is dark blue or nearly black on the back, with a good deal of red or orange on the underside of the body and limb-joints. The female Lobster produces immense numbers of eggs, which are attached to limbs, called 'swimmerets', on the under surface of her body, and are carried in that position during the whole period of incubation—some ten months. The young, on escaping from the eggs, are transparent, quite unlike their parents in appearance, and can swim actively in the surface waters of the sea by means of the swimming-branches attached to their legs. They do not pass through elaborate larval stages, but soon reach the adult form. Lobsters, like most of the larger Crustaceans, readily throw off a limb that is grasped by a foe or injured in the course of a fight The relinquished limb parts

company at a special fracture-point near the base, and later is replaced by a new one, which, after a series of moults, may attain almost the size of the original.

Closely related to the Common Lobster is the so-called Dublin Prawn or Norway Lobster, now chiefly caught in the North Sea. It is much smaller than the Common Lobster, from which it is easily distinguished by its long, slender claws, kidney-shaped eyes, and, when alive, by its beautiful orange colour marked with red and white. The little Freshwater Crayfish is closely related to the Lobster, but does not pass through a free-swimming larval stage; the young Crayfish hatches from the egg in a form differing very little from that of the adult, and remains clinging to its mother's swimmerets until sufficiently developed to fend for itself. In general appearance the Freshwater Crayfish resembles a lobster in miniature, measuring some 3 to 4 inches in length, and is usually of a brownish-green or olive colour. It digs holes in the earth, or hides in crevices in rocks along the edge of streams, and appears to be more active at night, when it goes out in search of food.

The large Spiny Rock Lobster or Crawfish is easily distinguished from the Common Lobster by its spiny carapace or upper shell, by the antennae (the second pair being stout and stiff, and the first pair having very thick basal joints), and by the total absence of the great claws. The pincer-claw of the lobster is replaced by a single short hooked claw, working against a knob or blunt spine—an arrangement very like that of the SHRIMP (q.v.). The larvae of the Spiny Rock Lobster have oval, flattened bodies, and are almost transparent—being popularly known as glass-crabs. They have long spidery legs, and large black eyes mounted on stalks. Full-grown specimens measure a little over an inch across.

See also Vol. VI: CRAB AND LOBSTER FISHING.

LOBSTER MOTH, see PROMINENT MOTHS.

LOCUSTS, see GRASSHOPPER; see also Vol. VI: INSECT PESTS.

LONG-HORN MOTHS. Over 200 species are known of these small, often brilliant, metallic, day-flying moths belonging to the family Adelidae, fourteen occurring in Britain. They are conspicuous for their extremely long,

thread-like antennae, which in males are sometimes four times the length of the body. The
males of some species also have enlarged eyes.
The Green Long-horn, one of the commonest
British woodland species, is a beautiful coppery-
green moth, with about ½-inch wing-span. On
sunny days in May and June, the males, in
swarms of twenty to thirty, dance above the
leafy branch of an oak some distance from the
ground, resting at intervals, and then resuming
the dance. The females sit about on neighbouring leaves and enter the swarms to mate.
The eggs are laid in the midribs of leaves, and
the caterpillars of most species mine in the
leaves or flower-heads, and then make flattish
cases from leaf fragments attached to fallen
leaves. British species occur on Black Hore-
hound, Scabious, Privet, Lady's-smock, Ger-
mander Speedwell, and other plants.

LOOPERS. These caterpillars, of which there
are some 3,000 species in the northern regions
of the Old World, lack abdominal legs, except
on the 6th and 10th abdominal segments (*see*
CATERPILLAR, Fig. 1 B). They walk by gripping
an object with their front legs, arching their

bodies to bring up their hind-legs, and then
holding on with these, extending themselves to
the fullest extent to obtain a new grip with the
front legs. The scientific name of the family
of moths, Geometridae, to which they belong,
and the common American names, 'measuring
worms' or 'span-worms', refer to this habit of
matching their length against the ground. The
slender, hairless caterpillars often resemble brown
or green twigs, and not only have rough processes suggesting buds or leaf scars, but assist
this deception by resting on real twigs, which
they grip with the hind-legs, while their bodies,
sometimes supported by a silken thread, are
held out rigidly at an angle (*see* CAMOUFLAGE).

Geometrid moths have slender bodies and
relatively large wings. They have conspicuous
openings in the sides of the first abdominal
segment, which leads to well-developed, sound-
detecting organs, to be compared with the ears
of vertebrates. Most of them fly by night, but
they will take to the wing in daylight when
disturbed. Most species rest with the wings flat
on either side of the body; but occasionally the
wings stand erect, as in butterflies, or slope
roofwise. Many rest by day on tree-trunks,

Left. WAVED UMBER LARVA IN TYPICAL LOOPING POSITION. *Right.* LARVAE OF LARGE THORN MOTH RESEMBLING TWIGS
OF THE OAK SPRAY. *S. Beaufroy, F.R.P.S.*

where their general resemblance to lichen-covered bark is enhanced by their habit of resting so that they cast no shadow, and so that the dark lines on their wings fit in with the vertical cracks in the bark. Some seek safety by resembling bird-droppings (some Carpets), or dead leaves (Thorns). A few, e.g. the Magpie, a common pest on gooseberry and currant, have bold warning colours, in this instance, white with black and yellow spots (*see* PROTECTIVE COLORATION).

Several Geometrid Moths have names reminiscent of butterflies—for instance, the pale-yellow Swallow-tailed Moth, with a wing-expanse of $1\frac{3}{4}$–$2\frac{1}{4}$ inches, and with a caterpillar which feeds on ivy; the smaller, bright-yellow Brimstone Moth, common in hawthorn hedges; and the still smaller and local, brownish-white Peacock Moth. The Yellow Shell, with its many narrow brown markings, is one of the commonest summer moths among bushes and hedgerows. The robust Pepper and Salt Moth is white, speckled with black; but recently it has been completely replaced in the smoky industrial areas of northern England by a black variety—less conspicuous in these sooty surroundings. The Emeralds are delicate shades of green, a rare colour in butterflies and moths. The caterpillar of the Essex Emerald achieves camouflage by covering itself with pieces of its food-plant, the sea wormwood. There are many species of Waves, whitish, yellowish, or brownish moths, with darker, wave-like patterns crossing the wings. The Pugs, easily recognized by their small size and long, rounded forewings, are brownish, greyish, or greenish. The Seraphims have glandular flaps on the hind-wings, suggesting an extra pair of wings. Though the male Winter Moth is on the wing from October to February, often to be seen in the beams of car head-lamps, the almost wingless female is unable to fly, but climbs the trunks of trees to lay her bright green eggs singly on buds and spurs or in cracks in the bark, where they soon turn brick red. The green-striped caterpillars hatch out in March and April, and start to feed on the opening buds, doing much damage to fruit trees. Other fruit pests with wingless females are the March Moth, Mottled Umber, and the Early Moth. The Vestal, a small, pale-yellow moth, with a pink or brown stripe on the forewings, is ordinarily only an occasional visitor to Britain from the Mediterranean region; but

in 1947 it reached the south coast in great numbers, and successfully bred there.

See also MOTHS.

LOUSE.

Lice are external parasites on birds and mammals, and for their size have very powerful claws, by which they cling tightly to feathers or hair. Some lice are eyeless, but others have well-developed compound eyes. All are wingless, and have very short antennae. There are two groups, Biting Lice and Sucking Lice, both of which have small, flat bodies. Biting Lice, of which we know about 1,700 species, use their mouth-parts for chewing, and feed on feathers, hair, and similar dry material. As they are much more often found on birds than on mammals, they are often called Bird Lice. All birds seem to be affected by these lice, and the habit birds

BITING LOUSE
× 10

have of taking dust baths is probably for the purpose of ridding themselves of them. Pigeons are almost always infested with a very slender louse, which looks to the naked eye like a dark line on the feather. It clings so tightly to the feathers that it is very difficult to remove without tearing off the claws. Sucking Lice, which puncture the skin and suck the blood flowing from the wound, are found only on mammals. As yet we know about 120 species; but it is probable that these are only a fraction of the total number. Two species are found on man, about a dozen on his domestic animals, and the remainder have been found on wild mammals.

HUMAN LOUSE
× 15

Lice have no METAMORPHOSIS (q.v.)—that is to say, the young are like their parents, except in size. The eggs are called 'nits'. The female of the Human Louse is able to lay some 300 eggs in the course of a month. Those of Biting Lice are cemented to the feather, and soon hatch out. There are several changes of coat during growth,

NITS ON PIG BRISTLE
Magnified

which lasts a few weeks. The whole life of the insect is spent upon the warm-blooded animal it parasitizes, and it soon dies if removed. Infection of one animal from another takes place very easily by contact. Lice of any particular species confine themselves to one particular species of animal, and will not remove themselves to another species. But this does not mean that one animal can be attacked by only one species of Louse: ducks, for example, are attacked by several different kinds of Biting Louse, and there are two different species to be found on the dog.

See also INSECTS. See also Vol. VI, ANIMAL PESTS. See also Vol. XI, HOUSEHOLD PESTS.

LUMPSUCKER. Known also as the Sea-hen, this rather curious-looking fish of the North Atlantic is quite common on some parts of the British coast. The pelvic fins form a sucking disk beneath the body, by which it attaches

LUMPSUCKER DEFIES THE SWIRL OF THE TIDE BY ATTACHING ITSELF TO A ROCK. *A. Fraser-Brunner*

itself firmly to rocks. The eggs are laid in spring, between tide-marks on the shore, in great masses averaging 100,000. The male, which is smaller and more brightly coloured than the female, guards the eggs faithfully, fanning them with his large pectoral fins to aerate them. Both fish and eggs are likely to fall prey to numerous enemies, for when the tide is out, they are exposed to attacks from sea-gulls, rooks, and rats, and when they are under water various other fishes feed on them. Nevertheless, the father will suffer death rather than leave his eggs. The Lumpsuckers grow to a length of about 18 inches. They are not much used for food.

LUNG-FISH. These are the only living survivors of a group of fishes that were numerous

THE SOUTH AMERICAN LUNG-FISH AND ITS TADPOLE-LIKE LARVA. *A. Fraser-Brunner*

in an earlier period of the world's history, and are believed to have been the ancestors of the Amphibia (Frogs, Newts, and Salamanders). The air-bladder of some of these fishes (the African ones) is double, and in many ways resembles the pair of lungs of higher animals—and this is why they are called Lung-fish. Besides this singularity, the Lung-fish have paired fins of a peculiar kind, which are borne on a fleshy lobe supported by bones which seem to foreshadow the leg-bones of higher vertebrates.

One species of Lung-fish valued as food is found in Queensland, Australia, where it is known as the Barramunda. Since its flesh is pink, it is often referred to as 'salmon'. It comes to the surface of the water to take air into its (single) lung, and when the used air is forced out through the gullet, it produces a loud grunting noise that can be heard for some distance. The Barramunda is a large, clumsy-looking fish, with big scales.

The Lung-fishes of Africa are more slender, with smaller scales, and in some ways look remarkably like SALAMANDERS (q.v.). Young ones have large, feathery, external gills, like those of tadpoles, which shrink as the animal grows up. The adult, therefore, has small gills, which are not sufficient to meet its needs, so that it has to breathe air by means of its lungs. The African lung-fishes are sluggish, moving slowly about at the bottom of swamps, using their paired fins like legs, to climb among the roots of vegetation. They burrow a great deal, their shape being well adapted for this. During the rainy season, when food is abundant, they feed heartily; but when the dry season comes, and the water begins to dry up, they burrow into the soft mud to await the return of the rains. Presently, the mud dries up quite hard, and the fish is then in a sort of earthenware cocoon. The natives often dig out these cocoons to use the fish as food—and lung-fishes have been sent long distances in this condition, afterwards to be liberated in water and exhibited in aquariums. Lung-fishes lay their eggs in underground burrows, the male remaining in the 'nest' to guard the eggs and aerate them.

LUNGS, *see* RESPIRATION IN ANIMALS.

LYNX, *see* CAT.

LYRE-BIRD. This Australian bird, slaty-brown in colour and nearly as large as a pheasant, is conspicuous for the development of the tail-feathers of the cock. These rise in a spectacular fan over the bird's back, the middle pair of feathers being narrow and curved, and the outer pair very broad, banded with chestnut, and shaped like the sides of a lyre. The inner plumes are lighter in colour, and very fine and hair-like. Lyre-birds have long legs and large, strong feet, well adapted for scratching up the grubs on which they feed. In the forests of south-eastern Australia, these birds used to be common; but the clearing of the forests, bush fires, and the depredations of foxes, who attack the nests, have reduced their numbers considerably.

Lyre-birds carry out a remarkable courtship display in the mating season. The cock-bird makes a mound in the forest; and there, throwing his wonderful tail forward over his head, he sings vigorously and performs a display dance. The Lyre-bird is a fine songster with rich and powerful notes. Young birds do not sing until they have grown their full tails—which is not, apparently, until they are 4 years old. Both cocks and hens are remarkable mimics of other birds' songs, their power of mimicry being greater, perhaps, than that of any other bird.

LYRE-BIRD OF AUSTRALIA DISPLAYING HIS MAGNIFICENT TAIL
Australian News & Information Bureau

During the mating season each cock has his own territory, and rarely infringes on that of another bird (*see* ANIMAL TERRITORY). He is accompanied by two or three females—though it seems likely that only one hen in each party lays in one year. The nest, placed on the ground, is made of small sticks interwoven with moss and roots; it is roofed over, the entrance being at the side. Only one egg is laid, a dark, blotched purple. The birds often build on the outskirts of a dense covert, where the nest can be clearly seen from the road. The birds themselves can also be seen roosting high up, generally in a gum-tree.

See also ANIMAL LANGUAGE.

M

MACAW, *see* PARROT.

MACKEREL. Among the loveliest fishes that swim in the oceans are the Mackerels. They are beautifully streamlined, with a widely forked caudal (tail) fin, and many are handsomely coloured. The rich, oily flesh of most of the species is excellent food.

The common Mackerel has a glittering green back with black cross-stripes; the two dorsal fins, the first with slender spines, are set far apart; and above and below the tail is a row of little extra fins. Mackerel run in vast shoals, feeding, as they swim at great speed through the surface water, on small crustaceans and other animals of the 'plankton' or floating ocean life. Spawning takes place not far from land, each female laying about half a million eggs per year. These are minute, and each is provided with an oil globule, which enables it to float for a time. Schools of Mackerel 20 miles long and ½ mile wide have been reported off the American coast, where the Mackerel is more numerous than in European waters—the American fishery for them being enormous (*see* FISHING METHODS, Section 1 *c*, Vol. VI).

The true Mackerels (there are other species in the East Indian and Australian regions) are quite small, rarely more than a foot in length; but some of their relatives are much larger. The so-called Spanish Mackerel of American coasts, for instance, grows to 12 pounds or more in weight, and is much sought after by anglers, to whom it affords great sport and good food. The Seer of India, one of the most esteemed food-fishes of that country, grows to a length of 4 feet.

The giants of the family, however, are the Tunnies, or Tuna, which have a band or 'corselet' of large scales round the shoulders, but are otherwise very much like overgrown Mackerel. Some of these grow to about 8 feet in length, and may weigh 800 pounds. The Atlantic Tunny, though a fish of the warm seas, follows the Gulf Stream from America in summer to feed on herring in the North Sea, where it has been caught by anglers off Denmark and the English coast. Others are said to reach Cornwall from the Mediterranean. The blood of Tunnies is generally warmer than that of other fishes, and the flesh is red in colour. There is a regular fishery for them in the Mediterranean, where the flesh is canned as 'Thon rouge'.

Similar to the Tunny, but not so large, and with longer pectoral fins and white flesh, are the Albacores, which are also canned, under the name 'Thon blanc'. Smaller still are the Bonito, which are usually about 10 lb. in weight. These beautiful fish move in immense schools at great speed—they are said to be the swiftest of all fishes. They are the 'tuna' of the canning industries in America and Japan (*see* BONITO FISHING, Vol. VI).

Nearly related to the Mackerel are some other giant fishes, that have the upper jaw prolonged into a sword or 'rostrum'. The most famous of

MACKEREL   *A. Fraser-Brunner*

SWORDFISH   *A. Fraser-Brunner*

these is the Swordfish, which has a flattened rostrum and no pelvic fins. It has a habit of attacking things larger than itself, such as big sharks, whales, and ships—for what purpose is not understood. There are many records of its sword having been driven right through the side of a wooden boat. It is much sought after by anglers, especially round New Zealand, and when hooked it takes great leaps from the water (*see* BIG-GAME FISHING, Vol. IX). Much the same may be said of the Spearfishes and Sailfishes which have a rounded rostrum and possess pelvic fins. The Sailfish gets its name from the high, sail-like dorsal fin, the use of which is not known.

Finally, mention should be made of certain species which, although related to the Mackerel, do not look at all similar. These are long, flattened fishes, with large mouths full of very strong teeth, a fin along the whole length of the back, and the tail ending in a fine point. The commonest is the silver Cutlass-fish, which grows up to 5 feet long.

MAGPIE, *see* CROW, Section 7.

MAGPIE MOTH, *see* LOOPERS.

MALLARD, *see* DUCK, Section 2.

MAMBA. This poisonous snake of southern and central Africa is greatly feared on account of its vindictive nature and deadly bite. The common belief that there are two species, a black and a green mamba, is not correct: they are colour phases of the same species, and many specimens that are green when young turn darker with age. The Mamba grows to 6 or 7 feet long. It is without doubt the fastest snake that we know of: there is good evidence to show that on suitable ground it can travel perhaps 20 miles an hour, and can keep it up for 100 yards or so. The fastest snakes in America are called the Racers, but experiments with them have shown that they do not travel more than 6 miles an hour. (*See also* SNAKES.)

MAMMALS. The Vertebrate (or Chordate) animals are divided into six classes, of which the mammals are the most highly developed. The term 'mammal' was introduced by LINNAEUS (q.v. Vol. V), and means an animal which has 'mammae', or milk-secreting organs, for suckling its young. Mammals first arose during the Age of Reptiles (*see* EVOLUTION)—before Birds, which are also descended from Reptiles. Man, the most highly organized of all animals, is a mammal.

The two main characteristics are the growth of hair and the secretion of milk. The purpose of HAIR, as of FEATHERS (qq.v.), is to keep up a constant body-temperature in the varying conditions of a mammal's environment. The velvety fur of a mole, the wool of a sheep, the spines of a hedgehog, or the bristles of a pig are all forms of hair. All mammals carry some hair, though Whales and Hippopotami have very little. Milk is the ideal food for the young, who, while they are suckling, remain dependent on their mothers for protection and generally, also, for training.

Mammals normally have two pairs of limbs, both in the majority of species being used for walking. In the Sea-cows and Whales the front limbs are modified for swimming, the hind legs being lost, and in the Bats the arms have been modified for flying. All mammals have tails, though in some species, such as Man, the tail is undeveloped, while in others it is prehensile and can be used as a fifth limb. The brain is more highly developed in this class than in any other, the higher mammals being better able than any other animals to condition instinctive behaviour as the result of experience, and so to change their behaviour patterns. Some, such as the Apes, show the beginning of the power of reason, which guides Man's intelligent behaviour (*see* INTELLIGENCE).

There are three sub-classes of mammals, the primitive egg-laying mammals, such as the DUCK-BILLED PLATYPUS and the ECHIDNAS (qq.v.); the MARSUPIALS (q.v.) or pouched mammals; and the placental mammals, in which the young remains within the womb of the mother until it has reached a comparatively advanced stage of development. This last group, which is much the largest, has proved the most successful in the struggle for existence —the first two groups being mostly found in regions, such as Australia and New Zealand, where members of the last group are not indigenous. The last group, the placental mammals, is sub-divided into nine main orders, of which the Edentata, or mammals without teeth, are the most primitive, and the Primates, including Man, the most developed. Two of the orders, the Sirenia or SEA-COWS, and Cetacea or WHALES (qq.v.), Dolphins, and Porpoises, contain mammals adapted for life in the sea. The Ungulata, or hoofed mammals, are those which specialize in running, the toes being reduced to two, in the case of the CATTLE and SHEEP, and one in the case of the HORSE (qq.v.). The Rodentia have special teeth for gnawing (see RODENTS), and the CARNIVORA (q.v.) for tearing flesh. The INSECTIVORA (q.v.) feed mainly on insects. The Chiroptera, (see BATS) contain the only mammals able to fly.

MANATEE, see SEA-COW.

MANDRILL, see BABOON.

MARMOSET, see MONKEY.

MARMOT. This small, stout rodent, related to the SQUIRREL (q.v.), is found in the northern parts of Europe, Asia, and North America. It is generally from 1½ to 2 feet long, and is covered with fairly long, coarse, reddish-brown fur, with tail, and short legs, and small ears.

Marmots live in large colonies in burrows, which they dig in open spaces. On fine days they sit on the observation-mound at the entrance of the burrow, or go for short distances in search of food—roots, leaves, and seeds. At the least alarm they rush back to the entrance of their burrow, where they sit up on their hindquarters surveying the scene and trying to detect the danger. If the enemy comes at all near, a loud, whistling scream from one of the party is a signal for all to dive headlong into their burrows. After a short time they put their heads out to see if the coast is clear.

In the autumn, marmots carry large quantities of hay into their burrows to make snug beds for their long winter hibernation. As they lay up no store of winter food, it is likely that their sleep is unbroken throughout the whole winter. The young are born in the early spring, and on warm days in early summer are to be seen outside their burrows in numbers.

The American Marmot, or Woodchuck, differs from the other species in occasionally climbing trees. The reddish-brown Prairie Marmot, or Prairie Dog, lives on the open plains east of the Rocky Mountains. The American Chipmunks, often called Ground-

ALPINE MARMOT
This squirrel-like little animal is on the look-out for possible danger. *Paul Popper*

Squirrels, are not, however, true squirrels, but are related to the Woodchucks and Prairie Dogs. They make themselves most comfortable three-roomed burrows, consisting of a living compartment, a food-store, and sleeping quarters. Realizing that he would be cornered were an enemy to find his way in, the Chipmunk provides a safety-exit by making a second burrow leading from his apartment to a back door, which is cleverly hidden under, for instance, a stone or log.

MARSH PLANT, *see* WATER PLANTS.

MARSUPIALS (Lat. *marsupium*, a pouch). This is the name for the Pouched Mammals, which are found only in Australasia and the Americas. Among the best known are the KANGAROOS, KOALAS, and OPOSSUMS (qq.v.).

The chief difference between the marsupials and other mammals is that young marsupials are born very undeveloped and extremely small. The only parts at all well developed at birth are the front feet and claws; and with these the tiny creature instinctively crawls through its mother's fur to her pouch, where it becomes firmly fixed to her nipple. It has no power to suck, but the mother injects milk into it by a muscular action. Some of the marsupials have no actual pouch, but the young, when clinging to their mother's breast, are hidden by her fur. Most of the Australasian marsupials are pouched; some, like the Kangaroos, Wallabies, and Wombats, are vegetarians; others are flesh-eaters; while others, including the Pouched Mice and the Banded Ant-eaters, feed on insects. The American marsupials are known as OPOSSUMS (q.v.), and are both flesh and insect-eaters. All, except the Water Opossum, live among the trees, most of them being excellent climbers, making use of their prehensile tails, which they can twine round the branches.

The name 'opossum' is also commonly used in Australia for a group of Australian marsupials, though it is perhaps more correct to call these Phalangers. The group is made up of many small and medium-sized animals, including the KOALA (q.v.). Some are vegetarian, while others also eat flesh. They live in trees, have thick woolly coats, and all except the Koala have long tails, which in most cases are prehensile. The Flying Phalangers (or Flying Opossums) have a membrane joining the fore

SHORT-HEADED FLYING PHALANGER
Paul Popper

and hind limbs, by means of which they can glide for great distances from branch to branch. One of these, popularly known as the 'Flying Squirrel', or 'Sugar Squirrel', is often kept as a pet in Australia.

The Wombats are a distinct group of Australian marsupials, which can gnaw like rodents and burrow with their feet. They are thick-set, about the size of badgers, and look rather like small bears. They sleep during the day in burrows, feeding at night on grass, leaves, bark, and roots. They walk in a peculiar shuffling way, and when irritated utter either a hissing sound or a short grunt. They are normally shy and gentle, but can bite savagely in self-defence.

Members of the Bandicoot family vary in size from that of a rat to that of a rabbit. These Australian marsupials eat both animal and vegetable food, and are detested by the farmer because of the great damage they do to crops. They are nocturnal, hiding by day in holes in the ground or in thick vegetation. The most distinctive member of the group is the Rabbit Bandicoot, which has long ears like a rabbit's, a fairly long tail, and long hind legs like a kangaroo's, and looks something like a cross between a rabbit and a rat.

Of the Australian flesh-eating marsupials the largest is the Tasmanian Wolf. It is very like a European wolf, though smaller, and it has dark bands across the hinder part of its greyish-brown body. It is now rare, as its night-time ravages among sheep and lambs have led to its extermination, except in the wild mountainous parts of Tasmania. The Tasmanian Devil,

TASMANIAN DEVIL
A nocturnal killer of sheep and poultry
Australian News & Information Bureau

about the size of a badger, has a short body, short legs, and a very large head. It has thick, black fur, with a white stripe across the chest. It hunts its prey at night, attacking any creature it can overcome, including sheep and wallabies.

The Native Cats of the mainland of Australia are about the size of a small ordinary cat—but are, of course, no relation to the real cats. They are either black or pale brown, spotted with white. They eat birds and small animals, and are extremely troublesome to poultry-keepers. They live in trees, behaving very much like MARTENS (q.v.).

Among the insect-feeding marsupials are the Pouched Mice, which vary greatly in size, some being about the size of a small squirrel, while the tiny Common Pouched Mouse is only 3½ inches long. Most of them keep to the ground, living in rocky caves or hollow banks; but some of them climb trees. As many as ten young may be born at a time, and are brought up in the pouch of their mother. Another insect-eater, the Banded Ant-eater, is one of the few marsupials in which the female has no pouch. It is about the size of a squirrel, with bands of white across the hinder part of its body, the ground colour of which is dark chestnut-red above and white below. It feeds chiefly on ants and termites.

See also MAMMALS.

MARTEN, *see* WEASEL, Section 4.

MARTIN, *see* SWALLOWS.

MAY-FLY. On warm summer evenings large numbers of May-flies appear suddenly over the surfaces of rivers and lakes, and perform an aerial wedding dance, in which they fly swiftly upwards and then sink slowly downwards again, wings and tails sloping upwards. Other peculiarities which make these insects particularly interesting are the facts that adult life in many species is very short, and that the adults do not feed. About forty species are found in Britain.

May-flies have two pairs of triangular wings, the fore-wings being large, the hind-wings very small, and both showing an intricate network of cross-veining. When the May-fly is at rest, it holds its wings vertically over its body, like a butterfly. At the tip of its abdomen are two, sometimes three, long, slender tails. Its mouth-parts are minute, and useless when it becomes adult. Most species live for only 4 or 5 hours as adults, though some live for several days.

The eggs of the May-fly are often very numerous—as many as 4,000 having been counted from one mother. The nymph lives entirely in the water, under stones, buried in mud, or freely swimming in swiftly flowing streams, for three or more years. Along its abdomen are plate-like gills. It is thought to cast its skin at least twenty-three times during its pre-adult life. Most are vegetarians. When it is fully developed, the nymph floats to the surface of the water, the skin cracks along the back, the May-fly emerges, and almost at once flies away. It looks exactly like the finished product; but in its present condition it is called the 'sub-imago'. The whole body, including the wings, is enclosed in an extremely thin, transparent sheath, which must be cast off before the insect becomes the true imago. The May-flies are the only insects which cast their skin after they are fully winged. The empty skins may often be found on tree-trunks, on the banks of rivers and lakes, or floating on the surface of the water. Once the skin is shed they begin their wedding dance. When the male has found a mate he flies beneath her, and takes hold of her with his long fore-legs. Grasping her body from below with a short pair of claspers, which (in males only) are at the root of his tails, he passes his outer tails between the hind and fore-wings of the female. Thus united, the pair float to the ground, where their union is completed. The instant they separate the female returns to the water and drops her eggs on its surface.

Then, their short life as 'spinners' over, they fall dead into the stream.

MERGANSER, see Ducks, Section 3.

MERLIN, see Falcon.

METAMORPHOSIS. This is the scientific name used to describe the very striking changes in structure which occur in the life-cycle of some animals, especially insects. Until we understand the process of metamorphosis, we can hardly credit the extraordinary fact that the gaudy Red Admiral Butterfly (q.v.), which we see flying over the flower border, is in reality the same individual as the slow, worm-like Caterpillar (q.v.), which was feeding on the nettles a few weeks back. Almost as unbelievable is it that the long-legged green Frog (q.v.), which hops out of the grass, is the same individual as the little black tadpole, seen a short time back in the pond; or that the magnificent sapphire-blue Dragonfly (q.v.) was once a drab, inconspicuous, and unlovely larva.

All Arthropods—that is to say, lobsters, crabs, scorpions, wood-lice, spiders, centipedes, as well as the insects—wear their skeletons on the outside, and can grow only by first climbing out of the skeleton and then, after an interval, hardening another, larger one—a process called the 'moult'. But most insects make a change in shape and appearance, also, at the time of some of these moults: this change is called a metamorphosis (or change of form). A few insects have no metamorphosis, but hatch directly from the egg to the adult; others have an incomplete metamorphosis—that is, they miss out one of the stages. The May-fly (q.v.), for instance, hatches from the egg, not into a 'larva' or grub, but into an incomplete fly, called a 'nymph'. The new-born nymph is without developed wings or sex-organs, and lives on the water; but it develops gradually into an adult May-fly without any further sudden change. Other insects have a complete metamorphosis—that is, they make the changes from egg to larva (caterpillar, grub); from larva to pupa (chrysalis); and from pupa to imago (butterfly, bee, ant, fly, beetle, and so on). This series of changes is very clearly marked, and most usually observed, among the Lepidoptera (butterflies and moths).

The female butterfly or moth lays her eggs, either singly or in batches, on the food-plant proper to the species. In about a week, the eggs change colour, often going dark grey or black as the tiny caterpillar shows through the semi-opaque shell. On hatching, the caterpillars usually make their first meal of the egg-shell, and then begin to feed on the food-plant where the eggs were laid—for instance, if they are Cabbage Whites, on the cabbage plants in our garden. The Caterpillar (q.v.) is a worm-like creature whose whole business in life is to eat and grow.

The end of the caterpillar or larval stage is 'pupation'—that is to say, the change to a chrysalis or pupa. Some pupate amongst the leaves or on the stems of their food-plant; some crawl away and hang up head downwards, attached by a pad of silk on their tails, from

FIG. I. SWALLOW-TAIL CATERPILLAR CASTING ITS SKIN AS IT PUPATES. *Natural size*
S. Beaufoy, F.R.P.S.

FIG. 2. YELLOW BRIMSTONE BUTTERFLY EMERGING FROM THE CHRYSALIS SHELL. *Natural size*
S. Beaufoy, F.R.P.S.

fences or under the guttering of a shed, summer-house, or farm building. Some crawl to earth and pupate amongst moss or tufts of grass, or bury themselves a few inches under the soil. Some spin a slender girdle of silk to support their bodies round the middle, before they cast their skin and change into the chrysalis. Some roughly fasten shreds of bark and other materials together with a little silk to form a protective case. Some moths, not only the domesticated SILK-WORM, but also the British EMPEROR MOTH (qq.v.) and a number of giant tropical moths, spin golden silk-cocoons; others make tough, water-proof cocoons, sometimes constructed of shreds of bark, fastened together with a glutinous substance, camouflaged with lichens, and fixed on tree-trunks.

To become a chrysalis, the caterpillar must cast off its skin—and this requires a series of muscular feats. The caterpillar's skin splits along the back from the head, and the pupa gradually draws out of it, sometimes leaving the cast skin clinging to the tail end of the chrysalis (*see* Fig. 1). The newly formed chrysalis has a soft outer shell, which hardens and darkens in a few hours. An immobile period, apparently for rest, then follows, and lasts for about 10 days—though some butterflies and moths will hibernate in this condition and not emerge till the following spring. Some moths will remain as pupae for a year—and have even been known to persist as long as 5 years in the chrysalis stage. Indeed, the 'Seventeen-year Locust' sometimes remains as a pupa for 17 years before it emerges as an adult.

Although during this period the insect inside the chrysalis appears to be quite inactive, in fact immense biological changes are going on, to prepare for the transformation that follows. The internal organs of the insect are broken down and then rebuilt within the chrysalis case. The strong jaws of the caterpillar are no longer wanted by the butterfly, and so a different mouth-part is built up, with a sucking organ, called a 'proboscis', to enable the insect to suck nectar from flowers. In insects which bite, the jaws are retained, and in other insects the proboscis can pierce like a beak, as well as suck. The rudimentary antennae of the caterpillar develop into the important sense-organs of the butterfly, and a pair of large compound eyes provide it with a wide range of vision for its new life. The thirteen segments of the caterpillar's body are retained in the butterfly's body; but the three segments of the thorax become separated from the ten segments of the abdomen by a slender waist. The embryo wing-buds, on the second and third segments of the thorax in the caterpillar, develop within the chrysalis into closely packed wings, ready to expand when the butterfly emerges. The three pairs of short front legs of the caterpillar develop, while the five pairs of abdominal legs disappear. The male and female sex-organs, entirely embryo in the caterpillar, develop in the butterfly, so that mating can take place, and the female lays eggs to produce the next generation.

When the insect finally breaks out of the chrysalis shell (*see* Fig. 2), it expands its wings and dries them, and within about an hour, after opening and closing its wings as if to test them out, it launches forth into the air to begin a new life. All insects which pass through a complete metamorphosis follow much the same pattern described here for butterflies, though different species vary the procedure in some minor respects.

Frogs and Toads (qq.v.), and some other amphibian reptiles, also go through a metamorphosis, but they omit the pupal stage. The adult frog lays eggs from which, after about 10 or 12 weeks, hatch tadpoles, the frog's larvae. The newly hatched tadpole appears to consist mainly of a round head with a tail. As it lives entirely in the water, it is provided with gills. After a period of growth, the tadpole gradually develops legs, its gills are replaced by the lungs of the adult frog, and it loses its tail. From now on it can breathe air, and can live on land or in water. The life-history of the toad follows much the same pattern.

See also Insects; Butterflies; Moths.

MIDGE. This small insect is very like the Mosquito (q.v.); but its wings have no scales. There are about 135 British species, in twenty-nine of which the females are bloodsuckers. Others are quite harmless, as they take no food at all in adult life. They are among the most irritating of all insects, as they usually emerge in the evenings in considerable swarms, which dance up and down in the air at about head height. In early life, midges are usually aquatic. Often the larvae are red, and are then called 'bloodworms'. The red colour is due to haemoglobin, the pigment that colours our own blood. It is usually considered that this red pigment greatly increases their breathing capacity below water—and, certainly, the haemoglobin is not present in those species whose larvae feed at the surface of the water. The pupae may be active and swim about, or they may stay at the bottom. At the end of the pupal stage, they come up to the surface, their skin splits open, and the adult emerges and flies off.

See also Flies.

MIGRATION. Many kinds of animals—mammals, birds, fish, crustaceans, insects, and others—move from one place to another at certain seasons of the year, returning at other seasons. These periodical movements are known as migrations. The term should not be used of those movements which are made in one direction only, without any return (usually spoken of as 'irruptions'), since these are generally prompted by some abnormal external circumstances, such as bad weather, lack of food, or destruction of normal habitat. True migrations take place in accordance with some inner need

RED LAND CRABS MIGRATING TO THE SEA TO SPAWN
C. A. Gibson-Hill

(physiological or psychological) of the animal—although the stimulus may depend upon some external condition, such as temperature.

Migration is often connected with the breeding cycle of the animal. Thus TURTLES, which live most of the year in the sea, must come to land to lay their eggs on the beach—afterwards returning to the sea. In contrast with this, EELS breed in the Sargasso Sea, but migrate as small elvers to the fresh water of European rivers. Some years later, when mature, they return to breed in the depths of the Sargasso Sea—and are seen no more. SALMON (qq.v.) follow the opposite course, coming up the rivers to breed, but passing down to the sea to feed and grow.

Many animals, and especially birds, breed in the cooler parts of their range, generally in the north. (The number of species which breed in the southern hemisphere and move to the south of their range to breed is far smaller; but a glance at a map of the world will show that there is far more land towards the north than towards the south.) In Newfoundland, the Caribou move south in winter, but in summer return to the north again. In mountainous country, many animals move to lower ground for the winter, returning to the heights in spring to breed.

A great many butterflies and moths, including several common British species, are regular migrants, and depend wholly or partly on migration to keep up their numbers. Both the Large and Small WHITES (q.v.), though able to winter in Britain, have their numbers increased by enormous migrations from Europe. Darwin, when he once witnessed their arrival, described it with the phrase 'snowing butterflies'—an apt description of their irregular flight, which resembles falling snowflakes. A record migration, seen at Dover in 1846, was said to have completely obscured the sun for hundreds of yards over the Channel. The RED ADMIRAL and the PAINTED LADY (qq.v.) cannot survive the British winter, and they arrive in spring in large numbers from the Continent. The Painted Lady, a large, delicately coloured, pink and brown butterfly, is very widely travelled. It is believed that it originally starts from the regions of the Atlas Mountains in north Africa. In 1869, a naturalist in the Sudan, on a sunny morning in March, watched thousands of Painted Ladies emerge from their chrysalises and almost at once take to the air to move off northwards in a mighty company. They usually reach the Mediterranean coast in April, continuing their journey through Europe to arrive in England in late May or June. Individuals have been known to reach north Scotland and even Iceland and the Arctic Circle—a journey of over a thousand miles. Among moths, the Death's Head Hawk, the SILVER Y MOTH, and the Humming-bird HAWK (qq.v.) are notable migrants.

The migrations of butterflies and moths are not regular, as are those of birds, and until recently there was little evidence of any return south in autumn—which is not surprising in such short-lived creatures. Hordes of them will set out on apparently pointless journeys across the sea, only to fall, exhausted, into the water. Their movements are, therefore, strictly speaking, irruptions. The movements of the huge, reddish-brown American butterfly, the MONARCH (q.v.) or Milkweed, are, however, true migrations, for they are observed in both directions regularly. The insects fly about singly until the autumn, when they begin to congregate, like swallows, and gradually move southwards in an ever-growing army of tens of thousands. They fly from 200 to 300 feet above ground, and when they settle for the night, they appear to change the colour of the vegetation. When they reach warmer lands, they cluster on the limbs of trees for the winter. In the spring, the multitudes break up and travel north again, setting off in ones or twos to re-colonize their old haunts. The Monarch is a regular migrant to and from Canada, and has also quite often crossed the Atlantic and reached Britain.

Still more spectacular are the migrations of many species of birds. The SWALLOW (q.v.), which breeds so commonly in the British Isles, and as far north as the Arctic circle, winters in South Africa. The huge flocks of STARLINGS (q.v.) that feed on our fields in winter are drawn from Russia and the Baltic countries, vastly augmenting the numbers of our own native Starlings, which, oddly enough, do not migrate south, but remain all winter. Some of the shore birds, Dunlin, Sanderling, and the rest, breed in the tundra of northern Europe and Siberia, and in autumn pass our coasts on their way to Patagonia or New Zealand (see WADING BIRDS). These birds travel for the most part along the coasts, though they must also cross great stretches of open ocean. The North

DUNLINS GATHERING ON THE SHORE PREPARATORY TO MIGRATING
Eric J. Hosking, F.R.P.S.

American Golden Plover, which breeds in the Canadian Arctic, flies direct from Nova Scotia across 2,000 miles of the Atlantic to the coasts of South America; while the birds of the same species on the Pacific coast fly an even greater distance from Alaska to their wintering grounds in Hawaii. Even the tiny Ruby-throated HUMMING-BIRD (q.v.) flies across the Gulf of Mexico, a non-stop flight of 500 miles.

Many birds migrate in large flocks, sometimes composed of several species flying together—and there is surely no more remarkable sight in the world to watch than the resolute progress of such a flock. Many birds migrate by day; but others, such as the small WARBLERS (q.v.), Duck, Snipe, and Woodcock, migrate at night, when the calls by which they keep in company are the only indication of their passing.

The birds which fly at night are often those which are most active during the day, and it is difficult to understand how they avoid hills, trees, and buildings in their way. Many young birds migrate quite independently of their parents, and find their way, without any form of guidance, from one end of the earth to the other. How they do this—how a young Swallow finds its way from a farm in England to a farm in Natal in its first autumn, and then finds its

way back in the following spring to the place where it was born—is quite unknown. More than this, no one has any plausible explanation as to why it should do so. It is of course absurd to say that a Swallow needs to go all the way to South Africa to find the food it requires: even if there is not enough in England in winter, it need go no farther than the Mediterranean. It is no less absurd to suggest that a Sanderling cannot find enough food on any shores till it reaches Patagonia, or that an Arctic TERN (q.v.) has any physical need (that we can discover) to winter in the Antarctic. Neither is it an adequate explanation to say that a Swallow, or a Sanderling, or an Arctic Tern must return north in the spring to find a suitable nesting-place. The truth is that we neither know how nor why migration takes place, and we probably never shall. We believe that it must somehow benefit the birds to undertake these arduous and perilous journeys—and that is all we can say.

Perhaps the most extraordinary and inexplicable of so-called migrations is that of the Lemmings (*see* VOLES), yellowish-brown rodents, about 5 inches long, which normally live in the mountains of Norway and other Arctic countries. Since this migration has no return, it

A SWARM OF LOCUSTS DESCENDING ON A PLANTATION IN
NIGERIA. *Anti-Locust Research Centre*

these strange migrations originated when physical conditions were different, and some benefit was to be gained. Now the impulse remains, though the results are disastrous.

The so-called migrations of LOCUSTS (q.v.) are similar. The purpose behind the movement of these terribly destructive insects is not fully understood, but food and temperature are probably the main causes. Locusts move in enormous swarms, far too great to make it possible to estimate their numbers. In the air, they look like black clouds, large enough to blot out the sun. The distance a swarm may travel varies a good deal: a thousand miles is often covered, and the journey may be much longer. They usually travel by day and rest by night; but they have been found over the Atlantic at least 1,200 miles from land, when they must have performed a non-stop flight of several days and nights.

The recording of the facts of migration, by the marking of individual animals, whether fish, or mammals, or birds, is a fascinating study. It is possible to discover what happens on migration—the speeds and heights at which the birds travel, the sort of weather and wind they prefer, the routes they take, and so on. Much is already known about these matters, and also about the astonishing ability of birds to find their way home to their nests, perhaps from hundreds of miles away, and from a district where neither they nor any of their kind have ever been. But the more information that is gathered, the less possible does it seem to account for the how and why of it all. It is likely that scientists will never discover these things, and that men will continue to wonder at the migrant birds that 'observe the time of their coming', as they have done since the days of Jeremiah.

should be called an irruption. It is probably caused in the first place by scarcity of food, though search for food is clearly not its purpose. In certain years there is an exceptional increase in the Lemming population, which is soon followed by a food shortage. Countless swarms of these little creatures make their way in a straight line across country. They climb mountains, swim rivers and lakes, eat their way through fields of corn and grass, perhaps taking up to 3 years to reach the sea. On that journey they are accompanied by great numbers of birds and animals who harass them continually, so that in all probability only a small proportion ever complete the journey. Even when they reach the sea, as they eventually must, they plunge in and continue their journey, swimming on till all are drowned. Why they do this no one knows.

A migration of the same kind is carried out by certain kinds of hairy caterpillars which, for no apparent reason, will start to walk towards a lake. They progress at a slow pace, often covering considerable distances—only at the end to drown themselves in the water. Perhaps

MILKWEED BUTTERFLY, *see* MONARCH.

MILLIPEDES, *see* MYRIAPODA.

MIMICRY, *see* PROTECTIVE COLORATION, Section 4.

MINK, *see* WEASEL, Section 6.

MISTLETOE. This is perhaps the best known amongst semi-parasitic plants. It is an evergreen plant, which grows on the boughs of many trees,

MISTLETOE
Eric J. Hosking, F.R.P.S.

MITES AND TICKS.

These belong to the same class of animals as SPIDERS (q.v.)—the Arachnida. The most familiar include the Cheese Mite, the Sheep-tick, and the Red Spider. Many of them are parasites; many help to spread diseases; and many injure our domestic animals (such as the tiny mite which causes mange in dogs), or spoil our crops (such as the mite which causes 'big bud' in currants). Because of their parasitic habits, they are rather different in structure from other arachnids—for example, they often have elaborate mouth-parts, which enable them to fix themselves to their victims. The bites of the 'Harvest-bug', which in the summer cause so much irritation to some people, are the work of mite larvae which have forced their probosces into the skin. Mites also produce galls on trees and other plants—as, for example, the 'witches' brooms'

although it prefers Apples, Oaks, Hawthorns, and Poplars. It rarely grows on the Beech, Birch, and Plane, probably because their smooth bark is unsuitable for the lodgement of the seeds. The white berries of the Mistletoe develop from yellowish flowers, which the plant produces in February and March. These berries contain a sticky liquid. Birds (particularly the thrush —hence Missel-thrush) are attracted to the white fruits; and in cleaning the sticky liquid off their beaks on the branches, they rub off seeds which become lodged in crevices in the bark. These germinate, and send out a sucker which penetrates the branch as far as the wood-vessels. From these vessels are obtained water and mineral salts, which are carried to the green leaves of the Mistletoe. There, by the process of PHOTOSYNTHESIS (q.v.), they are made up into sugars and starch—the plant's food. The sucker of the Mistletoe thus performs the functions of the root of a normal plant in the soil.

The Mistletoe was treated as a sacred plant by the Druids (*see* RELIGION, PREHISTORIC, Vol. I), and even to-day it is supposed to be lucky. In NORSE MYTHS (q.v. Vol. I) it was supposed to be the plant whereby the god Baldur was killed.

See also PARASITIC PLANTS.

CHEESE MITE   SHEEP TICK

often seen on the birch. The damage done by mites is generally the result of the large numbers which quickly appear in favourable circumstances; but, unlike insects, there seem to be no mites whose activities are in any way helpful to us.

See also Vol. VI, INSECT PESTS.

MOA, *see* OSTRICH.

MOCKING-BIRD. In the southern States of North America, this friendly, quiet-looking bird is well known for its power of mimicking the song of other birds, the cries of animals, or any other familiar sound which has attracted its attention. One species, known as the Cat Bird, utters screams and whistling cries like a tom-cat —though it has also a quite pleasant natural song. Another species makes a peculiar mewing kind of cry. Mocking-birds are very common in the southern States, where they frequent human dwellings. They build their thrush-like nests in vines, shrubberies, or piles of brush-wood, and will defend their young with great courage. The Mocking-bird is about 10 inches long, with a long tail, and plumage which is dove-grey underneath and brownish-grey above.

MOLE. This little, soft, velvety-furred, burrowing animal belongs to the order INSECTIVORA, as do HEDGEHOGS (qq.v.); but it eats insect larvae only occasionally, living principally on earth-worms. The Common Mole is found over most of Europe. It is about 6 inches long, and is usually covered with grey-black velvety fur. Its eyes are small, and deeply buried in its fur, thus being protected from the dust and grit thrown up when the animal is burrowing. Sight is not important to the mole: with its very sensitive nose it smells out its prey, and its small, sharp teeth crush it to pulp as soon as it is seized. Its forelimbs are armed with very strong claws which act as shovels, scooping out the soil with almost incredible speed.

THE COMMON MOLE
It has strong, digging, claws and a long, sensitive, nose. *A. R. Thompson*

Everyone is familiar with the mounds and ridges which moles make by burrowing under fields and gardens. The mole is a highly skilled engineer, making a carefully planned underground home from which several burrows radiate, and which is reached by one main and many side passages. The main run is rather wider than the animal's body. The usual way of catching a mole is to put a trap across this run. The many side tunnels are made in the search for worms and grubs. The mole needs constant supplies of food, being unable to do without it for much more than 4 hours on end. Wisely, therefore, it stores away any food which it does not need at the time. When it gathers earthworms, it bites off their heads and places them in its larder beneath its fortress home. The worms remain alive, but without their heads they are unable to dig into the earth and escape.

The females make extremely clever nest chambers. To provide against being flooded out, the nest chamber is higher than the tunnels leading to it, and has, as well, a small drainage tunnel. A gutter is made between the roof of the chamber and the surface of the earth to prevent the earthen roof from leaking or becoming so water-soaked that it might cave in. In the mating season, the males, who up till then have lived apart, fight fiercely amongst themselves for possession of a female. About May, from two to seven naked, pink-skinned young are born. Their skins darken and become hairy in about 10 days, and they leave home when they are about 5 weeks old.

See also Vol. VI: ANIMAL PESTS.

MOLLUSCS. These include the Cuttlefish, Octopus, Pearly Nautilus, Snails, Cockles, Mussels, Oysters, and other less familiar forms, with soft bodies usually enclosed in a shell. They are divided into five classes. First of the three most important classes is the Gastropoda —literally stomach-footed—all the members of which possess a broad, flat 'foot' on the underside of the body, by means of which they move about. Some, for instance most land and sea SLUGS (q.v.), do not possess a shell, though many of these are thought to be descended from shell-bearing ancestors. Those that are shell-bearers always have a single shell, more or less distinctly spiral and cone-shaped, and, because of this characteristic one-piece shell, they are called 'univalves': the SNAILS, WHELKS, and LIMPETS (qq.v.) are familiar examples. Another remarkable organ possessed by all Gastropods is a rasp-like tongue, or 'radula', which consists of a long, flexible, horny ribbon, bearing on its upper surface numerous minute and variously shaped teeth, arranged in close-set, transverse rows. The teeth are used to break up the food into small fragments, or in some species, to file neat round holes through the shells of bivalves so that the occupants may be eaten. The radula is moved backwards and forwards over a firm, fleshy cushion on the floor of the mouth by special muscles (if you watch a pond snail crawling up the glass side of an aquarium, you may sometimes see the radula at work). The shape and number of the teeth vary enormously in the different species—for instance, while one of the sea-slugs has only 17, the common garden snail can boast of no fewer than 135 rows, each consisting of 105 teeth, making a total of some 14,175 teeth.

The second great class all possess shells divided into two halves or valves, and are known as 'bivalves'. (The scientific name of this class, the Lamellibranchia, refers to the arrangement of their breathing gills.) All the bivalve molluscs feed on microscopic organisms and particles of

TYPES OF BIVALVE AND OTHER MOLLUSCS
1. Common Cockle; 2. Sunset Shell; 3. Smooth Venus;
4. Elephant's-tusk Shell; 5. Chiton

plant and animal matter floating in the surrounding water. They have no radula, no distinct head, and in many of the most sedentary species the foot is absent or but poorly developed. In the more active species, however, the foot is well developed—for instance, in the freshwater swan-mussel it is a ploughshare-like organ, by means of which the animal ploughs its way slowly through the mud; in the cockles it is rather like a flexible finger, which enables its owner to take short jumps over the sandy shore. To this class belong such familiar species as the OYSTERS, CLAMS, MUSSELS, COCKLES, and PIDDOCKS (qq.v.).

The third important class, the Cephalopoda, includes the OCTOPUS, the CUTTLEFISHES AND SQUIDS, and the PEARLY NAUTILUS (qq.v.)—the Giant Squids being the largest living backboneless animals. The name Cephalopoda literally means head-footed, for in these molluscs the flat foot of the Gastropoda has become converted into a circle of long, sucker-clad arms or tentacles surrounding the head. By means of these tentacles, the creatures can capture their prey, or even creep about head downwards on the floor of the sea.

The two remaining classes are smaller, and include less familiar creatures. They are the class Amphineura, containing the primitive Coat-of-mail shells or Chitons, and the class Scaphopoda, to which belong the Tusk-shells, molluscs that form a tubular shell open at both ends, and slightly curved and tapering, like an elephant's tusk.

Most molluscs possess eyes, ranging from the simplest eye-spots, capable merely of responding to changing degrees of light and shadow, to the large, well-developed eyes of the Octopus

TYPES OF UNIVALVE MOLUSCS
1. Auger Shell; 2. Pelican's Foot Shell; 3. Top Shell;
4. Dog Whelk

and Cuttlefish. A very large proportion of the univalves or Gastropods possess a pair of fairly well-developed, though rather short-sighted, eyes, and these may be placed on the top of the longer pair of 'horns' or on the head near their base. The bivalve molluscs, on account of their more sedentary habits, usually possess eyespots only, though in the SCALLOPS (q.v.), which are very active creatures, they are more highly developed.

In all molluscs, the shell, which consists chiefly of carbonate of lime, is formed by certain fleshy folds, called the 'mantle', containing the special shell-glands, and secreting also the exquisite colours with which many shells are tinted. All molluscs lay eggs; but out of the vast numbers produced by some species, only a very small proportion reaches maturity, for they are the food of many other animals. The land snails generally lay fewer eggs, and their young emerge completely formed, differing from their parents only in size. The majority of the marine and some of the freshwater species pass through a free-swimming, larval stage before they reach the adult form; and in these early stages of their life they are totally unlike their parents in appearance. They are little oval or oblong creatures, possessing a girdle of 'cilia', or hair-like organs, by the rhythmical movements of which they propel themselves through the water. At certain seasons of the year, these larvae appear in countless myriads in the sea.

Molluscs are an ancient group, the oldest fossil-bearing rocks being full of beautifully preserved shells which closely resemble in shape those seen on any sea-shore to-day. Very conservative in habit, only one group, the Gastropods, has ventured on land, the rest having kept to an aquatic life—the majority to their ancestral home in the sea. However, those which have established themselves on land have flourished to such a degree that the land snails to-day constitute one of the largest and most widely distributed groups of land animals. Nor must we regard molluscs entirely as slow-going, stupid creatures; for one whole class, the Cephalopoda, are extremely active—very powerful swimmers, and as fierce and savage in their ways as any lion or tiger. Even among the snails and whelks, we find active flesh-eating species. Only among the bivalve molluscs (and by no means in all of these) do we find a species that leads an entirely immobile life.

MONARCH (Butterfly). This huge butterfly, with a wing-span of nearly 4 inches, is reddish-brown with black veins and black and white margins to the wings. It is the only member of its family, the Danaidae, to reach Britain, which it only does occasionally: since 1876, only 150 specimens have been reported—mainly from coastal areas. Its home is in tropical America and in the southern states of the U.S.A., where it lays its eggs singly on the milkweed plant, on which the caterpillar feeds. To reach Europe it must cross the Atlantic, since, there being no milkweed, it cannot breed here. Whether it really crosses the Atlantic on the wing, perhaps helped by favourable winds, or whether it comes as a stowaway on a ship is still undetermined. As its occurrences in Britain appear to be mainly since the development of the trans-atlantic fruit trade, the likelihood of its coming by ship seems great (*see* MIGRATION).

In America, the Monarch migrates north-wards, and produces a succession of broods, some specimens penetrating far into Canada. In the autumn, there is a return migration, during which large swarms hibernate along the Californian coasts. The large, yellowish-green caterpillar has black bands and a pair of black filaments at each end of its body, which twitch when it is disturbed. The exquisite green chrysalis, ornamented with black and gold, hangs suspended head downwards. Both cater-pillar and butterfly are unpleasant in taste, and their distinctive colour patterns serve as warn-ings to would-be enemies to leave them alone (*see* PROTECTIVE COLORATION).

MONEY SPIDER, *see* SPIDERS.

MONGOOSE. This is, strictly speaking, the Indian member of the Ichneumon family—a small, carnivorous, weasel-like animal, with short legs and a bushy tail. In this article all the better-known Ichneumons are described under the headword, Mongoose. The largest of them are as big as cats; their heads have pointed muzzles with rather long noses, and their ears are small and round. They live in Asia and in Africa.

The best-known species is the Grey Mongoose of India (Kipling's 'Ricki-Ticki'), which is about 18 inches long, with a tail almost as long again, and a coat of fairly long, grey or reddish-grey hair. It lives in hedgerows, thickets, fields, and

THREATENING DISPLAY IN REPTILES

1. Frilled Lizard of Northern Australia erecting its 'frill' in defiance. 2. The Red-tailed Pipe Snake of
S.E. Asia rearing its tail and showing red in warning

A MEERKAT—AN AFRICAN MONGOOSE
The Meerkat uses its tail as a prop when it stands erect watching for enemies. *Harold Bastin*

near streams, and feeds on rats, mice, snakes, lizards, birds' eggs, and insects. It is a fierce little animal, quite ready to attack large poisonous snakes. By its quick movements, thick skin, and long, thick hair, it manages to protect itself from the snake's fangs until it is able to fix its teeth into the back of the reptile's neck. When captured young, it becomes tame, like a cat, and is often kept as a pet and as a protection against vermin.

One of the larger species is the Egyptian Mongoose of north-east Africa. This is particularly fond of crocodile eggs, which it digs out of the sand; and its usefulness in checking the increase of crocodiles led the Ancient Egyptians to consider it as a SACRED ANIMAL (q.v. Vol. I). Consequently it has gained its popular name, 'Pharaoh's Mouse'.

The Meerkat or Suricate is a small Mongoose found only in the Cape Colony, where it lives in colonies, burrowing into the sandy soil. It feeds on bulbs, which it scratches up with its long claws; and it loves to sit in the sun 'begging' like a small dog. It is a popular pet in South Africa.

MONITOR—the common name for the lizards of the family Varanidae. They are often called IGUANAS (q.v.), but should never be confused with them, as they are not closely related and live in different hemispheres—there are no Iguanas in the Old World, except in Madagascar; there are no Monitors in the New World. They are the largest of all lizards: the Common Asiatic Monitor may reach a length of 10 feet; the Komodo Dragon, although not quite so long, is a heavier beast, weighing up to a hundred pounds. With one exception, the Monitors are fond of water and are strong swimmers; some of them live by the sea. In spite of their bulk and somewhat clumsy form, they climb well. They are flesh-eaters, and are prepared to devour anything that they can overcome; some of them like carrion. Altogether there are some thirty species, ranging over the tropical parts of Africa, Asia, and Australia.

THE LACE MONITOR—A VERY LARGE LIZARD
Paul Popper

The Desert Monitor—the only species found in dry country—inhabits the sandy regions of south-west Asia and north Africa.

See also LIZARDS.

MONKEYS. These belong to the highest order in the animal kingdom, the Primates, to which belong also the APES and LEMURS (qq.v.), as well as man himself. Monkeys are the only mammals which, like human beings, have a good stereoscopic vision—that is, they can see objects in the solid, not merely flat, their two eyes being in the front of their heads, both looking forward.

BLACK MACAQUES OF TROPICAL ASIA
Paul Popper

The chief difference between Monkeys and the man-like apes, such as the Chimpanzee and Gorilla, is that the apes have no tails. Most monkeys live in warm climates or at least in climates with a very warm summer. Some of them can endure severe cold, and are found among the snows of the Himalayas, Tibet, and north-west China. There is only one species of monkey in Europe—the Gibraltar or Barbary ape, and in Australia none at all. Strangely enough, there are no monkeys in Madagascar, New Guinea, and the West Indies. Whilst most monkeys live in forest trees, the African BABOONS (q.v.) are an exception, as they spend most of their time on the ground, moving in troops from one place to another.

Monkeys show a great affection for each other —indeed very few sportsmen like to kill them because of the grief the rest of the troop show over their dead comrade. They all make excellent parents, nursing and fondling their babies with great care, and defending them with courage. So devoted are they to their babies that when one dies, it is often carried about by its mother for days, the bereaved parent making pathetic attempts to induce it to feed and play. Sometimes the mother steals another baby to take the place of the lost one. Young monkeys ride like jockeys on the backs of their mothers. Almost all monkeys can be tamed, but they never seem to lose their sense of mischief. Although they can be taught many amusing performing tricks, their intelligence is generally thought to be not as great as that of a dog.

The Asiatic or African monkeys are different in several particulars from South American monkeys. None of the monkeys of the Old World, the Simiidae, can swing from a branch by its tail, as can many of the South American monkeys, the Cebidae. Only the monkeys and baboons of the Old World have the peculiar patches of hard, naked skin on their buttocks, on which the monkey can rest completely when it is sitting upright. Another feature peculiar to the Old World monkeys, although by no means common to all of them, is the presence of cheek pouches in which the monkey stows away its food to be eaten at leisure in some safer place. The space between the nostrils of the American monkeys is much wider than that between the nostrils of the Asiatic and African monkeys.

One of the main groups of Old World monkeys is the Macaque genus. Most of these monkeys live in troops in the forests of tropical Asia. When a party is on the move, the leader, usually an

SPIDER MONKEY OF BRAZIL
Paul Popper

old male, stations himself at the head of the vanguard and marches majestically in front of his followers. If the younger members attempt to stray, the leader is at once among them, dealing disciplinary blows and bites. If the troop is attacked, the females and young ones are at once surrounded by the males, who attack the enemy with tooth and nail, fighting furiously. The Barbary or Gibraltar ape, the only monkey living in Europe, is also a Macaque. It is not clear how this monkey came to be on the Rock: it may possibly have arrived at a time in the distant past when Africa and Spain were connected by dry land, or it may have been brought over later by man. According to the legend, if ever these monkeys die out, Gibraltar will no longer belong to the British. There are many other species of Old World monkeys, from the remarkable-looking Proboscis Monkey of Borneo, with its long, drooping nose, to the slender, long-tailed, and attractive-looking Diana Monkeys of Africa.

In the New World, most species of monkeys are to be found in the forest regions of Brazil. There are many species in central America, as far north as Mexico. The most docile and easily taught of the American monkeys are the Sapajous and Spider Monkeys; and as they bear confinement and the European climate quite well, this is the kind of monkey which organ-grinders, for instance, carry with them. The Douroucolis, or Night Apes, are a group of small monkeys which are extremely active after dark. They have round, flattish faces, with very large eyes, and long, bushy tails. During the day they remain asleep in the hollows of tree-trunks, waiting till dark to hunt for insects and small birds. The Howlers differ from the other South American monkeys in having a large, hollow sound-box at the upper end of the windpipe, enabling them to produce a loud, discordant, howling cry from their homes in the tree-tops. The Capuchins (another name for the Sapajous) are small monkeys with soft, woolly coats and high-pitched, trilling voices, like a bird.

The Marmosets, elegant little monkeys about the size of a squirrel, also live in the forests of central and South America. Unlike the more typical monkeys, Marmosets have claws, not nails, on their fingers and toes, which enable them to get a firm hold on tree trunks. Their tails are not prehensile. Whereas other monkeys usually give birth to a single baby, Marmosets

MARMOSET OF CENTRAL AMERICA
Paul Popper

have litters of two or three. They are often kept as pets, but they are delicate, and do not keep healthy if they cannot get enough insects to eat.

MONK-FISH, *see* SHARKS and RAYS.

MOORHEN, *see* RAILS.

MOORLAND PLANTS, *see* HEATHS AND MOORLANDS.

MOOSE, *see* DEER, Section 5.

MOSQUITO (Gnat). This is a small, slender-bodied, long-legged, two-winged fly, with antennae which are plume-like in the male and hairy in the female. Along the edge of the wings, and usually also along each vein, is a row of scales. Many Mosquitoes, but by no means all, are blood-suckers, and of these not all attack man, some preferring other mammals, and others birds. In blood-sucking Mosquitoes, it is only the females that 'bite'; the males, not being able to pierce the skin, feed on the nectar of flowers or the juices of ripe fruits.

LARVA   PUPA   TIGER MOSQUITO

The eggs are laid either upon the surface of or near to water. The common Gnat deposits them side by side in floating egg-rafts, and may lay up to 300 eggs or more. Others lay them singly, each with a float on either side. The larva has a large head and thorax and a narrow abdomen, and has a thick tuft of bristles on each side of the mouth. The last segment but one of the abdomen carries a breathing tube, and the resting larvae hang head downwards in the water with the opening of this tube at the surface. They are to be found in lakes and streams, in small pools left after showers, in rain-barrels, and even in flower vases. Many feed on vegetable matter, but some are carnivorous and even cannibalistic.

The pupae are very active, though, of course, they take in no food. They are to be found, often in great numbers, in the same places as the larvae. The head and thorax together form a large globular front body, which carries a pair of breathing trumpets, and the pupa rests with the mouths of these trumpets at the surface of the water. The length of time required for a Mosquito or Gnat to go through all its changes varies with the temperature; it may be as short as 11 days. Thus, the rain-water in a discarded tin may be all that is necessary for development from egg to insect.

A few kinds of Mosquito are often exceedingly common within the Arctic Circle, but the greatest number of different species occurs in tropical countries. For a long time, most people were interested in them only because of their blood-sucking habits. Some species attack silently; others fly with a high-pitched hum. Some attack only by day; others only by night. Some Mosquitoes are now known to carry organisms which cause certain deadly diseases: a spotted-wing Mosquito, for instance, is chiefly responsible for carrying Malaria, and the Tiger Mosquito is the carrier of Yellow Fever, the disease which nearly prevented the construction of the Panama Canal.

Compared with many other insects, Mosquitoes are easily controlled. Mosquito-infested districts have been successfully cleared by draining swamps, by pouring oil on the surface of standing water so that the breathing tubes of the larvae and pupae are choked, by the removal of likely breeding-places, and even by the importation of fish that will eat the larvae and pupae (see MOSQUITO FISH). The Pontine Marshes south of Rome were for many centuries malaria-infested; but when, twenty years ago, the Italians drained the marshes, the malaria disappeared.

See also FLIES; INSECTS.

MOSQUITO-FISH. It is curious to think that the construction of the PANAMA CANAL (q.v. Vol. IV), one of the most valuable waterways in the world, was greatly assisted by small fishes. Yet it is a fact that the Panama region was so infested with fever-carrying MOSQUITOES (q.v.) that the cost in human lives would have been too high to make the canal a practical proposition, had not large numbers of small fishes been liberated in the stagnant waters to feed on the mosquito larvae.

Many different kinds of fishes include these larvae in their diet; but those found most useful to man, owing to their hardiness and the rate at which they breed, belong to the family of fishes referred to in America as Killifishes or Topminnows. Particularly valuable is the little Millions-fish, or Guppy, a native of Barbados in the West Indies, which has been introduced into many fever-stricken areas. The young of this species and its relatives are born alive. The male fish is very brilliantly coloured, though only an inch long and much smaller than the female. Guppies are great favourites in the home AQUARIUM (q.v. Vol. IX). Other species of the same family, as well as a variety of others, including Goldfish, Carp, Eels, and Gobies, are used to combat disease in Africa and Asia.

MOSSES AND LIVERWORTS are among the simplest plants, and are common throughout the world wherever there is an adequate supply of water. It is believed by most students of EVOLUTION (q.v.) that plant life originated in water, and that the ALGAE (q.v.), which still live in water, Liverworts, and Mosses, all of them simple in form, were among the first living chings. At a later period, it is believed, as land appeared above the surface of the ancient seas, more complicated plants began to appear, and slowly to colonize the land.

Liverworts—so called because, in former times, a 'wort' or brew made from the plants was used to treat complaints of the liver—often form green growths, like pancakes, on wet surfaces, such as shady banks, the sides of cuttings and ditches, neglected walls and fences, and the trunks of trees. Liverworts do not generally show divisions into true leaves, stems, and roots, like flowering plants, although they sometimes develop fine, hair-like, absorbing structures on their lower surfaces, and some kinds appear to have both stems and tiny leaves. These lowly plants propagate by means of spores (*see* PLANT REPRODUCTION), which are produced in rounded boxes or capsules at the ends of erect stalks. When these capsules are ripe, they burst, and the light spores are set free and carried away by the wind. Most of the spores die, but a few settle down and germinate.

Mosses are more complicated in structure than Liverworts, most of them showing simple divisions into stem, leaves, and root-like structures. They are generally small, though there is one Australian moss which grows to a foot or more in length. Although some mosses grow in dry places and withstand long periods of drought, recovering their activity when wetted, the majority prefer damp conditions, and are chiefly found on moist tree-trunks, banks and rocks, and on the floors of shady woods. Mosses reproduce themselves in the same way as Liverworts by means of spores. Some mosses actually grow in water, either entirely or partially submerged. One of the most common of these aquatic mosses in Great Britain is the Bog- or Peat-moss, called Sphagnum, which forms enormous areas of deep peat in moist, temperate, and cool regions. The Bog-moss is spongy in texture and absorbs water; it is therefore used for packing living plants to send by post and, in war-time, is also used for making surgical pads.

See also Vol. III: MOORLAND AND MARSH.

spore capsule

MOSS
(enlarged)

MOTHS

MOTHS. The insect order Lepidoptera is divided into about twenty super-families, one including the BUTTERFLIES (q.v.) and all the others the Moths. It is impossible to make a hard and fast distinction between the two. The moths are very much the larger group—for instance, there are about 60 species of butterflies in Britain and over 2,000 species of moths. In the world altogether there are some 100,000 species of moths. The most obvious distinction, which is true at least of British species, is that the antennae of butterflies are clubbed, while those of moths are not. The antennae of some species of moths, such as the Burnets, widen at the end, but they do so gradually. Moths have a variety of antennae, including many feathered types. (*See* Fig. 1.) In most, though not all, moths, there is a curious kind of hook-and-eye arrangement for fastening the wings together, which is never present in a butterfly. The bodies of most moths tend to be stouter and more hairy than those of most butterflies, and to be without any waist between thorax and abdomen. Most moths fly by night rather than by day, and these generally are duller coloured than butterflies. But on the other hand there are many brilliant-coloured, day-flying moths in Britain as well as in tropical countries.

The night-flying moths are obviously not so easy to find or to study as the day-fliers. Some

DIFFERENT TYPES OF MOTHS' ANTENNAE (MALE). ×3
1. Green Longhorn; 2. Elephant Hawk Moth; 3. Five-spot Burnet; 4. Brindled Beauty (*a*) female, (*b*) male; 5. Garden Tiger; 6. Leopard Moth; 7. Drinker Moth

A

B

C

D

FIG. 2. LIFE CYCLE OF DRINKER MOTH FROM (A) EGGS, (B) LARVA, (C) PUPA, TO (D) ADULT. *S. Beaufoy, F.R.P.S.*

species, however, can be located by searching in their day sleeping-places—the cracks and crevices of tree-trunks, old walls, or fences, lichen-covered rocks or stones, underneath loose bark on dead trees, or in poorly lighted barns or out-houses. Sometimes they can be persuaded to fly out of hedges or bushes if these are shaken or tapped with a stick. At night, they can be seen round street-lamps, or can be attracted to a strong light shone on to a white sheet spread in a woodland clearing or on a hill-top (*see* BUTTERFLY COLLECTING, Vol. IX).

Moths vary greatly in size. The largest of all the Lepidoptera is the great Atlas Moth of the Himalayas, which may have a wing-span of up to 12 inches (*see* Colour Plate op. p. 80); the smallest is the Midget Spotkin, one of the tiny leaf-borers, which has a wing-span of little more than $\frac{1}{12}$ inch. The main groups of moths are dealt with in separate articles under the head-words Emperor, Hawks, Prominents, Tussocks, Lackeys and Eggars, Tigers, Night-fliers (Owl Moths), Loopers, Burnets and Foresters, Goats and Leopards, Clearwings, Swifts and Ghosts,

Bagworm Moths, Gold and Purple Moths, China Marks, Leaf-rollers, and Silk Moths.

Like butterflies, moths have a complete METAMORPHOSIS (q.v.)—that is, they go through the stages of egg, caterpillar, and pupa, to reach the adult stage. This life-cycle is generally completed within the year—one month in the egg, two months as a caterpillar, two months as a pupa, and one month as an adult moth. The winter is spent in hibernation in one or other of these four stages, which is accordingly prolonged. Moths may produce three or four generations during the summer, all but the last being short-lived. In some species, such as the Clearwings, the caterpillars take much more than 2 months, sometimes 2 or 3 years, to make their necessary growth. In others, a year or more is spent in a resting condition as egg or pupa—this dormant stage having been known to last for 5 years or more.

The female moth lays her eggs, generally in small or large batches on the plant on which the caterpillars will feed. They are often stuck to the leaves with a gummy substance. The eggs of different species vary in shape, size, and colour. They are generally a plain colour, though those of the Lappet Moth are patterned with stripes of green and white. The Satin Moth lays eggs with a curious covering like candy sugar; and the pale green egg masses of the Small Emerald give off a pleasant scent—though what effect this has we do not know. A female moth lays anything from 100 to nearly 3,000 eggs; but only a very small proportion ever reaches maturity—for they have many enemies during their life-cycle. Once they have laid their eggs, moths are no longer concerned with them, though some species do, in fact, protect them by covering their egg batches with fluff from their tails.

When the caterpillars hatch, they make their first meal from the egg-shell, before turning to their food-plant. Most moth larvae eat leaves or flowers, some feeding on dead leaves. Some bore into timber, making a tunnel which widens as the caterpillar grows; some small species feed on woollen clothing, hair or skins (see CATER-PILLAR). Many moth larvae spin a cocoon in which to pupate, either with silk only, or with wood or some other hard substance, held together with sticky liquid secreted from the silk glands. Moth pupae are never suspended from their tails as are the chrysalises of many

butterflies. They generally lie in protected crevices, or on or under the ground, covered by dead leaves or some such protection. Growth is completed entirely in the larval stage. The adult moth has no jaws, and can only suck with its 'proboscis' or tongue. In many species the proboscis is reduced. The Gold Moth is exceptional in having no proboscis but jaws instead. Some species, such as the Convolvulus Hawk Moth, have a proboscis long enough to reach down the long tubes of such flowers as the Sweet-scented Tobacco Plant.

See also BUTTERFLIES AND MOTHS, TROPICAL; INSECTS; PROTECTIVE COLORATION (insects); MIGRATION; HIBERNATION.

MOULDS. Many organic substances (such as bread, jam, cheese, and leather), if left for some time, become covered with a dense network of threads called a 'mould'. This is a fungus, a SAPROPHYTE (q.v.), which obtains its food from dead organic matter. Some moulds, such as *Penicillium*, from which penicillin is obtained, are blue-green in colour; others are brown or black; while yet others are white. The white mould, called *Mucor*, is a typical mould, a description of which will serve to illustrate the main feature of all moulds.

Mucor can be easily obtained if damp bread is kept under cover at a moderate temperature

Spore capsules
(a) developing
(b) ripe
(c) shedding spores

hypha or thread

As seen under microscope

As seen under magnifying glass

PIN MOULD

for 4 or 5 days. The body of the plant, known as the 'mycelium', consists of long branching threads, each a continuous tube of fungus-cellulose, lined with protoplasm, in which smaller bodies called 'nuclei' are embedded. The mycelium penetrates the food material on which the fungus is living, and absorbs organic matter through its surface.

The mould reproduces itself in two ways, one a sexual and the other a non-sexual process. When *Mucor* reproduces non-sexually, it gives off upright branches about $\frac{1}{8}$ inch long. The top of each branch swells into a small black sphere, within which develop hundreds of spores. Each branch looks like a small pin—and so the plant is commonly called Pin Mould. The wall of each sphere eventually breaks, and the millions of ripe spores are shed into the atmosphere—minute, one-celled, reproductive bodies, having no reserve food material, but capable of withstanding a certain amount of dryness or change of temperature. Under favourable conditions on the right food material, a spore germinates to form a new mycelium.

Non-sexual reproduction in fungi takes place when food is plentiful; but when food becomes scarce, the plants reproduce sexually. In sexual reproduction, two young, actively growing threads approach each other and come into contact, either side by side or at their tips. When the branches are in close contact, small protuberances are put out, in which exchange and fusion of nuclei take place. Eventually a structure with a greatly thickened dark wall is produced. This can resist adverse conditions and remain dormant for several months. Under favourable conditions it germinates, and the life-cycle of *Mucor* begins again.

One species of mould is used in making the famous Gorgonzola and Stilton cheeses (*see* CHEESES, Vol. XI). A strain is inoculated into the cheese, eventually producing the characteristic green veins.

See also FUNGI.

MOUSE. The name 'mouse' is loosely applied to any or all of the members of the mouse family, which includes Mice, RATS, VOLES (qq.v.), and Lemmings. It is by far the largest group of RODENTS (q.v.), with representatives in nearly every part of the world. The true mice and rats always have long, scaly, and generally naked tails, bright, prominent eyes, and sharply pointed

muzzles, and their movements are quick and active. The most common mice in Great Britain are the House Mouse, and the Long-tailed Field or Wood Mouse.

House Mice are grey-brown, and weigh only $\frac{1}{2}$ ounce. They probably originated from central Asia; but they are now found all over the world in or near human dwellings and stores of food. They live only where there are human beings, as they depend for food entirely on man. They will eat practically anything; but their main food is grain and scraps of human food. They make their holes everywhere in houses—in the wainscoting, panelling, and floor. Their nests, which they place for preference in the wall nearest to stores of food, are made of chewed-up soft materials, such as wool, paper, linen, or straw. As a rule, House Mice are timid, only venturing out at night; but sometimes they become very bold and come out to nibble food in broad daylight, scuttling back to their holes only when someone approaches. They sit up to eat, holding their food between their forepaws. They can jump quite high, and can climb vertical wooden surfaces. When they run at full speed, they move like a cat by bounds of the hind legs and skips of the forelegs. In country villages, they take to the cornfields in the summer and to the stacks in the winter, riddling them with runways. House Mice usually have four or five litters a year, of from five to seven young, or more if there is plenty of food. The young mice can themselves breed at 10–12 weeks old—so, unless they are checked, their numbers increase enormously. White and coloured mice, so often kept as PETS (q.v. Vol. IX), are domesticated House Mice. The so-called 'singing mice', which sound not unlike a distant canary, and are said to have a range of a full octave, are ordinary House Mice suffering, it is thought, from a disease. Similarly, 'waltzing mice', which run round and round in circles, do so because they are affected with a tumour on the brain.

Harvest Mice are, together with Pigmy SHREWS (q.v.), the smallest of British mammals: they weigh only $\frac{1}{6}$ ounce. Their colouring is bright chestnut above and white below. In summer they are found among growing corn-crops, on which they feed. They move gracefully and actively from stalk to stalk with the help of their tails, which coil round anything they touch. They are playful animals, and may be

HARVEST MICE USING THEIR TAILS TO CLIMB THE WHEAT STEM
A. R. Thompson

HARVEST MOUSE ON HER NEST
A. R. Thompson

seen swinging from the stalks and performing gymnastic feats. Their summer breeding-nests are compact balls of grass, corn blades, or reed leaves, about the size of an orange, interwoven among the stalks a few inches from the ground and lined with chewed grass. The entrance, which is at the side, is closed when the mother goes out. During the winter, Harvest Mice sleep fitfully in moss nests inside ricks, or sometimes in nests attached to reeds above water. Besides eating grain, they like to eat flies and other insects, which they dig out of the ground or catch with their hands or mouth.

Long-tailed Field Mice or Wood Mice are a little larger than House Mice, and are reddish above and white below. They are by far the most numerous of British mammals, being found in almost every garden, hedgerow, and cornfield from sea-level to mountain top. They usually make their nests in burrows in hedgerows and fields; but they also nest in the open, sometimes high up in trees. They eat almost everything, and are probably even cannibals. They store corn, nuts, and seeds for the winter in their holes and burrows, and sometimes in an old nest of a thrush or blackbird. Although they

very rarely nest in human dwellings, they frequently invade country houses for shelter. They are timid, only venturing abroad in daylight if they are ill. When they are frightened, they sit up and wash thoroughly all over.

The Common Hamster, a rodent related to the mice, is found in Europe and Asia, but not in Britain. It is a stout animal, about one foot long, with thick, glossy fur, and a short tail. The male, female, and young Hamsters all have separate burrows. Each burrow consists of a dwelling chamber with smooth walls and a straw-covered floor, and a long gallery leading to a granary, where corn is stored for the winter. Young Hamsters have only one granary, but the old males often have several, and they spend the whole summer stocking them with corn. The burrows are kept scrupulously clean —in fact, the presence of any rubbish in a burrow shows that it is uninhabited. About October, the Hamsters close up their entrances and exits with earth, and feed for the next few months on their stores of corn. They venture out again about the middle of March, and soon build their summer burrows. Towards the end of April, the male visits the female, fiercely fighting any rival he may meet on the way. In May, there is a litter of from six to eighteen young, and yet another in July. The numbers of the Hamsters would increase, therefore, very rapidly were it not that they have a number of enemies to thin their ranks—buzzards, owls, ravens, polecats, and stoats, as well as man. Even as it is, swarms of Hamsters often damage the harvest.

MOVEMENT OF ANIMALS. In a biological sense the word movement has a slightly different meaning from that associated with it in everyday speech. So far as animals are concerned, we can distinguish three main types of movement, which are often related to each other, yet which belong to different aspects of life. To begin with, protoplasm itself exhibits a streaming movement. That is to say, under the microscope the substance of a living cell can be seen moving in a particular direction. If the cell is naked, as in Amoeba, or a white blood corpuscle, this streaming results in the pushing out of 'pseudopodia', or foot-like excrescences; and the streaming of the protoplasm becomes translated into a movement of the whole cell from one place to another —or in other words, it is translated into locomotion. In plants, where the cell wall is a rigid coat of cellulose (*see* MOVEMENT OF PLANTS), the streaming of the protoplasm does not result in locomotion, and the streaming itself is to some degree restrained. The same is the case in animal cells where the cell wall is itself rigid, or where the cell forms part of a tissue. The streaming of the protoplasm is an essential movement in the internal economy of cells, and assists in nutrition, respiration, and excretion.

The other two types of movement are those which affect parts of the body only, and those which affect the body as a whole, among the latter being included those that result in locomotion. Both are the result of activity on the part of special cells, known as MUSCLE cells (q.v.), which have the power of rapid relaxation and contraction.

Locomotion is the sum total of movement by means of which an animal travels from one place to another. In Amoeba and its relatives, this takes the form of a rolling movement, initiated by the streaming movement of the protoplasm. In other unicellular organisms, locomotion is due either to 'cilia', delicate hairs which beat rhythmically and in so doing push against the surrounding fluid, or to 'flagella', long single hairs which, by a lashing movement, create a vortex and so pull the organism forward. Locomotion depends, therefore, upon pushing or pulling movements, the majority of locomotory movements involving a push.

A few other examples of locomotion will illustrate how the push or the pull operates in animal movements. A worm makes first a push and then a pull. Along the belly of a worm each segment is provided with four pairs of bristles, or 'setae', which can be pushed out or withdrawn into the body. Two sets of muscles run the length of the body—circular muscles to make it fat or thin, and longitudinal muscles to make it long or short. The bristles at the tail end get a grip whilst the worm lengthens and stretches forward. Then the bristles in the front of the body get a grip, the hind ones are released, and the body is pulled up or hauled up, becoming short and fat, ready for the next extension.

Caterpillars have three pairs of jointed walking legs near the head, ending in curved claws. A varying number of claspers, provided with tiny hooks, is situated at the other end of the

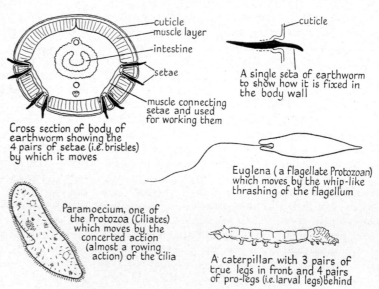

cuticle
muscle layer
intestine
setae
muscle connecting setae and used for working them

Cross section of body of earthworm showing the 4 pairs of setae (i.e. bristles) by which it moves

cuticle

A single seta of earthworm to show how it is fixed in the body wall

Euglena (a flagellate Protozoan) which moves by the whip-like thrashing of the flagellum

Paramoecium, one of the Protozoa (Ciliates) which moves by the concerted action (almost a rowing action) of the cilia

A caterpillar with 3 pairs of true legs in front and 4 pairs of pro-legs (i.e. larval legs) behind body. The legs pull and grip as the body goes forward, and the claspers push to prevent any slipping backwards. Looper caterpillars push their bodies forward by getting a grip with the two pairs of claspers at the end of the abdomen, the body being then hauled up into a loop ready for the next push.

When a snail comes out of its shell, its foot spreads out along the ground. Rhythmic movements of the muscles pass along its whole length and carry the snail forward. To ensure a good grip, a gland under the mouth secretes a slime, which is left behind as the familiar slimy trail.

A starfish uses suction in order to move itself from place to place. On the under-surface of its arms there are rows of tiny tube-feet. These are distended with water, which is drawn in through a perforated plate on the upper surface of the animal. When the starfish is moving forward, the foremost tube-feet are extended and pressed on to the solid surface to get a grip by suction. The body of the animal is then pulled forward. Then the hindmost tube-feet hold fast, while the front ones are released and advanced ready for the next pull. A leech moves in much the same way; but here it is a muscular mouth that grips whilst the body is hauled forward. An adhesive sucker on the tail prevents it from slipping back.

Snakes almost row themselves along on dry land. The scales of the back and sides are replaced on the belly by broad horny bands, each band attached to a pair of ribs that come down from the jointed backbone. The ribs are swung forward, the edges of the horny bands grip the ground, and as the ribs move backwards, the bands hold firm, and the snake advances. The movement of the ribs is so rapid that the snake appears to glide along.

There are a few animals that can make an emergency movement by means of an explosive recoil. The clumsy larva of the dragonfly crawls lazily at the bottom of a pond. In its tail it has a respiratory siphon which, during normal breathing, is filled and emptied quietly; but when it is emptied suddenly and quickly, the larva is shot forward to catch an unsuspecting victim. The cuttlefish also has a siphon through which water can be ejected with some force, and by changing the direction in which the siphon points, the animal can propel itself in the contrary direction. When in rapid movement, it always travels backwards.

Generally speaking, the larger the animal the more slowly it moves in proportion to its size. This is also true to some extent of different parts of the body. It is possible to move fingers or an arm about 10 times per second, but eyelids can move much faster. The wings of a dragonfly beat 28 times per second, those of a bee 190 times, and those of a housefly 300 times. The reason for this is that, generally speaking, long muscles cannot stand up to rapid movements as well as short ones. Muscle fibres, tendons, and bones, being delicate things, snap if overstrained, and the limit of safety depends to a great extent upon the length of the muscle.

See also MOVEMENT OF PLANTS; MUSCLES.

MOVEMENT OF PLANTS. 1. The common belief that plants are fixed, while animals can move, is not strictly true. Some plants, such as the green scum, which often appears so mysteriously in water-butts, are not fixed to one spot. On the other hand, some animals, such as the CORALS (q.v.), are stationary. And, even in plants such as shrubs and trees, the different organs often make movements in response to changes in their surroundings, although the plant as a whole remains fixed to one spot. For instance, many plants, when kept indoors, will in time turn their flower-heads or shoots towards the light.

Movement of living things is of two kinds. The movement of the whole organism itself (as of the dog towards the bone) is called a 'taxis' (Greek word meaning 'arrangement'). In the plant world this only occurs in the lowliest, such as the unicellular ALGAE (q.v.), which react to stimuli such as light, or to the presence of dissolved salts and gases in the water in which they live. In higher plants, these taxis movements occur only in certain reproductive cells. The other type of movement is that in which the living organism moves only a part of itself, as a response to a change in the external conditions. The stem of a potted house-plant turns towards the light; and a root curls round towards its water-supply. This movement of a single organ is called a 'tropism' (Greek *tropos*, a turn).

Taxis movements are not easy to demonstrate in plants; but it has been shown how various reproductive cells will react to certain chemical substances. In ferns, for example, the male reproductive cells or sperms will swim towards a drop of malic acid added to the water in which they are living. This is because the organs in the fern plant which bear the female reproductive cells or eggs also give off malic acid when the eggs are ripe. The sperms, therefore, swim towards the eggs, and fertilization is ensured. With certain seaweeds, too, ripe sperms and eggs are shed quite freely into the sea, with no obvious means of bringing them together. But the passive eggs give off a chemical substance which causes the sperms to swim towards them, and fertilization takes place (*see* REPRODUCTION IN PLANTS).

Tropisms in plants are much easier to demonstrate. They are caused by reactions of different plant organs to various influences, such as light, gravity, or moisture. These may result in change of direction and, sometimes, in rate of growth. Most shoots bend towards the light, in order to present the maximum amount of leaf-surface to the sun; but many roots are repelled by light. Most roots, however, since they grow in complete darkness, are not affected by light at all. If a Mustard seedling is fixed in a hole in a piece of cork and floated on water in an upright position in a vessel from which all light is excluded, except for one slit on the side, the root of the seedling is found to bend away from the light, and the shoot towards it.

The effect of gravity can be shown by placing a potted Geranium on its side in the dark for a few days. In due course the shoot will be observed to bend upwards, while the roots will turn downwards. This reaction to gravity explains why the young shoots grow upwards through the dark soil where, until they reach the surface, they are not being influenced by light at all. Some shoots arrange themselves naturally at right angles to the pull of gravity, and grow in a horizontal position. This is seen in the 'rhizomes' or underground STEMS (q.v.) of grasses, and in the runners of strawberries. Roots tend to grow towards moisture, even growing upwards to do so, if necessary.

Since tropisms are really growth-movements, the parts of the plant directly affected are the growing-points—that is, the tips of shoots and the parts just behind the tips in roots. If the tips of roots and shoots are removed, the plant will no longer respond to the influence of light, gravity, and moisture. In shoots, the response to gravity gets less the farther down the shoot until, beyond the growing region, it no longer exists. It is probable that the production of the growth-promoting plant hormones is in some way connected with outside stimuli, and that these hormones, in turn, affect the rate and direction of growth (*see* GROWTH OF PLANTS).

The value of these tropisms is clear. When the seed germinates, gravity draws the young root towards a greater supply of moisture and to strong anchorage; while the young shoot is drawn towards the light—a process which is continued later by the placing of its leaves in the best position for carrying out their work of food-manufacturing by PHOTOSYNTHESIS (q.v.). The Ivy-leaved Toadflax shows the importance of light-reactions particularly well: at first the flower-stalks grow out towards the light from the walls in which they live, and become prominently displayed; but later, when the fruit-capsule splits, the direction of growth is reversed —the stalks now turn away from the light, so that the seeds may be 'sown' in the crevices of the walls.

Gravity, light, and moisture are not the only causes of tropic movements in plants. The climbing organs or tendrils of some plants respond to mere contact. If the young tendril of the Passion-flower, for example, is rubbed or touched by a solid body—particularly one with a rough surface—the tendril will bend towards the stimulated side. As the tendril bends, it makes further contacts—and so the stimulus is continued until the tendril is coiled round its support. The tendril of a certain tropical Marrow will respond to the touch stimulus in less than a minute (*see* CLIMBING PLANTS).

2. SLEEP MOVEMENTS. Plants make other movements, as well as taxis and tropisms. Many flowers and leaves take up different positions by day and night. This is called 'sleep movement' —though it has nothing to do with the sleeping habits of animals, of course. Night and day movements are well seen in the flowers of the Daisy, the Water-lily, and the Lesser Celandine, which close up at night; while in the Evening Primrose, Salsify (popularly called John-go-to-bed-at-noon), the Bladder Campion, and some species of the Tobacco Plant, the flowers close in the day, and open at night (as we know by their scent). These flowers react mainly to changes in the intensity of light; but the Tulip, which closes at night and opens in the day, responds mainly to changes in temperature—as can easily be shown by experiment.

The reason for these night and day movements

SENSITIVE PLANT (*Mimosa pudica*) SHOWING 'SLEEP' MOVEMENT
Left, Plant before being touched; *Right*, Plant after being touched.   *Harold Bastin*

is far from clear, but may be associated with the way in which the plants are pollinated by insects. Those that open during the day are pollinated by day-flying insects such as bees and butterflies; while those that open at night are generally pollinated by night-flying insects, especially moths. The flowers of the Scarlet Pimpernel (or Poor-man's-weatherglass) close when the air gets damp: the petals close together, and the flower-stalk twists so that the flower hangs downwards. This may be a device to keep the pollen dry. Other flowers which close as a response to moisture are Poppies, Anemones, Rock Roses, and Herb Roberts.

Certain leaves also open and close in response to changes of light and darkness. The three leaflets of the Wood Sorrel leaf close together at night so that the three under-surfaces are flattened against one another. The leaflets of the White Clover, on the other hand, close so that the upper surfaces are brought together. Since the stomata, through which the leaf gives off water during the day by TRANSPIRATION (q.v.),

are found on the under-surfaces in the Wood Sorrel and on the upper-surface in the White Clover, the value of closing may be that it reduces transpiration at a time when it might do more harm than good to the plant; or perhaps, by preventing the stomata from being blocked by dew, it enables transpiration to begin as soon as the leaves unfold.

The most remarkable case of a sleep movement is that of the Sensitive Plant, a common tropical weed of the Mimosa family. In the 'sleep' position the leaflets are folded together and the whole leaf hangs down. This position is usually taken up in the evening; but it can be brought on at any time by striking or shaking the plant. If the touch is gentle, only the nearest leaflets will close at first; but if the stimulus is continued, the movement will spread downwards until all the leaflets are asleep and the plant looks almost dead. No reasonable explanation has been put forward to account for the natural closing-up at night.

See also GROWTH OF PLANTS; MOVEMENT OF ANIMALS.

MUD PUPPY, *see* SALAMANDER.

MULLET. This name is given to two very different kinds of fish, the Red and the Grey Mullets. The Red Mullets (sometimes called Goatfish) are sea-fishes, mostly small. They have on their chins a pair of stiff 'barbels' or feelers, with which they explore the bed of the sea for their food. When not in use, these barbels are packed away in a groove along the lower jaw. Freshly caught Red Mullet are brilliantly red, but the colour soon fades unless the scales are removed immediately. For this reason, the ancient Romans, who valued the Mediterranean species both for its beauty and its excellent flavour, had it brought to their tables alive, so that they could admire its colour before eating it. The Grey Mullets, which are not at all nearly related to the Red Mullets, are much duller in appearance. They are found chiefly in the estuaries of rivers, where they grow to a length of about 3 feet, feeding principally upon mud and algae (lowly aquatic plants), which they suck up by means of their thick lips. Grey Mullet are provided with a sort of gizzard, something like that of the fowl, and the eyes are partly covered with folds of skin, called 'adipose eyelids'.

MUSCLE. In all animals except the PROTOZOA and most of the SPONGES (qq.v.), certain cells take on the function of muscle-cells. These are responsible for movements within the animal's body, and also for the movements which carry the animal from place to place. Lean meat is a good example of muscle tissue. A peculiar feature of muscle-cells is their ability to relax and contract, being long and spindle-shaped when relaxed, but short and thick when contracted. Under the microscope, their protoplasm shows numbers of fine threads, like strands of elastic, which help them to contract. The cells themselves are very small; but where great numbers are grouped together, they may form conspicuous bands of muscle.

When a muscle contracts, it is obvious that, since both ends are fixed, something else must move if the tissues are not to tear. The ends are fixed by tendons (or cords of tissue) to bones, which the muscles can move, as the bones are hinged together by joints. It is possible to feel the contraction of muscles. When the arm is bent, the biceps muscle-cells contract, becoming like a hard ball; when the arm is relaxed, the muscles seem to disappear, as the cells become long, thin, and soft. Muscles are usually arranged in pairs with opposite actions. In the arm, for instance, the biceps contract to raise the forearm; and the triceps, on the opposite side of the arm, contract to pull it down.

Striped or voluntary muscle   Involuntary muscle

Biceps working

There are two types of muscles—those that are under conscious control, and those that continue to work without any effort on the part of the owner. When a dog wags its tail, or a man gets up from his chair, or a bird moves its wings to fly, 'voluntary' muscles are brought into action, and the movement can be brought to an end by an effort of will; while those movements of the digestive system, breathing, the pumping of the heart, and all those actions which continue even during sleep, when the voluntary muscles are still, are controlled by involuntary muscles. The voluntary muscles, which can be controlled by the brain, can be distinguished under the microscope by the dark and light bands or 'striations', which run transversely across the cells; the cells of the involuntary muscles have no striations, and are said to be 'unstriated'.

A muscle soon ceases to work properly without oxygen; so a regular flow of blood (which carries oxygen) is needed. The muscle contains a sugar 'glycogen', from which energy is liberated by 'oxidation', or uniting with oxygen from the air. A by-product of this oxidation is lactic acid, the presence and accumulation of which bring on fatigue; so that it must be removed. It may be reconverted into glycogen by the addition of more oxygen, and this in turn is used up producing energy (in the form of work and heat), carbon dioxide, and water. The carbon dioxide and water are removed by the blood through the veins.

It sometimes happens that muscles remain contracted and cannot be relaxed, causing cramp and pain. (Stitch in the side is a kind of cramp.) An unaccustomed amount of violent exercise or a continued muscular strain in an unnatural position will cause a lack of oxygen and, consequently, an accumulation of lactic acid in the muscle tissue, bringing on cramp. A swimmer sometimes gets cramp because the cold water causes the capillary blood vessels to contract, thereby conserving the heat of the body, but as a result the supply of oxygen and blood to the muscles is cut down to danger-point (*see* BLOOD SYSTEM).

Stiffness and soreness are usually the result of the tearing of some of the delicate fibres and membranes of the muscles. These fibres are very efficient; but to stand extra strain they have to be toned up gradually. Certain muscles are sometimes over-developed, while others may be seldom used. A professional cyclist, for example, with over-developed leg muscles, is not likely to be a good swimmer; because when he tries to bring the seldom-used muscles of his arms into action, they do not work efficiently, and he may become muscle-bound.

Plants have no muscles, and their movements are brought about in a different way (*see* MOVEMENT OF PLANTS).

See also MOVEMENT OF ANIMALS.

MUSHROOMS, *see* FUNGI; *see also* MUSH-ROOMS, Vol. VI.

MUSK OX, *see* CATTLE.

MUSK RAT, *see* VOLE.

MUSSEL. This is the common name for several species of bivalve MOLLUSCS (q.v.), some of which live in the sea, others in lakes and rivers. The Edible Mussel is one of the most familiar, large numbers being found closely packed on rocks and pier piles, each mussel firmly anchored by a tuft of tough threads, called the 'byssus', spun from special glands on the short, dark-brown foot. The mussel is not necessarily permanently fixed to one spot, for it has the power to cast off the byssus threads and change its surroundings. Large quantities of eggs are produced annually. The young are totally unlike their parents, emerging

EDIBLE SEA MUSSEL
ATTACHED BY BYSSUS
THREADS TO TIMBER

from the egg as tiny oblong-bodied creatures, furnished with a band of 'cilia', or hairlike organs, by means of which they can swim actively. Partly by their own efforts, partly by the ebb and flow of the tide, they are carried away to fresh unoccupied grounds, where they settle down and, changing in shape, soon begin to look like miniature mussels, very small indeed, but with the familiar deep purple shell.

Much more remarkable is the life-history of the Freshwater Mussels, of which the River Mussel and the large Swan Mussel are common British species, and which also include the Pearl Mussel. These Freshwater Mussels live half-buried in the mud, through which they slowly plough their way by rhythmic movements of their large muscular foot. The spawning season starts in May or June, large numbers of eggs being produced. These are kept within the shelter of the parent's shell. By October a minute mussel, which has formed inside the egg, emerges. It has a toothed beak at the tip of each triangular valve, and also a single, sticky, byssus thread, by which it glues itself to the mantle-folds of its parent, and there safely shelters throughout the winter months. In the following spring, in late February and March if conditions are suitable, the parent mussel discharges its numerous offspring in tangled wisps. The young mussels swim by clapping their valves vigorously. Should a fish pass within range, they moor themselves by their byssus threads to its skin. The instant that the toothed valves of the shell touch, they take a firm hold. The flesh of the fish, irritated by their presence, swells up round them so that the young mussel is entirely covered over. It is carried about as a parasite on the fish for 3 months, during which time it absorbs food from the tissues of its host, and undergoes further important changes. Finally, its development completed, the young mussel drops from its host into the mud, perhaps several miles from the place where it first took grip. Only certain fishes, such as stickle-backs and minnows, can serve as hosts; and if none of these is present at the right time, this strange life-history cannot be completed, and the mussel spawn will perish. The Pearl Mussel has an oval shell, which, in full-grown specimens, is about 4 inches long by 2 inches across, and pitchy black in colour. This mussel occasionally forms very perfect pearls in the folds of its mantle. The Swan

SWAN MUSSEL AND LARVA

Mussel is the largest of the river species, a fine specimen measuring 6 inches by about 3 inches. The valves of the shell are covered by a thin, yellowish-green skin, adorned with two or three broad bands of darker green. The soft body is grey, tinged with red or yellow, with the edges of the mantle tinged with brown, and the large muscular foot a yellowish-orange colour.

See also Vol. VI: SHELL-FISH FISHING.

MUTTON BIRD, *see* PETREL, Section 6.

MYRIAPODA (many-footed). This class of animals includes the Centipedes and Millipedes, animals related to INSECTS and SPIDERS (qq.v.), but differing from them in having elongated bodies composed of many segments, each of which bears one or two pairs of walking legs. Myriapoda have distinct heads and one pair of antennae. The several thousand species found throughout the world are all land-dwellers, though a few live on the shore between tide-marks. Most species feed by night, generally spending the day under such cover as stones or pieces of wood. They hatch from eggs, the young Centipedes having only six pairs of legs and the young Millipedes only three pairs. They add pairs of legs each time they shed their skin to make growth; but even when fully grown, many species do not have as many legs as their names suggest. There is, for example, the House Centipede of North America which has no more than fifteen pairs of legs altogether, though these are very long, so that the animal looks rather like a many-legged spider.

Centipedes have one pair of legs on each segment, whereas Millipedes have two pairs from the fifth segment backwards. Centipedes have flattened bodies, move quickly, and carry poison-fangs with which they attack their prey

MILLIPEDES UNDER THE BARK OF A DEAD TREE IN CHRISTMAS ISLAND, INDIAN OCEAN. *C. A. Gibson-Hill*

—for they are carnivorous. One tropical species, which reaches 10 or 12 inches long, has a poison-fang strong enough to kill small birds. Millipedes, on the other hand, have rounded bodies and no poison-fangs, move slowly, and feed on vegetable matter. One quite common English species, the Pill Millipede, defends itself by rolling into a ball, exposing only its outer shell. Another, *Iulus sabulosus*, makes a tight coil when disturbed.

The female Millipede constructs a tiny mud hut in which she lays her eggs, finally sealing its entrance with a daub of mud. The female Centipede coats her eggs with a sticky fluid, and rolls them in the earth until they are camouflaged to look like pellets of soil. This she does to prevent the male from eating them.

See also Vol. VI: ANIMAL PESTS.

N

NAILS AND CLAWS—the horny sheaths at the end of the fingers and toes. If they are broad and flat, as in a man or elephant, they are generally known as nails; if they are sharp-pointed, as in a lion, sparrow, or lizard, they are called claws. In birds of prey they are called talons. Nails or claws assist in grasping objects more firmly, in walking, perching, or seizing prey or food. They are used also in scratching and cleaning the body, and as weapons of defence.

FOOT OF OSPREY (BIRD OF PREY)

Many mammals have HOOFS (q.v.) instead of nails; but in the majority nails are present on all four limbs. Birds have claws on the hind limbs (feet), but very seldom on the fore limbs (wings). In a few species, however, the nail is present on the thumb and first finger, as in some Geese and Birds of Prey—though it seems to serve no useful purpose. The only bird to use these wing-claws is the South American HOATZIN (q.v.). The spur, or nail, at the back of the leg of many members of the PHEASANT family (q.v.) is used solely as a weapon.

The term nail is used also for the horny sheath at the tip of the beak of some birds, especially GEESE (q.v.).

NARWHAL, *see* WHALE.

NATTERJACK, *see* TOAD.

NERVOUS SYSTEM. In the lowest forms of animal there are no nerve-cells, the protoplasm of each cell being to some extent capable of nervous response. As the body grows more complex, so the need for an elaborate nervous system increases—just as in a small village there is no need for telephones because the inhabitants live close together, whereas in a large town an extensive network of telephone lines is needed. The nervous system is a means of communication between the sense organs (*see* SENSES), which receive messages (or stimuli) from the outside world, and the MUSCLES (q.v.), which must carry out the appropriate action.

The nervous system consists of a central nerve cord (called, in vertebrates, the spinal cord), which runs from one end of the body to the

TRANSVERSE SECTION OF A SPINAL CORD

other, and a number of main nerves running from it to the sense-organs, the limbs, muscles, and other internal organs. The ends of the main nerve split into finer and finer branches until all tissues are supplied with nerve fibres. The main nerves are divided into two groups: the sensory nerves, responsible for conveying the impulses (messages) from the sense organs; and the motor nerves, carrying the impulses to the motor organs (the muscles).

In the invertebrates, the central nervous system is ventral—that is to say it lies under the gut, in the lower half of the body. In vertebrates it is dorsal, and lies within and is protected by the skull and spine.

NETTLES, *see* PLANT DEFENCES, Section 5.

NEWT. This is a SALAMANDER (q.v.) of the genus *Triturus*, of which there are some twenty species—mostly found in Europe, although some of them inhabit Asia. North Africa has two species, and there are two in North America Britain has three newts, the Crested or Warty Newt, the Common or Smooth Newt, and the

CRESTED NEWT (MALE)

Palmate Newt. The first is easily recognized by its large size, black, warty skin, and orange belly with black markings. It grows to a length of nearly 6 inches. The other two species seldom exceed 3 inches in length; their skin is smooth, and usually spotted or marbled with black or dark brown. These two species are much alike;

PALMATE NEWT

but in the breeding season, the males can easily be distinguished, for then the hind feet of the Palmate Newt have broad black webs, and the end of the tail is cut off abruptly and ends in a black thread. The males of all three species develop a high crest of skin on the back and tail at this time. In the Crested Newt this is deeply notched. The female also has a crest, though hers is less conspicuous than the male's. At the end of the breeding season the crest disappears, and both males and females leave the water. Newts that are kept as pets should be allowed to leave the water as soon as the breeding season is over. The old English name for the newt, 'eft', is now seldom used.

Other well-known species of newt, often seen in captivity, are the Marbled Newt from the south of France and Spain, and the Alpine Newt.

NIGHT-FLYING MOTHS (Owlets). The families Caradrinidae and Plusiidae include over 20,000 species, of which over 350 occur in Britain. Their average wing-span is about 1½ inches—the largest British species, the Old Lady, being nearly double this, and the Black Witch of America about 4 times. Night-flying Moths usually rest by day on tree-trunks, walls, or in dark places, where their brownish, greyish, or blackish colour makes them difficult to detect. The Wainscots have little-marked, yellowish fore-wings—much the colour of the dead marsh reeds among which they live. The majority of Night-flying Moths, however, have a pattern of circular and kidney-shaped spots with five cross lines, the innermost being short and the outermost zigzagging. While resting, the moth holds its fore-wings roof-like over its stout body, so concealing the pale greyish or whitish hind-wings. Some—for example, the Yellow and Red Underwings—have brightly coloured conspicuous hind-wings, which disappear behind the sombre fore-wings when the insect alights. Such colours, temporarily displayed and serving to distract the attention of enemies, are known as 'flash colours' (*see* PROTECTIVE COLORATION). The moths are attracted to light and to 'sugar', a mixture of treacle, beer, rum and such things painted on trees to catch moths. They also visit sallow blossom in the spring, valerian and other flowers in the summer, and ivy in the autumn.

The eggs are usually spherical, slightly flattened, and fluted or netted. The caterpillars feed mainly on leaves, but also on flowers, seeds, and roots. Many species show considerable variation in their selection of food plants: the Wainscots tunnel in reeds; the Marbled Beauty, found commonly in towns on old walls, is a lichen feeder; and the local Waved Black feeds on fungi.

Caterpillars of Night-flying Moths are usually night-feeders, hiding by day, often on the ground under dead leaves, their coloration of green or brown with longitudinal stripes assisting concealment. When disturbed, they roll themselves into a ring and drop, remaining motionless in the herbage until danger has passed. Many have one or more pairs of abdominal legs reduced or missing, and are known as semi-loopers from their method of crawling (*see* LOOPERS). The majority are smooth, but a few, such as the scarce Merveille du Jour, are hairy. The Alder Moth caterpillar has long clubbed hairs and conspicuous warning coloration—though when young it resembles a bird-dropping. Although the moths are almost identical, the caterpillar of the Grey Dagger is easily distinguished from that of the Dark Dagger by the yellow instead of reddish stripe along the back, and a longer and thinner hump on the first abdominal segment.

The pupae of Night-flying Moths are usually shining mahogany-brown or black, and are generally formed in cells underground; though some spin cocoons among leaves or in crevices in bark.

One of the earliest British moths to emerge from HIBERNATION (q.v.) is the Herald; and one of the commonest in the autumn, often seen on the wing by day, is the migratory Silver-Y. Among other moths of this group are the Darts, Rustics, Brocades, Coronets, Gothics, Minors, Ears, Quakers, Drabs, Sallows, Chestnuts, Sharks, and Clovers.

Many species of this group are serious INSECT

Pests (q.v. Vol. VI). The moths of some Asiatic and Australian species damage oranges and bananas by piercing the skins with their strong tongues. They are themselves the chief food of the Long-eared Bat, which catches moth after moth in flight, returning between each catch to its sheltered retreat to strip off the wings and eat the body. Sometimes quite an accumulation of wings is formed. The larvae of many species are pests of corn, vines, and vegetable crops, particularly in America where they are known as Cutworms. In America, too, the Army Worm sometimes swarms over hundreds of square miles, devastating corn-fields. In Britain, comparable plagues of caterpillars of the Antler Moth occasionally occur in hilly parts, denuding whole districts of grass. The caterpillars of the Cabbage Moth are probably even more destructive than those of the White Butterflies (q.v.), as they eat into the cabbage itself instead of confining their attacks to the outer leaves. In Australia, swarms of the Bugong Moth were formerly used by the aborigines for food. Other common pests belonging to this group are the Turnip Moth, the Bright-line Brown-eye (known to market-gardeners as the Tomato Moth), and the Angle Shades, a catholic feeder, notably a pest of chrysanthemums and geraniums. The Angle Shades Moth closely resembles a withered leaf.

NIGHTINGALE. This rather insignificant, brown bird, not unlike a small thrush, has been the subject of more poetry, perhaps, than any other creature. According to the Greek legend, its breast is pierced by a thorn as it sings, and this is the cause of the famous melancholy note which occurs in its song. In fact, the song of the Nightingale might not have been noticed above some other British songsters, including its close relation, the Thrush, were it not that the bird sings by night, when there are fewer other sounds to distract our attention. It sings also by day, when it is by no means so easily distinguished.

Nightingales winter in Africa, migrating in April to Europe where they breed. The males arrive first, and each establishes himself in a territory, making his presence known to the females by his song. The main purpose of the song is to announce to other nightingales his right over the territory in which he and his mate will breed and find food (see Animal Territory). Nightingales frequent woods and thickets, never breeding north of Yorkshire, and being found most freely in certain localities in south-east England. They build their nests in undergrowth close to the ground, and lay four or five olive-brown eggs. They cease to sing after the eggs are hatched in mid-June, and by August they

NIGHTJAR ON NEST

The plumage of this bird affords it such efficient camouflage that it is very difficult to distinguish it from its natural surroundings. *Eric J. Hosking, F.R.P.S.*

are migrating to Africa for the winter. They feed mostly on the ground on worms, grubs, and insects.

There are several species of Nightingale. The Eastern Nightingale, which reaches eastern Europe, is a rather larger bird, with a more powerful, but less perfect, song. The Persian Nightingale, sometimes called the Bulbul, is distributed over central and western Asia; and there are two species in Africa.

NIGHTJAR (GOATSUCKER). There used to be an old country superstition that Nightjars sucked milk from goats—hence their name. The American Nightjar is often called Whip-poor-Will because of its call-note. Nightjars are to be found in most parts of the world. They are characterized by their nocturnal habits, and by their flat heads, small bills, but wide mouths with bristles at the sides, large eyes, and short legs. Both the birds and their eggs (which are laid on the bare ground with no nest) have a speckled coloration which makes them difficult to distinguish from their surroundings. Nightjars feed always at night, eating such insects as moths and cockchafers, which they catch on the wing. The European Nightjar, a bird about $10\frac{1}{2}$ inches long, winters in Africa and arrives in its summer quarters during May. It may be seen in Britain, especially in dry, heathy country and open woodland, hawking for insects at dusk. Its note is a sustained churring trill, with an occasional 'coo-ic' as it flies.

In northern South America there is a relative of the Nightjar, the Guacharo or Oil-bird, a much larger bird, some 17 to 20 inches long, which spends its days and makes its nest in caves, coming out only at night. The nestlings of these birds are covered in thick, oily, yellow fat, which the native Indians value, and collect in clay pots, calling it Guacharo butter. In tropical Asia and Australia are other relatives of the Nightjars, called Frogmouths because of their wide mouths. They are rather owl-like in appearance, and spend their days roosting on some dead tree-stump, their mottled brown plumage making them so like the tree that they are difficult to distinguish.

See also CAMOUFLAGE.

NITROGEN SUPPLY IN PLANTS. Next to water, the chief substance which a plant requires from the soil is nitrogen. This is necessary for the manufacture of proteins, which help to build up and maintain in good health the tissues of both plants and animals. Most plants obtain their nitrogen in the form of nitrates. Obviously, if all green plants were to continue absorbing nitrates from the soil, and there were no means of replacement, the soil would soon become impoverished and the plants would die of nitrogen starvation. In nature, however, nitrogen is constantly being restored to the soil, either as animal droppings, or by the decay of dead animals and plants. The nitrogen in this dead organic matter, or 'humus', cannot be used by plants until it has undergone various changes which turn it into nitrates able to be absorbed by the root-hairs. First, the proteins in the humus are broken down into ammonium compounds; and these are then acted upon by various bacteria in the soil, until they are built up into the nitrates which the plant can absorb. In this way nitrogen is constantly kept circulating. The farmer, however, who often cannot wait for these natural processes, replaces the nitrates which his plants remove by adding nitrates in the form of artificial manures, or by returning the proteins themselves to the soil in natural manures, such as dung, humus, or leaf-mould.

ROOT NODULES. Not all plants are dependent on soil nitrates for their supply of nitrogen. Leguminous plants, which include Peas, Beans, Clovers, and Vetches, possess certain swellings or nodules on their roots, which contain many thousands of a certain bacterium normally found in the soil. These bacteria infect the roots of a leguminous plant through the root-hairs, and pass to the cells underneath the skin of the root, where they multiply so much that the nodules are produced. The cells themselves enlarge to accommodate the bacteria, and even divide to produce new cells. These bacteria are able to act on nitrogen gas in the air spaces of the soil, and convert it into nitrogen compounds, such as nitrates suitable for absorption by the green plant. This 'nitrogen fixation,' as it is called, cannot

ROOT OF A BEAN SHOWING
NODULES

be performed by the green plant itself, and its importance to a plant growing in a soil deficient in nitrates is obvious. In return for the nitrogen compounds, the plant supplies the bacteria with sugar and similar compounds needed by them. This convenient arrangement, by which the bacteria and leguminous plants live on terms of mutual benefit to one another, is known as 'symbiosis'. The bacteria, of which there are several varieties, appear to be most particular: the bacteria from clover will not develop nodules in peas, nor vice versa. If a farmer has not cultivated a special kind of leguminous plant in a field for some time, he may take soil from a field where the plant has been growing recently to obtain the bacteria he needs. When crops of clover or other legumes are ploughed into the soil, they do so much to enrich the nitrate supply that the operation is called 'green manuring'.

There are other bacteria with this same power of converting gaseous nitrogen into the nitrates which the plant can absorb. These live freely in the soil, and do not enter into close relations with plants.

See also BACTERIA; NUTRITION OF PLANTS.
See also Vol. VI: MANURES.

NODULES, ROOT, *see* NITROGEN SUPPLY IN PLANTS.

NOTORNIS, *see* RAILS.

NUTHATCH. This small, plump, woodpecker-like bird has a short tail and long sharp beak. It has bluish-grey plumage on its back, a white throat shading to pinkish-buff underneath, and a black stripe under its eye. Nuthatches are found in many parts of the world, and are not uncommon in wooded districts of central and southeast England. They move easily up and down trunks and limbs of trees, making short hops in any direction as they tap the bark, probing the crevices for hidden grubs and insects. In the autumn they eat nuts, especially hazel-nuts, wedging them into crevices of the bark and smashing them open with powerful strokes of their bills, clapping their wings in time with each stroke. They make their nests of dry leaves in a hole in a tree, or in a nesting-box, carefully plastering the entrance with clay to ensure that it is exactly the right size. Their song has varied notes, especially in the spring, but their usual

NUTHATCH CARRYING INSECT FOOD TO ITS NEST
Eric J. Hosking, F.R.P.S.

call is 'chwit-it-it'—which sounds rather like the sound of a stone being thrown across an ice-covered pond. They fly with a slow and dipping motion, quite unlike that of any other British bird.

NUTRIA, *see* COYPU.

NUTRITION OF ANIMALS. All living things, whether plants or animals, need food in order to replace the matter used up by them in the process of living. Foods are classed as proteins, carbohydrates, and fats; and in some form or other these are all required by every living thing. Unlike plants, animals cannot make their food from raw materials—carbon dioxide, water, and mineral salts: they are dependent on the conversion of these into suitable forms by plants, largely through PHOTOSYNTHESIS (q.v.). Even a carnivorous animal, such as a cat or a lion, derives its food ultimately from plants, by eating a mouse that has fed on grain, or a zebra that has fed on grass. Without the power of green plants, therefore, to use light, life of any kind would be impossible.

An animal needs proteins, carbohydrates, fats, salts, and water in order to replenish the protoplasm, the living matter of the cells. When an animal feeds, the pieces of animal or vegetable matter it takes into its body are too large to be absorbed at once into the blood (which carries the food to the cells). These pieces must, therefore, be broken up and made soluble by the process of digestion, so that they may be built up again into the proteins, carbohydrates, and fats characteristic of the animal. Digestion is set in action by 'enzymes' or ferments, which are manufactured by many of the cells in the walls of the alimentary canal, especially in the stomach and intestines. There are also glands which pour into the small intestine secretions which continue the process assisted by the warmth of the body.

When the food is seized by the animal in its mouth or beak, it may be chewed (if the animal has teeth), or it may pass at once into a gizzard, where it is milled by the small stones and grit which the animal (bird, crab, or worm) swallows from time to time. Before passing into the gizzard, the food is softened in the crop, where some birds also store food to bring home to feed their chicks. A snail has a tongue with thousands of teeth, the 'radula', which it uses as a rasp, working it against the horny roof of the mouth. Some animals, such as spiders and many insects, are able to suck juices only, because they have no chewing or grinding mechanism. The amoeba has no alimentary canal, but merely surrounds particles of food with its body, and so breaks them down with digestive fluids in what might be called a temporary stomach.

Most mammals have a digestive system similar to man's, consisting of one stomach, and a small and a large intestine. But those which chew the cud, such as cows and deer, have a different arrangement: they have stomachs with four chambers. When the grass is swallowed, it passes into the first of these, the 'paunch'. From here the watery fluids from the grass pass into the 'honeycomb', or second chamber, while the solid parts of the grass are returned in balls back to the mouth to be thoroughly chewed. This chewed grass returns then to the third chamber, the 'manyplies', and thence to the fourth chamber, or 'reed', which is similar to the stomach in man. Finally it passes into the small intestine, as in other animals.

The value of food to the body is measured in calories, a calorie being the unit of measurement of the heat required to raise the temperature of one gramme of water one degree Centigrade. The number of calories needed to make up a satisfactory diet depends on the activity of the creature: the more active it is the more are needed. When too few calories are provided, the body begins to use up the stores of protein and fat contained in its tissues, until starvation takes place. If an animal over-eats, it has difficulty in getting rid of the excess of food, and the body suffers accordingly.

See also GROWTH OF ANIMALS.
See also NUTRITION OF MAN, Vol. XI.

NUTRITION OF PLANTS. The real difference between the nutrition of plants and animals is that, whereas plants can take inorganic materials and build up their own food substances, animals cannot, but must make use either directly or indirectly of the food which has already been made up by plants. Plants, like animals, need for good nutrition an adequate supply of water, carbohydrates (starch and sugar), mineral salts, fats, and proteins. To be well nourished, animals must have an adequate supply of the particular foodstuffs they require, whereas plants must have a supply of the raw materials from which the foodstuffs can be built up. And just as the mere supply of foodstuffs to animals is not enough to promote healthy nutrition and living, so in plants the conditions under which the raw materials are absorbed are of prime importance also.

Adequate supplies of water are, of course, essential to the plant, and water is always present in living plant-tissue. In many fruits it makes up 90 per cent. or more of the total weight; in green foliage leaves, the content of water may be as high as 80 per cent., and even dry seeds may contain 10 to 12 per cent. In most green plants the bulk of water is taken in by the roots, and, together with the mineral salts it contains, is carried right through the plant to the green leaves. There, in the presence of sunlight, and by the addition of carbon dioxide from the atmosphere, complicated food substances are built up by the process of PHOTOSYNTHESIS (q.v.). These made-up food substances, which provide the plant with its carbohydrate and protein foods, are then conveyed to those parts of the plant—root, stems, leaves, flowers, or fruits—where they may be needed. The entire tissues of the growing plant are thus bathed in a water-flow, either taking raw materials to the leaves, or made-up food substances from the leaves to wherever they are required.

Since the plant system is covered by an outer skin, it would seem that loss of water would occur only through evaporation, and would not, therefore, be very important. As in human beings, however, the solution of one problem in plants raises another. The carbon dioxide which is used in the leaves is known to be taken from the atmosphere in the form of gas. This enters through tiny pores on the leaf-surfaces, which regularly open and close. Since much of the water in the leaf is in the form of water-vapour, the opening of the pores to admit carbon dioxide simultaneously allows water-vapour to escape in considerable quantity. The loss of water-vapour is known as TRANSPIRATION (q.v.).

The protoplasm of the plant seems to exercise a considerable degree of discrimination, rejecting some salts and taking in others (*see* ROOTS, Section 2). It is easy to understand how water with the dissolved salts passes from the absorbing hairs of the roots to the nearby plant tissues. But how does a watery liquid get from roots many yards deep in the soil to the top of a tall beech tree? Several forces are involved, the most important being suction from the leaves, which are constantly losing water. Some water is probably also pushed up by ROOT-PRESSURE (q.v.). Substances are carried round the plant dissolved in this water; insoluble ones such as starch and proteins are first acted upon by enzymes and thus changed to soluble forms.

Finally, in considering the feeding of plants, its inseparable connexion with the process of RESPIRATION (q.v.) must be taken into account. In animals, we see the end-stage of a process in which food, which has been built up originally by plants, is acted upon by oxygen to release the stored energy necessary for all animal activities. This energy, which is derived from the sun, was in the first place built up into food in the plant's leaves. But the plant, also, needs energy for its successful working; so that besides the building-up process of photosynthesis, there is the breaking-down process of respiration, when complicated food-stuffs are oxidized to release their contained energy. The waste products of plants are given off in various ways by processes not fully understood.

See also NUTRITION OF ANIMALS; NITROGEN SUPPLY IN PLANTS.

NUTS, *see* FRUITS, Section 2c.

O

OAK, *see* WOODLANDS, Section 2.

OAK TORTRIX MOTH, *see* LEAF-ROLLERS.

OCTOPUS. This strange, sinister-looking creature, with its large unwinking eyes, grotesquely shaped body, and long sucker-clad arms, belongs to the same division of the animal kingdom, the MOLLUSCS (q.v.), as the familiar oyster and snail. However, the Octopus, together with the CUTTLEFISH and SQUID, and the PEARLY NAUTILUS (qq.v.), differ enough from all other molluscs to be placed in a class by themselves—the Cephalopoda, literally head-footed, so called from the fact that all are distinguished from other molluscs by having in the place of a foot a circle of sucker-clad arms growing out from the head. With the help of these arms, the Octopus both captures its prey, and literally walks head downwards on the floor of the sea. The Octopus swims by ejecting with great force a stream of water from a short siphon-tube which forms part of the mantle on the underside of its body, and this makes it shoot rapidly backwards through the sea. Moreover, when excited or alarmed, the Octopus discharges

AN OCTOPUS DISCHARGING ITS 'SMOKE SCREEN' FROM ITS 'INK SAC'. *Paul Popper*

through the same tube an inky fluid right into the face of its astonished foe, and, under cover of this effective 'smoke-screen', makes good its escape. The inky fluid is secreted within a special glandular organ, the 'ink-sac'. In the centre of the circle formed by the formidable sucker-clad arms is the mouth, with its stout pair of horny jaws shaped like a parrot's beak; while behind the jaws, the mouth has a long armoured tongue or radula, used for grating the food into fragments small enough for swallowing.

The Octopus spends most of the day-time quietly resting in some cranny among the rocks on the floor of the sea; as darkness falls, it becomes active and wanders in search of prey, returning to its favourite hiding-place at dawn. It has remarkable powers of adjusting the colour of its body and arms to harmonize with its immediate surroundings, and this chameleon-like

THE LESSER OCTOPUS
F. Martin Duncan, F.R.M.S., F.Z.S.

ability helps the Octopus to avoid the notice of large Dogfish, giant Conger-eels, and other hungry foes. Much information concerning the habits of the Octopus has been obtained from specimens kept under observation in large marine aquaria. It seems that the female is a model mother, watching over her rather grape-like masses of eggs with devotion, and furiously attacking any prowling creature that may venture near. On hatching, the young octopods are less than $\frac{1}{4}$ inch in length, with their future arms showing as a circle of budding outgrowths round the tiny head.

With few exceptions, the different species of Octopus live on or near the bottom of the sea, the majority being active, powerful animals. The Giant Octopus of the Pacific reaches a span of 30 feet across the outstretched arms; while our own British species, the Common Octopus,

SHELLS OF THE ARGONAUT OR PAPER NAUTILUS
F. Martin Duncan, F.R.M.S., F.Z.S.

occasionally spans as much as 10 feet, though most specimens measure only from 3 to 4 feet.

Quite different in appearance from all other members of the Octopus family is the Argonaut or Paper Nautilus. The female of this smallish creature possesses a most beautiful, slightly corrugated, fragile shell, which is held in position by the two uppermost arms. These not only clasp the shell, but are expanded and provided with glands that secrete the substance of which the delicate shell is composed. This shell is also used as a receptacle for the developing eggs, and there the baby Argonauts remain until they leave their mother. The male is very much smaller than the female, and has no shell. The Argonaut is found in nearly all warm and sub-tropical seas. It was well known to the ancient Greeks, who called it the Nautilus, or Sailor, because they thought that it used its shell as a boat and hoisted its expanded front arms as sails. Actually, the Argonaut swims backwards near the surface of the sea by ejecting water from its siphon like the Octopus, and it crawls about on the floor of the sea in as prosaic a fashion as any winkle.

See also Vol. VI: Octopus, Cuttlefish, and Squid Fishing.

OKAPI. This is a very shy creature living in the densest and least-explored forests of tropical Africa—in fact its very existence was not confirmed until as recently as 1901. Though closely related to the Giraffe (q.v.), it is unlike it in its habits. It differs greatly in appearance, also, being much smaller—about the size of a large mule. It has a short body, rather long legs and neck (though not nearly so long in proportion as the Giraffe's), and very large ears, which are sensitive to the slightest sound. Its eyes are large, its nostrils hairy, and its tail fairly long, with a small black tuft of hair at the tip. Full-grown

males have short horns about 3 inches long. The Okapi's colouring and marking are peculiar: it has white stripes on its hindquarters and the upper part of its legs only, while the rest of its body and neck is dark chocolate-brown, its face whitish, and the lower part of its legs mostly white. This colouring makes a perfect camouflage in the subdued light of its native forests.

Like the Giraffe, it feeds on the leaves of trees, stripping them off the branches with its long tongue and flexible upper lip. Okapis are rarely

seen in the wild by white men; but one has been kept with success in the London Zoo. An Okapi was first brought to the Antwerp Zoo in 1919.

OPOSSUM. This is the only Marsupial (or pouched mammal) (q.v.) found in the Americas, all others belonging to Australasia. There are several different species: in some the female has a fully formed pouch, while in others there is no pouch, or only a rudimentary one consisting of two folds in the skin of the abdomen. Opossums are rather like rats to look at (though some species are much bigger); but they have longer snouts, with quite naked muzzles. Their tails are very long, partially naked, and prehensile at the tips. Except for the Water Opossum they all live in trees, and are nocturnal, sleeping during the day among the leaves or in hollow trunks. Nearly all Opossums are expert climbers, helping themselves with their prehensile tails, which they can twine round the branches. Most of them eat every sort of food—flesh, insect, or vegetable. In those species in which the female has no pouch, the young, after leaving their mother's teats, are carried on her back, holding on by curling their tails round her tail, which she bends back for the purpose.

AN AUSTRALIAN PHALANGER CARRYING HER BABY ON HER BACK
These Marsupials are often, inaccurately, called Opossums. *Harris Picture Agency*

The best known, and much the largest of the Opossums, is the Common or Virginian Opossum—the only species found in North America, all the others belonging to central and South America. It is about the size of a cat, and has a tail some 14 inches long, and a coat of long, bristle-like grey hairs with very soft black and white under-fur. These Virginian Opossums are most destructive to poultry and game, for they eat birds and their eggs, as well as the usual food of Opossums. Six to sixteen young are born in a litter. The mother shows great devotion to her offspring, and will use every means in her power to prevent her pouch from being opened. When the little creatures become too big for their mother's pouch, they cling to her body, hanging on to her fur, legs, or tail, and are carried about with her wherever she goes. When caught, the Virginian Opossum invariably pretends to be dead—from which has originated the expression 'to play possum'.

The Water Opossum or Yapock, found from Guatemala to Brazil, has webbed hind toes, and spends much of its time in the water. It is about 14 inches long, with a tail even longer than itself. Its short, close, light-grey coat has a much darker stripe, expanding into blotches down its back. It is very like an otter in its habits, and feeds on crustaceans and small fishes. The female has a complete pouch.

ORANGE-TIP BUTTERFLIES, *see* WHITES.

ORANG-UTAN, *see* APE.

ORCHIDS. Though orchids are generally thought of as exotic hot-house flowers, there are about forty different members of the orchid family growing wild in this country. The vast majority, however, grow in warmer climates; and the remarkable flowers seen in hot-houses in this country grow equally luxuriantly and in

Orchis ericetorum
Harold Bastin

Butterfly Orchis
Harold Bastin

Fragrant Orchis
Harold Bastin

Spotted Orchis
Eric J. Hosking, F.R.P.S.

Dwarf Orchis
Harold Bastin

Bee Orchis
Harold Bastin

BRITISH ORCHIDS

great profusion in TROPICAL JUNGLES (q.v.), of which they are characteristic.

All orchids are perennial herbs. In the hot, steamy jungles, they grow perched in the crevices and crannies in trees, sending down twining roots which cling to the branches for support. Such plants are called 'epiphytes'. They do not absorb their food or water from the tree itself—for then they would be PARASITIC PLANTS (q.v.)—but from the humus, chiefly dead leaves, which collects around them. Besides the food-absorbing roots, many orchids have long aerial roots, which hang suspended in the humid jungle atmosphere. The outside layer of these roots is spongy, and offers a large surface on which moisture from the surrounding air condenses, thus providing the orchid with its water-supply. There are a great many species of tropical orchids: many books have been written on them, a glance at one of which would show the richness and variety of this strikingly beautiful group of flowers.

The flowers of most orchids have only one stamen. There are no true sepals or petals; but the petalloid structures are arranged in two sets of three, of which the three outer are usually equal in size and comparatively small. The three inner 'petals' are very unequal, both in size

stamen-bearing spur

labellum

FLOWER SHOWING METHOD OF CROSS-POLLINATION

and form, those in some of the tropical flowers being large and highly coloured. The lower front 'petal', called the 'labellum', is the largest, and is extended forwards to form a platform with drooping wings, and backwards to form a spur. The two inner 'petals' form an upright hood, which is fused with the style. Orchids have one of the most efficient and ingenious methods of cross-pollination in the whole plant kingdom. An insect, after alighting on the platform of the labellum, tries to force its mouthparts down the spur, and so brings its head in contact with the contents of the anther-lobes, which are called 'pollinia'. In withdrawing, it pulls with it these pollinia (really masses of pollen), which then stand erect, like two Indian clubs, on the insect's head. They soon curve forwards and downwards, however; and when carried to the next flower, they strike against the stigma, so causing cross-pollination to take place.

Most British orchids are normal, green ground-plants; but two of them have no green parts, and obtain their food from decaying organic matter (see SAPROPHYTES). One is the Bird's Nest Orchis, usually found in the decaying leaf-mould of beech woods. Its underground stem bears roots, forming a tangled mass surrounded by myriads of threads of a fungus, which help the plant to absorb foodstuffs from the humus—the whole looking very much like a bird's-nest. The upright stem grows about a foot high, and bears leaves which are no more than tiny, brown scales, and dull-brown flowers crowded together in a dense spike at the top. Another saprophytic British orchid is the Coralroot, a smaller yellowish plant, found rarely in the sandy woods of eastern Scotland.

One of the most common British orchids is the Early Purple Orchis, often seen growing among bluebells and cowslips in open pastures. The long green leaves are blotched with brown, and the reddish-purple flowers grow in loose spikes. Its food is stored in tubers which, in Shakespeare's day, gave the plant the name of Dead Men's Fingers. Another common orchid is the Spotted Orchis which, with its spikes of pink-purple flowers and spotted leaves, is common in moist meadows and marshes throughout Britain, flowering in June and July.

The Twayblade, a not-uncommon orchid, flowers in moist pastures and woods from May to July. This is easy to identify, because its stem, which grows up to 2 feet high, bears two large, oval, strongly ribbed leaves about half-way up. The small flowers are greenish-yellow. When touched by insect visitors, they rupture violently at one point, giving off a sticky fluid, which helps to bind the pollinia to the insect's head.

Three less common and beautiful orchids are the Bee Orchis, Fly Orchis, and Spider Orchis. They are local rather than rare, being confined to restricted areas in southern England. Many botanists have tried to find a reason for the remarkable resemblance of these flowers to the insects after which they have been named. According to one French scientist, the Fly Orchis resembles very closely the female of a particular insect, of which the male hatches some days before the female. He suggests that the male flies round looking for his mate, and finds the Fly Orchis instead—but before he can discover his mistake, his work of pollination is completed. Unfortunately for this idea, most of these orchids are seldom visited by insects, and they are usually self-pollinated.

Lady's Tresses is a fairly common orchid, found flowering during August and September in dry pastures. Each plant has three or four leaves, borne in a spreading tuft; while the small, white flowers, which smell like almonds, appear as a spirally twisted spike. Another rare orchid is the Musk Orchis, which has slender spikes of green flowers, smelling at night-time of musk. It is pollinated by small flies and beetles.

See also ORCHIDS: Vol. VI.

ORIOLE. Most Orioles, about the size of a thrush, are brilliantly coloured, yellow, green, and black predominating, though some species have crimson underparts. They are found in most tropical and temperate climates. The Golden Oriole belongs to Europe, Africa, and Asia, the Green Oriole to Australia, and the Mango Bird to India.

The Golden Oriole winters in central and southern Africa, but comes north to breed, visiting most parts of Europe and occasionally the southern counties of England. The male is a brilliant yellow and black bird, but is very shy and hides among the foliage, only revealing himself when he flies from one clump of trees to another. His loud, musical, flute-like whistle, however, often proclaims his presence. The female is of a much less showy greenish-yellow. Orioles build nests which are generally suspended like a hammock from the bough of a tree.

OSMOSIS, see ROOTS, Section 3.

OSPREY. This bird of prey—often called the Fishing Hawk in America—is related to the HAWKS and EAGLES (qq.v.), and is found throughout the greater part of the world, especially in northern America. It used to breed in Scotland, but now is a rare summer visitor. It is about 22 to 24 inches long, and has very long wings, and large powerful claws covered with rough, spiny scales. Its plumage is brown, the underparts white streaked with brown, and the head white.

Ospreys frequent large lakes or rivers in the neighbourhood of woods, and the sea-coast near cliffs. They feed on sea or freshwater fish, and can be seen sailing high above the water waiting for a catch. On sighting a fish, the Osprey drops suddenly and seizes the prey in its claws. It will then sometimes sail round and round for a long time, holding the fish in its claws before devouring it. It builds a large nest of sticks either in a tree or on a ledge of rock, and returns to the same nest year after year, adding to it till it becomes a bulky structure. It lays three or four eggs, and will protect the nest from attack with considerable ferocity.

OSTRICH. The Ratites or flightless birds include not only the Ostriches proper, of Africa and south-west Asia, but also the Emus and Cassowaries of Australasia, the KIWIS (q.v.) of New Zealand, and the American Rheas, as well as several birds now extinct, such as the Moas.

1. OSTRICH. This is the largest of living birds, a fully grown male standing 8 feet high to the top of its head, and weighing perhaps 300 lbs. It is unique among birds in having only two toes, one long, strong toe on which the whole weight rests, and one much smaller and almost useless. The male has magnificent, glossy black plumage with white tail-feathers; while the female, a rather smaller bird, is dusky grey. The Ostrich has a small and flattened head, with a short beak, a very long, powerful neck, and long, stout, muscular legs, able to deliver a powerful defensive kick, and to carry the bird at a very great pace. Ostriches can, in fact, run faster than an Antelope.

There are four species of Ostrich: one found in north Africa, Syria, and Arabia, and the other three in central and South Africa. Wild Ostriches are becoming scarcer; but the birds

MALE AND FEMALE OSTRICHES WITH THEIR NEST OF EGGS
Dorien Leigh

are now bred for their plumage on farms in Africa, America, and Australia. In the wild state, they generally live in parties of 10 or 20, often moving about in company with Antelopes or Zebras, and depending on their very keen sight and great speed for defence. They feed on grass, leaves, and fruit, as well as on small animals and insects. They will, in fact, eat almost anything, 'the digestion of an ostrich' being proverbial. They need a certain amount of salt and a good deal to drink, though they can travel through the desert for long periods without water. As the breeding season approaches, they break up into small parties, each cock having three or four hens. The cock Ostrich makes a very elaborate display during the courtship season. He dances with his neck upright and his feathers fluffed out, and then suddenly drops to the ground and fans his mate with his rudimentary wings, blowing out his neck and making a sound rather like the roar of a lion (*see* ANIMAL LANGUAGE). The hens generally have a communal nest in a hollow in the sand, in which

they lay as many as twenty eggs. The cock incubates the eggs at night; during the day either the hens take charge or the eggs are covered with sand and incubated by the sun. The young chicks are guarded carefully (and often savagely) by their parents.

Ostrich-hunting has been a favourite sport of African natives, many devices for catching them being used. Generally, parties of Ostriches are surrounded by huntsmen on horseback; sometimes they are run down by relays of mounted huntsmen; sometimes they are driven into pitfalls; the BUSHMEN (q.v. Vol. I) used to dress up in Ostrich-skins and, keeping on the leeward side, would mix with a party of the birds. The habit proverbially attributed to the Ostrich of burying its head in the sand when faced with danger would be less absurd than it sounds, for the Ostrich's skull is very weak, the most vulnerable part of its body.

2. EMU and CASSOWARY. Both these birds, rather smaller than Ostriches, belong to Australasia, the Emus in open country and the

Cassowaries in dense forests. Emus have light, mottled grey and brown plumage, with black tips to the feathers. They live in small parties, except in the breeding season, when they pair off. The female is often mistaken for the male, for she is the larger bird—and the cock incubates the eggs and broods the chicks. Emus protect their young fiercely, by kicking at any enemy, both outwards and backwards. They are unpopular with farmers, since they eat the crops, and their numbers have been very much reduced in consequence.

Cassowaries have blue-black plumage, and carry on their heads helmet-like prominences of bone covered with blue-green and red skin. These and the wattles on their necks are protections to the birds as they push through the thick undergrowth of the forests. Cassowaries live in parties of seven or eight, except in the breeding season, when they pair. They are shy birds and difficult to watch.

3. RHEA. The 'Ostrich' of the plains of South America is a much smaller bird than the real Ostrich, and has three toes instead of two, a longer beak, and no apparent tail. Its blue-grey-brown plumage makes an excellent camouflage in the grassy plains. Rheas live in large companies of as many as sixty or more, and break up at the mating season into small parties of one cock and five to seven hens. The birds are fond of water and are bold swimmers. The hens lay from 20 to 30 eggs, only a proportion of which are hatched. Rhea hunting is a skilled sport, generally consisting of throwing the 'bola' (a kind of ball on a rope) at the birds.

4. MOA. This was a very large flightless bird, which used to be common in New Zealand until it was exterminated by the MAORIS (q.v. Vol. I) some time before the white man appeared there. There were several species of Moa, some as small as turkeys, and one as high as 12 feet. The largest egg of which the remains have been found measured 10 inches by 7 inches.

OTTER. This carnivorous water-animal belongs to the WEASEL family (q.v.), and is found in most parts of the world, but not in Australia. The various species do not differ very greatly from each other, though albino, cream-coloured, and spotted varieties are known, as well as the common brown. The wild Otter, if captured young, is easily tamed and will follow its owner about like a dog. In India and China, Otters

AUSTRALIAN EMU
Australian News & Information Bureau

AUSTRALIAN CASSOWARY
Australian News & Information Bureau

OTTER ON THE LOOK-OUT FOR FISH
Harold Bastin

are often trained to catch fish. In Britain, OTTER HUNTING (q.v. Vol. IX) used to be, and in places still is, a popular sport—a special type of hound being bred for the purpose.

The Common Otter, widely distributed through Europe and Asia, is 4 feet long, and has webbed feet, thick, brown, waterproof fur, a long, tapering tail, and broad, flattened face. Both its nostrils and ears can be closed under water. It dives perfectly, and swims very fast, with muscular twists of its body and tail, and paddling with its fore-feet only. On coming out of the water, it shakes itself dry before lying up. On land it travels at a swift trot or gallop, frequently making journeys of up to 15 miles. When excited, it utters a yelping bark, and gives a sort of whistle as an alarm note to its fellows. Most Otters spend the year by streams or tarns, going to the sea in dry summers and returning up-stream for the breeding season in autumn. Some, however, spend all the year by the sea-coast, only going up-stream during storms.

Otters live mainly on fish, but also eat rabbits, frogs, ducks, moorhens, snakes, worms, grouse—and they have even been known to kill sheep. They delight in hunting fish; and can chase, tire, and kill salmon larger than themselves. They often hunt in couples and, by working in circles from the centre of a pool, drive the fish to the shores. Their cheek-teeth can hold slippery fishes and at the same time pierce their hard scales. They kill their prey by biting the back-bone, and then take it on land to eat. They are shy, elusive animals, hunting only at night. They spend the day in permanent resting and breeding places, known as 'holts', in the banks of streams or in old hollow trees with an underwater entrance. One chamber is normally used as an earth closet. On the Norfolk Broads, Otters build large nests of dry reeds; in other places, of dry grass and leaves. The female, or bitch, generally produces one to three whelps in the spring. The young are born with fine, silky coats, and are blind for 35 days. Before their eyes open, the mother carries them under water. At 8 weeks old, they reluctantly learn to swim and, gradually, to hunt for themselves.

The Sea Otter is quite unlike other members of the Otter family, and looks more like a Sea Bear (*see* SEALS). It is a larger and more massive animal than other otters, and has huge, webbed hind-feet. It used to be very common on the coasts of the North Pacific, but was very nearly exterminated by fur-hunters because of its soft, woolly, brown fur. Since 1910 it has been protected, and is now becoming re-established in its old haunts. It is a playful animal, and lies on its back for hours tossing bits of seaweed up in the air. Its quick hearing and acute smell are unequalled in any other creature, and it is so timid that it will not go anywhere near where man has been.

OUNCE, *see* LEOPARD.

OVEN BIRD. The Red Oven Bird, or Hornero, of central and South America is about the size of a thrush, with red-brown plumage above, shading to nearly white underneath, and with a bright, red-brown tail. It is most often to be found in the open country, parks, and gardens of Paraguay and Argentina. It is remarkable for its unusual nest, a large globular structure of clay, about a foot in diameter, and often weighing as much as 9 lb., which is shaped like a baker's oven—hence the bird's name. The nest is placed conspicuously on a bare branch or post, often facing a road, or on the roof or beam of a building. It consists of an outer vestibule, with a small entrance into the central chamber, where there is a soft lining on which the four or five white eggs are laid. This nest takes a long time to build, and the birds often start building in the autumn, resuming work in open spells through the winter.

OWLS. These birds of prey, of which there are some 200 species distributed over almost the whole world, form an order of their own. They all have the characteristic 'owl-face', due to the forward direction of their large eyes and to the circular disc of radiating feathers round each. As the eyes can move in their sockets to a very small extent only, the owl has to turn its head when following any wide movement. This it can do so far, that it can look over its own back. Owls have well-developed ears, and a keen sense of hearing as well as of sight. They have strong, hooked beaks, feathered legs, and toes furnished with sharp, curved claws, the outer claw of which can be directed backwards or forwards. Many species carry small erect tufts of feathers

BARN OWL
Eric J. Hosking, F.R.P.S.

on their heads. The plumage, usually a mottled blending of browns and greys, is very soft; and this enables the birds to make a practically noiseless, ghost-like flight, very useful in hunting prey by night.

Owls range in size from the Pigmy Owlet, no larger than a thrush, to the Great Eagle-owl, larger than a buzzard. Most species hunt only by night and sleep all day; some hunt by either day or night; while the Hawk-owls prefer the bright sunlight for hunting. All are carnivorous, eating small mammals, reptiles, birds, insects, worms, and snails. The large Fish-owls of India and Africa catch fish, crabs, and other water creatures. Most owls are beneficial to farmers, for they feed so largely on rats, mice, and other vermin; but the Eagle-owls, which will attack game-birds, hares, and rabbits, are more harmful. Many species are arboreal, often using the discarded nests of crows in which to lay their nearly round, white eggs. Some species roost and nest in clefts of rock or in buildings, especially barns, church towers, or ruins. They swallow most of their food whole, and throw up the indigestible parts in the form of pellets. Ornithologists, by examining these pellets, can tell exactly what the bird's diet has been.

The Barn-owls form a separate family in the Order. They are quite small—little over a foot long; but have larger eyes than any other bird. They are sometimes called White Owls, because their faces are white and their general plumage paler than the typical colouring. They are also called Screech-owls, because of the weird shriek which they make through the night, especially early in the year. They prefer to live close to human habitations, and their loud 'snores' have an almost human sound. Barn-owls frequently lay their eggs in pairs at short intervals, so that the young hatch at different times—birds at three different stages being sometimes in the nest together. Both parents incubate, and have been found sitting side by side, each incubating some of the eggs.

The Tawny, Brown, or Wood Owl, a rather larger bird, lives chiefly in woods. It continually utters its cry, 'too-whit, too-whoo'; and in the breeding season, when it is very noisy, it also utters a laughter-like cry. The Long-eared and Short-eared Owls carry tufts of feathers, not really ears, on their heads. They are nocturnal in their habits, and are shy, avoiding human habitation. If attacked, they are fierce and spit

TAWNY OWL USING THE DISCARDED NEST OF A BUZZARD
This owl has turned her head right round so that she is looking over her back
Arthur Brook

like cats. If caught in the open in the daylight, they are often mobbed by the small birds who by night fly in terror of them. The Little Owl, only 7 or 8 inches long, is a bold and savage hunter, sometimes attacking by day as well as by night, and flying rather like a bat. There are many other interesting species, including the handsome Snowy Owls of the Arctic with their white, slightly spotted plumage, and the large Horned Owls or Eagle-owls, found all over the world, except Australasia.

OX, *see* CATTLE.

OYSTER. If an unopened Oyster is carefully examined, it will be seen to have unequal shell-valves, the left or lower valve being more saucer-like in shape, stouter in build, and convex externally; while the right or uppermost valve is flatter and lighter, and therefore easier for the Oyster to raise when it gapes. It will also be seen that the surface of the valves shows many irregular narrow lines, which may be grouped into a few larger zones. These wavy lines are a record of the changes in the life of the Oyster, each zone indicating fairly accurately a year's growth; whereas the lines indicate the rhythmic seasonal alternation of periods of active growth and of inactivity, their distinctness being due to the fact that the Oyster practically ceases to feed during the winter, from about the end of November to the middle of March. As there can be no shell growth while the Oyster is fasting, what has already been formed during the spring and summer becomes slightly weathered and corroded, and this results in a distinct boundary-line showing where each new spring growth starts. Although the Common Oyster produces many thousands of eggs each year, only a very small number of the young Oysters survive, most of them being eaten by other animals. Even in later life, the growing Oyster, now settled on the sea-floor, has many enemies such as Starfishes and Dog-whelks.

What the fisherman calls 'white-sick' and 'black-sick' Oysters are not really 'sick' at all: the terms simply indicate two natural stages in the development of the young within the safe shelter of their parent's shell. When the young are ready, the parent Oyster slightly opens the valves of her shell and blows out the 'spat' (as the young Oysters are called) in jets, looking like miniature clouds, into the surrounding water. The young Oyster must then find some suitable ground on which to anchor itself, and unless it does so within 48 hours of its expulsion from the parent shell, it will perish. Once attached to some solid object, such as a piece of rock, growth is rapid, the young Oyster increasing from about $\frac{1}{20}$th inch in diameter to some $\frac{3}{8}$th inch in the first 5 or 6 months, and in a year to about 1 inch. Thereafter, its age may be roughly determined by the number of inches it measures across its shell. If left undisturbed on their natural breeding ground, Oysters become full grown in about 4 years.

See also PEARL OYSTER.
See also Vol. VI: OYSTER FISHING.

OYSTER-CATCHER, *see* WADING BIRDS, Section 6.

P

PAINTED LADY BUTTERFLY, *see* VANESSINAE.

PALMS, *see* DESERT PLANTS; *see also* Vol. VI: PALMS.

PANDA. Pandas are related both to RACCOONS and to BEARS (qq.v.), and are to be found principally in north-eastern India and western China. There are two kinds—the Red or True Panda, sometimes popularly known as the Cat Bear, and the Giant Panda, or Parti-coloured Bear, which was first shown at the London Zoo in 1939, and has since become very popular in Britain.

Red Pandas, which are about the size of large domestic cats, live in the south-eastern Himalayas and south-west China. Their long, thick fur is usually dark red on top of the body, and black below, including the legs; their faces are white with red stripes running from the eyes to the corners of the mouth; and their tails are marked with light and dark red rings. They move awkwardly on the ground, but spend most of their life in trees, using their sharp, curved claws for climbing. During the day they sleep in hollow trunks or between the branches. They normally sleep curled up sideways with their heads hidden by their tails; but they frequently rest by sitting down on their haunches with their heads tucked in between their forepaws. They generally eat in the early morning and evening, their food being various fruits, acorns, bamboo shoots, and sometimes eggs. They make their nests in hollow tree-trunks or in rock crevices,

in which two young are born in the spring. The Red Panda is a stupid, sluggish animal, which can be captured easily. Although it will hiss and spit like a cat, and growl like a young bear when angry, it seldom uses its strong claws in its defence. It is easily tamed at whatever age it is captured; but requires a great deal of care when kept in Zoos in Europe, as it is very sensitive to the cold.

Giant Pandas live in the large bamboo forests of western China. They are not at all like Red Pandas, but look more like bears, and have very short tails and large, broad feet. Their colouring is remarkable—mainly white, but with black ears, legs, and feet, black patches round their eyes, and a broad black band passing round the body from the front legs over the shoulders. They sleep during the day in hollow tree-trunks or in other secluded places, and come out at night to eat roots and bamboo shoots, or small mammals and fish, which they hold between their forepaws and chew with their very powerful jaws.

PANGOLIN (or Scaly Ant-eater). This mammal belongs to the order of animals called the Pholidota. At one time it was included with the ANT-EATERS and ARMADILLOS (qq.v.) in the order Edentata, simply because it, like the Ant-eaters, is toothless. In addition there is a superficial resemblance between the armour of the Pangolin and that of the Armadillo. Pangolins are found in various parts of Asia and Africa.

THE GIANT PANDA OF CHINA
'Picture Post' Library

THE SCALY ANT-EATER OR PANGOLIN OF CHINA
Harold Bastin

They are covered all over with large, overlapping, horny scales, which make them look much like elongated fir-cones with a head, legs, and, usually, a long tail. Like the Ant-eaters, they have powerful legs and claws, and long, elastic, sticky tongues, which they use to lick up the ants and termites on which they live. The largest species live on the ground and dig themselves burrows; the smaller species live in trees, using their long tails to support themselves in climbing, the sharp points of the scales being pressed against the trunk. All roll themselves up into balls when attacked, relying for their safety upon their hard, scaly covering and on a nauseous-smelling secretion which they can give out. The young Pangolins are carried around seated on their mother's tail.

PANTHER, *see* LEOPARD.

PAPER NAUTILUS, *see* OCTOPUS.

PARASITIC PLANTS. Nutrition in plants is normally by PHOTOSYNTHESIS (q.v.), in which food substances are built up from raw materials by the aid of the sunlight and the green colouring matter in the leaves. Some plants, however, derive their nourishment from the living bodies of other plants or animals, including even human beings. These are called Parasites, and should be compared with those plants called SAPROPHYTES (q.v.), which obtain their food, either directly or indirectly, from dead plants or animals.

Some parasites are totally devoid of green colouring matter (chlorophyll), and must get all their food from the bodies of other living creatures. These, known as 'complete parasites', include many FUNGI (q.v.), some bacteria, and a few flowering plants. Examples of parasitic flowering plants are the Dodder, Broomrape, and Toothwort; while Microsporon is a fungus which lives parasitically on human beings, causing ringworm. Other parasites contain some chlorophyll and nourish themselves partly by photosynthesis and partly from the bodies of other plants or animals. An example of these 'semi-parasites', which are generally flowering plants, is the MISTLETOE (q.v.). Other semi-parasites are partial root-parasites, of which the Yellow Rattle, Lousewort, Eyebright, and Cow-wheat, all members of the Foxglove family, are typical examples. Most of them live in pastures and meadows, and send out suckers from their roots to penetrate the roots of grasses, from which they absorb some of their food. The Lousewort can grow independently, but the others cannot grow apart from the grasses.

In many cases, parasitic plants kill the host plant or animal on which they live. In others, the parasites cause disease, so that the host plant becomes deformed, or has a reduced growth or production of fruit. They are a terrible pest to farmers and gardeners, and, in tropical countries, cause losses of many thousands of tons of valuable crops each year. Yet some plant parasites scarcely affect their hosts at all.

The Dodder is a flowering plant which is completely dependent for food on its host plants, Clover, Gorse, Hop, Thyme, Heather, Flax, or Nettles. The Dodder seed germinates late in the spring when the host plants have already de-

Toothwort   Broomrape   Dodder

veloped their shoots. The seedling is a delicate yellow thread, capable of standing erect, which sways in ever-widening circles as it grows. If, as it sways, it meets with a suitable host, it twines round the stem, and sends out suckers. These penetrate the tissues of the host until they reach the wood and bast tubes, and thus obtain supplies of organic food, as well as water and mineral salts. As soon as it is established on the host plant, the root of the parasite dies. The yellowish stem branches a great deal and produces minute scaly leaves and numerous small clusters of pink flowers. Dodder is common in meadows, especially in Clover fields. It seldom kills its host, which generally manages to produce enough food to supply both itself and the parasite.

Broomrapes, of which there are several species, are also complete parasites, obtaining their food from the roots of other plants. The Great Broomrape grows chiefly on the roots of Broom and Gorse, and the Lesser Broomrape grows on various plants, but more particularly on Clover. All the Broomrapes have colourless stems, bearing whitish-yellow, scaly leaves. The flowers are conspicuous, being borne at the top of the stem, and vary from brown to yellow and red, but never green.

The Toothwort is parasitic on the roots of Beech, Hazel, and other trees, and is therefore found chiefly in woods. It has a creeping underground stem or rhizome, bearing crowded fleshy leaves; and the erect stem carries a spike of purplish flowers. Like the Dodder, the Toothwort obtains its food by sending out suckers into the tissues of the host plant. The hollow leaves on the underground shoots were thought to be traps for insects (*see* INSECTIVOROUS PLANTS); but they probably serve to absorb water from the host plant.

PARROTS. This group of birds, which forms a separate order containing six families, includes Parrots, Macaws, Love-birds, Cockatoos, and Budgerigars. There are altogether more than 500 species, found mostly in tropical and subtropical regions. There are not many in India, and still fewer in Africa; while in Malaya, Australasia, and South America there are great numbers of very varied types. One species is found in the southern states of the U.S.A.; but there is none in Europe.

The most characteristic features of the Parrots are their feet and beaks, both of which are adapted for their life in trees, where they need to climb more than to fly. In the feet, the first and fourth toes are directed backwards, and the second and third forwards. The feet are covered with rough scales, and the legs are short—in some species extremely short. The beak is short, stout, and strongly hooked, the upper part having a hinged top which can be lifted at will. Parrots climb as much with their beaks as with their feet, clinging with them to the branches of trees—or to the bars of a cage. In the larger species, the beak is enormously strong—the Blue Macaw of Brazil, for instance, crushes to pulp in its beak palm-nuts which a man could break open only with a heavy hammer. They use their beaks also for hollowing out a suitable nesting chamber in a tree-trunk.

Parrots lay white eggs, the larger species producing only two or three in a season. Both parents generally take part in the incubation, and the young are fed by half-digested food disgorged from the parents' crops into the mouths of the nestlings. Parrots are vegetarians, feeding on various fruits and nuts. They generally feed in large and extremely noisy parties, and love to congregate in open, sunny gardens and orchards. One species, however, the Kea or Mountain Kaka of New Zealand, has gained a reputation for killing sheep in order to feed on the fat round the kidneys. The Keas have developed their carnivorous habits during the comparatively short period since sheep were introduced to New Zealand. Now they are a considerable menace to farmers. These birds are also unlike other Parrots in that they nest in mid-winter, high up among the glaciers and snowfields of the mountains.

Parrots vary greatly in size. The Great Black Cockatoo of New Guinea is a heavy bird, about 2 feet 6 inches long; while the Macaws of America are even longer, the brilliant Red-and-blue Macaw of central America being 3 feet long, nearly 2 feet of which is tail. On the other hand, the green and blue Parrotlets of central America and the vivid little Love-birds of Africa are only about 5 inches long, while the Pigmy Parrots of New Guinea are smaller than a sparrow—just over 3 inches. The best known of all Parrots, the African Grey Parrot, has grey plumage with a bright red tail. The prevalent colour, however, as is natural for arboreal, fruit-eating birds, is green, though many species have

A PAIR OF SOUTH AMERICAN MACAWS
Booth Steamship Co.

to rose-colour on cheeks, breast, and underwings, and a very showy crest with bands of vermilion and yellow.

One of the prettiest and best known of the Parakeets is the Budgerigar of Australia. It has a complicated colour-pattern of grass-green, blue, pale yellow, and black, and has a long tail, taking up more than half its length of 7½ inches. It is to be seen commonly in large flocks in the neighbourhood of Adelaide, perching on the gum trees, or hunting for the seeds on which it lives.

Parrots, as is well known, live very well in captivity, and become extremely tame and friendly. Their great powers of mimicry and their excellent memories enable them to repeat words and phrases taught to them (*see* CAGE BIRDS: Vol. IX). Parrots live to a great age, many of the larger species being known to have lived 60 to 80 years in captivity.

brilliant hues of blue, yellow, crimson, white, and occasionally black. Perhaps the Macaws are the most showy, as well as being the most noisy, of the group; though the Purple-capped Lory of Australasia is gorgeous—a scarlet bird with a golden throat, blue and green wings, and a deep purple cap on the head.

Cockatoos are characteristic of all Australasia, except New Zealand and the eastern islands. They bear a crest of feathers on the head; their skulls differ from those of other Parrots; and they have short legs, and short, deep beaks. The predominant colour, instead of green, is white, generally tinged with red or yellow, especially on the crest and tail. In one species the whole breast is red and the back is grey; another species is entirely grey except for its red head. The Raven Cockatoos are black, one species having a vermilion band across the tail. The Great Black Cockatoo, one of the largest of all Parrots, is slaty-black, with pale-red cheeks. This bird uses its enormously powerful beak for breaking open the very hard shell of its favourite food, the Kanary-nut. The most gorgeous of all Cockatoos is Leadbeater's Cockatoo of South Australia, a magnificent bird with white plumage, shading

PARTRIDGE. This member of the order of Game-birds is a relative of the PHEASANT and GROUSE (qq.v.). The common Grey or Brown Partridge is found throughout Europe and much of Asia; and its close relative, the Spur-legged Partridge, or Francolin, belongs to Africa. The Snow-partridge lives in the high mountain ranges of central Asia; and from there to south-east Asia are found the Tree-partridges, which, unlike typical Partridges, perch in trees. Wood-partridges rarely leave the jungle, where they live in parties of six to a dozen; some of them are glossy black, while others carry fan-shaped, maroon crests of hairy feathers.

The common Partridges are stocky birds about 12½ inches long, with the well-known horseshoe marking on their chests, the male and female birds being very much alike. They are found chiefly on arable land, and are useful to the farmer as, besides being valuable food themselves, they destroy insect pests. After the breeding season, they congregate in coveys generally composed of parents and young, two or more families sometimes joining together. At night, the covey 'jugs'—that is, they form a circle, nestling closely together in grass or growing crops. In the spring, the party breaks up with a good deal of quarrelling into pairs, and these remain together, nesting at the end of April or in May. The hen lays ten to twenty olive-brown eggs in a nest in the grass. The male has a loud, hoarse cry, 'caer-wit, caer-wit', which in still

RED-LEGGED PARTRIDGE AND NEST
Eric Hosking, F.R.P.S.

weather can be heard from a great distance. In the 18th century, the Red-legged or French Partridge was introduced into Britain, and is established in many places, though it never consorts with the common Partridge. There is evidence for believing that the hen French Partridge frequently lays two clutches of her yellowish-white, red-spotted eggs in separate nests, each parent incubating one clutch, and the two groups joining up when the young are hatched.

Quails are small, stout, partridge-like birds, which winter in Africa and southern Asia. In spring they migrate northwards in large flocks, the cocks generally arriving first. They breed in Europe, and occasionally in southern England and Ireland, among rough pasture and arable. The birds, which are good food, used to be netted in vast numbers on the Mediterranean coasts, until they came near extermination. Attempts are now made to protect them. There are several other species of Quails in India, tropical Africa, and Australia. The American Quail, although belonging to the same family, is a rather distant relative. There are several species, both in North and South America, one of which carries a handsome crest of black, club-shaped feathers.

See also Vol. IX: GAME SHOOTING.

PEACH-BLOSSOM MOTH. This medium-sized moth has olive-brown fore-wings with five pinkish patches clouded with brown. This color-

ation suggests peach-blossom—though the pink patches, in fact, make the moth resemble the fallen petals of its food-plant, bramble. The Peach-blossom Moth is common in many wooded districts in England and Ireland. The velvety reddish-brown and grey caterpillar has a series of humps on its back, and usually rests with its hind part raised. It pupates in September in a frail cocoon among dead leaves on the ground.

Other British moths of this small family are the Buff-arches, Figure of Eight, Poplar and Lesser Lutestrings, Lesser Satin, Satin Carpet, Yellow Horned, and Frosted Green. They superficially resemble Caradrinidae (*see* NIGHT-FLYING MOTHS), though they are not related to them, and differ from them structurally in many ways. The caterpillars usually hide by day among leaves held together with silk, and, like the Peach-blossom, frequently adopt curious resting positions. Their food-plants are bramble, poplar, birch, alder, and oak.

PEACOCK. Pea-fowl belong to the order of Game-birds, and are relatives of the PHEASANTS (q.v.). They differ from other game-birds in having the upper tail-coverts developed into a long train, which the cock can spread out into a magnificent fan. These long feathers are decorated with the well-known 'eyes'. The Pea-hen resembles the cock except for the train, which the cock himself does not develop fully until the third year. Pea-fowl also carry delicate, fan-like, erect crests. Peacocks are found wild from India to the East Indies, preferring jungle-land near water, and not reaching to the high altitudes inhabited by many pheasants. They have been domesticated since very early times, the Romans keeping them both for ornament and for food. A Peacock served whole in all its plumage was a characteristic dish for a medieval banquet.

Another pheasant, rather like a Peacock in appearance, and also decorated with the characteristic 'eye-spots', is the Argus-pheasant, the most spectacular of which is the Rheinhardt's Argus of Indo-China, which measures about

7 feet from head to tail. Argus-pheasants live in the depth of the evergreen forests, each male selecting for his own territory an open, level spot, which he clears of debris and undoubtedly uses as a dancing-ground. In his courtship he makes a magnificent display of his tail and spectacular wing-feathers (*see* ANIMAL LANGUAGE).

PEACOCK BUTTERFLY, *see* VANESSINAE.

PEACOCK MOTH, *see* EMPEROR MOTH.

PEARL OYSTER. The so-called Pearl Oyster, which produces the finest pearls and most valuable mother-of-pearl, is not an oyster at all, but belongs to another family of MOLLUSCS allied to the SCALLOPS (qq.v.). It is widely distributed in tropical seas, where the different varieties have received local names, such as the Black-edged Banda-shell from the seas of the Malay Archipelago, and the giant Silver-lip Shell, highly prized for its mother-of-pearl, from Australia and New Guinea.

In outline the shell somewhat resembles that of a Scallop, the upper valve being flat, and the lower slightly convex externally. Inside the valves there is a lining of nacre, commonly known as mother-of-pearl, which is the same substance as that from which pearls are formed. Pearl growth is started by the presence of some minute foreign body, frequently the tiny dead body of a parasitic worm, a grain of sand, or a fragment of shell, which has got lodged in the mantle tissues of the mollusc, and around which the nacre or pearl secretion has been deposited. The beautiful lustre is due to extremely minute wavy lines, which break up the light falling upon the surface of the pearl, and, in mother-of-pearl, produce delicate rainbow tints.

A perfectly spherical or 'orient' pearl as it is called is one that has remained throughout its growth enfolded in the fleshy tissues or mantle of the mollusc. Very often, however, the pearl in its early stages becomes cemented at one end to the inside of the shell, so that, when ultimately cut from the shell, it presents the appearance of a sphere that has been cut in half. The perfect pearl must be of fine texture, free from any visible speck or blemish, and of a clear, almost transparent white colour, showing a soft iridescent sheen; in shape it must be either perfectly spherical or symmetrically pear-shaped. Such a specimen, flawless and perfect in shape,

is rare indeed and, when found, is literally 'a pearl of great price'. What are known as 'blister pearls', hollow bodies of irregular shape formed on the inner surface of the shell, are caused by the pearl oyster protecting itself from an external boring foe by depositing nacreous material beneath the point where the enemy has started tunnelling inwards.

The Pearl Oyster is not the only mollusc capable of producing pearls: our British freshwater Pearl Mussel, the common marine Edible Mussel, the West Indian Great Conch or Fountain-shell, and the large Chank-shell all at times form pearls, while black pearls are chiefly obtained from a species of Pearl Oyster that lives in the waters of the Gulf of Mexico.

See also OYSTER : MUSSEL.
See also Vol. VI: PEARL FISHING.

PEARLY NAUTILUS. This MOLLUSC (q.v.) lives in the seas of the Far East, in the shallow waters round the Philippines, Moluccas, New Britain, New Guinea, and Fiji. It is of particular interest, because it belongs to the only surviving genus of an ancient and extinct race of Cephalopods (*see* MOLLUSCS) which flourished in the seas of past geological ages. It must not be confused with the Argonaut or Paper Nautilus (*see* OCTOPUS), to which it is only distantly related. The Pearly Nautilus has a large and handsome cream-coloured shell, the interior of which is divided by curved partitions into a number of chambers, each a little larger than the first. These compartments have been added one by one to accommodate the Nautilus as it increased in size, the last-formed and largest chamber being its final abode. The smaller, empty and

SHELL OF PEARLY NAUTILUS
F. Martin Duncan, F.R.M.S., F.Z.S.

shut-off compartments are air-tight, and contain a gas rich in nitrogen, secreted by the Nautilus, which helps to make the large and solidly built shell more buoyant.

The Pearly Nautilus, like the Octopus, swims by the rhythmic expulsion of water from its siphon-tube, and crawls head downward on the floor of the sea. The visible part of the animal is brownish, mottled with white. Round the top of the head, which has the mouth in the centre, is a large number of small, short tentacles, which take the place of the sucker-clad arms of the Octopus and Cuttlefishes. When the tentacles are extended beyond the mouth of the shell, the Nautilus resembles a queer kind of Sea-anemone.

PELICAN. This large bird, which is found in most tropical and warm regions of the world, belongs to the same order as the CORMORANTS and GANNETS (qq.v.). There are about ten species, which do not vary very much from each other. They have small heads, short legs, mas-

PELICAN DIVING AFTER FISH
Hugo H. Schroder

sive bodies, long necks, and thick, harsh plumage —generally dishevelled-looking. The most conspicuous feature is the Pelican's beak, which is enormous. It is very long, flattened, and deeply furrowed, and the lower half has a great pouch. The whole beak acts like a fishing-net with a lid.

The European Pelican, which is typical of the family, has white plumage tinged with pink, with some black wing-feathers and yellow neck-feathers. The great beak is pale red, shading to yellow, with a crimson line along the middle. The pouch and feet are flesh-coloured. The birds are about 5 feet long. They live in very large flocks near swamps, estuaries, or rivers, feeding on fish, which they catch by diving and by systematic fishing in companies in the shallow water. They appear to keep regular periods of fishing and resting. They nest generally in small groups, making flat, sometimes large, nests of sticks, and laying two or three eggs with thick, bluish-white shells. The female feeds the young by allowing them to thrust their beaks into her pouch, where fish is ready for them. Although Pelicans are clumsy birds, they dive gracefully and fly powerfully—a flock of them flying in a long line with their great necks bent back over their bodies is a very striking sight.

PENGUINS. These flightless birds, adapted for life in the sea rather than the air, form a separate order, which includes about seventeen species. Their wings, which are paddle-like, and used for swimming instead of flying, are small and stiff from the shoulder, with no elbow-joint —so that Penguins cannot fold up their wings as other birds can. They have no quills, but are covered with small, scale-like feathers. Their legs are short and very thick, and are set very far back so that they can walk in an upright position. Their beaks are strong and pointed. They are much more agile and graceful in the water than on land, swimming and diving with such proficiency that they have been mistaken for dolphins or porpoises. They live on weed and on fish and other marine animals, which they capture (and sometimes swallow) under the surface of the water. On land they have a quaint, waddling walk, and when frightened they help themselves along by flapping their little wings.

Penguins belong entirely to the southern hemisphere, though they range from the Antarctic to islands almost on the Equator. They breed in great numbers on most of the lonely islands of the southern seas. Their plumage on the back and wings is generally dark, sometimes black, and white on the front. The Blue Penguin has a pale-blue back, with a black line down each feather. Some species carry crests also, generally yellowish in colour. Penguins vary in size from the great Emperor Penguin of the Antarctic, which stands nearly 3½ feet high and weighs as much as 90 lb., to the little Blue Penguin of New Zealand, which is only 19 inches tall.

Their breeding habits vary a good deal. The Emperor Penguins and the King Penguins of the lonely islands in the Southern Ocean breed at the beginning of the winter. They make no nest, but protect the single egg by placing it in a sort of fold or pouch of skin in front of the body, where it keeps warm in the down feathers and rests on the bird's feet. The chick remains within this protection until it is developed enough to stand the cold. In spite of this arrangement, however, a great many chicks do die of cold.

The Jackass Penguins of the Falkland Isles make tunnels, sometimes 3 or 4 yards long, for their nests, burrowing into a sandy cliff or under thick bushes. While on shore, these birds keep up a strange donkey-like braying the whole day. Most Penguins breed in 'rookeries', thousands of them together, and lay their single egg in a slight hollow in the ground, both parents taking part in the incubation. They have well-beaten paths from the sea to their nesting colonies, along which they walk in solemn procession. The Black-throated or Adélie Penguins always make their nests up high cliffs reached by steep slopes, up which the birds must toil slowly every time they return from the sea—perhaps several times a day. The journey up is laborious for birds which cannot fly; but they make the return journey quickly by tobogganing down the slope on their chests. These birds carry out an amusing courtship. When they first come to the 'rookeries' in October, the sexes keep apart, the females seeking last year's nest, repairing it, and then sitting on it. After a time the males begin to get

GENTOO PENGUINS AND ELEPHANT SEALS ON THE COAST OF SOUTH GEORGIA
C. A. Gibson-Hill

A PENGUIN BRAYING

The egg is resting on the bird's feet, and is kept warm in the thick down. *C. A. Gibson-Hill*

excited, fighting among themselves by pushing their chests against each other and striking with their tiny wings. Then, after much bowing and curtseying, they finally pair off. As is the case with many birds, the females appear to pay little attention to the males' display.

PERCH. This fish of the freshwaters of Europe and America is olive-brown or yellowish in colour, with dark cross-bands on the back, and bright red lower fins and tail-fin. The back-fin

FRESHWATER SUN-FISH AND YOUNG OF NORTH AMERICA
A. Fraser-Brunner

consists of two parts, the front portion being supported by strong, sharp spines, the hind part by soft, jointed and branched rays. Perch generally move in shoals, and are very voracious, feeding on such small fish as Bleak or Roach— and even on smaller specimens of their own kind, difficult though these are to swallow because of the spiny fin on the back. Spawning takes place in April and May, the eggs being laid in long strings among weeds on the bed of the river. Very much like the Perch, and with similar habits, but much smaller, is the Pope or Ruffe of European and English rivers.

Perch-like fishes are very numerous, but most of them are marine, and are here described under the heading SEA PERCH (q.v.). Among the freshwater kinds, there are the Darters, of which there are about fifty small, brightly coloured species living in American rivers, sheltering under stones in clear running water, feeding on the larvae of flies, and darting rapidly when disturbed. Much larger are the Pike-perches, found in Europe and America, some of which are popular as food and game fishes. The Common Perch has been used to illustrate the anatomy of fishes in the article on FISHES (q.v.).

The Sunfishes of North American freshwaters are very closely related to the Perch. Most of them are small, deep-bodied, and handsomely coloured. Some have breeding habits similar to those of the CICHLIDS (q.v.), of South America. Some of the prettier kinds have been introduced into Europe as pond and aquarium fishes, notably the Common Sunfish, Diamond Bass, Long-eared Sunfish, Blue-green Sunfish, and the dainty little Black-banded Sunfish, which thrives well in a tropical AQUARIUM (q.v. Vol. IX).

Much larger and longer in the body are the so-called Black Bass, celebrated as sporting-fishes, which have been introduced into various parts of the world, though not always successfully.

PEREGRINE, *see* FALCON.

PERIWINKLE, *see* SNAIL, Section 4.

PETRELS. 1. These, and their relatives, the Albatrosses and Shearwaters, form the order of Tube-nosed birds, which contains a great many species of sea-birds, inhabiting most parts of the world, but especially belonging to the southern hemisphere. Birds of this order are distinguished from all other birds because their nostrils grow out as tubes along the surface of the beak, the tip of which is sharply hooked. The three front toes are webbed, and the back toe is very small or altogether absent. Petrels have long wings and are capable of strong and sustained flight. They are swimmers rather than divers. They are carnivorous, feeding on carrion, cuttlefish, and crustaceans, and any available refuse. Some petrels, especially the Fulmars, look much like gulls, having the typical gull colouring of grey and white. They are, however, quite different structurally, and differ also in being comparatively silent.

2. ALBATROSS. This is the largest member of the order, forming a separate family, and distinguished by the fact that the nostril tubes lie along the sides instead of on the top of the beak. Albatrosses inhabit the southern seas, spending the greater part of their lives in the air. They have extremely long, narrow wings, with a wing-span of 10 or more feet—an enormous stretch for a bird weighing only some 17 lb. The Wandering Albatross is the largest of ocean birds, having a wing-span of nearly 12 feet. The plumage is yellowish-white, with blackish bars on the wings. The young birds are brownish, with white faces. The smaller Sooty Albatross has a dark ashy-grey plumage. Albatrosses will follow ships for hundreds of miles as scavengers, a few strokes of their enormous wings carrying them great distances. They take every advantage of the wind, gliding, soaring, and making small quick movements with their wings. They only come to land at the breeding season, when they nest in colonies on lonely Pacific islands. They build a neat, conical nest of turf and clay, and lay one round white egg with a few reddish spots, as large as a swan's egg. In the Island of Laysan, the collecting of Albatrosses's eggs for the sake of their oil is an important industry.

3. STORMY PETREL. These are the smallest of the web-footed birds. No larger than skylarks, they are dingy blackish birds, with a white patch over the tail. Sailors often call them 'Mother Carey's chickens', and believe them to foretell stormy weather. When hunting for food on the surface of the water they have a habit of gliding

GIANT FULMAR, WITH CHICK, FROM SOUTH GEORGIA
C. A. Gibson-Hill

over the waves with feet dangling, looking as though they were walking on the water—hence the name 'Petrel' (or little St. Peter). Stormy Petrels breed in the islands off British coasts. They lay their single egg in holes in walls, or in burrows, the nesting bird entering or leaving the nest only after dark. The egg takes 5 weeks to incubate, and the nestling is fed by its parents for another two months, until it is extremely fat. When fully feathered, it is abandoned, and after a week or so of starvation, it finally leaves its burrow, and flies out to sea to look for a living.

4. FULMAR. This white and grey bird is much larger, being about 19 inches in length. It is a superb flier, sweeping in huge arcs and, like other petrels, gliding for long distances with its wings held stiff and straight. It is very common round Pacific and North Atlantic coasts, and often follows ships for food. Its name means 'foul gull', and it is so called because, like most petrels, it has a habit of squirting stinking oil from its mouth at any intruder to its nesting ledge. The people of the St. Kilda Islands, where the Fulmar nests in great numbers, used to catch the birds for the sake of this oil, which they used for lamps. They also ate its flesh.

5. SHEARWATER. The commonest member of this species in European waters is the Manx Shearwater, a bird about the size of a pigeon, dingy black above and white below. It is so called because of its habit of shearing the wave-tops with rapid gliding flight, tilting first to one side and then to the other. Like the Stormy Petrel, Shearwaters nest in colonies of burrows on lonely islands, and visit the nests only after dark. Then, the cries of thousands of birds, all calling at a slightly different pitch and rhythm, make a most weird din. The birds probably recognize their mates in the dark by the cry. The Great Shearwater from Tristan da Cunha, and the Sooty Shearwater from near New Zealand, often visit European seas in the summer.

6. MUTTON BIRD. This is the Australian and New Zealand name for the Short-tailed or Sooty Petrel, which inhabits the seas round those countries, nesting in vast colonies on the islands. They nest in burrows, sometimes as much as 6 or 7 feet long, and so numerous that the ground is completely honeycombed with them. Many of the nesting islands belong by tradition to the MAORIS (q.v. Vol. I), who run a flourishing trade both in the eggs and young birds for food. The young birds, just before they leave the nest,

are extremely fat, and have a flesh of much the same texture as mutton, with a flavour rather like that of a kipper. The birds are not seen during the day-time, but after dark the air is filled with their weird cries.

PHALANGER, *see* MARSUPIALS (picture on p. 298).

PHEASANT. The order of Game-birds contains a great many species, most of which belong to the Old World. It includes the GROUSE, PARTRIDGES, GUINEA-FOWL, PEACOCKS, and TURKEYS (qq.v.), as well as the Pheasants. Most species have naked legs and feet, and carry one or more pairs of spurs on their legs.

Pheasants belong essentially to southern Asia, especially to the Himalayas, Tibet, and the mountains of north Burma, north-west China, and Manchuria. The Common Pheasant is a native of central Asia and south-eastern Europe, and was probably first introduced to Britain by the Romans. It has been a common resident ever since. It is a magnificent bird, about 3 feet long, with brilliant metallic plumage and a long tapering tail. A cock-pheasant in full spring plumage, flying out of a cover in the spring sunshine, is a sight of startling brilliance. As with most game-birds, the female is smaller and carries much more sober plumage. Pheasants roost in trees, but otherwise are ground birds, feeding on roots, grain, berries, and insects. In the spring, the cocks fight fiercely for their mates. They fluff out their feathers and fly at each other, leaping in the air and striking with foot and beak. The hen lays about ten to fourteen eggs in a hollow on the ground. The chicks, which are covered with down, run out after the hen as soon as they are hatched.

Some of the Pheasants of south-eastern Asia are brilliantly coloured birds, living at very high altitudes in the mountains, and coming down to the lower forests in great numbers in the winter. The green, crimson, and grey Blood Pheasants are to be seen in packs of seventy to a hundred birds in the forests during December. Among the most gorgeous is the Monal Pheasant, which has a long tail of chestnut-red, and long, green crest-feathers above a head and body of metallic green, blue, and purple. In the mountains of eastern Tibet and in western and southern China are found the Golden Pheasants, with scarlet and orange-yellow bodies and crests, and chestnut-brown tails twice as long as their bodies.

The Amherst's Pheasant of the same regions has a dark bronze-green body, a blood-red crest, a mantle over neck and shoulders of white and blue, and an enormously long white tail, barred with black and tipped with scarlet.

The Jungle-fowl, a close relative of the Pheasant, which is common in well-watered jungle country in parts of India, Ceylon, Malaya, and the East Indies, is the only pheasant-like bird to produce a comb, a high fleshy protuberance, running from the base of the beak along the top of the head. The Red Jungle-fowl is the species from which domestic poultry have been derived (*see* POULTRY, Vol. VI), and itself resembles the Black-red Bantam.

See also Vol. IX: GAME SHOOTING.

PHOTOSYNTHESIS. By derivation, this means a 'building up by means of light'. In photosynthesis, the carbon dioxide and water absorbed by plants are converted into organic food substances by the green colouring matter (chlorophyll), with the help of radiant energy from the sun. If green plants ceased to photosynthesize, all living things—plant, animal, and man—would die, and so life on earth would cease. Life cannot continue without food; and all other feeding depends upon the green plant's ability to build up foodstuffs. Even flesh-eating animals, like lions, are dependent upon photosynthesis, since the antelopes and zebras on which they prey are grass-eaters. When human beings eat mutton and beef, they are eating grass—several stages removed.

Photosynthesis is dependent upon chlorophyll; but, in spite of a great deal of experiment in the last forty years, botanists are still far from clear about the exact nature of chlorophyll. In some way, chlorophyll acts as a hastener in bringing about the combination of carbon dioxide (from the air) and water (in the leaf) to form complex food substances, such as sugar and starch, without itself being materially altered in the process. If chemists were able fully to understand the chemical composition of chlorophyll, so that they could produce sugars and starches artificially, life might then be possible without photosynthesis; but although they have gained a great deal of knowledge about it, they cannot make chlorophyll or tell how it works. They have found, for example, that chlorophyll in solution separates into two kinds. In one, there are two pigments which they call A and B; the other contains two pigments which occur in other parts of the plants than green leaves. One (carotin) causes the red colour in carrots, and the other (xanthophyll) gives many petals their colour. But how A and B chlorophylls combine in photosynthesis is still unknown.

The foodstuffs formed during photosynthesis are really a means of storing the sun's energy. Later on, the foodstuffs are reconverted into energy, and used in the living processes of plants (*see* RESPIRATION OF PLANTS), or by animals, including human beings, directly or indirectly in the same way. In all animals, the joint processes of digestion and respiration combine to liberate energy required for heat and work from its locked-up state in foodstuffs. (*See* RESPIRATION OF ANIMALS.)

The stages in the process of photosynthesis are quite easy to work out by experiment. Water, containing mineral salts, is absorbed by the roots, and, by the processes of TRANSPIRATION and ROOT PRESSURE (qq.v.), is carried up the stalk or trunk to the green leaves—even to the top of the tallest tree. There the water and dissolved salts pass into the leaf-cells, where chlorophyll is contained in special structures known as 'chloroplasts'. Here it comes into contact with the carbon dioxide drawn in from the atmosphere, which also is dissolved in the water in the leaf. When this watery mixture is acted upon by sunlight, complex organic foodstuffs, called carbohydrates, are formed, oxygen being given off as a waste product. These carbohydrates are the basis of all food materials.

Although the air contains only three parts of carbon dioxide in 10,000, it is possible to prove by experiment that the carbon dioxide does, in fact, reach the leaf from the atmosphere. The gas gets into the leaf through thousands of tiny pores or 'stomata', which occur on both sides of the leaf, but are usually more numerous on the lower. They can be seen with a good pocket-lens. The entrance to each stoma is controlled by two guard cells, which, by alternate swelling and shrinking, can open and close the aperture, and so prevent the entry or escape of carbon dioxide or water vapour. Generally speaking, they open in the light and close in the dark; but they are affected also by changes of temperature, of humidity, or of concentrations of carbon dioxide in the atmosphere.

Sugars, among the simplest of organic food materials, are the first substances to be built up

Outer skin of a foliage leaf

TRANSVERSE SECTION OF A FOLIAGE LEAF

happens in flowering plants. If fats and proteins were built up in green leaves, they would certainly be converted into a soluble form, so that they could be transferred to those parts of the plants where they were most needed.

Photosynthesis can only take place, therefore, if there is light, chlorophyll, carbon dioxide, and water with its mineral salts. If a plant is grown entirely in the dark, chlorophyll will not develop, the plant will be a pale whitish colour, photosynthesis will not take place, and the plant will be spindly and weak, and finally cease to grow. Plants with variegated leaves, like the ivy or geranium, have chlorophyll only in the green streaks, and, in consequence, photosynthesis takes place in these only: the pale streaks, if tested, would be found to be without starch. In the case of coloured plants, like the Copper Beech or Red Cabbage, the green chlorophyll is in the leaves, although its presence is disguised by the red pigment.

The rate of photosynthesis is governed a good deal by temperature: in summer it is speeded up; in the winter, when plant activity is much less, it is greatly slowed down. In plants that die down altogether in the winter, it stops completely. Some experiments have been made by horticulturists to increase the yield of crops in green-house culture by the artificial control of the factors controlling photosynthesis.

See also NUTRITION OF PLANTS.

PIDDOCK. This mollusc is chiefly interesting for the ravages it makes on rocks and buildings on the sea-shore. Wherever limestone, sandstone, or other relatively soft rocks occur between tide-marks, their surfaces are likely to be pitted by its excavations. The burrow made by the Rugose Stone-borer, a mollusc of the same type, is shallow, never exceeding 6 inches in depth, while those made by the Piddock, particularly in the softer rocks, are much larger and deeper, for it is the larger animal. The breaking up and dispersal of large blocks of weathered stone which have fallen from the cliffs on to the shore is often largely effected by the activity of these molluscs.

A full-grown Piddock often measures 5 or 6 inches in length, and the surface of each valve of its creamy-white shell is covered with row upon row of short, sharp-pointed spines, which are thickened around the broad base. The shell, though a good deal harder than the rock

by the active green leaf. They are, however, immediately converted into the more complicated food-substance, starch; and so their presence is difficult to detect. The presence of starch, however, is easy to demonstrate, since it turns blue-black when brought into contact with iodine. If the chlorophyll is first removed from a green leaf by using a solution of acetone, the addition of iodine will show very clearly whether starch is present or not in the leaf—in other words, whether or not photosynthesis has taken place. The starch built up in the leaves is insoluble, and is therefore changed into soluble sugars before, for instance, it is carried down to the tuber of a potato or artichoke. There it is reconverted into starch and stored. The tuber, then, has the power of building up starch from sugar—but not, like the leaf, from the raw materials of water and air. It is known that fats and proteins also are built up in the plant; but how and where this occurs is not certain. It is recognized that in some lower plants, such as certain ALGAE (q.v.), fat is built up in photosynthesis; but it is not known whether this

PIDDOCK AND THE ROCK IN WHICH THE ANIMAL IS BORING
F. Martin Duncan, F.R.M.S., F.Z.S.

attacked, does in time show signs of wear, the rows of rasping spines becoming blunted in old specimens. The Piddock has a very strong foot, with which it adheres firmly to the bottom of the burrow it is excavating. While carrying out tunnelling operations, it adopts a rocking, twisting motion, ejecting the rock debris by the help of jets of water from its outbreathing siphon. Once the burrow has been driven to a sufficient depth to hide it completely from view, the Piddock ceases operations, confining itself in the future to such occasional deepening of the burrow as may be sufficient to meet increase in growth. Like many other marine animals, the Piddock is luminescent at night, particularly during the summer months, when its long respiratory siphons glow brightly.

The Rugose Stoneborer is much smaller, and the valves of its stout, coarsely wrinkled shell are generally oval in shape, whitish in colour, and rather opaque, the complete shell rarely exceeding 1 inch in length by about ½ inch in breadth. The front part of the body and the siphons are often bright orange-red in colour, on account of which fishermen, who use them for bait, call them 'Red-noses'.

See also MOLLUSCS.

PIG, *see* SWINE.

PIGEON. This group, of which there are a great many species, including the Doves and the now-extinct flightless Dodo and Solitaire, are found all over the world, often in great numbers. They have rather large heads and stout, compact bodies; and most species are strong fliers. They have large crops, into which they can cram an enormous amount of food—a Wood Pigeon's crop can hold as many as sixty acorns, and the bird can consume at one time a quantity of food amounting to more than its own weight. Their principal food is grain and seeds, berries, acorns, beechmast, peas, beans, clover, and turnip-tops—it is not surprising that they are unpopular with the farmer (*see* ANIMAL PESTS, Vol. VI). After an elaborate courtship, including much bowing and hopping, cooing, and flying in circles, pigeons mate for life. Both sexes take part in building the nest, generally a loosely constructed platform of twigs, and in incubating the two pure-white eggs. The young are fed on 'pigeon-milk', which they get from the parent's bill, pumped up from the crop. Later, this is mixed with half-digested food.

WOOD PIGEON AND NESTLINGS
Eric J. Hosking, F.R.P.S.

TURTLE DOVE BROODING
G. K. Yeates, F.R.P.S.

In Indonesia and Australia are the Crested and Bronze-winged Doves, with golden-green wings and black crests. In New Guinea are the largest of the pigeons, the Crowned Pigeons, splendid birds with erect, fan-shaped crests. The Tooth-billed Pigeon of Samoa forms a separate family from the rest of the pigeons, being in some ways more like the extinct Dodo. It has a remarkably strong, hooked beak. These rare birds used to live chiefly on the ground, where they fell victim to wild cats and other marauders; but they now appear to have taken to an arboreal life, and their numbers are again on the increase.

The Dodo of Mauritius and Réunion, and the Solitaire of Rodriguez Island, were very large birds, as big as swans, with large, hooked beaks and short, stout legs, the Solitaire having the smaller body, but longer legs and neck. They were still fairly numerous at the beginning of the 17th century; but the Dodo was extinct by the end of the century, and the Solitaire soon afterwards.

See also Vol. IV: Pigeon Post.
See also Vol. IX: Pigeon Racing.

Generally two or even three broods are reared each season.

Wood Pigeons (or Ring Doves) are very common in most wooded districts in Europe, western Asia, and north-west Africa, their numbers having increased since the larger birds of prey, their enemies, have become more scarce. They are, however, often reduced by a strange epidemic, a kind of diphtheria, which occurs in certain years in certain regions. In autumn and winter, pigeon-shooting accounts for a number of birds —though their erratic and swift flight makes them not easy to hit (*see* GAME SHOOTING: Vol. IX).

Doves are rather smaller than pigeons, but otherwise have much the same habits. Stock Doves are to be found over most of the British Isles; they nest in holes in trees or rocks, or in deserted rabbit-burrows or squirrels' nests. Rock Doves are the species from which most of the domestic breeds, such as Pouters, Tumblers, and Fan-tails, have been bred. In the wild state they reside chiefly on cliff coasts, nesting on rock ledges or in caves. The Turtle Dove, often referred to in poetry as the 'turtle', is the smallest of the group, and more slenderly built. It is a summer visitor to south-east England, preferring open woodland and plantations, and nesting in trees.

The Passenger Pigeons of central and North America, birds with much longer tails than the British species, were found in large numbers, but are now extinct. Many of the pigeons and doves in tropical regions are brilliantly coloured.

PIGMY MOTHS. These tiny, very primitive moths, including the smallest of all moths, range in size from 3 to 10 mm. Their family, Stigmellidae, is rather isolated from other moths, though perhaps most nearly related to the GOLD or LONGHORN MOTHS (qq.v.). They have a world-wide distribution, eighty species occurring in Britain. The narrow, pointed fore-wings are covered with fixed hairs and rather large scales, and have a peculiar arrangement of veins. They are usually dark and metallic, the fore-wings often tinged with purple, and sometimes with a silvery or golden band or pale spots. The hind-wings are generally grey. They fly erratically in sunshine, and hide on cold days, some species occasionally being found in great numbers in cracks on tree-trunks. The eggs are generally laid on leaves or leaf-stalks, the British species largely favouring birch, oak, hawthorn, apple, and willows, though others are attached to rose, bramble, or agrimony. The young larva eats

4852·2

M

its way out of the egg-shell directly into the leaf, and then constructs a characteristic mine near the upper surface, which may be straight, curved, twisted, wide, or narrow, or, in some types, a blotch. In autumn the part of a leaf surrounding a mine retains its green colour long after the rest has changed, even when it has fallen to the ground. The little flattened larva, as is often the case in leaf miners, has only rudimentary legs, or in some species none at all. The larva leaves the mine to pupate in a tough cocoon among litter or in the soil.

PIKE. Of all fishes, the Pike has the greatest reputation for greed and destructiveness, and has been called the 'river wolf'. It is rare to find more than one Pike in any stretch of water, for there would not be enough food to supply more —and, in any case, the larger one soon devours the smaller ones. There are records of Pike attacking and swallowing fishes as large as themselves. A good account describes how a small specimen seized a Salmon about its own size, and held on in a fierce tussle for two hours, at the end of which the Salmon was so exhausted that the Pike began to swallow it head-foremost. It was three days before the meal was finished, and then the Pike, looking very swollen, lay still for a week, almost unable to move.

The common Pike, which is found throughout Europe and in North America, reaches a length of about 5 feet and a weight of over 50 lb. There is an old legend in Germany about a specimen that was supposed to have been 19 feet long, weighed 550 lb., and to have been hundreds of years old. Imaginative paintings of this monster exist, and what was supposed to be its skeleton is preserved in Mannheim Cathedral; but a German scientist, who examined the bones, found that there were far too many vertebrae in the backbone for any one fish—so the skeleton had apparently been enlarged to fit the legend!

Pike spawn in the early months of the year, laying about half a million tiny eggs. These lie on the bed of the stream, where most of them are eaten by other fishes long before they can hatch out. Young Pike are usually called 'pickerel' in England. A fine account of the life of a Pike is to be found in a Scandinavian book (published in English) called *Grim*.

In America there is a larger species called the Muskallunge, which is greatly sought after by anglers, and has been compared to the Salmon as a sporting fish. It inhabits the Great Lakes region, and may weigh as much as 80 lb. A number of smaller kinds, known as Pickerel, are also found in the United States. All the Pike make very good eating.

See also Vol. IX, Angling, Freshwater.

PILCHARD, *see* Herring.

PILOT-FISH, *see* Sea Perch.

PINES, *see* Conifers.

PIPIT, *see* Wagtail and Pipit.

PITCHER-PLANTS, *see* Insectivorous Plants, Section 6.

PLAICE, *see* Flat-fishes.

PLANT. From a casual glance at the vegetation of a garden or meadow, it is clear that plants vary a great deal in size and form. Most people have little idea of the number of plant forms which do exist, and use the word 'plant' only for flowers, herbs, and, sometimes, for shrubs. Yet trees are plants, many of them flowering

THE VORACIOUS PIKE PURSUING ITS PREY
A. Fraser-Brunner

plants; and ferns, mosses, moulds, yeasts, and even the green scum which sometimes grows in water-butts, are all plants.

Perhaps the best way of grouping plants is into those which bear seeds and those which do not. The seed-bearing plants include CONIFERS (that is, cone-bearing trees like the Pine, Fir, and Larch) and FLOWERING PLANTS (qq.v.). Plants which do not bear seeds are FERNS, MOSSES, and LIVERWORTS, FUNGI, and ALGAE (qq.v.). (Algae are very simple plants: they include seaweeds and the green threads which grow in ponds.) The non-seed-bearing plants are much simpler in form than the seed-bearing plants. With this type of plant, new plants will often spring up from bits of the old ones which have become detached or broken off. The usual way in which non-seed-bearing plants propagate, however, is by the production of spores— delicate, one-celled structures which, unless they quickly find conditions favourable for germination, die. On the other hand, the SEEDS (q.v.) produced by the seed-bearing plants are tougher, many-celled structures, and often contain large reserves of food on which the young seedling can draw for its first supplies before the plant has become capable of making its own food. Plants which bear seeds have, therefore, a better chance of survival in the struggle for existence. All the most complicated plants, such as Pines, Spruces, Larches, Buttercups, Dandelions, Grasses, Elms, Limes, and Oaks, are seed-bearing.

See also NUTRITION IN PLANTS; GROWTH OF PLANTS; REPRODUCTION OF PLANTS; RESPIRATION IN PLANTS.

PLANT ASSOCIATION, *see* ECOLOGY OF PLANTS.

PLANT DEFENCES. 1. When we think of grazing herds, fruit-eating and seed-eating birds, leaf-eating insects, root-eating grubs, and all the other pests which prey upon plants, the question naturally arises: how do plants hold their own? Animals, like the field vole and the locust, often turn a green and pleasant land into a frowning desert. Why does this not happen more often? How is it that animals do not devour all the plants, and so sign their own death-warrant?

The main answer is that most plants can multiply so abundantly that they can stand a good deal of thinning out. Moreover, when herbivorous animals have eaten up the bulk of available plants, their numbers are automatically reduced by starvation. Also, few animals eat the whole plant and, even when they eat the fruit, this often results in scattering the seeds more widely (*see* SEEDS 2(*b*) Animal Dispersal). Yet, while the survival of plants depends mainly upon their abundant multiplication and on their almost inexhaustible food-supplies of air and soil-water, they are not without their defences also. Venus's Fly-trap, the Sundew, and other INSECTIVOROUS PLANTS (q.v.), are actually on the offensive in their attempts to capture insects. Most plants, however, rely on defensive mechanisms for protection.

2. PRICKLES, SPIKES, AND THORNS. A Rose-bush is covered with triangular-shaped prickles, which break off neatly when pressed sideways, showing that they are very superficial growths from the outer skin of the plant. In the Barberry, a whole leaf becomes hardened to form a spine; in the Holly, only parts of the leaf form spines; while in some Acacias, the spine is formed from a 'stipule', the name given to a small structure occurring at the base of a leaf-stalk. Plants such as the Hawthorn have hard, pointed thorns, which are formed from reduced and toughened shoots. That they are modified shoots is clear, because some thorns bear leaves—and only shoots can bear leaves. Gorse has both spines and thorns.

Spines, thorns, and prickles may have other and more primary purposes than defence. For instance, many sharp-spined plants, such as CACTUSES (q.v.), which grow in dry places, have soft leaves and shoot-tissues reduced in size in order to avoid excessive loss of water (*see* TRANSPIRATION). It has been found that young spiny and thorny plants, such as Gorse and Holly, if planted in a damp atmosphere and in the shade, produce fewer spines or thorns than those planted on dry soil, where there is much sun and wind. But it is probable that these defences do, to some extent, prevent the plant from being devoured by animals; and the position they occupy on the plant sometimes seems to indicate a defensive purpose. The spines on the under surface of the huge leaves of the Giant Water Lily, for example, apparently ward off the attacks of aquatic animals; and the thorns guarding the entrance to pitcher plants, such as Nepenthes (*see* INSECTIVOROUS PLANTS, Section 6), may baulk some insectivorous birds. Donkeys, however, enjoy thistles, and a goat will nibble off leaf after leaf from a thorny plant without once scratching its nose.

3. PROTECTIVE CHEMICAL SUBSTANCES. The Cuckoo-pint or, as it is sometimes called, Jack-in-the-pulpit—a common plant of shady places—has a different kind of defence. If a piece of one of the glossy, green leaves is broken off and nibbled, it causes a painful irritation on the lips and tongue. This is due to crystals of oxalate of lime, a waste product of the food-manufacturing process of plants, which serve to protect the plant from the attacks of snails and slugs. Indeed, if the crystals are washed away with hydrochloric acid, and the leaves then well washed, snails find them very attractive to eat. There are many other plants in which these crystals occur, notably the Wood-sorrel and the Docks. Other protective chemical substances found in plants are formic acid, tannins, oils such as eucalyptus and turpentine, and strong alkaloid poisons such as those of the Hemlock and Deadly Nightshade.

4. PROTECTIVE STRUCTURE. Some plants develop exceptional hardness of the leaves and shoots for the sake of protection: the hard envelopes of some seeds, for instance, save them from injury, since they pass right through the bodies of birds and animals which have eaten the fruits, and are then excreted.

In warm countries, it is often the custom to put the feet of table-legs into tiny jars of paraffin in order to trap white ants which come out of the floor and try to tunnel in the wood. In the same way, the 'cisterns' of the Teasel, formed where the leaf-bases embrace the stem, serve as moats to prevent the ascent of unwelcome insect visitors, and are often found to have trapped a number of insects. Some wild plants have defences on the same principle as the grease-bands placed around fruit-trees to prevent the ascent of injurious grubs. The Campion, for instance, has sticky rings on its stem which act

'CISTERN' OF TEASEL

as defensive moats. Ants, however, are sometimes known to make bridges over such moats, even using the bodies of their companions to make a living (but very soon a dead) ant-bridge. The Sensitive Plant (*see* MOVEMENT OF PLANTS, Section 2) also uses what appears to be a kind of plant protection. Although this plant grows freely in tropical countries, grazing animals will not eat it, presumably because, when they touch it, it collapses—an unexpected form of behaviour, which scares off the animals.

5. STING AND POISON. One of the best-known and most effective means of plant protection is the sting. On the Common Stinging-nettle, which grows densely in waste places along road-sides and in fields, the heart-shaped leaves and the younger parts of the ridged stems are covered with stinging-hairs. These hairs are single, superficial cells, which have become elongated and tapering, and possess a bulbous base. The tip contains silica, and is so brittle that, when touched, it breaks off, the sharp point entering the skin. The pressure set up causes the poisonous liquid in the bulbous part to be ejected into the puncture. The poison which causes the irritation is not, as was once thought, formic

STINGING HAIR OF NETTLE

acid, but is a protein of undetermined composition. If the leaf is firmly grasped, the nettle cannot sting, because the tips of the hairs break off, and the rest of the long hairs are bent over and crushed before they are able to make a puncture. Unlike Stinging-nettles, Dead-nettles have no stinging-hairs. It may possibly be more than coincidence that the Dead-nettles, which so much resemble the Stinging-nettles, are nearly always found growing near them. Their likeness to Stinging-nettles, and the fact that they grow in the same places, suggest that, by deception alone, the Dead-nettles may have acquired an effective means of defence.

The scientific counterpart to the Upas Tree of Java, which, according to the fable, is said to have had a fatal influence on people who came within its spell, is the Poison Vine or Ivy of sub-tropical regions. This plant, which looks like the Virginia Creeper, often has a harmful effect on susceptible people. It is not even necessary that they should touch the plant; for the poison, which is found in a milky juice, seems to be carried through the air on floating particles. A certain Primula, originally from China, called *Obconica*, also carries in the hairs of its leaves a poison, to which some people are so susceptible that they can be made seriously ill by touching the plant.

It is well to remember, however, that no matter how well a plant may be protected, some animal will always get the better of it. And those devices which we suppose to be defensive may have been produced for quite different reasons, their use in defence being only secondary.

PLATYPUS. The Duck-bill (or Duck-billed Platypus) is a very curious animal. It lays eggs, like a bird or reptile; yet it is a mammal, because the female suckles its young from milk secreted in its body. The only other mammal which lays eggs is the ECHIDNA (q.v.) or Porcupine Ant-eater; and these two together constitute the order Monotremata. The Platypus is found only in Australia and Tasmania. It is the most primitive of all mammals, its brain being of relatively low, simple type. Its jaws, which are the shape of a duck's bill, are also unique amongst mammals.

It frequents fresh waters in southern and eastern Australia and Tasmania; but being a shy animal, it is not very often seen. Its body is oval-shaped, covered with dark brown, mole-like fur, and from the tip of its beak to the tip of its short, flattened tail measures from 18 to 20 inches. It has short legs, and its feet, each

with five toes and strong nails, are webbed for swimming. The web on its forefeet stretches out beyond the tips of its nails, and as this would be an inconvenience when walking or burrowing, it folds back the web over its paws when out of the water. Even so, it shuffles along very awkwardly on land. The male has a poisonous spur on its heel, which it probably uses in fighting. The Platypus eats small aquatic animals, insects, crustaceans, and worms, for which it probes with its beak in the mud and sand. It stores this food in its cheek pouches, and eats it at leisure. The favourite haunts of the Platypus are where streams open out into wide, still pools. It burrows in the banks, making tunnels sometimes as much as 50 feet long, ending in a chamber lined with grass. Here, the mother lays two eggs at a time—each being about $\frac{3}{4}$ inch long and having a strong, white, flexible shell. The young are blind and naked when first hatched. Their beaks are short, with smooth, fleshy edges forming a nearly circular mouth for receiving milk from their mother. She has no teats, but ejects her secreted milk through a number of small pores into a small, cup-like hollow in her abdomen, from which the young lick the milk, instead of sucking it in the normal way.

See also MAMMALS.

PLOVER, *see* WADING BIRDS, Section 5.

PLUME MOTHS. These small moths, belonging to the family Alucitidae, are widely distributed over the world. Most species have several V-shaped notches in the outer margins of their wings, which extend, more or less deeply, between the long veins, and divide the wings into several long-fringed, plume-like lobes. The largest British species, the White Plume, with a wing span of about an inch, is found commonly in gardens and waste places, where its hairy caterpillar feeds on the bindweed. The majority are greyish, yellowish, or brown, their long, slender legs and long, narrow, pointed wings somewhat resembling those of CRANE-FLIES (q.v.). They fly chiefly at dusk, and are

THE AUSTRALIAN DUCK-BILLED PLATYPUS
Australian News & Information Bureau

relatively more frequent in mountain districts, occurring at altitudes of 15,000 feet. Their flight is so feeble that it seems likely that they are distributed largely by wind, for which their extreme lightness makes them well suited. The spiny pupae are attached by tail hooks, like those of butterflies, and are sometimes enclosed in cocoons. About 600 species are known, thirty-five occurring in Britain.

The caterpillars of the local Marsh Plume, the smallest British species, feed upon the Sundew, an INSECTIVOROUS PLANT (q.v.) long thought to be itself immune from insect attacks. The Marsh Plume lays its bright yellow eggs on the stalks of the marginal leaf-glands among other places. The young larva of the summer brood feeds upon these glands and their sticky secretion, clearing a space in the centre of the leaf, in which it rests, well camouflaged by its own reddish excrement, which is about the same colour as the reddish glands of the leaf. Larvae of the autumn brood make their way to the central buds, where they construct silken shelters in which to hibernate. The fully grown, reddish-brown and green caterpillar, nearly $\frac{1}{3}$ inch long, has long, flattened hairs which enhance its general resemblance to the Sundew leaf. It supports itself on a stalk or on the under-surface of the leaf, which it devours from the edge; and it also eats the flower-buds. The pupa is suspended from a stem, and the moth emerges in June and August.

The so-called Twenty-plume Moth, the only British representative of the small Oriental and African family Orneodidae, and not closely related to the other Plumes, has each yellowish-grey wing deeply divided into six lobes. Its yellowish caterpillar feeds among the flower-buds, and tunnels in the shoots of honeysuckle.

POISON-FISHES. Among the most unusual of all fishes are the members of a group called Plectognathi (which means plaited-jaws), found in tropical waters. Nearly all of them have poisonous flesh, and none of them has any ribs; but otherwise they vary a lot in their queer shapes and colours. For instance, there are the Trigger-fishes, which get their name from a little movable spine on the abdomen (all that is left of the pelvic fins), like the trigger of a pistol. The first dorsal or back fin consists of three spines; and when these are raised, the first big one is automatically locked upright, and cannot be lowered until the second is depressed. Many Trigger-fishes are beautifully coloured, and are commonly found about coral reefs. They have hard, rough scales on the body, a small gill-opening, and strong, chisel-like teeth, with which they can bore through oyster-shells. Some of them are scavengers, and are found around harbours.

More remarkable still are the Trunk-fishes, also called Box or Coffer-fishes, which have the body encased in a hard, firm box of six-sided, bony plates, pierced only by the jaws, eyes, small fins, and feeble tail. There are no spiny dorsal fin, and no pelvic fins. These curious creatures move about by using the dorsal and anal fins as propellors, helped by jet-propulsion through the small gill-openings—though they can use the tail as a stern-oar when in a hurry. Most of the Australian Trunk-fishes are oval in shape, with a ridge on the back, and an assortment of large flat spines at various strategic points; they are often brightly coloured. In the Indian and Pacific Oceans there are others, some with oblong boxes and four or five ridges, others triangular; while in the Atlantic there are four or five other triangular kinds, including the Cow-fish, which has a face with horns, strongly suggestive of a cow.

Puffer-fishes, Globe-fishes, or Blow-fishes are common in most tropical seas, and often in the estuaries of rivers, some kinds being able to live in fresh water. They are generally small, plump fishes, with rather small dorsal and anal fins and no pelvic fins. The teeth are united together to form a solid, parrot-like beak, which is in two pieces in each jaw, joined in the middle. The body is usually provided with small prickles,

WEST INDIAN COW-FISH
A. Fraser-Brunner

THE OCEAN SUN-FISH
A. Fraser-Brunner

which at ordinary times are sunk in pits in the skin. When alarmed, the Puffer-fish gulps water rapidly into a special bag connected with the front part of the stomach, with the result that the body swells up into a ball, and the prickles stand out, making the fish a much less attractive morsel to the would-be attacker. Very similar, but armed with long, sharp spines instead of prickles, are the Porcupine-fishes. When the fish is swimming normally, the spines lie flat on the skin; but when it blows itself up with alarm, they are raised as a very effective protection.

No fishes, perhaps, are more astonishing in appearance than the Ocean Sun-fishes, which look very much like the head of some large fish that has been severed from the body. The picture gives some idea of the appearance of one of them. They are related to the Puffer-fishes, and, like them, they have a parrot-like beak and no pelvic fins. What gives them their strange appearance, however, is that they have lost the tail fin, and the dorsal and anal fins have grown round the end of the body. This causes them to swim with a curious rolling motion. They may be 6 feet long, weighing several hundredweight,

and provide a remarkable sight when basking at the surface of the sea, as they are in the habit of doing in sunny weather. Sun-fishes are caught (never very commonly) in nearly all seas.

POLAR BEAR, *see* BEAR.

POLECAT, *see* WEASEL, Section 3.

POLLINATION, *see* REPRODUCTION OF PLANTS, Section 5, FLOWERS.

POLYP, *see* JELLYFISH.

POND SKATER, *see* BUG.

PORCUPINE. The name comes from the French, *porc-épic*, or spiny pig, a name given to the Porcupines because they make pig-like grunts. They are RODENTS (q.v.), gnawing animals, and are related to the CAVIES, CHINCHILLAS, and AGOUTIS (qq.v.). There are two main groups—those of the Old World, the True Porcupines, and those of the New World, almost all living in trees. All are covered with long, stout spines or quills, and are about 2 feet long, the American species being rather lighter in build than the Old World species. Porcupine flesh is excellent to eat, with a flavour something between pork and veal.

The True Porcupine is found over southern Europe, southern Asia, and most of Africa. It has the whole of its back, sides, and tail covered with a double coat of long, sharp, black and white quills. When frightened or angered, the

TRUE PORCUPINE OF THE OLD WORLD
Harold Bastin

BRAZILIAN TREE PORCUPINE
Paul Popper

SHRIMP

low down on the sea-shore; but a few are found in deeper waters. Practically all of them have remarkable, chameleon-like powers of colour-adjustment, which enable them to harmonize with their immediate surroundings (*see* CAMOUFLAGE). Some species pass through many changes of form before reaching the adult stage, and some of the deep-sea species are brilliantly luminescent.

It is easy to distinguish a Shrimp from a Prawn; for a Shrimp may at once be recognized by the two curious projections, rather like a rabbit's ears in shape, on each side of the head, by the pair of short, forked antennae just in front of the eyes, and by the pair of long, slender antennae near the 'rabbit-ears'. Moreover, the Shrimp's first pair of legs are broad and flattened, and terminate in a little hook-like claw, which can be closed against a short, sharp spine so as to grasp minute objects. The Prawn is quite different in appearance. From the front of its head there projects a single great serrated 'rostrum' or horn, while both pairs of antennae are long and slender, and the first and second

Porcupine erects its quills and rattles them together, at the same time stamping on the ground with its feet. If this is not enough to scare off the aggressor, the Porcupine turns round and rushes backwards at its enemy, inflicting severe injury with the long quills on its hindquarters. In Europe, Porcupines live alone or in pairs; but in India they are found together in large numbers. They hide during the day in burrows, in caves, or in clefts of rock, and feed at night on vegetable foods, mainly roots. The Porcupine's large teeth can gnaw through almost anything—it has even been known in the jungle to gnaw an elephant's tusks. The female gives birth to from two to four young in a nest made of leaves, grass, and root fibres. They have their eyes open when born, and are able to run about at once. At first their spines are soft and flexible, but they very soon harden.

The American Porcupines live almost entirely in trees, and range from the cold forests of Canada to the tropical forests of South America. Most of them have long tails by which they cling to the branches. They have also short spines with barbed tips, which dig into the flesh of an attacking animal and cause a festering wound. The Brazilian Tree Porcupine has a long tail, short fur, with very conspicuous white spines, and fleshy pads on its hind feet, which helps it to grasp boughs of trees. The Canadian Porcupine has a short tail and a thick coat of hair, which completely hides the spines.

PORPOISE, *see* WHALE.

PRAWNS AND SHRIMPS. These Crustaceans live mostly in the rocky and sandy pools

PRAWN

pairs of legs end in delicate little claws shaped like those of the lobster.

Many of the Prawns of tropical seas grow to the size of small lobsters. The little Aesop Prawn of British waters, which lives among the weeds in rock-pools and is hardly more than an inch in length, has gained its name from the hunchback shape caused by the sharp, downward bend of its abdomen (for Aesop of the fables was a hunchback). It is of particular interest, because it has the power to vary the colours of its body to match the hue of the particular seaweed to which it clings: thus on bright or dull green weeds, the prawn will be of that particular green tint, while on a brown or red weed, it will be olive-brown or red. Should the weed to which it is clinging be branched or feathery, the Aesop Prawn will be correspondingly lined with colour. The Aesop Prawn changes to a beautiful transparent blue at night, resuming the colour of the surrounding weeds with the return of daylight. Even the common Shrimp adapts its colour to suit its surroundings, its translucent greyish-brown colour, speckled with darker brown, closely resembling the sand in which it rests half-buried.

Most remarkable in appearance are the Mantis Shrimps, so called because of the resemblance of their great claws to those of the PRAYING MANTIS insect (q.v.). They have long and rather flattened bodies, and their stalked eyes are carried on separate movable segments of the head—a peculiarity not to be found in any other Crustacean. The large claws are not pincer-claws, but are so constructed that the last segment, edged with strong teeth, closes down on the preceding segment like the blade of a clasp-knife, making them most formidable weapons. Most of these Mantis Shrimps live in burrows in the sand or in crevices among the rocks, emerging to seize any small animals which pass within their reach. They pass through a long series of larval stages, in which they differ markedly in appearance from the final adult form (*see* METAMORPHOSIS). They are most common in tropical seas, where some species reach to more than 12 inches in length—veritable giants compared with the British species, occasionally found on the south coast of England, which rarely measure more than 3 inches in length.

See also CRUSTACEA.
See also Vol. VI: SHRIMPING AND PRAWNING.

MANTIS SHRIMP

A PRAYING MANTIS EATING ONE OF ITS FELLOWS (nat. size)
C. A. Gibson-Hill

PRAYING MANTIS. Mantids are widely distributed in tropical and warm countries generally, but are not found in cooler regions. The nearest area to Britain that they inhabit is central France. From the way in which the Mantis sits with its head and the first part of its thorax semi-erect, it has been given such names as Praying Mantis, Praying Insect, Soothsayer, and even Saint Teresa—there is nothing of the saint, however, about the Mantids. They are all carnivorous and cannibalistic, the larger attacking the smaller, and females often eating the males, after pairing. They wait motionless for long periods until their unsuspecting victims come near enough to be caught. Their colouring is so like that of their surroundings that it is almost impossible to detect them. Some Mantids even resemble flowers, and so attract flower-loving insects to their doom. They seize their prey with their fore-legs. These have grooved femurs, into which the tibiae fit, just like the blade of a penknife into the haft, and the edges of the groove have teeth that increase their effectiveness. The eggs are laid in egg-cases, like those of their relatives, the COCKROACHES (q.v.); and it takes about a year for the insect to mature.

PREHISTORIC ANIMALS, *see* EVOLUTION. *See also* Vol. III: PREHISTORIC ANIMALS.

PROMINENT MOTHS. When at rest, these medium-sized, white, greyish, or brownish moths conceal their stout bodies and pale hind-wings beneath their long, narrow fore-wings. The latter slope down on either side, the hind edges meeting along the back and bringing into prominence the middle tuft of marginal scales: it is this prominence which has led to their name. The family Notodontidae, to which they belong, has a world-wide distribution. The British species include thirteen Prominents, the Lobster Moth, three Marbled-browns, the Buff-tip, three Chocolate-tips, three Kitten Moths, and the Puss Moth. The caterpillars, which are found more often than the moths, are naked, except for the hairy Buff-tip and Chocolate-tips. Caterpillars of Prominents usually have one or more humps on their backs.

The Lobster Caterpillar, the most grotesque of all, has four of its front legs greatly lengthened, a double row of pointed humps on the back, and swollen end-segments bearing short processes. The young larvae are easily mistaken for ants, for they hold aloft a pair of their long legs and

PUSS MOTH CATERPILLAR AND MOTH
S. Beaufoy, F.R.P.S.

wave them—much as ants wave their antennae. Older caterpillars, while at rest, hold up their heads and turn their hind-parts back over their bodies to suggest crumpled dead leaves. When disturbed, they bend back their foreparts and rapidly vibrate their long legs, an action which is vaguely reminiscent of the behaviour of a lobster. The caterpillars sometimes (*see* p. 77) protect themselves by spraying formic acid, as do Puss Caterpillars. Lobsters are not common, and are found more frequently in beech-woods on the Chilterns than elsewhere. When full-fed, they spin a silken cocoon between two beech leaves, and pupate inside. The moths, which emerge in May or June, are brown with yellowish-grey markings.

The common Puss Moth, also found in May and June, is white, with dark veins, greyish wavy markings, and fluffy hair, like cat's fur, on its head and body. The female lays her brown eggs on poplars, willows, and sallows. The young caterpillar, which emerges in late May or early June, is black, though, when full-grown in August, it has changed to green, with a broad, purplish saddle-stripe edged with white on its back. This pattern so distracts attention from the caterpillar's real shape, that it is very difficult to recognize in its natural surroundings (*see* PROTECTIVE COLORATION). When disturbed, it assumes a threatening attitude, raising up the front of its body and inflating a fold of red skin bearing two black, eye-like spots, so that the head suggests a terrifying face. At the same time it sprays formic acid from its ventral gland, and bends the hindpart of its body over its back, lashing at the enemy with two flexible red threads, which shoot out from its tail-like hind claspers. The caterpillar pupates within a very well camouflaged cocoon fastened to the bark of its food-tree. This cocoon is as hard as a nut, for the silk is toughened by treatment with the same acid secretion that the caterpillar uses in defence. The adult moth breaks through the cocoon by moistening a thin window in the wall with caustic potash from its mouth. When the silk is softened, the moth breaks it with its head, and emerges.

The Alder, Poplar, and Sallow Kittens, named after the typical food-plants, are about half the size of the Puss Moth, and all have a distinct band across their fore-wings. Their caterpillars resemble those of Puss Moths.

The caterpillars of the Chocolate-tips hide by

day among leaves fastened together with silk. The Small Chocolate-tip may be found commonly during the summer on dwarf sallow in boggy places. The downy caterpillar of the Buff-tip is 2 inches in length when full grown, and yellow with interrupted black stripes. It feeds in groups on trees, stripping bare whole branches, and is frequently found in the autumn crawling on paths beneath lime-trees, seeking a suitable place to pupate in the soil. The moth emerges in June and July, and when resting, folds its silvery buff-tipped wings close to its body, so that it closely resembles a broken lichen-covered stick.

PRONG-BUCK (PRONG-HORN). This animal lives in the temperate regions of North America, where it is known by the name of 'Antelope'. It is not a true ANTELOPE (q.v.), however, because its hollow horns are branched, and because it sheds the sheaths every year, leaving a pair of hair-covered knobs on which the new horns grow. It stands about 3 feet high, and has a chestnut coat with white markings, and a brownish-black face. Usually only the males grow horns, and these increase in size year by year, reaching their full extent (12 to 17 inches) at about the age of 5. Until the middle of the 19th century Prong-bucks were numerous; but they have been hunted so much that now they are rare. They are shy, timid animals, very fast runners, but poor jumpers.

Sometimes, when the female is about to give birth to her young, she makes her way to the middle of a patch of cactus (prickly pear), in the centre of which, so it is said, she clears a space by a series of jumps and by means of her sharp hoofs. Here the young are born, and remain protected for some time from the wolves, which cannot easily penetrate the prickly cactus fence. Eagles, however, often attack the fawns, and the mother shows great courage in protecting them.

PROTECTIVE COLORATION (INSECTS). **1.** Travellers to foreign countries, especially tropical countries, often bring back with them insects which are remarkable either because they attract notice by their conspicuous colours and displays, or for the opposite reason, that they are seldom seen because their colours, form, and behaviour make them extremely like their surroundings, of earth, bark, sticks, or leaves. The result of such coloration is the same in both cases—neither is devoured by insect-eating animals. In the first case, 'warning coloration', the insect is easily recognized by possible enemies as having proved harmful or unpleasant to taste; in the second, 'cryptic coloration', the insect is protected because it is not discovered. A third type of protective coloration, 'mimicry', is achieved when the insect by its colouring deceives the enemy into mistaking it for a different kind, unsuitable for food.

2. WARNING COLORATION. Conspicuous colours are displayed as clearly as possible. The great naturalist, Wallace, explained the significance of this display when Darwin asked him why caterpillars were often so conspicuous. He replied that the body of a caterpillar was a thin-walled tube, containing fluids under pressure. If the skin were punctured by a peck from a bird, the juices would ooze out, and the insect would bleed to death. Even though the bird found it distasteful and did not eat it, the caterpillar would die. The bird might remember the association of the conspicuous colours of the caterpillar with its unpleasant taste, and the next caterpillar of the same kind might be left alone, at any rate so long as better food could be found. So the more conspicuous and easily recognized the insect is, the more likely the enemy is to remember what the bright colours mean. The insects, therefore, display their colours as well as they can. They fly or walk slowly, and sit about in conspicuous places. They make little effort to get away, for if they did so, the enemy, not recognizing them, might pursue and kill them to find out what they were. Such insects can be easily captured, and can put up with a fair amount of rough handling. A brightly coloured tropical grasshopper, for example, when handled, does not lose its hind-legs in the distressing way that an ordinary green grasshopper does.

The commonest warning colours are red and yellow; blue is rarely used, although *Euploea* butterflies often have a lovely blue or purplish sheen. Black and white is common, as is shown by *Amauris* butterflies and large Carabid beetles.

Two quite different kinds of insects, both unpleasing in some way, may have the same warning colours, each reminding the enemy of the other, and both gaining in consequence. Indeed, many insects with the same warning colours, so long as each is relatively nasty, may join in such an association for the benefit of all. A good example of such common warning colours is the simple orange-brown and black colouring of the Lycid beetles, closely allied to the GLOW-WORM (q.v.), which are found in all warm countries. The Lycid coloration is shared by hosts of other beetles, bugs, wasps—and even flies and moths —all of which are themselves objectionable; and all, therefore, benefit by their similar coloration.

Warning colours can be found in most of the higher groups of insects, including many tropical butterflies and moths. Many tropical grasshoppers show red or purple wings when disturbed, and emit bubbles of a bitter yellow froth. The BOMBARDIER BEETLE (q.v.), and others of the family Carabidae, have the power to eject a bitter fluid, capable of burning the skin, which blows off like a puff of smoke. LADY-BIRDS (q.v.) have typical warning colours—red or yellow with black spots—and they, also, give off an unpleasant-smelling juice. Everyone is afraid of touching an insect with black and yellow rings, because of the mental association with wasps.

Warning colours, it must be remembered, are only a safeguard to an insect so long as the enemy can find other, pleasanter food; when food is very short, the display colours are only a danger. So warning coloration is not seen very much in winter, or in the tropical dry season, when insects are few: it is best shown in the teeming life of the tropical jungle (see TROPICAL BUTTERFLIES AND MOTHS).

3. CRYPTIC COLORATION. The word 'cryptic' means secret or hidden. In this case the animal escapes being seen—and in consequence eaten— because its colours resemble its surroundings, and, so long as it keeps motionless, it appears to be part of them. Those creatures with cryptic coloration have, by the process of natural selection, tended to survive and grow more common —for it is safer not to be seen at all than to run the risk of being captured, examined, and partly eaten. All experiments so far show that a highly cryptic animal is good food. Insects, particularly, being generally small and defenceless, have developed cryptic coloration, together with special habits and attitudes which increase their likeness to their surroundings.

This likeness may be general, as in a green grasshopper, or special, when some particular

The long-horned grasshopper of Brazil (*left*) mimics the burrowing wasp (Pompilidae, *Pepsis*) both in colour and behaviour

leaf, stick, seed, or other object is resembled. The famous 'Dead Leaf Butterfly' (*Kallima*) of Asia is not only like a dead leaf in shape and colour when it settles, but it also reproduces the minutest peculiarities of the dead leaf, such as the marks made by tiny fungi, even the fungus growth itself, and the holes and cracks which let light through (see Colour Plate, opp. p. 336). The writer well remembers catching what seemed to be a bit of thistle-down drifting by, only to find it was a small thin bug, with many fine prolongations of its skin. The 'Stick Caterpillars' of the Geometrid moths have projections on their bodies, which are very much like those on the bark of twigs (see LOOPERS). Wallace tells of a stick insect brought to him by the natives of Borneo, who assured him it was covered with moss—and only by very careful examination could he discover that the 'moss' was part of the insect. There are some caterpillars, like those of the rare Essex Emerald Moth, which cut off pieces of their food-plant and attach them to their spines. The grubs of the Tortoise Beetles on thistles wear their discarded skins on their backs, and look like little bits of dead leaf.

Right, A two-winged fly (Asilidae, *Mallophora fascipennis*) mimics a bee (*Euglossa fasciata*) from the same part of British Guiana

A male Swallow-tail (*Papilio dardanus*) from Lagos, West Africa, carries black and yellow colours; but the female, heavy with eggs, mimics the black and white pattern of the distasteful Danaid butterfly (*Amauris niavius*) from the same locality

other hand, some insects which resemble dead leaves have been described as moving gently with a peculiar swaying motion, like that of a wind-stirred leaf.

4. MIMICRY. This term is used for an insect which achieves some degree of safety by resembling another, better-protected insect. This is in principle quite different from the resemblance which occurs when two or more insects make use of the same warning coloration. The mimicking insect is not protected by sting, spines, or unpleasant taste, but deceives its enemy into mistaking it for another insect with these protections, whose warning coloration serves to keep the enemy at a distance. Were the enemy to investigate closer, it would find that the 'mimic', in fact, did not resemble its 'model' in structure, but only in deceptive coloration. This form of protective coloration is found chiefly among insects.

The naturalist Bates studied mimicry very thoroughly among butterflies in South America. He suggested that the resemblance which, of course, is unconscious on the part of the mimic, must have grown up gradually through the working of the law of natural selection. One insect, perhaps, differs slightly from its parents, and by this difference happened to resemble slightly some common, well-defended insect in the locality. An insect-eating animal, looking for the nicest food when choice was plentiful, might leave the doubtful specimen in favour of another which did not suggest an unpleasant taste. The insect, therefore, would survive, and some of its offspring might inherit to a greater degree this variation from the normal. This process, continued through many generations of successful survival, would produce a 'mimetic' resemblance. The mimic now looks different from its relations (although it remains like them in other ways), but so much like another unrelated insect, whose unpleasant qualities are advertised by its warning colours, that the enemy is deceived into avoiding it.

Mimetic resemblance is produced in different ways. The characteristic narrow waist of ants and other stinging insects is often mimicked: the thicker body of the mimic is made to look narrow by a 'painting out' of part of the body by white, so that a narrow dark stalk shows up, and the white part looks like white light in the herbage. Many insects mimic ants, bees, and wasps—among them flies and beetles, such as

In cryptic coloration, as in warning coloration, we find that the insects develop habits and take up positions which have no purpose except to add to the effectiveness of their disguise. The wonderful 'Stick Caterpillars' are able to fix themselves like a twig at an angle with a branch, and to stay there during long resting periods. A moth settles on the bark of a tree in such a way that the main dark lines of the pattern on its wings fit in with the lines on the bark. It would be of little use for a caterpillar which resembles a bird-dropping to move about restlessly—and, in fact, such caterpillars are sluggish. On the our Wasp-beetle. Beetles mimic other beetles, and some Cockroaches mimic Lady-birds. Large caterpillars of Hawk-moths wonderfully resemble small snakes, having false eyes on the swollen front part of their bodies to mimic the snake's head.

As in the case of warning and cryptic coloration, the mimicking insect develops habits which help in the deception. This is clearly shown by certain spiders which mimic ants. A spider is very different in structure from an ant. It has, for instance, four pairs of legs, but no antennae; whereas the ant has only three pairs of legs. Now an ant-like spider, when active, does not use its front pair of legs for walking, but waves them in the air in front, so that they look like the always-moving antennae of the ant. Many spiders, such as the Zebra spider, catch their prey by jumping on it. Now, if a mimetic spider jumped, the deception would be found out, for ants do not jump. Therefore ant-like spiders suppress the jumping habit, except as a last resort. The writer, in Africa, seeing some ants on a branch, put some in a box; but to his astonishment, one leapt out—and proved to be a mimetic spider. The grasshopper shown in the picture on page 332, which is mimicking a wasp, does not fold its wings along its body when on the ground, as grasshoppers usually do, but keeps them spread out, as a wasp would carry them.

For successful mimicry, the mimic must occur with a model which is more common than itself: if an edible mimic were as common as the distasteful model, the enemy might find it worth while to catch and examine every one; but if only one out of a hundred were edible, the enemy would not investigate. Therefore, true mimics wearing false warning colours are generally among the rarer insects only, their models being among the more common.

Mimicry has been most thoroughly studied in butterflies and moths; but it occurs in many of the main groups of insects, and all over the warm parts of the world.

See also INSECTS; BUTTERFLIES; MOTHS; CATERPILLARS.

PROTOCOCCUS, *see* ALGAE.

PROTOZOA—or 'first animals' (from the Greek words *protos*, first or original, *zoon*, animal). This is the name of a group or phylum of animals consisting of several thousand different species, in all of which the body consists of a single cell. They are all similar in structure to AMOEBA (q.v.), and the differences in them are best explained by describing the four classes into which they are divided. Like Amoeba, they are all found in moist or wet places, in fresh water or in the sea, and some live in the bodies of larger animals.

The first class is the Rhizopoda, or root-footed animals, with a body consisting of the usual living cell, with its central nucleus. When the animal moves, parts of its body flow out into finger-shaped, thread-like, or root-shaped 'pseudopodia', or false feet. Many of the Rhizopoda have, like Amoeba, completely naked bodies; but some make a small house of minute sand-grains or other materials. Some of them, such as *Entamoeba*, live in the bodies of other animals—one species of this genus living in the human intestine is responsible for the disease known as dysentery.

One order of the Rhizopoda, the Radiolaria, take up silica from the sea-water and lay it down around their bodies in the form of glassy shells of exquisite beauty. The shell of a Radiolarian is usually spherical or helmet-shaped, perforated with numerous holes, through which the pseudopodia (or false feet) protrude, and usually ornamented with radiating spines. The animals swim in the sea in myriads, and the shells of dead Radiolaria have sunk to the sea bottom over millions of square miles to form the mud on the ocean bed (*see* OOZES: Vol. III).

Another order, the Foraminifera, also manufacture shells for the protection of their bodies; but these are made of lime. Although these are not so intricate in design as those of the Radiolaria, they, also, are very beautiful. Foraminifera shells can often be seen in the sand of the seashore—but a hand-lens is needed, as they are no bigger than the sand-grains. Often the sand is made up mainly, and in some places exclusively, of Foraminifera. The shells are usually rounded, flask-shaped, or oval; sometimes they are multiple, consisting of several rounded or oval shells joined together. In some cases, the walls of the shells are pierced with numerous minute holes, or 'foramina', through which the pseudopodia project; in others, there is a single opening at one end. Fossil Foraminifera and Radiolaria are commonly found in rocks, and there is no doubt that they have contributed largely to the formation of certain kinds of rock, especially LIMESTONE (q.v., Vol. III).

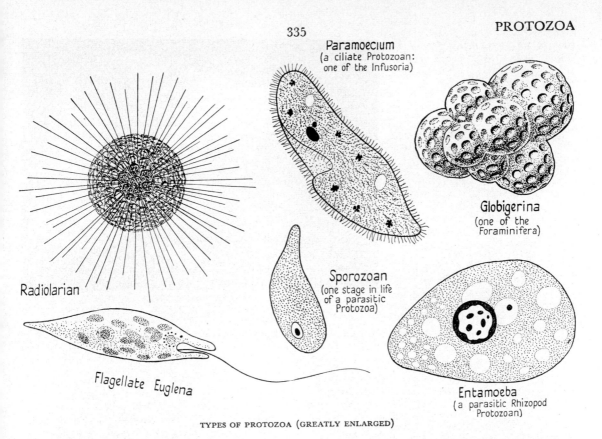

Paramoecium
(a ciliate Protozoan:
one of the Infusoria)

Globigerina
(one of the
Foraminifera)

Radiolarian

Sporozoan
(one stage in life
of a parasitic
Protozoa)

Flagellate Euglena

Entamoeba
(a parasitic Rhizopod
Protozoan)

TYPES OF PROTOZOA (GREATLY ENLARGED)

The next class of Protozoa is called the Masti-gophora, or Flagellata, both words meaning 'whip-bearers'. The animal's body, which is usually oval, carries at one end one, two, or four protoplasmic threads, like the lash of a whip, called 'flagella'. By the lashing movements of the flagella, the animals are drawn through the water. The Flagellates may be found in fresh water and in the sea. Some are parasites in the bodies of other animals, and are responsible for certain diseases—for instance, for the African sleeping-sickness in man.

The next class, the Sporozoa, are all para-sitic. Like all internal parasites, they have degenerated, and feed by absorbing fluid from the body in which they live. Sporozoa have a life-cycle which consists of three stages. In the first stage, the animal feeds and grows. In the second stage, two of the animals come together and join, or conjugate. The body formed by the conjugation then divides into numerous small spores, each with its nucleus, and each protected with a tough coat. In the third stage, the spores pass from the body of their host, and have to await the chance of being picked up by another

host. They may be transferred to the second host by being accidentally swallowed in its food; or they may be swallowed by an intermediate host and transmitted when the intermediate bites the real host. Malaria is passed on in this way. A particular species of mosquito bites a person who has had malaria, and takes into its body the blood containing the spores which cause the disease. The insect then bites another person, and, along with its own saliva, injects the parasite into the blood of the new victim.

The next and last class is the Ciliophora, or Ciliates, both of which words mean cilia-bearers —for the body of these animals is covered with short protoplasmic hairs or 'cilia'. The Ciliates used to be called Infusoria, because they were found in infusions or water containing much decayed vegetable matter. The Ciliates show a considerable advance in organization on the rest of the Protozoa. They are still microscopic, or nearly so; but instead of the simple body with a changeable shape, and organs which arise as wanted, they have a definite shape, and a num-ber of permanent organs. Two types of Ciliates, found in ponds and streams, either on water-plants or swimming freely in water containing dead vegetation, will illustrate what the members of this order are like.

The Slipper Animalcule, or *Paramoecium*, is shaped like the sole of a slipper. The surface of the body is coated with a great many short cilia, which propel it through the water. On one side of the body there is a groove leading into a mouth, from which a gullet runs into the body. Food, caught in this groove, is passed on through the mouth into the gullet, from which it passes round the body, being digested as it goes, the undigested remains being passed out just behind the groove. It differs from the rest of the Protozoa in these ways: instead of one, it has two nuclei, a large and a small one; the cell consists of an inner granular layer, surrounded by a clear outer layer, and, in addition, there are two permanent contractile cavities for excretion.

The Bell Animalcule, or *Vorticella*, has a bell-shaped body on a long stalk. It has few cilia, but these are long and bristle-like, and are arranged round the mouth of the bell. It has the same physical features as the Slipper Animalcule; but its most remarkable feature is that it is fixed by its stalk, which can be pulled down in a spiral until it looks like a tightly coiled spring. If disturbed, it pulls itself back rapidly on its stalk, and after a time slowly stretches out again to its full length. Bell Animalcules are unusual in that they grow bunched together, looking, when fully expanded, like microscopic and very delicate flowers.

One unusual group of Ciliates, the Suctoria, have the cilia converted into suckers for catching their prey—usually other Ciliates.

PTARMIGAN, *see* GROUSE.

PUFFIN, *see* AUK, Section 4.

PUMA. The Puma and the JAGUAR (q.v.) are the two great CATS (q.v.) of America. The Puma is generally smaller and slimmer than the Jaguar. It has a far greater range, being found over a vast area stretching from Canada to Patagonia. In North America, where the Puma

A PUMA WITH KITTEN
Paul Popper

is known as the Mountain Lion, it is sometimes nearly as big as a small lioness; but in the forests of tropical South America it is very much smaller. The adult is usually a uniform tawny-brown; but the cubs, until they are 6 months old, are heavily spotted with black.

Pumas are most destructive beasts of prey, and frequently kill horses, cattle, and sheep by springing on their shoulders and dislocating their necks. In the wilder parts of South America, where there are no domesticated animals, they eat Guanacos (wild Llamas) and deer; and in the dense forests of the Amazon and Orinoco, they hunt in the trees, chasing monkeys from bough to bough. If they are very hungry, Pumas will eat almost any flesh. Nevertheless, they have hardly ever been known, even in self-defence, to attack a human being: even in places where they are very numerous, it is considered perfectly safe for a child to wander alone. Many sportsmen have said that they would never again kill a Puma because of its unwillingness to defend itself, and the distress it shows—it is even said to weep tears, though this we can doubt. Pumas can leap amazing distances—indeed, when pursued by dogs, they have been known to spring upwards to reach a bough 20 feet from the ground, and they can leap down from a height of 30 or 40 feet. In the breeding season their penetrating, screaming 'yowl' has often scared travellers.

PUPA, *see* METAMORPHOSIS.

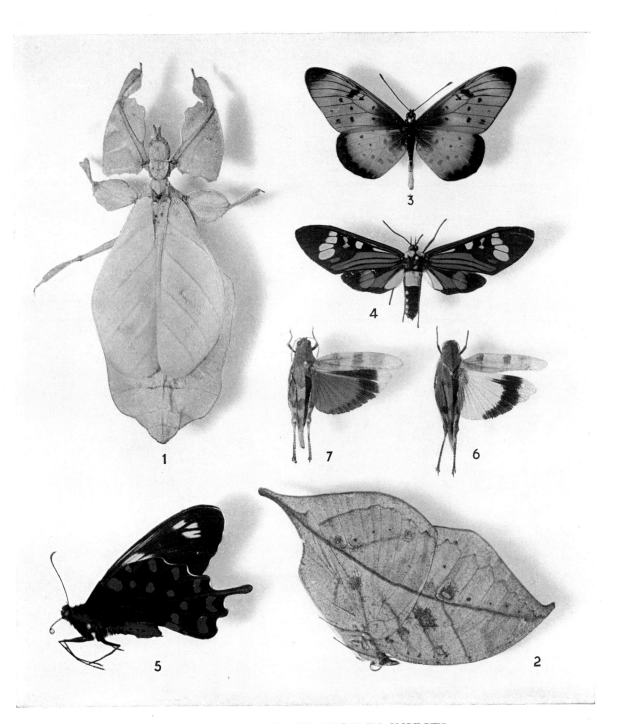

PROTECTIVE COLORATION IN INSECTS

A. Cryptic coloration. 1. Asiatic 'Leaf Insect' (*Phyllium*). 2. Asiatic 'Dead Leaf Butterfly' (*Kallima*)

B. Warning coloration. 3. Tropical African Butterfly (*Acraea*). 4. Tropical American Syntomid Moth (*Histioea*). 5. Asiatic Swallow-tail (*Atrophaneura*)

C. Flash coloration. 6 and 7. European Grasshoppers (*Oedipoda*)   (*about ⅘ nat. size*)

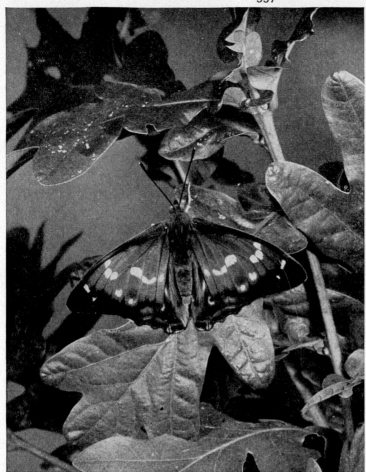

PURPLE EMPEROR BUTTERFLY
S. Beaufoy, F.R.P.S.

which it is restricted. The females, which are brown and white with no purple sheen on their wings, frequent the undergrowth, and lay their eggs singly on sallow bushes.

The green caterpillars look rather like slugs, and in contrast to other Nymphalids are solitary in their habits, and have no spines—though they have two horns on their heads. In the autumn they spin a pad of silk in the fork of a branch, where they retire into hibernation, gradually changing to an olive colour to complete their camouflage. Sometimes they hibernate on a leaf, in which case they fasten the leaf securely to the stem with silk. In the spring their colour changes to brighter green to match the young sallow leaves on which they feed. The pupa is attached by its tail to a leaf secured by silk to the stem. It closely resembles a sallow leaf in shape and colour, its bulk being disguised by numerous small white spots which break up the dark shadows. The butterflies emerge in July. Although seldom seen because of their habit of flying round the tree-tops,

PURPLE EMPEROR BUTTERFLY. The Emperor butterflies of the family Nymphalidae are found in nearly all parts of the world but not in Africa. The only British species is the brilliant Purple Emperor, so called because of the iridescent flush of imperial purple on the wings of the male. It has a wing-expanse of about 3 inches, and is sometimes called the 'King of the Forest', as it flies round the highest oak-trees in the woodlands of the south and midlands, to they can sometimes be attracted near the ground by a flashing mirror, a bright piece of cloth, or a sheet of newspaper spread out in a clearing where they occur. They are also attracted by waste or decaying animal substances.

PUSS MOTH, *see* PROMINENT MOTHS.

PYTHON, *see* BOA (picture, p. 398).

Q R

QUAIL, see PARTRIDGE.

QUEEN OF SPAIN FRITILLARY, see FRITILLARIES.

QUEZAL, see TROGON.

RABBIT. This very common British mammal is a RODENT (q.v.), belonging to the same family as the HARE (q.v.). It is found all over Europe, except in the extreme north and east, and in many other parts of the world, generally having been originally introduced by man. As rabbits eat almost any vegetable matter and have an alarming rate of breeding, they are a serious menace to farmers, and are classed as vermin (see ANIMAL PESTS, Vol. VI). The doe (female) produces four to eight litters of five to eight young in a year. These are blind, helpless, and nearly naked at birth; but in 2 weeks' time they are able to run, and by a month can fend for themselves. At the age of 6 months they are themselves able to breed. Given favourable circumstances, it is reckoned that a single pair of rabbits would in 3 years have a progeny numbering 13,718,000. Three pairs of rabbits were introduced in the 18th century into Australia, and in a few years had multiplied and, with the addition of others similarly introduced, have spread over most of the continent. Since then, in spite of all attempts to exterminate them, they have caused damage costing millions of pounds each year to farmers. Export of the skins has, however, proved very profitable.

Unlike hares, rabbits live together in large numbers in burrows under the ground. The burrows are often connected by long passages, so forming a warren. Rabbits generally come out at dusk and in the early morning to feed and play, rushing out in a line, after first peering cautiously round to see if the coast is clear. They are less fleet of foot than hares, and tire easily after about 70 yards. When chased, the rabbit runs very fast, with its ears back and its scut (tail) up.

Just before breeding, the doe leaves her burrow and digs a new hole, in which she makes a nest 2 feet long and lined with leaves, fern fronds, and fur plucked from her own body. The buck (male) sometimes helps with these preparations. When the doe leaves her young in the nest, she covers over the entrance with earth. After man, the wild rabbit's chief enemies are foxes, stoats, cats, buzzards, weasels, and polecats. Rabbits become paralysed with fear when hunted by any of these animals—so much so that they are unable to run more than a few yards before they stop and await death, screaming with terror. Recently, the virus disease myxomatosis, transmitted by insect bites, has greatly reduced their numbers.

Tame RABBITS (q.v. Vol. VI) are all descended from the wild rabbit. They are bred for their fur and meat, and also as PETS (q.v. Vol. IX); and a large variety of breeds has resulted.

RACCOON. This thick-set, carnivorous (flesh-eating) mammal, found only in the North and South American forests, is closely related to the BEAR (q.v.). It does not look very like a bear, but it walks in the same way on its soles, and eats much the same kind of food. Raccoons spend most of their life high up in trees, but they hunt their prey on the ground. There are few wild animals so expert at concealing their presence. During the day they lie curled up in a hollow tree or in a hole among rocks, out of sight. Again, there are few animals which can use their front paws so skilfully as Raccoons: not only do they use their paws when eating, but they can pick up very small objects, and will lift a cup just as a human would. When taken young, they make interesting and, usually, gentle pets. They are very inquisitive creatures, for ever investigating anything new or strange.

The North American Raccoons are about 2 feet long, covered with soft, grey fur, and with thick, short tails, marked with black rings. Their faces are white, with large black patches under the eyes. They are excellent climbers, and also good swimmers. After dusk, they climb down from their resting-places in the trees and go in search of food. In order that their tracks may not betray their presence, they will follow cattle

THE RINGTAIL, A NORTH AMERICAN RACCOON
E. O. Hoppé

trails, well-trodden pathways, or even a paved road, in the course of their hunting. Birds, small mammals, reptiles, aquatic animals, and insects are all welcome food. Like the bears, they will sometimes capture fish by scooping them out of a pool or stream with a quick sweep of their paws. Before putting their food in their mouths, Raccoons have a curious habit of moistening it in some water. They sometimes use the deserted nests of large birds for shelters; but the young, usually four to six in a litter, are born in hollow trees or holes in rocks. In the Adirondack region in north-east U.S.A., where they are fairly numerous, Raccoons hibernate during the severest part of the winter; but elsewhere they usually remain active the whole year round. They are hunted a great deal for the sake of their fur.

The Crab-eating Raccoon, found in South America, is smaller and lighter in colour than the North American species; but its habits are very similar. The Coatis are related to the Raccoons, and very like them, except for their long, bushy, pointed tails, and peculiar, rubber-like snouts. Unlike Raccoons, which are usually unsociable, Coatis go about in troops of from eight to twenty strong. Frequently, when they are hunting the large lizards known as Iguanas, they divide the troop into two sections, one of which makes its way through the branches, while the other hunts on the ground, so that any prey which falls from the trees has a poor chance of escape. The Cacomistle or 'Cunning Cat Squirrel', of the forests of Mexico, Texas, Nevada, and Oregon, is another relative of the Raccoon. It is about the size of a domestic cat, with soft, yellowish-brown fur; and, although bold and ferocious for its size, it is easily tamed and sometimes kept as a pet.

Kinkajous are the only members of the family which have prehensile tails. The tip curls round the branches of the trees, holding so firmly that it is able to support the whole weight of the animal. Kinkajous have small, round heads with flat faces and large eyes, giving them an owlish expression. Their tongues are enormously long and flexible, enabling them to lick honey from the comb, or termites and ants from holes and crevices. The Kinkajou is the most 'handy' of all the Raccoons, even using its tail to hold things, or inserting it into deep holes to grasp birds' eggs or young birds in their nests.

RAILS. This group of birds includes Water Rails, Land Rails or Corncrakes, Moorhens, and Coots, species of which are found all over the world. The greater number of them live in wet and marshy localities. They are characterized generally by having long legs and toes suitable for walking on marshy land, by their loose, hairy plumage, feeble wings, and short tails. Some species, such as the Weka Rails of New Zealand, have lost the use of their wings altogether, and some, in consequence, have become or are

CORNCRAKE ON HER NEST, IN THE REEDS
Eric J. Hosking, F.R.P.S.

THE COOT NESTS IN A REED-BED NEAR THE WATER
G. K. Yeates, F.R.P.S.

becoming extinct. Even such species as the Moor-hen, which can fly strongly, do not take readily to the air. Rails generally fly with their legs dangling down. Most Rails have narrow bodies, convenient for threading their way quickly through long grass and reeds. They do, in fact, tend to take cover as soon as anyone approaches, many species, such as the Corncrake, being known better by their cry, 'crek-crek', than by their appearance. Most species have rather small heads, longish necks, and long beaks. The majority build deep, cup-shaped nests of grass and reeds—often substantial and very firmly woven. The Clapper-rail of North America, an inhabitant of salt-marsh country near the Atlantic coast, lays up to fifteen eggs; but most other species generally lay seven or eight. The large Weka Rail breeds in burrows in the ground, and lays only two or three eggs. This bird, unlike most Rails, is fearless and sometimes very pugnacious, being known even to attack fully grown rats. One species of New Zealand flightless Rails, *Notornis*, believed to have been extinct since 1898, has reappeared lately, a colony of at least 100 birds having been found near Lake Te Anau, in the South Island.

The Moorhen, easily recognized by its yellow and red beak and green legs, is a common bird throughout Europe, Asia, and Africa, living on 'meres' or marshy lakes rather than moors. It is a strong swimmer, the nestlings taking to the water as soon as they are hatched. It feeds on weed and on small water animals, and in the breeding season is an unscrupulous robber of other birds' eggs or even nestlings. It often produces as many as three broods in a season, the young of the first brood often helping to rear the last. The Coot, a sooty-black, rather larger and heavier bird, with a bald white patch on its forehead, lives on large stretches of reed-encircled, fresh water, and often goes to the sea-coast in very frosty weather. It has lobed toes, and swims and dives like a duck. Like most of the Rails, it has a harsh cry.

RAT. This very unpopular animal is a RODENT, of the same family as the MOUSE (qq.v.). Rats are found in most parts of the world, especially wherever humans live, as they eat all kinds of human food, as well as grain and potato stores, and young game and poultry. Indeed, when really hungry, they will eat almost anything—their strong teeth being able to gnaw through the toughest fibre. Not only are they a menace for what they eat, but also they carry diseases, such as bubonic plague, by means of parasitic fleas. Every effort, therefore, is made to exterminate them with traps and poisons. The modern version of the rat-catcher is the local rodent officer. Rats, unfortunately, breed very prolifically indeed: the female can have a litter every six weeks, and she produces usually eight, but sometimes as many as twenty, at a birth.

Rats are difficult to trap, and, if caught, will frequently bite off a limb so as to escape. They run away from human beings unless they are cornered or starving, when they will attack fiercely. If driven from their homes by fire or shortage of food, they migrate in hordes. They need a lot of water, and have been known to gnaw through a 2-inch lead pipe to get it. They come out mainly at night for their food, much of which they take back to their nests to be eaten. In Great Britain there are two species, the Black or Old English Rat, and the Brown or Sewer Rat, sometimes called the Norwegian Rat from a mistaken belief that it originally came from Norway.

Black Rats are from 7 to 9 inches long, with

an equally long tail. They are believed to have been brought unintentionally to this country during the 11th century by ships returning from the East, and for 500 or 600 years they were the only rats in Britain. They ran riot in the old wooden buildings, carrying the germs of the plague from one house to another. Brown Rats are thought to have arrived in the same way from the East in about 1728. They are larger and more powerful than Black Rats, which they soon began to oust from their haunts, until they became the more numerous of the two and are now the common rats of the country generally. Black Rats still infest ships and dockyards, being much more active climbers than Brown Rats. In cities they frequent sewers, docks, warehouses, and old houses, and in the country hedgerows, ricks, and coverts.

See also Vol. VI: ANIMAL PESTS.

RATTLESNAKE, *see* VIPERS, Section 3.

RAVEN, *see* CROW, Section 3.

RAYS, *see* SHARKS and RAYS, Section 3.

RAZOR-BILL, *see* AUK, Section 2.

RAZOR-SHELL. This mollusc is one of the most interesting of the sand-burrowing molluscs. The two valves of the shell are often 6 or 7 inches in length, and are either quite straight or slightly curved; it is their resemblance in shape to the protecting handle of a razor that has given them their popular name. When perfect, the valves of the shell are covered externally with an olive-green skin, mottled with bright orange; but this skin is so thin that it peels off very easily, leaving a whitish surface beneath, streaked with purple, pink, yellow, or brown. The Razor-shell lives in a vertical tunnel, which it usually makes low down on sandy shores, the entrance, something like a keyhole in shape, being only uncovered for a short time at low tide. Just before the tide begins to flow in again, the Razor-shells may often be seen sticking up 2 or 3 inches above the

RAZOR-SHELL WITH FOOT EXTENDED

surface of the damp sand—but they are very wary and any nearby movement, or the passing shadow of a low-flying gull, is quite enough to make them disappear instantly from view. They have good cause to be on the alert, for hungry gulls and shore-frequenting crows are only too ready to pounce on and eagerly devour any loiterer. It is possible, however, by the exercise of a little patience and caution, to grab one and pull it out of its burrow. The Razor-shell may be so alarmed as to contract altogether within its shell for a time; but, if placed on the damp sand, it will, if uninjured, and after a little delay, set to work to rebury itself—a process well worth watching. First, the mollusc will cautiously push out its foot, and feel about for a soft spot; then the foot is lengthened, and the pointed tip thrust into the sand. In a few seconds, the shell is pulled forward gradually into an upright position. A series of rhythmic jerks follows in quick succession, and with each jerk the shell is drawn down, until it finally disappears from view. The way in which the Razor-shell uses its foot to do this is really very remarkable. When first pushed into the sand, it is tapered to a sharp point; then, when it has stretched down as far as it will go, the mobile tip is turned to form a hook with which to anchor, while the shell is hauled into the upright position. The foot is again tapered and thrust still deeper into the yielding sand, and then, suddenly, its base swells out until it looks like the clapper of a bell, which wedges tightly against the sides of the shaft, while the upper part contracts and drags the shell downwards with a jerk. This process is repeated again and again, until the Razor-shell feels itself sunk to a depth well out of reach of danger.

See also MOLLUSC.

RED ADMIRAL, *see* VANESSINAE.

REDBREAST, *see* ROBIN.

REDSHANK, *see* WADING BIRDS, Section 3.

REDSTART (or REDTAIL). This small migrant bird, which visits Europe in the summer months, is a member of the THRUSH family (q.v.). It has a bright orange-chestnut tail, which is constantly quivering from side to side. Of the two species which visit Great Britain, the Common Redstart male bird has a bright orange breast and rump,

THE REDSTART BRINGING A FLY TO HIS NEST
(Flashlight photograph.) *Eric J. Hosking, F.R.P.S.*

and a white forehead, contrasting with black cheeks; while the Black Redstart has a black breast and throat, and an orange rump.

The Common Redstart frequents old woods and parklands, well-timbered gardens and orchards, as well as stone walls, quarries, and ruins. Its song is a high warble, ending rather abruptly, as if the singer had been surprised and stopped short. The female lays her delicate, pale-blue eggs in a hollow in a tree or hole in a wall. When the nestlings are hatched, both parents guard them anxiously, often uttering their alarm note, a hurried 'Whee-tic-tic'.

The Black Redstart is a common Continental bird, generally frequenting the neighbourhood of buildings. It used to be chiefly a winter visitor to Britain; but in recent years it has visited and even bred in the south of England, especially in bomb-damaged areas in large cities. The males are very pugnacious in the mating season, though they are not such fighters as the Robins. Black Redstarts like fine weather, and tend to mope with their feathers puffed out when it is wet.

The Blue-throat, a relative of the Redstart, is a fairly regular passage migrant in the autumn to the east coast of Britain. It breeds in central and western Europe, but winters in Africa. It has a russet tail, a whitish stomach, and a large patch of azure blue with a white spot in the middle on its throat. Another race, the Red-Spotted Blue-throat, breeds in the mountains of Norway. Both birds have a very striking song, which sounds like the tinkling of silver bells.

REDWING, *see* THRUSH.

REINDEER. These are members of the DEER family (q.v.), especially adapted for living in cold climates. They are to be found in northern Europe, Asia, and America; but fossil remains show that they were once more widely distributed, and were common in the British Isles. As a protection against the Arctic climate, their noses and small ears are covered with soft hair, and their entire bodies with a woolly under-fur. They have very broad hoofs, which spread out sideways, enabling them to travel at great speed over the snow. They eat leaves, grass, water-plants, and lichens (reindeer moss) on the mountains, using their hoofs and noses to clear away the snow. Reindeer are unique amongst the deer in that both male and female have antlers. They shed them annually, the hind keeping hers longer than the buck, so as to be able to protect her fawn against the attacks of wolves. The different races vary in size: the large American stags are, for instance, about $4\frac{1}{2}$ feet high, with antlers often from 4 to 5 feet long; whereas the Swedish reindeer are about a foot smaller.

In Spitzbergen, although they have been much hunted, reindeer are still fairly numerous. During the summer they live on the grassy plains in the ice-free valleys; in the autumn they frequently go to the coast in order to eat the sea-weed thrown up on the beach. In the winter they return to the lichen-covered mountains in the interior. When the snow freezes, they find it almost impossible to get anything to eat, and so grow very thin; but they soon fatten up again during the summer. In Siberia, the reindeer migrate in huge herds in the autumn from the hills to the forests, where they spend the winter. The wild reindeer of America, called Caribou, live as far north as the borders of the Arctic Ocean, and they, too, migrate south in the autumn to regions where food can be found.

Reindeer have been domesticated for a very

A HERD OF REINDEER
These animals are nosing aside the snow to reach the lichen underneath. *Paul Popper*

long time, and various SIBERIAN PEOPLES and many of the LAPPS (qq.v. Vol. I) still rely on them almost entirely for their food (milk, cheese, and meat), transport, and clothing. The breed kept by the Lapps is much smaller than the wild race, and is used chiefly for pulling sleighs; but in Siberia the tame reindeer are large enough for riding. At the end of the last century the Siberian domesticated reindeer were introduced into Alaska, and have proved invaluable to the ESKIMOES (q.v. Vol. I), now that whales, seals, and bears have become more scarce.

See also Vol. IV: BEASTS OF BURDEN.

REMORA. From the earliest times the Remoras, or Sucking Fishes, have excited interest and wonder for their power of attaching themselves to sharks, large fishes, turtles, or even to ships. The ancients believed that the Remora could act as an anchor and stop a ship—indeed, the defeat of the Emperor Caligula was said to have been due to one of these fishes holding his galley. The natives of several tropical countries have for centuries employed the sucking powers of the Remora for the purpose of catching turtles. They tie a strong cord to the Remora's tail, and when the Remora attaches itself to a turtle, the fisherman hauls in the cord, bringing both Remora and turtle ashore. This method of fishing, when described by the son of Christopher Columbus, was thought to be just a traveller's tale; but now it is known to be in fact practised (*see* TURTLE FISHING: Vol. VI).

The sucking apparatus consists of a disk on the top of the head—really the first dorsal fin, the spines of which are split into halves, as it were, each half being laid sideways on the flat top of the skull. By the slight raising of these rays, a series of vacuum spaces is created, producing a suction so powerful that the fish cannot be removed by pulling it backwards. It is said that it will allow its tail to be torn off rather than release its hold; but a slight sliding movement forwards will loosen the grip. Usually one or

REMORAS ATTACHING THEMSELVES BENEATH A SHARK
The sucker-like fin on top of the head shows clearly in the
Remora which has not yet attached itself
A. Fraser-Brunner

more of these fishes may be found accompanying large sharks in the tropics, or sometimes attached inside the mouths or gill-cavities of large fishes. They gain by this habit in two ways, firstly by being carried from place to place without effort, secondly by securing scraps of food left from the meals of their large host.

REPRODUCTION IN ANIMALS.

In animals, as in plants, there are three methods of reproduction. In the lowest animals, parts of the parent are separated off and begin an independent existence. In some, such as the AMOEBA (q.v.), the animal simply splits in half. In others such as HYDRA or the SEA-ANEMONE (qq.v.), buds are formed which, when large enough, detach themselves as separate animals. It is obvious that in all these creatures there is a continuity of life between parent and offspring; and this continuity exists even where more complex methods of reproduction tend to hide it.

The higher forms of animals develop reproductive cells (gametes) at the stage known as maturity—a stage reached by some animals a few hours after birth, and in others not for many years. Generally speaking, the larger the animal the longer it takes to reach maturity. These reproductive cells are of two kinds—the egg (ovum) or female gamete, and the sperm (spermatozoon) or male gamete. To enable a new life to begin, union must take place between one gamete of each kind—and this usually involves the union of two adult individuals.

REPRODUCTIVE CELLS

Even in the lower animals, such as SPONGES, JELLYFISH, WORMS, and most MOLLUSCS (qq.v), which are hermaphrodite (that is, both kinds of gametes are contained in the one individual), self-fertilization is rarely possible. In the higher animals, including most of the vertebrates, and most of the higher invertebrates, such as CRUSTACEANS, SPIDERS, and INSECTS (qq.v.), the sexes are separate, which means that two individuals, usually unlike and known as male and female, must contribute. Often union of the two cells, known as fertilization, takes place outside the body of the female. This is the case with most fishes, the unfertilized eggs being shed into the water, where the male later pours on to them his 'milt' (sperms contained in a fluid). In the case of the SEA-HORSE (q.v.), the female injects the eggs into a pouch in the underside of the body of the male, where they are fertilized. As they remain there till they hatch, it appears to be the male who finally gives birth to the young. In many REPTILES, and in BIRDS (qq.v.), the egg is fertilized within the body of the female, afterwards being deposited and incubated—in other words, developed through the warmth of the parent's body, of the sand, of the sun, or in some other way.

In MAMMALS (q.v.), except for the Duck-billed PLATYPUS and the Spiny Ant-Eater or ECHIDNA of Australia (qq.v.), the egg, after fertilization, remains in the body of the female, and develops there during the period of gestation or preg-

HYDRA ATTACHED TO A WATER PLANT AND BUDDING

nancy. This period may last a few weeks (in a mouse), several months (in a dog), 9 months (in a human), or as long as 2 years (in an elephant). The young animal is then born, more or less well developed, to be fed with milk by the mother for a further period. The foal or calf is able to stand and walk almost as soon as it is born; but puppies, kittens, and other animals are born blind and helpless—though they develop quickly. The human baby is intermediate between these extremes, but develops very slowly.

The MARSUPIALS (q.v.) are a special class of mammals in which the young animal is retained within the body of the mother for only a short time. When born it crawls into a pouch, where it is carried and suckled until ready to live an independent life.

See REPRODUCTION IN PLANTS: HEREDITY.

REPRODUCTION IN PLANTS. 1. This may occur in three ways: by vegetative, asexual, or sexual propagation. In the vegetative form, part of the parent plant becomes detached and grows into a new plant. In lower plants, like algae or fungi, this may happen with any part of the plant; but in the higher flowering plants, the agent for vegetative propagation is usually a special part of the plant—the tuber of the potato being a typical example. In the asexual process, separate reproductive cells, usually known as spores, are formed, and these develop into new plants without sexual union. In the sexual process, special male and female reproductive cells are formed, which fuse together to form a new young plant or embryo. Asexual reproduction by spores enables the plant to spread very quickly in favourable conditions, since spores are produced in large quantities and are light enough to be disseminated widely by the wind. However, these spores are not able to resist adverse conditions, such as lack of moisture, and low or high temperature, for more than quite short periods. Seeds produced by flowering plants by sexual reproduction usually have hard protective coats which enable them to live through difficult times. Some seeds have been known to remain dormant for many years, protected by their hard coat.

2. VEGETATIVE PROPAGATION takes place in many ways. With seaweeds, new plants may be budded off from the parent near the base; while in the green pond-scums, short pieces, consisting

Leaf of 'Life-plant' (*Bryophyllum*) with young plants growing direct from it

of a few cells, may break off and rapidly grow into fresh filaments. YEASTS (q.v.) are propagated vegetatively by a process known as budding: small protuberances or buds grow out from the parent plant, and eventually break off to form independent plants. Vegetative propagation occurs in mushrooms every time a cake of spawn is grown in a mushroom bed. The cake of spawn is made of numerous threads of mycelium of the plant, and these, under the right conditions, soon grow out and branch to form new threads. New moss and liverwort plants may be grown either from detached pieces or from separate buds on the old plant. In some ferns, little buds may be produced on the leaves, and these grow out into small plants—so that each leaf may produce dozens of individuals. In higher plants, vegetative propagation may take place by the production of underground stems, such as rhizomes and tubers, or when BUDDINGS, CUTTINGS, or GRAFTINGS (qq.v. Vol. VI) are made.

3. ASEXUAL REPRODUCTION by means of spores occurs only in the lower plants, such as algae, fungi, mosses and liverworts, and ferns, and not in flowering plants. In the algae, spores formed by rapid divisions of the cells are shed freely into the water, to begin life as new plants. In fungi,

A. Section through fern frond showing sporangia (spore cases) on underside; B. Single sporangium splitting to release spores

the spores are borne on fruiting bodies, such as mushrooms, toadstools, and puff-balls. The clouds of spores which come from a dry puffball show what prolific numbers are produced. In mosses and liverworts the spores are carried in little boxes or capsules; while in ferns the brown lines or clusters on the under-surfaces of the leaves are collections of spores.

4. SEXUAL REPRODUCTION occurs in almost all types of plants, but becomes more complicated and efficient in the higher flowering plants. As in animals, the climax of sexual reproduction occurs when the male reproductive cell or sperm fuses with the female reproductive cell or egg. In passing from the lower to the higher plants, we see the development of devices to ensure that the sperm is brought to the egg. In algae, such as the seaweeds, the sperms and eggs are shed freely into the water, and whether or not they meet with one another is largely a matter of chance—although it is believed that the eggs give off some chemical substance which attracts the sperms (*see* PLANT MOVEMENT). The pinmoulds (*see* MOULDS) have a form of sexual reproduction in which two threads grow together and fuse at their tips; while in other fungi no form of sexual reproduction appears to occur. In mosses, liverworts, and ferns, the eggs are not shed freely as in seaweeds, but are protected in fixed organs, which grow near to the structures containing the mobile sperms. Here, too, the eggs give off a chemical substance which attracts the sperms. In all lower plants the product of the sexual union between sperm and egg is a one-celled structure which has no reserves of food, and so is unable to withstand adverse conditions.

The most efficient form of sexual reproduction occurs in the seed-bearing plants. SEEDS (q.v.) are many-celled structures, usually with thick, toughened coats containing food reserves, such as starch and oil, to give the seedlings a good start in life. The sperms are cells within the pollen grains, which are produced in great profusion. These are transferred to the eggs by air-currents, there always being tremendous wastage. In CONIFERS (q.v.), the least specialized of the seed-bearing plants, sperms and eggs are produced in cones, and the seeds are not protected by a fruit wall, but remain naked. In FLOWERING PLANTS (q.v.), the seed produced after union of the sperm and egg becomes protected by the growth of part of the flower to

form a fruit-wall, within which the seed may remain protected for many years (*see* FRUITS).

5. POLLINATION. This is the process in flowering plants whereby the pollen, containing the male reproductive cells, and the ovules, containing the female reproductive cells, are brought together to make the eggs fertile. As in most kinds of sexual reproduction, this happens by the movement of the male cell, the pollen being transferred from the stamens to the tip of the carpels or stigma of the stationary female. Generally, pollination is dependent upon pollen from another flower (cross-pollination), though sometimes pollen may reach the ovule from the stamen of the

CROSS SECTION OF FLOWER

same flower (self-pollination). Both self- and cross-pollination may be brought about by the wind or by insects; and sometimes birds or even water may cause pollination. Wind-pollination is a purely chance process, the dry pollen being caught up in currents of air, and some of it happening to alight on the stigma of a similar flower. Wind-pollinated flowers, therefore, produce large quantities of pollen to allow for the wastage. Wind-pollination is found in many British trees and most grasses, but few of the smaller flowering plants could survive by so haphazard a method.

In self-pollinated flowers such as the Chickweed, the exposed pollen merely passes to the stigma of the same flower, sometimes being carried there by the wind. Some flowers rely on self-pollination when cross-pollination has failed. In

FLOWERS OF HOLLY
Left. Male flower with stamens. *Right,* Female flower with pistil.   *Harold Bastin*

HAZEL FLOWERS, MALE AND FEMALE
The catkins are the male pollen-bearing flowers. The inconspicuous, female, nut-producing flower is seen on the lower part of the stem. *Harold Bastin*

the Sweet Violet, for example, cross-pollination usually takes place; but certain of the flowers do not open, and in these, when the pollen is ripe and the anther becomes ruptured, self-pollination takes place. If the Scarlet Pimpernel has not been cross-pollinated, the flower closes up and remains closed for 2 or 3 days, while self-pollination takes place. The petals of the Garden Pea flower are so firmly interlocked that no insect can force an entry, and self-pollination must take place.

Insects visit flowers for food or shelter, or to lay eggs. The food they seek is pollen and 'nectar' (a solution of sugars produced in little sacs called 'nectaries'). When insects, such as bees, visit flowers in search of nectar, parts of their hairy bodies become dusted with pollen, and this easily rubs off on the stigmas of that flower or the next one they visit. Insects seem to be strongly attracted by certain colours, but to pay little attention to others—though scents probably attract them more surely than do bright colours. In fact, some flowers—e.g. Meadow Sweet—are so strongly scented that insects are attracted to them though they have no nectar to offer.

Most insect-pollinated flowers have wonderful devices for guiding the movements of the insect and turning them to the best account. Sometimes, as in Dead-nettles and some members of the Pea family, and particularly in the Sage, the insect can enter the flower in one way only, and in consequence must push against special outgrowths which move the stamens and dust the pollen over its body. The Primrose has two types of flowers—the pin-eyed, in which the stigma is above the stamens, and the thrum-eyed, in which the stigma is below the stamens. When a bee alights on a thrum-eyed flower, it pushes its proboscis down to the bottom of the petal tube to obtain nectar, and in doing so, the top of its head touches the ripe anthers and is dusted with pollen. This part of the bee's head later comes into contact with the stigma of the pin-eyed flower, so ensuring cross-pollination.

6. FERTILIZATION. The union of the male and female reproductive cells, after the transfer of pollen from the stamens to the stigmas of the carpels, is known as fertilization. After pollination, the pollen grain containing the male reproductive cell is held on the stigma, which is often sticky. There it absorbs moisture, swells, and its outer coat bursts, allowing the more delicate inner one to protrude. A pollen tube then grows down through the tissue between the stigma and the ovary, and through a minute hole in the ovule to reach the female cell. The two then fuse, and the process of fertilization is completed. This union of male and female reproductive cells is essential to sexual reproduction, and, when it has taken place in flowers, the SEEDS (q.v.) develop. The seed contains a minute plant packed in a small space, usually with enough stored food to nourish it until the seedling is established. Within each carpel there are as many seeds as there were fertilized ovules. During the development of the seeds, the walls of the carpels also change in various ways, the completed structure with its enclosed seeds forming the FRUIT (q.v.).

7. GERMINATION. Seeds need moisture, oxygen, and warmth to germinate; so they remain dormant in winter, becoming active in spring. The majority of seeds do not appear to be much affected by the presence or absence of light. The seeds of some plants, however, such as Purple Loosestrife, Rhododendrons, Mistletoe, and certain of the Speedwells, are 'light-sensitive'—that is, they will not germinate until they have been exposed to the light. The seeds of other plants, such as the Tomato and cultivated plants such as Phlox and Love-lies-bleeding, are 'light-hard'—that is, they will germinate only in the dark.

Some seeds must germinate immediately they are shed from the fruit, or they will die; in others, germination can be delayed from a few days to several weeks or longer. Packets of garden seeds can be kept for several years, the seeds remaining in a resting state until conditions suitable for germination arise—though the longer they are kept the fewer will germinate. Species of Clover have remained in this resting state for 50 years, and the Indian Lotus for 250 years. Seeds can be made to germinate more quickly by being soaked in water for a day or so before sowing, or, in the case of large seeds like the bean, by having their seed-coat pierced to allow the water to enter.

See also REPRODUCTION IN ANIMALS.

REPTILES. It is most probable that reptiles first appeared on the earth at a time subsequent to the Carboniferous Period when the climate of the world was growing warmer and drier. When water was becoming scarcer, animals not dependent on life in water were at an advantage. It is not always easy to distinguish the first reptiles from the AMPHIBIA (q.v.); but during the Mesozoic Period, 70 to 170 million years ago, before the appearance of birds and mammals,

the reptiles were the dominant animals on land. Some were gigantic animals, the largest being the *Diplodocus*, which reached a length of 84 feet (*see* PREHISTORIC ANIMALS, Vol. III).

Reptiles are cold-blooded animals; that is, their blood takes on the same temperature as their surroundings. When this temperature falls, they become less active, until in very cold temperatures they become torpid; and so they are never found in arctic regions. They flourish best in tropical conditions, where they can be active enough to compete successfully with other animals. In temperate climates such as Britain, they spend about half their time in HIBERNATION (q.v.). The skin of reptiles is protected by bony scales. The female lays an egg which is encased in a porous shell of a rather leathery consistency, and this in most species is incubated by the heat of the sun or the warmth generated by decaying vegetation. In some species of lizards the eggs are retained in the mother's body until the young are ready to hatch.

Reptiles may be divided into five main groups, and these differ considerably from each other. The first group, of which the only surviving species is the TUATARA (q.v.) of New Zealand, represents an early group of reptiles now extinct, except for this one species. The next group consists of the TURTLES AND TORTOISES (q.v.), reptiles well protected by bony shells. The next two groups, which contain the LIZARDS and SNAKES (qq.v.), have proved the most successful, a great many varied species having been evolved. The last group, the CROCODILES (q.v.), includes the largest living reptiles. These spend the greater part of their lives in water, and are found in warm climates only.

RESPIRATION IN ANIMALS. After food has been digested and passed into the blood, it is transported to all the living cells of the body (*see* NUTRITION OF ANIMALS). To use the energy locked up in this material, oxygen is needed—for only with oxygen can the protoplasm break up the digested food into simpler compounds. In this process, energy is set free, and carbon dioxide is produced as waste. The intake of oxygen and the getting rid of carbon dioxide is known as breathing.

DIPLODOCUS CARNEGII, THE LARGEST OF THE EXTINCT GIANT REPTILES, 84 FEET LONG

In those animals which have no blood, such as SPONGES, JELLYFISH, and SEA-ANEMONES (qq.v.), the sea-water circulates instead, carrying with it the needed oxygen, and removing the waste carbon dioxide. Most animals, however, are supplied with a blood system; and it is by breathing in that they charge the blood with oxygen, and by breathing out that they remove the carbon dioxide. The exchange of these gases can take place only through a moist surface.

Not all animals breathe in the same way as man and the vertebrates. WORMS (q.v.) breathe through the skin, which is very thin and moist, rather like the membrane lining our lungs. INSECTS (q.v.) breathe through tracheal tubes, which run throughout their bodies from external openings or 'spiracles'. SPIDERS (q.v.) breathe through very thin sheets of skin on the underside of the body, arranged like the leaves of a book, and hence known as the 'lung-book': the air passes over these leaves, and thus exchange takes place. FISHES, CRABS, WATER SNAILS (qq.v.), and other aquatic animals breathe through gills, which are areas of skin rich in blood-vessels. A fish takes in water through its mouth, and passes it out at the side of the head through the gills, the covers of which may be seen opening and closing with a regular rhythm, showing, when open, the very red, thin skin of the gill openings. In CRABS and LOBSTERS (qq.v.), which have the gills at the bases of the legs, and in many other water animals, the gills are fine and hair-like. The gills of Tadpoles (see FROGS) and other young amphibians are on the sides of the head; they are then replaced by internal gills, like those of a fish; and finally by lungs when the animals emerge for their life on land.

On land, provision must be made for keeping moist the surface of the skin through which respiration takes place. In some of the more lowly animals, such as the earthworm, this is done by the secretion of slime all over the body; most animals, however, possess lungs, which are kept moist inside the body. Air is brought to the lungs from the nose or mouth through the wind-pipe (trachea), which is kept permanently open by means of rings of gristle. The windpipe divides into two smaller tubes (bronchi), one of which goes to each lung. In the lung, these tubes divide and re-divide many times, thus conveying the air to the thin, moist skin of the lung's surface. The air sacs, in which this exchange of oxygen for carbon dioxide takes place, are so designed as to present as large a surface as possible to the air. A man's lungs have normally a capacity of about one gallon of air; but athletes and men engaged in heavy manual work develop larger lungs, so that the blood may be oxygenated more quickly. When we get 'out of breath', it is because we are unable to take in air as quickly as the body requires for the strenuous work we are doing. BIRDS (q.v.) have the most perfect system of respiration of any animals, and they need this because of the immense amount of energy used in flying. In addition to their lungs, they have air-chambers, into which pure air passes, and from which the lungs are filled also. Because of this economical arrangement, and also because the expulsion of the air is assisted by the strokes of the wings, a bird does not get out of breath.

RESPIRATION IN PLANTS. 1. Growth in both plants and animals depends upon two things: (i) a liberal supply of building materials, such as sugars, starches, fats, and proteins; (ii) enough oxygen to release energy from these materials. Plants make their building material by PHOTOSYNTHESIS (q.v.), which takes place in the green leaves. The release of energy, seen in animals in the forms of heat and movement, is not so obvious in plants. Respiration in both plants and animals, however, releases energy in the same way as the combustion of coal releases heat. And respiration gives rise to carbon dioxide as a waste product, just as in the burning of coal. It is an old custom to remove plants from the wards of hospitals at night, because the plants, through respiration, remove from the atmosphere oxygen needed by the patients, and at the same time, return to the atmosphere carbon dioxide, which helps to make the room stuffy.

In plants, photosynthesis and respiration are often going on at the same time. In photosynthesis, carbon dioxide is taken in and oxygen given off; whereas in respiration, oxygen is taken in and carbon dioxide given off. Photosynthesis usually takes place in daylight only; but respiration proceeds at all times, oxygen being taken in to react with the made-up foodstuffs to release energy. It is not easy to demonstrate the process of respiration, because photosynthesis uses much more carbon dioxide than is released by respiration—and, consequently, it releases much more oxygen than respiration uses. To demonstrate

THE ALPINE SOLDANELLA FLOWERS MELTING THEIR WAY THROUGH THE SNOW
Albert Steiner

respiration, we have either to use active parts of the plant which have not yet begun to photosynthesize, such as growing seeds, or else to make our experiments with green plants under conditions in which photosynthesis cannot take place, such as in complete darkness. Thus, if some germinating seeds, opening flower-heads, or ripening fruit are put, with a thermometer, into a vacuum flask (which prevents radiation of heat), the temperature within the flask will be seen to rise—showing that some energy has been liberated as heat. Or if some peas are put into water to soak for about 24 hours, the temperature of the water will increase perceptibly—absorption of water by the peas will have increased the active processes in them, and heat will have been set free by respiration.

An exceptional but most interesting example of excessive respiration producing heat is shown by a plant, *Soldanella alpina*, which is common in the Swiss Alps. In the autumn this plant develops thick, leathery leaves, which build up reserves of starch. During the winter the plant becomes covered with snow and ice to a depth of several feet. When spring comes, the sun melts all the snow and some of the ice, and water trickles down to the roots. The plant revives, and food is passed to the flower-buds—which therefore respire so actively that they give off enough heat to melt the remaining ice around them. The developing flowers thus actually melt their way through, and whole blue patches of them may be seen, as if they were growing on and in ice. By the time the flowers have forced their way out of the ice, the leaves have used up so much of their stored food in this great respiratory activity that they have become as thin as paper (*see* ALPINE PLANTS).

The rate of respiration in plants, as in animals, varies greatly according to the activities of the cells. A deciduous tree, for example, grows more rapidly, and therefore respires more, during the summer than during the winter, when it is mainly resting. In dry seeds, living processes are reduced to a minimum, and respiration is very low; but when they germinate, the living processes quicken, and the rate of respiration is speeded up accordingly. Respiration is affected by temperature also—a rise in temperature of 10° approximately doubles its rate. At 35° C., however, the living processes of plants begin to fall off, as does the rate of respiration, also.

2. ANAEROBIC RESPIRATION. Although the release of energy from foodstuffs is nearly always dependent on a regular supply of oxygen (aerobic respiration), there are cases where respiration goes on in the absence of gaseous oxygen (anaerobic or 'without air' respiration). If germinating seeds, for example, are kept under conditions in which they can get no free oxygen, respiration will still occur, and carbon dioxide be released. In respiration of this kind, the chemical reactions which take place are different: instead of being completely broken down to carbon dioxide, the foodstuffs form other breakdown products, one of which is alcohol. This is made use of in the formation of beer from malt by the fungus yeast, this process of FERMENTATION (q.v.) being really an example of anaerobic respiration. Some bacteria and fungi are able to live and grow only in situations where oxygen is completely absent, and die when they are exposed to oxygen. One of these

is the soil bacterium called tetanus, which, when it gets into open wounds, may cause the disease known as lock-jaw. If the existence of tetanus in a flesh wound is suspected, therefore, the doctor at once uses an antiseptic with strong oxidizing properties, such as hydrogen peroxide.

RHEA, *see* OSTRICH, Section 3.

RHINOCEROS (from a Greek word meaning nose-horn). This huge, ungainly beast can claim to be the largest of the mammals after the Elephant, with the Hippopotamuses but very little smaller. Rhinoceroses belong to the same section of the great order of mammals, the Ungulata or hoofed mammals, as do HORSES and TAPIRS (qq.v.). There are five distinct species, three of which are found in Asia and the other two in Africa. They became extinct in America in very early times, and are becoming much scarcer in the Old World. They are all enormous creatures, with bulky bodies on comparatively short legs. Their heads are large and elongated, and their erect, oval ears are set very far back. They have small eyes and weak sight,

WHITE RHINOCEROSES IN UGANDA. *Dorien Leigh*

and their upper lips generally protrude beyond the lower. Some of them have prominent canine teeth in their lower jaw. The horns are composed of matted and compressed hair: some species have one, others two, usually of unequal length.

Rhinoceroses are found both in open plains and in grassy jungles and swamps. They feed chiefly at night, and eat only vegetable food, some species living almost entirely on grass, others eating mainly twigs and small boughs of trees. They are harmless, even timorous creatures; but their short-sightedness makes them inclined to charge blindly at anything arousing their suspicion. The African species rely entirely on their horns as weapons of defence, whereas the Asiatic kinds, having smaller horns, defend themselves mainly with their canine teeth, which can inflict enormous gashes.

The great Indian Rhinoceros is the largest of the Asiatic species, its height at the shoulder being from 5 to $5\frac{3}{4}$ feet, its length from its nose to the root of its tail about 10 feet 6 inches, and its girth about 9 feet 8 inches. It has a single horn on its nose, usually up to 1 foot long, and two long canine teeth in its lower jaw. Its thick hide is hairless, except at the ears and tail, and it is studded all over with large tubercles, looking rather like rivet-heads on an iron boiler. At the joints are huge folds of skin, which divide up the body into shield-like sections, and form great rolls at the neck. The animal generally moves at a long, swinging trot; but if disturbed it breaks into a rapid but awkward gallop. When excited it makes a curious grunting noise. It is generally solitary, feeding mainly on grass, and preferring swampy districts, where it likes to wallow in the mud. In captivity it often loses its horn by rubbing it away against the brickwork of its house.

The names of the two African species, the Black and the White Rhinoceros, are misleading, for, in fact, they differ very slightly in colour, both being a slaty grey. The White Rhinoceros is the largest of all the species, being over 6 feet in height. Both species have two horns. The front horns of some of the Black Rhinoceroses are as much as 44 inches long; while the record length for those of a White Rhinoceros is $62\frac{1}{2}$ inches. They have no protruding canine teeth, and no folds of skin like the Indian Rhinoceros. The Black Rhinoceros inhabits river valleys and thick jungles, feeding on young shoots and branches of trees. The White Rhinoceros keeps to the open plains, where it feeds only on grass; it walks with its head close to the ground. The mother always follows her calf, guiding it, apparently, with her long horns.

RHIZOME, *see* STEMS, Section 2*b*.

RIBBON-FISH. These oceanic fishes are very long, flattened from side to side, and very fragile. Except when washed ashore in a much-damaged condition, they are seldom observed clearly; so that, when seen from ships, they have usually been mistaken for the mythical sea-serpent. They are quite inoffensive. They inhabit the open sea, usually swimming close to the surface with a side-to-side movement of the long, flexible body. There is no anal fin, and the caudal (tail) fin is either bent upwards at a sharp angle, as in the Deal-fish, or is absent, as in the Oar-fish. The jaws slide forward by means of a very curious arrangement of the bones.

The great Oar-fish, which may grow to a length of more than 20 feet, was long known to the Norwegians as the 'king of the herrings'; and they believed that, if harm was done to the Oar-fish, the herring would move away to some other coast. Its body is semi-transparent, and light blue in colour; the dorsal fin rises like a crest on the head, bearing tufts of bright red; and the pelvic fins are long filaments, thickened at the tips.

The so-called Deal-fish, sometimes called Vaagmaar, are very similar. These have a long, streamer-like fin above the head, and the tail fin is developed and turned upwards. In the young, the crest on the head is composed of

THE OPAH, ONE OF THE RIBBON-FISHES
A. Fraser-Brunner

about six long filaments, with shining tassels at intervals along them. Deal-fishes do not grow so large as the Oar-fish, and more varieties are known. They are said to be strong and swift swimmers, in spite of their flimsy appearance.

Despite its very different appearance, the Opah or Moonfish is related, having the same curious sliding arrangement of the jaws. This beautiful fish reaches a large size, sometimes weighing 500 lb. or more. The sides are tinted with lilac, shading to rich blue on the back, and are scattered with silver spots, each surrounded by a golden ring; the jaws and fins are bright scarlet. The Opah is rather rare, but is very widely distributed through the seas of the world, odd specimens turning up every now and then at widely separated places. The flesh is firm and pink, and is said to be very good eating.

RINGLET, *see* Browns (Butterflies).

RING-OUZEL, *see* Thrush, Section 3.

ROACH, *see* Carp.

ROBIN (Redbreast). Common over the greater part of Europe, this member of the large Thrush family (q.v.) is among the best known and favourite of British birds. Some are resident all the year round, some migrate farther south for the winter, and a number come to winter in Britain from northern Europe. Some frequent human habitations, breeding in gardens and orchards, others breed in lonely woods.

Although so friendly to man, the Robin is among the most aggressive and pugnacious of small birds. In the spring the cock lays claim to a definite estate, singing boldly and displaying his red breast as a warning to other Robins to keep away. He will attack and fight with great ferocity any rival to his territory or mate. Unlike other birds, however, the Robin continues to hold his territory after the breeding season, and in the winter the female also claims a territory and sings to maintain it (*see* Animal Territory). In the spring, during the courting season, the cock Robin's breast is a brilliant colour. He puffs out his feathers, sways and bobs his head, and flirts his tail in his courtship (*see* Animal Language). The hen also has a red breast, though not so brilliant; but the young birds do not show red in their first season. The Con-

THE ROBIN AT ITS NEST BUILT IN A PIECE OF PIPING
Eric J. Hosking, F.R.P.S.

tinental Robin is paler in colour; but the Ruby Throat, a species of Robin which breeds in the arctic tundras of Siberia, and winters in southern Asia, has vivid red colouring.

The name 'Robin' is used for several foreign birds with only a superficial resemblance to the Redbreast, such as the American Robin, a larger, heavier bird, and the New Zealand Robin. The Indian Dhyal Bird and Indian Shama, found in most parts of south-eastern Asia, are like Robins in structure, but are distinguished by long black and white tails. The Dhyal Bird, in particular, is much like the Robin also in behaviour, being confident and friendly with humans, and exceedingly pugnacious in the breeding season. Both birds have a charming song, with an even greater compass than the European bird.

'ROCK-SALMON.' There is no living fish to which this name is properly applied: the name is given by the fish trade to any kind of fish that is not easily sold under its real identity. Wolf-fish, Monk-fish, and Dog-fish, which are too large and ugly to display complete on the fish-monger's slab, are beheaded and skinned, and the flesh, cut up into suitable sizes, is labelled 'Rock-salmon'.

RODENT. The order of Rodents (gnawing animals) is the largest group of mammals, and also the most extensive, rodents being found all over the world except in the extreme polar regions.

Members of the order all have characteristic teeth. There are two front teeth, the incisors or biters, in both the upper and lower jaws. These are large and prominent, and grow continuously throughout the animal's life. They have a hard enamel surface on the front, and little or no enamel on the sides and back, so that with use each constantly wears the other sharp. To keep them in condition, all rodents must gnaw. If one of these teeth is broken or lost, the opposite one continues to grow unopposed, finally killing the animal, either by preventing it from feeding, or by turning a full circle and piercing the brain. There are no canine teeth, a wide gap separating the incisors from the cheek teeth. The cheeks close into this gap forming two hairy packs which help to keep such things as earth and other matter out of the mouth when the animal is gnawing or burrowing. The cheek teeth crush and grind food, but do not have cutting edges. The cheek teeth of some rodents, VOLES (q.v.), for instance, are also permanently growing and rootless, like the incisors.

Rodents nearly all live on dry land; but some, such as the BEAVER and MUSK RAT (qq.v.), live mostly in water, and others, such as the SQUIRRELS (q.v.), spend most of their life in trees. Most rodents are vegetarian, and they do much damage, especially by eating grain and stripping bark off trees. Because they have an enormous birth-rate, they are able to hold their own in the face of countless enemies which prey on them. They also show great wariness and skill in hiding. Most are timid, but some—as, for example, rats—attack fiercely if they are cornered.

The Cape Jumping Hare or Spring Haas, a South African rodent, which looks like a hare, measures about a foot in length, with a bushy tail of about the same length. It progresses by a series of leaps of some 20 to 30 feet. Large colonies of these animals live on the rocky plateaux of South Africa.

The Gophers of America, burrowing, mole-like rodents about the size of a squirrel, with very short tails, live in holes in the ground. The Pocket Gophers have large pouches in their cheeks, which they use for carrying food to their underground store-rooms. They have great, sharp, digging claws, and can travel with ease and speed either backwards or forwards, their short, sensitive tails guiding them when running in reverse. They are vicious, surly beasts, and fight savagely with each other.

ROOK, see CROW, Section 4.

ROOT PRESSURE. When young saplings are felled or pruned in the spring and early summer, a liquid collects at the cut ends, and the 'bleeding' goes on for some time, especially in plants such as the young vine, suggesting that water is being forced up from below. This force, known as root pressure, varies with the season of the year, being much more vigorous in the spring, when the plant's water requirements are at their highest, and falling to a minimum in the autumn and winter, when its water requirements are lower. It also varies on different days, and is less by day than by night, suggesting that it is affected in some way both by the intensity of light and by the temperature. The cause of root pressure is far from clear. It results partly from water being forced under considerable pressure from the absorbing cells of the root into the woody vessels, up which sap is carried to the leaves to take part in the food-manufacturing process known as PHOTOSYNTHESIS (q.v.). Root pressure varies greatly, as can be seen in the amount by which different plants 'bleed' when their stems are cut. In conifers, such as Pine and Larch, root pressure hardly exists.

In some plants, root pressure exerts a considerable force. A cut Stinging-nettle was found

THE HOUSE MOUSE USING ITS INCISORS
Harold Bastin

to give off 17 pints of water in 40 hours; and a potted Fuchsia produced a pressure so great that it would have been able to force a column of water up to a height of 25 feet. As root pressure has never been found to raise water higher than about 30 feet, it seems clear that this would be incapable of raising water to the top of the tallest trees; though it may account for the upward movement of water to the leaves of some herbaceous plants. How water is raised to the top of a tall tree is a mystery yet to be solved: but probably it is due to the combined effects of many forces, mainly TRANSPIRATION (q.v.), or water-loss through the leaves.

The drops of 'dew' to be seen on grass and other plants early in the morning, especially on 'steamy' spring days, are often due to root pressure. (DEW (q.v. Vol. III) is, of course, also caused by condensation of water vapour in the atmosphere.) Since the air in the early morning is usually saturated with water vapour, transpiration from the leaves does not occur. But absorption of water continues through the roots, and the water continues to be forced upwards, where it appears as liquid drops at certain points on the leaves. This giving off of water occurs particularly in the Garden Nasturtium and in certain Saxifrages. Some Saxifrages give off water containing calcium salts in solution, and, when the water evaporates, the salts are left as a white coating on the margins of the leaf. In humid tropical forests, the oozing of water from the leaves is common, some plants giving a constant drip. One leaf has been known to exude 190 drops a minute.

Root pressure is made use of commercially in Canada, where incisions are made into the trunks of Sugar Maples in the spring before the leaves are fully formed, and the liquid, a sugary syrup, oozes out and is collected (*see* MAPLE SYRUP, Vol. VI).

ROOTS. The two main functions of roots are to anchor the plant firmly in the soil, and to absorb water containing dissolved mineral salts, which form the raw materials of plant foodstuffs. They may also serve as a food storage. Plants of the Legume family have root nodules, housing BACTERIA (q.v.), which hold nitrogen to be used by the plant.

1. ANCHORAGE. Roots have to resist a pulling strain from above, caused perhaps by the wind or by the tugging of an animal. This is particularly true of the long, firm, main roots known as tap-roots, and the deeper these grow, the more (other things being equal) they can resist such pulling strains. Plants with stout tap-roots, such as Dandelions and Parsnips, will often resist a tug until the root tears, usually near the base of the shoot.

The other type, the fibrous root, is equally efficient for anchorage. Fibrous roots are much too branched for a main root to be distinguishable; they cover a surprising amount of space in the soil. When a plant with a fibrous root is pulled up, a large amount of root is usually left behind. The roots of oak-trees, for example, often penetrate as far down as the tree is high. The roots of wheat go down 5 feet deep or even farther. If the soil is rocky, however, and the roots cannot go down, they spread out sideways.

2. WATER ABSORPTION. This is the most important function of the root. Soil is made up of tiny particles of various shapes which, although close together, have many air spaces between them. The water in the soil forms a film round each soil particle, and in order to get at this water film, a plant has special absorbing

adventitious roots of ground ivy

buttress roots of bean

tuberous roots of lesser celandine

tap root of spinach

fibrous roots of nasturtium

TYPES OF ROOTS

structures, called root-hairs, which generally grow near the tip of the root. Each root-hair is composed of one cell with a very thin cell-wall, a thick lining of protoplasm, and a space in the middle filled with fluid. Water is absorbed from the soil by 'osmosis'. When a living cell is surrounded by water, or by a solution less concentrated than its own sap, water is drawn into the cell, which then swells until its walls are fully extended, its cell-sap meanwhile becoming diluted by the addition of water. Dried prunes or currants put to soak take up water by this same osmosis. We can also demonstrate it for ourselves by taking half a peeled potato, scooping a hole in the middle, putting a lump of sugar in the hole, and standing the potato in water. The sugar soon becomes dissolved by water drawn in through the tissues of the potato. Sugars and other substances in the currant, the prune, and the root-hair behave in the same way. From the root-hair, the water containing mineral salts passes into the roots, and thence up the shoot to the leaves, where the plant's food is made.

It is useless to look for root-hairs on an uprooted plant. They have either been destroyed during the pulling up, are hidden by the clinging particles of soil, or have shrivelled in the dry air. They can easily be seen, however, by allowing some seeds to germinate on paper in a damp atmosphere. The number of root-hairs varies greatly on different roots and under different conditions of humidity. In a maize plant grown in a moist chamber, 400 to the square millimetre were counted under a microscope. Water-plants do not need them.

When root-hairs are in contact with soil particles, the wall of the hair becomes soft and gummy and sticks fast to the particles. That is why roots cling so tenaciously to the soil, and why so much soil comes away with an uprooted plant.

There is a close connexion between the way the roots of a plant spread and the arrangement of its leaves. This is especially obvious in trees. After rain, the soil beneath the outer edge of the tree is wet, while that under the crown remains comparatively dry. The branches of the roots extend in the soil as far as the leaf-branches overhead, so that, as the water from the dripping leaves passes downwards to the soil, the root-hairs at the tips of the root-branches can absorb it. This co-ordination between leaves and root occurs in other plants besides trees. In the Arum Lily, for example, the tips of the downwardly pointing leaves are directly over the ends of the spreading roots. In the Rhubarb, however, where there is a tap-root with few branches, the water travels towards it by way of the groove in the leaf-stalk. All plants have some such arrangement for conducting rain or dew towards the root-hairs.

3. FOOD STORAGE. The third function which some roots perform is to store food which the plants have manufactured in excess of their immediate needs. Thus, in the Dahlia, Lesser Celandine, and Orchids, some of the roots, which have become very thick, are found to contain stored-up starch; these are called Root-tubers. In Carrots and Beets, the swollen tap-root stores up sugar; in other root-crops, such as the Parsnip and Turnip, it stores starch. Some of these underground storage organs, however, such as Potato tubers, Iris rhizomes, and bulbs, are not roots, but underground stems (*see* STEMS, Section 2).

4. ADVENTITIOUS ROOTS. Some roots have other special functions. It is difficult to tear Ivy from a wall or tree because of the presence of hundreds of tiny roots which fix the plant securely to its support. Because they grow from the stem, these roots are called 'adventitious roots'. In the case of the Ivy, they are also called 'climbing roots'. The root-tubers of the Dahlia, Lesser Celandine, and Orchids are also, in fact, adventitious; for they, too, grow from the stem at about ground level. Some orchids and other tropical plants, which grow on the branches of trees and never come into contact with the soil, have 'aerial roots' which remain suspended in the air, and are able to supply the plant with moisture absorbed from the saturated atmosphere of the forests. These are supplemented by similar adventitious roots. Their outer surfaces are of a spongy texture, and consist of specially modified cells. In Maize and Bamboo, where the plant is large and has only a comparatively thin stem to support it, adventitious roots, called 'buttress' or 'stilt roots', grow out from the bottom of the stem to prevent the plant from being blown over. They are not unlike the flying buttresses seen in some churches and cathedrals.

5. RESPIRATORY OR BREATHING ROOTS. Like other living structures, roots must breathe. This they can usually do by absorbing the air trapped in the small spaces between the soil particles,

unless the soil becomes waterlogged. In the waterlogged mangrove swamps of the tropics, many of the plants have special root modifications by which, instead of growing downwards in the usual way, many of the roots grow upwards into the air. Those parts of the roots exposed to the air have patches where the cells are loosely joined, and through these spaces exchange of gases takes place. Breathing or respiratory roots are only occasionally adventitious.

ROSES. Some of the loveliest of our countryside flowers belong to the very large rose family. Of the roses themselves there are the pink Dog-roses, the white Burnet-roses, the hairy Sweet Briar or Eglantine, and the white, scentless flowers of the Trailing or Field Rose. Among the wild relatives of the roses are the shrubby Blackberry, Raspberry, and Dewberry, the tree-like Blackthorn, Wild Cherries, Hawthorn, Crab-apples, and Rowan or Mountain Ash, as well as herbaceous wild plants like the Silver-weed, Wild Strawberry, Cinquefoil, Tormentil, Meadow-sweet, and Herb Bennet. Besides these British species, members of the rose family are to be found in all parts of the world, although they occur most abundantly in northern temperate regions. In warm climates, the leaves of roses are often tough, leathery, and evergreen—very different from the fine, delicate rose-leaves of Great Britain.

The flowers of roses and related plants are made up on the same general pattern. Each flower has five green sepals, five large free petals of varying colours, and many stamens. Some flowers have only one carpel, while in others the number may be indefinite. Sometimes the carpels are free, and sometimes joined (*see* FLOWERS).

The most common British wild rose is the popular Dog-rose, so called because, since the days of the Ancient Greeks and Romans, it was believed to cure the bite of a mad dog. Its leaves are compound, being divided into seven serrated leaflets, and having two pronounced

THE ENGLISH WILD ROSE
Harold Bastin

leaf-structures or 'stipules' at the base of the leaf-stalk. The stems and leaf-stalks are covered with prickles, which curve backwards. The delicate perfume of the flowers attracts bees and other insects, which collect the pollen and, incidentally, help to cross-pollinate the flowers. After fertilization, the fruits develop into scarlet 'hips', so attractive to birds, which unwittingly help to distribute the seeds.

The Burnet, or Scots Rose, is a much smaller shrub than the Dog-rose, and is fairly common near the coast. During the summer, it develops handsome, white flowers, with stamens which form a well-marked golden boss in the centre of the flower. The hips are large and globe-shaped, sometimes dull red, but more usually a rich black. Easily recognized by the fragrant smell of its rubbed leaves, the Sweet Briar or Eglantine has sticky, fragrant, reddish glands on the lower sides of the leaves. It is a more slender plant than the Dog-rose, and its pink flowers are seen in hedgerows in early summer, generally solitary. The Field Rose has slender, trailing branches, which often extend for many feet. Its shiny leaflets are common in hedgerows and thickets, and the white flowers, in bunches of three or four at the ends of the branches, appear in the summer. They last much longer than those of the Dog-rose.

See also HEDGEROWS.
See also Vol. VI: ROSES.

RUFF, *see* WADING-BIRDS (picture, p. 14).

RUMINANTS. These are animals which 'chew the cud', a process most highly developed in CATTLE, SHEEP, and DEER (qq.v.). The stomach of a ruminant is divided into four parts, as shown

in the diagram. The food is cropped, and then swallowed, unchewed and in bulk, into the paunch or rumen, where it is stored until the whole paunch is filled. The beast then begins to ruminate. During this process, the food passes from the paunch into the honeycomb bag, where it is squeezed into round 'boluses' or balls of 'cud'. The balls are regurgitated, one by one, up the gullet into the mouth, and there they are mixed with saliva and chewed until they become soft and liquid. Each ball is now swallowed again, and goes direct to the manyplies. The form of the gullet is such that dry bulky food closes the entrance to the manyplies and opens that to the paunch, whereas liquid and pulpy chewed food follows the other passage and closes the entrance to the paunch. The manyplies allows only well-chewed material to slip between its filter-like leaves into the belly, and the residue alone passes on to the gut. The process of chewing the cud allows a shy animal to swallow a large amount of food in a very short time, and to digest it at leisure.

See also MAMMALS; NUTRITION OF ANIMALS.

S

SABLE, *see* WEASEL, Section 4.

SALAMANDER. The term 'salamander' has been applied to many creatures, all belonging to the Caudata or tailed AMPHIBIA (q.v.), but scientifically not closely related to one another. It includes the true Salamanders, represented by the Spotted Salamanders of Europe and the Newts in England; the Mexican Axolotl and the Marbled and Tiger Salamanders of North America; the Red, the Dwarf, and the Slimy Salamanders of the U.S.A.; and the Giant Salamander of Japan. Any of the Amphibia, provided it has legs and a tail, might be termed a Salamander, if we use the word in a popular sense. All Salamanders pass through a larval stage; but their tadpoles throughout their lives are much more like their parents than are those of TOADS and FROGS (qq.v.)—tailless Amphibia. Some species never lose their gills, and spend their whole lives in the water.

Salamanders are found mainly in northern countries, except for a few species which inhabit the mountainous regions of central America. North America has many more species than Europe, Asia, and Africa. Europe has some twenty species, and there are fifteen or more in eastern Asia; but the dry regions of south-western Asia are without them. The NEWTS (q.v.) are the only members of the Salamander family which are found in Britain. The belief that the Salamander can stand fire is, of course, a legend (*see* FABULOUS CREATURES, Vol. I).

The Spotted Salamander, the common Salamander of central Europe, lives in hilly districts, and hides by day under stones or fallen timber or among decaying leaves. It is black, with large, irregular spots and patches of bright yellow on the back and limbs. The secretion from its skin is poisonous to small animals, and for this reason it has few enemies in nature. It is frequently kept as a pet in England, and will live for years, feeding on worms or pieces of raw meat.

The Axolotl, a Salamander of Mexican origin, is greyish or whitish, sometimes pure white, with small yellow spots, and grows to a length of 6 or 7 inches. In the Mexican lakes, it permanently retains its larval form, with branching external gills and crested tail, and breeds as if it were fully developed. But in other parts of North America, it undergoes a METAMORPHOSIS (q.v.) or change of form, as do all other Salamanders. If the larval form is kept, and the amount of water in its tank is reduced little by little, it will gradually turn into the mature, lung-breathing Salamander. Axolotls live well in captivity, and are often kept as pets.

The Giant Salamander of Japan is the largest Salamander known, growing to a length of 3 feet or more. It has a heavy body, with a large head and bluntly rounded muzzle, and a dark-brown or black, thick, warty skin. It lives in mountain streams, usually fairly high up, and although found originally in both China and Japan, is now probably extinct in China. Its flesh is eaten by the country people. The Hell-bender, sometimes called the Mississippi Salamander, is of the same family as the Giant Salamander, differing mainly from the true Salamander in that it has no eyelids. The Hell-bender inhabits the rivers of the mountainous districts of the eastern States of North America, and lives entirely in the water. It has a stout body, short limbs, and a short and crested tail. Its skin is glandular and slimy to touch, and forms a thick fold along the side of the body. It is a voracious creature, being much disliked by fishermen, whose bait it often steals.

Another interesting Salamander is the Olm, a primitive, blind creature, living in the subterranean waters of the mountainous districts of south-eastern Europe. It is 10 inches long, and has a smooth, eel-like body ending in a crested tail. It is greyish in colour, except for the gills, which are coral-red. The limbs are small and feeble, with three toes on the fore-feet and two on the hind-feet. Another species belonging to the same family is the Mud Puppy or Furrowed Salamander, which is found in fresh-water in the U.S.A. and Canada, living in the mud at the bottom of streams. It has eyes, and is extremely resistant to cold.

The Siren or Mud Eel, an eel-like creature

AXOLOTL

OLM

SIREN OR MUD EEL

SPOTTED SALAMANDER

TYPES OF SALAMANDER

with external gills, belongs to the class of two-legged Salamanders, for it has two small fore-limbs, but no hind limbs. It lives in the swamps of southern U.S.A.

SALMON. 1. This fish justly deserves the title 'king of fishes'. It is certainly the most valuable of food-fishes, and supports an important industry wherever it is found (*see* SALMON FISHING, Vol. VI). Anglers have always counted it as their richest prize, and have developed its capture into a fine art (*see* ANGLING, FRESHWATER, Vol. IX). In strength and beauty it has few superiors. So important a fish has, of course, been carefully studied, and a great deal has been written about it. There are two main strains of Salmon, an Atlantic species and a group of Pacific species.

The Atlantic Salmon is found on the western coasts of Europe, but not in the Mediterranean, and on the eastern coasts of North America. So far as we know, there is only the one species, which, however, varies in appearance in different places or because of different habits. There is some difference of opinion as to whether Salmon are sea-fishes that breed in fresh-water, or fresh-water fishes that go down to the sea to feed. The latter is probably correct; but it is an unimportant matter compared to an understanding of the life-history of these fine creatures.

The eggs of Salmon are laid on the gravelly beds of rapid streams, where the female hollows out a shallow trough, or 'redd', and then covers the eggs with fine gravel. They take a long time to hatch out—anything from 5 weeks to 5 months, according to conditions. When they hatch out, the baby fish, or 'fry', are tiny and transparent. They carry part of the yolk of the egg beneath the body, and this is gradually absorbed during the first few days, before the fish have learned to feed by mouth. They grow rapidly, and are soon recognizable as little Salmon, called 'parr'—though at this stage they have dark bands across the body. They remain in fresh-water for about 2 years, feeding on insects, crustaceans, and so on. Then a change occurs in their make-up, and a beautiful silver sheen develops on the body, covering up the parr-marks. The 'parr' have now become 'smolt', and they move down the river to the sea.

Here they remain, feeding in the rich store-house of the ocean, and growing large and beautiful, for a varying period of time, until they are ready to return to the river to breed. This happens usually during the autumn, when the fish are about $3\frac{1}{2}$ years old. These Salmon, entering the rivers to spawn, are called 'grilse'; after spawning, they return to the sea the following spring, when they are called 'grilse-kelts'. Some, however, do not move up the rivers until the spring, when they are about 4 years old: these are known as 'small spring salmon'. Others may not leave the sea until they are 5 or 6 years old, when they are called 'maiden' fish.

Fresh from the rich feeding in the sea, the Salmon is plump and active, its flesh firm and red, and it is at this period that the fishermen set their nets or cast their lines to catch it. With the approach of spawning-time, however, the female turns to dull brown, spotted with red and orange, and with white-edged black spots, while the skin of the male becomes thick and spongy, and the jaws grow longer, especially the lower jaw, which becomes hooked at the end. After spawning, the Salmon are exhausted, and many of them are unable to reach the sea alive. Those that do, however, soon recover, and regain their bright silver coats. Some Salmon pass up the rivers to breed every year, others only occasionally.

The life-history of a particular fish can usually be found out by 'scale-reading'—that is, by examining one or more scales from the side of the body. The edges of the scales grow, rings being added at fairly regular intervals by growth outwards. Since the fish grows more rapidly in the sea, the rings are spaced farther apart during this period, whereas in freshwater periods they are very close together. So we find alternate 'zones' which, when added up, tell us how old the fish is, how many times it has been to the sea, and roughly for how long. Moreover, the changes that take place in the body at spawning-time leave a scar on the scale, so by these 'spawning-marks' we know how many times the fish has bred. This scale-reading is useful for many kinds of fish, but is particularly valuable when studying Salmon and Trout.

The rapid rivers up which the Salmon moves to spawn often have waterfalls or weirs; and to get over these into the peaceful waters above, the fish often makes enormous leaps—in fact, the name Salmon comes from a Latin word meaning 'to leap'. To encourage the valuable Salmon up difficult rivers, 'salmon-ladders' are often built, or by-passes cut, to enable them to get past waterfalls that would otherwise be impassable. Not all Salmon go to the sea, however: a few are 'land-locked'—that is, confined to lakes that have no outlet to the sea.

Of the Pacific Salmon, there are several species. The King Salmon, or Quinnot, of the north, runs up rivers in enormous numbers in the spring, at the age of about 4 years, and may travel over 2,000 miles to reach its spawning-ground. The Blue-back has similar habits. The Silver-dog, and Humpback Salmon, on the other hand, run in the autumn. Once having spawned, the Pacific Salmon never reach the sea again: they are so feeble that they fall a prey to parasites and disease, and the banks of the streams are littered for miles with their bodies.

2. TROUT. Closely related to the Salmon is the Trout, which alters so much in different circumstances that its study has proved very difficult: indeed, for a long time it was thought that there were many different species. Almost every stream

SALMON LEAPING UP A WATERFALL TO REACH ITS BREEDING-PLACE

A. Fraser-Brunner

has its own variety of Trout, some of them being very beautifully coloured. Those of mountain streams are generally only a few inches long, while those of great lakes reach a large size. In addition, some of them, called Sea-trout, have a silver livery like the Salmon, and feed in the sea in much the same way. Nevertheless, they are all the same species, their differences being the result of the different conditions of life.

To distinguish a Trout from a Salmon it is necessary to examine the little fleshy fin, or 'adipose fin', above the tail, behind the true dorsal fin. In a Salmon, the scales, counted downwards from the hind edge of this fin to the lateral line, number ten to thirteen; while in a Trout, the number is thirteen to sixteen. The number thirteen, which might be either Salmon or Trout, is fortunately not common.

The Trout is not so important a food-fish as the Salmon; but it is a highly prized sporting fish, and has been introduced into other countries for the benefit of the angler, notably to New Zealand, where it is now more common than many of the native fishes.

The Rainbow Trout of America is very similar, but can be recognized at once because it has many black spots on its tail. Finally, mention should be made of the exquisitely coloured Char, of which there are many kinds in America and Europe. Many lakes in Britain have their own distinct varieties.

See also Vol. VI: SALMON FISHING.
See also Vol. IX: FISHING.

SALT-MARSH PLANTS, see SEASHORE PLANTS, Section 3.

SAND-DUNE PLANTS, see SEASHORE PLANTS, Section 4.

SAND-GROUSE. These birds are not GROUSE (q.v.), but belong to a separate order of their own, showing some relation to Pigeons on the one hand and Game Birds on the other; their strong flight is rather like that of the Plover. They inhabit the desert regions of Africa and western and central Asia, one species belonging to Madagascar, and another spreading to southern Europe. Their plumage is of a colour and pattern to make them very difficult to see in their sandy surroundings. They have plump, compact bodies, long, pointed wings and tails, and feathered legs which are so short and have

such short toes that the birds cannot perch. They associate in flocks, often going long distances across the desert to their drinking pools. They will scratch themselves comfortable hollows in the sand, and there bask in the hot midday sun; but they also can stand severe cold. They nest in slight hollows in the ground, the hen always incubating the eggs by day and the cock by night.

One species, the Pallas's Sand-grouse, occasionally makes freak migrations from its natural home in central Asia to Europe. These migrations, from which there is normally no return, are, strictly speaking, irruptions (see MIGRATION). On certain years, the last occasion being in 1888, enormous flocks of Sand-grouse have arrived in the spring on the east coast of Britain, and have spread over the whole country, even as far as the western isles. They have attempted to breed, but sooner or later the damp cold of the north-western European climate has proved too much for them. Small invasions have been recorded in other years.

SANDPIPER, see WADING BIRDS, Section 3.

SANDWASP, see WASPS, Section 2.

SAPROPHYTES. Green plants obtain food by PHOTOSYNTHESIS (q.v.)—that is, by building up sugars and starch from raw materials acted upon by their green colouring matter, or chlorophyll, in the presence of sunlight. Some plants, however, contain no chlorophyll, and so cannot feed in this way. They obtain their food either directly from the living body of another plant or animal, when they are described as PARASITES (q.v.), or

STUMP FLAP (*Polystictus versicolor*)
A saprophytic fungus growing on a dead stump of wood
Harold Bastin

from dead organic matter, when they are called saprophytes.

Saprophytes are of great importance to the farmer and gardener, because of the part they play in promoting decay. Many types of saprophytic bacteria live on dead plant and animal matter, causing it to decay, until it is reconverted into the original chemical elements from which it was formed (*see* NITROGEN SUPPLY IN PLANTS; CARBON IN LIVING THINGS). Another big group of saprophytes are the FUNGI, of which the MOULDS and YEASTS (qq.v.) are well-known examples.

A few flowering plants also live as Saprophytes, examples in Britain being *Monotropa*, the Yellow Bird's Nest, which belongs to the heather family, and *Neottia*, the Bird's Nest Orchid. Both have at the base of the stem a mass of short, thick roots (tangled like a bird's nest), and the fleshy upper part of the stem bears small, yellowish-brown scales, instead of green leaves. The Yellow Bird's Nest grows in beech-woods, and probably obtains its food-supply from the decaying beech leaves. The exact way in which these plants feed is not known, but an excess of organic matter is necessary to them.

See also BACTERIA.

SARDINE, *see* HERRING.

SAW-FISH, *see* MACKEREL.

SAWFLY. This insect is so called because its ovipositor, or egg-laying tube, is toothed like the edge of a saw, for cutting into the plant tissues where it lays its eggs. It has a large, square head, broad, ample wings, and a stoutly built abdomen. The absence of a narrow 'waist' just below the thorax will distinguish a Sawfly from its relative, the ICHNEUMON FLY (q.v.).

The larvae or CATERPILLARS (q.v.) are vegetarian, feeding mostly on trees and shrubs. They differ, as a rule, from the caterpillars of butterflies and moths in having more pairs of claspers behind the three pairs of jointed legs. In some species there is a pair on each segment of the abdomen. Caterpillars of Stem Sawflies, which bore up the stems of plants, have only vestiges of legs. Of these, the Wheat Stem-borer is destructive to wheat, though much less so in Britain than in some other countries. Some Sawfly caterpillars are covered with a white or bluish bloom, which gives them a very mealy appearance. Others have a slimy, brownish or greyish covering that makes them look like slugs, but they shed this before they pupate. Many others are quite clean on the surface: the caterpillar of the Currant Sawfly, for instance, is pale green dotted with tiny black spots.

Most Sawfly caterpillars feed openly by daytime, but some feed only at night; others, such as the Apple Sawfly, hide in fruit, and there are some which hide in plant-stems or in galls (growths of plant tissues), which they have caused to grow round them. A few are leaf-miners, boring galleries between the upper and lower surfaces of leaves. The pupae are usually enclosed in tough silken cocoons, and often buried below ground. Some adults are short-lived, the males dying within a few hours of pairing, and the females after laying their eggs, a process which takes only a few days. They are sluggish fliers, not usually flying more than a few yards. On hot summer days they may be seen resting on flowers.

See also Vol. VI: INSECT PESTS.

SCALE INSECT. Some of these bugs, closely related to the APHIDES (q.v.), are serious agricultural pests; but others are of some use to man. For instance, a Scale Insect, called the Cochineal Insect, which lives on species of cactus and prickly pear, provides a red dye, used among other things for soldiers' tunics. Dyes and artists' pigments, as well as a resinous varnish called shellac, are obtained from the Lac Insects of India; and the Chinese at one time used to get much of their wax for candles from another Scale Insect, the Chinese Wax Insect, that feeds on the ash tree.

In most species of Scale Insects, the males have wings; but only the first pair is fully developed, the hind-wings being very small. During their change from larvae to adults, their mouth parts disappear, and, as adults, the males take no food. They are always smaller than the females, sometimes extraordinarily so. The females are always wingless, and often without any legs. Some, such as the Cochineal Insect and the Mealy Bugs, retain their legs and are active throughout life; but other adult female Scale Insects show almost every stage of degeneration, some being found without antennae or legs, firmly attached to their food-plant by means of their mouth parts. Because of this habit of clinging to their food-plant, many Scale Insects have been transported all over the world, especially in the export of nursery plants. The females always provide themselves with some special covering of their own making. In the Mealy Bugs, for instance, this is a fine powdery wax, and the crimson Cochineal Scale Insect excretes a white mass of waxy threads. As soon as the Lac Insects hatch, they begin to suck the juices of their food-plant and then to exude a resinous covering. When large numbers feed together, the twig becomes encrusted with this substance, and here and there are little cavities, in each of which a young Lac Insect is growing up, and in which, when fully grown, she lays her eggs. Most female Scale Insects retain the discarded skins of their two larval stages, and increase the covering by an additional secretion. In some of these, the resulting 'scale' looks like an oyster or mussel shell, and beneath it the imprisoned insect lives her life, sucking the juices of the plant tissues beneath her, and eventually laying her eggs there. The eggs are never openly exposed: most Scale Insects cover them with the 'scale'; but in the Cochineal Insect they are protected by the dead body of the female parent.

There are some 150 kinds of Scale Insects in the British Isles, the Mussel Scale being a well-known pest on apple, pear, and plum trees (*see* INSECT PESTS, Vol. VI).

See also BUGS.

SCALES. The scales of fish develop from small, nipple-like protuberances, called 'papillae', in the skin. Their roots are so arranged that the scales overlap, like tiles on a roof. The scales of fish such as COD, HERRING, and SALMON (qq.v.) are called 'soft', because they are completely covered with a thin, slimy epidermis or outer skin. Fish such as SHARKS (q.v.), skate, and dog-fish have bony scales, with enamel tips that come through the surface like tiny teeth. The scales of reptiles are securely fixed in the skin, and covered over with a hard, horny layer. The 'slough' of a SNAKE (q.v.) is not a shed skin, but is this outer covering, which bears the imprints of the scales. The scales on the wings of insects such as butterflies and moths fit together so closely that they look like one complete surface. These scales are responsible for the patterns and colours on the wings (*see* BUTTERFLIES).

SCALLOP. These molluscs are of interest on account of their habits, their food value, and the

SCALLOP (PECTEN) SHOWING ROW OF GREENISH-BLUE EYES ROUND THE EDGES OF THE MANTLE. *M. Burton*

beauty of their shells. Perhaps the most familiar species is the Great Scallop, so often seen upon the fishmonger's slab. It is the largest British species, average specimens measuring about 6 inches in length by 5 inches in width. There is a striking inequality between the two valves of the shell, the lower being more deeply convex than the upper, which is almost flat. The rather thick shell is further strengthened outside by regularly spaced broad ribs, which in turn have a corrugated surface. While the lower valve generally has a whitish ground, showing delicate tints of pink and creamy yellow, the flat upper valve is more brightly coloured, the ribs often showing a rich dark-red ground with the finer corrugations brown, both colours grading to a lighter hue towards the apex. But quite the most remarkable feature in the Scallop is the row of iridescent, greenish-blue eyes, which shine like precious stones. These are placed along the two edges of the mantle, so as to receive the light when the shell is open, and they are almost as complex in structure as the eyes of the higher vertebrate animals. How much or what exactly the Scallop sees it is difficult to estimate; but undoubtedly these remarkable eyes are capable of warning their owner of approaching danger, so giving the Scallop time either to beat a rapid retreat, or to close the valves of its shell tightly. Normally, Scallops rest on the floor of the sea, with their shells slightly gaping; but when alarmed, or if they wish to seek another resting-place, they shoot through the water in a curious zigzag manner achieved by the rapid alternate opening and closing of their shells.

The Quin, or Queen Scallop, is a slightly

smaller species than the Great Scallop. The shell averages about 2 inches in breadth, both valves being slightly convex, and it is not so thick as that of the Great Scallop. Different specimens vary considerably in colour, from pure white to pale pink, yellow, red, brown, or purple. The Quin is commonly found round the coasts of England on sandy bottoms offshore, sometimes in large numbers. The shells of many smaller species, some hardly measuring ½ inch in width, but beautifully coloured, may be found stranded on sandy shores as the tide goes out.

See also MOLLUSCS.
See also Vol. VI: SHELL-FISH FISHING.

SCARAB. The celebrated beetle, to which the great naturalist Linnaeus gave the name *Scarabaeus sacer*, and others of the same kind, are called Scarabs. These insects were held sacred by the ancient Egyptians on account of their strange habit of fashioning perfectly round balls from the animal-droppings upon which they feed. These they roll about, pushing them backwards by thrusting their heads against the ground. This curious habit has aroused attention and wonder for many centuries. It was supposed that the ball contained the insect's egg, which could only be hatched in this way; but we now know that most are used for food and are generally eaten in the end by the insect itself. The female beetle, however, digs a hole in which she places a ball, and then, opening it, deposits an egg in the cavity, and carefully closes it again. The interior is eaten by the soft-bodied grub which emerges from the egg, while the outer crust becomes the cell in which it undergoes its

SACRED EGYPTIAN SCARAB PUSHING ITS FOOD-BALL
G. J. Arrow

transformation into a winged beetle. Egyptian sculptures and paintings are full of representations of these beetles in all sorts of curious forms, sometimes holding a ball and sometimes with their wings spread in flight. Models of them, usually of baked clay, were also made in immense numbers—probably because healing virtues were attributed to them. These, also called scarabs, are still manufactured and sold to-day, and a few superstitious people still credit them with mysterious properties.

See also BEETLES.

SCIENTIFIC NAMES. The biological sciences are unique in having an international language, so that any living creature, whether plant or animal, has a scientific name by which it is known throughout the world. The criticism is often made that the use of 'difficult' names is unnecessary, the common names being quite sufficient. A single example will meet this criticism. We are familiar in this country with the robin, a small bird with a red breast; but there are many other birds in different parts of the world, each having a red breast, each known by the common name of 'robin', and yet none related to the other. The only way any of these 'robins' can be accurately described is by its scientific name, which shows its true relationship. Thus, the British robin is *Erithacus rubecula*, the robin of North America is *Planesticus migratorius*, of South Africa *Caffrornis caffra*, of India *Saxicoloides fulicata*, of Australia *Petroica phoenieca*, and of New Zealand *Miro longipes*. If these universal names were not used, then the word 'robin' would become entirely meaningless, except in local use. And there are many other similar cases.

Scientific names consist of two, or three, parts. The scientific name of the common English House Sparrow, written in full, is *Passer domesticus domesticus* (L.). The first name (*Passer*) is the generic name, and shows the genus to which this and other sparrows belong. The second name (*domesticus*) is the specific name, and shows the species of Sparrow (i.e. House Sparrow, not Tree Sparrow). The third name is the subspecific name, and shows the sub-species or geographical race—that is, the European race (not the Syrian or Algerian). The letter (L.) shows that LINNAEUS (q.v. Vol. V) first gave one of these names to this bird. But Linnaeus considered the sparrow to be related closely to the

Finches, and called it *Fringilla domestica*. Had he called it *Passer domesticus* as we do now, the letter L. standing for his name would not have been enclosed in brackets. Thus the scientific name for the Skylark remains the same as Linnaeus gave it—*Alauda arvensis*, and is written in full *Alauda arvensis arvensis* L. (In Linnaeus's day the three-name system, with a third name to indicate sub-species, was not used.) These names are normally written *Passer d. domesticus* (L.) or *Alauda a. arvensis* L., where the specific and the sub-specific names are the same. (Such races are known as the 'typical' race.) Where the names of the species and sub-species differ, they must both be written in full. So the Eastern Skylark (from Asia) is *Alauda arvensis intermedia* Swinhoe. (This was first named in 1863 by an ornithologist, Swinhoe, who believed the bird to be a different species, not merely a different sub-species.)

See also CLASSIFICATION OF ANIMALS AND PLANTS.

SCORPION. This animal belongs to an order of the class known as Arachnida, to which belong also SPIDERS, MITES, and TICKS (qq.v.). There are about 600 known species, found in most warm parts of the world, but not in New Zealand, Patagonia, and the oceanic islands. They are generally about 2 to 4 inches long.

In ancient times they enjoyed a reputation, not wholly deserved, for ferocity and venom, owing to the facts that they can run at a great speed, that they possess large, powerful claws called 'pedipalpi', and that they carry, and

A FEMALE SCORPION CARRYING HER NEWLY BORN YOUNG ON HER BACK.   *Edmund A. Robins*

freely use, a poison-bearing sting at the end of the tail. When a scorpion strikes, it arches its tail over its back and then thrusts it forward; at the same time, muscles squeeze the poison-gland, and force the poison into the wound made by the tail. The sting of a scorpion is much more virulent than the bite of a spider, and is instantaneously fatal to insects, spiders, and centipedes. Some scorpions are more dangerous than others: many are quite harmless to man; others may produce pain and swelling, more or less serious, and very occasionally death follows. A scorpion, however, cannot poison itself—a fact which contradicts the popular fable that a scorpion, surrounded by fire, will commit suicide.

Most scorpions are more active at night than by day. They never attack unprovoked, and, when disturbed, they generally much prefer to escape unnoticed. They lead solitary lives, and are said to be found together only when mating or when one is eating another. They seem never to drink: evidently their food provides them with all the moisture they require—so that they are well adapted to the hot sandy places in which they are usually found. Like spiders, they can survive prolonged fasts. Like spiders, too, they are slow eaters, and will spend more than an hour consuming one cockroach.

All scorpions are born alive, not in eggs, and the newly born young, like young Wolf Spiders, are carried on their mother's back until their first moult, after which they can feed themselves.

See also SPIDERS; FALSE SCORPIONS.

SCORPION-FISH. This name is given to a number of warm-sea fishes, which have the sharp spines of the first dorsal fin on the back provided with a poison that causes very painful wounds. Needless to say, they are much dreaded by fishermen. Many of them are quite fantastic in appearance, and are often beautifully coloured, generally being marked to resemble their surroundings. One kind, found in the South Seas, is black when living among dark volcanic rocks, mottled with deep red when found among red sea-weed, and bright yellow when caught in deep water—yellow because concealment is not necessary in the dark of the deep ocean, and because yellow colouring matter will develop in the dark better than black or red. Another kind of Scorpion-fish, found in Indian waters, is always covered with colonies of small polyps (relatives

A SEA BULLHEAD
A. Fraser-Brunner

of the Sea-anemones), only to be found growing on this fish. The polyp does the fish a good turn by concealing it from enemies, while in return it gets transport from place to place.

A species of Scorpion-fish, bright red in colour, is sometimes seen in American and British fish-shops, where it is called Norway Haddock, or the more fitting name Rose-fish. One species is often called the Lion-fish, and is found in reefs of the Indian and Pacific Oceans.

Related to these are the Bullheads, a large family of small fishes inhabiting seas north of the Equator. Most live near coasts, but a few species are found in deep water. They have two dorsal fins, the first with spiny rays, and a large bony head, usually provided with sharp spines above the eyes, on the nose, and on the gill-covers. Some of them are able to make a loud noise by moving one bone of the gill-cover against another. There is one freshwater species, the Miller's Thumb of Europe, common in England and Wales, a small fish about 3 inches long. Its head is broad and flattened, the same shape as the thumb of a miller, which is flat from continually testing the texture of his flour.

Bullheads, in common with certain other

RED GURNARD
A. Fraser-Brunner

fishes, show their feelings by sudden changes in colour, generally turning pale with anger and dark with fear. Most of them have a pattern consisting of irregular blotches that help to conceal them among the weeds and corals where they live. Many of them take good care of their eggs, placing them under stones, inside broken bulbs of the bladder-wrack, inside empty mollusc shells, in crevices of rock or coral, or even making a crude sort of nest among seaweed. Sometimes the male will take the whole egg-cluster under him, embracing it with his pectoral and pelvic fins, which have numerous prickles underneath, enabling him to get a firmer grip; and there he will rest, aerating the eggs by fanning every now and then with his large pectoral fins, until they hatch out.

Gurnards, similarly, have large, bony heads, often armed with ridges and spines. The pectoral fins are long, the lowermost rays being separate, strong, jointed, and movable like fingers. By their aid, the Gurnards are able to walk about on the bed of the sea, and to feel about in the sand or explore inside shells for food. Many Gurnards have strong, thorny plates of bone along the side, and sometimes a pair of long, bony, sword-like growths, pointing forwards above the mouth, which they use, maybe, for digging out worms and other creatures on which they feed. These fishes are quite well known among fishermen for the loud grunting noises they make when caught. The larger kinds are useful as food.

SEA-ANEMONE. These gaily tinted, almost flower-like, animals are abundant in the deep rock-pools exposed at low tide all round our coasts; but they may very easily escape the untrained eye of the casual visitor, for, when alarmed or left exposed by the receding tide, they contract their graceful tentacles and bodies until they look like rather uninviting blobs of jelly. They are found in all climates, from the cold seas of the Arctic and Antarctic to tropical regions, where they attain their greatest size and magnificence.

Anemones vary greatly in colour, shape, and size. The soft body is called the 'column'; it may be long and slender, or short and fat, and it is capable of changing considerably in a single individual—for the Anemone can expand, contract, and alter the shape of its body at will. At the top of the body-column is the 'disk', with the

tentacles

tentacles

mouth

partition wall

stomach

apertures in wall

aperturesin wall

column or body.

column or body

partition wall.

muscle

muscle

A

B

A. SEA-ANEMONE WITH EXPANDED TENTACLES.
B. CROSS-SECTION OF SEA-ANEMONE

slit-like mouth at the centre, encircled by one or several rows of tentacles. The tentacles vary considerably in size, shape, and number in the different species. They are hollow, extremely sensitive, constantly on the move, expanding and contracting, and are armed externally with many minute, complex, stinging-thread cells used for defence and for the capture of prey. The Anemone attaches itself to the rocks by its base or foot, and normally sticks to one spot, though it sometimes glides slowly over the surface or, relinquishing its hold upon the rock, trusts to the flow of the tide and the waving of its tentacles to carry it to a more congenial spot. The minute oval larvae emerge from the mouth of their parent, and by the rhythmic lashing of their hair-like cilia, swim freely through the water. They soon settle down on the floor of the sea and change into very small Anemones. The mouth of an Anemone is very elastic, and comparatively large animals are sometimes swallowed, so that the body becomes very much distended. How long they live under natural conditions is difficult to estimate, but one particular specimen is known to have lived more than 100 years.

While some species live attached to the rocks in the tidal pools and at greater depths, others live half-buried in the sand, and others are almost invariably found attached to a whelk-shell inhabited by a hermit-crab (see CRAB). One group of Anemones, known as *Edwardsia*, is of special interest, because in their structure they make a connecting link between the Anemones and the true CORALS (q.v.). There are six British species of *Edwardsia*, all small in size and with long, slender bodies, which do not end in a flat disk, but are rounded. They live with their bodies entirely buried in the sand, only their tentacles being expanded at the sur-face. When the tide is out, they disappear from view, the only guide to their presence being a small roundish hole in the sand.

The largest and handsomest of our British Sea-anemones is the Dahlia Anemone, which measures sometimes as much as 8 inches across its expanded disk. It has a stout body-column, and its tentacles, though short, taper gracefully to a point, and are arranged in five rows round the mouth-disk. The Dahlia Anemone varies much in colour—pinkish-red, crimson, purple, or deep orange, while the tentacles may be snowy-white or banded with delicate shades of red, white, and orange. Those that live low down on the shore among the rocks often hide themselves under a covering of fine shingle and fragments of shell; but those living in the deep rock-pools do not trouble to camouflage themselves in this way, and remain fully expanded. The Beadlet Anemone may often be found in the rock-pools between mid-tide and low-tide levels. Crimson and green are its commonest colours, but there are many intermediate tints. Generally, the base is edged by a narrow blue line, and the short, stout column is purplish-brown, with a band of brilliant azure-blue spots round its upper margin, which give it the appearance of a bead necklace—hence its popular name. It was one of these Beadlet Anemones that was taken from the Firth of Forth by the famous old Scotch naturalist, Sir John Dalyell, in 1828, when it was judged to be not less than 7 years old: it not only survived its captor, but continued to flourish in captivity until 4 August 1887, when it died. The Plumose Anemone is one of the most grace-ful and exquisitely tinted inhabitants of the deep rock-pools. It has a tall, moderately slender column, crowned with innumerable tentacles, and it varies considerably in colour. The Snake-lock has long slender tentacles, and looks rather like a shaggy chrysanthemum.

See also COLOUR PLATE, opp. p. 400.

SEA-BREAM, *see* SEA-PERCH.

SEA-COW. The Dugong and the Manatee are the two members of the Sea-cow family. They are MAMMALS (q.v.), but are not related to whales, although they have horizontal tail-fins, no hind-legs, and flipper-like fore-legs. They live in shallow waters, never venturing out into the open sea. The Dugong is found along the coasts of the Indian Ocean and Australian

Seas, and the Manatee in tropical rivers on both sides of the Atlantic. Sea-cows have small eyes and mouths, and tiny holes for ears; their thick skin is either finely wrinkled or rugged like bark, and is sometimes sparsely covered with fine hairs. They are sluggish, harmless, and not very intelligent creatures, living on seaweed and other water plants. The female produces one baby at a time, which she looks after with great care. When suckling she raises her head and breasts above the water, showing her baby clinging to her, supported by her flippers. It has been suggested that this human-looking sight was the origin of some of the stories of the legendary MERMAID (q.v. Vol. I).

Manatees (except for one species) have three rudimentary nails on their flippers: this pecu-

A DUGONG

liarity, and the way they use their flipper-like hands when nursing their young, account for their name (derived from the Latin *manus*, a hand). They grow up to 8 feet long. They have remarkable mouths, with prehensile upper lips, with which they can grasp and eat food without any help from their lower lips. They are now rather scarce, as they have been much hunted for their oil and hides.

The Dugong is generally smaller than the Manatee, its average length being from 5 to 7 feet. It has a crescent-shaped tail, and is without the nails on its flippers. Formerly Dugongs used to be seen in large herds of several hundreds, and they were so fearless of man that they would allow themselves to be touched. Now they are found in small parties only, and have become much more wary.

SEA-CUCUMBER (Holothurian). Although totally different in shape and appearance, the Sea-cucumbers are really close relatives of the STAR-FISH and SEA-URCHIN (qq.v.), and have derived their popular name from the tough, warty skin covering their somewhat sausage-shaped bodies. Like the starfishes, Sea-cucum-

A SEA-CUCUMBER OR HOLOTHURIAN

bers possess tube-feet; but the number and position of these vary considerably in the different species: they may be present as five regular zones, running down the entire length of the animal, or scattered over the surface of the body, or again reduced, as in the slender worm-like *Synapta*, to a circle of oral tentacles.

The Sea-cucumbers have no continuous limy skeleton, like that of the Sea-urchins; but instead they have innumerable microscopic spicules or rods and plates embedded in the tough skin. These are often of great beauty, resembling miniature anchors, or perforated oval plates. Some species are found round the coasts of Britain, among the seaweeds, or with their bodies partly buried in the sand and mud. One of the commonest is the Cotton Spinner, which may measure nearly 12 inches in length when fully expanded. It is so called because of the mass of long whitish threads, composed of mucus combined with parts of its inner organs, which the animal spouts into the surrounding water when alarmed or injured. In tropical seas, the Sea-cucumbers grow to a large size, and, under the name of Trepang or *Bêche-de-mer*, are sold as food in the markets of the Far East. The giant of the tribe is the tropical Bessel's Sea-cucumber, which grows to 6 feet in length.

SEA-HORSE. The quaint Sea-horse, shaped very much like the knight in a set of chess-men, is the only fish that can use its tail for holding on to stems of seaweed. Many different species, varying from 2 to 12 inches long, are found in all warm seas, all looking very much alike, except for certain Australian kinds. These latter are among the most fantastic of all fishes, for they are provided with long bony outgrowths from the body, upon which are flaps of skin; so that the creatures look exceedingly like bunches of seaweed, being similarly coloured. They are often called Leafy Sea Dragons.

Sea-horses are close relatives of the Pipe-fishes, which do not have the head bent at an angle to the body, and do not use the tail in the

SEA-HORSE AND PIPE-FISH
A. Fraser-Brunner

of these large water mammals are quite active on land on their flippers, but others have greater difficulty once they are out of the water.

The Sea-lions and Sea-bears are the most active, and spend a good deal of time on land. By turning their hind flippers forward, they can walk and even run and climb rocks almost as easily as land animals. The Sea-lions or Hair Seals are the largest—a very big one being 12 to 13 feet long. These seals, however, do not have the soft, woolly underfur which makes the skins of the smaller Sea-bears or Fur Seals so much sought after by the fur-hunter.

Sea-lions and Sea-bears go to their breeding places in the spring. The first to arrive are the males, who at once select stations for themselves. They fight fiercely amongst themselves for the best positions; and some of the early arrivals, which took up stations near the shore, become so exhausted that they have to yield and move farther inland. When the females arrive, each male tries to capture as many as possible for himself. In order to guard their harems, often of from ten to fifteen females, the bull seals have to be continually on the watch. Throughout the breeding season, therefore, which lasts for several weeks, they neither eat nor drink, with the result that, though at the beginning of the season they are fat and in good condition, by the end they become thin and weak. The cubs are born on land, generally one only at a birth, weighing from 3 to 4 pounds.

Walruses, which live in the Arctic Ocean, are bulkier and less active than the Sea-lions and Sea-bears. Both male and female grow powerful tusks 20 inches or more long. As a rule, Walruses collect in herds; and when they are on shore or on an ice-floe, they huddle together like

same way. They are mostly small, worm-like creatures, with a long, tubular snout, at the end of which is a small mouth. The body is encased in rings of bone, somewhat after the fashion of flexible gas-piping. Sea-horses and Pipe-fishes are feeble swimmers, moving about by a waving motion of the small fin on the back, and being carried from place to place by currents. The males have a pouch on the underside of the tail, into which the female injects the eggs. When the eggs hatch, it is apparently the male which gives birth to the young. Even after hatching, the young remain near the father, darting back into his pouch if danger threatens.

SEAL. There are three separate families of seals: the Sea-lions and Sea-bears (or Eared Seals); the Walruses; and the True or Earless Seals. The Walruses live entirely in northern waters; but the other two families live on both sides of the Equator, though they are found in the greatest numbers on northern coasts. Some

FEMALE CAPE SEA-BEAR AND CUB
C. A. Gibson-Hill

COLONY OF ALASKAN FUR SEALS ON THE COAST OF ST. PAUL ISLAND, BERING SEA
E. O. Hoppé

pigs. They feed mostly on shell-fish prised off the rocks with their tusks. They are very devoted to their young, and also show great sympathy with each other: the whole herd, for instance, will unite in an intelligent defence of a wounded companion. Although not at all aggressive, they will fight fiercely if attacked, and use their great tusks with considerable effect. They have a deep, full roar, and a bark which they repeat several times in succession.

The True Seals are not very active on land. They have thick, close fur, and a large reserve of fat (blubber) under the skin. The largest species is the Elephant Seal, which is also the largest of all the seals, growing to 20 feet or more in length, with a girth of about 15 feet. It gets its name from the male's short, movable trunk. The Grey Seal lives in the north Atlantic, and is fairly common off the shores of northern Europe. It breeds on the Scilly Isles and several of the Scottish Isles, and is very common off south and west Ireland. Its voice is a gloomy 'hoo', often accompanied by angry, bear-like growls. During the breeding season the males fight fiercely amongst themselves for the females, often severely wounding each other with their teeth. One, or sometimes two, young are born after about $11\frac{1}{2}$ months. The baby has a white, woolly coat, which is shed at the end of 3 weeks and is replaced by a slaty-blue coat. At 4 weeks old, the cubs are weaned, and the mothers go off to sea leaving the young to find their way to the water unaided and unattended. The slaty-blue coat is gradually replaced by the adult coat, which varies a great deal from brown to grey.

The smaller Common Seals are found also off the coasts of the British Isles, especially on the smaller Scottish isles. They spend much of their life ashore, coming to rocks or sand-banks, usually at half-ebb, to bask in the sun and sleep. Apparently they post a sentinel, and then all lie, head to sea, ready to dive on any alarm. The young take to the water as soon as they are born, and swim with ease. Common Seals are very easily tamed, and will often follow their owners about like dogs.

SEA-LILY, *see* STARFISH.

SEA-LION, *see* SEAL.

SEA-PERCH. This name is generally applied to a large number of different fishes, all having the front portion of the dorsal or back fin supported by sharp spines; and all with one spine and five soft, branched rays on the pelvic fins. Many of them are very valuable as food. Only a few of the most important can be described here.

On the Atlantic coasts of America and southern Europe are found the Sea-bass, which often enter the mouths of rivers. They are good food, and also very good sporting fish, being much prized by anglers, particularly in Britain. They are caught with fine tackle, somewhat after the fashion of salmon. Very much larger are the so-called Groupers, of tropical seas, which are often brightly coloured. One Indian species, for instance, is vivid red with many blue spots. Some of them, usually called Jewfish, grow to 6 feet or more, and weigh 500 or 600 lb., while the biggest, found in the south Pacific, is said to reach 12 feet in length. Various other handsome kinds, such as those known as Snappers, and a multitude of small, brilliant species, are found throughout the warmer seas of the world.

A small, brightly coloured species of Sea-perch, called the Comber, lives in the Mediterranean, and sometimes strays to the coast of Britain. The remarkable thing about this fish is that it is hermaphrodite—or both male and female in the same fish.

The Cardinal-fishes are related, but differ in having two separate dorsal fins. Most of them are small and handsomely marked, and live among rocks and corals. They have the habit of taking their eggs into their mouths to protect them until they hatch out. One species, found

recently on the coast of Florida, lives inside the mouth cavity of a large sea-snail, popping out every now and then in search of food. Strongly marked and often brilliantly coloured species belonging to a family called the Pomacentridae are found in coral-reefs. The most famous is a small fish with a bright orange body crossed by pearl-blue stripes and edged with velvety black. It lives inside the body-cavity of a giant sea-anemone, darting out and in for food—quite unharmed by the anemone's stinging-cells or digestive juices. It is sometimes called the Clown-fish, or Anemone-fish.

The Horse-mackerels, so called because many of them resemble Mackerel, although there is no relationship, are particularly common in tropical seas. Some of them, the Cavallas or Pampanos, grow very large. Most are silvery in colour, and have two small separate spines in front of the anal fin. They change very much with age, the fully grown fish being very different from the young (which have, in most cases, thread-like filaments on the fins). Some of the larger kinds, notably the Yellow-tail of America, are well-known sporting fishes; while others are of value as food.

The young of many kinds of Horse-mackerel live in the open sea, where they seek refuge from their enemies beneath the 'umbrellas' of the larger kinds of medusae, or jelly-fish, protected by the deadly stinging-cells. One species of Horse-mackerel, often called the Scad, is found in British seas, sometimes in great abundance, but is of no use as food, for it is lean and bony, with a row of strong armour-plates along the side.

The famous Pilot-fish belongs to the Perch family. It is found nearly always in the company of sharks, and was once believed to lead them to their food—hence its name. It will often travel alongside ships in the same way, from which arose the idea that it could pilot vessels safely into harbour. In fact, it follows sharks simply in order to pick up the scraps left over when these large creatures devour their prey, trusting only in its swift movements to escape being eaten itself. Similarly, it no doubt accompanies ships to feed on the 'leavings' thrown overboard, and not in any spirit of benevolence. It is a bluish fish with dark cross-bands, and has a keel on each side of the tail.

The Sea-breams are a family of perch-like fishes, not at all like the freshwater Bream, which

MALE CARDINAL-FISH CARRYING THE EGGS IN HIS MOUTH FOR SAFETY. *A. Fraser-Brunner*

SOUTH SEA BUTTERFLY-FISHES
A. Fraser-Brunner

belongs to the CARP family (q.v.). There are many kinds of Sea-bream, some of them, such as the Porgies of America and the Schnappers of South Africa and Australia, being valued food-fish. One species, the Red Bream, is often sold in London markets. These fishes have very strong teeth, the front ones being pointed for grasping, the back ones blunt and smooth for grinding, admirably suited for crushing the shells of molluscs and crabs on which they feed. Perhaps the most famous species is the Red Tai, of Japan, which is as much a national emblem as the rising sun. Ebisu, the fish-god, is always shown in pictures and sculptures with a Red Tai under his arm.

Another group of Perch-like fishes is the tropical Butterfly-fishes—short and deep fishes, flattened from side to side, and with fins covered with scales. Their bright markings serve as camouflage, so that they are not easily seen in a coral-reef, with its strong light and shade. All these fishes have many close-set, bristle-like teeth in their jaws, with which they browse among the coral. Some of them, Angel-fishes, have a strong spine on the gill-cover. The best-known is the Emperor Fish of Indian seas, a very gaudy fish, with its yellow stripes crossing a blue or brown body, and blue and white markings on head and fins. These fishes change a great deal with age. When very small they have tough bony shields on the head, often with big spikes jutting out over the eyes; these they lose as they grow up. Some of the Angel-fishes, when young, have a black-and-white pattern, quite different from the gaudy adult.

SEA SERPENT. As with the Loch Ness Monster, there is no real evidence that the Great Sea Serpent exists. Many people claim to have seen it, and have described it, but it has never yet been caught. It is possible that the sea contains many large creatures that we know nothing about, but the larger they are, the less likely are they to have escaped capture—particularly if they are air-breathers, and must therefore come to the surface at frequent intervals. From time to time large sea creatures have been cast ashore, and have been claimed by the less reputable newspapers to be the Sea Serpent. But expert examination has shown that they are either well-known mammals or fish, generally in varying stages of decay. That some Plesiosaur-like creature still survives in the ocean is perhaps within the bounds of possibility, and were it to be seen swimming with its head and neck showing above water, it would be not unlike some pictures drawn of the Great Sea Serpent. But until a specimen or some part of this unknown monster is available for examination, the scientific world cannot accept it and give it a name.

See also Vol. I: FABULOUS CREATURES.

SEASHORE PLANTS. 1. Although the sea-shore constitutes one large association of animals and plants, there are many separate communities, the rocky shores, the salt-marshes, and the sand-dunes each having a characteristic vegetation. The seaweeds, which must be included, can best be seen during the period of low-water on the three days before and after new moons. At these times the tides flow to a much higher, and ebb to a much lower level than at other times (*see* TIDES, Vol. III).

2. SEAWEEDS, or ALGAE (q.v.), are plentiful where the rocks run out to sea, and also on

Sea Aster

Glasswort

Bladderwrack

Sea Holly

Sea Lettuce

Coralline

scattered rocks on the beach, and at the foot of cliffs washed by the sea. Seaweeds grow in three levels on the shore. Green seaweeds are found highest up the beach, and are exposed to the atmosphere at all low tides, brown seaweeds are found between high and low water-level; while red seaweeds are found growing in deeper water, and are usually never exposed. Among the greens are the Sea-lettuces, with their flat, wide 'fronds'; and where fresh water runs over rocks or over the beach, grows the green, streaky *Enteromorpha intestinalis*, consisting, as its name suggests, of tubes varying in length from 1 inch to 1 foot, the ends of which are inflated into bags.

Of the brown seaweeds, the leathery Channelled-wrack or *Pelvetia* grows the highest on the shore, and is usually only reached at high-water spring tides. When dry, it is tough and brittle, but becomes soft and supple when moistened. The most common of the brown seaweeds, the Bladderwrack, grows lower on the shore. It consists of flat, forked branches, each with a definite vein, and with round air-bladders on either side, which buoy up the plant

when it is floating in water. Still lower grow the long, strap-like fronds of the Knotted Wrack, with forked branches swollen in places to form large oval air-spaces; the flat, forked branches of the Serrated Wrack, which have toothed edges, can be recognized because they bear no air-bladders and retain their glossy olive colour when dry. Farther seawards are the large, light yellow-brown straps of the Oarweeds or Tangle weeds. These are uncovered at the lowest spring tides only; at other times their leathery fronds may be seen at low water, rising and falling with the waves, the stems remaining attached to the rocks. They can be picked up on the beach after a gale.

Beyond the brown seaweeds, below the limit of the lowest spring tides, the red seaweeds are found. Their colour is due to a red pigment, which increases in intensity on exposure to light. Most of them have a light, airy appearance, and usually consist either of delicate plumes or of flat, fan-like membranes. The Coral Seaweed, one of the most common, owes its coral-like appearance to a coating of lime. It is purple, but fades to white when dry. Red seaweeds may be found in rock-pools or thrown up on the shore.

3. SALT-MARSH PLANTS. A salt-marsh is formed where a river meets the sea, its rate of flow being slowed down so that the silt is deposited as mud. Along these estuaries, as well as in sheltered bays, the mixture of mud and sand supports a special type of vegetation. These salt-marsh plants or 'halophytes' are occasionally immersed entirely in salt water, and at all times there is a high percentage of salt in the soil. Consequently, they have to adapt themselves not only to the movement of the mud, which makes rooting difficult, but to the lack of oxygen in the waterlogged soil.

The roots of halophytes are able to absorb water from a strong salt solution; and the presence of many water-storage cells in their fleshy leaves enables them to conserve this water. The lack of oxygen is overcome by the development of large air-spaces; and to meet the shifting state of the mud the plants have long roots, or underground stems, which act as anchors. A characteristic halophyte is the Glasswort, which has a branched, rounded, fleshy stem, and resembles a CACTUS (q.v.). It is one of the first to colonize the open beach. Masses of dead seaweeds accumulate around the Glasswort plants and help to manure the mud. The mud gathers around the hummocks so formed, which then become colonized with other halophytes such as the Sea Aster, Sea Lavender, Seablite, Sea Plantain, and Seaside Arrowhead. As the mud becomes built up, it becomes further invaded by plants such as the Sea Thrift, Sea Purslane, Scurvy Grass, Sea Beet, and Sea Milkwort. A grass which plays an important part in the stabilization of moving mud is a species of *Spartina*, a cross between the American and European species, first known in this country about 1870, since when it has spread rapidly round the south and west coasts of Britain.

4. SAND-DUNE PLANTS. Sand-dunes are found above the high-water mark on seashores. They

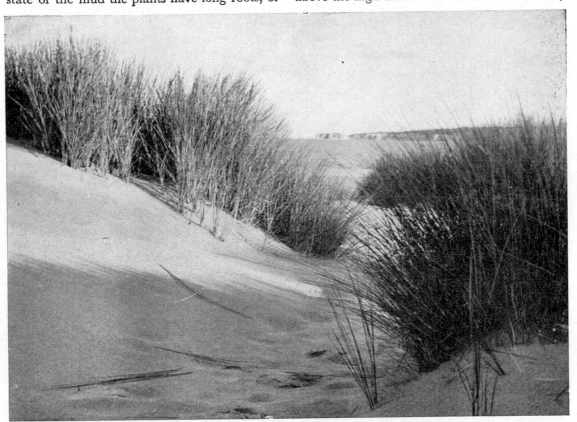

SAND DUNES WITH MARRAM GRASS—STUDLAND HEATH, DORSET
Harry Meyer

are built up by accumulations of blown sand, and are as constantly being blown away by the wind, so that they are always shifting. If there is nothing to stop their progress, sand-dunes may be blown far inland—indeed they have been known to overlie whole districts. One of the most powerful checks to the movement of sand-dunes is the growth of Marram Grass, a plant with upright shoots and sharp narrow leaves. Marram Grass has long, perennial 'rhizomes', or underground stems, as well as deep-growing, fibrous roots, which help to bind the sand together. Although the shoots are constantly being buried by the sand, they have the power of being able to force their way again to the surface. The roots are renewed at higher levels, too, the old ones remaining in the sand and helping to bind it below. In this way the level of the dune is built up—in some cases as high as 80 feet—humus being added to the soil by the decay of the roots and shoots of the grass itself. In south Lancashire, the Sea Couch Grass acts as a dune-former. It grows nearer the sea than Marram Grass, and has the advantage of being able to endure immersion in sea water. It has, however, only a limited power of upward growth through sand, and the dunes formed from Sea Couch Grass are usually smaller than those formed from Marram Grass. As the dunes are built up, the sheltered landward slopes become invaded by such plants as are able to face a deficiency of humus. At the higher levels of the dunes there is little moisture, although the sand may be quite wet at the bottom. The dunes become very hot, also, during the day, and cold at night. Among the plants which have become adapted to these conditions are the Stork's Bill, Ragwort, Cat's Ear, Sea Purslane, Sea Holly, Sea Bindweed, Sea Spurge, Sea Buckthorn, the Red Fruited Dandelion, and the Sand Sedge. When the dunes have become fixed, they are invaded by other plants, such as Dutch Clover, Bird's-foot Trefoil, and Rest Harrow.

See also ECOLOGY OF PLANTS.

SEA-SLUG, *see* SLUG.

SEA SNAKE.

Except for one species which inhabits a fresh-water lake in the Philippines, Sea Snakes live entirely in salt water. They can be distinguished at once from all other snakes by their paddle-shaped tails. There are two sub-families: the one with ventral shields—that is, enlarged scales which enable them to move on the ground, and the other without proper ventral shields. They range from the Persian Gulf to the shores of Japan, and south through Malayan waters to the north coast of Australia and western Polynesia. One species has extended its range to the east coast of Africa, and has crossed the Pacific to the Gulf of Panama.

The first sub-family spend a good deal of their time among rocks on the sea-shore. They lay eggs—whereas the second sub-family bring forth their young alive. These latter live entirely in the water, and are active and graceful swimmers; on land, owing to the absence of proper ventral shields, they are almost helpless. They prefer sheltered waters, and are seldom found many miles from the coast. On days when the sea is quite calm, they may be seen in hundreds basking on the surface of the water. They feed upon fish, some species living mainly upon eels.

All Sea Snakes are poisonous, the venom of some being very deadly. There are no records of bathers ever having been attacked by them; but the native fishermen, when hauling in their catches, often come into contact with them and get bitten. Some fifty species are known, and it is unlikely that many more will be discovered. The majority do not exceed 3 or 4 feet in length; but two species reach 7 or 8 feet, the most massive being Stokes's Sea Snake from Australian waters, which is 6 feet in length and has a girth of 10 inches. Sea Snakes have nothing to do with the great SEA SERPENT (q.v.), which has not yet been proved to exist.

See also SNAKES.

SEA SQUIRT.

On the rocks and on pier-piles at low tide may be found tough, jelly-like bags, from half an inch to 2 or 3 inches long, which, when touched, squirt out a fine jet of water. These are the Tunicates or Sea Squirts. There are two holes in each bag, one at the top and one at the side. The water, bringing food and oxygen to the animal, is drawn in at the top and ejected at the side. Although the adults are fixed and unable to move about, the larvae are free-swimming. They resemble the tadpoles of frogs, with round bodies and long tails. Some Sea Squirts, such as the Golden-star Sea Squirt, live in colonies, the jelly-like covering containing many small animals arranged in rosettes. One colonial form, the beautiful *Pyrosoma* of the tropics, is long, tubular, and luminescent, and floats in large numbers near the surface of the sea, lighting it up at night.

SEA-URCHIN. These belong to the same division of the animal kingdom—the Echinodermata or prickly-skinned animals—as the STARFISH and SEA-CUCUMBER (qq.v.). With the exception of the so-called Leather-urchins, Sea-urchins possess a skeleton formed by a complete armour of plates of hard carbonate of lime, and an outer covering of skin. They are more or less globular, heart-shaped, or disk-shaped animals, and they pass through free-swimming larval stages before becoming adult. All live in the sea. Their bodies are thickly clad with spines, varying considerably in length, thickness, and number in the different species. There are five broad bands of large spines, and five narrow bands on which the spines are in smaller numbers, and where the plates of the skeleton are pierced by small holes, through which the long

BLUNT-SPINED SEA-URCHIN IN A POOL ON THE COAST OF THE KEELING ISLANDS, INDIAN OCEAN.   *C. A. Gibson-Hill*

and slender tube-feet are extended. The spines are attached by muscular fibres to round knobs or bosses on the close-fitting plates of the skeleton, so that they can be moved in all directions; and it is by the combined movement of the spines, together with the dragging or hauling action of the tube-feet, that the Sea-urchin is able to move about on the floor of the sea. Scattered over the body are large numbers of specially modified spines, some of which have glands secreting a poisonous fluid, and are used as weapons of defence. In most species, though not in all, the mouth is provided with a complicated arrangement of teeth, called the 'lantern of Aristotle', after the famous philosopher, who was the first to give an accurate description of the Sea-urchin.

The different species vary greatly in size, form, and colour. Some have bodies reaching fully 7 or 8 inches in diameter. The Common or Edible Sea-urchin, which may grow to the size of a big Jaffa orange, is usually pale ruddy-brown or purple, covered with pink or purplish spines, sometimes with white tips, of moderate length and thickness. Another fairly common species, the Purple Egg-urchin, lives in holes among rocky ledges, exposed, or only partially submerged, at extreme low-tide. This has much longer spines, of a fine purple colour, though its

COMMON SEA-URCHIN MOVING ACROSS A ROCK
M. Burton

body is smaller than that of the Common Sea-urchin. On wide sandy shores near extreme low-tide mark, the brown, heart-shaped Heart-urchin forms burrows in the sand to a depth of 8 to 10 inches, communicating with the surface by a narrow, somewhat cylindrical shaft. Occasion-ally, as if impatient for the return of the tide, the urchin emerges from its burrow and slowly makes its way toward the incoming waves. The popularly called Cake-urchins are flattened in form and more or less oval in outline, resembling, as their name suggests, little flat cakes. They frequent shallow inshore waters, where they live half-buried in the sand, their flat shape and multiplicity of tube-feet preventing them from sinking too deeply in the sand or being turned over by the waves. A very flattened form, almost circular in shape, is the Sand-dollar urchin, common on the east coasts of North America. The curious Leather-urchins of the deep sea are generally large and brightly coloured, and have thin strips of soft flesh between the hard skeletal plates. They are also rather flat and cake-like in shape. They are capable of inflicting very pain-ful wounds with their poison spines.

SEAWEED, *see* ALGAE; SEASHORE PLANTS, Sec-tion 2.

SECRETARY BIRD. Although this large, pearl-grey and black African bird belongs to the Birds of Prey, it differs from the others in appear-ance and behaviour. It stands some 4 feet high on long grey legs, and has two long tail-feathers, barred at the ends with black and white. It has an eagle-like, hooked beak, and ten long feathers projecting from the back of its head, like quill pens behind the ears of a clerk.

Secretary Birds are fairly frequently seen, generally in pairs, on the plains of South Africa, and are found as far north as Abyssinia on the east and the Gold Coast on the west. They spend most of their time on the ground, and can walk faster than a man can run. But they can also fly strongly, and will soar high in the air, with head stretched forwards and legs back-wards. They attack their prey—lizards, snakes, small mammals, and birds—with their strong feet, striking them so quickly that they have no time to retaliate. Although their propensity to attack large snakes is probably exaggerated, they are considered sufficiently valuable as destroyers of poisonous snakes to be protected by law.

SEEDS. 1. STRUCTURE. Inside the protective coat, or 'testa', of a seed there is a complete plant in miniature, called an 'embryo'. This can grow only if it has enough food to give it a start in life; therefore the seed contains a reserve of food, stored either within the embryo itself or outside it. The Broad Bean is a good example of a seed with a large store of food. On the flattened edge is a long black band, a scar show-ing where the seed was joined to the fruit. Near this is a triangular bump, and between the two is a tiny pore or 'micropyle', through which water can pass. Most of the space in the seed is taken up by two large seed-leaves, called 'cotyle-dons', which contain the food reserves in the form of starch and a little protein. Where these join, there is a tiny root (the 'radicle'), and a tiny shoot (the 'plumule'), destined to bear the leaves, flowers, and fruit.

Protected by its hard coat, the dry bean-seed passes the winter in a resting condition. With the coming of the warmth and moisture of spring, the embryo gives off enzymes, which so act on the starch and protein that they become suitable for nourishing the growing seedling. The plumule and radicle, therefore, begin to grow. The radicle passes through the tiny pore or micropyle, splits the coat or testa at its point of weakness, penetrates into the soil, and begins to form branch roots. At the same time the plumule grows up. Until it has passed through the soil its tip remains bent like a crochet-hook, so that the delicate growing-point is not harmed. When it reaches the surface of the soil, the stem straightens out and continues growing into a shoot, bearing foliage leaves. Until the young

SEEDS SHOWING GROWTH

seedling is established, and has developed green leaves to take over the duties of food manufacture, food is supplied from the reserves in the cotyledons. These remain below ground, gradually shrivelling up as the starch and protein are used, and finally disappearing.

Seeds such as the Broad Bean, the Scarlet Runner, and Pea remain below ground to nourish the young seedling. When the French Bean germinates, however, the cotyledons are carried above ground, and after their contained food has been used to nourish the young seedlings, they remain as two shrivelled organs at the bottom of the stem. The seeds of the Mustard and Cress differ from the French Bean in that the cotyledons, once they reach the air, soon open out and turn green, to begin the work of PHOTOSYNTHESIS (q.v.) or food manufacture. In the Castor Oil seeds, the cotyledons are thin and tissue-like, and do not store food; but instead an oily type of food is stored inside the seed, not directly connected to the young plant. When the seed germinates, the cotyledons remain inside the seed for some time, absorbing the food material over their whole surfaces. Then, as the shoot grows, the cotyledons are carried above ground, become green, and begin to manufacture food.

All the seeds so far described have two cotyledons, and are typical of one of the two big groups of FLOWERING PLANTS (q.v.), the 'dicotyledons'; but in the other group, the 'monocotyledons', there is only one cotyledon. To this group belong the Lilies, Daffodils, Crocuses, Tulips, and Grasses, including all the cereals. The grain of Maize or Indian Corn is a good example of the second group. This is not a true seed, but a fruit in which the fruit-wall and seed-coat are fused. On one side of the flattened grain there is an oblong area of pale colour, which indicates the position of the embryo. The rest of the grain is filled with reserve food material—chiefly starch, but a little protein. One part of the embryo is somewhat shield-shaped, and is pressed against the reserve food: this is the cotyledon. The remaining part consists of the plumule and the radicle. On germination, the cotyledon gives off enzymes, which act on the starch and protein to convert them into food suitable for the growing seedling. The leaves of the plumule are enclosed in a sheath, which splits as it appears above ground. The radicle has only a short life, and before it dies

off adventitious roots spring from the base of the stem, and grow into an extensive fibrous root system (*see* ROOTS, Section 5).

Seeds, therefore, possess either one or two cotyledons. In some seeds the cotyledons remain below ground, in others they appear above ground. There are many other variations, however. In the Sycamore, for example, the cotyledons are long, tightly coiled, and green—which, as they have been enclosed in a dark seed, is rather surprising. The Date-stone is a seed in which the reserve food material is cellulose—the material characteristic of the cell-walls of plants.

2. SEED DISPERSAL. It is clearly of advantage to plants that the seeds should be carried some distance from the parent and be widely dispersed, so that overcrowding is avoided; and various special devices help to achieve this end. The four chief methods are dispersal by wind, animals, or water, and by explosive or ejection mechanisms in the fruit itself.

(*a*) *Wind Dispersal.* The seeds of some plants, such as the Orchids, are so small and light that when they are set free, they are freely blown by the wind. Others have hairs or wings which enable them to float on the wind. The winged fruits of the Sycamore, Elm, and Ash are good examples, and also those of the Hornbeam and Lime, where the 'wings' are formed from bracts. In Traveller's-Joy or Old Man's Beard (Clematis), the fruit consists of a collection of seeds (achenes) on each of which, as it ripens, the style remains as a long white plume which helps the fruit to float in the air. The Willow, Poplar, and Willow-herb have plumed seeds. Other plumed seeds develop a ring of hairs, or a feathery appendage called a 'pappus', as in the Dandelions, Hawkweeds, Thistles, Groundsel, and other members of this family of flowers. In the Dandelion, the pappus acts as a parachute, and is often carried for miles through the air. In Thistles, the pappus with its branched hairs is attached so delicately to the fruit that a light breeze is enough to separate them; the fruit falls to the ground, and the pappus, as thistledown, floats away.

Plants in which the seeds are borne in capsules bearing teeth or pores are also distributed by wind. The capsule of the Poppy, for example, is borne at the end of a long stalk which is easily shaken about in the wind, and the seeds are shaken out through the pores. Wind dispersal is probably the best method of distributing seeds

Campion
(with capsule)

Burdock
(with hooks)

Willow Herb
(with plumed seeds)

Violet
(with explosive pods)

Marsh Marigold
(with explosive
follicle)

TYPES OF FRUIT SHOWING DIFFERENT FORMS OF SEED DISPERSAL

over large areas; but it is probably also the most wasteful.

(*b*) *Animal Dispersal*. Seeds and fruits may be distributed by animals, either by sticking to their coats or by being eaten and then excreted by them. Some seeds have hooks which catch in the fur or wool of browsing animals, or to the clothing of human beings; so that they are carried and dropped elsewhere. The Goose-grass, Burdock, Teazel, Wood Avens, and Enchanter's Nightshade all have such hooks, and are sometimes carried great distances from the parent plant. Birds, in particular, carry seeds over wide areas —web-footed water-birds, for instance, carry seeds in the mud that clings to their feet. Charles Darwin (q.v. Vol. V) once removed 6¾ ounces of mud from water-fowls, and mixed it with sterilized soil—from this mud no less than 537 plants germinated. Animals sometimes distribute fruits and seeds by dropping them accidentally. Squirrels, for example, when carrying nuts for their winter hoards, often drop some on the way; rooks and jays distribute acorns in much the same manner. Even the ant is responsible for seed dispersal: it carries off oily seeds such as the Violet, Periwinkle, and Greater Celandine, not all of which reach their destination.

When fleshy fruits, such as drupes, berries, and pomes, are eaten by animals, the seeds either pass out in the droppings or are rejected by the animal after the juicy part has been eaten. In the Blackberry, for instance, the seeds pass through the animal unharmed; but in the Cherry, the hard stone is rejected by the bird and dropped.

(*c*) *Water Dispersal*. This is the least common method, and is confined to a few plants growing in or near water. The seeds of the riverside Alder, for example, have spongy coverings filled with air, and these drop into the water and float away. When the spongy covering becomes saturated with water the seed loses its buoyancy and sinks—to germinate in the bed of the stream or river. The Coconut has a fibrous mesocarp enclosing a large number of air spaces, which make it buoyant. The coconut palm grows chiefly along the seashore or along the banks of rivers; and the fruit, when ripe, usually falls into the water. There it floats until it is washed up on dry land or is caught in the mud, where it develops into a new plant. The Water-lily, also, is dispersed by means of a floating seed.

(*d*) *Ejecting and 'Explosive' Fruits*. Some fruits catapult their seeds away. When the pods of Gorse and related plants ripen, they dry and shrivel. The shrivelling takes place unequally, with the result that the two halves of the pod separate, and then twist. All this takes place so rapidly that the seeds are shot out to a considerable distance. On a hot still day, the gentle 'pop, pop' from a group of Gorse or Broom bushes can easily be heard. The Geranium is another example of an ejecting fruit: so sudden is the splitting of the fruit that the five portions into which it divides are flung to some distance.

Probably the best example of an explosive fruit is the Squirting Cucumber. When ripe, the rough, hairy, almost prickly berries become detached from the stalk, leaving only a delicate skin at the base. The pressure of the juice inside the skin causes the berry to burst at this weak spot, and the juice containing the seeds is shot out of the hole to some considerable distance.

See also Fruits, Reproduction of Plants.

SENSES. 1. Our contact with the world around us is entirely through our senses, a fact which is too often overlooked. The same is, of course, true of every animal. The five senses are those of sight, hearing, touch, taste, and smell. In addition, it is usual to speak of a sixth sense whenever we find ourselves doing something that is not obviously dependent upon one of those five. This fact alone is sufficient to warn us that we have not explored completely the field of sensory experience, even so far as human beings are concerned. Much less fully do we understand the senses of animals—indeed, so long as we are unable to get inside the mind of an animal, so long shall we be unable to understand fully its sensory experiences in relation to our own.

Let us see how little we know of an animal's sensory experiences by comparing the behaviour of a man and a dog. A man is more aware of the world from what he sees than from what he feels, hears, tastes, or smells. Next in order of importance comes touch, with hearing following third: smell and taste have but a limited importance to him. To a dog, however, smell appears to be far and away the most important sense, with hearing second, sight a poor third, and touch of little importance. Taste is so closely linked with smell that it is often difficult to tell where one begins and the other ends. If, then, we had the sensory experiences of a dog, the world would probably appear as a place in which every object had its characteristic scent or perfume. We should recognize each other by smell. We should find our way home by smell. We should not eat without first smelling our food. We should know if our companions were pleased or angry, sad or happy, tired or energetic, by the scent they gave off. Again, we should be much more aware of sound: we should be aware of noises now too highly pitched for us to hear, just as we should recognize smells which, as human beings, we are not aware of. Our sight, on the other hand, would be defective compared with what we have now. Our appreciation of colours would be limited; the outlines of common objects would be blurred: only things close at hand would be at all clearly seen. Touch would be limited to a gross appreciation of solid objects, although the lips would probably be more sensitive as tactile organs. Therefore, though a dog has a brain, eyes, nose, tongue, and so on, very like those of human beings, the world must appear to him very different. We can be reasonably sure that even greater differences must exist between our own experiences and those of other vertebrates, such as birds, reptiles, and fishes, even though their brains, nervous systems, and sense organs are built on essentially the same pattern as our own. It is of supreme importance to recognize this great difference between the sensory experiences of man and animals, and also between one animal and another; otherwise our interpretation of behaviour will be seriously at fault. Nevertheless, it must be recognized that all behaviour and all sensory experiences have a common origin and fit neatly into an evolutionary sequence.

The senses, and as a consequence the sensory experiences, of the invertebrates depart even more widely from those of human beings. While it is true that the higher invertebrates, such as insects, crustaceans, and molluscs, have eyes comparable with those of vertebrates, though of different structure, the other senses are very different. Most invertebrates have no ears, but some, such as crickets, which produce sound, have auditory pits. For the most part, however, the antennae are the main sensory organs, and probably in them are lodged organs of smell, taste, and touch, and even, it may be, senses which have no parallel in the vertebrates. In the lower invertebrates—sponges, sea-anemones, worms, and starfish—sensory appreciation is limited to an ill-defined touch, taste, and light-perception. In the lowest animals of all, the protozoa, although the protoplasm appears to possess the dawning senses of taste (ability to select food-particles from among indigestible matter), sight (reaction to light stimuli), hearing (sensitivity to vibrations), touch (reaction to changing temperatures, chemicals, or electric currents), all responses are on the part of the protoplasm as a whole. With the evolution of the multicellular animal, certain cells began to take on separate functions, and the senses tended more and more to be localized in special organs; and the more highly the animals evolved, the more localized and specialized the organs became.

2. SIGHT. The eye in its most highly developed form may be compared with a camera. Both possess a LENS (q.v. Vol. VIII) through which rays of light are allowed to pass and strike upon a sensitized film. In both there is a shutter for controlling the passage of light, and also a diaphragm for cutting down the amount of light when it is too intense. In dealing with the eye, we use the term retina for the sensitized film, eyelid for the shutter, and iris for the diaphragm. There is, however, one important difference between the eye and a camera: whereas the sensitized plate or film of a camera can produce a negative image only after further treatment

CROSS-SECTION OF MAMMALIAN EYE

by chemicals, and can be used only once, the eye is able to produce a never-ending series of positive images which, in the higher animals, are stored up in the brain as memories.

The eye and its function of sight in the highest animals can be best understood by seeing how the eye is evolved from the lowest animals to the highest. In the most primitive animals, the protozoa, there is an obvious response to light, some moving away from light and some towards it. In some protozoa, however, there is somewhere in the body a pigment spot, usually black, brown, or red, the possessors of which always react more strongly and rapidly to the stimulus of light. This same tendency is seen more and more marked as we pass from the unicellular protozoa to the multicellular metazoa, and upwards through the metazoa from the less highly organized to the more highly organized animals. Thus, in the jellyfishes and the worms, the pigment spots are already becoming larger; and in the mollusca, crustacea, and insects, a definite eye has been formed.

There is a considerable variety of eye-pattern in the animal kingdom, the eye becoming more complex the more highly organized the animal. From the simple pigment spot of the protozoa, a retina slowly evolves by the laying down of more and more pigment granules. At a later stage, a lens is added; and this has the effect of concentrating the light rays on small areas of the retina, thus producing on it an image of the object from which the rays have been reflected. In general terms, sight in the lowest animals is no more than a vague reaction to the stimulus of light; but in the higher animals there is also the formation of an image. The degree to which this image is formed varies from one type of animal to another: fishes and reptiles, for instance, can probably appreciate only vague shapes and, more particularly, movement in objects around them.

The best-developed sight is 'stereoscopic sight' —that is, sight capable of seeing things in the solid. This is possessed by man and certain birds and mammals with eyes close together instead of one on each side of the head. An elephant, with an eye on each side of the head and directed away, can almost certainly see only a flat picture of the world around; whereas a cat, with the eyes close together and pointing in the same direction, as are human eyes, must be able to appreciate solid forms as we do, and therefore has stereoscopic vision. A bird, to whom sight is perhaps the most important of the senses, has very highly developed and efficient eyes.

3. HEARING. The ear, the organ by which we hear, is not the fleshy flap on the side of the head, although in everyday speech we are accustomed to speak of it as such. This is merely the instrument for catching the sound waves and directing them towards the *tympanum*, or ear-drum. The middle and inner ear, the mechanism by which the more highly developed animals hear, consist of a complicated apparatus of small bones and cartilages, lodged in a cavity in the skull, from which a nerve, the auditory nerve, runs to the brain, enabling us to translate vibrations of air into what we call SOUND (q.v. Vol. III). Similar sound vibrations will travel through air, water, and earth; and almost all animals respond to one or other of these vibrations, according to whether they live on land, in the water, or under the earth.

SECTION OF THE MAMMALIAN EAR

In the animal kingdom, hearing has a different meaning according to the group of animals with which we are dealing. As the protozoa are sensitive to light even though they have no eye, so some animals—for example, earthworms—are sensitive to vibrations, whether of air, water, or land, without showing any sign of a structure which could be called an ear. The sensitivity of earthworms, for instance, to vibrations in the ground makes them withdraw into their burrows when a thrush runs across the lawn. The simplest form of ear known, in some of the lowest animals, is a minute pit in the skin, known as an auditory pit, lined with sensitive protoplasmic hairs, and containing a tiny pellet of lime. This is connected to the nervous system by one or more nerve-fibres. The ears of the higher animals are in structure the same as those of humans. The bigger outer ears of many animals make effective instruments for catching the sound waves.

Closely related to hearing, whether through the highly organized ear of a higher animal or through an auditory pit, is the sense of balance, both hearing and balance being perceived through the ear.

4. FEELING (TOUCH). The 'tactile' or touch sense was the first sense to appear in the course of EVOLUTION (q.v.). It is located throughout the skin, although it is more highly developed in some parts than in others. The human finger-tips, for example, have a more highly developed tactile appreciation than, say, the back of the neck; and the palms of the hands are more sensitive still. The sense is conveyed by means of fine nerve fibres ending just under the skin; and in the higher animals, especially in those parts more highly sensitized, such as the finger-tips, their minute touch-corpuscles are made up of highly branching nerve-fibres encased in cushions of tissues. In such animals as insects, where the body is covered with a horny layer, the sense of touch works through sensory hairs projecting from the surface—in particular, through the antennae; and in mammals where the body is covered with fur there are long, very sensitive hairs, such as those on a cat's face, which perform the same function.

5. TASTE. The taste-buds, the special organs of taste, consist of groups of narrow, rod-shaped cells in the skin of the mouth and, more particularly, of the tongue and soft palate. In fishes, they are found on the outer surface of the gills also. They are comparable with the touch-corpuscles, and like them are connected by nerve-fibres to the central nervous system.

6. SMELL. The sense which enables us to perceive a scent or perfume is spoken of as the 'olfactory' sense. In the vertebrates this is lodged in the nose, and is dependent upon a mucous lining richly supplied with nerve endings derived from the olfactory nerves in the brain. In only a few vertebrates, notably the whales, is there no sense of smell; in fact, in many animals it is the most developed of the senses. In invertebrates there is no organ which may be called a nose, although it is clear that some, such as insects, have a sense corresponding to the sense of smell, which is probably located in the antennae. The mechanism of smell is very imperfectly understood, but probably scent or perfume is the result of stimulation by minute particles which bombard the mucous membrane.

See also NERVOUS SYSTEM; BRAIN.
See also Vol. XI: SENSES (human).

SHARKS AND RAYS (Selachians). **1.** These are not true FISHES (q.v.), but represent an early stage in the evolution of fishes. Many fossil Selachians have been discovered; and their position in the record of the rocks shows that we are right in believing them to be related to creatures that existed long before modern fishes were evolved (*see* FOSSILS, Vol. III). They are not the ancestors of fishes; but a study of their anatomy helps to explain what the ancestors of both sharks and fishes were like. In many ways they link up the LAMPREYS (q.v.), with their very primitive supporting-rod or 'notochord' of gristle, and the true fishes, with their back-bones. In other ways, some of the Selachians have progressed even farther than many of the fishes. Therefore they are considered to be a distinct class, equivalent to Fishes and Amphibians.

The skeleton, though still formed only of gristle (cartilage), is much more complete than that of the Lampreys, and the gills are supported on jointed rods of cartilage, called gill-arches. Except in the Chimaeras, each gill has a separate opening at the side of the head. In most cases there are five openings on each side (though occasionally there are six or seven); and just behind the eye there is a valved hole, called a 'spiracle'. This has no respiratory function but probably contains a sense organ.

Most sharks grow new teeth continually, these

being simply implanted in the gums, not in sockets, like those of human beings. They lie in rows one behind the other, the new ones being formed at the back. The front teeth, which are the largest, are used for biting; as these are worn out or lost, those behind move up to replace them.

The fins of Selachians are supported by numerous horny rays, upon a complicated skeleton of gristly rods; but these are not visible from outside, as they are completely covered by skin and muscle. A Selachian can be easily recognized by the shape of its tail, the end of the body being turned upward, so that most of the tail fin lies beneath it. It is easy to distinguish the male from the female, also, since he has a pair of stiff finger-like 'claspers' attached to the pelvic fins.

Most Selachians bear their young alive, some-

what after the fashion of mammals; but a few, such as the Port Jackson Shark and some of the Rays, lay a sort of egg, encased in a strong, horny capsule.

2. Sharks. Most sharks are rather long-bodied, fish-shaped animals, with the eyes and gill-openings on the side of the head. They have two pairs of fins, the pectoral fins behind the head corresponding to our arms, the pelvic fins, farther back on the belly, corresponding to legs. They have one or two dorsal fins on the back, an anal fin below the tail, and the typically shaped caudal fin at the end of the tail. The body is covered with denticles pointing backwards, so that the skin feels fairly smooth if rubbed towards the tail, but very rough when rubbed in the opposite direction. This skin, when dried, is called 'shagreen'. Sharks usually swim with a side to side bending of the body. They feed for the most part on fishes.

Many different kinds of shark are known in the various seas of the world, a few entering fresh water. The most primitive kinds are the rare Frilled Shark of the North Atlantic and Japanese waters, and the more common Cow-sharks. Among the more developed sharks are the fierce Mackerel-sharks, including the well-known Porbeagle, sometimes caught off the coast of Britain during the summer months, when it may damage the nets of fishermen. This shark, which grows to about 12 feet long, has a large mouth full of frightful teeth, and a keel on each side of the tail, to help its swift surface-swimming. The famous Man-eating Shark of tropical seas, a relative of the Porbeagle, grows much larger, often as long as 30 feet. It is by far the most voracious of all, and there are many stories of its attacks on bathers and pearl-divers. The great naturalist Linnaeus considered it to be the animal, wrongly called a

VARIETIES OF SHARKS AND RAYS

1. Spotted Dogfish—a small species of shark; 2. A 'Mermaid's purse'—the horny egg-case of the Dogfish; 3. The Skate swimming with its broad 'wings'.   *A. Fraser-Brunner*

whale, that swallowed the prophet Jonah. Other large sharks have also been responsible for the death or injury of men, particularly some of the Cub-sharks of the West Indies. Related to them is the Blue Shark, a handsome species that follows the mackerel to the British coast during the summer.

The Hammerhead is a strange creature, much like a Cub-shark, but with the sides of the skull so drawn out that the eyes, fixed on broad stalks, are wide apart. The Thresher, another curious species, has a tail-fin as long as the rest of the fish. It is said to beat the water vigorously with this long tail to round up schools of fishes so that it can charge into the terrified mass and eat its fill. Quite different are the Carpet-sharks, harmless creatures, broad-bodied, with large heads provided with fleshy fringes. They live at the bottom of the sea, having a complicated pattern for concealment, the best-known species being the Wobbigong, of Australia.

The various Dog-fish, also known as Cat-sharks or Roussettes, found throughout the temperate seas, are quite small and harmless—some being useful as food (see ROCK SALMON). They lay eggs which are protected by horny oblong capsules attached to weeds by means of tendrils at the corners. These are occasionally found washed up on the shore after a storm.

Some sharks have a strong spine in front of each dorsal fin. One of these, the strange Port Jackson Shark of the Pacific, has a big, clumsy head, and heavy, scroll-like teeth for crushing shells. It lays its eggs in spiral cases that spin round and round in strong currents instead of being washed away. The common Spur-dog, or Picked Dog-fish, is another of these spiny Sharks. This and its relatives usually have no anal fin, and do not grow very large; some of them are jet-black, with luminous areas on the body, and inhabit very deep water. Their young are born alive (see DEEP-SEA FISHES).

The largest of all sharks is the great Whale-shark, which may be as much as 40 feet long. This rather rare monster is quite harmless, however, having very feeble teeth, and feeding mainly on very small creatures. Several have been caught off Florida during recent years. Almost as large and equally harmless is the Basking Shark, which is remarkable for its very long gill-openings. The Basking Shark is so called because, when not feeding, it spends much time merely floating, or basking, on the surface of the ocean. Occasionally, when a Basking Shark dies or is killed, its decomposed remains are washed up on shore, the jaws and gills having nearly always fallen away, leaving the small skull on the end of what looks like a long neck. When this happens, it is almost certain that a news-paperman will photograph it, and it will be described in the papers as a SEA SERPENT (q.v.). It is happenings such as this that keep the old legend of the Sea Serpent alive.

Among the curios often brought home by travellers are the 'saws' of the Sawfish. This is a rather wide, flattened shark of the tropics, which may grow to a large size. The snout is lengthened into a long, flat blade, on each side of which is a row of teeth (really altered denticles) set in sockets. With this weapon the Sawfish drives into shoals of fishes, making great havoc, after which it feeds at leisure on the bodies. Another flattened shark is the Monk-fish, or Angel-shark (often marketed as 'Rock Salmon'), which has only one gill-opening on each side, and rather broad pectoral fins, something like those of a Ray.

The flesh of many kinds of Shark is eaten in different parts of the world, and the Chinese value the dried fins of some species very highly, making them into soup.

3. RAYS AND SKATES. These are like Sharks, but are very much flattened, the pectoral fins being joined on each side to the head, so that the fins and head together form a disk. The eyes and spiracles are on top of the head, the nostrils, mouth, and gills underneath. The tail is usually slender, and there is no anal fin. The most Shark-like kinds are the curious Guitar-fish, with a small disk and pointed nose, and the Torpedoes, or Electric Rays (see ELECTRIC FISHES) which have a round disk. Both these have rather thick tails, and bear their young alive.

The Skates have bigger pectoral fins, and a slender tail, bearing the little dorsal fin near its end. They lay eggs in horny cases, called 'skate-barrows', which are oblong in shape, with a stiff tube at each of the four angles. Some of the Skates grow very large, and are valuable as food.

Sting-rays have tails drawn out into long whip-lashes. Instead of a fin at the end, there is a strong spine, with a groove that contains poison, and this can inflict a very painful wound. Sting-rays are found in warm seas, and are dangerous to fishermen.

Largest of all is the great Devil-fish or Manta of tropical waters, which has the pectoral fins

CHIMAERA OR RABBIT FISH (MALE ABOVE, FEMALE BELOW)
A. Fraser-Brunner

drawn out to points, like great wings, and may be as much as 20 feet from tip to tip. On each side of the very big mouth is a sort of tentacle, which is used like a hand to push food into the mouth. Devil-fishes seem to be fairly harmless creatures, unless attacked.

Skates and Rays live on the bed of the sea, feeding mostly on molluscs, crustaceans, or carrion, which they crush with their flat teeth. They swim by wavy movements of the edges of their great pectoral fins.

4. CHIMAERAS. These silvery-coloured creatures, often called Rabbit-fishes, are among the most extraordinary in appearance, and belong to a very ancient family. They are found mostly in deep water. They have long tails, drawn out to a fine point, and teeth quite unlike those of Sharks, consisting of flat, bony plates called 'tritors', which form a sort of beak. In addition to the usual claspers, the males have small extra ones on the front of the pelvic fins and above the eyes. The dorsal fin extends along the back, and has a strong spine, which is said to be poisonous, at its front end. Chimaeras feed on a great variety of worms, molluscs, and crustaceans, and are themselves eaten by many larger fishes. They lay eggs in horny capsules, one end being drawn out into a long point, which sticks in the mud, serving as an anchor.

See also Vol. VI: SHARK FISHING.
See also Vol. IX: BIG-GAME FISHING.

SHEARWATER, *see* PETREL, Section 5.

SHEEP. These belong to the order of animals called Ungulata, or hoofed animals. They are hollow-horned RUMINANTS (q.v.), as are also ANTELOPES, CATTLE, and GOATS (qq.v.). They eat mostly grass, which they digest at leisure by 'chewing the cud'. Both sexes of wild sheep usually have horns, those of the males being much larger than those of the females, and, as a rule, curved outwards from the side of the head in more or less of a circle. Their outer hair is short and stiff and not woolly, as is that of the domestic breeds; but they have an undercoat of wool.

There are nearly a dozen wild species, all essentially mountain animals, mostly living in Europe and Asia. There is one species in the Rocky Mountains of North America, and one, unlike all the others, in North Africa. Among the best known of these wild species are the fine American Bighorns, which stand about $3\frac{1}{2}$ feet high, and have massive horns. Some of these sheep are remarkably agile, making tremendous leaps from rock to rock. The lambs, when only a few days old, can follow their mothers up the steepest cliffs. In the great heights of the Altai and Pamir Mountains of central Asia live the Argalis, great wild sheep as large as donkeys, with massive horns sometimes nearly 5 feet long, measured along the curve. The Pamir Argalis are also known as Marco Polo's Sheep, for he first wrote about them in the 13th century. In the mountains of Corsica and Sardinia live the Moufflon, which are about 2 feet 3 inches high, and have dark reddish-brown coats with a white saddle-patch. The Barbary Sheep, or Udad, of Africa are 3 feet or more high, and have a great mass of long hair on their throats, chests, and fore-limbs, and thick, hairy tails. They live in the Atlas Mountains, and are said to be able to go for several days without water. The rams of these wild

THE MOUFFLONS OF CORSICA
Paul Popper

sheep, with their massive horns, are magnificent animals, very different from the domestic sheep.

It is difficult to trace the origin of the domestic sheep, as they do not appear to be directly descended from any of the wild species existing to-day. But as they were domesticated so very long ago, they may well be descended from species that no longer survive. Domestic sheep differ from wild sheep, not only in having wool instead of hair coats, but also in having naturally long tails—though these are usually docked. The only wild sheep to have long tails are the African Barbary Sheep.

See also Vol. VI: SHEEP.

SHEEP MAGGOT-FLY, see BLOWFLY.

SHELDRAKE, see DUCKS, Sections 1 and 2.

SHIELD BUG. There are thirty-eight species of Shield Bugs in Great Britain, very flat, broad insects, and amongst the largest of British Bugs. They are often extremely handsome and brightly

coloured, and easily recognized by this from other Bugs. The triangular horny plate, covering the third segment of the thorax, extends backwards until it reaches the point at which the wing-cases ('elytra') cease to be stiff and become flexible. Sometimes the thorax grows outwards on each side into a sharp spine. The growing Shield Bug casts its skin five times before it assumes its adult, fully winged condition. Much of the handsome appearance of the adults is due to the colours of their fore-wings, and the fully grown Bug is often greatly changed in appearance from its early forms.

Shield Bugs are not molested very much by other animals, probably on account of an unpleasant odour they give off; but toads, which so often attack insects that other animals reject, seem to like them quite well. Shield Bugs generally feed on plant juices, but some attack animals, especially other insects. Some are found on trees, and others on low-growing, herbaceous plants; but none of those in Britain seems to do any serious damage. One of our British species, a deep metallic blue insect, is found on a variety of trees, and is said to feed on other insects, especially on Flea-beetles and their larvae. Two very beautiful species, one

shining black with white mottlings, the other purple-bronze, are often found where nettle and dead-nettle grow together. Another species is scarlet and black, and several are bright green. Others, of various shades of brown, may often be seen on tree-trunks.

See also BUGS.

SHIPWORM. This mollusc lives in the timbers of ships and the wood of breakwaters and harbour works. At first sight it is hardly recognizable as a mollusc, for it has a long, slender, worm-like body, from 6 inches to a foot long. At one end of the body are the pair of small, globular-shaped valves of the shell, while the other end carries a curious pair of small, racket-shaped plates, which are probably used to close the entrance to the burrow in which the Shipworm lives. The outer surfaces of the valves of the shell have a file-like texture, and as the animal can rock them from side to side, giving a grinding action to the series of toothed ridges,

ADULT SHIPWORM   *Robert Clarke*
The shell is in front, and at the hind end of its long, wormlike body are its two breathing syphons.

they form a very effective tool for boring. As it bores, the Shipworm lays down a shelly lining to its tunnel. The female Shipworm sheds her eggs into the sea, and the larvae, hatching from them, can swim freely to fresh timbers, where they start boring operations on their own account.

No kind of timber seems to be entirely immune from the attacks of the Shipworm: pine and other relatively soft woods are rapidly destroyed, while even teak and oak do not escape. The tunnel is always bored in the direction of the grain of the wood, only swerving to one side when an extra hard knot or an iron nail is encountered. In the days of wooden sailing-ships, the depredations of the Shipworm were an ever-present danger; but the practice of sheathing a ship's timbers with metal below the water-line gave safety from this menace. In the 18th century, the havoc wreaked by Shipworms on the piles and timber-work of the sea-dykes often caused serious damage and inundations along the coast of Holland. As an example of the speed at which Shipworms work, a piece of pine-wood pile measuring 9 inches in diameter, after being in use for 5 years, had become so bored away as to contain barely one inch of solid timber. Indeed, 4 to 5 years' submergence in the sea is generally enough to destroy any wooden piles, unless they have been well studded with broad-headed iron nails. But no matter how tortuous or crowded together the tunnels of the Shipworm may become, they rarely, if ever, invade each other, the boring molluscs being guided either by the sense of hearing or by the yielding of the wooden sides.

Another mollusc which causes extensive damage to marine timbers is the Wood Piddock, which shows a marked preference for birch, pine, and oak. Unlike the Shipworm, however, it generally bores against the grain, in a slightly diagonal direction, and goes only deep enough to bury itself in the timber; nor does it secrete a shelly lining to its burrow. It has a small rather globular-

shaped shell, composed of two glossy, semi-transparent valves. It is always to be found at work on the timbers of old groins and breakwaters.

See also MOLLUSC.

SHREW. Although they are often called Shrew-mice, shrews are not mice, but belong to the INSECTIVORA (q.v.), or insect-eating order of mammals, as do MOLES and HEDGEHOGS (qq.v.). They eat a variety of food, such as worms and slugs, as well as insects. Shrews can be recognized by their long, sensitive snouts, small eyes, and soft, silky fur. They live in Europe and the temperate and semi-tropical parts of Africa, Asia, and America. The four species found in Great Britain are the Common Shrew, Pigmy Shrew, Water Shrew, and Scilly Shrew.

Common Shrews are about 3 inches long, with tails 1½ inches long. They have thick, velvety coats, brown on top and whitish below. They are extremely greedy, foraging for food unceasingly by day and night, and eating an amazing amount—four times their own weight in 36 hours. They die if they are without food for more than a few hours. The foul, musky smell which they give out from glands on each flank protects them from certain of their enemies; but, nevertheless, they are killed and eaten by moles, stoats, weasels, owls, and kestrels. Dogs

THE LESSER SHREW

This is the smallest British mammal and is shown here at life-size

John J. Ward, F.R.E.S.

and cats also kill, but do not eat them. Shrews can run at a speed of about 2½ m.p.h., and they can also leap a distance of some 2 feet. They climb up trees in search of insects, and also swim.

Shrews are always very quarrelsome among themselves, but particularly so in March, when they often kill and eat each other. They build their breeding-nests under logs, in tree-holes, and in banks. These are woven of dry grass, shaped like a cup, and have a loose lid. Litters of from five to seven young are born in the spring and summer. They stay in the nest, and are fed by their parents until they are almost fully grown. In summer, shrews live in grass or thick cover, either making nests of their own or using those of mice and voles. In the autumn they migrate to other ground, and in winter retreat to hedgerows, gorse, and piles of leaves and sticks. In the autumn, very large numbers are found dead. This abnormal mortality at only one season may be on account of a shortage of food; but it is now thought that it is due merely to their normal span of life being only 18 months. They are said to die also in thundery weather.

Pigmy or Lesser Shrews are smaller than Common Shrews, being only 2 inches long. There are not so many of them in Great Britain, although they are by no means rare, and they are the only shrews found in Ireland. Scilly Shrews or Blair's Shrews are the same size as Pigmy Shrews and, as their name denotes, are found in the Scilly Isles.

Water Shrews are a little larger than Common Shrews, and have shiny, velvety fur which throws off water without becoming wet. Their colour varies from blue-black to dark brown. On the underside of their tails they have a 'keel' of stiff hairs which helps them in swimming, and they have a fringe on the side of the hind-foot for the same purpose. They are about day and night, winter and summer, spending most of the time in the water, and preferring clear, slow streams and backwaters to muddy and swift waters. They come up every half-minute to breathe, and rarely venture far from the bank. Instead of using all four legs when swimming, like most mammals, they wriggle their bodies like fish and use their forelegs only to steer. On rising to the surface, they often leap clear of the water. Like all shrews, they have large appetites. In the water they turn over the stones in search of fish-spawn, small fry, caddis-flies, and other insects and larvae. As this food does not always

satisfy them, they search for food on land, even killing and eating each other. They make their nests of grass, moss, roots, or oak-leaves, deep down in small, mole-like galleries in the banks of streams, with entrances above and below water. A litter of from five to eight young is born in May, and probably a second litter later on in the year. In autumn Water Shrews travel away from their usual homes, and sometimes live away from water. Like the Common Shrews, large numbers die each autumn.

SHRIKE (Butcher Bird). This large and varied family includes the scarlet Minivets of India and east Asia, the black and white Magpie Larks and Piping Crows of Australia, as well as the typical Shrikes, among which are the Red-backed Shrike, the British species, and the European Great Grey Shrike, a winter visitor to Britain. Of the 200 or more species, however, the majority are found in Africa, where they are, perhaps, the most characteristic bird of the open thorn-scrub country. There are only two species in North America, and none in South America.

The Red-backed Shrike is not uncommon in localities in the southern half of England. It winters in Africa, and is one of the latest birds to arrive in Britain, and one of the earliest to

COCK RED-BACKED SHRIKE FEEDING HIS FAMILY
Eric J. Hosking, F.R.P.S.

depart. The cock bird has a blue-grey head, reddish-brown back, white throat, and pinkish underparts. It and other members of the family earn their name of Butcher Birds because of their habit of neatly impaling their victims on thorns or spikes in a sort of larder near their nests. They have powerful bills, the upper part being hooked and toothed, and with this strong weapon they attack not only insects, but small birds, field-mice, frogs, and lizards. They are very agile and quick in their movements, shooting out like an arrow on their prey, and very seldom missing their mark. They build a largish nest in a hedge or low bush—not in a tree, as do most members of the family.

The Great Grey Shrike, a rather larger bird, some 10 inches long, breeds in central and northern Europe. It builds in forest trees, often in an oak-tree on the outskirts of a wood. It lines its large nest with a great deal of soft material—feathers, fur, wool, and hair. It visits the east coast of Britain fairly regularly in the winter. The Woodchat Shrikes of central and southern Europe also occasionally visit Britain.

SHRIMP, *see* PRAWNS AND SHRIMPS.

SHRUBS, *see* FLOWERING PLANTS.

SIGHT, *see* SENSES, Section 2.

SILK MOTHS. The common Silkworm (belonging to the family Bombycidae) is the only insect that has been entirely domesticated by man, and it is doubtful whether it exists anywhere in the wild state now. For thousands of years it had been bred in captivity for the silk the caterpillars produce when they spin their golden cocoons. The moths have lost their power of flight, although they still retain their wings, and the caterpillars have no inclination to wander, relying upon man to feed them daily with mulberry leaves. The story of how two Persians, nearly 1,500 years ago, stole some of the precious eggs from a 'silk farm' in China, and smuggled them into Europe hidden in hollow staffs, is too well known to be told in detail here. But from this small stock it is said that the great silk industries of France and Italy have sprung into being (*see* SILKWORMS, Vol. VI).

Each female silk moth lays 200 to 400 eggs, which lie dormant all the winter, and hatch in the spring, when the mulberry leaves burst from their buds. Sometimes in late springs it is necessary to keep the eggs in a cold place to prevent their hatching before the leaves are ready; and at other times they can be forced in special incubators. The caterpillars, or silkworms, which are smooth and putty coloured, crawl about from leaf to leaf on the tray where they are fed, never moving more than a few inches in search of food. If mulberry leaves are short, they can be fed on lettuce, though lettuce is not suitable for commercial purposes. They change their skins several times, until they reach a length of 2 to 3 inches. When they are ready to spin their cocoons, the yellow silk begins to show through their skins. The worms attach their cocoons to bunches of straw, twigs, or spirals of paper. When finished, the cocoons are about $1\frac{1}{2}$ inches long, and golden-yellow or sometimes pale green, light apricot, or white. Each cocoon consists of an outer case of coarse silk (called floss silk in commerce), and inside this is a closely woven sheet made from a continuous double thread of silk. The brown chrysalis lies inside the cocoon. Except for a few that are kept for breeding purposes, the pupae are killed inside the cocoon before the silk is wound off. One cocoon may yield as much as 2,400 feet of silk.

Many moths belonging to the family Saturniidae are also silk producers. The EMPEROR MOTH (q.v.) is the only British representative of this group, which includes such giants as the Atlas Moth (*see* COLOUR PLATE opp. p. 80), the Tussore Silk Moth, the Indian Moon Moth with long sweeping tails to its wings, and the lovely North American Robin Moth. In contrast to the common silk moth, which is insignificant and of a plain creamy colour, the other large silk moths are strikingly beautiful, most of them having characteristic large eye-spots on their wings. Their caterpillars, too, are marked in brilliant colours and decorated in surprising profusion with bright tubercles, warts, and hairs. Although some of them are bred in captivity, notably the Tussore Silk Moth and the Chinese Oak silkworm (which produces light buff shantung), none has ever reached anything like the commercial importance of the Chinese Mulberry Silkworm.

The silkworm of Greek and Roman times is a relative of the LACKEY (q.v.). It was cultivated in Persia for over 2,000 years before the introduction of these Chinese species.

See also Vol. VIII: SILK INDUSTRY.

SILVERFISH. This insect is about a third of an inch long, wingless, and covered with silvery-white scales. At the end of its body are three slender, antennae-like tails, on account of which the name 'Bristle-tail' has been given to the Silverfish and its near relatives. METAMOR-PHOSIS (q.v.) does not occur, as the newly hatched insects are like their parents, except in size. They have six changes of coat as they grow up. Silverfish move with great speed, and are often seen skimming quickly over the floor as they make for cover. They are most likely to be found in old houses, especially in kitchens near bread-bins. A liking for starchy food may make them a nuisance in libraries, as they will attack the bindings of books for the sake of the paste.

The Firebrat is another species, larger and with dark markings on top. It has similar habits, but is even more fond of the warmth of fire-places and ovens.

SILVER-Y MOTH, *see* NIGHT-FLYING MOTHS.

SISKIN, *see* FINCHES, Section 3.

SKATE, *see* SHARKS AND RAYS, Section 3.

SKELETON, *see* ANATOMY.

SKIN. This is the flexible covering of the body of the higher animals, from which grow the HAIR, FEATHERS, SCALES, HOOFS, NAILS AND CLAWS, and HORNS (qq.v.) with which it is wholly or partly concealed or adorned. (The hard external skeleton of crustaceans, and the chitinous covering of insects are not, strictly speaking, skin.) The skin produces Vitamin D3 when exposed to the sun, and this vitamin is also produced in the fur of animals and the feathers of birds. In some animals, notably the amphibia, the skin also assists in RESPIRATION (q.v.), and in other warm-blooded animals, through the presence in it of sweat-glands, it assists, through perspiration, in keeping the body at a uniform temperature.

The skin is not a single, simple covering, but consists of a number of layers, the outer of which are periodically renewed. In some animals, the outer covering (fur, feather, scales) is moulted annually, or even more often; but in others the

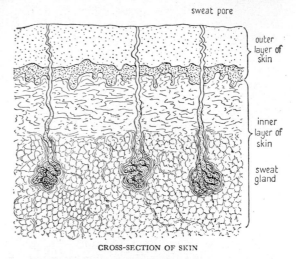

CROSS-SECTION OF SKIN

process is much more gradual, and so less obvious.

Skin may be hard, thick, and opaque, as in the elephant and rhinoceros, or it may be soft, thin, and semi-transparent, as in many mammals, including man, and in birds. In most animals it cannot be moved independently of the part of the body which it covers; but a dog coming out of the water can shake his fur dry while standing still, a horse can twitch off flies by means of his fly-muscle, and man can wrinkle or smooth out his brow.

SKIPPERS (BUTTERFLIES). These small insects, so called because of their habit of skipping swiftly from flower to flower, are traditionally regarded

SMALL SKIPPER (× 2)
S. Beaufoy, F.R.P.S.

as butterflies, though they differ from true
BUTTERFLIES (q.v.) in many respects, and are
probably best classified by themselves. They
have large heads, prominent eyes, and thick,
often very hairy bodies. Their antennae are
clubbed like those of butterflies, and sometimes
hooked. Their rather small wings are usually
brown, orange, black, or grey, with lighter or
darker patterns. Some, e.g. the Dingy Skipper,
rest with their wings sloping downwards,
like moths; but most hold their hind-wings
horizontally and tilt their fore-wings upwards.
The Regent Skipper of Australia, more primitive
than any other butterfly, has the front and
hind-wings in the male coupled together by
means of bristles, as have most moths. The
simply-formed caterpillars of Skippers often feed
on grasses, but also on some other plants such
as irises, lilies, and palms. They shelter beneath
silken webs or spun leaves, as do those of many
moths, a few being stem-borers. The smooth,
long-shaped pupa lies in a loosely spun cocoon—
another difference from true butterflies which
do not spin cocoons.

About 3,000 species are known, many of which
are South American. Of the eight species
breeding in Britain, four, the Dingy, Grizzled,
Large, and Small Skippers, are quite common
and fairly generally distributed. It has been
recently discovered that the Chequered Skipper,
long thought to be confined to a few Midland
woods, has a darker and more greenish variety
on the west coast of Scotland. The Lulworth
Skipper is confined to parts of the Dorset and
Devon coasts, and the Silver Spotted Skipper to
chalk or limestone country. The Essex Skipper
occurs on both sides of the Thames and in
Bedfordshire and Somerset.

SKUA, see GULLS, Section 5.

SKUNK, see WEASEL, Section 5.

SLATER, see WOODLOUSE.

SLAVE-MAKER ANT, see ANTS, HABITS OF.

SLOTH. This is a South American mammal,
about the size of a fox-terrier, belonging to the
same order as the ANT-EATERS (q.v.)—the Edentata—the members of which have no front teeth.
Its name 'sloth' arose because its ungainly, slow,
cautious movements give an impression of in-

THREE-TOED SLOTH OF SOUTH AMERICA
C. S. Webb

dolence. In fact, it is not particularly more
slothful than any animal living in rather pre-
scribed surroundings. It is found only in the
tropical forests, where it lives high up in the
trees, hanging upside-down from the branches,
and never coming down to the ground except
to pass from one tree to another. Its body is
adapted for this kind of life: it has very long
front legs, and its feet end in long, hook-like
claws, by means of which it hangs from the
branches.

Sloths have very thick coats of long, coarse,
brownish-grey hair, which grows in the reverse
direction from that of other animals, corresponding to their normal upside-down position. Their
fine under-fur is striped brown and orange. The
most extraordinary thing about their coats is
that a microscopic plant grows in grooves on the
longer hairs, giving the coat a greenish tinge. In
consequence, the animals look very like the
lichens which grow on the boughs of their native
tropical forests; and when they go to sleep rolled
up in a ball, their heads tucked between their
arms, they look amazingly like the lichen-covered
knots. This camouflage is, in fact, their only
defence, for they are harmless, unaggressive
animals.

Sloths live in pairs or in small families. They
move and eat at night, living on leaves and
fruit, which provide them with so much moisture
that they do not need to seek water. The young
are born singly, and the baby sloth clings to its
mother's hair with its claws, its arms round her
neck. There are two main types of sloth—those

with three toes on the fore-foot, and those with only two. Some prefer dry districts, and others those which are permanently flooded; but otherwise their habits are much the same.

SLOW-WORM. This legless lizard of England and Europe belongs to the family Anguidae. Because it has no limbs, it looks like a snake; but it is a true LIZARD (q.v.) with eye-lids, a fleshy tongue, ear-openings, and vertebrae of the lizard type. It has the vestiges of a pelvis, but no shoulder girdle. As in many other lizards, the tail is fragile; and if the creature is carelessly handled, it will be cast off—hence its scientific name *Anguis fragilis* (fragile snake). The tail can be regrown, but it has never the same length or appearance as before.

The Slow-worm is common in many parts of England and Scotland, being found on heaths, in open woods, and in gardens. On fine days it may be seen basking in the sun; but those looking for it will more often find it hiding under stones or fallen timber. It is easily caught, and has never been known to bite. It feeds mainly on worms and slugs, particularly the small, white kind. The young are born alive in September, and are beautiful little creatures, striped lengthwise with gold or yellow on a black background. The adult is brown, with or without darker stripes, and sometimes with blue spots. When fully grown, it reaches a length of 14 inches, of which the tail forms about one-half.

The so-called Glass Snakes are members of the same family, being lizards, not snakes, in spite of their legless, snake-like form. They differ from snakes in having a deep fold of skin along the side of the body. Four species are known: one inhabits south-east Europe, two the Indo-Chinese region, and one North America. They live on small rodents, other lizards, and sometimes snakes.

See also LIZARDS.

FAMILY OF SLOW-WORMS
The young Slow-worm is about 6 weeks old.   *A. R. Thompson*

SLUG. These are molluscs very similar in structure and habit to the land SNAILS (q.v.), and they are, in fact, probably descended from shell-bearing ancestors, although only a few species now develop a small single shell. While many species seriously damage crops and garden plants, others are harmless or even mildly beneficial, as they feed on their own vegetarian relatives, on worms, and insects. Some 600 species are known, of which nineteen are British.

One of the most interesting of the British species is the Carnivorous Slug, which is about 3 inches in length, and has a small oval shell at the hind end of the body. It is yellowish-brown, and at once attracts attention by the shape of its body, slender in the fore-part and increasing in girth behind—exactly the reverse shape of ordi-

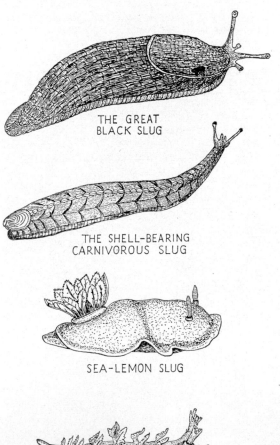

THE GREAT
BLACK SLUG

THE SHELL-BEARING
CARNIVOROUS SLUG

SEA-LEMON SLUG

A CRESTED SEA-SLUG

nary garden slugs, whose bodies always taper away to end in a slender tail. The Carnivorous Slug spends most of its time beneath the surface of the soil, where it hunts for worms, being able to elongate its body so as to enter their burrows. It also preys upon some of the caterpillars and beetle larvae which feed upon plant roots.

The Great Grey Slug, measuring 5 or 6 inches in length, has a small oval shell, hidden beneath the mantle and covering the breathing apparatus. It usually keeps its spotted and yellowish-grey body fully stretched out when at rest, with the tail-end slightly curved towards the mantle. It often haunts larders and dairies, as it likes cream, milk, butter, and other animal food, while fresh green plants are distasteful to it. On the other hand, the Tree Slug, which to look at might easily be mistaken for a half-grown Great Grey, is totally different in habit, living chiefly among the branches of trees, particularly beech and walnut, and also frequenting lichen-covered rocks, its colour harmonizing wonderfully with its surroundings. It descends from one branch to another by means of a thread of slime secreted from its slime-glands.

In the slugs belonging to the genus *Arion*, which includes many garden and field pests, the shell is represented by a few disconnected granules of limy substance. Of these, a familiar example is the large Black Slug, which is by no means always black—brown, red, and yellow specimens being not at all uncommon, while even white ones are sometimes found. This slug grows to fully 5 inches in length, the red and dark-brown ones being really handsome creatures. They devour ripening fruit and tender vegetables, and, when green-food is scarce, eat almost anything they can find, from smaller slugs to dead birds and mice, and even stray pieces of damp paper. The smaller Garden Slug is all too common and familiar a native of our gardens, hiding away during the day-time under damp stones or boards and garden rubbish, and coming forth as night descends to start upon its nocturnal raids among the garden crops and flowers (*see* GARDEN PESTS, Vol. VI).

Very different in appearance are the Sea-slugs. Most of these have rows of plume-like papillae arranged along their backs, and the majority are truly elegant creatures, their varied shapes and soft lovely colours in some cases being protective, and in others conspicuous and warning (*see* PROTECTIVE COLORATION). Some feed entirely upon seaweeds; while others are more or less flesh-eating, browsing upon living sponges, hydroids, sea-anemones, and corals. Some frequent the deep rock-pools exposed at low tide, and shallow waters off-shore; while some, such as the Gulfweed Sea-slug, are found only in the open sea, where they live on floating seaweeds. A familiar British Sea-slug is the Sea-lemon Slug, which both in colour and shape is rather like a lemon that has been cut in half lengthways. At one end of its body it has a pair of ear-like tentacles, and at the opposite end a circlet of plume-like gills, which can be withdrawn into a special body-chamber. It is found near low-tide mark, feeding upon living sponges.

See also MOLLUSCS.

SMELL, *see* SENSES, Section 6.

SMOOTH SNAKE. This is the rarest of the three British snakes—indeed not many people in England have ever seen it. It is restricted to the heather country of the south, particularly that of Hampshire and Dorset. It can be distinguished from the ADDER (q.v.), which in general appearance it resembles most, by its more slender body, and the absence of a defined neck. Its colour is different, also, being grey or reddish above, with dark-brown or black transverse bars or paired spots, and no zigzag marks. The belly is brown, grey, or reddish, either uniform, or speckled with black. The pupil of the eye is round, instead of slit-like as in the Adder. It grows to a length of 2 feet. The Smooth Snake feeds mainly upon lizards and slow-worms, but will also eat small mammals, which it kills by constriction—for it is not poisonous. It will bite when first caught, but is easily tamed and can be trained to feed from the hand, and, for a snake, shows much intelligence. It is widely distributed over Europe, but was not recorded in England until 1859.

Related to the Smooth Snake is the beautiful Leopard Snake of southern Europe. The particular colour-variety from which it derives its name is greyish or pale brown above, with a series of large, dark brown or bright red spots with black edges, arranged transversely with the smaller ones on the sides of the body. Underneath it is white chequered with black, or nearly all black. This snake, which is about 3 feet long, feeds on small creatures, which it kills by crushing them in its coils.

SNAIL. 1. There are hundreds of different kinds of snails to be found on land, in fresh water, and in the sea. All possess a well-developed head, which usually bears a pair of small eyes, and one or two pairs of horns, or tentacles, which can be pushed out or withdrawn. Inside the mouth, there is a rasping tongue-ribbon, or 'radula', for breaking down the plant or animal matter upon which these molluscs feed. The spiral shell is secreted by glands on a part of the body called the 'mantle', the fleshy folds of which are also arranged to form a chamber containing the breathing organs. In many of the marine species the hind end of the foot carries a structure called the 'operculum', which forms a perfectly fitting lid when the animal retires within its shell. It is a permanent structure, and increases in size as the snail grows. The land snails have no operculum; but in late autumn, when about to retire for their winter sleep, they secrete from their foot-glands a temporary lid, composed of a mixture of hardened slime and lime, which closes the mouth of the shell and shuts out the winter cold. When they awaken in early spring, this temporary door is moistened from within and dissolves away. The land snails generally lay eggs. In some species these are enclosed in hard shells, and the young, on hatching out, are already completely formed, only differing from their parents in size. The majority of marine snails, however, pass through a larval stage, and at first are totally unlike their parents in appearance, being minute oval creatures, with a girdle of fine hair-like cilia which, by rhythmical lashing movements, enable them to swim about.

2. LAND SNAILS. The different species of land snails have become accustomed to live under the most varied conditions, so that there are few places, from the ice-bound lands of the Arctic and Antarctic to the humid swamps and sun-scorched deserts of the tropics, where some kind of snail is not found. Because of their nocturnal

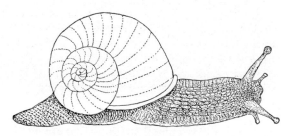

ROMAN SNAIL

habits, however, they are apt to escape notice, for most of them have their regular hiding-places, to which they return after their nightly foray, and there, safely hidden from view, they sleep away the hours of daylight. They vary greatly in size, and many possess beautifully coloured shells. Our two largest British species are the common Garden Snail and the Edible or so-called Roman Snail. (Whether the latter was introduced into Britain by the Romans is extremely doubtful.) It is restricted to the chalk hills and downs of southern England. It has a large handsome shell, usually creamy-white, marked with three to five spiral bands of a pale-brownish tint.

In South America, the West Indies, and Tropical Africa, there are giant land snails with shells measuring over 6 inches in length. Many of these giant snails live in the forest trees, and some lay hard-shelled eggs nearly as large as those of a pigeon.

3. FRESHWATER SNAILS. These abound in rivers, ponds, and lakes all over the world. There are two British species, which must be familiar to anyone who has gone pond-hunting or kept an aquarium—the Great Pond Snail, which has a large greyish or yellow-brown spiral shell, and the Ram's-horn Snail, which has the whorls of its reddish-brown shell coiled in the same plane, and measures about an inch or more in diameter. Several

GREAT POND SNAIL

species serve as the intermediate hosts for parasitic worms which cause various diseases in cattle, sheep, horses, and man.

4. SEA SNAILS. Strictly speaking, the term 'Snail' should not be applied indiscriminately to the hosts of marine molluscs possessing spiral-shaped shells, for many of them are quite unlike the land snails both in habit and appearance, while all are 'water-breathers', obtaining their supplies of oxygen from the water bathing their gills. The round-mouthed sea snails most nearly approach the true land snails. They are nearly all vegetarians, and are therefore found only

between tide-marks on shore, and in the shallow waters off-shore where seaweeds abound. Familiar examples are the Periwinkles, which in many ways resemble their cousins, the true, air-breathing land snails. Indeed, one species, the Rough Periwinkle, prefers to be out of the water for long periods at a time, and lives so far up the shore that even at the highest tides it is not completely immersed in water. In contrast to the dull-coloured common Periwinkle, there are some members of the family with yellow, red, white, orange, or pale-green shells of smaller size and smoother surface. Another familiar family of sea snails is the Top-shells, to be found feeding on the seaweeds in the rock-pools. Their shells are cone-shaped, something like a peg-top, and, in the common British Top-shell, are creamy flesh-coloured, with deeper pink or red wavy markings, the animal itself being bright ruddy-brown, with long and slender, pinkish horns.

See also MOLLUSCS.

SNAKES. These are reptiles of the order Squamata, which includes also the LIZARDS (q.v.). Many lizards with elongated bodies and no limbs, such as the SLOW-WORM (q.v.), look like snakes; but snakes have certain characteristics which, when taken together, will always distinguish them. The eyes of snakes are without lids, the eyeball being covered with a transparent skin shaped like a watch-glass; there is no ear opening; the body is greatly elongated and is without limbs, except in some of the BOAS (q.v.) and other primitive snakes, in which there are tiny vestiges of a hind pair protruding from the body on each side of the vent; the tongue is long, deeply forked, and can be drawn back into a sheath.

Altogether, some 2,500 species of snake are known. They are found all over the world except in Polar regions. Some, for example the English

SKELETON OF A SNAKE
By permission of the Trustees of the British Musuem (Nat. Hist.)

KING COBRA   *Zoological Society of London*

and are freely movable. The size of some of the objects devoured by snakes is almost incredible. The Egg-eating Snake of Africa, with a neck no thicker than the little finger, can swallow a fowl's egg. It has a mouth and gullet specially modified, so that when the snake's mouth closes over the egg, the muscles of the gullet contract, and small teeth in the neck break the shell. The snake then swallows the contents and ejects the fragments of shell. A python in Australia has been known to devour a kangaroo, and an Indian python, a leopard. Some snakes kill their prey by constriction—that is, by squeezing them in their coils so that they suffocate, no bones being broken in the process. To help them in swallowing their enormous meals, most snakes are well provided with salivary glands, from which the saliva is poured out during the process of swallowing—they do not lick their food all over before starting a meal, as is often stated. All snakes are flesh-eaters. The Milk Snake of eastern North America, and some other snakes, are accused by farmers of sucking the milk from cows; but it is doubtful if any snake could do this, even if it wanted to.

snakes, live in fields, woods, and on heaths; some live in the desert, others in the thickest jungle; some pass their lives in fresh water; while the SEA SNAKES (q.v.), with one exception, live in the sea. Some live on the ground; others, such as the Cat Snakes of south-west Asia and north Africa, live in trees; others again, such as the Blind Snakes, spend their lives underground, and have bodies adapted for this life. Snakes are most numerous in tropical countries, and those that live in temperate climates spend the cold months in a state of torpor. They have been found in the Himalayas and in the Andes at heights of 10,000 feet.

Scientifically, the snakes are divided into eleven families, three of which are poisonous and eight non-poisonous. The non-poisonous can be divided again into the Solid-toothed Snakes, which are harmless, and the Back-fanged Snakes, whose bite is poisonous to the creatures they feed on, but hardly ever to man. The division between these two groups is, however, not clearly defined. The Back-fanged Snakes are so called because the back teeth of the upper jaw are enlarged and grooved to carry the venom, which comes from a special gland, originally part of the upper labial gland. The majority of non-poisonous snakes belong to the family Colubridae. It is by far the largest of the families, including some two-thirds of all the snakes known. The three families of poisonous snakes are as follows: the Elapidae, which include the COBRAS and KRAITS; the SEA SNAKES (Hydrophiidae); and the VIPERS (Viperidae) (qq.v.).

The ability of snakes to swallow food much exceeding their own girth is well known. This is possible because the bones of the jaws are only loosely attached to the skull and to one another,

The tongue of a snake is an organ of touch and smell, and when it is seen flickering, in the way we know so well, it is collecting scent particles which are then passed on to the organ of scent, a structure lying above the palate, close to the nostril. From there, the sensation passes by means of a thick bundle of nerve fibres to that part of the brain concerned with the sense of smell.

All snakes are covered with SCALES (q.v.), which on the head are large and usually regular in shape and position, but on the body are smaller, and vary in shape, numbers, and arrangement. The number of scale-rows on the body is a valuable means of identification. The scales on the belly, known as 'ventral shields', are broad—in most species nearly as broad as the body. Only in the Sea Snakes and some burrowing snakes—Blind Snakes, for example—are they absent or very small. The Wart Snake, which lives in brackish waters in Malaya, has small, hard, rough scales, and no proper ventral shields, so that it is almost helpless on land. There are two kinds of viper—the Rattlesnake of North America, and the Viper of south-western Asia—both known as Side-winders, for they are able to travel in a sideways as well as in a forward direction. They do this particularly when trying to escape. Some snakes are known

YOUNG PYTHON SWALLOWING A MOUSE
Douglas Fisher, A.R.P.S.

as Flying Snakes—and the term is not entirely incorrect. No snake can fly in the real sense of the word; but some can plane through the air from a higher to a lower altitude, in the same way as the Flying Frog, the Flying Lizard, and the Flying Squirrel (*see* FLIGHT). The snakes known to be able to do this are the Golden Tree Snake and the Painted Bronze-back, two well-known snakes of the East. In 'flight', the scales of the belly are contracted to produce a concave surface, the body is straightened and made rigid, and the creature planes through the air at a steep angle.

The largest snakes in the world are the Pythons and the Boas, both of which are known to reach 30 feet in length; the smallest, the burrowing snakes *Typhlops* and *Leptotyphlops*, are only a few inches long. Most snakes lay eggs; but a few produce their young alive. All embryo (un-hatched) snakes are provided with an egg-tooth to enable them to break the 'shell', which is of whitish, parchment-like skin, containing only a small amount of lime.

There are some 600 species of poisonous snakes, of which about 150 carry a poison strong enough to kill a man. The poison of snakes is injected into their victims through specialized teeth, known as fangs. These convey the venom from the poison gland (a modification of the salivary gland) either through a tube or along a groove in the fang. To provide an antidote to snake-bite, snakes are kept in captivity, and the venom is periodically extracted, to be used in the making of anti-venine. The first 'snake park' was opened at São Paulo, Brazil; and there are now others at Johannesburg and Port Elizabeth in South Africa, at Kasauli in India, at Nha-Trong in Indo-China, and at Bangkok in Siam. The snakes are kept in open-air enclosures, provided with shelters or retreats, into which they can retire during the day-time. Periodically they are 'milked' by pressing on the venom gland so that the venom is discharged into a small dish. When dried, it becomes crystalline, and in that state will remain unchanged for years. Venom kept for 40 years has been shown experimentally to be just as active as when fresh.

The distribution of snakes is interesting. There are no snakes in Ireland (from where, according to the legend, they were cast out by St. Patrick), or in New Zealand. There are no poisonous snakes in Madagascar. The majority of the snakes in Australia belong to the family Elapidae, the family which includes the Cobras and Kraits, and are therefore poisonous; but there are no Vipers there. There are no Elapid snakes in Europe, where the only poisonous snakes are the Vipers. In Britain there are only three Snakes: the GRASS SNAKE, the SMOOTH SNAKE, and the ADDER (qq.v.).

SNIPE, see WADING BIRDS, Section 4.

SOLAN GOOSE, see GANNET.

SOLE, see FLATFISHES.

SONG, see ANIMAL LANGUAGE.

SPARROW. This name has been given to many small brown birds, including the Hedge Sparrow, which is not a sparrow at all (*see* WARBLERS). It belongs properly to a group of thick-billed, finch-like birds, of which the House Sparrow is a typical example. Sparrows are natives of almost every part of the Old World, but not Australasia. They were, unfortunately, introduced into America, because it was hoped that they would keep down noxious insects—but they are so much more seed-eaters than insect-eaters that any good they may do is far outweighed by their depredations on seeds and grain-crops (*see* BIRD PESTS, Vol. VI). They increase in numbers very fast, for they generally produce three broods in a season. They build rather untidy nests, generally placed in some part of a building. Occasionally they build in a hedge or tree, and then they construct a dome to protect the nest from the weather. Sparrows are very particular to keep their plumage in good order, not only taking frequent water-baths, but also, in summer, enjoying dust-baths.

Another species, the Tree Sparrow, found locally in Britain, is much less inclined to frequent human habitations. It is rather differently marked, having a chestnut crown and black patches on the cheek. In the Mediterranean countries the Spanish Sparrows are serious pests. They nest in very closely packed and noisy colonies. In South Africa the Black-breasted Sparrow, in West Africa the Grey-headed Sparrow, and in Arabia the Golden Sparrow are the common species.

See also FINCHES.

SPIDERS. These are not insects: they form the largest and most widely distributed order of the class of animals called Arachnida, which also includes the SCORPIONS, HARVESTMEN, FALSE SCORPIONS, MITES AND TICKS (qq.v.), as well as the marine King-crabs and several less important creatures only to be found in the tropics. The bodies of all these animals are in two parts: in front, the head and chest closely joined, forming the cephalo-thorax, and behind, the abdomen. They have a pair of jaws, a pair of 'pedipalps' or pincer claws, and four pairs of legs, all of which are attached to the cephalothorax. These features, and their lack of antennae, distinguish the Arachnida from INSECTS (q.v.). Spiders secrete silk through tubular spinnerets, usually six in number, placed at the tip of the abdomen. They use the silk for a variety of purposes, the most characteristic being the spinning of a web to ensnare their prey.

Not all spiders spin webs: many hunt for

DIAGRAM OF SPIDER

WOLF SPIDER

ZEBRA SPIDER

their food in quite an ordinary way, usually at night. Others have developed particular habits, usually shared by all members of a family, which help them in hunting. For example, the Wolf Spiders—the small brown spiders so common in woods and pastures from spring to autumn—run fast enough to pursue their quarry and overtake it. Crab-spiders lurk among fallen leaves and pounce unexpectedly upon their victims. Their popular name is descriptive, for they are flattened in form, with crab-like legs, and a habit of darting sideways. A few of them lie hidden in flowers, and seize the butterflies and other insects which alight on the petals. Jumping-spiders have better eyesight than other spiders; they stalk their quarry, approaching it stealthily until near enough to leap upon it. The little Zebra Spider, common all over Britain, is often to be seen hunting on walls and fences in bright sunshine. It has a habit, common to all spiders, of trailing behind it a drag-line of silk, fastened at intervals. If the spider misses its footing, the drag-line, like a mountaineer's rope, saves it from falling to the ground.

The drag-line habit is important, because it suggests a possible explanation of how spiders first started to make webs; and the web is interesting because it is almost the only trap constructed by any animal. If a spider continued to use the same hiding-place, the approaches to it must soon have become coated with threads of silk—and as soon as the spider had learnt that the trembling of these threads gave notice of the passing of an insect, the 'web-idea' had come into being (*see* INTELLIGENCE). The webs of the most primitive spiders do, in fact, consist of a roughly circular mat surrounding a hole, in which the spider waits: the rough, bluish-looking webs, to be seen, for instance, in the corners of windows, are familiar examples of this primitive type of web. The spider will obviously catch more if he extends the area of the 'mat'; and the house-spiders, which spin 'cobwebs' in the corners of our rooms, illustrate this development,

The spider lives in a silk tube, the trap part of the web being a hammock-like sheet, sometimes—as in the space between two rafters of a shed roof—of a great size. The web-forms which evolved from this are often seen in hedges and on bushes.

Most of the small spiders of Europe belong to the family Linyphiidae, which includes the 'Money-spiders'. These do not use the tubular shelter, but hang themselves upside-down under a sheet or hammock—a characteristic which makes the family easily recognizable. Above the sheet is a supporting maze of threads, which checks the flight of insects and throws them down on to the sheet beneath. The spider seizes them from below and drags them through it. A family of small, brightly coloured spiders, known as Theridiidae, use the superstructure without the sheet for their irregularly tangled webs. Lastly, the perfection of web-spinning is found in the cart-wheel, or orb-web, spun by the Garden Spider, and other members of its family, Argyopidae. This has been so successful that it is found all over the world, sometimes reaching a large size.

A SPIDER'S WEB
Zoological Society of London

BRITISH ROCK POOL

From left to right

Above water: Mussels; Rock Whelks; Bladderwrack Seaweed; Winkles. *Below water*: Common Anemone; Blenny; Prawns; Hermit Crab, Velvet-fiddler Crab, and Shore Crab sharing a meal; Opelet and Dahlia Anemones; Sea Lemon

TROPICAL SPIDER CARRYING HER COCOON OF EGGS
C. A. Gibson-Hill

climbs upon the female and tickles her; and the Web-spider drums on the sheet of the web or tweaks its threads. The result of these peculiar actions of the male spider is to suppress the female's usual inclination to leap upon, kill, and eat any moving creature that approaches her. Hence a male, as soon as he begins his courtship, is comparatively safe, and often he lulls the female into a passive trance. After mating, he usually escapes at his best speed. The popular belief that female spiders always eat their mates is an exaggeration; but it sometimes happens towards the end of autumn, when the females are likely to be hungry and the males less active.

In addition to all these there are spiders, not to be found in Britain, which dig a hole in the ground, line it with silk, and close it with a silk trap-door, covered with earth and other materials so that it exactly resembles its surroundings. These Trap-door Spiders include the largest species known, and are sometimes misnamed Tarantulas. Some are also called Bird-eating Spiders, for they are able to attack and consume small humming-birds. Ordinarily, however, spiders eat insects; and the stories told of their killing mice, snakes, and fish are either chance occurrences, or are records of the special habits of peculiar species.

It is clear that, to be able to detect their prey by the vibrations of the threads of their silk webs, spiders must have an extremely delicate sense of touch—as indeed they have. Their bodies and legs are covered with hairs (or 'setae'), many of which are perhaps merely protective, but some of which are certainly sensitive organs of touch. The finest of them are believed to respond to the air-waves which convey sound, and to provide the spider with its only means of 'hearing'. There are organs on the legs which appear to detect scents; but, on the whole, a spider leads a life in which almost every sensation is of touch, every event a vibration.

Among the most remarkable of spiders' habits are their peculiar methods of courtship, different in different families. The male Jumping-spider performs a kind of dance in front of the watching female; the Wolf Spider waves his decorated forelegs in front of her; the male Grab-spider

All spiders start life as eggs, usually laid in masses in a silk cocoon. Generally, the female pays little attention to her cocoon after it is completed; but the female Wolf Spider fastens her cocoon to her spinneret and drags it about with her. Newly hatched Wolf Spiders ride for a time on their mother's abdomen. Spiders do not go through a larval stage, as do most insects, but resemble their parents when they hatch. They grow by periodic castings of their skins, and the sex of a spider is usually impossible to tell until it is mature.

When spiders bite they paralyse their victims with poison secreted from glands in their jaws. The venom has an effect on such small animals as mice, moles, or sparrows; but only a few spiders, and no British spiders, are dangerous to man. The largest spiders are not the most

BLACK WIDOW (× 2)

dangerous: the most poisonous spiders are the American 'Black Widow' and its relatives in other countries (*see also* TARANTULA).

The well-known phenomenon 'gossamer' is produced by young spiders of many species, and adults of a few, in their peculiar method of MIGRATION (q.v.). When the weather is suitable, they climb up fences and railings, turn their heads towards the wind, raise their abdomens, and exude silk. The drop of silk is drawn out by the breeze into a long thread, and when sufficient buoyancy is attained, the spider lets go and drifts away. These aerial journeys may reach heights of several thousand feet, and cover distances of hundreds of miles. Similar to this, but nothing to do with migration, is the rarer 'rain of wool'. Sometimes a sudden rise of temperature stimulates the many thousands of spiders on the ground to secrete silk, and the earth becomes carpeted with a sheet of silk. Rising currents tear this, and pieces are borne into the air—but not carrying spiders.

There are about 22,000 different species of spiders, of which about 500 are British. The largest are found in central America, and have a body-length of about 3½ inches: the smallest species are less than a twenty-fifth of an inch long.

SPIROGYRA, *see* ALGAE.

SPONGE.
This animal holds a peculiarly isolated position in the animal kingdom; for its exact relationship to other forms of animal life is very obscure, and there are many problems concerning its daily life and reactions that remain to be solved. Indeed, although a few species grow to a great size—for example, the Neptune's Cup Sponges which reach 3 feet in height—they appear in many respects to be most nearly allied to those microscopic single-celled animals known as collared-monads, which belong to the simplest forms of animal life, the PROTOZOA (q.v.).

Some sponges, such as the common Bath Sponge, build a skeleton of horny fibres, others, a more elaborate skeleton of silica, or of carbonate of lime. Scattered over the entire surface of a sponge, in addition to the easily recognized large holes or vents, are thousands of tiny pores, opening into equally minute canals, which branch and pierce the tissues of the sponge in all directions. Each fine division of the branching canals ends in a spherical chamber, the walls of which are lined with special collared cells. These cells carry a protoplasmic collar or funnel, with a whip-like 'flagellum' or slender outgrowth, springing from the base inside the collar. By the lashing of the flagella of hundreds of thousands of collared cells, a continuous flow of water is drawn through the body of the sponge, entering at the pores and leaving by the vents, bringing food and oxygen, and carrying away waste matter. The fine canals, travelling inwards to the chambers, carry the inward flow of water, and are known as 'inhalant canals'; those carrying the water away from the chambers to the exterior are called the 'exhalant canals'.

It is possible, by squeezing a living sponge enclosed in a piece of very fine silk, to separate the tissues into their component cells, and to observe under the microscope their movements in a small glass dish filled with sea-water. The separate living cells are seen for a time to move about freely, but gradually to draw together until they form a little mass, which is the beginning of a new sponge. Because of the behaviour of its cells, a living sponge must be regarded, not so much as a single individual, but rather as a colony of cells, in which each cell is more or less independent of the rest, and is capable of changing its form and function as occasion may demand—and yet as one in which a bond of union exists, so that all work together to make one harmonious whole. No less wonderful are the skeletons built up by certain of the sponge cells. The spicules from which they are formed are composed of silica, or of carbonate of lime, extracted from the water which passes through the canals. These take on the most beautiful and varied shapes, such as slender needles, stars, forks, hooks, or anchors, mostly microscopic in size, though in some species they may be several inches, and in one species nearly a yard long.

Sponges are divided into the following four

Left, Collared cell (each flagellated chamber is lined with collared cells). *Right,* Section of a sponge showing canal system

THE THREE COMMON BRITISH SPONGES.   *M. Burton*

Left, The Purse Sponge growing on seaweed; *Top right*, The Crumb-of-bread sponge growing on rock; *Bottom right*, *Hymeniacidon sanguinea*—a brick-red or tan sponge, growing on rocks

orders: (1) the Calcarea, which have spicules of carbonate of lime, and are found mostly in shallow seas; (2) the Hexactinellida, which have skeletons composed of six-rayed spicules of silica, and are mostly deep-sea forms. They include the beautiful Venus's Flower-basket, the Glass-rope Sponge, and the curious Single-stem Sponge, which has one great spicule, over a yard in length, standing erect with its base buried in the mud, and the sponge itself embracing it at the middle; (3) the Tetraxonida, which have four-rayed spicules of silica. They include the common Crumb-of-bread Sponge, which grows in green or yellowish-white masses on rocks, sea-weeds, and shells, between mid and low-water mark all round our coasts; the large goblet-shaped Neptune's Cup Sponges from the warm sea around the coasts of the Dutch East Indies;

and also the Freshwater Sponges, which form greenish, slimy masses on lock-gates; and the burrowing Cliona Sponge, which is a shell-boring pest of the Oyster; (4) the Keratosa or Horny-skeletoned Sponges, which include the Bath Sponge and other commercial sponges, all possessing skeletons composed of a network of spongin-fibres, and chiefly obtained from the eastern Mediterranean and the West Indies.

SPOON-BILL, *see* STORK.

SPORES, *see* REPRODUCTION IN PLANTS, Section 3.

SPRAT, *see* HERRING.

SPRINGBOK, *see* ANTELOPE.

SQUID, *see* CUTTLEFISH AND SQUIDS.

RED SQUIRREL
Dorien Leigh

They sleep with their heads covered by their tails. Although they can swim well, they do not much care for water.

In the British Isles, there are both red and grey squirrels. The native Red Squirrel used to be much more numerous than it is now; but its numbers have been reduced by epidemic diseases, and it is being replaced in many districts, particularly in southern England, by the more robust American Grey Squirrel, which was introduced into England at the end of the last century. The Red Squirrel changes colour a good deal during the year, owing to two moults, one in October and another in May. Its tail starts dark, but gradually bleaches and thins through the year. Squirrels are very active during the day; but, being timid, they usually dart behind a trunk and climb up the far side of a tree at the sight of a human being. When they are scared, they scold and chatter. They eat acorns, beech-mast, haws, bark, fungi, fruit, seeds, and, very rarely, eggs and young birds. They sit up to eat, holding their food in their hands, and wasting a good deal of it. In autumn they spend a lot of time on the ground, picking up food to be stored for the winter. In very cold climates, Red Squirrels hibernate for some of the winter; but in England, they take only a few long sleeps. At the mating season in early spring, the males fight amongst themselves; but by February or March both sexes are busy building nests, called 'dreys', of sticks, bark, and moss. They

SQUIRREL. This RODENT (q.v.) belongs to a sub-family of the large family Sciuridae, the other sub-family of which includes the MARMOTS (q.v.). Squirrels are found in wooded districts of most parts of the world, except Madagascar and Australia. They range in size from as small as a mouse (Borneo and west Africa) to as large as a cat (Malaya), and in colour from bright chestnut-red to deep, blackish-grey or clear, pale grey. There are some very beautiful striped species in tropical countries, among the commonest of which are the little Indian Palm Squirrels, to be seen in large numbers running about most Indian villages. In general, they have slender, agile bodies, long, bushy tails, well-developed, pointed ears, and feet adapted for climbing. They mostly live in trees, leaping from branch to branch and running down the trunks head-first; the heavier-built tropical squirrels are less arboreal. Squirrels are among the most thrifty of animals, and are for ever storing food away for future consumption. They make holes in the ground to hold hundreds of nuts— though they often forget where their stores are.

GREY SQUIRREL
Harold Bastin

usually make these in conifers or in hollows in other trees, sometimes using as a foundation an old crow's, sparrow-hawk's, or wood-pigeon's nest. The nests, unlike most birds'-nests, have roofs and side entrances, like those of magpies. Additional nests are built close by, so that the young can be transferred to them in case of danger. As a rule two or three young are born, naked and blind, in March or April, with often a second litter in August.

Grey Squirrels (sometimes called tree-rats) are larger than Red Squirrels. They cause a great deal of destruction by eating buds and young shoots, and by stripping the bark off deciduous trees. They tear off ripe and unripe fruit in gardens, and also eat grain, nuts, seeds, young birds or rabbits, and carrion. In consequence, farmers kill them whenever they can. Unlike Red Squirrels, Grey Squirrels usually live in deciduous woodland, and in the autumn often leave the woods for hedgerows and fields. Their nests, which are domed, with hidden entrances at the side, are usually built in deciduous trees. The first litter of young is born between March and May, and a second litter appears in June or July, with possibly a third in August or September. The parents turn their young out of their nest before the coming of the winter.

Flying Squirrels, most of which belong to south-east Asia, have flaps of skin joining their limbs so as to form a parachute, by means of which they can glide 60 or more yards from one tree to another. As they always lose height when they glide, they have to climb to a considerable height before attempting to fly to the lower branches of the next tree. They are very playful creatures, delighting in racing up and down the trees and chasing each other about.

STABLE FLY. This bloodsucking insect, sometimes called the Biting House-fly, is common in most country places throughout the summer. It frequents outbuildings on farms, and also comes into houses. It inflicts wounds on human beings and beasts by piercing the skin with its proboscis, which points downwards and forwards from the head. The Stable Fly can be easily distinguished from the HOUSE-FLY (q.v.) by this proboscis. It breeds chiefly in horse manure, and completes its development from egg to adult in from three weeks to a month.

See also FLIES.

THE COMMON STAG BEETLE, MALE AND FEMALE
G. J. Arrow

STAG BEETLE. The largest beetle found in the British Isles, and the most remarkable in its appearance, is the common Stag Beetle, *Lucanus cervus*. It is not known in the north, but is quite common round London. Its grubs, which take 3 years to reach maturity, feed upon old decaying tree-stumps or at the base of rotting posts. The beetles emerge to fly about in early summer; but their adult life lasts only for a few weeks. The enormous, antler-like horns, peculiar to the male, are really its jaws. The females are so unlike the males that they were once thought to be quite different insects. Their small jaws are really more useful instruments than the formidable-looking horns of the male. Four different kinds of Stag Beetle inhabit Britain, all of them passing their early stages in rotting wood. In the whole world nearly 1,000 kinds are known.

See also BEETLES.

STARFISH. The common Five-fingered Star-fish may be found in the rock pools or stranded on the sands near low-tide mark on most shores round British coasts, and must be one of the most familiar members of that great and remarkable division of the animal kingdom, the Echinodermata, or spiny-skinned animals, which also includes the SEA-CUCUMBERS and SEA-URCHINS (qq.v.). The body is disk-shaped, and from it grow out five symmetrically arranged arms,

COMMON STARFISH (*Asterias rubens*) SHOWING STAGES IN
THE REGENERATION OF THE ARMS.   *M. Burton*

which gradually taper to their blunt-pointed
ends. The upper surfaces of both the body and
arms are pink, red, or purple. If the starfish is
turned over on to its back, it is possible to see the
mouth, from which radiate five narrow grooves,
one along each arm. These grooves are crowded
throughout their length with tubular bodies
with sucker-like ends—the tube-feet, by means
of which the starfish creeps about and also
grasps its prey. The tenacity with which these
tube-feet can adhere to any object is remarkable.
The whole of the upper surface of the starfish is
covered by a network of somewhat rod-like
plates embedded in the tough skin, forming a
partial skeleton; while scattered over both the
upper and under surfaces are numerous very
minute, pincer-like organs, which keep the surface of the body clean by grasping any minute
organisms or floating particles that otherwise
would settle on the skin. The mouth is very
elastic: the degree to which it can be stretched
to take in some extra large object is quite
remarkable.

The sex of the starfish is difficult to discern
without dissecting the animal. At the spawning
period, the female lays a great mass of minute
eggs into the sea, where they are fertilized by
the sperm of the male. From the egg develops a
larva, quite unlike the parent. After some weeks
of free swimming, the larva fixes itself to a rock
or seaweed by little sucker-like disks at its front
end, and then a series of changes takes place,
transforming its body into that of a baby starfish, with the five-ray shape.

Of the many other species of true starfishes to
be found in British waters, it is possible here to
mention only one or two of the more interesting.
The Lingthorn, a large and handsome starfish
with five to seven long, flat, and rather slender
arms, is fairly abundant in shallow waters off-
shore. It has a habit of parting rather readily
with one or more of its arms when in danger, or
if roughly handled during capture. This violent
dismemberment is common among starfishes,
though it happens to some more easily than to
others. The loss of one or two arms causes only
temporary inconvenience, as new limbs are
gradually grown. The Rosy Cribrella is a fine
rosy-red, and has five rounded, tapering arms
with narrow grooves on their under-surface, the
tube-feet being arranged in two rows. Very
handsome and striking in appearance is the
common Sun-starfish, so named because of its
resemblance to the conventional drawings of the
sun seen on such places as the signboards of
ancient country inns. It varies a good deal in
colour from the typical fine orange-red to a
somewhat purplish-red tint. The arms are quite
short and stout, and number from eight to sixteen. The common Cushion-starfish, found on
the south, west, and northern coasts of England,
has such short arms that the starfish really looks
like a small five-cornered cushion, bright red,
yellowish-white, or mottled. The Bird's-foot
Starfish, another of our British Cushion-star-
fishes, is thin and flat, and the narrow deeply set
grooves spreading across the under-surface help
to intensify its resemblance to the webbed foot of
a wading bird.

The Sand and Brittle Stars all have small,
disk-like bodies and long slender arms composed
of a number of joints. The common Brittle Star
is one of the handsomest of our British species.
The upper surface of the body-disk is covered
with short spines, except for five pairs of bare,
almost wedge-shaped plates, standing out in
marked contrast to the darker portions of the
body, which may be rose-red with grey scales,

THE SUN-STARFISH.   *M. Burton*   THE BRITTLE STAR.   *M. Burton*

white spotted with red, or brown with ruddy markings. The long arms are covered with stout, short spines growing out at right angles, and the animals move about by snake-like movements of these arms. The Sand Stars have very short spines, lying close to the sides of the slender arms and making each look like the tapering end of a lizard's tail. The remarkable Gorgon-head Brittle Stars are the largest of Brittle Stars, and their long, slender arms repeatedly fork so as to form a regular crown of interlacing branches. The giant Arctic species measures more than a foot from tip to tip of its many-branched, out-stretched arms.

The Feather Stars and the Stalked Crinoids or Sea-lilies are so distinctive in character as to be placed in a separate division, called the Pelma-tozoa—literally, stalked animals. Instead of crawling about mouth downwards by the aid of their tube feet, like all other starfishes, they remain more or less permanently fixed in one spot, mouth upwards, the Sea-lilies growing on long, slender stalks, and the graceful Feather Stars being anchored by little clawed hooks to seaweeds and stones. They are the only living representatives of a great group which swarmed in the seas of past geological ages. The Rosy Feather Star is not uncommon in shallow water off British coasts. It has a small disk-shaped body, from which arise five arms, each divided almost at its base into two—giving the little starfish the appearance of possessing ten slender rays. From the middle of the back of the body-disk arise the clawed hooks, by means of which the creature anchors itself to the weed or stone upon which it rests.

The stalked Crinoids or Sea-lilies are all cup-shaped animals with slender branching arms; they grow on long jointed stems, permanently attached to some suitable base on the floor of the sea. They are found in most parts of the world, and often live at considerable depths.

STARLING. Until the second part of last century, the Starling was not a common British bird; but it has increased enormously of late, and is now found in large numbers in all parts of the country, even more migrating from northern Europe to winter in Britain. Although flocks of Starlings do great damage to fruit-orchards, as a whole the Starling is a useful bird, for it destroys the larvae of harmful insects. It not only searches assiduously for grubs in the grass and earth, but it also picks parasites off the backs of sheep. One species of African Starling, the Ox-peckers, feed mainly on the ticks which they peck from the backs of animals—cattle, elephants, rhinoceroses, and antelopes; and they have feet provided with sharp, curved claws which enable them to keep their hold on the animals' backs.

From a distance the common Starling appears to be a dull, black bird; but seen close to, in the sunlight, its dark plumage is seen to be shot with brilliant greens and purples, and spotted with buff. It has a song of its own, heard all the year round; but it is a very good mimic, also, imitating not only the songs of other birds, but any other sound which has caught its attention. It builds a large, untidy nest in any suitable sheltered situation, a crevice in a cliff, wall, or building, a hole in a tree (hollowed out, perhaps, by a Woodpecker for its own use), a Sand-martin's burrow enlarged, or even the entrance to a rabbit-hole. After the nesting season is over, Starlings band together in flocks, sometimes of many thousands. A huge cloud of birds can often be observed in the evening, circling and wheeling in the air about their chosen roosting place, and then suddenly dropping down to their perches.

Among the other species of Starlings is the Rosy Starling, or Rose-coloured Pastor, a lovely bird, with a black crest, head, wings, and tail, and a rose-coloured back and breast. This bird sometimes visits Britain from southern Europe. The Indian Mynas are the common Starlings of southern Asia. The Glossy Starlings of Africa and the Grackles of Asia are near relatives of the true Starlings. They are mainly forest birds, feeding on fruits among the highest branches of trees, and rarely coming to the ground. Several species have been kept in zoos, where they have learnt to repeat words and tunes perfectly.

The Crested Cassiques of tropical America are sometimes called the Starlings of the New World, though perhaps they are more closely related to the ORIOLES (q.v.). They are small, black and citron-yellow birds, which live in colonies, hanging their long, bag-shaped nests in groups from the twigs of tall forest trees, or even sometimes from telegraph wires. These nests are made of closely woven grass, and have long narrow necks, on the side of which is the entrance.

STAR SLIME. This whitish, jelly-like substance is sometimes found lying on the ground in open places in the country, particularly in late summer and autumn. Popular legend has for years associated it with 'shooting stars'—Pembroke-shire shepherds being said to have called it 'pwdre sêr', the 'rot of the stars'. Actually, the jelly is formed from the gelatinous lining of the oviducts (egg-passages) of frogs or toads which may have been devoured by birds, possibly crows, the internal organs having been left untouched. When exposed to moisture, the jelly swells to such an extent that the oviducts are split open. With advancing decomposition, the jelly sometimes persists for some time after the tissue from which it originated has become unrecognizable.

STEMS. 1. (*a*). The main work of stems is to support the leaves and to display them so that they gain the maximum benefit from the light of the sun. Roots have a fairly constant environment; but the shoot is exposed to wind and rain, to the heat of day or the chills of night, and must adapt itself to meet these different conditions. Whereas most kinds of roots look much alike, the shoots—stem and leaves—differ so greatly that plants can generally be identified from them.

A second function of the stem is to display the flowers and, later, to suspend the fruits and seeds. The stem also acts as a connecting-link between root and leaves, all the water and dissolved salts absorbed by the root from the soil passing up through a passage in the stem, called the 'xylem' or wood, into the leaves. If a green stem is stood in red ink for a few hours, and then cut across, this passage will be seen to be stained red. Some of the foodstuffs manufactured in the leaves, too, pass down the stem to the roots through a separate series of vessels called the 'phloem' or 'bast'. So the stem is like a seaport where raw materials and manufactured products are constantly crossing each other.

Besides the ordinary aerial stems which grow erect, some stems, such as those of the Moneywort, Creeping Jenny, and Ground Ivy, grow along the surface of the ground; and some grow underground. In addition, some act as storage organs for food: some, such as those of the CACTUS and other succulent plants which live in dry regions, store water. In some plants, such as many ALPINE PLANTS, the stems are so short as to be almost non-existent, and the leaves are arranged in a tight rosette. CLIMBING PLANTS (qq.v.), on the other hand, have long, weak stems which are able to grow upwards only by using supports.

(*b*) BUDS. The stem bears buds, which grow into flowers and leaves. As buds are delicate,

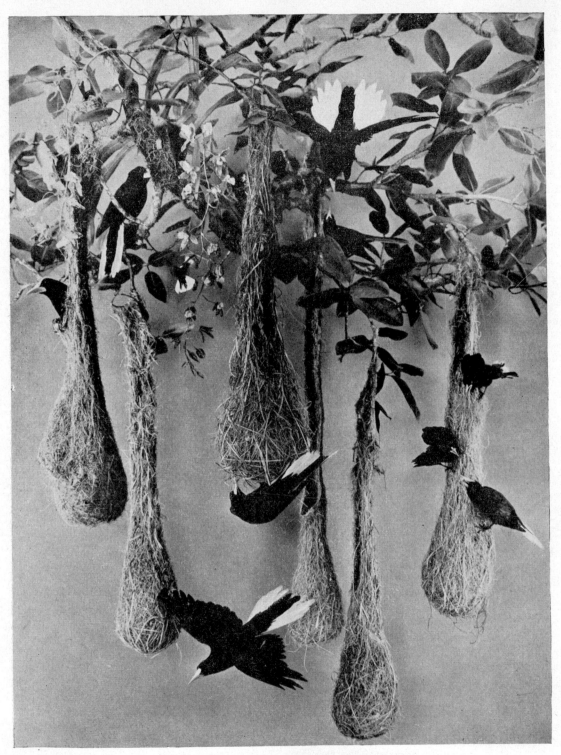

A NESTING COLONY OF CRESTED CASSIQUES FROM TRINIDAD

New York Times

there are often elaborate devices to protect them from the weather, from insects, or from fungal diseases. The arrangement of the growing leaves inside a bud shows it to be no more than a condensed shoot—as can be seen if a big leaf-bud, such as a Brussels Sprout, is carefully unravelled, or if small buds are uncoiled with needles and tweezers. Leaf-buds appear at the growing-tip of the stem, which is concealed and protected by the young leaves, and also in the angle (the 'axil') made by last year's leaves with the stem. These side buds often do not develop unless something happens to injure or check the growth of the bud at the tip. The 'dormant' buds, for example, on a hedge or fruit-tree are stimulated to growth when the tip-buds are trimmed or cut off by PRUNING (q.v. Vol. VI).

(c) AGE OF A STEM. This, and the amount of growth a stem has made in a season, can be told in the following manner. Young buds are covered with tiny scale-leaves, which drop off as the bud unfolds and the shoot begins to grow.

scale leaf scars

foliage leaf scars

When they drop, they leave scars, called 'girdle scars' because they run around the stem. As each girdle scar shows the beginning of a new year's growth, the length of the stem between two adjacent sets of scars shows the amount of growth in any one year. In the branches of trees (for these, also, are stems) the scars are, of course, shed with the bark; but as long as they persist on a branch, the age can be calculated. These girdle scars are very plainly seen on the Beech and Horse-chestnut twigs. In one British tree, the Wayfaring Tree, there are no scales to the buds, for these are well protected by hairs; and so the age of the twigs cannot be calculated in this way. Naked buds occur also in tropical lands, where there is no unfavourable season from which the buds must be protected.

(d) CORK. Stems are liable to become infected by myriads of moulds, mildews, and other fungal diseases, either from the air, or indirectly through attacks by insects. Just as animals are covered with a SKIN (q.v.), one of the functions of which is to keep out diseases, so young plants are covered by a compact layer of cells which forms a skin, or 'epidermis'. As the plant gets older and its girth increases, this epidermis is often replaced by a layer of cork, formed from a row

Bark { Epidermis
{ Cork

Bast

Wood

Vascular bundle

SECTION OF STEM OF HERBACEOUS PLANT

of cells situated below the epidermis. The walls of the cork cells become impregnated with a material through which water or water vapour cannot pass—a fact made use of in ordinary bottle-corks, which are made from the corky tissue of a Mediterranean tree called the Cork-oak.

(e) BARK. Since water cannot pass through the corky layer, all the cells outside it die off. In places, however, small gaps called 'lenticels', consisting of loosely packed collections of cells, occur in the cork, and allow air to pass in for the respiration of the tissues beneath. Lenticels can be seen clearly as pale spots on the shoots of the Elder, and the dark streaks on bottle-corks mark the lenticels in the bark from which they were made. Each year, a new cork layer is formed just below the old, and the layer of tissue outside the cork, already dead because it is cut off from the plant's food and water supply, becomes a little thicker. This dead layer is the bark of a tree. When a tree is wounded, as, for instance, by the breaking of branches or the cutting of initials, a special process of cork-formation takes place to heal the wound. Owing to the formation of successive layers of cork round the wound, the initials (often cut on the smooth surface of a beech trunk, for instance) become more and more indented as the years go by.

2. UNDERGROUND STEMS. (a) Tubers. The colourless appearance of the tubers of potatoes, and the branches which bear them, suggest that they are typical underground roots. But those who have stored potatoes know that the potato produces shoots—a function performed only by

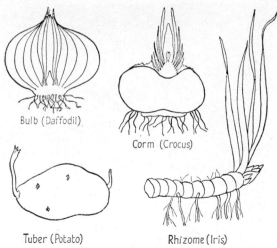

Bulb (Daffodil)

Corm (Crocus)

Tuber (Potato)

Rhizome (Iris)

TYPES OF UNDERGROUND STEMS

stems. The potato tuber, then, although it develops underground, is a stem, not a root. Its shoots develop from the 'eyes', which are young buds arranged in the axils of very much reduced scale leaves, and which, when the potato is planted, grow upwards and become leafy stems. The potato tuber is a stem which has become greatly swollen to act as a storage organ, storing chiefly starch, with a little protein. This nourishes the plant until the leaves are sufficiently formed to manufacture food for themselves (*see* PHOTOSYNTHESIS). Other examples of stem tubers are the Chinese and Jerusalem Artichokes, though they differ slightly in structure, and contain different food materials.

(*b*) The RHIZOME (as seen on the Iris, for example) is another type of underground stem. Superficially, rhizomes appear to be roots; but examination shows that they bear leaves and buds. They grow almost horizontally, just below the surface of the ground; but during the spring and summer, the tip turns upwards, carrying the leaves and flowers above the soil, where they continue at first to be nourished by food stored in the thick, fleshy rhizome. So the direct onward growth of one year's length of rhizome comes abruptly to an end; and, next year, the rhizome grows in a slightly different direction. Since they are stems and cannot absorb solutions from the soil, rhizomes produce adventitious roots underneath, which serve both for absorption and for anchorage. Solomon's Seal has a fleshy, food-storing rhizome in which the round scar or 'seal' is left by the decay of a whole shoot,

lately the bearer of foliage leaves and flowers. Slender rhizomes are found in Wood Anemone, Reeds, Sedges, and Grasses—those of Couch-grass (Twitch) being only too well known because of the difficulty of getting rid of it from the garden.

Some plants with sturdy tap-roots, such as Carrots, Primroses, and Radishes, appear to have their leaves growing from the top of the root. This topmost part, however, is not a root, but a short, thick, vertical stem or rhizome, known as the root-stock.

(*c*) CORMS. The Crocus supplies another example of an underground stem modified for food storage—the corm. Here, the main stem is round and globular, and is surrounded by a number of loose, scaly leaves, which, when removed, reveal small buds in their axils. In early spring, one of the uppermost buds bursts forth and produces a flower and green foliage leaves, while the base of one of the other buds begins to swell, eventually forming the corm for the following year. During the spring, food manufactured by the foliage leaves is stored in this young, developing corm, the old corm shrivelling up. In late spring, when growth has ceased, the new corm remains in the soil in a resting condition until the following spring. Corms occur also in Gladiolus and Montbretia. The roots of some corms have a special structure which enables them to contract and pull the corm into the soil to the most suitable depth.

(*d*) BULBS. In the corm, the stem portion is by far the most prominent and important part, the leaves being merely protective scales. In bulbs, however, the swollen, fleshy, pale-coloured leaves which act as storehouses of food form the bulk, the stem being a relatively insignificant, small, bun-like structure, which gives off adventitious roots round its edges. The bud grows from the centre of the upper surface, and finally produces the foliage leaves and flowers, nourishment for the growing shoot being supplied from the fleshy leaves. In Tulip bulbs, the stored food is starch; in Onions, sugar. In Lily bulbs, the fleshy leaves overlap at their margins and are called scaly bulbs. Like corms, bulbs have contractile roots, able to pull the bulb down to the required depth in the soil.

See also PLANTS; ROOTS; LEAVES; FLOWERS.

STICK CATERPILLAR, *see* PROTECTIVE COLORATION, Section 3; LOOPERS.

STICK INSECT AND LEAF INSECT. These are remarkable creatures, nearly related to our COCKROACHES (q.v.). They closely resemble either the twigs of their food-plant or its leaves, and are therefore good examples of animal CAMOUFLAGE (q.v.). The bodies of Stick Insects are brown or grey-brown, cylindrical and stick-like; often they have projections, like thorns, and a few species even have grey-green lumps giving the effect of moss-grown twigs. They are natives of tropical and semi-tropical countries, but they can be reared easily enough at home on privet and ivy. They are not very entertaining pets, however, for during the day-time they cling quite motionless to their food-plant with two or three of their legs, the rest being either pressed close to the body, or stuck out in an angular manner. It is, of course, important for an insect relying on concealment to escape its enemies, that it should act its part well—and a stick that started to walk about would very soon attract attention. Stick Insects, therefore, move and feed only at night. In many species, including that reared in Britain, males are very rare indeed, and many generations can be raised in succession without producing even one. The eggs seem to be dropped to the ground at random. Each is enclosed in a hard capsule with a lid, through which the newly-hatched insect escapes.

Leaf Insects are no less flat and broad than Stick Insects are long and narrow. Their wings are bright green, and ribbed so as to resemble very exactly the veins of leaves. There are growths on the sides of their legs, also, which are flat, green, and leaf-like (see COLOUR PLATE, opp. p. 336). They, too, remain still during the day. Leaf Insects inhabit the Far East, especially the islands of the Indian Ocean.

See also PROTECTIVE COLORATION (INSECTS).

STICKLEBACK. The three-spined Stickleback, known to most people as the 'Tiddler' (or perhaps by some other name, such as Sharpling or Bandie), is a very common freshwater fish in Britain and Europe, and is found across Siberia,

THREE-SPINED STICKLEBACK
The male is swimming round to keep intruders away from his nest.   *A. Fraser-Brunner*

in Japan, and in northern America. It is equally at home in the sea, and in the far north is a marine fish. Sticklebacks are small fishes, with the first dorsal fin composed of separate, stout spines, and the pelvic fins on the abdomen composed of one strong, sharp spine each, and one small soft ray. The tail is very slender, and along the side there is a series of large plates of bone, which vary in number, fish from inland waters having as few as three near the shoulder, those near the sea having a complete set.

At mating time, the male Three-spined Stickleback develops a brilliant dress of shining green, with a bright red chest, in order to attract the female, and he fights fiercely with any other male who intrudes. He builds a round nest among the water-plants, with an opening on each side of it, and, after the eggs are laid, he guards them, and he also protects the young when they hatch out.

A less common kind, found in more southern localities, is the Ten-spined Stickleback, a freshwater fish which has similar habits, but which, as its name indicates, has ten spines on the back instead of three. Another and larger kind, the Fifteen-spined Stickleback, which sometimes reaches 7 inches long, lives only in the sea or in brackish water at the mouths of rivers.

STOAT, *see* WEASEL, Section 2.

STORK. This very long-legged, long-beaked bird is a relative of the HERON (q.v.), and also of the Ibis, the sacred bird of ancient Egypt, and of the strange-looking Spoonbill. There are about 20 species, spread over most of the world, other than very cold regions, and generally living and breeding in communities. They have plump bodies, with large wings and short, rounded tails; long, strong, naked legs; long beaks with sharp points; and a plumage which is predominantly white and black. They have no song, their only noise, often surprisingly loud, being made by the snapping of their beaks. They are strong fliers, and frequently soar to great heights. In many places they are looked upon with great favour, almost reverence, not only because they are useful scavengers, but because they are proverbial for

A SPOONBILL STANDING ON A TURTLE
Booth Steamship Co.

the care of their young—from which reputation, perhaps, has grown the nursery legend that the stork brings the baby.

The common European White Stork, a typical stork, is a handsome bird about 3 feet 6 inches long, with pure white plumage, long black wing-feathers, and a red beak and legs. It is particularly common in Holland, Germany, and Poland, and spreads also over western and central Asia and parts of India. It is an occasional visitor to Britain. It migrates in vast flocks to Africa for the winter. The White Stork frequents human habitations, standing on roof-tops and building its flat nest of sticks on chimney-tops and roofs. The birds, which mate for life, return to the same nest year after year, adding to it until it becomes a bulky structure. Three to five pure white eggs are laid. The Black Stork is a smaller, much less common, and much shyer species, which frequents secluded swamps, and nests in tall trees. Another species closely related to the White Stork is the African White-bellied Stork, a still smaller bird, found very commonly in the Sudan and farther south, and much venerated by the natives of the Sudan.

The largest of all the Storks are the huge, ugly Adjutant Storks, or Marabou, of Africa and southern Asia. They are over 5 feet long, with enormous, thick, wedge-shaped beaks, bare heads and necks, and long pouches hanging from the throat. The Indian Adjutants are common in some parts, especially in Calcutta, where they used to perch in numbers on the parapets of Government House during the rains. In many places, they are protected because of their good

EUROPEAN WHITE STORKS AT THEIR NEST
Arthur Brook

THE HUGE ADJUTANT STORK
Harold Bastin

neck, and tail-feathers. Other species are found in Madagascar, Australia, New Guinea, and eastern Asia. The Glossy Ibis is a species belonging to Europe and western Asia, occasionally visiting Britain, and found also in North America. The Scarlet Ibis is a brilliant bird, with scarlet plumage and black tips to the wings, found in tropical America and the West Indies.

The Spoonbill is a white bird, rather over 2½ feet long, with a long, drooping crest, black legs, and an enormous, wide, black beak. It used to breed in Suffolk and Sussex some 300 years ago, and is still a fairly frequent visitor to the east coast in the summer. It lives near marshy lakes or sandbanks on rivers over most of the world, using its great, broad, spoon-shaped bill for fishing up small aquatic animals in the shallow water.

STURGEON. These are mostly large fishes which resemble SHARKS (q.v.) in the shape of the tail, in having the mouth underneath, as well as in other features in their anatomy. But they have a bony skeleton (which Sharks have not), and a single gill-opening protected by a gill-cover, besides having fins and many other characters that show them to be true FISHES (q.v.). They are clumsy, sluggish creatures, with a long, bony snout, below which are barbels or 'whiskers' for feeling in the mud. The mouth, which has no teeth, can be stretched out like a telescope to suck up the small creatures on which they feed. The skin is rough, and along the back is a row of very large bony plates, or 'bucklers', while on each side are two rows of smaller ones.

There are many kinds of Sturgeon found in Europe, northern and central Asia, and North America. Many of the larger ones are marine, moving only a short distance up rivers to spawn; but some of the smaller kinds spend their lives in fresh water. The common Sturgeon of the Atlantic sometimes visits Britain. In this country it is called a royal fish, since, according to an old law, any Sturgeon caught is theoretically the property of the King. The flesh is good to eat, though coarse and beefy, and in places where Sturgeon abound they provide a very important fishery. Their eggs are prepared as the highly prized delicacy called caviare.

In the Mississippi Valley of America is found a very curious Sturgeon, called the Paddle-fish, Spoonbill, or Shovel-fish, because of the shape of its snout. This is expanded to form a large,

work as scavengers. The tropical regions of America, Africa, and Australia have other very large Storks, about 5 feet long, with very long beaks.

The Ibis, which belongs to a different family related to the Storks, is a smaller bird, with much shorter legs, and a long, slender, slightly curved beak. The Sacred Ibis is now no longer found in Egypt, but belongs to the swampy regions of the Sudan near the Upper Nile, where it nests in colonies. It is white, with a black head,

THE STURGEON
A. Fraser-Brunner

paddle-shaped blade, nearly as big as the body. Another, with a somewhat similar snout, is found in the great rivers of China.

SUNDEW, *see* INSECTIVOROUS PLANTS, Section 3.

SURINAM TOAD. This primitive AMPHIBIAN (q.v.), not really a TOAD (q.v.), inhabits central America and the Guianas. It lives entirely in the water, and is tongueless and toothless. Its fingers end in star-shaped tips, and its toes are broadly webbed. It is remarkable for the way in which its young are produced—the eggs, when laid, being placed on the back of the female by the male, where they sink into wrinkles of the skin and develop in the pouches thus formed. The tadpoles do not leave their cells until they have completed their METAMORPHOSIS (q.v.) into the adult, after 80 days. The Surinam Toad stands captivity well.

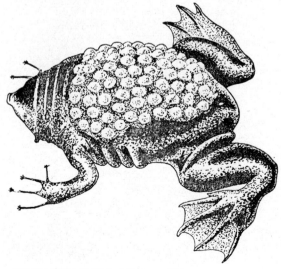

FEMALE SURINAM TOAD CARRYING HER EGGS ON HER BACK

SWALLOW. The Swallow tribe includes not only the Swallow, but also the House Martin and Sand Martin. They are all birds with stream-lined bodies, long wings, and long, generally forked tails; and all feed on insects, which they catch on the wing. They are found in most parts of the world, those species that breed in the cooler regions of both hemispheres migrating to warmer climates for the winter.

The Swallow is the largest of the group, being about 8 inches long. It is distinguished from the House Martin by its more deeply forked tail and its chestnut-red forehead and throat. It winters in South Africa, and the earliest specimens reach the south of England towards the end of March. During April they come in great numbers, returning usually to the same district in which they spent the previous summer. As soon as they are mated the pair begin to build their nest of mud and straw, a task which sometimes takes several weeks. The nest is a saucer-shaped structure, made by the plastering on of tiny beakfuls of mud with water and saliva. The inside is shaped and polished with the beak, and lined with wool and feathers. Swallows prefer to build under cover and in the dark, the rafters of farm buildings or the wide chimneys of old-fashioned houses being favourite sites. Four or five white eggs with reddish spots are laid, and sometimes as many as three broods are produced. The fledglings of the latest brood sometimes fare badly, as their parents' migratory instinct proves stronger than their parental instinct, and they desert the nest to join the noisy gatherings collecting on telegraph wires, trees, and fences, ready for the autumn flight. Strangely enough, the young swallows of the earliest broods are the first to migrate, setting off some two or three weeks before their parents, and finding their way by some uncanny instinct to the winter quarters, to which the older birds soon follow.

The House Martins usually arrive in their breeding quarters a little later than Swallows. They are rather smaller birds, with more white in their plumage, and a rather heavier flight. They build cup-shaped nests of mud, which they fasten on the wall of a building under the shelter of the eaves, or in the angle of a beam. The entrance is by a small hole near the top. In coastal districts colonies of Martins often build against the cliff face under the shelter of an overhanging rock. Their nests are sometimes attacked and taken over by Sparrows, against whom the

PAIR OF SWALLOWS AT THEIR NEST
Eric J. Hosking, F.R.P.S.

HOUSE MARTIN
Eric J. Hosking, F.R.P.S.

Martins can put up no fight. The Martins gather for flight in the autumn, often making the migratory journey in company with Swallows.

Sand Martins, the smallest, least conspicuous, and least noisy of the group, do not frequent human dwellings, as do their relatives, but seek nesting sites in sand-pits or quarries, railway cuttings, or steep, sandy river-banks. They prefer to live near water where flies breed freely. They dig a nesting tunnel in the sand, generally some 3 feet long—though much longer tunnels have been found. The tunnel usually slopes slightly upwards towards the nest for the sake of drainage. It is said that, after two or three years' tenancy, the nest becomes so foul and flea-infested that a new tunnel has to be dug. The Sand Martin is more vigorously attacked by these parasites than the Swallow, partly accounted for by the fact that it does not take the continual plunging baths that Swallows enjoy, nor even dust baths.

The Crag Martin of the Alps and southern Europe resembles the Sand Martin. In America the Purple Martin is a well-known bird, which generally nests in hollows in trees.

SWALLOWTAIL BUTTERFLIES. This family is characteristic of tropical forests, the Bird-wings of the East Indies, for instance, being some of the largest and finest butterflies known (*see* BUTTERFLIES AND MOTHS, TROPICAL). Of the 850 known species, however, 25 occur in

North America and one in the British Isles. Male and female Swallowtails often differ considerably in form and colour, the females being without the tails, and often achieving safety by mimicking several different species (see picture, p. 333). The wide-ranging African *Papilio dardanus*, for instance, has so many different guises that it has aptly been described as the most wonderful butterfly in the world.

The English Swallowtail, which has a wing-span of 3 inches, is pale yellow, with black bands and blotches on the fore-wings, and a broad band of dark blue and two red eye-spots on the hind-wings near the two 'tails', which occur in both sexes. The butterflies fly during May and June, and often again in August, at Wicken Fen and along the Norfolk Broads. The females lay their spherical eggs singly on milk parsley, a plant almost restricted to the marshes of eastern England. There is also a Continental race of this Swallowtail, which occasionally migrates to the southern counties of England, particularly Kent, and in favourable seasons has been known to breed, though it never establishes itself. It lays its eggs on wild or cultivated carrot. These two races of the same species, therefore, not only differ in appearance, but also in locality, habitat, and habits: it is from such differences that new species of butterflies evolve. This insect ranges through Europe as far as India and China, and shows many slight variations in pattern, different from the heavily marked British race.

SWALLOWTAIL WITH WINGS CLOSED
S. Beaufoy, F.R.P.S.

SWALLOWTAIL WITH WINGS OPEN
S. Beaufoy, F.R.P.S.

The young black and white caterpillars resemble bird droppings so closely that they are likely to be passed over by insect-eating enemies as objects unsuitable for food. Later, they assume strong warning colours, vivid green with black bands and orange spots. These, together with the unpleasant smell coming from a fleshy, forked organ extended repeatedly from behind the head, serve to remind would-be enemies that the caterpillar's body is unpleasant to taste and is best left alone (*see* PROTECTIVE COLORATION, Section 2). The chrysalis is found on the stem of a reed, attached by the tail to a silken pad and supported round the middle by a silken girdle. This silk represents the remains of a cocoon similar to that made by the caterpillars of many moths.

See also BUTTERFLIES.

SWAN. This close relative of the GEESE and DUCKS (qq.v.) is found in the wild state in many parts of the world, and in all types of climate. Excepting the Black Swan of Australia, swans all have white or mainly white plumage. In summer they live near inland waters, but in the winter they frequently seek the sea. Swans feed chiefly on water-plants, insects, and small molluscs. They feed by dipping their long necks under the water, sometimes standing straight on end, as ducks do, to reach down far enough.

Swans mate for life, and return yearly to the same nesting site. Their nests are untidy erections of sticks and vegetation, often several feet across and 3 or 4 feet high. They are placed near the water, sometimes on an islet. Generally about eight large, greenish-white eggs are laid, which the 'pen' (female) incubates for 5 weeks, while the 'cob' (male) guards the nest with great ferocity. While he is 'busking'—that is, swimming with wings raised and head thrown back in an aggressive attitude, it is unwise to go near him, for a swan can kill a dog or seriously cripple a man with blows from its open wing or elbow-joint. The 'cygnets', or young swans, are covered with dark greyish down, which lightens as the birds grow older. They soon take to water, following their mother in search of food; but if danger threatens, the mother takes them on her back, holding up a foot for them to scramble up by. She cleans and dries them very thoroughly when they return to the nest. When autumn comes the swans migrate southwards, flying in large groups, generally in a deep **V**-formation, very high and very fast.

The European wild swans are called the Mute Swan, the Whooper, and Bewick's Swan. The Mute Swans are supposed to have been brought to England by Richard I when returning from a crusade. They live here now in a partly domesticated state, though they breed in a wild state over much of the Continent. For many hundreds of years in England, swans were called 'birds royal', because only the king or those with a licence from the Royal Swineherd might keep them. An individual or a city company with a licence to keep swans received a special 'upping mark', which had to be cut on the bill of every swan once a year. The ceremony of 'swan upping' is still held on the Thames every year, for the swans on the Thames are still regarded as the property of the King and of the Dyers and Vintners companies.

The Whooper Swan nests in Iceland, Scandinavia, and within the Arctic Circle, and visits the coasts of Britain in the winter. It is often called the Whistling Swan from the curious noise its wings make as it flies. Bewick's Swans, rather smaller birds, are rarer winter visitors. All three species are rather alike; but the Mute Swan has an orange beak with black at the base, and carries its neck in a graceful curve, and its secondary wing feathers raised over its back; while the other birds have yellowish beaks with black tips, hold their necks more stiffly, and carry their wings flat on their backs.

There are two species of swans in North America, the Trumpeter Swan, the largest of all, and the Whistling Swan. In South America, especially in Chile, is the Black-necked Swan; and in Australia lives the Black Swan, first discovered in 1697 by a Dutch explorer. This bird is completely black, except for its white flight-feathers and its coral-red bill.

SWIFT. It is common to associate this bird with the SWALLOW (q.v.) which it superficially resembles. Like the Swallow, it has a streamlined body, long wings, and a forked tail. It is almost always seen on the wing, using its short beak and wide gape to catch its insect food. It

is, however, no relation to the Swallow, being actually more closely related to Humming-birds and Nightjars. As well as the typical Swifts which visit Europe, there are several other species widely distributed in America and Asia.

The Swifts are among the latest of the migrant birds to arrive in Britain and the earliest to depart, spending less than 4 months here. They winter in South Africa, and arrive in Britain about the beginning of May, announcing their arrival with their loud, harsh, screaming cry. They build their nests in crevices in walls or holes under the eaves, constructing them of straw, dead leaves, or any other material which they can pick up in the air, bound together with their own saliva. Swifts, as their name suggests, are perhaps the fastest fliers of all British birds. The Alpine Swift is even more rapid than the British variety. They twist and turn in the air like bats, and soar very high up into the sky. It is said that the male birds even sleep floating in the air—a suggestion which has arisen because of their habit of disappearing up into the sky in the fading evening light. Though so agile in the air, their long wings and very short legs make them extremely awkward on the ground. They never come to the ground if they can help it, but if brought down, they have great difficulty in rising again. Neither can they perch, for all their four toes are directed forwards—an arrangement which, however, makes them well able to cling on to vertical surfaces. When ready to migrate

WHITE-BELLIED SWIFTLET ON ITS NEST IN A CAVE ON CHRISTMAS ISLAND. *C. A. Gibson-Hill*

NEST OF THE EDIBLE SEA SWIFT
Harold Bastin

in the autumn, they do not gather in swarms on telegraph wires, as swallows do.

The most interesting of the Asiatic Swifts are the Edible Swifts, which build nests composed mainly (with one species, entirely) of their own saliva, and fasten them on to the walls of caverns. The nests of the Borneo Edible Swifts are highly prized by the Chinese, who use them for soup. The Asiatic Tree Swifts make tiny nests of bark and saliva, large enough to hold one egg, and fasten them on to the side of a thin bough.

SWIFT AND GHOST MOTHS. These are the most primitive of all moths except the GOLD AND PURPLE MOTHS (q.v.); but in spite of this, they are highly specialized. Their long, narrow fore-wings have a small flap, which projects beneath the smaller hind-wings to couple the two together, and this takes the place of the bristles by which the fore and hind-wings of most moths are linked. The larvae bore in roots, stems, and trunks, attacking a wide range of plants, and often taking 2 years to complete development. The pupae have flexible abdominal segments bearing spines, which enable them to push their way out of the soil when the moths are ready to emerge.

Of some 250 known species the majority are in Australia and New Zealand, and include some of the largest and finest moths—the Bent-wing of New South Wales, for example, having a wing-spread of 9 inches. The Bent-wing is orange-brown, patterned with silver, and has a raised eye-spot on each fore-wing, so that, when at rest, it closely resembles a lizard's head. Its giant caterpillar bores in the trunks of eucalyptus trees, causing much damage.

The largest of the five British species is the Ghost Moth, the silvery-white males measuring nearly 2 inches across, and the pale yellowish-brown females half an inch larger. In June the males perform a 'ghostly' dance at dusk, swaying to and fro a few feet from the ground in rough meadows. Here they are sought by unpaired females, who thus reverse the usual role of the sexes. After mating the female scatters her eggs while hovering. The whitish larvae feed on the roots of grasses, dead nettle, dock, or dandelion.

The Gold Swift, common in woody districts in June, is not quite so large. Both sexes are yellowish-brown, the male being distinguished by silver spots. Although less conspicuous than the Ghost Moth, it hovers in the same way, and emits a pineapple scent attractive to females. The females of the Common Swift sit on grass stems in rough meadows on fine summer evenings, vibrating their wings as they await the yellowish-brown males. Their whitish caterpillars have shining brown heads, and brownish raised dots with a few hairs on the body. They normally feed for 2 years, either on the roots of weeds, or sometimes on lettuce and root crops.

The name Swift refers to the rapid flight of the moths. The most active British species is the Map-winged, which flies in June and July on heaths and in wooded districts, particularly in northern Britain, north Devon, and Somerset. The Orange Swift, a late-summer species, flies in early evening among bracken, or among the higher branches of trees. Though widely distributed in Britain, it is more common in the south and east.

SWINE. These animals belong to the order of Ungulates, or hoofed mammals. There are two main branches of the Swine family—the true pigs of the Old World, and the Peccaries of America. The HIPPOPOTAMUSES (q.v.) are fairly closely related, but are not included in the family. Many species of swine have become extinct, and in many places where they used to be common they have been exterminated by man.

EUROPEAN WILD BOAR AND FAMILY. *Dorien Leigh*

A FAMILY OF WART HOGS IN THE KRUGER NATIONAL PARK, TRANSVAAL. *Paul Popper*

The best known of the true pigs is the wild boar, which is still common in the larger forests of Europe and in parts of North Africa and Asia. There used also to be many in the British Isles, but the last was killed before 1600. The European wild boar is a powerfully built, blackish-grey animal, about 4½ feet long, standing nearly 3 feet high. The male has formidable tusks, growing from the lower jaw and projecting beyond the upper lips, the edges of which are sharpened against the upper tusks. They are powerful weapons, capable of ripping open a horse at a single stroke. Like all wild pigs, the wild boars like to wallow in mud, turning up the ground with their snouts in search of food. The female has one or two litters a year, of from six to ten. The young of all wild swine are lightly striped.

The Indian wild boar is one of the fiercest animals in the world. It will charge men, horses, even elephants, without a moment's hesitation, however badly wounded it may be. It can run very fast, but cannot keep up its high speed for very long. These wild boars make their lairs in any convenient covert, in tall grass, reeds, sugar-cane, in bushes, or in the forest. In the mornings and evenings they go out to look for food, devastating the crops in cultivated districts, but elsewhere eating roots and the carcases of dead animals. The old boars lead a lone life, while the females and young collect in droves of usually from ten to twelve head. PIG-STICKING (q.v. Vol. IX) is still a favourite and often dangerous sport in India.

In the damp forests of Celebes and Borneo in the East Indies live the Babirusas or Pig Deer, so called because of their long, curving tusks and long, slender legs. The male has four curved tusks, one pair growing from the lower and the other from the upper jaw, projecting through the skin. They are excellent swimmers, not only entering lakes to feed on water-plants, but also crossing the small channels of the sea which separate one island from another.

In Africa, south of the Sahara, live the Bush Pigs (or Bosch-Varks). These have rather long, greyish-brown hair—the Red Bush Pig or River Hog of West Africa being certainly the most handsome member of the swine family.

The most hideous wild pig is the African Wart Hog. It has an enormous head, with a huge warty protuberance below each eye, huge tusks growing from the upper jaw, a massive, almost cylindrical body, and a long tail. Very often a Wart Hog will occupy the deserted burrow of an AARD-VARK (q.v.), and before going down it he always turns round and goes in backwards so as to be ready with his tusks to gore any pursuing enemy. As recently as 1904 another large black wild pig, named the Forest Hog, was found in the forests of Equatorial Africa.

The wild pigs of America are called Peccaries. There are two kinds: the Collared Peccary and the larger White-lipped Peccary, both of which eat mostly fruit and roots, and live in the hollows of trees or in burrows dug by other animals. The White-lipped Peccaries are beasts of uncertain temper, and have been known to rush at human beings, squealing with fury and gnashing their sharp, razor-edged tusks. Their tusks are capable of inflicting terrible wounds, and dogs used in hunting them are frequently cut to ribbons by the vicious creatures. When food is scarce, large herds of the Peccaries make long migrations.

See also Vol. VI: PIGS (DOMESTIC).

SWORDFISH, *see* MACKEREL.

T

TADPOLES, *see* FROGS.

TAPEWORM, *see* WORMS, Section 6.

TAPIR. This animal, which belongs to the same section of the Ungulate order of mammals as do the RHINOCEROS and the HORSE (qq.v.), has kept much of the original characteristics of the primitive ancestors of the Ungulates, having changed hardly at all in the course of thousands of years. Though it must once have had a much wider distribution, it now lives in the jungles of the Malay Peninsula and Borneo, and in central and South America. It is a very strange-looking, ungainly beast, with an elongated snout, with which it hooks foliage into its mouth. Its legs are short and stout, and its tail short and thin. It has a thick, smooth skin, scantily covered with very short hairs.

The single species living in the Malay region is coloured black and white. The newly born young are brown or velvety black, with very vivid, yellow, longitudinal stripes on their sides, and white stripes beneath their bodies. This striking colouring makes an effective camouflage on the occasions when they are left alone by their mother in the thick vegetation. They take on the colour of the adults when they are from 4 to 6 months old. Malayan Tapirs are very seldom seen, and little is known of their habits, because they remain hidden in the interior of the country, avoiding inhabited parts.

MALAY TAPIR

There are four species of Tapir in central and South America, the best known being the Brazilian Tapir. The adults are blue-black or brown all over; but the young have the same conspicuous striping as those of the Asiatic species. They live in the thickest parts of the forests, avoiding all open spaces, and journeying in search of food and water along regular pathways made by themselves. They eat palm-leaves and young plants, fallen fruits or swamp grasses, beginning their feed in the early evening and probably continuing throughout the greater part of the night. In the early morning they go to the banks of the river to drink. They are fond of gambolling in the water and rolling in the soft mud, until their hides become thickly plastered —which probably protects them against insect bites. Except in the mating season they are nearly always about alone, walking slowly, deliberately, and quite silently, with their snouts close to the ground. If frightened, however, they will rush blindly forward, crashing through the bushes, or splashing through water. They swim and dive, and have no difficulty in crossing the largest rivers. As a rule they are perfectly harmless animals; but when they do attack—for instance, in protection of their young—they do so fiercely. The only sounds they make are a shrill whistle, of little volume in comparison with their size, and a loud snort when disturbed.

TARANTULA. This name (from the town Taranto in south Italy), was given in the 16th century to a spider, common in Europe, and now known as *Lycosa tarantula*. The bite of this spider was traditionally believed to be peculiarly dangerous: it was supposed to induce a general melancholy which would prove fatal, unless a cure could be achieved in time—the only cure being said to be music. The victims, known as *tarantati*, used to summon a musician, who would play a selection of tunes, or *tarantellas*, until he found one which inspired them to dance. They went on dancing for a long time with increasing speed and vigour, until at last they were exhausted—when the poison was supposed to have been sweated out of their bodies. During the Middle Ages, when whole communities were at times affected by what is now known as mass-hysteria, their peculiar behaviour would usually be ascribed to the local spider.

There is, in fact, no support for the belief that *Lycosa tarantula* is more venomous than any other

BLACK-BELLIED TARANTULA SPIDER AT THE MOUTH OF ITS
BURROW

small European spider. In America, the name is commonly applied to all the larger 'trap-door spiders'—those which live in silk-lined burrows, closed by a trap-door. These, again, are not necessarily more venomous than the rest. Dangerous spiders do exist—the best known being undoubtedly the Black Widow, a spider more conspicuous for its red and black colouring than for its size. The bite of this beast can have painful and even fatal effects, but it certainly does not induce any desire to dance.

See also SPIDERS.

TARPON, *see* HERRING.

TARSIER, *see* LEMUR.

TASMANIAN DEVIL, *see* MARSUPIAL.

TASTE, *see* SENSES, Section 5.

TEAL, *see* DUCK, Section 2.

TEETH AND TUSKS. Teeth are used to tear off and break up food in the first process of digestion; tusks are greatly enlarged teeth which, in such animals as wild boar, have developed as weapons, and no longer serve to break up food.

As animals feed on a great variety of foods, from grass and flesh to seeds and nuts, it is to be expected that their teeth will be of many different kinds. In RODENTS (q.v.) or gnawing animals, such as rats, rabbits, or beavers, the teeth are slender and sharp, and they grow continuously from the base as they are worn away at the top. So if a rodent loses a tooth, the one opposite the gap, having nothing to grind against, will grow abnormally long, and in the course of time will prevent the animal from feeding, and so starve it to death. In horses and other grass and grain-eating animals, the back teeth are broad and flat, and act as millstones (as the name molars indicates), the front teeth being sharp for biting off the grass. CARNIVORA (q.v.), or flesh-eating animals, such as dogs and cats, have sharp front teeth for killing, and knife-edged molars for tearing the flesh, which is very little chewed. In animals using a mixed diet, such as man, the teeth are adapted for tearing, biting, and grinding.

Teeth are modified in various ways to meet the special needs of particular animals. The hollow poison fangs of poisonous snakes are modified teeth; and the teeth of snakes in general point backwards, so as to prevent their victims from escaping while being swallowed. Some reptiles and fishes have several rows of teeth in either jaw; and the frog has teeth in the upper jaw and on the palate, but none on the lower jaw.

Most mammals are born without teeth, so that the mother can suckle the young without injury; but in some young seals the canine teeth are already developed and extremely sharp, so that they would hurt the mother were they not very much to the side. Mammals normally have two sets of teeth: the small 'milk-teeth', which are soon lost, and the permanent teeth which last throughout life. In other animals, such as fish and reptiles, there are no milk-teeth, the young animal being born with a permanent set. Many animals, including some of the Edentata (*see* ANT-EATER) and all birds except fossils have no teeth—the serrations on the edges of some birds' beaks being merely horny projections.

SECTION OF MAMMALIAN
MOLAR TOOTH

Teeth are made of a hard white 'dentine', a substance much like bone, and, like bone, composed largely of calcium. The outer covering, known as enamel, is derived from the epidermis, or outer layer of skin. The teeth of mammals have a fleshy central pulp containing the nerve.

See also Vol. XI: TEETH (Human).

TENDRILS, see CLIMBING PLANTS.

TERMITES. These insects are often called 'White Ants'; but this is a most misleading name, as Ants and Termites have little in common, excepting that they are both 'social insects' (see ANTS).

There are many colonies of termites in the tropics and in warm temperate countries, but none in the British Isles. They make nests of various types, the simplest being galleries in decaying tree-trunks. The species tunnelling these often attack also the dry timber of buildings and furniture: thus a table, apparently perfectly sound, may be so riddled inside that it is a mere shell, ready to collapse almost at a touch. Other species throw up 'termitaria', large structures of earth, excavated below ground and cemented together by saliva. These buildings are usually from 6 to 12 feet high (though they may reach even 20 feet), and are so hard that they are difficult to break open, even with a pickaxe. Other termites have their nests below ground—all that can be seen from above being a number of small mounds.

Termite communities, often composed of thousands of individuals, are divided into four groups or 'castes'. Only two of these are able to breed, but all four include both males and females. The first of the two reproductive castes is believed to be the original stock from which the other castes have sprung. Its members have two pairs of large, elaborately veined wings. At certain times, when the weather suits them (as, for example, during a rainy season), they leave the nest in very great numbers, to form new colonies. They are not good fliers, and it is unusual for a swarm to travel any great distance. As several colonies generally swarm at the same time, this allows interbreeding to take place. Of these large swarms very few individuals survive, most being destroyed by birds, lizards, and mammals; but of the few who remain alive, each pair tries to form a new colony. The first action of the 'royal pair', as they are called, is to break off

their wings along a line near the base. Both take part in building, as the beginning of the future nest, a small underground cavity called the nuptial chamber; and here they remain for the rest of their long lives. A queen of this caste may live in the chamber till she is about 10 years old. She devotes herself entirely to laying eggs, the enlargement of the nest being carried out by certain of her offspring. She increases enormously in size, being said to grow to about 20,000 times the bulk of one of her worker offspring. This enormous increase in bulk is made possible by the stretching of the softer cuticle between the hard plates, which, fitting close together, formed her protective covering when she was her original size. These plates now appear as small, widely separated, dark brown rectangles upon her pale-coloured, swollen body. The head and thorax keep their original size and appearance; the increase is in the abdomen. At the height of her activity she may be producing a million eggs a year—and this is a modest estimate.

ROYAL QUEEN

The second reproductive caste is made up of individuals whose wings never develop beyond the rudimentary stage. The members of this second, small-winged caste do not mate for life, as do the royal pair. Their use in the community may be to assist in maintaining it at full strength, to increase its numbers, or to continue the colony if the royal queen dies, either of old age or by accident. It is certain that the colony can outlast the life of its foundress, and can be maintained solely by the small-winged caste. In a very few species there is a third reproductive caste, a completely wingless one. Though the females of these two castes may increase in size, they never grow so enormous as the original queen. It seems that she, only, is able to produce new members of her own caste; and, so far as we know, it is members of her caste only which leave the habitation to start new colonies.

The other two castes, both wingless, consist of 'workers' and 'soldiers'. Though these, too, include both males and females, the development of their reproductive organs is arrested at an early stage, so that they are sterile. The workers

WORKER

are the most numerous. They are the first to be produced by the royal queen, and are fed to begin with on her saliva. They become adult after about 7 months, and do not partake of their normal food until well developed. As the queen increases in size, and in consequence becomes more and more helpless, she is tended by workers. Her diet is changed to soft food, which the workers specially prepare. They enlarge the habitation, building it up to its great size, and also look after the eggs and young nymphs.

The soldiers have very large heads and strong horny armament. They are of two types: one with very robust jaws, and the other with small jaws and a long horny projection. The soldiers are regarded as the defenders of the colony. The worst enemies of termites are ants, and the soldiers attack these and prevent them from entering the colony. (Some writers, however, say they are the first to run away when the habitation is broken open, though others maintain that they act with courage, adopt threatening attitudes, and attack intruders.) Apart from their stout armour and strong jaws, certain types of soldier are provided with poison glands, the contents of which can be discharged through a 'frontal pore' at approaching enemies. Ants are said to be put completely out of action by this means.

SOLDIER

When the large-winged offspring of the royal pair are ready to make their flight, the workers bore holes in the wall of the habitation to let them out, and many workers and soldiers assemble as if to bid them a ceremonious farewell. It is not yet clearly known what determines which of the offspring of the royal pair shall become members of their own caste and which will belong to the other castes, though it is possible to tell, when they leave the eggs, what they are going to be when they grow up. Occasionally, members of the sterile castes are known to have partly recovered the lost characters of the reproductive castes. Thus, egg-laying female soldiers have occurred, and their offspring have become workers; and soldiers have sometimes been found with small, undeveloped wings.

Adult termites live on wood and other vegetable matter, as well as upon refuse; but the young nymphs are fed on saliva. Foraging to bring food into the habitation from outside is an important duty of the workers. During these forays, there is a guard of soldiers on either side of a long procession of workers. They set out in the evening, collect all night, and return in the morning. The collected material may be taken straight into the habitation, or stored outside in mounds from which it is removed later into the nest. In some nests, there are special granaries for storage.

Certain species of termites have taken to what might be called horticulture. In their nests are special chambers, called 'fungus gardens'. The floor of these consists of decaying wood, well manured by the termites themselves. This manure apparently contains the spores of timber-attacking fungi, which pass unharmed through the bodies of the termites and then germinate in the decayed wood on the floor. The gardens, which are usually near the chamber where the royal pair remain imprisoned, form nurseries for the young nymphs, which graze upon them almost like sheep. Some of this fungus material is used also by the workers to make up the food upon which the old queen is fed.

TERN, *see* GULLS, Section 2.

TERRAPIN, *see* TURTLES AND TORTOISES, Section 3.

TERRITORY OF ANIMALS, *see* ANIMAL TERRITORY.

THORNS, *see* PLANT DEFENCES, Section 2.

THRUSH. 1. This very large family, closely related to the WARBLERS (q.v.), is distributed all over the world, and contains many of our best-known British birds. The ROBIN, REDSTART, NIGHTINGALE, and BLUE BIRD (qq.v.), all members of the thrush family, are described in separate articles. The family also includes the Blackbirds, Fieldfares, Chats, and Wheatears, as well as the Redwings of northern Europe, the Dhyal Birds of south-east Asia and Madagascar, and the Shamas of southern Asia.

The thrush family as a whole have rather delicate, slender bills, suitable for collecting their food of insects, grubs, and berries. The nestlings always have a speckled plumage, and this speckled pattern sometimes remains in the adult stage—as, for instance, in the Thrushes

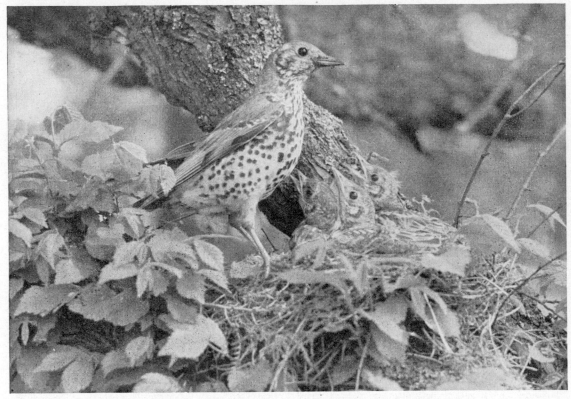

MISSEL-THRUSH AND FLEDGLINGS. *Eric J. Hosking, F.R.P.S.*

themselves. Many members of the family are migratory, though some make only short journeys. Great numbers of Thrushes and Blackbirds come to Britain every autumn from northern Europe to winter in the milder climate, and the Fieldfares and Redwings are winter visitors only. Practically all the family are fine songsters, their song being their means of declaring to other members of their species their claim over the territory in which they breed and find their food (*see* ANIMAL TERRITORY). The family may be divided into several groups: the Thrushes themselves; the Blackbirds, which are very closely related; the Chats and Wheatears; the Robins, Redstarts, and Nightingales; and the Hedge Sparrow, which is often classified as a Warbler.

2. THRUSHES. The Song-thrush (or Mavis) has a song as rich and varied as the Nightingale's, though in the opinion of many people, hardly as finished and perfect as that of some Warblers. It feeds mainly on the ground on slugs and worms—its method of cracking the shells of snails against a stone being well known. Near the sea, thrushes often eat sea-molluscs, such as whelks. The Song-thrush builds a characteristic cup-shaped nest, made chiefly of grass, and lined with mud and decayed wood. It is one of the earliest British birds to start breeding, and rears several broods in a season. The Missel-thrush, a larger bird, its breast spotted rather than speckled, is so named because it eats mistletoe berries, which other birds reject. It is also often called the Stormcock, because its loud song is heard on stormy days in winter. It builds its nest in a fork of a tree, the nest being, as are most nests of this family, a cup-shaped structure of materials such as grass on a mud foundation, but without the mud lining of the Song-thrush. When the young are fledged, they gather in family parties to hunt for feeding grounds, until the autumn, when they migrate.

Fieldfares are common in northern Europe, where they breed in colonies, nesting frequently in birches and fir-trees. Redwings, also northern birds, make migratory flights in large flocks, flying chiefly by night, across the North Sea to Britain or central Europe. They feed very much more on worms and insects than on berries, and therefore are apt to suffer badly during a protracted period of hard weather. It is, in fact, their flanks, not their wings, which are red. In southern Europe, southern Asia, and Africa are the Rock Thrushes, among them the Blue Thrush, shy birds which nest in remote places in holes in rocks or walls.

3. BLACKBIRD and RING OUZEL. The Blackbird, Shakespeare's Ouzel Cock 'with orange-tawny bill', does not breed as far north as many of the thrushes, and often migrates to a milder climate for the winter. The cock is a fine songster and a good mimic. The Blackbird's loud, cackling alarm-note is frequently to be heard, especially during that anxious period when the fledglings are making their first flights. The Ring Ouzel, in appearance like a Blackbird with a white patch on the chest, is a mountain-loving bird, much more shy and wary than its relation, and breeding in solitary places among rocks and heather. In Switzerland it nests in fir-trees, feeding on the berries of the mountain ash, and making raids on cherry orchards and vineyards.

4. WHEATEAR and CHATS. This group contains the smallest members of the family, the little Whinchat and Stonechat, each about half the size of a Blackbird. They inhabit open country, especially that covered with gorse or broom. The Wheatear and Whinchat migrate for the winter; but the Stonechat is a resident. These birds are not shy; but they are restless and very careful not to reveal the whereabouts of their nests. The Wheatears build in suitable crevices in banks or walls or among rocks; the Chats generally build under a whin or gorse bush a most skilfully concealed nest, which the female bird approaches through the grass from some little way off. The cock of the Stonechat is a brightly coloured little bird, with a shiny black head and a bright red-brown breast. The name Chat has come from the sound, like the clash of two pebbles, which the bird makes; it has also a sweet but short song. The Chats are typical birds of Africa, where there are several species. There are other species in western Asia and Europe; and the Black Chat is a common bird in India and Burma. North America also has a species.

5. The HEDGE SPARROW (Dunnock) belongs to the accentors, which are closely related to the thrushes and also to the warblers: it is no relation to the House Sparrow, which is a finch. Its shallow nest of roots and moss is usually placed low in a hedge or bush—so poorly concealed that it often falls victim to the birds'-nester. Cuckoos also frequently make use of it, though the Cuckoo's egg rarely matches the light-blue eggs of the Hedge Sparrow. Another species, the Alpine Accentor, occasionally wanders as far as Britain.

6. DHYAL BIRD and SHAMA. These graceful little birds, to be found especially in India, are closely related to the Robin, which they resemble in much of their behaviour and in their charming song. Their plumage is mainly black and white, the Shamas having chestnut under-parts and long tails.

TICKS, *see* MITES AND TICKS.

TIGER. The Tiger and the LION are the two largest members of the CAT (qq.v.) tribe. Most tigers are smaller than lions, but some—for instance, a full-sized Bengal Tiger—are actually larger. Tigers range over a vast area in Asia: from Mongolia, south-west to the Caucasus, and southwards to Java and southern India, but not Ceylon. The Mongolian Tigers, some of the largest, grow thick, rather pale, woolly coats; while those of Sumatra and Java are very much smaller, and have deep, rich-coloured coats.

WHEATEAR COCK BIRD
Arthur Brook

A TIGER COMING OUT OF THE JUNGLE TO A WATER-HOLE
Ewing Galloway, N.Y.

The big cats of Africa, the LEOPARDS, and those of South America, the JAGUARS (qq.v.), must not be confused with tigers.

The tiger's yellow coat striped with black, although so vivid when seen in the zoo, is a wonderful camouflage in the animal's native surroundings. Tigers generally lie concealed in long grass or in the forests until evening, when they start out on their nightly prowl. The Indian Tiger generally hunts alone. During the very hot season he takes up one definite 'beat', haunting river banks and patches of fresh, long grass close to swamps. He shelters from the burning rays of the sun in caves, or among the grass-grown ruins of deserted cities. Sometimes he takes a mud-bath in the shallow waters at the river's edge, and afterwards rolls in the dry sand. Very often he swims a river in search of prey. Tigers are very poor tree-climbers; but when attacking hunters they will spring as much as 18 feet from the ground into the fork of a tree.

The tigress is a devoted mother, and will protect her young with great ferocity. The number of cubs in a litter varies from two to six. As soon as they are old enough, she trains them thoroughly in the technique of hunting, and they generally stay with her until they are nearly 2 years old. Young tigers are more wanton in their killing than old ones, often destroying much more than they need to eat. Very young cubs are easily tamed; but tigers do not breed as freely as lions in captivity, and the cubs are more difficult to rear.

A typical jungle tiger lives chiefly on deer, wild pigs, and antelopes; but he sometimes eats cattle, and small animals such as porcupines, monkeys, and peafowl. He kills large prey by dislocating their necks. A wild bull buffalo is about a match for him; but he occasionally kills a young elephant or an adult bull gaur. He will eat his kill even when it has become putrid. In captivity, if not properly fed, he has been known to eat his own offspring. Tigers living near a village feed almost entirely on the small native cattle—unless, of course, they are man-eaters. Between meals they are sluggish and stupid and rarely show fight.

A regular man-eater is usually an old tiger which has grown too feeble to hunt other food; or, if there is a scarcity of food for their cubs, the females will attack humans. Cattle-stealers sometimes become man-eaters after they have got used to the sight of man and have lost their fear of him. A man-eater will seize an unsuspecting native by the neck, and drag the body to a quiet spot where it can eat it at leisure, without fear of interruption. It eats only the fleshy parts, and then goes out to get a fresh victim for its next meal. Man-eaters are very wary, and big-game hunters find them the most difficult of all tigers to kill (see BIG-GAME HUNTING, Vol. IX).

In many parts of India and in Burma, tigers are regarded with superstition, and the natives will not kill them.

TIGER BEETLE, *see* BEETLES, Section 3.

TIGER MOTHS AND FOOTMEN. The family Arctiidae contains some 3,500 species, of which 29 occur in Britain. The Tigers, with which are grouped the Ermines, Clouded Buff, Muslin, and Flunkeys, are usually larger and more robust, have wider wings, and are more brightly coloured than the Footmen. Their caterpillars are 'woolly bears', most of which hibernate and complete their development in the spring. Most insect-eating animals quickly learn to associate the conspicuous colours of these moths and their larvae with distasteful qualities, and consequently leave them alone (*see* PROTECTIVE COLORATION). Cuckoos, however, eat hairy caterpillars freely.

The largest British species is the common Garden Tiger, the female sometimes measuring 3 inches across the wings. The fore-wings are cream with large, dark-brown markings, and the hind-wings are deep reddish-orange with blue-black spots. These spots are sometimes so large that they are almost blotches, or sometimes so small that most of the wings are clear red. All-black specimens occur, and also others with the red colour of the fore-wings replaced by yellow, or with almost pure white, and with sooty-brown hind-wings—but they are very rare. The caterpillars, most easily seen on sunny days in April and May, when they are nearly full-grown, occur in most country lanes along the foot of hedgerows, round haystacks, or in farm-vards where nettle patches grow. They are jet-black, with numerous white spots or tubercles, each bearing tufts of long, black, silky hair tipped with white, while along the sides and by the head the hairs are reddish-brown. They feed on low-growing weeds such as stinging-nettle, dead-nettle, dandelion, plantain, and dock, and spin a loose cocoon of silk before turning into the chrysalis. The moths emerge in June and July, about 3 weeks after pupating; but as they fly only at night, they are not as well known as the caterpillars.

The Cream-spot Tiger has velvety-black upper-wings with about eight cream-coloured spots, butter-yellow hind-wings with five or six black spots, and a patch of red on the body near the tail end. The caterpillar, a less striking 'woolly bear' than the Garden Tiger, feeds in much the same sort of places and on the same

CATERPILLAR OF GARDEN TIGER MOTH
S. Beaufoy, F.R.P.S.

GARDEN TIGER MOTH
S. Beaufoy, F.R.P.S.

ance and habits: the yellowish-white males have dark central spots and pink edges to both fore and hind-wings; the females are orange with a central spot on the fore-wings and heavy black markings on the hind-wings. Though the males fly by day when disturbed, the females are rarely seen until the evening.

The black and yellow banded caterpillar of the Cinnabar Moth feeds on ragwort in waste lands and fields, the caterpillars being sometimes so abundant that they completely strip the ragwort. An unsuccessful attempt was made about 1930 to introduce the Cinnabar to New Zealand, so that it might control the weed. The Cinnabar Moth has sooty fore-wings with a vermilion stripe and two vermilion spots, and vermilion hind-wings.

The Feathered, Speckled, and Crimson Speckled Footmen, better known as Flunkeys, are nearer to the Tigers than to the true Footmen. The Speckled Flunkey is restricted to parts of Dorset and Hampshire; the other two are rare immigrants, the wide-ranging Crimson Speckled now extending into Africa, India, Australia, and New Zealand.

The British Footmen, of which there are 16 species, are mostly yellowish or greyish in colour. They have long, narrow fore-wings, which they fold along the body when resting—so presenting the stiff appearance which has suggested their common name. They mostly have a wing-expanse of about an inch, though the largest British species, the Four-spotted, measures $1\frac{3}{4}$ inches. Their hairy caterpillars feed on lichens. There are many of them in Australia, where they largely replace the Tiger Moths.

The Scarlet and Jersey Tigers are the only British representatives of another family with warning colours, the Hypsidae. The Scarlet Tiger has blue-black fore-wings with nine or ten creamy spots, and rich scarlet hind-wings dotted and banded with black. Though very local, it has occurred in many counties as far north as Staffordshire, most frequently on river banks on the chalk, but also on sandstone, on sand-dune marshes, and in clearings in woods. The yellow-spotted, black caterpillars feed on comfrey, nettle, and other plants, and hibernate when quite small in curled leaves on the ground. They feed up rapidly in the spring, and pupate low down amongst withered grass or dead leaves, emerging during June. A Berkshire colony of Scarlet Tigers, which was under observation for

kinds of weeds. It is most frequent in the southern and south-western counties of Britain. The much smaller Wood Tiger has yellow and black patterns on all four wings, the under-wings of the female being sometimes flushed orange or red. The moths are usually found in late May and early June in clearings in woods or on mossy moorland banks, and the caterpillars, rather gay-looking with their russet hairs, hibernate in thick, soft tussocks. The Ruby Tiger of southern England is crimson-rose, with black dots and a black border on its hind-wings. In the north, darker and duller varieties with little or no ruby colouring are found on moorlands where, in spring, their light brown, silken cocoons can be picked off heather stems. The quite common brownish caterpillars are thickly tufted with dark hair. They feed on a variety of weeds, and hibernate when fully fed.

The White, Water, and Buff Ermines, and the Muslin Moth are about $1\frac{1}{2}$ inches across, and white or buff with black spots. The Water Ermine is restricted to fens and marshes; but the others are common garden species, the hairy caterpillars feeding on mint, lily of the valley, and many other low-growing plants. The male and female of the Clouded Buff differ in appear-a period of years, was estimated to vary from 1,000 to 10,000 individuals. The Scarlet Tiger is exceptionally suitable for such population studies because of its restricted habitat and conspicuous coloration. The Jersey Tiger, common in the Channel Islands, but in Britain restricted to south Devon, is a gaudy moth, the fore-wings being metallic blue-green with 'tiger' stripes of pale cream, while the under-wings vary from scarlet to orange or yellow, with three or four dark blotches. The caterpillars, also, are brighter than other Tigers, being greyish-brown, striped with orange and yellow, and covered with short, bristly, brownish hairs.

TITS (TITMICE). These small birds, with short, strong bills, are to be found in most parts of the world. The family includes many species, several of which are common British birds. They feed principally on insects, which they hunt for in places such as the bark of trees and fruit buds, often perching with great agility upside down or in other odd positions.

Tits build lovely cup-shaped nests of moss and other soft materials, lined with feathers and wool —that of the Azure Tit of Siberia is chiefly of fur. The nests are generally placed in well-covered holes in trees or walls; but the Great Tits and Blue Tits specialize in finding odd places, such as upturned flower-pots, letter-boxes, or the base of a discarded Crow's nest. Some tits, such as the Long-tailed Tit of Britain, the Penduline Tit of South Africa, and the New Zealand Creeper, build much more elaborate nests. The Long-tailed Tit builds, in a tree or bush, a deep, domed, bottle-shaped nest, woven of materials such as moss, lichen, wool, and spiders' webs, and lined with a great number of feathers. The entrance is by a small hole high up on one side. When incubating, the bird sits with her long tail bent backwards over her head, sometimes even sticking out through the entrance-hole. The Penduline Tit hangs her woven nest like a deep hammock from a branch (*see* picture, p. 46). The New Zealand Creeper's nest is rather like that of the Long-tailed Tit—wool, moss, and vegetable fibre felted together into a pear-shaped bag, with a small entrance on one side. Many of the tits lay large clutches of up to twelve or fourteen white eggs, speckled with red. They generally rear two broods in a season.

The Great Tit, Coal Tit, and Blue Tit are all common residents in Britain, generally spending the winter in parties. These three species, although very closely related, have sufficiently different feeding habits to enable them to inhabit

LONG-TAILED TIT AT ITS NEST
Eric J. Hosking, F.R.P.S.

CRESTED TIT
Eric J. Hosking, F.R.P.S.

the same territory without interfering with each other. The Great Tit can eat larger insects than the other two, and occasionally even kills small or weak birds. The Coal Tit eats seeds as well as insects, and hunts its food on the ground as well as among the trees. The Blue Tit uses its delicate little bill to extract minute insects and grubs from the bark of trees or from fruit-tree buds. The Marsh Tit frequents woods near marshy country or along river banks; while the Crested Tit lives farther north and feeds partly on pine-seeds.

The Bearded Tit (Reedling or Reed-pheasant) is not very much like a typical tit—indeed it has more the build of a finch, and is often classified separately. Its name comes from the long, beard-like feathers on the sides of the throat. Its blue-grey, chestnut, and buff colouring makes it blend well with its surroundings in the reed-beds and marshes of Norfolk. A few breed in Norfolk, where they build nests of reeds and flat grasses lined with reed-flowers, and placed in the reeds near the water.

TOAD. The name, if strictly used, applies only to members of the family Bufonidae (Latin *bufo* a toad); but it is used for many different kinds of tailless AMPHIBIA (q.v.). The general opinion that toads have thick-set, rather clumsy bodies, and a dry, warty skin is not true of all members of the family. The majority of the *Bufo* genus live on the ground; some (*Nectophryne*) live in trees, and have adhesive pads on their fingers and toes, like the Tree Frogs; while the Malayan *Pseudobufo* spends most of its life in water.

The genus *Bufo*, with more than 100 species, is found all over the world, except in Australia and Madagascar. Identification of many of the species is often difficult, for the differences between them are slight. England has two species, the Common Toad and the Natterjack. Other well-known species are the Green Toad of Europe and north Africa (closely related to the Natterjack), the common Asiatic Toad, the Malayan Giant Toad, which reaches a length of 8 inches and is the largest of all the toads, the Common American Toad, and the Giant Toad of tropical America. This large toad, up to 6 inches in length, has now been imported into sugar plantations to destroy insect pests.

Toads lay their eggs in strings—as opposed to frogs, which lay them in clusters. The tadpoles of the English toad can be easily distinguished from those of the FROG (q.v.) by their smaller size and blacker colour. Toads breed in deeper ponds than do frogs. The larval stage lasts about 2 months. When first the baby toads leave the water, they measure little over $\frac{1}{2}$ inch in length, and for some time they live near the pond, hiding under leaves or stones by day. A sudden shower of rain will bring them out of their hiding-places —and this occurrence has given rise to the stories of 'showers of toads'.

The Natterjack is distinguished from the larger Common Toad by its smoother skin, which is greenish in colour and has a yellow stripe down the back. Also, having shorter hind legs, it usually runs rather than hops. It is much the rarer of the two species, being found only in certain localities—particularly sandy places, where it is often found in numbers. In the breeding season, male Natterjacks are very noisy, and on still evenings their loud calls can be heard a long way off.

The tadpole of the Natterjack is very small, about an inch in length, and it remains a tadpole for only about 6 weeks. When they leave the

NATTERJACK TOAD

Burrowing

SPADEFOOT TOAD

TOADSTOOL, *see* FUNGI.

TORTOISE, *see* TURTLES AND TORTOISES.

TORTOISESHELL BUT-TERFLIES, *see* VANESSINAE.

TOUCAN. This fantastic-looking, brilliantly coloured bird is an inhabitant of the tropical forests of South and central America, spreading as far north as Mexico. It is a relative of the Wood-pecker. Toucans have beaks out of all proportion in size to the rest of their bodies. The Toco Toucan of South America, for instance, a bird of about 2 feet long, has a beak which extends a quarter of its total length. This beak, which makes the bird look top-heavy, is actually very light, being made of a fine network of bony fibres which give strength without weight. It is generally highly coloured, as are the naked parts of the bird's head. The plumage in most species is predominantly black and green. Toucans are mainly fruit-eaters, living in large or small flocks in the high forest trees, and flying with ease

water, the young toads measure only $\frac{3}{8}$ inch in length; by the end of the second summer they are still less than an inch long, and they do not reach maturity until the fourth or fifth year. The average length of the fully grown toad is $2\frac{1}{2}$ inches. Natterjacks stand captivity well, and will become very tame.

The Midwife Toad, a native of central and western Europe, is so named because of the way in which the male carries and cares for the eggs during the early stages of their development. After the eggs are laid, the male pushes his legs through the mass so that they become wound round him in a sort of figure-of-eight. Then, leaving the female, he carries the eggs about with him for the next 3 weeks or so, moistening them regularly with dew or even immersing them in water. At the end of that time he takes them to the nearest water, and the young, already partly developed, escape from their covering membrane and continue their lives as tadpoles in the ordinary way.

Spadefoot is a name applied to the toads of two genera inhabiting Europe and North America. The foot is provided with a strong, shovel-shaped tubercle, by which the creature can dig itself into the soil, where it remains concealed during the day. The skin exudes a secretion which smells like garlic—and in Germany they are sometimes called Garlic Toads.

TOUCAN OF TROPICAL AMERICA
Booth Steamship Co.

and grace over the tops of the forests. During the heat of the day they rest motionless in the branches, but otherwise are constantly on the move. They nest in hollow branches of fruit-trees.

TRANSPIRATION OF PLANTS.

During cold weather the insides of greenhouses are often covered with water; and if a potted plant with a leafy shoot is put under a glass jar for a few hours, water will appear on the glass. This condensed water may have come either from direct evaporation from the soil, or else from the plants themselves. All land plants give off water-vapour which in certain circumstances, such as in the greenhouse, may condense as liquid drops. A fair-sized oak-tree may give off as much as 150 gallons of water a day, while a plant of Indian Corn, during its life of 26 weeks, may give off 20 lbs. of water. The process of giving off water is known as transpiration.

That green plants should transpire is natural, since the cells of their leaves are saturated with water, which, with its dissolved mineral salts, is constantly being supplied by the roots for the process of food manufacture or PHOTOSYNTHESIS (q.v.). The air surrounding these leaves is more or less dry. The thousands of tiny pores or 'stomata' on the leaves take in from the atmosphere the carbon dioxide necessary for photosynthesis, and at the same time let out water-vapour.

The leaves are almost entirely responsible for the loss of water-vapour from green plants. If, for instance, the leaves are greased on both sides, so that water cannot escape through them, transpiration will practically stop. In normal leaves, which lie horizontally to the ground, most transpiration takes place from the lower surfaces, where the majority of the stomata are found. The Lilac leaf, for example, has 160,000 stomata per square inch on the under and only six on the upper surface; whereas the Holly leaf has 63,000 per square inch on the under-surface and

water vapour given off at surface of leaf through stomata.

water passes up stem through wood vessels as sap.

water enters at roots.

none on the upper. As might be expected, leaves such as Grasses and Irises, which grow upright, have an equal number of stomata on each surface. Some WATER PLANTS (q.v.), however, the leaves of which lie out on the surface of the water, have all their stomata on the upper surface.

The passage of water-vapour through each of the stomata is controlled by two guard cells. As these swell or shrink, the pores automatically open and close. As a rule the stomata are open in the light and closed in darkness, and so transpiration takes place mostly during the day and practically ceases at night. In time of drought, when the soil is dry, the guard cells shrink, closing the stomata, and transpiration is reduced. When there is plenty of water in the soil, however, transpiration occurs freely.

The intake of water through the roots is not the only factor which affects transpiration. The humidity or amount of water-vapour in the atmosphere, for instance, is a consideration. Water evaporates much faster in a dry atmosphere than in a damp one, and at first transpiration continues rapidly in a dry atmosphere, until the air becomes so dry that the guard cells shrink and close the stomata. Wind, also, by drying the atmosphere increases transpiration, so that plants in exposed places often suffer from excess of transpiration, and need shelter. The intensity of light, by affecting the rate of photosynthesis, also affects the rate of transpiration. It is probable that humidity, temperature, light-intensity, wind, and the amount of water available in the soil, all interact together to control the rate of transpiration—although it has recently been shown that slight changes in the degree of opening of the stomata affect the rate of transpiration much less than was formerly supposed.

Transpiration is not, however, a purely wasteful process. The reason for the flow of water from deep roots to the top of a tall tree has never been satisfactorily explained; but transpiration probably plays a most important part in bringing this about. As water is lost by the cells bordering a stoma, so it is absorbed by these cells from the surrounding ones. This loss and absorption proceeds as a chain process in the leaf-cells until the veins are reached. These veins contain the wood vessels, which stretch in long tubes down to the roots, and make what amounts to a closed system of pipes. As water is sucked out of these vessels at the top, it is probable that a state of tension is set up, which causes water to be sucked in by the root-cells from the soil. Thus, by continual loss of water, transpiration is probably the means of starting a flow of water containing mineral salts from the roots to the leaves, where it is indispensable for photosynthesis. But the flow of water through a plant is also thought to be helped by a force exerted from below, a force the existence of which is known, and which is called ROOT PRESSURE (q.v.).

The upward transpiration stream in plants is closely associated with the transport of water containing the food substances made by photosynthesis. This 'translocation stream', as it is called, goes out to all parts of the plant, taking with it food for immediate use or for storage, as well as water and dissolved gases for respiration and other purposes. Together, the transpiration and translocation streams correspond to the BLOOD SYSTEM (q.v.) of animals.

See also RESPIRATION IN PLANTS.

TREE-CREEPER. This inconspicuous little brown and greyish-white bird has a long, curved bill, strong, curved claws, and a long, stiff tail. It spends much of its life running up the trunks of trees with quick, jerky movements, probing the crevices of the bark for insects. As soon as it has crept up one tree, it flies down to the base of the next tree and starts again. Insects form the bulk of its food, though it also eats some seeds and grain. This bird is to be seen fairly commonly in all wooded districts of Britain, and during the winter it often joins bands of Tits and Goldcrests in search of food. It nests in a crevice of a tree, often between the trunk and a piece of loose bark, or a thick ivy stem. There is a closely related species in North America.

The Wall-creeper is a larger relative, almost unknown in Britain, but to be found in the mountains of central and south Europe. It has a grey head and back, and large, rounded, blackish wings, marked with a crimson band and white spots. It spends its time hunting for insects over the faces of rocks or among boulders, climbing about with jerky hops, and helping itself by opening and closing its wings.

TREES, see FLOWERING PLANTS, Section 4; CONIFERS; WOODLANDS. *See also* Vol. VI: FORESTS; TREES, BROAD-LEAVED; TREES, CONIFEROUS.

TREE SHREW (TUPAI). This insect-eating mammal of Asia, though it looks very like a Squirrel, is not related to it. It is usually placed among the INSECTIVORA (q.v.); but in the opinion of some scientists is related more closely to the LEMURS (q.v.) and Primates (*see* MONKEYS). Tree Shrews have the long, sensitive snouts peculiar to the Insectivora; but, like Squirrels, they have bushy tails as long as their bodies, and live in trees. They show the same movements as Squirrels, too, often sitting up to eat and holding their food between their forepaws. They usually find enough insect food in the trees; but sometimes they hunt for it on the ground—in Malaya often entering houses for the purpose. Their rat-like heads and thievish expressions make them not very attractive. Among themselves they are quarrelsome—though, in fact, they are quite easily tamed. Their usual call is a short, peculiar, whistling sound which, when they are angry, changes to a loud, shrill cry.

TROGON. These tropical forest-birds carry, perhaps, more brilliant plumage than any other birds. The skins of the American Trogons, in particular, have been sought after so keenly that some species have been almost exterminated. The majority of Trogons belong to South and central America, one species reaching as far north as Texas and Arizona. Another species belongs only to San Domingo, and one only to Cuba. There are four species in tropical Africa, and others in south-east Asia.

One of the most spectacular of the Trogons is the Quezal of Guatemala. The male bird has a brilliant metallic green head, chest, back, and wings, deep blood-red underparts, and some white and black on the outer tail-feathers. It carries a large, rounded crest, long, drooping wing-plumes, and a very long tail, with the two middle plumes extended about four times as long as the rest—some 6 feet altogether. The female is much less adorned. The characteristic colouring of the typical Trogons, birds which range

RESPLENDENT QUEZAL

from southern Brazil to Mexico, is metallic blue and green above, and yellow, scarlet, and crimson beneath. They live, generally in pairs, in the forest, feeding on fruit and berries, and uttering at intervals their curious cries.

The African Trogons are shy birds, and not a great deal is known of their behaviour. One species belongs to East Africa, another to central Africa, a third to West Africa, and a fourth to Zanzibar. They are said to lay four white eggs in a hole in a tree. One of the Asiatic species, the Red-headed Trogon, eats insects rather than fruit, catching its prey on the wing, as a Fly-catcher does.

The Colies or Mouse-birds, exclusively African birds, and closely related to the Trogons, live generally in small flocks, and creep about fruit-trees with the help of their claws and beaks, hanging head downwards to reach the fruit. They are said even to sleep in that inverted position.

TROPICAL JUNGLES. The vast forests of the tropics form a girdle round the globe, and, whether in Africa, America, or the East, are in many ways alike. In some regions, where there is a definite dry season, the trees shed their leaves and have a resting-time (like our own trees in winter) till the rains return and the new leaves appear. But in hilly areas near the equator, where there is almost daily rain, there are great stretches of evergreen forest. Here the climate is one long moist summer, always hot and always damp, providing ideal conditions for the exuberant growth of plants. The trees grow to immense heights, often to 300 feet, forming a dense canopy, under which the air is always heavy with moisture. The light is dim, and there is a weird stillness below the canopy. The forest seems to be built on different levels. On the ground are the shade-loving shrubs; and above them woody climbers (*see* CLIMBING PLANTS) struggle ever higher towards the hidden sun— many of them beginning their race for light and air, not from the ground, but from nooks and crannies in the trees. Among the rope-like stems of the climbers are layers of filmy FERNS (q.v.), and perched plants or 'epiphytes', or even parasites, fastened on the branches of the trees (*see* PARASITIC PLANTS). MOSSES (q.v.) and lichens shroud the stems and branches; and even the leaves are veiled with minute ALGAE (q.v.). Seen from below the canopy looks green and brown; but in reality it is the home of many

vivid and striking ORCHIDS (q.v.) which, hoisted on the shoulders of the giant trees, flaunt their glowing blossoms.

Sometimes the plants which grow on other plants and live at their expense become so strong that the overburdened tree beneath gives up the struggle and dies. The parasitic fig-tree, for example, sprouts from a seed lying in the fork of another tree, and begins to send long roots to the ground. These long suckers form a network round the trunk of the supporting tree, and after they have reached the ground, they become strong and woody. The smothered supporting tree dies at last, leaving a trellis-work fig-tree in its place. The strands of the trellis fuse together gradually, till the fig-tree has developed a huge solid trunk, and becomes one of the forest giants.

A particularly interesting example of a tropical parasitic plant is Rafflesia, a native of the Malayan forests, which grows on the roots of vines. The roots, stems, and leaves of the plant become reduced until they are little more than colourless threads growing through the soil and piercing the roots of their vine host to extract food. The flower, on the other hand, is far from reduced—one species, in fact, has the largest-known flower in the world. This is usually red, measures 30 inches across. It has a repulsive smell, rather like that of decaying fish.

In those jungles where the sky cannot be seen at all because of the dense canopy, the undergrowth is usually scanty, the forest floor being covered merely with a carpet of pale FUNGI (q.v.) and with a scattering of dead leaves from the giants overhead. But where the sunlight can penetrate, the undergrowth becomes so thick that one can only see a few feet ahead. There is no grass in the true tropical forest, owing to the lack of sunshine; but where a stream flows or there is a clearing from a fallen tree, there is a rich plant life, with coarse grasses, like those of the bushlands, at the fringes of the forest.

The inexhaustible variety of plants found in the hot, damp climates of these forests grows with such incredible rapidity that areas which have been cleared and then neglected become completely grown over and unrecognizable within a few years. Although evergreens predominate, there is also a considerable proportion of deciduous trees, many of which burst into flower twice, and several even as much as four times, in a year. The mighty Teak of the Indian and

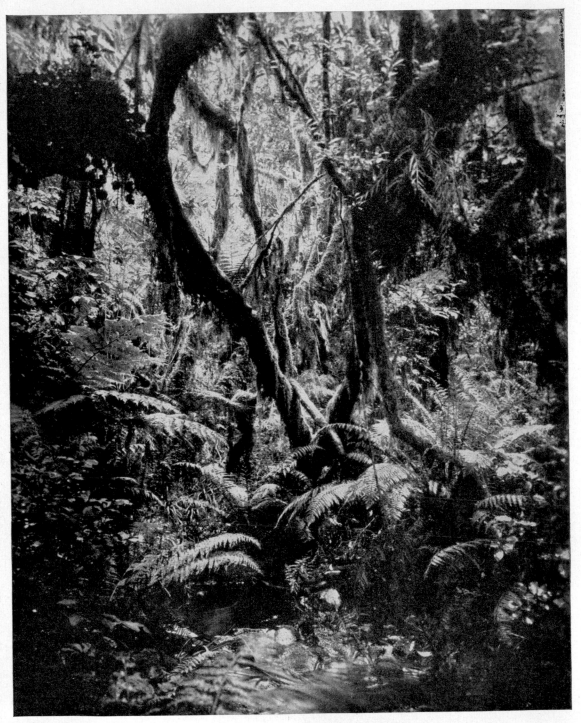

TYPICAL TROPICAL JUNGLE IN EQUATORIAL AMERICA
E. O. Hoppé

Burman jungles sheds its leaves in the dry season. With the evergreen trees, leaf-shedding occurs in a sporadic fashion; and also—which is more remarkable—flowering takes place sporadically throughout the year, instead of at any fixed season. In consequence, fruits also, including pulpy fruits, are available for animal food at all seasons. The flowers are often borne directly on the older stems or trunks of the trees and occasionally even on the roots. The flowers of the COCOA tree (q.v. Vol. VI) of West Africa, for example, are borne on the trunks.

The number of different trees to be found in these forests is immense: there may be as many as 400–500 different kinds to the square mile. They include a large number of such important trees as the Camwood, Ebony, Rubbers, and Mahoganies of enormous size, scented and otherwise, which are distributed in tropical forests throughout the world. Banana Palms are typical of the tropical forests of the Old World; the Ginger plant occurs in the Indo-Malayan forests; while the American forests contain Arrowroots. Coniferous trees occur only on the higher lands. (*See also* ECOLOGY OF PLANTS.)

See also Vol. III: FORESTS, Section 2 and 3 (*a*).
See also Vol. VI: FORESTRY; RUBBER; BANANAS.

TROPIC-BIRD. Called by sailors the 'Boatswain', this ocean bird, rather smaller than a common gull, frequents the tropical regions of the Atlantic, Pacific, and Indian Oceans. It

RED-TAILED TROPIC-BIRD OF THE INDIAN OCEAN
C. A. Gibson-Hill

belongs to the same group of birds as the CORMORANT, GANNET, PELICAN, and FRIGATE BIRD (qq.v.). It has predominantly white plumage, some species having red bills and black on the wing-feathers, and others yellow bills and a little red on the tail-feathers. All have webbed feet and two very greatly elongated tail-feathers. Tropic-birds often follow in the wake of ships for long periods, showing boldness in pursuing food. They breed in large companies on the Bermudas and Pacific Islands, nesting in holes in the rocks or in trees, and laying one dark-brown, mottled egg.

TROPISM, *see* MOVEMENT OF PLANTS.

TROUT, *see* SALMON, Section 2.

TRUFFLES, *see* FUNGI.

TSETSE FLY. This blackish, dark-brown, or yellowish-brown insect is found only in tropical Africa. It is about the size of its near relative

the HOUSE-FLY (q.v.); but it can easily be distinguished by the way it shuts its wings—folding them flat, one exactly over the other, upon the abdomen, beyond which they project considerably. Its skin-piercing and blood-sucking organ stands out a short distance in front of its head. The female produces one larva at a time, which drops, fully grown, on to the ground and burrows at once into the ground to pupate. The pupa is enclosed in a puparium, the last larval skin.

Tsetse Flies occur from the Congo on the west to Uganda and the Great Lakes of East Africa; but they are confined to patches of forest, where they have moisture, warmth, and shade. The tracts they inhabit are called 'fly-belts'. They carry protozoa which cause deadly tropical diseases, the most serious to mankind being 'sleeping-sickness'. 'Nagana' is a devastating cattle disease also carried by Tsetse Flies.

See also FLIES. See also Vol. XI: TROPICAL DISEASES.

TUATARA. *Paul Popper*

TUATARA. This solidly built reptile, somewhat lethargic in its movements, grows to a length of 2 feet. Although externally shaped like a LIZARD (q.v.), it differs in so many structural characters that it cannot be placed even in the same order. It digs a burrow in the ground, with a spacious chamber at the end, and this it shares with a bird, usually a species of PETREL (q.v.). The birds are allowed to breed there; but no other Tuatara is allowed to enter the burrow. It remains at home through the day, coming out after dark to hunt for its food, of small vertebrates, insects, and whatever it can pick up on the sea-shore.

It is of particular interest to scientists as being the most primitive of all living reptiles: it is the sole survivor to-day of an order—the Rhynchocephalia—that was once spread widely over Europe. At the beginning of the last century, the Tuatara was common on the main islands of New Zealand; but with the advance of the white man it has vanished, and is now found only in some of the islets in the Bay of Plenty, where it is preserved by Government order.

TUI, *see* HONEY-EATERS.

TUNNY, *see* MACKEREL.

TURBOT, *see* FLAT-FISHES.

TURKEYS. These birds, originally natives of North and central America, form a small group of the order of Game Birds. The Aztecs of Mexico had domesticated Turkeys long before the arrival of the Europeans, who introduced them into Europe after the Spanish conquest of Mexico, about 1500, and into England at least as early as 1541. The Turkey soon became a favourite table-bird, quite displacing the PEACOCK (q.v.). Mexican and North American species are still to be found wild in the eastern states of North America, from Mexico to Canada. It was found there by the 17th-century pioneers to North America, and has since then been the traditional dish for the American feast of Thanksgiving Day. How the name 'Turkey' originated is uncertain: perhaps the bird, being introduced to Britain from southern Europe, was thought to have come from Turkey. Turkeys of central America are resplendent birds, with plumage of green, bronze, blue, and gold, and 'eyes' on the tail-feathers like those of peacocks; but are too delicate to be domesticated. Cock Turkeys perform elaborate dances, with spreading of the tail and fluffing of the plumage, as part of their courtship display in the spring (*see* ANIMAL LANGUAGE). The Mexican Indians, thinking that the Turkeys danced to bring rain to the dried-up country, invented a 'turkey dance' themselves, which they performed as part of the magic to bring rain.

See also Vol. VI: TURKEYS.

TURTLES AND TORTOISES. 1. These creatures belong to the Order Chelonia or Testudines (Latin, *testudo*, a tortoise), which includes all the shelled reptiles, such as the Marine Turtles, the Mud or Soft-shelled Turtles, the Land Tortoises, the Freshwater Tortoises, the Terrapins, and the Side-neck Tortoises. The Chelonians differ from all other reptiles in having a more or less developed bony shell enclosing all the organs of the body, and into which the head and limbs can be withdrawn. Classification is based partly on the method of withdrawing the head, which can be done either by bending the neck vertically in an S-shaped curve, or by bending it sideways.

The shell can be divided into two parts, the upper being called the 'carapace', and the lower the 'plastron'. The two meet along the side of the body (the junction being called the 'bridge'), leaving a large aperture in front and behind for the passage of the head and limbs. The ribs and vertebrae of the back are solidly joined to the carapace, with the result that the upper bones of the limbs lie inside the ribs, instead of outside them, as in all other animals. In most species the bony shell is covered with horny plates. None of the Chelonians has teeth, the jaws being furnished with horny cutting margins. They lay rounded or oval white eggs: in the Marine Turtles these have a parchment-like covering; in all the others, there is a hard, chalky shell.

2. TURTLE. The name covers two very distinct groups—the Marine Turtles, which inhabit the oceans, and the Mud or Soft-shelled Turtles, which live entirely in fresh water.

The Marine Turtles can be recognized by their broad, paddle-shaped limbs, often furnished with claws, but without distinct digits, the fore-limb always being longer than the hind. They live entirely in the sea. There are five species, four belonging to one family, the Cheloniidae, while the fifth, the Leathery Turtle, which differs widely in structure from the others, forms a sub-order by itself.

The members of the Cheloniidae are the Green Turtle, the Hawksbill Turtle, the Loggerhead, and Kemp's Turtle, the latter a rare creature found only off the east coast of North America. The Green or Edible Turtle gets its name from the green colour of its fat. Except in the form of soup, obtained by prolonged boiling, its flesh is not usually eaten by Europeans. From the horny shell of the carapace of the Hawksbill is obtained commercial tortoise-shell. The flesh is not usually eaten; but the eggs of both species, and also those of the Loggerhead, are eagerly sought after as food, and the collecting of them is a regular industry, often under Government control. The eggs, as big as golf-balls, are laid on sandy beaches in holes dug by the female. Usually several batches are laid, the Green Turtle and the Loggerhead laying between 300 and 500 each season, the Hawksbill not so many. They are sold in the native markets, but to European taste are flavourless and rather gritty in texture. The Green Turtle is a vegetarian, living largely on sea-grasses; the Hawksbill and the Loggerhead are mainly flesh-eating. The shell of the Hawksbill seldom exceeds 34 inches in length; that of the other two reaches 40 inches. The home of all three is in tropical waters; but they occasionally find their way to the coasts of England.

The Leathery Turtle (or Luth) is the largest of all the living Chelonians, reaching a length of between 6 and 7 feet and an estimated weight of 1,000 pounds. It is not edible. It differs from all other Chelonians in the construction of its bony shell, this being composed of small, interlocking plates, not connected with the backbone

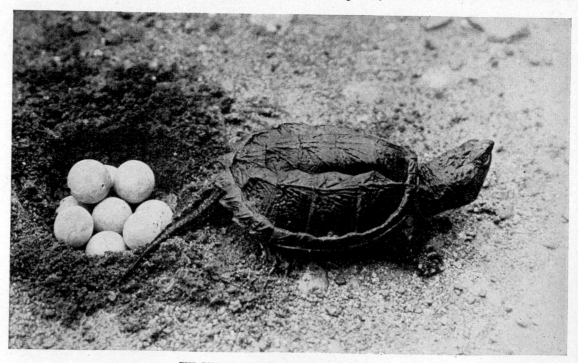

THE COMMON SNAPPER TERRAPIN OF THE U.S.A.
The Tortoise has just laid her eggs in a hole in the sand. She will cover them with sand, and then the hot sun will incubate them. *Dorien Leigh*

or ribs. It is generally found in tropical waters, but appears to be scarce everywhere, except on the coasts of Ceylon and southern India. It is an occasional visitor to English shores. It feeds mainly on shell-fish and marine plants; but, as it spends most of its life in the deep sea, very little is known of its habits. Like the other marine species it comes ashore to breed; but the young, once they are hatched and have escaped to the sea, are not seen again until they are ready to breed.

The Mud or Soft-shelled Turtles are so called because their bony shell is covered with skin instead of with horny plates. They live in slow-flowing rivers with muddy bottoms, and may be found also in lakes. The limbs are not flipper-shaped; but the toes are broadly webbed and are provided with sharp claws. The bones of the carapace and plastron are smaller than in other Chelonians, and there is no bridge holding them together. The snout is long and tubular in shape, with nostrils at the end which enable them to breathe in the water without exposing any other part of the body. The neck is long, and the head can be shot out and withdrawn with lightning-like rapidity. Most of the species are fierce in disposition and, when fully grown, are dangerous to handle.

Mud Turtles are found in many parts of Asia, Africa, and North America. They feed on fish, frogs, and molluscs, and are not particular whether their food is alive or dead. In captivity they will eat rice, bread, and other vegetable food. In many of the Indian and Indo-Chinese temples, they are kept in a semi-domesticated state, soon learning to come for food when called.

3. TORTOISE. The term tortoise is a useful name for all those Chelonians which cannot be included under the word turtle. It covers the Freshwater Tortoises, the Terrapins, the true Land Tortoises, the Side-neck Tortoises, and many others with more specific names, such as the Snappers, the Box Tortoises, the Painted, and the Musk Tortoises.

The name Terrapin covers all edible species (eight or ten) of Freshwater Tortoises inhabiting the U.S.A., the best known being the Snappers and the Diamond-back Terrapin. The Snappers, including two species, the Alligator Terrapin and the Common Snapper, have large heads, long tails, rugged shells, and fierce dispositions. When interfered with, they stand on the defensive with open mouths, looking as fierce as they can, and ready to bite anyone who tries to handle them. The Alligator Terrapin grows to a length of 15 inches, the Common Snapper not quite so long. They live in fresh water, and eat both animal and vegetable food. Another species of Terrapin common in the U.S.A. is the Painted Turtle, which has an almost black carapace, handsomely margined with yellow; the plastron is entirely yellow or marked with black or dark brown. The name Musk Tortoise is given to three species of Terrapin on account of the unpleasant odour which, on the slightest provocation, they give out from glands by the thighs. They are known also as Stinkpots.

Land Tortoises, as their name implies, live entirely on land—some in desert regions far from water. They are all vegetarians. The limbs are club-shaped, the digits compactly joined to one another and provided with sharp claws. The carapace in most species is deeply convex, and is united to the plastron by a solid bridge. The family, the Testudinidae, includes the Greek Tortoise from the Mediterranean, often seen in captivity in England, the Giant Tortoises of the Galapagos and Mascarene Islands, the Hinged Tortoises of South Africa, and the Gopher Tortoises of North America.

The long life of the Giant Tortoises is proverbial: it is beyond doubt that one of them has lived for at least 150 years; and it is said, though there is no authentic record, that they have reached 200 or 300 years of age. The Hinged Tortoises are so called because the hinder part of the carapace is joined to the front part by a hinge of gristle, enabling the creature, when the legs are withdrawn, to close that end of its house. A similar but much more perfect modification can be seen in the Box Tortoises.

Side-neck Tortoises are freshwater tortoises scientifically known as the Pleurodira. They are found only in the southern hemisphere, in Australia, South Africa, and South America; and, except for the marine turtles, they are the only turtles or tortoises in Australia and New Guinea The name Side-neck has been given to them because, when attempting to conceal the head under the shell, the neck is bent horizontally sideways, instead of in the more usual S-shaped curve. As most of the species have very long necks, the attempt is not very effective. There are also other characteristics in the skull, vertebrae, and shell, by which they differ from other Chelonians. Not many of the species have popular names. Some of those in Australia are called Snake-necked Tortoises, and perhaps the best known of all is the Mata-mata of South America. The largest member of the group is the Giant Amazon Tortoise, with a shell measuring 30 inches in length.

Box Tortoise is a general term given to certain species of Tortoise which can close their shells both in front and behind, so that the head and limbs are completely hidden—a very effective method of defence against their enemies. So perfect is the closure in some species, that the blade of a knife cannot be passed between the two portions of the shell. None of the Box Tortoises grow to more than 7 or 8 inches in length. Some are found in open woodland country; others spend most of their lives in rivers, lakes, and ponds. They are natives of the East and of North America.

See also REPTILES.
See also Vol. VI: TURTLE FISHING.

TUSSOCK MOTHS.

TUSSOCK MOTHS. Under this heading are grouped the members of the family Lymantriidae, which include the Tussocks themselves, the Vapourers, the Gypsy Moth, the Gold-tail, and the Black Arches. They are medium-sized brown, grey, or white moths with strongly combed antennae—especially in the males. Their mouth-parts are degenerate so that they cannot feed, and the females of some species are quite unable to fly, having only tiny undeveloped wings. Others have tufts of hair at the end of their bodies, which they utilize to cover their eggs. The caterpillars are always hairy, and some bear conspicuous tufts or brushes. They feed mainly on broad-leaved trees, some species being serious pests in Europe and America. Eleven species have been recorded in Britain; but now the Reed Tussock and Gypsy Moths are extinct, and the Black V-Moth a very scarce immigrant.

The common **Pale Tussock** is a drab, greyish moth, with darker cross-bands on the fore-wings; but its caterpillar is an exquisite shade of primrose-yellow, with whitish or greenish hairs, four thick brushes of yellow hairs on its back, and a larger, thin, reddish tuft at its tail. Between the brushes are velvety-black areas clearly displayed when the caterpillar, on being disturbed, rolls into a ring. This caterpillar is common in hop-fields, though it attacks the hops too late in the season to do much harm. The moths fly

in May and June. The Dark Tussock is chiefly a northern and Scottish species, but also occurs in Dorset and Kent.

The male Vapourer, a small, foxy-brown moth, with a white spot on each fore-wing, is frequently seen in towns, flying in the sunshine during July and August. When the grey, almost wingless female emerges, she lays her batch of eggs on her empty cocoon, which is attached to a twig, or some such support. The caterpillars, which hatch in the spring, are brightly coloured smoky-blue, dotted with red, and have four thick brushes of yellow hair on the back, a pair of fine pencils of black feather-like hairs in front, and a dark-grey or brownish tuft behind. They feed upon a variety of trees and bushes, and sometimes swarm in London parks. The Scarce Vapourer, which is very local, has more white on the wings of the male, but is otherwise like the Vapourer in appearance and habits.

The pure-white Brown-tail is a coastal species occurring in Kent and Sussex. The female lays her eggs on various trees in clusters of 200–400, and covers them with hairs from her tail. The young larvae make a tent by drawing together several leaves with silk, and there they hibernate. In the spring they quit the old shelters, constructing new ones, and feeding on buds and young leaves, sometimes completely stripping the trees. The full-grown caterpillar is blackish-brown, with an interrupted white line on each side, and two vermilion spots near the hind end. Its hairs are barbed and hollow, and contain a poisonous substance which causes an irritating rash on the human skin. In badly infested areas

CATERPILLAR OF PALE TUSSOCK MOTH
S. Beaufoy, F.R.P.S.

PALE TUSSOCK MOTH
S. Beaufoy, F.R.P.S.

introduced into Massachusetts, U.S.A., in the 19th century in an attempt to cross them with the Silkworm Moth; but some escaped and spread so fast that in 20 years they were a serious nuisance over 350 square miles. The steps taken to exterminate them were not persistent enough, and by 1905 they were defoliating trees over 2,200 square miles. It has cost millions of dollars to get the pest under control, and constant vigilance is still necessary, as the young larvae are very buoyant and easily carried by the wind, as well as being transported by man.

Both sexes of the common Gold-tail are silky-white. The female measures nearly $1\frac{3}{4}$ inches across, the male slightly less, but has one or two black spots near the hind margins of the fore-wings. The Gold-tail caterpillar is black, with a red stripe down the back and white tufts at the side. It hatches in August, hibernates, and in the spring is a familiar sight on hawthorn, fruit-trees, and roses. It pupates in a cocoon made of silk and barbed hairs from the caterpillar's body. When the female emerges in June or July she sweeps up many of these hairs with her golden tail, and then, when she lays her eggs, the hairs, as well as part of her own tail-tuft, stick to the eggs and serve to protect them. Both male and female Gold-tail raise their golden tails when disturbed.

The black and white caterpillars of the White Satin Moth hibernate, and in the spring feed on poplar, sallow, and willows, becoming full grown in June or July. The moth, which measures about 2 inches across, has also been introduced into the United States, where it is now a pest.

The Black Arches or Nun Moth, ranging from $1\frac{1}{2}$ inches across in the male to 2 inches in the female, has white fore-wings with zigzag black markings, greyish hind wings, and an abdomen tinged with pink. The eggs are laid on the bark of trees such as spruce, pine, oak, and apple, and the vari-coloured caterpillars hatch in the spring. Though widely distributed in Britain it has never become a serious pest; but the spruce plantations of central Europe are periodically defoliated.

The caterpillars of another member of the family, the Mexican Silk Moth, construct nests of silk which the natives spin into cloth (*see* SILK MOTHS).

the poisoned hairs are sometimes carried by the wind and may lodge in clothing. Brown-tails are spread over most of Europe. Some 50 or 60 years ago they were introduced into the eastern United States, where they caused much damage to fruit and oak-trees. They became such a menace that action had to be taken to reduce them—the most successful method being the destruction of the winter webs in which the larvae hibernate.

The female Gypsy Moth, measuring $2\frac{3}{8}$ inches across, has creamy wings marked with black. Her body is so large that she cannot fly, and she usually lays her eggs in July in a cluster near the cocoon from which she has emerged, covering them with brownish down from her tail. The smaller, brown male is a strong flier. The Gypsy Moth is common on the Continent, even in Paris, where its hairy caterpillars, which are brown, with blue and red warts arranged in two rows down the back, feed from May to July on the plane trees of the boulevards. They were

U V

UMBRELLA BIRD, *see* CHATTERER.

UNDERGROUND STEMS, *see* STEMS, Section 2.

UNDERWING MOTH, *see* NIGHT-FLYING MOTH.

VANESSINAE (Butterflies). These form a sub-family of the Nymphalidae, to which family also belong the FRITILLARIES, PURPLE EMPEROR, and WHITE ADMIRAL (qq.v.). The Vanessinae include some of the most gaily coloured butter-flies seen in the British Isles, the Peacock, Comma, and Tortoiseshells being permanent residents, while the Camberwell Beauty, Painted Lady, and Red Admiral are immigrants. The caterpillars are shiny, and often live in colonies until nearly full grown. The pupae, which hang by their tails, usually bear gold or silver spots —because of which the name 'chrysalis', meaning 'golden', came to be used for the pupae of all butterflies.

The Red Admiral is a gay, black and red im-migrant from North Africa and the Mediter-ranean coasts. The female lays only a few eggs, one at a time on each patch of nettles visited. The caterpillar folds the nettle-leaves over in a flap and secures them with fine threads of silk. When ready to pupate, it fastens itself by a silk pad to the top of a little 'tent' of folded leaves, within which it turns into a chrysalis. The butterflies emerge in late July, and compete with other Vanessinae for the best positions on the buddleia bushes and, a little later, on Michaelmas daisies. In autumn they are often seen feeding from rotting fruit in orchards, or from sap exuding from trees. They then attempt to hibernate, but few survive the winter; and the species would soon become extinct in Britain, but for the arrival of further migrants.

The strongly flying, pink and brown Painted Lady is the most cosmopolitan of all butterflies, and has been seen in most parts of the world where butterflies can live. It breeds continuously along the Mediterranean coast, and periodically migrates—though what causes these large-scale movements is unknown. Most years a few are seen in southern England, two or three influxes occurring during the summer; though some-times they appear in large numbers. On arrival, the females lay their eggs on thistles, nettles, or burdock leaves. The caterpillars are spiny, with streaks of lemon-yellow on their greyish skins. They feed singly, and are often found on thistles, each one lying along the mid-rib of the leaf, covered by a few threads of silk hooked on to the prickles. They crawl away from the plant to pupate, and hang up amongst thick undergrowth. The pupa is ash-grey and studded with golden

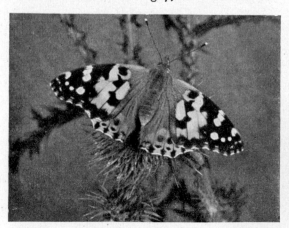

PAINTED LADY BUTTERFLY
S. Beaufoy, F.R.P.S.

CAMBERWELL BEAUTY BUTTERFLY
S. Beaufoy, F.R.P.S.

dots, which sparkle in the sunshine. The butter-flies fly in the evening long after most butterflies have settled down. They do not survive the winter.

The rich reddish-brown Small Tortoiseshell is one of the commonest hibernating butterflies in the British Isles, its dark underside being well adapted for concealment. It often spends the winter in houses, sleeping in a corner, behind a picture, or in the fold of a curtain; but on sunny winter days it may become active, and is some-times found fluttering in a window. If the butter-fly is allowed to fly out into the cold it will almost certainly die, for it does not normally leave its winter quarters until March. The females lay their eggs in large batches on the undersides of stinging-nettle leaves, several genera-tions appearing throughout the summer. On hatching, the tiny black caterpillars spin a web between the stems, and live together until they reach the last skin—when they are over an inch long, and have changed to greenish-grey with yellowish stripes along their back and sides. They then wander away and bask in the sun-shine in groups of two or three. They wander still farther to pupate, the chrysalis being dirty brown, ornamented with gilt points (*see* pictures, p. 63).

The Large Tortoiseshell is more nearly related to the Peacock and Camberwell Beauty than to the Small Tortoiseshell. Once common in most southern counties of Britain, it became increas-ingly scarce in the early part of this century. Recently, however, it has been seen in some numbers in Essex, Suffolk, and Norfolk. The females lay their eggs in batches round the twigs of elm trees or the stems of sallow bushes, and the caterpillars usually feed in large colonies on the upper branches. They frequently drop to the ground when ready to pupate, and then wander in search of a suitable site. Large num-bers of pupae have been found hanging in rows under the eaves of sheds or woodland cottages.

The Peacock is easily recognized by the four large 'peacock eyes' on its brilliant plum-red wings, and by its black undersides. The cater-pillars, which have inky black, spiny bodies, feed only on stinging-nettles, and live in large colonies in a common web. In the autumn, the butterflies haunt buddleia bushes, feasting on the rich nectar before retiring into hibernation in late September. Although sometimes found in-doors, Peacocks usually spend the winter in old

PEACOCK BUTTERFLY
S. Beaufoy, F.R.P.S.

barns, outhouses, hollow trees, or rabbit burrows, where they remain until the first warm days of spring. Peacocks have recently been found in many parts of Scotland, where they have long been absent.

The Camberwell Beauty is most often seen along the east coast of England, to which it occa-sionally migrates in the autumn from Scandi-navia. It has never been known to breed here, for only a scattered few succeed in surviving the winter. The butterfly, which is dark purple with a yellow edge to its wings, is called in Scandinavia the Mourning Cloak butterfly. The females lay their eggs on sallow bushes. The spiny black caterpillars are curiously marked with eight large, round, red patches on the back. In Scandinavia the butterflies hibernate among stacked pine-logs.

The Comma is so called because of the little white marks, like commas, on the underside of each orange-brown hind-wing. No other British butterfly has such ragged wings, which make

Commas resemble the dead leaves, among which they usually hibernate. In the spring they may be seen feeding from sallow catkins. The females lay eggs on a variety of plants, including elm, red currant, hops, and stinging nettles. The caterpillars are the brightest of British Vanessine larvae, being patterned in reddish-brown on the back for the first five segments, then in white to the tail. The butterflies mate after hibernation, some of the first brood of caterpillars producing butterflies in early summer. These early summer offspring are more tawny and less ragged than the late summer ones. They pair immediately and produce a second brood in September. During the 19th century the Comma declined, and became extinct in most districts, though it still survived in Hereford and neighbouring counties. Recently, however, it has increased again, and now even reaches into Scotland.

See also BUTTERFLIES; HIBERNATION.

VAPOURER MOTH, *see* TUSSOCK MOTHS.

VENUS'S FLY-TRAP, *see* INSECTIVOROUS PLANTS, Section 5.

VIPERS. 1. These poisonous snakes of the family Viperidae are distinguished from other poisonous snakes by having the poison-fangs attached to a moveable bone, the 'maxillary'. When not in use, the fang lies backwards in the mouth in a horizontal position. The vipers are divided into two sub-families: the true Vipers and the Pit Vipers—so called because they have a pit in the side of the face between the eye and the nostril. To the Pit Vipers belong the Rattlesnake of America and a large genus inhabiting south-west Asia and South America.

The typical viperine head, bluntly triangular and mounted upon a narrow neck, is fairly distinctive of the whole group; but it is found on many other snakes besides vipers, some quite harmless. Snakes of the Viper family are mostly thick-bodied, with shortish tails, slow in their movements, and when molested they will often stand their ground rather than retreat. The bite of many of them, particularly the larger species, is often fatal to man; the bite of others results in pain and swelling round the bitten place, but will not cause death.

2. TRUE VIPERS. The only British Viper is the ADDER (q.v.); but there are other kinds in

GABOON VIPER

southern Europe. Most vipers are to be found in the warmer parts of the world. Among these are many so-called Horned Vipers, which have extensions of the scales projecting from the head or snout. The Egyptian Horned Viper, like the African Egg-eater and the Saw-scaled Viper of India, has the scales on the side of the body placed obliquely and roughened like the teeth of a saw. By throwing the body into folds and rubbing these scales against one another, the snake can produce a hissing sound. The Saw-scaled Viper is very common in some of the dry areas of north-west India, and causes many deaths each year by its bite. In an attempt by the Government at the end of the last century to reduce the numbers of this deadly snake, nearly a quarter of a million were killed annually for several years, but without any apparent effect upon their numbers. On one occasion, when the reward was raised from 6 pies to 2 annas a head, 116,000 specimens were brought into Government offices in 8 days.

Largest of all the African Vipers is the gorgeously marked Gaboon Viper, which grows to a length of 5 feet, and bears the longest fangs—well over an inch—of any snake known. In spite of these, it is said to be quiet, and will even allow itself to be picked up without attempting to bite. The Night Adder of South Africa is remarkable in that the poison gland, instead of being at the back of the head as in most snakes, is in the forepart of the body. A long duct connects it with the fang. The Puff-adder of Africa has a thick body, and may reach 5 feet in length.

3. THE PIT VIPERS include a number of well-known species. One of the largest of these is the Fer-de-Lance of central America, which has a body as thick as a man's arm and is up to 7 feet in length. It is sluggish, and will strike rather than try to escape, its bite being said to be very deadly. Another species, much feared by the natives of the Amazon forests, is the red, brown, and black Jaracara. The Bush-master, which may reach 12 feet in length, lives in thick forest in tropical South America, and is reddish-yellow above, with a longitudinal series of large brown spots, each of which contains two light spots.

The Water Moccasin of North America has the unusual habit among Vipers of spending much of its time in the water. The Bamboo Snake of India, another Pit Viper, often seen in bamboo clumps in gardens, is green with a yellowish tinge; but, though its bite may be painful, it is not dangerous to man. Among the best known of the Pit Vipers is the Rattlesnake, some twenty-five species of which are known, inhabiting central and North America, especially the U.S.A. Rattlesnakes are so called because their tails end in a series of horny, interlocking segments—the rattle—which, when vibrated rapidly, produce a dull, hissing sound. The number of segments varies greatly, because the end ones are continually getting damaged and dropping off. Six to ten is a common number; more than fifteen is rare. A new segment is added every time the skin is cast—or, more precisely, a new one is revealed—for fresh segments are being continually formed at the base of the rattle, but are not exposed until the skin is cast. As a group, Rattlesnakes are heavy-bodied reptiles, slow in their movements, and, when menaced, often prepared to stand their ground rather than retreat. Their fangs are very large, and the larger species can inject a powerful dose of venom. In the northern part of the U.S.A., where the weather is cold enough for them to hibernate, they often congregate in hundreds, and, coiled together in masses, spend the winter in sleep. They often return to the same place year after year, and have been known to travel many miles to reach it.

Many theories have been put forward to explain the function of the rattle; but the answer really is that we do not know. That it acts as a warning to creatures near is generally recognized; that it was originally designed for that purpose is not so easy to believe. The habit of vibrating the tip of the tail when alarmed is common to many other snakes, both poisonous and non-poisonous; but having no rattle, they do not make a noise. Moreover, if, as we now believe, snakes have little power of hearing, the Rattlesnake cannot even be aware of the sound it is making.

See also SNAKE.

VIRUS. Very little is yet understood about viruses. By the end of the 19th century, it was known that certain diseases, such as measles and mumps, yellow fever, small-pox, foot-and-mouth disease, and the common cold, were caused by some substances too small to be seen by the strongest microscope. These substances appear to be on the border between living and non-living matter. Like living BACTERIA (q.v.), they appear to be able to absorb other substances, to grow, and to reproduce themselves. Yet they seem not to have a cellular structure, as have the simplest living organisms, and appear to be able to crystallize like a chemical compound. In recent years, the largest viruses have been seen with an ELECTRON MICROSCOPE (q.v. Vol. VIII). It seems likely, therefore, that more will soon be known about them.

See also Vol. XI: VIRUS DISEASES.

VOLE. This rodent is related to the MOUSE (q.v.); but it has a short tail, small eyes and ears, and a blunter head. Its teeth are also different, being typically herbivorous—that is, adapted to bite the toughest fibres and grasses on which voles feed, rather than the seeds and softer vegetable foods eaten by mice. The word 'vole', a Norse word meaning 'field', was first used for all field mice; but it is now strictly used for mice with herbivorous teeth. There are many different species of voles, including the Musk Rat and Lemming, in Europe, North America, and northern Asia, three, the Bank Vole, the Field Vole, and the Water Vole, being common in Britain.

Bank Voles are the most like mice. They are very active, and can climb nimbly, swim, and jump out of a box over 9 inches in depth. Though they are mainly nocturnal, they come out into the sunlight, especially in spring; and though they spend most of the winter in their burrows, they do not hibernate. They particularly like to live in ivy-clad banks, where they dig shallow burrows under the ivy or exposed roots of bushes. They often use mole-runs, sharing them with mice, shrews, and even rats. The Bank Voles drill smaller burrows leading from the mole-runs

Rattle enlarged

DIAMOND RATTLESNAKE

BANK VOLES
A. R. Thompson

into sleeping-rooms and stores, which they line with chewed grass. They are quarrelsome animals, and will kill and eat the less bold Field Vole; but they do not defend their young. The female has from two to four litters of from four to eight young a year.

Field Voles or Short-tailed Voles live in rough grassland and moorland. They are much less active than the other voles, neither jumping nor climbing. They make a burrow in the ground, at the bottom of which they construct the nest, and store tight balls of grass for winter food. Normally, they have about the same number of litters and young as the Bank Vole; but in certain years, generally following mild winters, they reproduce at an abnormal rate. In these years the 'vole plagues', as they are called, are responsible for the devastation of large areas, especially on the Continent. In one district in Germany, for instance, two million Field Voles were destroyed during one of these plagues.

Water Voles (often mistakenly called Water Rats) are not unlike Brown Rats, but their muzzles are blunter. They live by sluggish rivers and dykes, and make long, rambling burrows in the banks. They are almost entirely vegetarian, feeding on water-plants. They usually dive with a loud plop to avoid the pursuit of some of their enemies, and rise to the surface of the water under cover of leaves brought from the bottom.

Musk Rats or Musquashes of North America are as much as 11 inches long, with long, scaly tails, which they use as rudders when swimming. They dig their burrows in banks, hiding the entrance beneath the surface of the water. The tunnel turns upwards until it reaches above high-water level, where a large chamber is hollowed out. Here the Musk Rat lives and rears his family during the summer. With the approach of cold weather, he begins to build a winter home. This is a large, dome-shaped structure of mud, sticks, and reeds, resting on the bottom of a shallow pond or swamp, and rising several feet above the surface. In some winters dozens of these houses are to be seen; but in others there are few or none—for the Musk Rats seem to know if there is going to be a severe or mild winter, and make their plans accordingly. Some years ago Musk Rats were imported to a fur farm in Britain. A certain number escaped and became wild, causing considerable destruction to river embankments. A law now orders their destruction wherever they are found, and forbids any further importation.

The Lemmings of the mountains of Scandinavia are also voles. They are about 5 inches long, with soft, yellow-brown coats marked with dark-brown spots. They select dry places for their burrows, and during the day sit quietly in or near the entrance. If a human being appears, they become very excited, sitting up on their hindquarters and making ready to attack—and, indeed, they have been known to bite the legs of intruders coming too close to their holes. They eat grass, reindeer moss, birch catkins, and roots, and build nests of dry grass lined with hair, in which litters of five or six young are born. Lemmings are best known for their remarkable 'migrations'. Periodically they, like Field Voles, increase enormously in numbers; and, following such a period, they set off in huge numbers across the country, finally reaching the sea and drowning (see MIGRATION). Why they do this no one knows—but presumably scarcity of food is the basic reason.

VULTURE. This large Bird of Prey is closely related to the EAGLE and HAWK (qq.v.), but differs from them in having a more or less bare head and neck, blunter claws, and the habit of feeding upon the carcasses of dead animals. True Vultures are restricted to the warmer regions of the Old World. American Vultures, the largest of which is the enormous CONDOR (q.v.), belong to a different family, although their habits are much alike.

The best-known Vulture is the Griffon Vulture, which is found in the greater part of Africa and Asia, as well as in eastern and southern Europe. This large, brown bird, with a ruff of white feathers round the lower part of the neck, is $3\frac{1}{2}$ feet or more in length, with enormous, powerful wings. The Griffon Vulture finds its food by the aid of its keen sight. It circles high up in the air, scanning the ground

LAMMERGEYER VULTURE
Zoological Society of London

below over a wide area. When it sees a carcass, it begins a rapid, plunging descent, which is observed by other vultures at a distance. Soon a number of these great birds are gathered round the carcass, gorging their fill. They can go for long periods without food, but on making a good find they will stuff themselves until they cannot fly—and, indeed, can hardly stand. Griffon Vultures build very large nests of sticks and grass on an overhanging ledge of a cliff, several nests often being placed close together They lay one greyish-white egg. The young bird often stays in the nest until it is 3 or 4 months old, growing extremely fat on the food brought by its parents.

Among other true Vultures is the Black Vulture, to be found in Mediterranean countries and eastwards to India and China. Unlike the Griffon, the Black Vulture prefers wooded country, and usually nests in trees. This repulsive and ungraceful-looking bird serves a very useful purpose as a scavenger in hot countries where, without its services, disease might arise from putrefying carcasses. The white Scavenger Vulture of Egypt, a smaller bird, little more than

VULTURES ASSEMBLING TO GORGE ON A CARCASS ON THE PLAINS OF INDIA
Paul Popper

2 feet long, inhabits the Mediterranean countries and western Asia, and has occasionally wandered as far north as the British Isles.

The huge Lammergeyer or Bearded Vulture, found from southern Spain to China, seems to form a link between the true Vultures and the Eagles. Its habits are those of Vultures, but it is more eagle-like in appearance. It dwells in mountainous regions, building its huge nest of sticks on a rock ledge. It appears to be very fond of bones, which it cracks by dropping them on rocks from great heights. It also eats tortoises, breaking their shells in the same way. It is now becoming very scarce.

W

WADING BIRDS. 1. Plovers and plover-like birds form the order of Wading Birds, almost all of which belong to one family and have many characteristics in common. They include the Plovers; the long-legged Stilts and Avocets; the Curlews; the Sandpipers, Redshanks, Greenshanks, Dunlins, Godwits, and Phalaropes; the Snipe and Woodcocks; and the Oyster-catchers. Some waders belong almost entirely to warmer countries—the Pratincole, for instance, inhabits the Mediterranean countries and parts of Asia, and the beautiful Sun Bittern inhabits tropical America.

All these birds are migratory to a greater or lesser extent. Some only migrate from their inland breeding-quarters to spend the winter on the coasts; others migrate from their summer quarters in the tundra lands of arctic Europe and Asia to winter in tropical Africa. Many species which breed in Britain have their numbers greatly increased in the winter by flocks migrating from farther north (*see* MIGRATION). During the winter, therefore, members of this family are to be found in almost all parts of the world. Long legs, suitable for wading in the watery land where they generally live, and long, thin bills, suitable for probing in the sand or mud for food, are their characteristics. Most species prefer open marshy or boggy moorland, some live on the banks of rivers or lakes, and others on river estuaries or low sandy coasts. Almost all nest on the ground, generally making very little in the way of a nest, and laying four eggs, pear-shaped and with reddish-brown markings on an olive-greenish or buff background—an excellent protective coloration for moorland country. Most wading birds also are themselves equipped with a speckled plumage of reds, greys, and whites, which makes them able to depend on CAMOUFLAGE (q.v.) as their principal protection from enemies. All waders can walk and run with great ease, the chicks being able to run from the time they are hatched. The chicks are hatched with a good covering of down, and also with very effective protective coloration.

Most wading birds have a characteristic cry, generally a clear, wild, often melancholy note. The Curlew's plaintive 'Cur-lew' reaches far over the moors. The Redshank, a noisy bird, keeps up a continuous 'Too-oo-ee'. The Common Sandpiper calls 'Wheet, wheet, wheet'. The Golden Plover makes a clear 'Tlu-ee', and the 'Pee-wit' of the Lapwing is well known. The Oyster-catcher makes a shrill 'Kleep-kleep', which changes to 'Pic-pic' when the bird is alarmed. Most waders are noisy in their courtship, the male having a piping, trilling nuptial song. During the courtship season, the males have a variety of display habits. The Lapwing

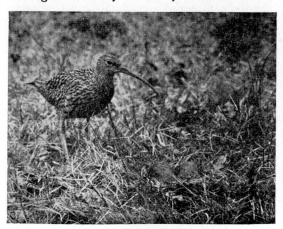

THE CURLEW OF MARSH AND MOORLAND
Arthur Brook

THE GREENSHANK WITH ITS NEST IN THE HEATHER
Arthur Brook

makes a series of bowings and short erratic flights, and also fight each other. The Redshank and the Curlew raise their wings before the female, and then, half lowering them, beat time with rapid quivers. Then they hover in the air, uttering a bubbling song. The Woodcock makes a slow flight with plumage fluffed out, uttering at the same time a deep, repeated croak, varied by a shrill screech. In the spring the Ruff grows ear-tufts and a remarkable ruff of feathers around the neck, the colour of this courtship adornment varying considerably from bird to bird. The Ruff spreads out his gay plumage before the female, the Reeve, and runs round with quick steps, or spars with a rival. In contrast to other members of the family, the Ruff is often polygamous, there being generally more Reeves than Ruffs. The female of the little Red-necked Phalarope is larger and more brightly coloured than the male, and it is noteworthy that the roles of the sexes are partly reversed, the female taking the more active part in the courting, even fighting other females, and keeping guard over the nest while the male does the incubating.

2. The CURLEWS, the largest of the family, vary from 21 to 26 inches in length. They are marsh and moorland birds, keeping away from cultivation. In winter, they can be seen flying in a V formation from the moors to sandy coasts. Great numbers of them migrate from Arctic Europe to winter in northern Britain. They are graceful birds with very long, slender, turned-down bills, which they use to probe for insects and worms in the sand or soft soil. The Whimbrel is a smaller Curlew, which breeds to some extent in the Outer Hebrides, Orkneys, and Shetland Isles.

3. The SANDPIPERS, smaller, gracefully built birds with long, slender bills, form a very large group of the waders. The Common Sandpiper is a lively, restless little bird, which lives on banks of rivers or lakes, or on river estuaries. It continually bobs its head and jerks its tail, and makes frequent flights across the river. It is a very common bird in Scotland. The Redshanks and Greenshanks, found on coastal marshes and lakes, are larger relatives, distinguished by their long red or green legs. The little Dunlins are among the commonest of all birds of the sea-shore, where they probe for worms in the wet sand or mud. They breed on high moors farther north. Like many members of this group, such

THE OYSTER-CATCHER OF THE SEASHORE
Arthur Brook

as the Sanderling, Knot, and Godwit, the Dunlin has a marked change of plumage between summer and winter, being much paler in the winter.

4. SNIPE and WOODCOCK are both valued as table birds. Snipe are difficult to hit, for when 'flushed' (roused to flight), they make a very swift, corkscrew zigzag for some 50 yards before flying straight. In the nesting season, cock snipe sometimes make wide, circular flights ending in a sudden descent, with wings half-closed and tail spread out. During the descent, the vibration of the stiff outer tail-feathers makes a curious noise known as 'drumming', somewhat like the bleating of a goat. Snipe are common on boggy moors in Scotland and north Britain, but less often seen in the south. Woodcock are heavier, larger birds, with shorter legs. They live in open woodlands, where some are resident, and to which others migrate in large flights for the winter. They are nocturnal birds, feeding in marshes and ditches at night, and sleeping among low trees by day. A Woodcock is known to be able to carry a chick, held between its thigh and body, when it is flying.

5. PLOVERS have shorter, stouter bills than other members of the family. Golden Plovers mostly spend the summer in the tundra lands of northern Europe and Asia, often wintering in Britain or passing on their way farther south; but one species is a resident of Britain, chiefly in the north. Like other waders, they are quick runners, and can be seen running sideways or backwards on the look-out for enemies. The little Ringed Plover is a very common shore-bird, and associates with the Dunlin and other waders. The Lapwing, Peewit, or Green Plover is common throughout Great Britain. It is a handsome bird, carrying a long, turned-up crest on the back of its head. The female uses many tricks, as do other waders, to distract enemies from her nest. She runs some distance before rising, and then sometimes feigns an injured leg or wing.

6. The OYSTER-CATCHER, a rather stouter, shorter-legged bird with a long, thickish bill, is black and white, with dull red legs. It inhabits shingly river-banks or seashores, feeding on shell-fish, sea-worms, and shrimps—but not, as one might expect, on oysters. Its main food is mussels, the shells of which it prises open with its beak. Oyster-catchers are very noisy birds, and in winter form small flocks, gathering on reefs and islets. The little red-legged Turnstone is an exclusively seashore bird, spending most of its time on the very edge of the waves, turning over stones in search of food.

7. The STILTS and AVOCETS are distinguished from other members of the family by their very long legs. Neither is resident in Britain, though one species of each is a very rare visitor. Both birds are essentially marsh-birds, often standing in water up to their knees on the look-out for food. When they fly, they stretch their necks out in front and trail their long thin legs behind.

WAGTAILS AND PIPITS. These birds have slender bodies, slender, insect-eating bills, and longish tails. Wagtails generally have longer legs and tails and brighter plumage than Pipits. They are distributed over most of the world, the majority belonging to Europe and Asia. Several species are resident in the British Isles, though most make at least short southward journeys in the autumn: the Grey Wagtail, for instance, rarely nests in the eastern or southern districts of England, though it may often be seen there in the winter. Some migrate long distances in flocks.

Wagtails are conspicuous for their characteristic run and flight. They walk or run, instead of hopping as do most birds, making a quick, sudden dash to catch an insect, and, when they

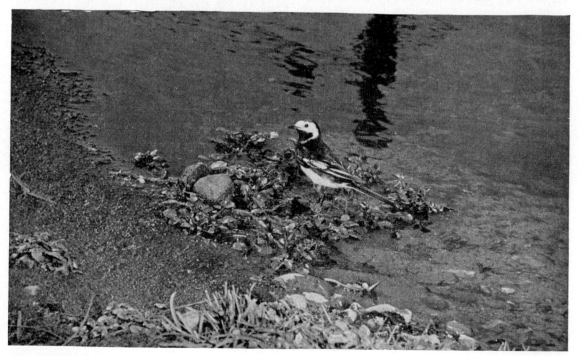

THE PIED OR WATER WAGTAIL
Eric J. Hosking, F.R.P.S.

stop, wagging their long tails up and down many times. Their flight is quick and erratic, with graceful dippings and risings in quick succession. They feed on insects and small aquatic animals—for most Wagtails like to live near water. They generally nest on or near the ground, in a hole in a bank or wall, among rocks, or in a hollow tree. Pied Wagtails sometimes nest in a thatched roof. The nest is made of grass and moss, lined with hair and feathers. Four to six eggs are laid, and two broods are often reared in a season.

The best-known Wagtails are the Pied or Water Wagtail, the Grey, and the Yellow Wagtail. The Pied Wagtail is the most common, frequenting not only rivers and pools, but gardens and farms. Its near relative, the White Wagtail, is well known on the Continent. The Grey Wagtail, with its blue-grey back, black throat, and yellow underparts, is essentially a water bird, frequenting rocky mountain streams, and uttering its short, pretty song from the tops of willow trees. In the summer, the cocks will attack fiercely any intruder on their territory. The Yellow Wagtail is a smaller, very graceful little bird, with brown-grey back and bright yellow throat and underparts. It is somewhat local in distribution, frequenting damp meadows rather than streams. Its close relation, the Blue-headed Wagtail, rarely visits Britain, but is found commonly in meadows and cornfields in most parts of Europe. Both these species nest in tussocks of dry grass. Another relative, the Yellow-headed Wagtail, belongs to Siberia and east Russia, and winters in India.

Pipits have predominantly brown and buffish-white plumage. They are not unlike LARKS (q.v.) in appearance and way of life. The Tree Pipits are not arboreal birds in spite of their name; but they often perch on high trees to sing. They also have the habit of rising from a tree into the sky about 40 feet, and then sailing down in spirals with tail spread and wings partly extended, singing as they come. In the late summer, they gather in flocks to feed in stubble-fields, and then migrate in flocks.

The Meadow Pipit, or Titlark, prefers moorland country, peat bogs, and rough, undrained meadows, and nests in holes in the grass or heather. Meadow Pipits have the same habit of singing on the wing as have Tree Pipits. The female, if disturbed when brooding, never rises straight from the nest, but runs some little distance through the grass first. Cuckoos very often lay their eggs in Pipits' nests (*see* pictures, p. 111). The Rock Pipit lives near rocky sea coasts, and nests among the rocks.

WAINSCOT MOTH, *see* NIGHT-FLYING MOTHS.

WALLABY, *see* KANGAROO.

WALRUS, *see* SEALS.

WAPATI, *see* DEER, SECTION 5.

WARBLERS. As their name indicates, these birds are noted for their fine song: in particular the Garden Warbler and the Blackcap have lovely, ringing, lively songs, thought by many people to be as fine as that of the THRUSH or NIGHTINGALE (qq.v.) to which they are closely related. Warblers are little birds with, for the most part, a sober brown or greenish plumage. The rare Dartford Warbler is exceptional in having a rufous breast. They are of slender build, with slender, insect-eating bills. They feed mainly on insects, which many of them catch on the wing, rather in the manner of

CHIFFCHAFF AT ITS NEST
Arthur Brook

Flycatchers. Since an insect diet is not available in northern countries, such as Britain, in the winter, almost all Warblers migrate southwards. Species of Warblers are to be found over most of the world, though there are very few in the Americas. The family includes the White-throats, Chiffchaffs, Blackcaps, Wood Wrens, and GOLDCRESTS (q.v.). Some of them, especially the Whitethroat and Willow Warbler, are among the commonest of British birds.

The Whitethroat, rather larger than many of the family, can be heard from mid or late April till early September singing its hurried, lively song, and can be seen making its quick, jerky movements and short flights in gardens, orchards, and any rough ground covered with rank vegetation. It nests for preference in a bank of thick nettles, but low bushes or brambles will serve instead. It shares a habit with other members of the family of feigning lameness to distract attention from its nest or fledgelings. The Lesser Whitethroat, a rather smaller bird, is much less common.

The Blackcap and Garden Warbler are much alike in habits, though the Blackcap is the earlier to arrive in the spring. They frequent woods, orchards, and rough common land—being no commoner in gardens than any other Warbler. The male Blackcap, in particular, is a pugnacious bird, and protects his own territory fiercely, especially against the intrusions of the Garden Warbler. Both are shy birds, and will stop singing if disturbed.

The very common, yellowish-green Willow Warbler is to be found in most localities in Britain—even in London parks—and has no particular connexion with willows. The Chiff-chaff is common also, and is to be heard singing its little song, 'chiff-chaff', all day long from the tree-tops. Another lover of trees is the Wood Warbler or Wood Wren, which delivers its song of a few clear notes with a hurried end from high up in tall oak or beech-trees. It nests on the ground, often among dead bracken.

The Sedge and the Reed Warblers are quite common near slow-flowing, reed-grown streams. The Sedge Warbler, as well as singing its own charming song, mimics the songs of other birds. It nests in dense, tangled vegetation. The Reed Warbler builds a deep cup of grass and moss, which it suspends between four reeds, where it sways with the wind. The Grasshopper Warbler has a curious 'reeling' cry, except for which it would be little noticed, because it takes cover quickly, hiding in the undergrowth.

WART HOG, *see* SWINE.

WASPS. 1. All Hymenoptera with stings, except BEES and ANTS (qq.v.), are included among the Wasps. An important thing to remember is that only the females sting.

Like bees, wasps may conveniently be divided into two groups, those which are social in habit and those which are solitary. The social wasps are those which live in an organized community, consisting of a queen and a large number of daughters, the workers, who are usually smaller than their mother. These tend the offspring of the queen, but produce none of their own. The solitary species, on the other hand, do not live in communities: a single female wasp builds a protected cell, places food in it, lays an egg on or near the food, and then takes no further interest in it. The vast majority of wasps are solitary in habit.

Adult wasps are very fond of sweet things, and visit certain flowers in search of nectar. The spring-flowering Cotoneasters attract large numbers of queen wasps, and later in the season the flowers of Figwort and Snowberry attract their workers. But wasps, unlike bees, usually have short tongues, and can get nectar only from flowers with shallow corollas. In late summer, ripe fruit will attract large numbers of the social wasps. The larvae, however, must have animal food, and to get it the female wasps prey mostly upon other insects—though some hunt only spiders.

Social wasps use their sting only for defence, and rely on their powerful mandibles and strong legs for killing and overpowering their prey. The Common and German Wasps of this country may often be seen hawking amongst low vegetation in search of flies and caterpillars. They are clumsy hunters, striking at far more flies than they are ever able to seize and destroy. Once she has caught a fly, the wasp bites off its head, legs, and wings, and chews the body up into a pulpy mass, which she carries to her nest to divide among the hungry grubs. She swallows the more liquid part of the prey, and later regurgitates it from her stomach to feed the grubs. The solitary wasp, however, although she stings in defence, uses her sting chiefly for injecting into her prey a minute quantity of poison, which paralyses but does not kill her victim. She then carries or drags the helpless victim to her burrow, where it remains alive until the tiny wasp-grub hatches and begins to devour it.

2. SOLITARY WASPS: Solitary wasps are found all over the world, especially in the tropics, and there are many British kinds. Of these, one of the so-called Potter Wasps, *Eumenes coarctata*, is a small, black and yellow insect, with a long, slender waist. The female builds a little hollow mud cell, about the size of a pea, with a small hole in the side, and attaches it, if possible, to a twig of heather. Then she catches and paralyses some small caterpillars, which she stuffs into the cell. Finally, she lays an egg among them, and closes up the hole with mud. As soon as the tiny grub hatches, it begins to eat the caterpillars. When it is full grown, it turns to a pupa (chrysalis). The following summer, as an adult wasp, it gnaws its way through the hard wall of the cell, and flies away.

A very common British wasp, of which there are several kinds, is *Odynerus*. Most of them nest in holes in walls or in the deserted burrows of other insects, especially in wooden posts. They all collect caterpillars as food for their young.

The name 'Sand Wasp' is used rather loosely for a vast number of wasp-like insects which move extremely rapidly, enjoy very hot sunshine, and nest in sand or dry soil. The Spider-wasps, Pompilidae, are among the best known of the Sand Wasps. They move in a quick and jerky manner, darting swiftly over the ground in short spurts, and will not fly unless hard pressed. The females store their burrows with spiders. On a hot day, one of these little wasps may often be seen dragging along a big spider to her burrow. In some tropical countries, especially South America, the Spider-wasps are often very large, with a wing-expanse of 3 to 4 inches. These amazons of the insect world are able to attack some of the largest-known spiders and, because of their agility, are almost always victorious. The Sphegidae, another large group of Sand Wasps, select their prey from a great variety of insects, including flies, beetles, grasshoppers, caterpillars, and cockroaches, though any one species of wasp confines itself to one kind of prey. Whatever insect happens to be used, the wasp paralyses it with her sting before carrying it off to her burrow.

Some of the best-known Sand Wasps belong

SOLITARY WASP, *Cerceris*

to the genus *Cerceris*, mostly black and yellow insects with a preference for dry, sandy regions. So far as we know, nearly all the species attack weevil beetles, stinging them and carrying them off to their burrows. *Cerceris arenaria*, a British species, is found in July and August on the sandy commons of southern England. It makes vertical burrows, often in very hard ground, and stores its cells with weevils. Another British species, *Cerceris rybyensis*, uses the small bees known as *Halictus*—a good example of how the habits of closely related species of Sphegid wasps can differ.

One of the most interesting Sand Wasps is *Ammophila*. This is a large, black, slender-bodied insect, with a partly red abdomen separated from the rest of the body by a long, thin stalk or waist. These wasps build their cells in burrows in dry, sandy places, and stock them with caterpillars. Where a species uses only one caterpillar for each cell, its victim is so large that the wasp cannot fly with it, but must drag it over the ground, often as far as 250 feet, to her burrow. On her way home, she often leaves her prey for a moment to take a short flight to survey the ground, so that she may be able to continue her journey on foot in the right direction. When she reaches her burrow, she leaves her prey at the

Female *Ammophila* carrying paralysed caterpillar to her burrow

Left, Sand Wasp, *Mutilla europaea,* or velvet-ant
Right, The ant-like Wasp, *Methoca ichneumoinides*

entrance, disappears into the burrow for a final inspection, and then, reappearing, seizes the caterpillar in her long, sickle-shaped jaws, and slips backwards into the hole, dragging her victim after her. Having laid an egg on the caterpillar, she reappears, and with rapid movements of her front legs scrapes the surrounding sand to fill the mouth of the burrow. And now a remarkable performance takes place: the *Ammophila* finishes her job with a tool! She selects a small pebble or stone and uses it as a mallet to ram down the sand at the mouth of the burrow, until all trace of its exact position has been smoothed out.

Under this general term 'Sand Wasp' are included the elegant little insects known as Mutillidae. The females are, without exception, wingless; the males are fully winged, much larger, and unlike the females in shape and colour. The females are brightly coloured, their abdomen being sharply marked with spots and bands of dense white hair. They are said to sting fiercely. They usually lay their eggs in the cells of other solitary wasps or of solitary bees; but one African species lays its eggs in the pupae of the harmful TSETSE FLY (q.v.), which the grubs destroy. Only two species of Mutillidae occur in the British Isles, one of which, *Mutilla europaea,* lays its eggs in the nests of certain species of Bumble-bees.

The Methocidae, a small family of blackish wasps with wingless females, related to the Mutillidae, has particularly interesting habits. The single British species attacks the fearsome larva of the common Tiger-beetle in order to lay her eggs on the grub's body. This grub lives

in a burrow in the ground, the mouth of which it blocks with its flattened head and thorax. Any passing insect which crawls over the flattened head is immediately seized by the larva in its sickle-like jaws and dragged down into the burrow to be eaten. How then can the little wasp lay her egg on the body of this ferocious larva? She allows herself to be caught in the grip of the beetle grub's jaws, and then, at the moment when she is being held aloft, before being dragged down into the burrow, she drives her sting home between the legs of the larva, so that it sinks back paralysed into its burrow. After laying an egg on her victim, the wasp fills up the burrow with sand, and goes forth in search of another beetle larva. But things do not always turn out according to plan, and occasionally a wasp has been seriously mutilated by a Tiger-beetle larva.

3. SOCIAL WASPS (VESPIDAE): these include the common wasps of the British Isles. There are seven species in Great Britain, the largest, but by no means the most vicious, being the Hornet. Their life-history is very like that of the BUMBLE-BEES (q.v.), the main difference being that wasps need animal food, such as flies and caterpillars, and build a nest of wood-pulp or papier-mâché. After sleeping through the winter, hidden away among dry leaves or beneath loose bark, or even among the folds of a window curtain, in late spring the queens seek out places in which to build their nests. Some British wasps, such as the Tree Wasp, *Vespula sylvestris,* and the Hornet, *Vespa crabro,* nest in hollow trees; others build their nests in the open, on the branch of a tree, or in a bush. But the wasps which are such a nuisance in late summer, such as the Common Wasp, *Vespula vulgaris,* are nearly always underground builders.

The wasps' building material consists of wood fibres scraped by their powerful mandibles from

Queen wasp hibernating under piece of bark

A. NEST OF TREE WASP. B. CROSS-SECTION OF TREE WASP NEST

wooden objects, such as posts. The fibres are mixed with saliva and worked to a pulp, which is then applied by a worker to the rim of a cell, and drawn out between the two edges of the wasp's mandibles to form a thin strip of paper, like a ribbon. The queen wasp builds a tiny nest in a suitable hollow under the ground—a beautifully made and fragile piece of work, about the size of a golf-ball. The Common Wasp uses soft decayed wood for her nest. This has two or three outer covers, which give it its familiar spherical shape, and a tiny comb, securely fastened by a short central stalk of hardened wood-pulp to a rootlet, or some other object, sticking out from the roof of the chosen cavity.

The comb consists of a single layer of cells, with their mouths opening downwards. At any one time it contains eggs, larvae, or grubs at different ages, and pupae hidden beneath white silken cappings. The queen toils from dawn until dusk to provide food for her large family. If there is a long spell of very cold or wet weather, she and her brood may die of starvation; but if all goes well, the first workers appear some time in June, about 4 weeks after the eggs are laid. They soon take over the tasks of fetching wood-pulp for nest-building and food for the larvae; while the queen, her wings frayed from long use and her bright colours faded, devotes herself to laying eggs. The little colony grows rapidly, reaching perhaps 2,000 workers towards the end of the summer. In late August and early September the workers begin to build combs composed of larger cells, in which the queen lays eggs. From these the workers rear perfect females or queens, perhaps several hundred, though only

a few of them will survive to found nests the following summer. The workers also rear a great number of males, who leave the nest with the young queens on fine days in autumn for mating. The males can often be seen flying around the tops of trees or up and down hedgerows, looking for the females. After pairing has taken place, the queens at once search for a sheltered spot in which to hibernate; but the males continue to fly about in large numbers on sunny days, jostling each other for a place at the ivy blossom. When hard weather comes, they soon die of cold and starvation. The old queen mother, exhausted from her labours of egg-laying, drags herself about feebly among the empty, mouldering combs until she, too, with her few remaining workers, falls a victim to the cold and damp of the last autumn days.

The Hornet, the largest British wasp, has a similar life-history to that of the common social wasps. It usually nests in hollow trees; but often it will hang its nest from the rafters of an outhouse or shed. Besides those described here, there are other sorts of social wasp, especially in South America, many having interesting habits which are not yet fully understood. But the social wasps, taken all together, form only a small part of the total wasp fauna of the world.

WATER-BEETLE, *see* BEETLES.

WATER-BOATMAN. Two different kinds of aquatic bug are known as Water-boatmen. One, *Notonecta,* is a strongly built insect about half an inch long, often seen resting with its head downwards, the tip of its abdomen at the surface of the water, the rest of its body submerged, and its two long hind-legs stretched straight out like a pair of oars. Several deliberate strokes with its legs will take it rapidly below water. In America it is known as the Back-swimmer.

The *Notonecta* should be handled with care because if it stabs the skin with its beak the wound may be very painful. It attacks tadpoles and small fish, and can make a shambles of an aquarium in a very short space of time. Its arrangements for breathing under water are interesting. There is a keel running along the middle of the under-surface of the abdomen, and from this, on each side, arises a row of stiff hairs. These meet other hairs that arise from the sides of the body. There is thus on each side of the keel a roofed-over space, and it is the air imprisoned in this space that is breathed by the submerged Boatman. Eggs are laid in notches cut in the stems of water-plants, and the young Boatmen can be found in all stages of growth in the same ponds as the adults. Except for the size and the absence of wings, they look very like their parents.

In America, and by some writers in Great Britain, the name Water-boatman is reserved for the other type, called *Corixa*, which is much less formidable and has a very much softer body. *Corixa* can be seen when the water is clear, paddling about near the bottom of the pond by means of a gentle movement of the hind-legs, very different from the vigorous, purposeful strokes employed by *Notonecta*. One British species is about half an inch long; but most of the others are much smaller. Their reserve air-supply is held between the wings and the abdomen. So far as we know, they are vegetarian in their diet.

See also Bugs.

WATER-PLANTS. The majority of these, such as the Bladderwort and Water-milfoil, have greatly reduced roots, and can absorb water all over the surface of the plant. Roots, when present, serve mainly for anchorage. Water-plants have no need of woody tissue for support or for conducting water from the roots; but many of them, especially in their under-water parts, possess large air-spaces in the tissues, so that a supply of oxygen for breathing is assured, even to the submerged organs. Many water-plants, such as the Water-lily and the Pondweed, have leaves which float on the surface of the water,

Victoria regia, THE GIANT WATER-LILY OF THE AMAZON.   *Harold Bastin*

YELLOW WATER-LILIES (*Nuphar lutea*)

The flowers of the Yellow Water-lily are raised on thick stalks a little above the water, while those of the White Water-lily float on the surface.   *John Markham, F.R.P.S.*

and differ from those of most other plants in having pores (or stomata) on the upper surfaces only (*see* LEAVES). Thus they can take in the carbon dioxide needed for building up food-stuffs. To prevent the stomata from being flooded, these floating leaves have long stems, which allow for changes in the water-level. Some tropical water-plants have leaf-stalks shaped like corkscrews, which stretch or twist to keep the leaves floating at the right level. The Giant Water-lily of the Amazon has leaves large enough to support the weight of a baby, with the edges upturned all round to prevent flooding.

Shallow water-plants often have two kinds of leaves: normal leaves growing above the surface of the water, and others growing below the water, with no stomata, which absorb gases from solution in the water. Many plants living sub-merged in flowing water have finely divided leaves which expose a far greater surface for the absorption of gases. Some Water-crowfoots, for instance, have both lobed floating leaves and thread-like submerged leaves. The Arrowhead of the ponds has arrow-shaped leaves growing above the surface, and ribbon-shaped leaves below, which spread freely in the water.

Some water-plants live in marshes, and some in ponds and streams. The soil in marshes, though waterlogged, is not peaty and sour as in bogs; but it is deficient in oxygen, and so marsh plants usually have large leaves with big air-spaces for the passage and storage of oxygen. In some marshes the dominant plant is the Osier Willow, while in others it is the Rush. Other marsh-plants are the Meadow-sweet, Ragged Robin, Wild Iris, Marsh Mallow, Water Mint, Water Forget-Me-Not, and the Marsh Marigold. The latter, with its sturdy rootstock holding the plant firmly in the soil, is a typical marsh-plant. Because of its large air-spaces, the whole shoot is spongy, while the yellow flowers are large, and readily attract insects.

The nature of the soil, the depth of water, and the position with regard to trees, affect the sup-ply of mineral salts to pond-plants, as well as affecting the temperature and the amount of light which they get. Some plants live in shallow water with their roots in mud and their leaves above or floating on the water; others live in deep water, are not rooted at all, and float freely on or just below the surface of the water. There are also plants which are rooted in the mud, but whose leaves are entirely submerged. Shallow water-plants are much like those in marshes, but may include others—Reeds, Sedges, and Bul-rushes, Arrowheads, Water Plantains, and Horse-tails, for example. Freely floating plants include the insectivorous plant, the Bladderwort (*see* INSECTIVOROUS PLANTS, Section 4), the Frogbit, with its rosette of leaves, few hanging roots, and starry white flowers, and the Duckweeds, with their small leaves and long white roots hanging freely in the water. Examples of plants rooted in the mud but with submerged leaves are the Water-violet, the Water-milfoil, the Water-star-wort, and the Canadian Pondweed. The latter is well known as a nuisance in reservoirs: it reproduces itself simply and very freely, since any detached piece becomes a new plant. It was introduced to Britain about 100 years ago, and now inhabits practically every expanse of water in the country.

The plants of streams and rivers differ with the strength of the current, though some, like the Floating Meadow-grass and Water-crowfoot, occur both in swiftly running water or almost dry mud, their leaves being long and narrow when in swiftly flowing water, and short when in mud. All marsh and pond-plants may also occur in sluggish streams and rivers, the banks of which are often lined with alders and willows (*see also* ECOLOGY OF PLANTS).

WATER SCORPION. The two types of this aquatic bug do not look at all alike, although they have exactly the same structure. In one, called *Nepa*, the body is broad and extremely flat; in the other, called *Ranatra*, it is a long and very narrow cylinder. Both types are found all over the world. In spite of the difference in their appearance, the more we compare them the more closely they are seen to resemble each other—so that we could almost imagine them to have resulted from accidents in which the one was squeezed flat and the other pulled out long-ways. The name of Water Scorpion is given more particularly to the *Nepa*.

Though these bugs spend their time in the water, their second and third pairs of legs are better fitted for walk-ing than for swimming.

Water Scorpions are the only aquatic bugs with legs not adapted for swimming. The front pair of legs is used neither for walking nor swimming, but for catching prey. They are distinctly 'elbowed', and the part farthest from the body can close down at the 'elbow' to fit into a groove in the nearer part, in exactly the same way as the blade of a penknife fits into the haft, so that any victim captured between the two is helpless.

At the other end of the body is a breathing-tube made up of two slender pieces, each of which is grooved on its inner side, the tube being formed when they come together. The mouth of the tube can be pushed to the surface when the insect is resting in shallow water, so that it can obtain air. At the base of the tube are two 'spiracles' or breathing-pores, by which the air is passed into the body.

These insects are carnivorous, feeding upon what they capture alive, and they obtain their food by stealth, relying greatly on concealment. The broad, flat, brown *Nepa* lies well hidden in the mud at the bottom of the pond. The olive-brown *Ranatra* may be found in similar places, its long legs and cylindrical body looking like the stalks of decaying vegetable matter. It often clings to aquatic plants and submerged grass, where it is equally well protected. If Water Scorpions were unable to harmonize completely with their surroundings, and so conceal themselves, they would be helpless. They can swim when necessary, but only slowly, and chiefly by means of the hind-legs, which act together like the legs of a frog. On land, they crawl awkwardly by means of the second and third pairs of legs, which move alternately, as is usual in walking animals; and they wave the first pair in front as they do so. They are said to be able to fly quite well, but as a rule fly only at night. The surface of the body that is exposed during flight, but concealed by the wings at all other times, is bright red—the one patch of colour on an otherwise uniformly brown body.

See also BUGS.

WAXWING. This small bird, of which there are about ten species, is to be found in the northern regions of Europe, Asia, and America. The Japanese Waxwing breeds in parts of Siberia, and winters in China and Japan. The Bohemian Waxwing breeds in Scandinavia and other northern countries, and comes south for the winter, in some seasons crossing the North Sea in large flocks to winter in the eastern counties of Britain. The Cedar Bird belongs to North America.

Waxwings are small birds with long wings, short legs, short, slightly hooked beaks, and silky plumage. The inner quills of the wings are tipped with red, horny appendages, almost like sealing-wax. The Bohemian Waxwing is a colourful bird, the male having a reddish-chestnut head and crest, grey-brown back, blackish wings tipped with white and yellow, a blackish tail ending in a broad band of yellow, and purplish-red underparts. Waxwings perch in an erect position, and if startled, raise and spread out their crests. These gay little birds, feeding in flocks on the red berries of the mountain ash above a snowy ground, are a most attractive sight. The Cedar Birds of America, smaller and less colourful, come down to the lower lands in the winter to feed on the berries of the red cedar, on which they become very fat. Waxwings make nests of coarse, dry grass in the fork of a tree, the eggs being pale blue, marked with purple-black spots. (See picture p. 465.)

WEASEL. The Weasel family belongs to the CARNIVORA (q.v.) or flesh-eating order of mammals, and is distributed widely over the northern hemisphere. The most important members are the Weasel itself and its close relatives, the Stoat, Polecat, Marten, Skunk, and Mink, as well as the WOLVERINE, OTTER, and BADGER, which are described in separate articles. Most of the family are greedy, bloodthirsty animals, and several of them have a vile smell, which they use as an excellent weapon of defence, giving it out whenever they are attacked or annoyed. Weasels and their near relatives all have long, slender bodies

WEASEL. *Eric J. Hosking. F.R.P.S.*

STOAT. *Harold Bastin*

and short legs. The family includes some of the most valuable fur-bearing animals in the world.

1. WEASELS are the smallest of the British carnivora, but are most savage hunters, probably even more courageous than Stoats. The males are 6–8 inches long, with short tails, and the females are somewhat smaller. Their coat is chestnut with white underparts, sometimes becoming entirely white in the winter in very cold climates. Weasels and Stoats look very much alike; but the Weasel is the smaller and has a less bushy tail, while the Stoat is the browner and has a black tip to its tail. They both give out a vile smell.

Weasels are widespread in country districts, living in hedgerows, woods, and among stones. Mice, voles, and rats form their main food; but although so small, they sometimes kill game, hares, and rabbits. They will continue to hunt and kill their prey long after they have satisfied their hunger. When out hunting, they advance by small leaps, stopping at intervals to sit up on their haunches and have a good look round. With their snake-like bodies, they can follow most of their smaller prey into their holes and hiding-places. They usually make their nests in holes in banks, dry ditches, or in hollow trees. The female has a litter of four or five young, which, if necessary, she will defend with fury and desperation, risking her own life rather than leave them. The young family is taken out regularly on hunting excursions, after having first been taught to use their teeth on half-dead mice and other small creatures.

2. STOATS normally have a brown coat tinged with yellow; but in Scotland and all very cold regions it becomes white in the winter, where-

upon the Stoats are known as Ermines. The white winter coat not only makes the Stoat inconspicuous in the snow, but also helps to conserve the heat generated by its body—for white fur is a bad conductor of heat. The winter coat of Scottish Stoats is too coarse to be of any commercial value; but Ermine from the very cold, northerly regions is highly prized.

Stoats will go almost anywhere after their prey—they will enter rats' and moles' burrows, climb trees, and even cross very wide rivers. In order to attract birds within their range, they tumble and writhe like snakes on the ground. When moving in packs, they have sometimes attacked dogs and even human beings. They overcome their prey by a final rush, seizing the victim by its throat or on the artery behind the ear. They then drag it back to their nests to be eaten, often pulling and pushing beasts as much as four times their own weight. They carry back stolen eggs by holding them under their chins, and rolling them on the ground. In Britain, a litter of from five to eight young is born in April or May.

3. POLECATS are also savage, evil-smelling creatures, the males being about 22 inches long, with longish tails, and the females always a few inches smaller. The Polecat's fur is almost black with a purple sheen, and through it shows a buff undercoat. They live in woods and hilly thickets, sleeping by day in their nests, and hunting by night. Small prey, such as rats and mice, rabbits, lizards, and snakes are their main victims, though sometimes they will attack geese, turkeys, and hares, biting them on the throat or at the back of the neck. Very occasionally they have been known to attack human beings. The sexes

POLECAT. *Harold Bastin*

live together for most of the year, and during the mating season (February to April) they make long night journeys. Their nests have two chambers, one lined with leaves for the young, and the other used as a larder for storing food. A litter of four or five young is born in April or May, and there is often another litter later in the year. The young are very pale when born, and do not become the colour of the adults until about 8 months old, though they are fully grown at 3 months. In winter, Polecats sometimes nest in deserted buildings.

Polecats live in Europe, Asia, and America. They used to be quite common in certain parts of the British Isles, but are now almost extinct, except in the remoter parts, especially of Wales. The domesticated FERRET (q.v. Vol. VI) is believed to be descended from the Asiatic Polecat, and although its domestication took place a very long time ago, the dark-coloured Ferret still looks much like a Polecat.

4. MARTENS do not have the unpleasant smell of the first three animals. They are found in many parts of Europe, Asia, and America, the different species varying very little. The only one now to be found in the British Isles, and that only rarely, is the Pine Marten. It is about 18 inches long, with a thick, bushy tail, and fur which is rich brown, except on the chest, where the colour varies from yellowish-white to bright orange. Pine Martens are wild and shy, and, as they mostly live in trees, are rarely seen. They creep swiftly from branch to branch in pursuit of birds and squirrels, but also come down to the ground to kill small prey and to raid the farmyard. When they are being chased they travel by long leaps, spitting and hissing like cats or uttering shrill, loud cries. Four or five cubs, with fine, white hair, are born once a year. They remain blind for about 3 weeks.

The Beech or Stone Marten and the Sable are found on the Continent and in Asia. The largest species is the fine, black-grey Fisher Marten of North America. All Martens are trapped for their fur, that of the Sable being so much sought after by fur trappers that the animal has now become very rare.

5. SKUNKS, which live only in America, have by far the most nauseous smell of all the weasel family. Whenever they are provoked or irritated, they discharge an amber-coloured liquid with a vile odour from a pair of glands under the tail. The Canadian Skunk, the best-known species, is about the size of a small cat. It has jet-black fur, with broad bands of white from head to tail, a white line down the face, and a black, bushy tail. The Skunk is not afraid to walk abroad, because this conspicuous colouring warns other animals off, reminding them of the Skunk's smell. The Skunk walks very slowly and deliberately, and, because of its fearlessness, is very easily trapped.

6. MINKS are small amphibious animals about 16 inches long, with thick, bushy tails, and a smell almost as bad as that of the Skunk. Their thick, glossy fur varies in colour from dull yellowish-brown to rich chocolate-brown. There are three species found in North America, eastern Europe, and Siberia. Minks never live far away from water, making their nests either in a hole in the bank of a river or lake or in a hollow log. They eat frogs, crayfish, mussels, water-birds, and various small water mammals, following their prey almost entirely by scent, and hunting them both by day and by night. Although Minks frequently make attacks on poultry, they are not nearly as destructive as some of the other members of this family. For many years now, Mink fur has been very highly valued, the best skins being obtained from the American species. When caught alive in a trap, the Mink's face, never very prepossessing, is said to take on an almost diabolical expression.

See also Vol. VI: FUR HUNTING; FURS.

WEAVER BIRD. Weavers form a large group of small, finch-like birds, found principally in Africa, but also in parts of Asia and Australasia. They are so named because of their elaborate and beautifully made nests, which they generally place close together in large communities. The majority build nests of grass and twigs suspended from trees or between the stalks of two or three reeds. The exclusively African Sociable Weaver Birds carry community building much farther. A flock of birds builds one enormous, umbrella-shaped erection of grass, difficult to distinguish at a distance from the thatched roof of a native hut, and fixed among the branches of a large tree. Under its shelter are constructed numerous little tunnels, leading to individual nesting chambers lined with feathers. The birds use these chambers not only for nesting, but also during other seasons as shelter against the violent tropical rains. The structure lasts from year to year, being repaired by the community as need arises.

MEXICAN DESERT

The thick leaves of the Cactus plants store moisture and resist heat. The colouring of the Horned Toads
makes them difficult to see against their background

LITTLE SKUNK
Paul Popper

MARTEN
Paul Popper

WAXWING
Paul Popper

LONG-TAILED WEAVER-BIRD
Zoological Society of London

The African Whydah Bird is included among the Weavers. There are several species, the Paradise Whydahs, in particular, being remarkable for the extremely long tails and brilliant plumage of glossy black and scarlet or crimson which the cocks carry in the mating season. During the rest of the year the cocks carry a much less conspicuous yellowish-brown plumage, like that of the hens.

Not very distantly related are the Tanagers of tropical America. There are altogether some 400 species of these finch-like birds, most of which are very brilliantly coloured, the typical colouring being blue and yellow. The splendid Scarlet Tanager, the 'Red-bird' of America, has a scarlet body and black wings. This bird winters in tropical America, but goes northwards in the summer, and is to be seen occasionally even as far north as Canada. Tanagers are very shy, and it is generally easier to hear their pleasant song than to see the birds themselves.

WEEVER-FISH. These small fishes of European and African coasts have two dorsal fins, the first with five grooved spines, and also a large grooved spine on the gill-cover, all provided with poison-glands. The sting of these spines is much dreaded, especially by shrimpers—for, as the Weevers feed principally on shrimps, they are often found in their company. Since the Weever has the habit of burying itself in the sand, with just the tips of the dorsal spines above the surface, it is liable to be trodden on, with painful results to a bare foot.

WEEVIL. This beetle has a head drawn out to form a snout, at the end of which is the mouth, with its tiny jaws. The snout may be either short, long, or very long. It often serves as a kind of gimlet to bore a hole in which the female places an egg. For instance, the Nut-weevil bores into the growing nut, and inserts an egg, which becomes the familiar fleshy white grub. There is an enormous number of different kinds of weevil, all feeding upon vegetable food of some kind, and many being extremely destructive. The tiny Rice weevils destroy great quantities of stored rice and grain, and the big Palm-weevils kill the trees which produce coco-nuts. Very common in Britain are the Leaf-rolling Weevils, pretty little beetles which cut and roll the leaves of birches and other trees to form the funnel-shaped or barrel-shaped objects so often found hanging

from them. The mother-beetle cuts with her jaws from the edge of the leaf to the midrib, and then rolls up the partly separated half, laying an egg inside the roll. The grub is protected by the roll, upon the interior of which it feeds until it drops to the ground, later emerging as a beetle. The little barrel-like cases, skilfully shaped from oak-leaves, are the work of a bright red weevil.

Some kinds of weevil have lost through disuse the wings which they formerly carried beneath their wing-covers. The wing-covers have now become firmly joined together, forming a solid armour, sometimes so hard that a child could stand on it without injuring the insect. Such weevils have the advantage that most birds find them too indigestible to eat. Many weevils have their bodies covered with extremely minute stalked scales, rather like the feathers of birds. These are often a brilliant green; but sometimes they are golden-green, blue, or red, mixed together or combined to form lovely patterns. The scales, like those of butterflies' wings, are very easily rubbed off.

Bark-beetles are weevils of a special kind, which burrow between a tree and its bark, causing the latter to fall off and reveal, at times, curious patterns traced in the wood. The female penetrates the bark and then gnaws a tunnel beneath it, laying eggs at regular distances along each side. Each little grub eats its way straight into the soft layer beneath; so that many side-galleries grow steadily outwards from the mother-tunnel. These increase in size as the grubs grow larger, and are made to diverge more and more in order to keep separate. The result is a very pretty pattern. Each grub, when it reaches full size, changes to the beetle-form at the end of its gallery; and then biting a round hole through the bark, it makes its escape.

See also BEETLES.
See also Vol. VI: INSECT PESTS.

WHALES. The whales are mammals—warm-blooded animals that suckle their young—and they belong to the order Cetacea, which includes Porpoises and Dolphins. Many of the young ones still have a few bristles round their mouths; but, otherwise, whales have lost the thick fur coat that most mammals wear in order to keep in the body heat. Instead, they have under the skin a thick layer of a very oily substance called blubber. They have become fish-shaped because this is the best shape for an animal that spends its

SPERM WHALE CATCHING A GIANT SQUID
The picture shows the used air coming out of the animal's nostril
A. Fraser-Brunner

life in the water. As whales never leave the water, they are more perfectly streamlined than the SEALS (q.v.), which spend part of their time on land. Their front legs have become 'flippers', somewhat resembling in shape the breast fins of fishes, and to all outward appearance their hind legs have become completely lost.

The most noticeable feature distinguishing whales from fishes is that the great tail-flukes are placed horizontally, whereas the tail-fin of the fish is upright, its movement being from side to side. Although some fishes bear living young, none suckles them, as do the whales. The whale has a double heart with four chambers, just like the human heart. It breathes, not by gills, but by lungs; and its skeleton is very much like that of other mammals, and quite unlike that of a fish. Because whales breathe by lungs, they have to come to the surface of the water every so often to get a supply of fresh air, and to rid themselves of the old used air. This is called spouting. The breath is puffed out from the nostril as a warm vapour—but it immediately condenses in the cold air into a sort of mist, and looks like a fountain of water.

All whales eat living animal food: some feed on small creatures such as prawns; many on fish; some on cuttlefish; but only one, the Killer Whale, attacks other warm-blooded animals. Most whales are harmless, timid creatures, showing great affection for one another, as well as for their young, which are both born and nursed in the water. Most pairs have one baby about once a year. Whales are found in all the oceans.

They generally swim together in herds known as 'schools', often numbering several hundreds. The two main groups into which they can be divided are, firstly the Toothed Whales, which include the Sperm Whale, Narwhal, the Killer Whale, and the Dolphins and Porpoises; and, secondly, the Whalebone Whales, one of which is the giant Blue Whale, the largest animal alive to-day.

The Toothed Whales, as their name suggests, all have teeth in their jaws. The largest is the Sperm Whale, the males of which are sometimes 60 feet long. When attacked, the Sperm Whale is a very dangerous creature, and in the old days, when harpoons were thrown by hand from small craft, it used often to upset the boat by its furious charge. Melville's Moby Dick, which bit off a man's leg, was a Sperm Whale. These whales are so valuable that they have been killed in large numbers, and are now less common. The head has a huge hump, consisting mainly of a reservoir for spermaceti. In the living animal this is a liquid oil; but it turns solid on being cooled, and is used for making ointments and candles. An even more valuable occasional product is ambergris, which is used for making perfumes. It appears to be formed in the intestines of the whale, and is sometimes found floating on the sea, looking rather like a dirty grey sponge, but a real treasure for the lucky finder. The ferocious Killer Whale feeds on seals, porpoises, and sea-birds, as well as on large quantities of fish. Occasionally Killers are seen off the coast of Britain. They hunt in packs, swimming at great speed. On more than one occasion they have been known to leap half out of the water on to ice-floes in an attempt to seize the sledge dogs of polar explorers.

The Narwhal, only about 18 feet long, lives in the Arctic Seas. In the male, one of the two teeth develops into a slender tusk, twisted in a left-handed spiral, often 9 feet long. This great spear may possibly be used in fights with other whales. A number of the small Toothed Whales, especially those with beak-like jaws, are called Dolphins. They are found in nearly all the seas of the world, and occasionally off the coasts of

WHITE ADMIRAL BUTTERFLY ON BRAMBLE FLOWER
S. Beaufoy, F.R.P.S.

LARGE CABBAGE WHITE BUTTERFLY WALKING ON ITS
SIX LEGS. *S. Beaufoy, F.R.P.S.*

haunt the tangled masses of blackberry blossom for nectar, and are often seen in company with Silver-washed Fritillaries. On hatching, the caterpillar makes its way to the tip of a honeysuckle leaf, and eats part of the leaf away from each side of the midrib. When it is not feeding, it lies along the midrib, where it can easily be found before it retires into hibernation in the autumn. Its winter shelter, a folded honeysuckle leaf, is prevented from falling by being attached to the stem with silk. In the spring the caterpillars cast off their dark olive-green winter coat, and appear in a brilliant light-green coat, matching the young growth of the honeysuckle. On their backs they have long, reddish spines. They pupate on the food-plant, hanging head downwards suspended from a silk pad. The chrysalis is green with beautiful shining silver markings, and is unique in shape, being grotesquely swollen in places and having two sharp projections on its head.

WHITE ANT, *see* TERMITE.

WHITE-FLY, *see* Vol. VI: INSECT PESTS.

WHITES (Butterflies). These largish butterflies, together with the YELLOWS and WOOD WHITE (qq.v.), belong to the very large family Pieridae. Two, the Large and Small Cabbage Whites, are among the most common butterflies in the British Isles. All Whites and Yellows have six fully-developed legs, all of which they use for walking. The Marbled White, in spite of its name, is a member of the BROWN family (q.v.).

The male Large Cabbage White has no markings on the upper side of his wings, except for a black tip. The female, however, has two large, black spots on each top wing, and a streak running towards her body. The British-bred Whites, which have two broods a year, are often reinforced by enormous migrations from the Continent. The female lays her eggs in batches of a dozen to a hundred on the underside of a cabbage leaf, and also on nasturtium, rape, jack-by-the-hedge, and mignonette. The caterpillars, which are greyish-yellow speckled with black, and have an unpleasant smell, live in communities. When they are in their last skin, however, and fully fed, they leave the food-plant and crawl away to a wall or nearby fence. There, they pupate, attached by the tail to a silken pad and supported by a girdle.

This butterfly is a great pest in the vegetable garden—indeed, were it not that only a small proportion survive to reach maturity, the cultivation of cabbages would be impossible. In some years, as it is, they do cause serious devastation. Many larvae die from bacterial diseases, and others are infested by Braconid Wasps, which pierce the newly hatched caterpillar and lay 20–100 eggs within its body (see ICHNEUMON FLY). The pupae, also, are freely eaten by birds.

The Small Cabbage White is almost an exact miniature of its large relative, except that the male usually has two spots, one on each top wing. (In the spring brood the spots are often missing.) The caterpillars, however, are quite different. The Small Cabbage White caterpillar is green with a fine yellow line along its back and sides, and it feeds alone, not in exposed colonies like the Large Cabbage Whites. There are three distinct broods, in spring, summer, and autumn;

but they usually overlap, and are frequently reinforced by immigrants from the Continent— so that the butterfly appears to be breeding continuously from March to early October. It was introduced into America about 1860, and within 30 years had spread all over the United States. In 1930 it was accidentally imported into New Zealand, where it rapidly increased. In both countries the Braconid parasites have been deliberately introduced in order to control the spread of the Whites.

The Green-veined White, although often confused with the Small Cabbage White, is not a garden butterfly, but frequents damp places, country lanes, open glades, and ridings in woods, where the markings on its underside harmonize well with the grasses among which it rests. The green colour is due to the intermixing of black and yellow scales. The males produce a scent, like lemon verbena, which appears to attract the females. The caterpillars, much like those of the Small Cabbage White, feed mostly upon jack-by-the-hedge and horse-radish. A brilliant lemon-yellow Irish form has been bred in captivity for many years.

The Orange Tip has blotched green and white undersides, which harmonize well with green and white flower heads. The male alone has the brilliant orange tips to the wings. A yellow form occurs in the Isle of Man. The female lays her eggs in May amongst the flower-clusters of jack-by-the-hedge, charlock, or cuckoo flowers. These are at first cream-coloured, change within a few hours to bright orange, and then fade until, as the tiny caterpillar begins to show through the semi-transparent shell, they appear almost black. The caterpillars may often be found during the day resting lengthways upon the long pods of jack-by-the-hedge. They are bluish-green, finely dotted with black, with a white stripe along the sides. Young larvae are often carnivorous, attacking others of the same kind. They also, like the BLUES (q.v.), secrete a sweet fluid attractive to ants, whose attendance gives them considerable protection. The extremely angular chrysalides may also be found attached to the stems of jack-by-the-hedge.

The Bath White derives its name from a piece of needlework executed at Bath in the 18th century, which portrayed a specimen said to be found near that place. This species is a rare migrant, and has only appeared in 27 years from 1824 to 1944, not more than 370 individuals

GREEN-VEINED WHITE BUTTERFLY SHOWING UNDERSIDES OF WINGS. *S. Beaufoy, F.R.P.S.*

altogether being recorded. In 1945, however, it reached the British Isles in unprecedented numbers, along a 500-mile front from Kent to Co. Kerry. At a distance the Bath White can easily be mistaken for the Green-veined White. Both sexes, however, have a large square black spot on each upper wing, and the female has a band of black markings on the outer margin of the lower wings. It may be distinguished from the female Orange Tip by the less complete black tips to the forewings and the more compact green marbling on the underside. The orange eggs closely resemble the pollen-bearing anthers of the mignonette, the most usual food-plant. The lilac and yellow caterpillar has been known, especially in 1945, to feed also on mustard and sea-radish.

The Black-veined Whites have been extinct in the British Isles for more than a quarter of a century. They were last seen in any numbers in the Canterbury district of Kent about 1912, but were previously known to breed in the New Forest and other parts of southern England and Wales. The butterfly is quite unmistakable, being larger than the Cabbage White, and with its wing-veins heavily etched in black—as the name of the butterfly suggests. The wings are semi-transparent, especially in the female, and, unlike most butterflies, they have no fringes round the edges. The caterpillars live in colonies in a slight web, and on the Continent feed on plum, blackthorn, and others of the prunus family.

ORANGE TIP BUTTERFLY SHOWING UNDERSIDES OF WINGS
S. Beaufoy, F.R.P.S.

WHITETHROAT, *see* WARBLERS.

WHITING, *see* COD.

WIDGEON, *see* DUCK.

WINKLE, *see* SNAIL; Section 4.

WIRE-WORM. This is the grub of certain of the Click-beetles or Skipjacks (so called from their habit of jumping into the air by striking the surface on which they lie). Click-beetles are narrow-bodied insects, generally found amongst herbage. When they are alarmed, they draw

WIREWORM

their legs close to their bodies and slip to the ground. If they happen to land on their backs they cannot easily get on their feet again as their legs are so short. They get out of this difficulty, however, by bending the body until it rests upon the head and the tip of the tail, and then straighten out so suddenly that they strike the ground and spring upwards, turning over at the same time—and so regaining their feet.

The grubs of the Click-beetles are slender, whitish creatures, some kinds feeding upon rotting wood and some devouring other insects, while some are the hated wire-worms —amongst the worst enemies of our crops. These love cultivated soil, where, unseen, they can feed upon the roots of corn, potatoes, vegetables, strawberries, and almost anything we grow for our own food. Fortunately, we are befriended by many kinds of birds

CLICK-BEETLE (ADULT OF WIRE-WORM)

which prey upon the wire-worms, and search the fields for them or follow behind the plough, devouring those which it brings to the surface.

See also BEETLES.
See also Vol. VI: INSECT PESTS.

WOLF. Wolves belong to the same group as the DOG, and are therefore close relatives of the FOX and JACKAL (qq.v.). They are widely distributed over Asia and North America; and

GREY OR TIMBER WOLF OF AMERICA
Ewing Galloway, N.Y.

though they have now disappeared from Britain and most of Europe some still live in the wilder and more mountainous districts, especially of eastern Europe. They are very numerous in many parts of Russia, but are not to be found in Africa or Australia. Wolves live both in forests and in open country. They hunt by day and by night, generally alone or in pairs, but sometimes, especially in winter, in family parties. Normally they are shy, suspicious, and cowardly animals; but when they are hungry, or when hunting together in parties, they grow fierce and aggressive. Wolves have on frequent occasions attacked and killed human beings, and in America they will attack animals as large as the bison or moose. They do not stalk their prey and then spring on it, as do the cat family, but run it down in the open. Their long, elastic gallop is deceptive—indeed few people would think that a wolf could out-distance a very fast horse. They have, too, a wonderful power of endurance, running for miles without slackening their pace. The cry of a wolf is a loud, prolonged howl. A single wolf can make so much noise that many a traveller has thought himself surrounded by a pack of wolves, when there was but one a couple of miles away.

A wolf's lair is usually either in a rocky cavern, in a hole in the ground, or in the hollow of a fallen trunk. The she-wolf generally produces from three to four cubs in the spring, and while they are young, she feeds them with the flesh of animals which she herself has swallowed and then regurgitated, partially digested.

In North America live the Grey Timber Wolves, the White Arctic Wolves, and a small wolf called the Prairie Wolf or Coyote. The Coyote is a crafty and cunning, but very cowardly, animal, which lives in burrows and feeds on various small mammals and birds. Cubs, captured young, become very tame, but never lose their shy, skulking habits. In the open bush country of Brazil and the Argentine lives the Maned or Red Wolf, which is rather like a large fox on stilt-like legs. It towers above the tufted grass, and so is able to follow the movements of its small prey.

Wolves can rarely be tamed so as to eradicate their wild instinct—sooner or later they nearly always attack their owner. Domestic dogs and wolves are very closely related; but it is not at all certain that the wolf is the only ancestor of the domestic dog: it may well be a product of several wild species (*see* Dog Breeds, Vol. IX).

WOLF SPIDER, *see* Spiders.

WOLVERINE. This mammal, also known as the Glutton, is a very strong and fiendishly savage, bear-like relation of the Martens, Stoats, and Weasels (q.v.). It is powerfully built, almost 3 feet long, with a short, bushy tail, and it has a smell almost as bad as that of the Skunk. Its dark-brown fur is rather coarse, long, and thick. Wolverines live in the forests of northern Europe, Asia, and America, rarely stirring abroad before nightfall. On the very few occasions when they have been seen about during the day, they were reported as sitting up and shading their eyes with their paws, as if suffering from the unaccustomed light. In spite of their clumsy-looking appearance, they run fast, climb trees with ease, and swim rivers in chase of prey. Generally they live alone in underground holes —frequently the deserted lairs of bears. The four to five young, which are born in June or July, remain with their mother until the following winter, after which they have to shift for themselves.

Wolverines are extremely greedy, and will devour any animal they can kill. Their sharp teeth and claws enable them to bring down a deer or caribou, although they prefer smaller game, and would far rather steal from others than hunt for themselves. They rob traps set for other animals, pulling the trap to pieces and removing the bait or the captured animal. After they have satisfied their hunger, they bury the rest of the booty, defiling it with their nauseating scent so that no other animal will touch it. They have also a curious habit of stealing and hiding things for which they could have no possible use—they have, for instance, been known to remove and hide the entire contents of an uninhabited hunting-lodge, including such articles as guns, axes, knives, cooking utensils, and blankets.

WOMBAT, *see* MARSUPIAL.

WOODCOCK, *see* WADING BIRDS, Section 4.

WOODLANDS. 1. Two thousand years ago most of Britain was covered by vast forests of different types. To-day, most of the land has been cleared for agriculture or for towns; but all the main types of woodland are still represented, some being dominated by a certain type of tree, such as the Oak, Beech, or Pine. The woodlands of Britain are made up either of deciduous trees, the most common being Oak-woods, Beech-woods, Ash-woods, and Birch-woods, or of coniferous trees, which are generally found at high altitudes and with pines as their dominant trees.

2. OAK-WOODS. There are two types of oak-wood in Britain, damp oak-woods, generally found in the south of England on clay or loam soils, and dry oak-woods, which are usually on the drier, shallower, and more sandy soil of the Pennines and other places. The typical damp oak-wood tree is the Pedunculate Oak, which can be recognized by its stalked acorns and by its shining, peculiar-shaped leaves. The typical tree of dry oak-woods is the Durmast or Sessile Oak, in which the flowers, and consequently the acorns, have no stalks, and the leaf-blades taper to the stalk and have star-like hairs on their under-surfaces. There are many crosses between the two kinds of oak, however, and the two sometimes live in such close association that it is difficult to distinguish a true damp oak-wood from a dry oak-wood. Durmast oak-woods are

found extending up hill-sides to altitudes of between 1,200 and 1,500 feet. Up to a height of 800 feet the trees grow to a moderate size; but above this they are stunted by the wind, and increasingly sparse.

Whether the Pedunculate or Durmast Oak is dominant in a wood, the plants found with them are much the same—although in the damp woods there is usually a greater profusion of undergrowth and of shrubs. Among the oaks are often found the Ash, Field Maple, Birch, Wild Cherry, Alder, Wych Elm, Rowan or Mountain Ash, and, sometimes, Hornbeam; but these usually grow on the edges of the wood and in the more open glades, as they are not able to compete with the oaks when these grow closely together. The rich shrub population of the damp oak-wood is made up of Hazel, Hawthorn, Blackthorn, Dogwood, Privet, Guelder Rose, and Willows. Most of these also occur in dry oak-woods, but not so profusely. The carpet plants in oak-woods vary according to the type of soil. In woods of Pedunculate Oaks, where the soil is light and dry, large areas may be covered with Bracken, Bluebells, Wood Sanicle, Dog's Mercury, Anemones, Primroses, and Meadow-sweet; in open places Foxgloves often flourish. In the south of England, these plants occur also in the Durmast woods; but in the more hilly regions of the north the ground flora is of a heathy type, and includes Bilberry, Ling, Heath Bedstraw, Wild Sage, and Tormentil.

3. BEECH-WOODS occur mainly in the south of England, their chief need being a warm, dry, well-aerated soil, preferably chalk or limestone: they never flourish on waterlogged ground. The finest beech-woods in Britain occur on the southern slopes and escarpments of the chalk hills of the North and South Downs, and of the Chilterns, as well as on the limestone ridges of the Cotswolds. The most striking feature of a beech-wood is the dense shade made by the leafy canopy, and consequently the scarcity of ground vegetation—unlike the abundant carpet vegetation found in oak-woods. Beech-woods are the home of the characteristic SAPROPHYTES (q.v.), such as Bird's Nest Orchid and the Yellow Bird's Nest, which get their nourishment from the decaying beech leaves. On the outskirts of beech-woods and in glades where light penetrates, considerable sheets of Dog's Mercury, Wood Sanicle, and Bluebells may occur, the former being better able than most plants to flourish in shade. The

OAK-TREE ON ASHTEAD COMMON, SURREY. *The Times*

POLLARDED BEECHES IN THE WOODS AT BURNHAM BEECHES, BUCKS. *The Times*

three kinds of Violet—Hairy, Wood, and Dog—Wild Strawberry, Arum Lily, Herb Bennet, and Enchanter's Nightshade may also be found. Very few trees can compete with the Beech; but Ash, White Beam, Yew, and Wayfaring Tree sometimes occur in clearings.

4. ASH-WOODS are found on chalky soils, particularly those which are poor in humus. They occur on the limestone hills of the north and west of England, and grow particularly well in the Peak District of Derbyshire. Where the chalk soil is damp, as in the Isle of Wight, they may replace beech-woods. Ash-woods extend well up hill-sides to a height of 1,200 feet, above which they merge into a zone of hawthorn scrub. Ash trees cast less shade than either oaks or beeches, and so their ground vegetation is often extensive. With the Ash grows a great variety of lime-loving, woody plants, including Wych-elm, Hawthorn, Yew, Juniper, Aspen, Hazel, Bramble, Ivy, and, in the south of England, Traveller's Joy. Where Hazel occurs, it often forms dense thickets, the shade of which hinders the growth of floor plants. Ash-woods in well-drained soils have carpets of Dog's Mercury and Moschatel, Ground Ivy, and Hairy St. John's

Wort. Those soils which are wet in the spring but drier later, have Garlic, Wild Strawberry, Globe Flower, and Red Campion; while in marshy places ash-woods have a ground vegetation of Meadow-sweet, Kingcup, Great Butter-burr, and Valerian. The floor carpet of ash-woods, especially in summer, often consists of one dominant herb—there may be nothing but patches of Dog's Mercury or Ground Ivy.

5. BIRCH-WOODS occur in both chalky and non-chalky soils above the limit of oak-woods on hill-sides—and Birches will grow farther north than most trees. In the moorland peat of the Pennines, and in Scotland, the remains of birch trees show how widely they once spread. The Rowan or Mountain Ash is frequently present in birch-woods. Quite often, especially on sandy soils, the Birch accompanies the Oak, and the abundant supply of light seeds also enables it to invade heaths. The Birch does not produce dense shade: and the well-developed ground vegetation is heathy in nature, including Bracken, Ling, and Bilberry, as well as MOSSES (q.v.), which tend to accumulate moisture.

6. PINE-WOODS. Most of the pine-woods of Britain are the descendants of trees originally

PINE-WOOD (ROTHSEN FOREST, INVERNESS)
Eric J. Hosking, F.R.P.S.

BIRCH-WOOD (FRILSHAM COMMON, BUCKS.)
The Times

imported from abroad, the original primitive pine forests being restricted to a few areas in the central part of Scotland. The dominant pine of these original Scottish pine-woods is a variety of the imported pine, and both have come to be called the Scots Pine or Scotch Fir. Provided the roots of the Pines can get a hold, pine-woods are found on all dry soils, on ground that is deep and sandy as well as on partially drained bogs.

When pine-woods are thick, the shade is so dense that all the lower branches, except at the edges of the wood, die off. There is little ground vegetation, the only plants to be found being a few Mosses, Fungi, and the Yellow Bird's Nest. In such woods there is a natural scarcity of nitrates, which are usually formed from decaying humus—and the Pine gets its necessary nitrogen through those peculiar FUNGI (q.v.), or *Mycorrhiza*, which infest its roots, and pass on to the tree the organic matter they use as food. At the edges of these dense pine-woods, Bracken, Bilberry, Ling, Bell-heather, Bramble, and herbs such as Tormentil, Heath Bedstraw, and Wood Sorrel may occur, and these are also found in pine-woods where the trees are more widely spaced (*see also* ECOLOGY OF PLANTS).

See also CONIFERS.
See also Vol. VI: FORESTS.

WOODLOUSE (Slater). Woodlice are common in every garden, where they hide during the hours of daylight under flat stones and rotten wood. They are the only members of the Crustacea completely adapted for spending the whole of their lives on land, and they possess the beginning of a tracheal system for breathing air, as is found in insects. They are active creatures when disturbed, crawling rapidly away in search of a fresh hiding-place—though one species, the Pill or Armadillo Woodlouse, has the habit of curling up into a ball when alarmed. The two other species common in our gardens are the Brown Woodlouse, which has a brownish body with two rows of yellowish spots on the back;

and the Grey Woodlouse, which is greyish-blue. The largest British species, nearly an inch long, is the Sea Slater, commonly found on the seashore in rocky places well above high-water mark, where only the salt spray will reach it.

See also CRUSTACEA.

WOODPECKER. There are many species of Woodpeckers distributed over most of the world but not Australasia and the Pacific Islands. Woodpeckers vary in size from the Great Grey Woodpecker of Malay, which is 18 inches long, to the tiny Piculets of tropical America, some of which are as small as 3 inches. Most of them spend their lives in trees, hunting for insects and grubs; but some, such as the Ground Woodpeckers of Africa, the Golden-winged Woodpeckers (or Flickers) of the U.S.A., and the Pampas Woodpeckers of Argentina, find most of their food on the ground—in river banks, hillsides, or the mud walls of buildings.

The typical Woodpeckers have short legs and strong claws adapted for climbing; stiff, pointed tail-feathers on which the birds support themselves when climbing; strong chisel-shaped beaks for digging into the wood and ripping off bark; and long tongues which the birds can shoot out to catch an insect. Woodpeckers have sticky tongues, like those of ANT-EATERS and CHAMELEONS (qq.v.), very convenient for licking up insects. Although they eat a certain amount of other food, such as fruit, berries, and nuts, their main food is insects and grubs—and they are particularly fond of ants. They breed in nesting holes in trees, laying pure white eggs, generally four or five in number, on nothing more of a nest than the wood-chippings left over from the excavation. The entrance hole is only just large enough for the bird to enter, and is marvellously symmetrical. The fledglings stay in the nest a long time, and are conspicuously noisy. Woodpeckers are shy birds, more often heard than seen. They quickly put the trunk of the tree between them and any intruder. Their general practice when hunting food is to start at the bottom of a tree and work upwards. They tap the trunk to see whether the wood is sound or not, and then rip off the bark from any likely sounding spot, to excavate for grubs and insects beneath. One group of Woodpeckers, the Sapsuckers of America, tap trees such as birches and maples, and feed on the sap which they draw. In the course of 2 or 3 years' such tapping, a family of Sapsuckers will kill a full-grown tree.

In Great Britain there are three species—the Green Woodpecker and the Greater and Lesser Spotted Woodpeckers. The quite common Green Woodpecker is conspicuous with its parrot-like colour of green, with crimson head, and yellow rump. It is often called the Yaffle,

GREEN WOODPECKER OR YAFFLE
G. K. Yeates, F.R.P.S.

GREAT SPOTTED WOODPECKER AT NESTING HOLE
Eric J. Hosking, F.R.P.S.

because of its cry like a harsh laugh, which it utters continuously as it makes its rather heavy, dipping flight from tree to tree. The Greater Spotted Woodpecker, a smaller bird with bright pied plumage and crimson crest, is less rare than is usually thought, but it is so shy that it is not easy to see. The Lesser Spotted Woodpecker is still smaller, about as large as a Chaffinch. Both birds in the spring make a curious jarring noise, almost like a rattle, by tapping their beaks very rapidly against a bough. This is quite unlike the normal tapping in search of food.

The Wrynecks, grey-brown birds about as big as Larks, are close relatives of the Woodpeckers, with the same long, sticky tongues, but with less strong beaks. Their plumage is mottled, their backs marked with little wavy black lines. They winter in tropical Africa and India, but breed in Europe, visiting many parts of Britain. They are often called Snake Birds, for they twist their long necks in a snake-like fashion and hiss like snakes when disturbed. Their cry is a monotonous, piercing, 'guee-guee-guee'.

WOOD WASP (Horntail). People who live near places where timber is stored are often surprised by the entry into their houses of a large, black and yellow insect. It looks like a huge wasp, and, because it seems to possess an extremely powerful sting, it causes considerable alarm. It is, however, quite harmless, and is one of the two species of British Wood Wasp, the other being steel-blue. Its body is about $1\frac{1}{2}$ inches long, and has a horn ending in a slender tail—to which it owes its name of Horntail. Its body is black, except for a yellow patch on each side of the head, a yellow band just below the wings, and the bright yellow colour of the lower half of the abdomen, including the 'horn'. Its wings are rich amber-brown, and have an expanse of about $2\frac{1}{2}$ inches. Its ovipositor, or egg-laying organ, the so-called tail, which gives the appearance of a sting, extends below and beyond the 'horn', and is continuous with the lower surface of the abdomen for about half its length. It is used to drill through the bark of a tree and deep into the wood beyond, an egg being inserted each time this **is** done. The larvae burrow into the heart-wood, and live there for about 2 years, after which they pupate in the galleries they have formed, each in a silken cocoon in which are entangled particles of the wood it has chewed up.

At the base of its ovipositor the Wood Wasp has a pair of cavities containing a fungus that attacks wood, but not sound timber. When the

insect lays its eggs deep in the timber, it also leaves there some of this fungus, which eats its way through the timber, and the larva, when hatched, travels in its wake, feeding upon partially digested material prepared, as it were, in advance. We have here an interesting example of what is called symbiosis, in which two living things are acting together for the benefit of both. In this instance the fungus gains entry by the drilling operations of the Wood Wasp, and the larva of the Wood Wasp finds its route and its food prepared for it by the fungus.

Now, although this particular fungus will not attack sound timber, its invasion of the tree is probably prepared for it by another fungus, the Honey-fungus. This is probably the most deadly foe of our forest trees: it attacks their roots, and so alters the timber that it becomes suitable for attacks by the fungus carried by the Wood Wasp.

It is not possible to say whether our two species of Wood Wasps are natives of Britain or whether they were introduced from abroad in imported timber; but they are quite at home here now, and not uncommon in the neighbourhood of pine-forests and fir-plantations.

See also Vol. VI: TREES, PESTS OF.

WOOD WHITE BUTTERFLY. This small, delicate butterfly has dead-white, black-tipped wings, and a long, thin, pointed body. It is the only British representative of the sub-family Dismorphinae, belonging to the WHITE family (q.v.), of which 98 out of the 101 species live in central and South America. It is extremely local, but, although it disappeared from many of its haunts at the beginning of this century, there are numerous signs of its revival. The male butterflies appear in sunny woodland glades in May, and a few form a second brood again in July. The females usually remain in the shade of the undergrowth, only coming out to lay their eggs on clumps of bird's-foot trefoil or tufted vetch. The caterpillar is vivid green with a yellow stripe above the legs. The narrow, angular chrysalis is brownish-yellow with a pinkish stripe along the sides.

WOOLLY BEAR CATERPILLAR, *see* TIGER MOTH.

WORM. 1. The word 'worm' is really only a convenient descriptive term for a large assortment of animals possessing more or less elongated bodies. In the higher forms they are composed of a series of rings or segments, as in the common Earthworm; many of the lower forms, however, are unsegmented, in some cases leaf-like, and often have complex life-histories. These include Flatworms, Ribbon-worms, and Roundworms, all parasites in the bodies of other animals. The higher forms, the ringed worms or Annelids, include the familiar Earthworms, the Freshwater Worms, and the very numerous and beautiful marine Bristle Worms. These latter rank among the highest forms of worm-life, possessing paired appendages called false-feet, and a more or less highly developed head, often bearing 'jaws', tentacles, and feelers.

2. EARTHWORMS. These are of considerable importance to agriculture, for by their constant burrowing and their habit of breaking and carrying down fallen leaves in autumn, they help both to turn the soil and to make it fertile. At the same time, earthworms can become a nuisance to those who like a tidy lawn—although their casts make an admirable top-dressing. The body of the Earthworm is covered from end to end by a smooth cuticle, which helps it to glide between the particles of soil. On each segment of its body are tiny bristles, called 'setae', normally eight to each segment. These enable the worm to fix one part of its body securely

PEACOCK WORM—A TUBE-DWELLING BRISTLE WORM
M. Burton

familiar of the freshwater worms. It often occurs in such numbers as to give a red tinge to the mud. About half the body is hidden in the little mud tube which the worm has formed as its home, the remainder protruding into the water and constantly waving backwards and forwards.

4. MARINE WORMS. The marine Bristle Worms (*Polychaeta*) form a large and very important group, the members of which are characterized by possessing bodies externally divided into a series of rings or segments, bearing numerous bristles. These may grow out on projections, called false-feet, on each side of each body-ring, or from depressions in the tissues of the skin. Bristle Worms also possess tentacles and external breathing organs, called 'branchiae'. There are two main groups, the wandering worms, with well-developed false-feet, and the tube-forming worms, which lead a more or less sedentary life in tubes constructed from various materials. All pass through a series of transformations before reaching the adult stage, the larva being quite unlike its parents, and possessing one or more girdles of hair-like structures, called 'cilia', by which it swims through the water. At certain seasons of the year these larvae swarm in immense numbers in the surface waters of the seas, providing some of the food of various larger sea animals. One of the most familiar of the wandering sea-worms is the common Lug-worm, which throws out from its burrows the little mounds composed of ropes of sand and mud so often seen on flat, sandy shores when the tide is out. It has a long, cylindrical, blackish or bronzy-green body, measuring up to 10 or 12 inches in length, the first thirteen segments bearing bright-red, branching gill-filaments. The so-called Red Cat-worm, used by sea-anglers for baiting their lines, is a typical example of the wandering worms, and is charac-

to the ground while another part is being moved. The Earthworm also helps itself through the soil by the sucking act of its pharynx. This draws some of the earth into its body, the digestible parts being absorbed as food, and the rest passed through the body and ejected, forming little heaps called worm-casts.

There are many different species of Earthworms, varying considerably in size, colour, and choice of dwelling-place. The Brandling, which every angler values for use as bait, lives in manure heaps; the less familiar Tree-worm climbs trees; while other species frequent the roots of certain plants growing in swamps or on the banks of streams. Java is the home of a very large earthworm said to grow to several feet in length; it is called *Perichaeta musica* from the fact that, as it creeps about on the surface of the earth at night, it produces a sharp clinking sound, probably caused by the bristles of its body striking against stones lying in its path. Tasmania possesses a giant Earthworm which sometimes reaches close upon 6 feet in length; it is said to make a gurgling noise as it slithers back into its burrow in the ground.

3. FRESHWATER WORMS. The common little pond Blood-worm, measuring from half to nearly 2 inches in length, is one of the most

VARIFOOTED SEA-WORM

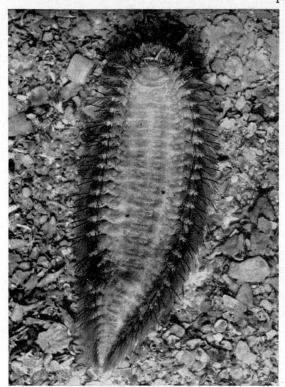

SEA-MOUSE, SHOWING RINGS AND BRISTLES OF A WORM
M. Burton

terized by its long, slender, segmented body, flat head, and large, horizontally moving jaws. It varies a good deal in colour, from a fleshy-red to a yellowish-brown or greenish hue, and burrows in the sand and mud on shore between tide-marks. Among the giants of the family is the Creeper, which grows to 18 inches in length, and lines the walls of its burrow in the sand or mud with mucus secreted by the large, leaf-like lobes of its false-feet. One of the most unworm-like of the wandering worms is the Sea-mouse, often found on wide, sandy shores at low tide. Its body, which may be 10 or 12 inches long, is oval in outline, the whole of the back being covered by a soft, dense, mouse-grey felting; while down each side of the body runs a prickly armature of bristles and compound hairs, displaying the most beautiful iridescent hues; in addition, its numerous false-feet bear long, stout, sharp-pointed bristles, which may be of service as weapons of defence.

The tubes formed by the sedentary marine worms are very varied, both in structure and composition. In some species they may consist merely of hardened mucus secreted by the worm; while in others the mucus forms a lining, as well as a natural cement by which particles of mud, sand, minute fragments of shell or small pebbles are held together so as to form an elaborate tube; in a few species, a single coiled or slightly curved tube of carbonate of lime is secreted. On shores where there is a mixture of sand and mud the Fan Sabella builds a tube which looks like a piece of narrow-bored rubber tubing sticking out of the sand. Sometimes the Fan Sabella may be seen at work in a pool, lengthening its tube; and then the worm, with its red or brown, feathery gill-tufts fully expanded and banded with bright colours, looks like some delicate flower on a slender stalk. Sometimes, near low-tide mark on a clean sandy shore where there is an admixture of sand and fragments of shells, one may see what look like miniature trees, their trunks and branches coated with glistening sand-grains, fragments of shell, and pebbles: these are the work of another tube-building worm, the Shell-binder, which selects and collects the materials for its elegant tube with its long, slender tentacles. In a similar place the Sand-mason worm uses nothing but carefully selected sand-grains of a certain size for its tiny tube. This is slightly conical in shape, and only one sand-grain in thickness, the grains being embedded in a liberal cementing of mucus, which makes both the inner and outer surfaces quite smooth.

Sometimes at the bottom of rock pools, on stones or on old scallop or oyster shells, one may see pinkish or greyish tapering tubes composed of carbonate of lime, about 3 inches long, marked at irregular intervals with encircling ridges, and slightly coiled at the narrow end. These have been formed by a Serpulid worm, which possesses special lime-secreting glands for the purpose. It is a small but very handsome worm, with

FAN SABELLA

magnificent plume-like gills which spread out like broad fans on the head, and are composed of bright red, slender filaments. One of its horns, or antennae, is transformed into a brightly tinted conical-shaped plug for closing the entrance of its tube.

5. LEECHES, animals used in the old days by surgeons for 'bleeding' (see Vol. XI, MEDICINE, HISTORY OF), also form a group of the Annelids. Leeches live on the blood or juices of other animals. They carry suckers at either end, by which they attach themselves to their hosts, the mouth being in the front sucker. They pierce the skin of their victims with saw-edged jaws, and inject into the wound a fluid which stops the blood from coagulating. They store the blood they suck in a large pouched crop to await digestion. Some, such as the Medicinal Leech, live in fresh-water; some, such as the Horse-leech, live also in damp places on land, and prey on earthworms and other invertebrates; others, such as the Warty Rock-leeches which infest sharks and rays, live in the sea.

6. PARASITIC WORMS. These are small, usually slender animals, such as Ribbon-worms, Flat-worms, and Roundworms, which dwell as parasites in or on the bodies of other animals or plants.

The Ribbon-worms are mostly marine, ranging from a fraction of an inch to several yards long, living in the mud, and feeding on Bristle Worms. The Flatworms include the Planarians, Flukes, and Tapeworms. The Planarians are small, flat, and unobtrusive animals, living among decaying vegetation and feeding on small molluscs and insects. The Flukes are small, leaf-like Flatworms, which cling by suckers to the bodies of larger animals, and may be found, in some cases, on the outside of the body, in other cases, in the internal organs where their presence is the cause of a variety of diseases. The Tape-worms are usually parasitic in the stomach or intestines, and are of particular interest since, while all parasitic worms have undergone degeneration to a greater or lesser extent, the Tapeworms represent the most extreme case. A typical Tapeworm consists of a cylindrical head, armed with a crown of hooks and several suckers. Although this part is spoken of as the head, it is no more than an organ for clinging to its host and budding off at the free end a never-ending series of segments each filled with eggs. There are no sense-organs in the head, and no mouth, nor does the animal possess limbs. In fact, it possesses very few organs other than those devoted to reproduction. The mouth, stomach, and intestine are unnecessary, for the parasite feeds on the fluids of its host, which it absorbs over its whole surface.

The Roundworms are mainly free-living, but some are partially or wholly parasitic. They are found in almost all situations on land, in fresh-water, or in the sea. Some attack animals, some cause disease in plants, whereas others merely feed on decaying matter.

See also Vol. VI: ANIMAL PARASITES.

WREN. About 100 species of Wrens are known, a great many in South America, and others in North America and the Old World, principally in the cooler regions.

The common European Wren, to be found in nearly every hedge and garden in Britain, is a tiny, russet-brown bird, with a pointed, slightly curved bill, a compact little body, and short, rounded wings and tail, the latter carried tilted up over its back. For its size it has a powerful and sweet song, which can be heard at all seasons and in all weathers. It is an insect-feeder. Wrens nest in thick bushes or hedges, in sheltered banks or ivy-clad walls, or in the thatch of cottage roofs. The nest is a domed construction, rather large for the size of the bird, with a neat hole on one side. The outside is made of dry leaves felted together with moss and lichen, and the inside is lined with finer moss and feathers. Six or eight eggs are generally laid—though much larger clutches, up to 16, have been known. The pair bring up several broods in a

TAPEWORM OF DOG
Maurice G. Sawyers

WREN AT ITS NEST IN THE IVY
G. K. Yeates, F.R.P.S.

season, and care for them assiduously. The cock has a curious habit of building the framework of several nests—these unfinished nests, called 'cocks' nests', being probably used for shelter in cold weather, when the birds will creep into any convenient hole and huddle together for warmth.

There are different races of the common Wren in the Scottish Isles and on St. Kilda's Isle, these being larger and of varying shades of plumage. The St. Kilda Wren has a very loud, penetrating song.

The Warbling Wren or Organ Bird of the Amazon forests has a lovely and peculiar song. Sometimes the notes sound unmistakably like those of a boy's voice, at other times like the notes of a flageolet. The Cactus Wrens are a larger group, species of which are to be found from California and Texas to South America. They build large, pouch-shaped nests in cactus plants. These nests are made of twigs and dry grass, lined with feathers, and measure as much as 10 or 12 inches from the narrow entrance-passage to the end. The Willow Wrens, Wood Wren, and Golden-crested Wrens are not true Wrens, but belong to the WARBLER group (q.v.).

Y Z

YAFFLE, *see* WOODPECKER.

YAK, *see* CATTLE.

YEAST. If some baker's or brewer's yeast is examined under the microscope, it will be seen to consist of oval cells, separate or loosely joined in long chains. Each cell is composed of a mass of protoplasm containing a small central body or nucleus, and is surrounded by a thin cell-wall. Yeast is a fungus, and, like all FUNGI (q.v.), it contains no green colouring matter, or chlorophyll, and so cannot build up its own food from raw materials by PHOTOSYNTHESIS (q.v.). Since yeasts obtain their food by absorbing dead organic matter, they are called SAPROPHYTES (q.v.).

The common method of reproduction in yeasts is by budding. When the cell has reached a certain size, a small outgrowth appears, gradually swells, and finally separates off as another yeast cell. At maturity each bud has the same structure as the parent cell, and repeats the process of budding. In this way colonies of yeast cells, looking like bunches of grapes, may be built up. When conditions are unfavourable to this method, another process of reproduction begins. The cell contents divide into four portions. Each portion, or spore, as it is called, surrounds itself with a thick wall, and later, when the wall of the original cell breaks down, it escapes to form a new yeast plant. With this thick wall, spores can withstand frost, drought, or other adverse conditions, and, being small

YEAST CELLS

and light, they are easily blown about in the atmosphere, which contains many millions of them. In the brewing industry, where specially cultivated yeasts are used, great care is taken to see that spores from other yeast strains do not fall into the fermenting material from the atmosphere, and so spoil the flavour of the beer.

Yeast is of enormous use to man, for every year tons of yeast cells are used to promote fermentation necessary for the making of bread, beer, wine, and other things. Its value lies in its peculiar method of anaerobic respiration (*see* RESPIRATION IN PLANTS), by means of which it is able to oxidize sugars into alcohol and carbon dioxide. It is this carbon dioxide, given off in great quantities, which causes bread to rise.

There are several kinds of yeasts. That used in beer-making is known only under cultivation, but wine yeast is found in the soil in vineyards. Most fruits have wild yeasts growing on them and feeding on their sugar. Wild yeasts are used in making cider. Yeast also contains relatively large quantities of Vitamin B2, and is often used as a tonic. It also produces valuable plant proteins; and factories have been set up in the West Indies especially to manufacture these yeast proteins on a big scale.

See also FERMENTATION.

YELLOW-HAMMERS, *see* FINCHES, Section 7.

YELLOWS (Butterflies). These largish butterflies belong to the same family as the WHITES (q.v.), and have many of the same distinguishing characteristics, including six fully developed legs. The Brimstone is a common British resident, but the Clouded Yellows are migrants.

The Brimstone is one of the first hibernating butterflies to awaken in the spring. It has often been suggested that the word 'Butterfly' takes its origin from this 'Butter-coloured fly', so conspicuous because of its early appearance. The male is brilliant yellow, and the female the lightest shade of pale greenish-yellow, the most conspicuous marking being an orange spot near the centre of each wing. Both sexes have hooked tips to the fore-wings and points on the hind-wings, making them quite distinct from other British butterflies. The undersides resemble the yellowing ivy leaves among which they winter. In the spring the females fly for miles in search of buckthorn bushes, the only food the caterpillars will eat. The caterpillar lies along the

CLOUDED YELLOW BUTTERFLY
S. Beaufoy, F.R.P.S.

upper surface of the leaf's midrib, and is exceptionally difficult to see, as it is the same colour as the buckthorn. It has a white line running the length of the body just above the legs, which decreases the intensity of shadow. It pupates underneath a leaf or on a twig, attached by a silken girdle. The butterfly emerges in July. Hibernated individuals are sometimes still on the wing in July, making a span of life of about a year—the longest of all British butterflies. Before going into hibernation the Brimstone haunts fields of clover and lucerne, or flower gardens, apparently without the urge to wander.

Clouded Yellows are rich orange-yellow butterflies, with deep black-bordered wings. They migrate to the British Isles from the Mediterranean region, usually arriving in late May and early June, and in some years spreading over southern England in vast numbers. The females immediately disperse in search of clover or lucerne fields on which to lay their eggs, while the males chase over hills and downs, soon wearing themselves out and dying. In warm weather the dark-green caterpillars, which have conspicuous side stripes of alternating yellow and orange, are fully grown within six weeks. In another fortnight the butterflies emerge, beautifully fresh-looking as compared with their parents. Sometimes the Clouded Yellows do not reach England until the end of August or September, in which case the young caterpillars have no time to feed up before being nipped by

early frosts. A variety of the female Clouded Yellow, called *helice*, prized by collectors, has white or cream wings, instead of orange-yellow.

The Pale Clouded Yellow is primrose-yellow, the paler female bearing a strong resemblance to the *helice* just described, but being less heavily marked with black. Its caterpillar resembles that of the Clouded Yellow and feeds on the same plants. Another much rarer species, *Colias australis*, sometimes confused with the true Pale Clouded Yellow, *Colias hyale*, has the tip and front edge of the fore-wings rounded and the black markings of both wings less extensive. It is said to be faster and wilder on the wing, and to be attached to chalky or limestone areas where the Horseshoe Vetch, its only food-plant, grows. The caterpillars are green, streaked with yellow, and spotted with prominent black dots—very different from those of the Pale Clouded Yellow. They visit Britain less frequently than the Clouded Yellow and penetrate less far north.

YELLOW UNDERWING MOTH, *see* NIGHT-FLYING MOTHS.

YEW, *see* CONIFERS.

YUCCA MOTH. The Yucca Lily plant of Mexico and the southern United States produces seeds only after pollination by the small white Tineid moth; and this moth depends on the seeds of the Yucca plant as food for its larvae. The female moth flies by night from flower to flower. When she has collected the sticky pollen from the stamens by means of a pair of peculiar scrapers in her mouth-parts, she visits yet another flower to lay her eggs. She inserts her long flexible ovipositor into the ovary, and there she lays one or more eggs. She then climbs up the style of the flower to the funnel-shaped opening of the stigma, which she fills with pollen from the compact mass carried under her head, pressing it down firmly. As a result the ovules are fertilized and develop into seeds—enough both to feed the Yucca moth caterpillars and to propagate the plant. The special adaptations of the Yucca moth in structure and behaviour, so that it is able to serve the Yucca plant and, incidentally, provide for its own sustenance, are unparalleled in insects, except among BEES (q.v.). Usually the association of insects and flowers leads to much greater modification of the flower than of the insect.

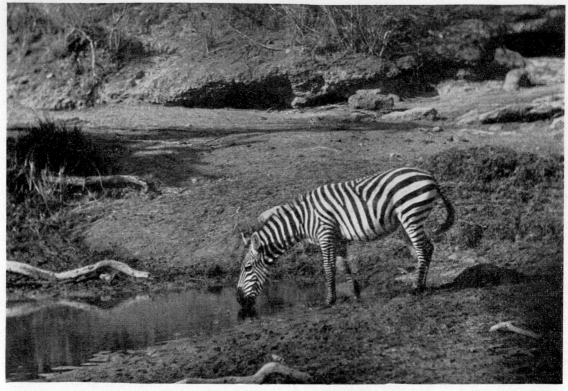

SOUTH AFRICAN ZEBRA AT WATER-HOLE
Dorien Leigh

ZEBRA. These animals, which are found only in Africa, are closely related to the HORSE (q.v.) and the Ass, the main difference being their striped coats. They are declining in numbers, two species being already extinct.

The largest species is Grevy's Zebra, which lives in droves in the open plains of Abyssinia, Somaliland, and northern Kenya. It stands about 13 hands, and has wide ears and rather narrow stripes down to its feet. The mare carries her young for about 12 months. When the foal is born, its mane extends from its shoulder to the tuft of its tail. The Mountain Zebra, once common in the mountainous districts of Cape Colony, but now almost extinct, is a small, sturdily-built animal, standing about $11\frac{1}{2}$ hands. It is striped all over, the stripes on its hindquarters being broad, and the horizontal ones meeting the tranverse ones to form a distinct pattern known as the 'gridiron'. A fold of loose skin at its throat forms a dewlap. A slightly different type of this Zebra is found in South-West Africa.

A long time ago in Cape Colony there were vast herds of reddish-brown Zebras with very few stripes and rather upstanding manes. They were called Quaggas, in imitation of their cry. So ruthlessly were they hunted for their flesh and hide, however, that they became extinct in the wild state about 1870. They had several near-relatives, among them being Burchell's, Chapman's, and Grant's Zebras. Burchell's Zebra, an animal with a striped body but white legs, used to be common north of the district occupied by the Quagga; but it, too, has now been exterminated. Chapman's Zebra of Bechuanaland is a similar type, but is striped all over; while Grant's Zebra, still quite common in East Africa, has very distinct black and white stripes. Many efforts have been made to break in and train Zebras, but in general these have not been successful. One pair of Zebras, however, were trained and driven in Hyde Park in the early years of this century.

ZOOLOGICAL GARDENS, *see* ZOOLOGICAL GARDENS, Vol. IX.